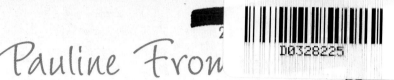

Pauline Fron

WALT DISNEY WORLD® & ORLANDO

SPEND LESS ★ SEE MORE ™

1st Edition

by Jason Cochran

Series Editor: Pauline Frommer

BICENTENNIAL
1807
WILEY
2007
BICENTENNIAL

Wiley Publishing, Inc.

Published by:

Wiley Publishing, Inc.

111 River St.
Hoboken, NJ 07030-5774

ISBN: 978-0-470-12535-9

Editor: Naomi P. Kraus
Production Editor: Michael Brumitt
Cartographer: Elizabeth Puhl
Photo Editor: Richard Fox
Anniversary Logo Design: Richard Pacifico
Interior Design: Lissa Auciello-Brogan
Production by Wiley Indianapolis Composition Services

For information on our other products and services or to obtain technical support,
please contact our Customer Care Department within the U.S. at 800/762-2974,
outside the U.S. at 317/572-3993 or fax 317/572-4002.

Wiley also publishes its books in a variety of electronic formats. Some content that
appears in print may not be available in electronic formats.

Manufactured in the United States of America

5   4   3   2   1

Contents

A Note from Pauline 1

1 America's Playground 2
The Sights You *Must* See 3
The True Character of the Place. 5
Lodging to Make It Possible 5
Food, Beyond the Chains 5
The Best "Other" Experiences 6

2 The Lay of the Land 7
Getting Around Orlando 8
Getting to Know Orlando's Layout 13

3 Where to Stay, in or out of the Parks 20
Home Rentals 20
Orlando's Hotels 28

4 Dining Options Around Town 60
Walt Disney World 61
Universal Orlando 67
U.S. 192 & Lake Buena Vista. 70
International Drive & Convention Center. 74
Downtown Orlando 79
Winter Park 85
Dinnertainment. 86
Character Meals. 90

5 Walt Disney World............... 93

Ticketing 94
Eating on Site 98
Navigating the Parks 100
Optional Park Services 101
The Magic Kingdom 102
Epcot........................... 129
Disney–MGM Studios 147
Disney's Animal Kingdom 158
The Water Parks 166
Downtown Disney 169
Disney's Wide World of Sports ... 171

6 Universal, SeaWorld & Busch Gardens 172

Universal Orlando 172
SeaWorld Orlando 201
Discovery Cove 213
Busch Gardens Africa 215

7 Beyond the Major Parks 221

International Drive Area.......... 221
U.S. 192 Area 225
Downtown Orlando............... 226
South of Orlando............... 231
East of Orlando 237

8 The Other Orlando 242

How Orlando Works 242
How Orlando Plays.............. 253
How Orlando Learns............. 256
How Orlando Lives............. 257

How Orlando Prays. 260

How Orlando Helps 261

9 Outdoor Orlando 263

Gardens 263

Natural Springs 264

Nature Reserves. 266

Golf. 271

Horseback Riding. 274

Hot Air Ballooning and Hang Gliding 275

10 Orlando After Dark—and in the Dark. 276

The Theme Parks' Entertainment Districts 278

Professional Sports 285

The Performing Arts. 285

Dance Clubs, Bars & Live Music Venues. 289

11 Shopping: The Good, the Bad
& the Discounted. 295

Retail Malls 295

Outlet Malls 297

Flea Markets 298

Antiques 299

Other Interesting Stores 300

12 The Essentials of Planning 302

Where to Find Tourist Information 302

When to Visit 304

Entry Requirements for Non-American Citizens 310

Customs Regulations for International Visitors. 311

Getting to Orlando. 312

Travel Insurance—Do You Need It? 316

Traveling from Orlando to Other Parts of America 316

Money Matters 317

Health & Safety. 318

Packing 321

Getting Attraction Discounts. 321

Specialized Travel Resources 323

Staying Wired 326

Recommended Books & Films 327

Index 331

Accommodations 340

Restaurants 341

List of Maps

Orlando Neighborhoods 15

Walt Disney World Area
   Accommodations 34

U.S. 192 Area Accommodations. . . 45

International Drive Area
   Accommodations 53

Walt Disney World Area
   Dining 62

International Drive Area
   Dining 75

Downtown Orlando Dining 81

The Magic Kingdom 104

Epcot 131

Disney–MGM Studios 149

Animal Kingdom 159

Universal Studios Florida 178

Islands of Adventure 191

SeaWorld Orlando 203

International Drive Area
   Attractions 223

Orlando Area Attractions 227

Downtown Disney 279

CityWalk. 283

About the Author

Jason Cochran is also the author of *Pauline Frommer's London*. He has written for publications including *Entertainment Weekly, The New York Times, New York Daily News, New York Post, Travel + Leisure* and *T+L Family, Budget Travel, Newsweek, TravelAge West, City, Inside.com, the South Florida Sun-Sentinel, Arena* (U.K.), and *Who* (Australia), as well as *Scanorama* and *Seasons* (Sweden). His writing has been awarded the Golden Pen by the Croatian government and was selected to appear in a permanent exhibit in the National Museum of Australia. He also devised questions for the first American season of *Who Wants to Be a Millionaire* (ABC) and, before that, spent nearly 2 years backpacking solo around the world. As a commentator, he has appeared on CNN, CNN Headline News, CNNfn, Australia.com, WOR, Outdoor Life Network, and MSNBC.com. He is an alumnus of Northwestern University's Medill School of Journalism and New York University's Graduate Music Theatre Writing Program.

Photo credit: Photo of Jason Cochran by Maia Rosenfeld

Acknowledgments

Although many people helped support and shape this book, I can't imagine the final product without the help of several in particular. Amy Voss and Alyson Gernert of the Orlando/Orange County Convention & Visitors Bureau for their unquestioning support; Rick Sylvain (dude!); Holly Ambrose for the pancakes; Shanon Latimer for the sharks; Jill Revelle for the giraffes; Tom Schroder for the fries; Ingrid Rodriguez, Lisa Holroyd, and Chris Blanc for the advice; Pam Brandon for the gelato; Julie Norris; David Landsel; Sara Moore; Mike McDonnell; Theresa Lowe; and Gary Shires. I can't imagine having as much fun as I did without the company, wit, and energy of the incomparable Katie Elliott. Thanks, as always, to Arthur Frommer for always having the courage to tell it like it is in a guide book, and to Pauline Frommer for knowing just how to put it. Praise also belongs to Naomi Kraus, who knows Disney better than just about anyone, and who kept me honest. Finally, my family and friends (including Michael, Laura, Mike, Kaitlin, Tony, Curtis, Jessica, Bryan, and Dwayne) made this exhausting effort possible—how I did two in 1 year is a testament to their support. Julie Morris practically raised her kids on Disney soil, and her input was indispensable. Love also to my mother, Tracy, who, like me, remembers the Magic Kingdom before the trees grew in. I raise a chocolate-covered frozen banana to them both.

An Invitation to the Reader

In researching this book, we discovered many wonderful places—hotels, restaurants, shops, and more. We're sure you'll find others. Please tell us about them, so we can share the information with your fellow travelers in upcoming editions. If you were disappointed with a recommendation, we'd love to know that, too. Please write to:

Pauline Frommer's Walt Disney World & Orlando, 1st Edition
Wiley Publishing, Inc. • 111 River St. • Hoboken, NJ 07030-5774

An Additional Note

Please be advised that travel information is subject to change at any time—and this is especially true of prices. We therefore suggest that you write or call ahead for confirmation when making your travel plans. The authors, editors, and publisher cannot be held responsible for the experiences of readers while traveling. Your safety is important to us, however, so we encourage you to stay alert and be aware of your surroundings. Keep a close eye on cameras, purses, and wallets, all favorite targets of thieves and pickpockets.

Star Ratings, Icons & Abbreviations

Every restaurant, hotel and attraction is rated with stars ★, indicating our opinion of that facility's desirability; this relates not to price, but to the value you receive for the price you pay. The stars mean:

No stars: Good

★ Very good

★★ Great

★★★ Outstanding! A must!

Accommodations within each neighborhood are listed in ascending order of cost, starting with the cheapest and increasing to the occasional "splurge." Each hotel review is preceded by one, two, three, or four dollar signs, indicating the price range per double room. Restaurants work on a similar system, with dollar signs indicating the price range per three-course meal.

Accommodations
$ Up to $75 per night
$$ $76–$125
$$$ $126 to $175
$$$$ Over $176 per night

Dining
$ Meals for $9 or less
$$ $9–$15
$$$ $15–$21
$$$$ $21 and up

In addition, we've included a kids icon 🧒 to denote attractions, restaurants, and lodgings that are particularly child friendly.

Frommers.com

Now that you have this guidebook to help you plan a great trip, visit our website at **www.frommers.com** for additional travel information on more than 3,500 destinations. We update features regularly to give you instant access to the most current trip-planning information available. At Frommers.com, you'll find scoops on the best airfares, lodging rates, and car rental bargains. You can even book your travel online through our reliable travel booking partners. Other popular features include:

- Online updates of our most popular guidebooks
- Vacation sweepstakes and contest giveaways
- Newsletters highlighting the hottest travel trends
- Online travel message boards with featured travel discussions

A Note from Pauline

I STARTED TRAVELING WITH MY GUIDEBOOK-WRITING PARENTS, ARTHUR Frommer and Hope Arthur, when I was just 4 months old. To avoid lugging around a crib, they would simply swaddle me and stick me in an open drawer for the night. For half of my childhood, my home was a succession of hotels and B&Bs throughout Europe, as we dashed around every year to update *Europe on $5 a Day* (and then $10 a day, and then $20 . . .).

We always traveled on a budget, staying at the mom-and-pop joints Dad featured in the guide, getting around by public transportation, eating where the locals ate. And that's still the way I travel today, because I learned—from the master—that these types of vacations not only save you money, but give you a richer, deeper experience of the culture.

I've conceived these books as budget guides for a new generation. They have all the outspoken commentary and detailed pricing information that you've come to expect from the Frommer's guides, but they take bargain hunting into the 21st century, with more information on how you can effectively use the Internet and air/hotel packages to save money. Most important, we stress the availability of "alternative accommodations," not simply to save you money but to give you a more authentic experience in the places you visit. In this Orlando book, for example, we tell you about dozens upon dozens of cushy rental homes (p. 20) where you and your family or a whole lot of friends could stay, with private pools, pool tables, full kitchens, and even flatscreen TVs (all common amenities) for less than you'd pay for the average hotel room. We also tell you how you can find the best inexpensive hotels throughout Orlando and Kissimmee, and which of the theme park digs are actually worth the cost.

Because time is money in Orlando, we don't pull our punches about which rides are worth the wait and which are skippable, which are best for teens and which will delight toddlers. We understand that many different types of people come to play in Orlando and we've done our best to speak to them all.

Chapter 8, "The Other Orlando," immerses you in Orlando, behind the scenes. Page through this section and you'll find tours that take you deep into the hidden city under the Magic Kingdom and you'll be introduced to the "Imagineers" who created these marvels of engineering, city planning, and awe-inspiring creativity (p. 242); programs at Cape Canaveral that allow you to dine with an astronaut or undergo modified space training (p. 251); and "trainer for a day" experiences at SeaWorld that get you up close and personal with Shamu or a dolphin (p. 250). We also go deep into the topic of Spring Training for baseball fans, and explore the oddities of the area, such as a planned community entirely inhabited by psychics. These are just a few examples.

The result, I hope, is a valuable new addition to the world of guidebooks. Please let us know how we've done! I encourage you to e-mail me at editor@frommers. com or write me in care of Frommer's, 111 River St., Hoboken, NJ, 07030.

Happy traveling!

Pauline Frommer

Pauline Frommer

1 America's Playground

IN 1886, A YOUNG UNMARRIED MAILMAN, FRUSTRATED WITH HIS FRUITLESS endeavors in the Midwest, moved to the woolly wilderness of Central Florida to make a better go of life. The land was no one's friend. Summers were oppressively hot, the lightning relentless, and the tough land, by turns sodden and scrubby, seemed to defy clearing. The only domestic creatures that thrived in Central Florida, it seemed, were the cattle, and even they turned out stringy and chewy. Undaunted—and in love with a girl from a neighboring farm—the young man planted a grove of citrus trees and waited for things to get better. They didn't. His trees died in a freeze and the young man was forced to return to delivering the mail to support himself. By 1890, the young man gave up. He moved, defeated, to Chicago to seek work. He was joined by his new bride, whose father had been injured clearing Florida pine and died. Back in the smoke of the Midwest, they had children and settled for what was to be an anonymous existence.

One day, 8 decades later, long after the young man and woman had lived full lives and passed away, two of their sons would return to Central Florida, that land that broke their father, and together, they would transform the recalcitrant swamp into the most famous fantasyland in the world.

The American Dream appeared to fail for Elias Disney. Little did he know it was only skipping a generation, and that his sons Walt and Roy would become synonymous with the very land that rejected him. Had he known that the Disney name would in due time define Central Florida, would he have been so despondent? Even if he could have had a fleeting vision of what was to be, and what his family would mean to this place and indeed to the United States, could he even have believed it?

The Disney brothers turned a place of toil into a realm of pleasure, a place where hard-working people can put their entertainment in reliable hands. The English have their Blackpool; Canadians have their Niagara Falls. Orlando rose to become the pre-eminent resort for the working and middle classes of America, and the breathtaking ingenuity of its inventions now inspires visitors from everywhere on Earth. While other countries segregate their holiday destinations by income or some other petty quality, Orlando, in the classic American egalitarian style, is all things to all people, from all countries and backgrounds.

This guide is written with a keen awareness that Orlando represents something even more powerful to American culture and history than merely being the fruit of a dream. It's something we all share. No matter who you are, no matter where you grew up, no matter what your politics, you probably went at least once to Walt Disney World and Orlando, and if you didn't, you desperately wanted to. What other thing in our culture can we all claim to share? What else has given children for the past two generations such sweet dreams? I've always said that if somehow Walt Disney World went out of business tomorrow, the National Park Service would have to take it over. It means that much to us.

So don't think of the amusements of Orlando as mere moneymaking enterprises. Of course they are, and it's easy to name legitimate issues with how they're run. But Walt Disney World, and by extension Orlando, is also Americana incarnate. The taste for showmanship and fantasy that Walt Disney World crystallizes, now known as *Disneyfication,* has become the defining mind-set of modern culture, in which even local grocery stores and shopping malls are dressed up like film sets and the "story" of your local burger joint is retold on the side of its soda cups.

Orlando tells us about our own culture, and it defines who we are and who we dream of being. Virtually nothing about today's Orlando is natural or authentic, and yet there may be no more perfect embodiment of our national culture. To understand this invented landscape is to understand our civilization and our generation. And if you observe Orlando with a long view—starting with young Elias Disney cutting his hands trying to budge a tough Florida pine—you will be a part of the explosive, unexpected powers of the American Dream.

And one more thing: As you'll soon see, it's a hell of a lot of fun.

THE SIGHTS YOU *MUST* SEE

Walt Disney World operates four top-drawer theme parks every day of the year: **Magic Kingdom,** the most popular theme park on Earth, is an improved iteration of the original Disneyland and the park that started it all; **Epcot** is a new-brew version of an old-style world's fair; **Disney's Animal Kingdom** blends animal habitats with theme park panache; and **Disney–MGM Studios** presents a show-heavy salute to the movies. Every bit as elaborate and cunning, Universal Orlando's two parks, **Universal Studios Florida** and **Islands of Adventure,** command great respect and get the adrenaline pumping a bit stronger. The gardens and marine mammals at **SeaWorld Orlando** serve to soothe. Those seven parks, all of which are in the top 10 most visited in the world, would take over a week to see fully, but there are still a few more. Busch Gardens Africa provides animal sightings with coaster after celebrated coaster, and three water parks combine cooling water with kinesthetic energy: **Typhoon Lagoon** for family-friendly slides, **Blizzard Beach** for more aggressive ones, and **Wet 'n Wild** for no-holds-barred thrills.

IF YOU HAVE ONLY 1 DAY IN ORLANDO   Well, I'm sorry for you. Just as it's impossible to eat an entire box of Velveeta in one sitting, you can't get the full breadth of Orlando in a day. But there is a must-see attraction: Walt Disney World's **Magic Kingdom** (p. 102). There is enough diversion at every Orlando theme park to keep you busy from morning to midnight—it's all a matter of willpower, and at what point you can tear yourself away. Ride the great Disney Audio-Animatronic odysseys, **Pirates of the Caribbean** and **Haunted Mansion,** and **"it's a small world"**; and brave the drops of **Splash Mountain** and **Space Mountain.** While you're there, take a free spin on the **monorail** through the iconic **Contemporary Resort,** and then connect for the free round-trip ride to **Epcot** (p. 129) and back, where you'll see the other top Disney park from above. Stay until closing, through the **fireworks** and the **parade,** or, if you've had enough, head to a quintessentially kitschy dinner banquet spectacle such as **Dolly Parton's Dixie Stampede** (p. 87). Hope you're not hungry for subtlety!

IF YOU HAVE ONLY 2 DAYS IN ORLANDO   Do the **Magic Kingdom** for sure, but for your second day, drop into **Epcot** and pass the morning hours seeing **Future World,** and then have lunch at one of the ethnic eateries of **World Showcase,** such as in **Morocco** or **Japan.** Hopefully, you bought an admission ticket that allows for park hopping, so you can duck into **Disney–MGM Studios** (p. 147) to try the superlative **Twilight Zone Tower of Terror,** or as long as it's before 5pm, into **Disney's Animal Kingdom** (p. 158) to sample the newly built **Expedition Everest** roller coaster.

IF YOU HAVE 3 OR 4 DAYS IN ORLANDO   Now it's time to consider branching out beyond the Mouse. If you're here for theme parks, you should go directly to **Universal Orlando's Islands of Adventure** (p. 189), one of the most elaborate amusement parks in the world, and don't neglect some of its most celebrated rides, **The Adventures of Spider-Man, Incredible Hulk Coaster,** and **Popeye & Bluto's Bilge-Rat Barges.** If you have small kids or you don't like thrills, then **SeaWorld Orlando** (p. 201), with its **Shamu** show and multiple marine animal habitats, makes for a soothing change of pace. Fill in spare time by visiting the secondary Disney theme parks (Animal Kingdom and Disney–MGM) or by spending a few hours at **Universal Studios Florida** (p. 176). During the evening, spend 1 night at the shopping-and-clubs zone of **Downtown Disney** (p. 169) and another among the nightlife of Universal's **CityWalk** (p. 282), or for an experience that's a little less canned, hit a pedestrian zone such as **Old Town** (p. 225) in Kissimmee, **International Drive** north of Sand Lake Road (p. 221), or the beer halls of **Wall Street** (p. 290) downtown. You might need a fine art fix, too: The **Morse Museum's** (p. 234) dazzling collection of Tiffany glass, followed by a boat cruise past the mansions of **Winter Park** (p. 268), might be just the ticket. At the moment you get sick of roller coasters—or when the temperature cracks the boiling point, whichever comes first—head for a water park: **Blizzard Beach** (p. 166) for a heavily themed experience, or **Wet 'n Wild** (p. 221) for unvarnished thrills.

IF YOU HAVE 5 OR MORE DAYS IN ORLANDO   Finally—you're approaching a vacation long enough to enable you to actually relax, and to take time to sit by the pool. Of course, if you stuck to a schedule as rigid as one major theme park per day, it would still take you 8 days to knock down the biggies, and that's before setting your belly on a single water slide. Take a day to drive out to **Kennedy Space Center** (p. 237), or if you need some peace, take a dip in a natural spring, such as **DeLeon Springs** (p. 265).

IF IT'S RAINING   Universal Studios Florida, with its many air-conditioned shows, waiting areas, and its covered parking, is the best choice. SeaWorld Orlando, where you'll spend lots of time walking outside, is the worst in rain. If it's a **scorcher,** both Universal Studios and Disney–MGM Studios have lots of sheltered activities, but you'll be best served by one of the three water parks (Wet 'n Wild, Blizzard Beach, or **Typhoon Lagoon** [p. 167]) which get crowded, but are fine choices—though, of course, your hotel pool holds water as a heat reliever, too. The worst park on hot or wet days is the exposed **Disney's Animal Kingdom.**

THE TRUE CHARACTER OF THE PLACE

Of course, Orlando's identity as a theme park mecca only began in 1971. The city has a deep culture of its own. Sample the high art collected by its high-society settlers at Winter Park's **Charles Hosmer Morse Museum of American Art** (Tiffany glass by the shelf; p. 234), the **Cornell Fine Arts Museum** (lush decorative arts of every description; p. 235), or the **Orlando Museum of Art** (fine works from every era; p. 229). The reason all those blue-bloods migrated here? The fine weather and the beautiful water. While some people rave about the horticultural achievements at botanical gardens such as the **Harry P. Leu Gardens** (p. 263) or **Historic Bok Sanctuary** (p. 264), I personally crave swimming in the 72-degree natural springs at **DeLeon Springs State Recreation Area** (where you can make your own pancakes and then have a swim in pure water; p. 265); a canoe paddle at **Wekiwa Springs State Park** (just north of downtown; p. 265); or, in winter, watching some of the area's original residents, wild manatees, swim at **Blue Spring State Park** (p. 265). Even Orlando tourism has its antecedents: **Gatorland** (p. 231) and **Cypress Gardens** (p. 232) are pleasing, corn-fed throwbacks from another era. And modern history has fewer finer monuments than the still-active launch pads at the **Kennedy Space Center** (p. 237), where America accomplished the impossible, over and over again.

LODGING TO MAKE IT POSSIBLE

Although pretty much everyone comes here to see Disney, not everyone can afford its prices, which start at $82, in the best of times, for a mediocre room in its **Pop Century** or **All-Star** resorts (p. 37). So rent an entire house instead. **All Star Vacation Homes** (p. 23) decorates its properties, all within 4 miles of Disney, to the highest design standards from as little as $109 for two bedrooms, plus a living-room pull-out—and companies such as **Alexander Holiday Homes** (p. 23) and **Oak Plantation** (p. 25) do it for as little as $65 a night. Other affordable hotels such as **La Quinta Calypso Cay** (p. 46) and **Rodeway Inn at International Drive** (p. 54) get you a straight-ahead standard room for nostalgic prices. Of course, many people have saved up all year for the chance to splash out on their Orlando hotel experience, and for them, there are places where you can get a better-than-average experience for market value. The **Courtyard at Lake Lucerne** (p. 32), set in the city's oldest documented home, is impossibly romantic; the **Nickelodeon Family Suites** (p. 51) entertains kids with the flamboyance of a theme park; and the downtown hideaway **Grand Bohemian Hotel-Orlando** (p. 59) is decorated by original fine art, including drawings by Klimt. Let no one say Orlando lacks sophistication.

FOOD, BEYOND THE CHAINS

Orlando is one of those places where even blasé restaurants are priced like splurges, but I sort the wheat from the chaff and tell you which special-occasion tables get you the most for your buck, including **California Grill** (overlooks the Magic Kingdom fireworks from atop the Contemporary Resort; p. 64), **bluezoo** (impeccable fish by chef Todd English; p. 65), and **Primo** (modern Italian by whiz chef/author Melissa Kelly; p. 78). More importantly, I point out fabulous restaurants, many family-run, that have been elbowed into the background by the proliferation of also-ran chains. These guys could put Epcot's World Showcase to shame, and at a fraction of the price: **Bruno's Italian Restaurant** (*abbondanza!* Right in the franchise zone of Disney, too! p. 70); **Rice Paper** (Thai fusion, rich and addictive; p. 76); **Asia Bagus** (Indonesian, smartly done, also near Disney; p. 72); **Memories of India** (Indian, done lightly and with nuance; p. 76); and **Seasons 52** (no dish will hit you for more than 475 calories and desserts are served by the shot glass; p. 77). And a selection of little places will put you in touch with the locals: The hummus at the friendly **Dandelion Communitea Cafe** (**p. 79**) comes in a teacup, while **Little Saigon** (p. 83) feeds the resident Vietnamese community. Bet you didn't know there was one!

THE BEST "OTHER" EXPERIENCES

There's no better way to get under the skin of Orlando than to sneak backstage. Far from spoiling the show, behind-the-scenes tours only enrich your understanding and appreciation for the feats of urban planning that have been achieved here, and what's being accomplished every single day in the name of your entertainment. Walt Disney World's **Backstage Magic** (p. 245) is a 7-hour primer on the resort's operational secrets, from the secret utilidors underfoot at the Magic Kingdom to the warehouse where the Audio-Animatronic figures are repaired. You fulfill the childhood fantasy of having an empty theme park all to yourself, paired with the pleasure of learning to ride a Segway scooter, on **Around the World at Epcot** (p. 247). SeaWorld's **Dolphin Nursery Close-Up** (p. 250) is a rare chance to feed a dolphin family by hand, and at Busch Gardens Africa, you can do the same thing with nosy giraffes from a flatbed truck on the **Serengeti Safari** (p. 252). For even deeper learning, Kennedy Space Center's **Astronaut Encounter** (p. 251) affords the opportunity to meet and talk with a real NASA astronaut who has been to space, while Disney's **Dine with an Imagineer** (p. 245) program puts you in touch with the engineers who make fantasies into reality. Outside the theme parks, Orlando is rich with more opportunities to see how people live, from unusual planned communities (the picture-perfect Stepford town of **Celebration** [p. 257] and the psychics of the haunted 19th-century hamlet **Cassadaga** [p. 258]) to some of the most vital Christian evangelical projects in America (such as the **WordSpring Discovery** Bible translation center; p. 260). When you're worn out from thinking, take a night off to kick back at a **spring training** (p. 254) baseball game or a **drive-in movie** (p. 253)—Orlando is one of the only places in America that can boast both options.

2 The Lay of the Land

Orlando's not such a small world, after all

THERE ARE TWO KINDS OF AMERICAN CITIES: THOSE CONCEIVED BEFORE the proliferation of the automobile—with walkable distances and manageable transit links—and those spread-out sprawls laid after the car took over. Because its development took a hairpin turn in the 1950s, Orlando is two cities, one of each type.

Back when only cargo trains had much business in Central Florida, Orlando fashioned itself as a prosperous small city—some derisively called it a cow town—well positioned to serve the citrus and cattle industries as they shipped goods between America and Cuba. The city remained that way, buffered from the rest of the country by irrelevance, until the middle of the 20th century. The great cross-state cattle drives ended in 1943.

That was when Orlando developed its split personality. The turning point wasn't the arrival of Walt Disney on his secret land-buying trips. It came a decade earlier, when NASA settled into the Space Coast, 45 minutes east, and the local government, spotting a golden opportunity, invited the Martin Marietta corporation—now Lockheed Martin—to open a massive facility off Sand Lake Road, east of the present-day Convention Center. The compound, opened in 1957 on what was then barren land far south of the city, was at the time the largest building in the state, and to seal the deal, the government promised unprecedented civic improvements, including a still-unrealized high-speed rail system. Mostly, though, politicians built roads for what they hoped would be the city of the future. Florida's Turnpike to Miami was sliced past the Martin plot, S.R. 50 was hammered through downtown to link the coasts, and soon after, the city saw the construction of Interstate 4, linking it to Tampa on the west coast and Daytona Beach (then one of America's premier vacation towns) on the east coast. By the time Walt hungrily eyed the swamps, Central Florida's government (cheered along by Martin Anderson, the 30-year publisher of the *Orlando Sentinel*) had proven its skill in luring high-powered projects.

Walt's new kingdom was constructed 20 miles southwest of the city in scrubland, where his planners could forever keep the outside world at bay. The resort was intended to be an oasis in the citrus groves, but instead, a satellite town (outside the city limits but indivisible from Orlando in most visitors' minds) sprouted around the park's border, just as one had in Anaheim. For the last two generations, the space between the two disparate Orlandos has vanished, consumed by developments where "real" Orlando residents live, so that the old-fashioned, "traditional" city has come to be dwarfed, as it were, by family-friendly honky-tonk and idealized suburbs. Few casual visitors know the original Orlando—a lovely downtown of repurposed bank buildings and hollow, forgotten department stores—even exists.

As a city whose population explosion was enabled in no small part *because* of major highways, Orlando is combed by them. I would estimate that 90% of what a tourist wants to see or do lies within a 10-minute drive of Interstate 4, or I-4, as it's called. (This simplicity is a contributing factor to Orlando's tourism success.) I-4 runs diagonally through the city from southwest to northeast, linking Walt Disney World, SeaWorld, the Convention Center, Universal Orlando, downtown Orlando, and countless other attractions. The only trick to navigating I-4 is understanding that by federal definition, it's an east-west road, linking Florida's coasts, so although it indeed runs north-south through Orlando, all directions are listed as either west (toward Tampa and the Gulf of Mexico) or east (toward Daytona Beach and the Atlantic Ocean). Once you've got that down, you'll be set. Exits are numbered according to the mile marker at which they're found. Therefore, the Walt Disney World exits (62, 64, 65, and 67) are roughly 10 miles from Universal Orlando's (74 and 75), which are about 9 miles from downtown (83). If you have an exit number, you'll also have your distance.

Traffic on I-4 tends to be worse in one direction at a time. Blockage builds in the westbound lanes in the morning, when people who live in downtown and northern Orlando commute to the theme parks, and the eastbound lanes clog up when they drive home in the late afternoon.

Most of Orlando's other principal highways are toll roads. You'll probably use them to drive in and out of the airport, but not very many times otherwise.

Beyond the area's highways, planning hasn't been very successful. Particularly east of Disney, the curving roads, the most major of which appear to be lined by identical condo-hotel developments and go by several names, can be confusing; so if you stray too far from I-4, it's a good idea to carry a map. Disney World itself is a particular disaster, since its signage is incomplete. You won't be at a loss to find maps containing all the roads, though, as nearly every free coupon brochure has one, as does every car-rental agency. There's also one in this book.

Get several maps, though; it's hard to trust any single one. It seems that half the maps distributed for free are sponsored, and they leave off the locations of whichever amusement area is deemed a rival. Laughably, some maps provided by Universal don't acknowledge that Disney exists at all. Should this situation frazzle you, every convenience store sells area maps for about $8; **Map & Globe** (☎407/898-0757; www.mapandglobestore.com) is a local cartographer and its products are widely available. Look for a map that doesn't give the Walt Disney World/Kissimmee area short shrift by popping it into an inadequate inset box—a common shortcoming proving again that locals give the resort no respect. Also, the rental-car agencies give out excellent overview maps for free, as does the website of the **Orlando Convention and Visitors Bureau** (www.orlandoinfo.com/maps), which has printable, interactive maps that highlight the major avenues you're likely to use.

GETTING AROUND ORLANDO

The biggest issue with Orlando isn't its size—that is manageable enough, so you won't need to put much homework into studying maps and orienting yourself. Where you should do some planning is in choosing your transportation method. Far too many people don't think about it, or they choose to rely on free buses and shuttles, assuming those go everywhere worthwhile. Picking the wrong method for your particular itinerary means you could end up wasting accumulated hours waiting for rides, or worse, you could be effectively shut out from seeing stuff you wanted to see.

RENTAL CARS

I have yet to encounter someone who rented a car in Orlando and regretted it. Quite simply, it should be a part of your budget. The only people who need not apply are the ones who have no intention of leaving Disney property for their entire stay. And people who do that will leave town having missed much.

If you want to try the area's non-Disney attractions and shops, get a car. If you want to save huge amounts of money on meals both at cheap restaurants and through grocery shopping, get a car. If you intend to experience any of the "real" Orlando and its rich natural wonders and history, get a car. It opens up an entire world to you, loosens your schedule, and ultimately eliminates much of the frustration that you'd have to deal with if you were constantly waiting for communal buses and shuttles. Trust me—after a full day of waiting on your feet in line after theme park line, the last thing you want is to wait again for the bus to slowly wend its way back to your room. Gathering cobwebs at the many shuttle stops of Orlando, I've seen many family members that looked like they wanted to throttle each other. Some vacation.

I recommend cash-strapped parents make room in their budgets for a car by choosing to stay off Disney property. The amount you'll save on the room rate is usually more than enough to cover the car, but the happiness such freedom buys can literally save your vacation.

Another budget-saving solution for people staying on Disney turf is to rent a car for only the days you'd like to venture off property. To that end, **Alamo** (☎ 800/462-5266; www.alamo.com) operates two satellite agencies within the Walt Disney World Resort: one at the Dolphin hotel and one at the Car Care Center, which is located in the parking lot of the Magic Kingdom. In my experience, renting a car for, say, a 2-day stint is cheaper if you pick up and return to Alamo's airport location; I'm usually quoted about $40 per day, including taxes, that way. The same rental costs about $55 a day if you pick your car up within Disney. Renting at Disney and dropping off at the airport is another option that doesn't incur a scary surcharge; it adds about $5 on top of the rent-at-Disney price. A similar pricing pattern is true at most of the area hotels that have small rental-car desks (and there are many). Using Priceline.com, you might be able to obtain quotes as low as $16 a day in low season, and about $26 when business is better.

The legal age minimum in Florida for a rental driver is 21. Agencies will usually slap those aged 21 to 25 with a hefty surcharge of $25 a day, regardless of how trustworthy you look. Enterprise charges lower fees ($15), depending on the office (such as at the airport). **Continental Rent-a-Car** (☎ 800/656-4223; www.continental.com), a privately owned outfit located 4 miles from the airport by shuttle bus, also charges $15 a day. On the flip side of generosity, National has been known to charge up to $50, so watch out and ask what the fee is before committing. Most companies won't rent to anyone older than 85.

Money-Saving Tip: Always fill up your car before returning it at the airport. One gas station at the airport's entrance was recently nabbed by the *Orlando Sentinel* for charging a full $1.40 more per gallon than the going rate. You might be surprised to learn that the Hess stations inside Walt Disney World actually charge a competitive price—many times, less than other stations outside the World.

Parking charges can also add up. If you're staying at a Disney resort, it's free at the Disney parks, but otherwise you'll pay $10 to $11 a day. If you pay for parking once at any Disney park, you won't have to pay it again on the same day, even if you drive to a different park later on. Outside of the theme parks, parking is usually free, plentiful, and off the street.

Remember that the city is full of tourists who don't know where they're going. Many of the drivers you'll encounter aren't from Orlando, and these lost souls will weave, halt, and cross three lanes of traffic without thinking of consequences. Check your own maps before setting out, and keep a safe distance from the car in front of you.

SHUTTLE BUSES

There are three varieties. One is the Disney comprehensive resort shuttle system, the **Disney Transportation System (DTS),** which even non-guests can use for free. Curiously, the 230-bus fleet qualifies as the third-largest bus system in the state, after Miami and Jacksonville's public services. Taking DTS to a theme park eliminates the old parking tram rigmarole, and during the Magic Kingdom's operating hours, the bus stops at its doorstep, eliminating the need to take either the monorail or ferry from the Ticket and Transportation Center. However, once you add on the time spent waiting for a bus, which can be 20 to 45 minutes, plus the commute itself, which can be just as long and may require a transfer, you'll find that in almost every conceivable instance, having a car of your own will always get you there faster and is worth the expense.

The system is particularly overwhelmed during the opening and closing times of the theme parks, so dispatchers run extra buses around those times and keep routes rolling for about 2 extra hours before opening and after closing. If you're staying at a Disney resort that offers another kind of transportation—say, the monorail to the Magic Kingdom—then a bus won't be available for the same route. Also, since the system operates with a hub-and-spoke design centered around the theme parks and Downtown Disney, you will often have to transfer if you're going between two other points, like two different hotels or a hotel and a water park. The sprawl of the resort means that only in very few cases will you be able to walk instead of hailing a bus; for most trips, hoofing it is simply impossible. A benefit of the system is that parents can feel mostly confident in allowing their teenagers to take it alone, which makes for flexible scheduling.

On balance, DTS can save you from having to rent a car *if* you only plan to go to Disney attractions and nothing else (which would be a shame for you—thumb through the rest of this book) and *if* you're a patient soul who can face a potential 1-hour-plus commute after spending 11 hours swimming upstream in the parks. But if you're choosing to stay on Disney property because DTS will save you the price of a car rental, get some prices and do some math first. Given the price of many off-property hotels compared to Disney-run hotels, you could rent a car and *still* save money and *still* make door-to-door trips to the parks in less time. Because it can be frustrating and excludes everything non-Disney, I recommend DTS as a supplement to a rental car, but not as a replacement for one.

The second shuttle variety is the **hotel theme park shuttle.** These are addressed in chapter 3, "Where to Stay, in or out of the Parks," on p. 58, but the upswing is that, yes, you can save a lot of money on car rental by using them, but there are strong downsides including inadequate scheduling and rambling routes. These also only go to the parks' gates, completely excluding inexpensive restaurants, shopping, and all natural and historic attractions.

The third option is the **I-Ride Trolley** (☎ 407/354-5656; www.iridetrolley. com; adults over 12 $1 per ride, seniors 25¢, kids age 12 and under free; day pass $3, 3-day pass $5, 7-day pass $9; 8am–10:30pm), an excellent shuttle bus with plenty of clearly marked and well-maintained stops, benches to wait on, and genuinely useful routes. There are two of them. The Main Line (every 20 min.) plies International Drive from the shops and restaurants just north of I-4's Exit 75 all the way to Orlando Premium Outlets, near Disney and Dolly Parton's Dixie Stampede; along the way it touches down at SeaWorld and Wet 'n Wild, and comes within a long block of the entrance to Universal Orlando. Take this one if you want to shop at Prime Outlets and Festival Bay. The second route, the Green Line (every 30 min.), is more of an express route, taking in Wet 'n Wild, heading down Universal Boulevard, stopping at SeaWorld, and turning around, also, at Orlando Premium Outlets. Passes are sold at most of the area's hotels and attractions. You'll find free route maps wherever you find a rack of brochures, or you can plan by using the maps on I-Ride's website. Because of its routes, visitors may find it feasible to stay on I-Drive, use this $1 shuttle to see nearly everything, and then tack on the hated hotel shuttle or a city bus for Disney days.

CITY BUSES

There's not a lot to love about public transit in Florida. Buses are infrequent (usually one or two an hour), and shelters inadequate (often, nonexistent), and when the sun's strong, the combination is miserable. Distances are also fairly great, so journeys can take a while. Still, people have been known to use the buses on vacation, although I have to wonder how much fun they're having. The Central Florida Regional Transportation Authority runs the **LYNX system** (www.golynx.com), on which one-way fares are $1.50, day passes cost $3.50, week passes are $12, and transfers between lines are free. Kids 6 and under ride with adults free, and you have to pay with exact change.

If you plan on using the buses, go online ahead of time and download free system maps, because bus shelters lack complete information. Note that because the buses are designed for locals to use for commuting, tourist areas are not easily linked by single routes—you'll have to transfer. For tourists, the most convenient routes are:

◆ **Route 56** heads down U.S. 192 from the Osceola Square Mall in Kissimmee and straight to the front gates of the Magic Kingdom, where you can catch free Disney transportation to the other parks. This makes U.S. 192 east of Disney the only major hotel zone that provides transfer-free bus access to Walt Disney World. Buses run every 30 minutes, but the last one leaves at 9:45pm even if Disney's open later.

◆ **Route 8** does most of International Drive, including the Convention Center and a stop at SeaWorld. It duplicates the service offered by the I-Ride Trolley, above.

◆ **Route 50** goes from the central Lynx station in downtown Orlando, down Interstate 4, to the gates of the Magic Kingdom. It stops at SeaWorld where passengers can connect to I-Drive by transferring to Route 8.

- The lesser Disney areas are served by the 300-series lines. Number **300** goes to Hotel Plaza Boulevard from downtown; **301** to Disney's Animal Kingdom from Pine Hills; **302** to the Magic Kingdom from Rosemont; and **303** to Disney–MGM Studios from the Washington Shores area. These link up at a bus transfer point at Downtown Disney before getting on Interstate 4 and bypassing the rest of the tourist areas. Bus **304** is the only one that connects with another tourist zone; it trawls Sand Lake Road, which bisects I-Drive, before heading to Downtown Disney. Once they're off I-4, 302 and 303 pass within a few blocks of Universal Orlando, on Kirkman Road, so if you toss in about 15 minutes of walking, they could technically be used for Universal, too, but it wouldn't be fun.
- **Route 21** goes up Universal Boulevard from Sand Lake Road, past Wet 'n Wild, to the Universal Orlando park, and links with the downtown depot.
- **Route 42** starts at Orlando Premium Outlets (a few miles northeast of Disney), up International Drive, and nearly 2 hours later, reaches the airport.

TAXIS

Only tourists use taxis in Orlando. They're just not part of the fabric of locals' lives. You will, however, almost always find a cluster waiting outside of the major theme parks' gates, waiting to take fares to their hotels.

The going rate is $2 for the first ⅖ of a mile or the first 80 seconds of waiting time, followed by 25¢ for each ⅛ of a mile and 25¢ for each additional 40 seconds of waiting. Airport trips incur a 50¢ surcharge. Taxis carry five passengers.

Those planning to rely on taxis to get them to the parks should balance that decision with a hotel booking that's near the action. For Walt Disney World, a hotel in Lake Buena Vista would cut down on transport costs, and for Universal, the northern bend of International Drive is best. But if you spend more than $30 a day on taxis (a one-way ride from the Magic Kingdom to the hotel stretch on

---

I Speak Mouse

Orlando, like all good Utopian communities, has its own vocabulary:

At Disney, a staffer of any kind is a "cast member."

You're not a customer. You're a "guest."

The work areas where guests don't go is called "backstage."

What you and I call rides, they call "attractions" or "shows."

Disney parks were designed by "Imagineers."

Disney's robot figures are "Audio-Animatronics."

Shamu doesn't do tricks. He does "behaviors."

Indoor rides are "dark rides" or "flat rides."

The business/line area you see before a show is the "pre-show."

U.S. 192 east of Disney would cost about $20), smack your forehead, because you could have rented a car for that amount.

- ◆ Diamond Cab Company: (☎ 407/523-3333)
- ◆ Star Taxi: (☎ 407/857-9999)
- ◆ Yellow/City/Checker: (☎ 407/422-2222)

Many companies accept major credit cards, but ask when you summon a ride, because your payment may need to be processed by phone.

GETTING TO KNOW ORLANDO'S LAYOUT

In 1970, before the opening of Walt Disney World, the area was still a tourism center, attracting 660,000 people a year. But by 1999, the place was a power-house, with 37.9 million people visiting. During the same period, the area popu-lation skyrocketed from 344,000 to 860,000, soaring past such old-guard American cities as St. Louis; Washington, DC; Boston; Baltimore; and Portland.

However, for all that growth, and despite the fact the amusements are critical to Orlando's economy, most of the population still lives north of both Walt Disney World and SeaWorld, so visitors won't always find themselves in the thick of authentic Floridian life. The tourist zones aren't grafted into residential ones, so visitors will have entire areas to themselves. Huge chunks of your time, days at a stretch, will be spent in just a few carefully sculpted districts. Here are the ones you'll most probably visit:

WALT DISNEY WORLD

Best for: Space, theme parks, a sense of place, greenery, proximity to His Mouseness

What you won't find: Inexpensive food or lodging, a central location for anything except Disney attractions

When Walt Disney ordered the purchase of these 27,000 acres mostly just west of Interstate 4, he was righting a wrong he committed in the building of Anaheim's Disneyland. In commandeering as much land as he did, he ensured visitors would not be troubled by the clatter of motel signs and cheap restaurants that abut his original playground. "Here in Florida," he said in a promotional film shot months before his death, "we have something special we never enjoyed at Disneyland . . . the blessing of size. There's enough land here to hold all the ideas and plans we can possibly imagine." You could technically spend your entire vacation without leaving the greenery of the resort, and lots of people do, although those who do usually cite the advertising-copy word "magic" (whatever that means) in their rea-soning, and they're missing a great deal. Still, there's an awful lot to do spread around here, starting with four of the world's most polished theme parks, two of the best water parks, four golf courses, two miniature golf courses, a racecar track, a sports pavilion, and a huge shopping-and-entertainment district. Every inch was crafted with crowd control and profit in mind, and no opportunity is missed to open a gift shop crammed with Mickey Mouse– or princess-themed souvenirs.

First-time visitors aren't usually prepared for quite how *large* the area is: 47 (roughly rectangular) square miles. Only a third of that land is truly developed, and another third has been set aside as a permanent reserve for swampland. Major elements are easily a 10-minute drive away from each other. The Magic Kingdom is buried deep in the back of the park—which is to say, the north of it, requiring the most driving time to reach. Epcot and Disney–MGM Studios are in the center, while Disney's Animal Kingdom is at the southwest of the property.

For its convenience, Disney signposts hotels and attractions according to the major theme park they're near. If you are staying on property, you'll need to know which area your hotel is in. For example, the All-Star resorts are considered to be in the Animal Kingdom area, and so many signs on Disney highways will simply read "Animal Kingdom resort area," and leave off the name of your hotel. Ask for your hotel's designated area when you reserve.

Getting into Disney is easy. Every major artery near it is exhaustively sign-posted for "Disney World." Most of the signs leading out of the park are also straightforward, but a few useful secret exits are not marked on official Disney maps. One is the newly laid **Western Way,** which turns past Coronado Springs resort and skirts the back of Animal Kingdom to reach the many vacation home communities southwest of Disney. If you take it, ignore the big green signs telling you to take 429 to U.S. 192. That route will cost you $1 in tolls despite the fact it runs for scarcely a mile. Instead, go forward to the next left, and take that. It ends up at U.S. 192 soon, too, and without a fare. As of this writing, this egress from Disney World remains on the down low, appearing on none of the official maps, but it's a quick way to get to the cheap restaurants and grocery stores of western U.S. 192 in an area that, up until a few years ago, was mostly empty but is now a booming housing zone. Word has it Disney will begin developing this western plot of land with hotels and shopping in the coming years.

There's a second useful shortcut out of the resort that Disney doesn't label on its official maps: **Sherbeth Road,** just before the entrance to Animal Kingdom Lodge, winds its way to the thick of the cheap restaurants on western U.S. 192, about a mile west of the thronged main entrance to the park. Taking it could save a little time if traffic on U.S. 192 is bad; and if you're staying on western U.S. 192, it's definitely the quickest path to Animal Kingdom or Blizzard Beach.

Walt Disney World is at the southern end in the chain of Orlando's main attractions, so to see Universal, SeaWorld, and downtown, you'll always be heading north on I-4.

It's interesting to note that when you're at Disney, you're in a separate governmental zone. The resort's bizarre experiments in building methods (such as fiberglass-and-steel castles) are partly enabled, as is often pointed out, by the fact Disney runs its own government entity, the Reedy Creek Improvement District, which can set its own standards. Even its mundane buildings have been imbued with a fantasy twist: Not far down the road between Downtown Disney Marketplace and the Grosvenor hotel—a road not otherwise used by many resort guests—make a pass by the R.C. Fire Department, a toylike engine house with a one-of-a-kind outdoor fountain that looks like a spouting fire hose. Farther down the road, you'll find yourself among the drab warehouses that serve the facilities.

Disney owns a little bit of land east of Interstate 4, too, which it has largely forged into the New Urbanism town of Celebration (p. 257). As a residential center with upscale aspirations (golf and an expensive hotel), there's not much to do except shop and eat a bit in its town square.

Orlando Neighborhoods

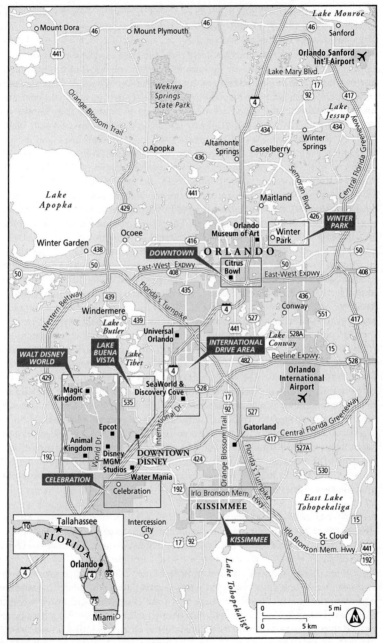

U.S. 192 AND KISSIMMEE

Best for: Value, dining and hotel options, family entertainment
What you won't find: High art, subtlety

No matter how Orlando changes, it's Kissimmee, its pipsqueak little sister, that remains the biggest news in saving money. Walt's master plan succeeded only in keeping tacky motels and buffets at a modest distance. Where the southern edge of the main resort zone touches Highway U.S. 192, the noise begins, stretching about 4 miles west and a good 10 miles east. This ostentatious drag, known also as the Irlo Bronson Memorial Highway (after the state senator who sold Walt a lot of his land to make the park possible), is the spine of Kissimmee, and it's your budget salvation for food and beds. It's also the best place to find that all-American kitsch you might be looking for—nowhere else in town will you find a souvenir store shaped like a giant orange half, and I call that a shame.

In the early 1970s, Kissimmee was the prime place to stay if you were visiting Disney World, because the resort operated just a few pricey hotels of its own and there just wasn't anything else built yet. The motels weren't flashy then, and they still aren't, but they're ever-affordable—$50 to $80 is the norm, and some fleabit places go down to $39 single/$45 double. Kissimmee itself, about 10 miles east of Disney, is a typical Florida small town with a main street by a lake, and its quickly growing subdivisions have become popular among Hispanic families, although that doesn't translate into accessible restaurants serving ethnic cuisine. U.S. 192 is mostly about the big chains. Motor east from Disney for a few miles, and if your family can't find something to agree on, no one's really hungry.

The best way to get your bearings on U.S. 192 is using its clearly signposted mile marker system. Disney's southern entrance (the most expedient avenue to the major theme parks) is at Mile Marker 7 and I-4's Exit 65 connects with it around Mile Marker 8. Numbers go down to the west and they go up to the east, as you drive toward the city of Kissimmee. Western 192, where the bulk of the vacation home developments are found, tends to be slightly less downscale than eastern 192, but neither stretch could be termed swanky or well planned. Although Osceola County has spent $29 million to beautify the tourist corridor, it's been pretty inept in the effort; in late 2006, the county cut down several stands of myrtle trees in the median of U.S. 192 because they blocked the view of the billboards. That should tell you what you need to know about how the road looks and where its values lie.

LAKE BUENA VISTA

Best for: Access to Disney, I-4 and chain restaurants, some elbow room
What you won't find: Non-Disney evening entertainment, the lowest prices, a sense of place

Lake Buena Vista is essentially part of Walt Disney World, on its eastern fringe. Because Disney bought property that straddled two counties, it had to create two corporate-run "towns," now Bay Lake and Lake Buena Vista, through which it could administer its land. You will rarely see much about Bay Lake because it's mostly an organizational entity. Lake Buena Vista, nicknamed LBV, is more prominent, mostly because it's also the name of a hotel zone east of Downtown Disney. LBV may technically be a town, but it doesn't much look like one, really, unless a town is supposed to be just hotels and restaurants on slightly winding streets.

The bottom line is that LBV is less tacky and higher-rent than Kissimmee's 192, but it's also under the sway of everything Disney, which some visitors will find tiresome.

If you stay in LBV, you can also (if you're hardy) walk to the Downtown Disney development, where you can then pick up Disney's free DTS bus system. You'll also be right next to Exit 68 of I-4, making it easy to get around town.

Vista Way, the housing development used by college-age and international Disney employees, is south of I-4 on Apopka Vineland Road. Because of its reputation as a party zone, the development is nicknamed Vista Lay. Tourists can't get in without a cast member; meet some of them at one of their hangouts, Miller's Orlando Ale House (p. 71).

INTERNATIONAL DRIVE
Best for: Walkability, cheap transportation, inexpensive attractions and food, family entertainment, proximity to Universal and SeaWorld
What you won't find: Space, style
Although a still-developing stretch of this street winds all the way south to U.S. 192, when someone refers to International Drive as an area, they mean the segment between SeaWorld Orlando and Universal Orlando, just east of I-4 between exits 71 and 75.

I-Drive, as it's called, is probably the only district where you might comfortably stay without a car and still be able to see the non-Disney attractions, since it's chockablock with affordable hotels (which are, on the whole, not as ratty as some of the U.S. 192 choices can be) and plenty of crowd-pleasing touristy things to see such as shopping malls, arcades, T-shirt shops, all-you-can-eat buffets, and dinner theatres. The cheap I-Ride Trolley, described earlier, trawls the area on a regular schedule.

I-Drive's touristic street life is varied. North of Sand Lake Road, within the orbit of Universal Orlando and Wet 'n Wild, it tends to host foreign visitors, particularly English families whose childhood holiday towns have acclimated them to promenades along touristy drags. Here, the midway games and the ice cream shops are where the action is. South of Sand Lake, closer to SeaWorld, you're more likely to find groups of domestic visitors, as the mighty Orange County Convention Center, located on both sides of I-Drive at the Bee Line Expressway/528, keeps the surrounding hotels full. On this part of I-Drive, the hotel cocktail lounge is king. North of Universal Boulevard, though, there's no street life to speak of—mostly giant malls separated by distance. Just over I-4 at Universal Boulevard, Universal Orlando's park-and-entertainment complex draws plenty of locals.

Because it runs parallel to I-4, I-Drive has excellent transport connections. Hotel and restaurant discounts may be posted on the area's business association and promotional website: **www.internationaldriveorlando.com**.

DOWNTOWN ORLANDO
Best for: Historic buildings, cafes, museums, fine art, wealthy residents
What you won't find: Theme parks, easy commutes
As much as I would like to tell you that downtown Orlando is one of America's great cityscapes, where you can park your car and stroll from boutique to restaurant, I'm afraid it simply isn't the case. Not yet, anyway. Like so many American

cities, residents fled downtown in the 1960s through the 1980s, although the city is gradually being rediscovered by young, upscale residents. Here are the highlights:

Downtown: Beneath the city's collection of skyscrapers (mostly banking offices), you'll find municipal buildings (the main library, historic museums) and a few upscale hotels (the Grand Bohemian, Courtyard at Lake Lucerne), but little shopping. Orange Avenue, once the city's main street of proud stone buildings and bustling department stores, now comes alive mostly at night, when its former cinemas and vaudeville halls essay their new roles as nightclubs. The 43-acre Lake Eola Park, just east, is often cited as an area attraction, but in truth it's just your average city park, although the .9-mile path around its 23-acre sinkhole lake is good for joggers who want to gauge distance. Just east of that, the neighborhood of **Thornton Park** (along Washington Street, Summerlin Avenue, and Central Boulevard) is noted for its alfresco European-style cafes, none especially inexpensive, where hip locals spend evenings and weekend brunches. A mile north of downtown, Loch Haven Park contains a wealth of the city's most important museums and theatre companies.

Vimi: Some old-timers might call this area **Colonial Town,** but more and more, it's known as the Vietnamese district, or Vimi. Just north of downtown, at Colonial Drive and Mills Avenue, in a mid-century neighborhood with the whiff of a faded 1950s Main Street, park your car behind any of the mom-and-pop-style eateries (advertised by cheap stick-on letters and neon, but with food far more delicious than their limited budgets would suggest) and have a stroll. Here, you'll find several omnibus Asian supermarkets stocked with exotic international groceries and unique baked goods—grab a baguette with meat and pâté, a common Vietnamese meal called *bánh mi*—for a quick $3 meal. Side by side with Asian staples, you'll find the hobby and art supply shops patronized by a burgeoning bohemian community of middle-class, suburb-raised kids who are tired of Orlando's overly corporate ethos. In some places, such as on the exterior walls of the Phó 88 restaurant on Mills Avenue, which local artists regularly beautify with changing folk-art murals, the two marginalized communities collaborate beautifully together.

WINTER PARK

Best for: Fine art, cafes, strolls, galleries, lakes
What you won't find: Inexpensive shopping

One of the city's most interesting areas, and one of the few that hasn't taken pains to cover or erase its history, Winter Park was where, 100 years ago, upstart industrialists built winter homes at a time when they couldn't gain entrée into the more exclusive, more WASPy enclaves of Newport or Palm Beach. The town, which blends seamlessly with northern Orlando (you can drive between them in a few minutes without getting onto I-4), is still pretty full of itself, but cruising on its brick-paved streets, gawking at the mansions, will always be fun. The town's long-running boat tour (p. 268) through its chain of lakes is probably the best way to see the opulence. The shops of Park Avenue, its main thoroughfare, aren't what they used to be—you'll find mostly jewelry, art, women's clothes, and at least three places selling artisanal chocolates—but a stroll down it, and into the country-club campus of Rollins College (at its southern end), are among the finer pleasures in town. Few people actually base themselves here on a theme park–centric vacation, because it'll take a half-hour to drive to the tourist district from here. The best art museum in the region, the Morse (p. 234), holds the most comprehensive collection of Tiffany glass you will ever see. West of Winter Park, over I-4, the up-and-coming district of College Park, centering around Princeton Street and Edgewater Drive, hosts restaurants and boutiques that are slowly bringing the area favor.

NORTH OF ORLANDO

Most visitors who venture into the suburban towns north of Winter Park do so to visit some of the area's natural springs or state parks (p. 234) or to connect with the spirits in the hamlet of Cassadaga (p. 258). After you've seen these places, there is little to engage you until you hit the Atlantic Coast on I-4. I know I may get angry letters for saying that. Many guidebooks will suggest you go to Mount Dora (picket fences, Victorian charm, and antiques; 40 miles northwest), but although they're nice enough, I personally don't think they rate beside the world-class attractions that should fill your itinerary. Every American city is surrounded by pleasant little towns, but that doesn't mean they're worth making up to an hour's drive to see.

SOUTH OF ORLANDO

Although the land north of Walt Disney World was long ago developed and joined with greater Orlando, only in the past few years has the swampland southwest of the resort and Kissimmee begun to be built upon in earnest, and the 65-mile run along I-4 to Tampa is gradually filling in with developments and golf courses. This patch of the Green Swamp, in which the two cities will one day merge into a megalopolis, even has a tongue-in-cheek nickname: Orlampa. A few specialty tourist sights, including Fantasy of Flight (p. 234) and Dinosaur World (p. 234), claimed land before prices got steep. Straight south of Orlando, in the town of Winter Haven, is Cypress Gardens (p. 232), Florida's most historic amusement park. Northeast of Tampa, in the part of town closest to Orlando, you'll find the excellent Busch Gardens Africa (p. 215), a worthy addition to an amusement park itinerary.

EAST OF ORLANDO

Most visitors will find themselves east of town for two reasons: to catch a flight or to watch NASA prepare theirs. The entrance to Orlando International Airport is 11 miles east of I-4, webbed into the city network by toll highways and surrounded by golfing developments at which the paint is still drying. Across empty swamp from there, the so-called Space Coast, of which Cape Canaveral is the metaphoric capital, is a 45-minute drive east of Orlando's tourist corridor via 528, also known as the Bee Line Expressway.

WEST OF ORLANDO

Because the Green Swamp commands the area, there simply isn't much west of the tourist corridor save a few small towns and some state parks like Lake Louisa (p. 268).

3

Where to Stay, in or out of the Parks

The town's best beds in hotel rooms, B&Bs, and home rentals

ORLANDO HAS MORE THAN 113,000 HOTEL ROOMS, ABOUT 20,000 SHY OF Las Vegas's record-breaking inventory, and by 2009, it will add 16,000 more. Close to 50 million visitors come here every year for theme parks, conventions, and outdoor recreation, unquestionably qualifying the city as the world's most popular family vacation destination.

As you can imagine, with numbers that large, price competition can be fierce, particularly in the budget range, where hotels regularly cut prices to the bone during lean times. But there are also plenty of places that rely on the steady stream of customers yielded by their corporate loyalty programs and don't bother to strive for excellence. Although the city hosts some incredibly elaborate resorts that, for a high price, can add to the escapism of an Orlando visit, you may be surprised to learn that, especially in terms of spaciousness, hotels are not the best accommodation value at all.

Most of Central Florida's monolithic hotel architecture steals and inflates European traditions, often on such a scale that even a Texan would blush. You'll find arcades, frescoes, columns, Spanish tiles, arched windows, and marble . . . but knock on the columns. They're hollow. Get close to the marble. It's often painted on. That's why Orlando's resorts, as much as they charge, rarely achieve true opulence. They're made by theatrical set designers, not artisans. Here, when you pay more for a fine hotel, you're mostly paying for dramatic flourishes in the public spaces that won't necessarily translate into heightened glory for your room.

Because of fierce competition from the growing condo-hotel/home rental sector, Orlando's hotels saw an occupancy decline in 2006. (That's non-Disney hotels; the Mouse doesn't release figures, although it's safe to say its occupancy rate is still the envy of the industry.) That means many off-property hotels are scrambling to fill space, and scoring deals can be easy for those who scratch around.

HOME RENTALS

It's a tradition in the Pauline Frommer series to lead off with what amounts to the most illuminating, most edifying, and most economical way to see any city in the world. Well, no, I'm not talking about staying with friends, although that's a really good idea, and if you can arrange that, you're way ahead of the game. Kindly skip this chapter. No, I'm talking about renting a home of your own.

In most guidebooks, the home rental option is relegated to a single box or a few wan paragraphs. That makes zero sense to me. For value, renting a home is quite simply the best way to go. The very first night I spent at a vacation home, stretching out on a leather sofa and watching a TV as big as a lap pool, speaking as loudly as I wanted and heading to the kitchen for periodic snacks, I dreaded having to return to the battery hen arrangement of a hotel ever again. Frankly, I'm not sure why people still want to use hotels. Probably because they don't know how sublime vacation homes are, or that many can be rented by the night. They seem too good to be true. Probably because most guidebooks only give the option a single box or a few wan paragraphs.

In recent years, the zone south of Walt Disney World has mushroomed with new housing developments. There are dozens of gated communities with street after street of shiny new two-story McMansions, each with its own pool and yard. These neighborhoods throb with activity—a line of cars pulls out of the driveways each morning and returns after dark, when the grills in the backyard fire up and the sounds of children splashing in pools drift across the green Florida lawns.

But look closely and you'll notice something strange about these neighborhoods. The homes don't have mailboxes. The garbage cans are pulled, like clockwork, to the curb by unobtrusive uniformed staff. And the residents change every week or two.

These neighborhoods are almost entirely for tourists. Developers built the first few, optimistically, to house locals, but it turned out that Orlando residents would rather live away from the tourist zone. So instead, out-of-town families purchased the homes—a British family, perhaps, that flies in for their 2 weeks a year—and they pay a management company to rent them out for the rest of the year. Each management company requires the homes it rents to meet a certain standard, which could mean cable TV in every room, high-speed Internet, a screened-in pool, or a garage converted into a screening room or game room. And every management company takes care of the nitty-gritty for you, such as laundering sheets before your arrival or wheeling out the trash bins on garbage day.

Relax. Staying in a vacation home in the Orlando area isn't like crashing in someone's house; rather, properties are usually decorated with the simple elegance of a hotel room, an empty shell waiting for (in fact, designed for) you to fill.

Almost all of these homes are located just a few miles from the property line of the Disney resort—most rental companies have a policy dictating just how far from Disney their homes are permitted to be (but do ask, just in case). Many homes take about as long to reach by car as Disney's cheapest motel rooms at the All-Star and Pop Century resorts, except for about the same amount of money, you get an entire home and not a dorm room packed with two double beds. You will also often find lifesaving perks such as video game consoles, entertainment centers, billiard rooms, and heated pools and hot tubs—often included in the price.

There are generally two kinds of homes. **Condos** are units that are attached to other units; these may have their own plunge pool, but more often they share a communal, hotel-style pool at a common clubhouse. **Houses** are free-standing and are generally about 30% more expensive than condos. They will almost always have private full pools, usually screened to keep out insects.

A good home rental is not to be confused with a timeshare. These are truly homes you rent, no strings attached. If you go with the following companies, you shouldn't have to endure a pitch to buy real estate (although most of them will be happy to tell you how to buy one of their houses if, and only if, you approach them for information on your own).

RENTAL AGENCIES

When it comes to renting a home, your biggest concern should be whether your chosen company is reputable. Shoddy maintenance is bad enough, but giving your money to an outfit that doesn't deliver anything would be a catastrophe.

In addition to being selected for their reputations, longevity, and inventory, every company listed in this guide has a satisfactory listing with the Better Business Bureau of Central Florida. Check on any company's background for the past 3 years at www.orlando.bbb.org. Another excellent resource is the Central Florida Property Managers Association, a self-policing organization for rental agencies and property managers that holds its members to high professional standards. It operates a clearinghouse website (www.vacationwithconfidence.com) through which its members rent to the public.

Rental companies represent properties in various neighborhoods, and none of them expect you to instantly know which area is best for you. A good rental agency will match your needs and budget to the most suitable property. All of these companies have pictures of each individual property available online, so all you really have to do is see something you like, point at it shouting "That one!," and then make sure it's in a location that you approve of. Don't let them talk you into something 10 miles from Disney if you'd rather be 3 miles away.

Your credit card will usually be charged a deposit ($300 is standard) about a month ahead of time. You'll also have to pay a one-time fee before your arrival that goes toward insurance or cleaning; $50 to $80 is normal, which makes stays of a single night less economical. Because it's not as easy to rent out a house as it is a hotel room, some companies are pretty tight about cancellations, too, so make sure you know if there will be a deadline for changes.

Ask your rental agency what it supplies and what you'll need to bring. Typically, you'll be given a roll or two of toilet paper per bathroom, a starter garbage bag, and maybe a packet of detergent, and you'll be expected to buy your own after those run out. Clean bath towels and sheets are supplied, but daily maid service won't be unless you pay extra for it. Restaurants and grocery stores will be no farther than they probably are from your own home—less than a mile in most cases—and certainly closer than they'd be if you were staying on Disney property. Mostly, you'll be left undisturbed to play as you wish.

When you check into a home, you will probably need to pick up your keys from the agency's main office, which will also be your contact point for problems and questions. Most of these companies are located within a few miles of the southern entry to Walt Disney World along U.S. 192 west of Interstate 4. If you arrive at night, you'll likely be asked to retrieve your keys from a lockbox; make sure you know your arrangements and have good directions before leaving home.

All of these companies provide plenty of photos of each property online. There's no reason you should rent a place without seeing it first; make sure you're satisfied that it's what you want. Some companies only post photos of their best houses and tell you that everything they rent is just as good. Those companies did not make it into this guide.

Everything represented by **All Star Vacation Homes** (7822 W. Irlo Bronson Hwy., U.S. 192, Kissimmee; ☎ 800/572-5013, 800/592-5548, or 407/997-0733; www.allstarvacationhomes.com; AE, DISC, MC, V), a thoroughly professional company, has a pool, even the condos, and everything is within 4 miles of Walt Disney World (although the company is opening units near the Convention Center, too, making it a rare outfit that caters to Universal devotees as well). Furnishings, by an in-house design team, are handsome, with lots of woods and fabrics that make most of its properties feel notably clean and new. Three-bedroom units sleeping up to eight, with a dedicated kids' room and flower beds out front, start at an incredible $119 a night, or about half of what it costs to squeeze six into Disney's cheapest family suite. Its website has ample information about each property, including photos and floor plans. Its cheapest options are its Condos and Town Homes (two to three bedrooms, tons of space, from $109), and of its three categories of stand-alone houses (Estate, Resort, and Luxury), Luxury is the most affordable, with a three-bedroom, two-bath house starting at $189, and a giant five-bedroom running $219. Full six-bedroom Luxury houses are $249—you can split that among 14 people if you've got a full house. Homes in the Windsor Hills area generally have an equal number of bathrooms to bedrooms, and the Formosa Gardens homes sit on a third of an acre, which is spacious for Florida. Prices go up as you add treats such as indoor/outdoor stereo systems, whirlpools, multiple master bedrooms, and so forth. To sweeten the deal, All Star often offers a free rental car with a 7-night stay, which takes care of another major expense, and its website frequently spotlights new properties that are going for 10% off.

Because of its attention to detail, All Star is my favorite rental agency in Orlando, and although its prices are slightly higher than its competitors, they're still far lower than most hotels. Check the remaining renters if you don't find something suitable. These companies have slightly less rigorous standards in terms of furnishings, reflected in slightly lower prices. These renters also may each represent houses in the same developments, so be sure to shop around as you may get different prices at the same developments.

The family-run **Alexander Holiday Homes** (1400 W. Oak St., Suite H, Kissimmee; ☎ 800/621-7888 or 407/932-3683; www.floridasunshine.com; AE, DISC, MC, V) has been renting since 1989, when the industry was in its infancy. It reps around 200 properties now, all of them within 12 miles of Disney, but most much closer. All of its privately owned homes come with at least two TVs and a DVD player or VCR. Its three-bedroom, two-bath homes start at $132 a night, and no property will deprive you of access to a pool, be it shared or private. Although its website spotlights deals as low as $65 for two-bedroom condos with shared pools and $80 for three-bedroom private homes, normal rates are more like $95 and $127, respectively. During peak season, it requires bookings of at least a week; otherwise, stays of 3 to 4 nights are often possible.

Another up-front business, **Florida Sun Vacation Homes** (7802 W. Irlo Bronson Hwy/U.S. 192, Kissimmee; ☎ 800/219-1281 or 407/938-0228; www.florida sunvacationhomes.com; AE, DISC, MC, V) rents homes ranging from two to seven bedrooms in the Disney area (the Windsor Hills and Windsor Palms developments in particular), with prices stating at $69 in low season and popping to $139 in high season. Three-bedrooms start at $89. All of its properties have a pool or a spa (or both). Its website is refreshingly frank about extra fees (one-time clean fees of around $75 are usually mandatory) and any minimum stays that exist for each property (3 nights is common). The company also rents condos in the Vista Cay development near the Convention Center. Like many companies, it asks that you reserve and pay at least 6 weeks in advance.

In business since late 1999, **Award Vacation Homes** (2303 Hamlin Terr., Clermont; ☎ 800/338-0835 or 352/243-8669; www.awardvacationhomes.com; AE, DISC, MC, V) has an inventory that is thickest around Highway 27, a newly developed corridor found 10 to 15 minutes west of Walt Disney World via U.S. 192 (via the Western Way back entrance, completed in 2006). Its houses are relatively new, which is an advantage, and their neighborhoods are serviced by grocery stores that are not overpriced for tourists, which is another perk, though they're also just a twitch farther from Disney than some people prefer. Strangely, European tourists don't seem to mind, so your temporary neighbors may be from overseas. For three-bedroom, two-bath places, rates start at $132 and peak at $155, depending on the week. Six-bedroom homes are $200 to $236.

Founded in the late '90s, **VillaDirect** (6129 W. Irlo Bronson Hwy., Kissimmee; ☎ 877/259-9908 or 407/397-1210; www.villadirect.com; AE, DC, DISC, MC, V) now claims some 550 Orlando-area properties of varying styles and quality on its roster. Its office is open 7 days a week, and about 70% of its inventory is located within 4 miles of the border of Disney property, particularly along the U.S. 192 corridor southwest of Animal Kingdom.

IPG Florida Vacation Homes (9550 W. U.S. 192, Clermont; ☎ 800/311-7105 or 863/547-1050; www.IPGFlorida.com; AE, DISC, MC, V) deals mostly with homes in Legacy Park, Highlands Reserve, Windsor Palms, and the Villas at Island Club, south or west of Disney. I find its furnishings a little cheaper and its service a little more mechanical than its competitors, but I can't fault the company for its 24-hour welcome center, or its comparable value: two-bedroom condos from $120 to $160, and three-bedroom homes with private pools from $140 to $200. With this company, "luxury" homes cost less than "exquisite" ones.

Although I find its website lacking in that it won't give a price breakdown until very late in the booking process, **Lowery's Vacation Homes** (7864 W. Irlo Bronson Hwy., Kissimmee; ☎ 866/397-0088; www.moremouse.com; AE, MC, V) has plenty of inexpensive and tasteful properties in the same developments as the companies above. It's a good fallback in busy seasons.

HOME RENTAL DEVELOPMENTS

Instead of dealing with rental agencies, you can also rent a home directly from the housing development that controls it. These developments, most of which consist of tightly packed but artfully situated condo units, cater to tourists and rent directly to the public. There's not really a solid reason to choose one rental style over another. Compared to dealing with rental agencies, dealing directly with these neighborhoods simplifies the selection process; if you like the location and amenities of any of these developments, your search will be over. These developments are also more likely to accept bookings for a night or two than are rental agencies. Rental agencies, on the other hand, represent properties in many different neighborhoods, which gives you more choice at the outset, and their homes tend to offer more elbow room. Rental agencies are also more likely to match you with a property that's the best fit for you.

As with rental agency houses, assume that housekeeping is not part of the bargain at developments, although your place will be clean when you check in. Some rental agencies also represent properties in these developments; such overlap is common and shouldn't alarm you. Just go with whomever offers the best deal.

At the bottom of the price range but top of the class for value, **Tropical Palms FunResort** ★ (2650 Holiday Trail, Kissimmee; ☎ 800/647-2567 or 407/396-4595; www.tropicalpalms.com; AE, DISC, MC, V) isn't a strict condo development, the way so many Orlando developments are, but a collection of pastel-colored, open-plan "cottages" that will remind you somewhat of mobile homes, and everything could use a new coat of paint. Who cares, when they start at $59 ($79–$99 is more common, but call to bargain) and include everything you need, from a full kitchen to room for four adults and four children (that's in both studios and two-bedroom cottages, although the former would be a very tight squeeze) and a sleeping loft for kids. There's also a communal heated pool, a playground, and a general store. The property is also remarkably close to Disney, on the eastern side of I-4 from it, close to all the offerings of U.S. 192.

For less of a camping vibe and more of a resort feel, the 242-unit, gated **Oak Plantation** ★★★ (4090 Enchanted Oaks Circle, Kissimmee; ☎ 407/847- 8200; www.oakplantationresort.com; AE, DISC, MC, V), a mix of one- and two-bedrooms in condo-style buildings, dates to the early 1990s, so it isn't as white-hot as some of the newer, closer developments. That makes it a terrific value. Spread around a pond as if it were more expensive, with true-as-advertised oaks, the gated Oak Plantation is popular with young families not just because it's affordable but also because it's got a warm personality. Amenities go beyond the expectation for the price level, including a free Internet cafe/kids' center, a big pool area with a tiki bar, a game room, a gym, and tennis and basketball courts. Each day, there's usually a cheap ($1–$3) family activity such as ice cream socials or cookie decorating. Units come standard with dishwashers, single-chamber washer/dryers, kitchens, and pull-out sofas. "Augusta" units (one-bedroom, sleeps four, 677 sq. ft.) are least expensive (around $109 a night). Things aren't perfect; if your upstairs neighbor is lead-footed, you'll feel it, and light sleepers should request rooms away from the pool area, which has piped-in music that starts at 7am. Its website has a specials page where deals are as low as $79 a night. The same company also operates the motel-style **Inn at Oak Plantation** (4125 W. Vine St., Kissimmee; ☎ 407/944-5600; www.theinnatoakplantation.com; AE, DISC, MC, V), right on U.S. 192, with prices from $69 to $89; be careful you're booking the right place. Both are about 6 miles east of Disney.

South of the intersection of U.S. 27 and U.S. 192, a few miles west of Walt Disney World's southern entrance, the gated community of **Bahama Bay Resort** ★ (400 Grand Bahama Bay Blvd., Davenport; ☎ 866/830-1617 or 863/547-1200; www.bahamabayresortorlando.com; AE, DISC, MC, V) is a complex of 38 two- and three-story buildings, each painted in soothing, washed-out Caribbean tones. The resort has a total of 498 condos of two or three bedrooms. Every condo has its own balcony, and many overlook Lake Davenport, a typical pond. There's a clubhouse with a fitness center, a DVD-rental desk, and an Internet cafe, plus three heated pools scattered around the property for guest use. Two-bedroom condos sleep six and cost about $99, while three-bedroom options sleeping eight go from $109 to $229, depending on how much space you want (although even the smallest condos are many times larger than a hotel room) and whether it's peak season. Its sister property, **The Enclave Suites Resort** (6165 Carrier Dr., Orlando; ☎ 800/457-0077; www.enclavesuites.com; AE, DISC, MC, V), a high-rise, is more densely packed but it's within walking distance of International Drive and close to Universal Orlando. It's also more expensive, with studio apartments that sleep four starting around $99 and two-bedroom units starting around $149 (although rates of $139 and $219, respectively, are more common).

The gated **Village at Town Center All Suite Resort** ★ (200 Village Blvd., Davenport; ☎ 800/425-7680 or 863/424-7606; www.villageattowncenterresort.com; DISC, MC, V) is neither a village nor near a town center, but at least it's "all-suite," as everything has a kitchen. You'll find this highly developed pod of three-story condo buildings one exit south of Disney on I-4 in an area that, until a few years ago, was swamp. Being slightly out of the action, even if only by a single exit, makes it more peaceful and more affordable: One-bedrooms, which have dining areas and laundry closets (something most competitors lack), cost $500 per week in low season to $750 per week in high season. Two-bedrooms are $600/$1,000 and three-bedrooms $675/$1,100. The architecture is a little Main Street–generic and buildings are too close together for my taste, but it's a good value for the location.

Encantada Resort (3070 Secret Lake Dr., Kissimmee; ☎ 800/520-8070 or 407/787-0770; www.orlandoescape.com/encantada/encantada.htm; AE, MC, V) is managed by the concern that built it, and especially in the fall and spring, it offers prices as low as $99 a night for its three-bedroom, Spanish-style town home units (at the most, prices jump $80). The development's layout of mostly straight streets is unimaginative, but in many units (which would cost around $350,000 if you bought one), first-floor rooms have 9-foot ceilings, and the decor is generally tropical and cheerful. Its "Sunrise Plan" units (three bedrooms, 2½ baths) have about 1,300 square feet and its "Tall Palm" units are four-bedroom, 3-bath and measure about 1,500 square feet (around $109). The palm-lined pool, shared by all guests, could belong to a fancy hotel.

At **Holiday Villas** (2928 Vineland Rd., Kissimmee; ☎ 800/344-3959 or 407/397-0700; www.holidayvillas.com; AE, DISC, MC, V), two-bedroom, two-bath villas sleeping six cost around $99 to $119, depending on the time of year; and three-bedroom, two-bath ones go for just $10 more. Splash out on a three-bedroom place with a computer and high-speed Internet access and prices rise to $134, while fully kitted out homes (plasma TVs, DVD players in all bedrooms, daily housekeeping) can be swung for around $229 for three bedrooms. Units have washer/dryers, two TVs with cable, and an in-room safe. The decor is plain, and the condo-style buildings date to the mid-'80s, but the location leaves little to be desired; they're 4 miles from the Disney gates by the intersection of Vineland Road and 192, near plenty of affordable restaurants and grocery stores. One downer: Every reservation gets hit with a $50 cleaning fee.

Windsor Palms ★★ (☎ 888/426-0472; www.globalresorthomes.com; AE, DC, DISC, MC, V), 10 minutes west of Disney, just off western U.S. 192, is a gated development of condos and freestanding identikit homes with as many as six bedrooms. For rentals of 5 nights or longer, it'll give you a free car rental. Two-bedroom units sharing a community pool go for $106. For the same price, you can also rent a place in the same company's Windsor Hills project, also gated and located in the same general area. All of its private homes have a private screened pool, and its condos all promise a private plunge pool. Also standard: washer/dryers and (in more expensive homes) game rooms. The layout has slightly more space than developments such as Village at Town Center, but the vibe is very much of a generic, newly built housing community.

Not gated but located on a tree-lined hotel avenue a 4-minute drive from Downtown Disney, **Celebrity Resorts Lake Buena Vista** (8451 Palm Pkwy., Lake Buena Vista; ☎ 866/507-1429; www.celebrityresorts.com; AE, DC, DISC, MC, V) is much more of a hotel-style setup than a condo rental development; from the outside, in fact, it looks like an upscale motel, which means there's less public space to play around in than other villa resorts, and the small pool is nothing posh. Units, which are comfortably shopworn, have large windows and come in either one-bedroom or three-bedroom varieties. "Mini Suites," from $53 low season/$109 high, have kitchenettes but no stoves; for cookers, you have to move up to a one-bedroom unit, which costs $79/$118. Three-bedroom units, with some 1,200 square feet accommodating up to 10 people, start at $109/$135. These are technically timeshares; just ignore any entreaties to buy.

TIMESHARES

Because this isn't a guide to real estate, I'm not going to wade into the sticky topic of timeshares. Suffice to say that there are plenty of developers and corporations (including the Walt Disney Company itself) that would love to take tens of thousands of dollars from you in exchange for the right to dwell in one of their apartments for a week or two a year. If you decide to enter into such an arrangement, then you don't need a guidebook as much as you do a good lawyer who can ensure that you can get out of the deal if you tire of it someday. You should also know that timeshares are not a sound investment because they're nigh impossible to sell for the price you paid for them (that's if you buy from a timeshare corporation; re-sales are another story).

In fact, Disney rents its timeshares to walk-up customers who have no intention of signing any dotted lines. This class of accommodation is called the Disney Vacation Club, or DVC, and it's heavily promoted to prospective buyers around the resort and even inside the theme parks themselves, which Walt surely would have detested. There are five DVC resorts: Beach Club Villas, Old Key West Resort, Boardwalk Villas, Saratoga Springs Resort and Spa, and the Villas at Disney's Wilderness Lodge. Another outpost by the Animal Kingdom Lodge is also in the works. All of them are outrageously priced. During value season, the simplest studio with a kitchen costs an insane $279, and in high season, it costs $359 a night. For that money, you could get a whole six-bedroom palace 3 miles away using a company like All Star, so I proclaim DVC a savings dud.

A few developments, particularly those with the Westgate name, will rent to temporary vacationers and then corner them with pitches to purchase time. Although I think it's acceptable for developers to let you know about the option, I don't think you should ever feel goaded or pressured into subtracting precious hours from your vacation when there are plenty of comparably priced accommodation options that don't require such a sacrifice, and for that reason, I haven't included in this book any developments with a reputation for the hard sell.

ORLANDO'S HOTELS

You'll arrive at the very first decision you need to make by answering this question: How much space would I like to have? If you have kids with you—and most visitors to Orlando's theme parks do—will a single hotel room supply the elbow room everyone needs? Does anyone in your group have funky feet or snoring issues? Does anyone hog the bathroom for 3 hours each morning? Disney hotel rooms, for example, typically have a maximum occupancy of four people in two double beds, so if your group exceeds that number, you'll have to rent two rooms or upgrade to something more expensive. For most families, renting a home or condo solves the space issue, and usually for less money than a hotel. I strongly advise that you turn back a few pages to the Home Rentals section and give some of those options a gander.

There's a second important question that will dictate your choice: Will I have a car? Unless you're a Disney-only type of person, I think you should have one, as they can speed you away from the theme parks' clutches, saving your sanity, your pocketbook, and your ability to see other parks and glimpses of the authentic city of Orlando. The cheapest hotels are only accessible by car (or by infrequent shuttles). With few exceptions, the only hotels that enable you to vacation easily without a car are the ones located on theme park property. These hotels are at least 40% more expensive than off-property ones, so often, whatever you save in not renting a car, you pay again in higher hotel tariffs, so don't be lulled by false economy. And after the fourth straight day of dwelling in the relentless theme park world, most people find themselves screaming for a break, which cars provide.

A final question helps you know which room to go for: How much time do I plan to spend at my accommodation? The things you need out of your Orlando hotel room will not be the same things that you'd need out of a hotel room on, say, a business trip. If your schedule is going to be full, and you're planning to return home only to pour yourself a bath and hit the sack, then you don't need a premium room. Staying at a pricey resort or shelling out for something with a view won't make sense because if you're in the theme parks for 12 hours a day, you won't be around to milk your purchase. Do you *really* need a fitness center after slogging around the 1.3-mile path of Epcot's World Showcase? No.

A Plan for All Seasons

Ask any hotel what it charges, and you're unlikely to get a straight answer. Almost all hotels in Orlando delight in changing their rates according to how full they are, and how much they can squeeze from tourists. As a rule of thumb, prices are highest during the holiday season, followed by all other periods in which kids are unlikely to be in school (summers, spring break), and followed by the light periods in late January, September, October, and early December. The emptier the hotel is, the more likely it'll be that rates are at their lowest. A few hotels charge a little bit more on weekends than they do on weekdays. The prices in this guide represent an average rate, and so they're typical for a night of average occupancy in a moderately busy month such as April, May, or November.

GETTING THE BEST RATES

One of the best ways to extract minimum rates from the hotels is to check the major Web discounters, including **Hotels.com**, **Priceline.com**, **Expedia.com**, **Orbitz.com**, **Skoosh.com**, and **Travelocity.com**. **Kayak.com**, **Sidestep.com**, and **Travelaxe.com** compare multiple sites simultaneously, and you'll often discover that most of the discounters offer the exact same price, across the board. Using these aggregator sites is an ideal way to get a grasp of the playing field. Also check **Hotelcoupons.com** for current discounted rates for some of the cheapest motels in town (no promises about their quality, and be forewarned that hotels frequently refuse to honor the lowest rates if they hit 75% to 80% occupancy).

Another reliable way to get a cheaper room is to buy your reservation along with an **air/hotel package.** With low-cost carriers as cheap as they are, no domestic company operates charter flights to Orlando anymore, but several packagers buy cheap hotel rooms in bulk and sell them with scheduled airfare. Whenever using these dealers, you should always do some price checks of your own to make sure you're getting a true bonus, but deals do exist. For example, **Vacation Express** (☎ 800/309-4717; www.vacationexpress.com) can do 1-week trips in March, including round-trip scheduled airfare and hotel room at a budget property, for around $525 per person. **eLeisureLink** (☎ 888/801-8808; www.eleisurelink. com) has a famous deal that pops up periodically and combines car rental, 5 nights in a non-Disney hotel, and airfare from New York or Chicago for only $399. You can also find deals from **Apple Vacations** (book through travel agents; www.applevacations.com), **Funjet** (☎ 888/558-6654; www.funjet.com), **Site59** (www.site59.com), as well as some of the vacation wings of major airlines such as **Southwest Vacations** (☎ 800/243-8372; www.southwestvacations.com), **Delta Vacations** (☎ 800/654-6559; www.deltavacations.com), **American Airlines Vacations** (☎ 800/321-2121; www.aavacations.com), and **Northwest Airlines Vacation Packages** (☎ 800/800-1504; www.nwaworldvacations.com). Increasingly, these websites will even sell hotel-only deals; American Airlines Vacations, for example, was recently selling 3 nights at the four-star Omni Orlando Resort at ChampionsGate, a golf resort a few miles south of Disney, for $285—which was equivalent to the walk-up price for just a single night.

Few of these players will truly discount a Disney hotel, although they may package Disney products without discounts. If they do, be careful to parse the pricing and compare it to a la carte options—Disney packages are notorious for including more than you could possibly need, which ends up wasting money. They're also not usually the cheapest; Southwest Vacations charges about $450 for round-trip flights from Chicago and 5 nights at a Disney Value resort, which sounds pretty good until you price-check non-Disney hotels and find out the same vacation would cost under $300. Even if you do want a Disney hotel, price be damned, I'm a big proponent of booking your Disney hotel separately from tickets or airfare; see "Inside Walt Disney World," below for more information about getting around Disney's rigged package system. When it comes to non-Disney hotels, though, package away, because that's where some great deals live. Internationally, **Virgin Holidays** (www.virginholidays.co.uk) is a huge player, with lots of customer service reps available on the ground should things go wrong.

Whenever you encounter a deal that seems to good to be true, trawl a few of the popular message boards to see who else has stayed at the motel in question and what they thought about the joint. It's the best way to make sure there's not a very unpleasant reason the price is so low. The review forums at TripAdvisor.com are active for Orlando, although I have noticed its reviews of Disney hotels tend to gush more about the Disney brand than truly appraise the quality of the rooms. (*Tip:* When a poster uses the word "magic" unironically, you may not be getting a clear-eyed appraisal.) When reading traveler review sites, I discard the out-and-out raves (which could be planted by the hotels themselves) and the venom-spitting pans (often the work of customers or competitors with a grudge) and use the middle-of-the-road reviews to glean the facts. The Yahoo! travel boards (http://travel.yahoo.com) and the message boards at Frommers.com are also smart places to collect unvarnished gossip. If all else fails, turn to the message boards at the Disney fan sites listed in chapter 12, "The Essentials of Planning" (p. 303); those posters are also more likely to be generous, but at least you'll get some feedback.

Some people trust the multitude of free newspapers and coupon books that are distributed at virtually every restaurant, rest stop, and gift shop within a 50-mile radius of Orlando. They're useful for finding the names and addresses of some of the cheaper hotel options. But don't assume that the appealingly low rates advertised in those publications are the lowest available. For example, one week in October, the Comfort Inn Lake Buena Vista was advertising a weekday rate of $59 in the free *Traveler Discount Guide.* Its own website confirmed that price, but a spot check of the major discounters (Priceline, Hotels.com, Expedia, Travelocity) yielded a price of $45, and when I showed up in its lobby and told them what I'd been quoted online, I was offered the same rate on the spot.

It's a valuable lesson. Once you've got a low quote in hand, check your hotel's website for a better deal. If the prices aren't budging lower after that, call the hotel directly to see if they will match or beat the Web discounters' quotes—after all, if properties rent directly to you, they can avoid paying commission to a middle-man. I've listed each hotel's direct number, where it's available (it usually begins with the 407 area code), right after its toll-free number (which often connects to a less helpful national reservations office), if it has one.

The major exceptions, as always, are Disney-run properties, which don't sell through third-party discounters. Disney's hotels are priced uniformly according to the season. There are sometimes some deals on offer, especially for annual pass-holders and Florida residents, and to find them, check the alerts at special web-sites including **TheMouseforLess.com** (you'll have to join the free mailing list for the scoop) and **MouseSavers.com**. If you have a AAA membership, inquire whether a hotel has special deals for you.

A warning: Don't wait until you arrive to find a room. While, yes, many hotels will be thrilled to make a deal rather than allow a room to go empty, you run the risk of sellouts. Orlando hosts some mighty big conventions, and during vacation periods, Disney itself is booked solid. That said, the **Orlando Official Visitor Center** (8723 International Dr.; ☎ 407/363-5872; www.orlandoinfo.com; daily 8am–7pm) will help you find something, but you have to go to its office in person.

WHAT TO EXPECT

If you have ever stayed in a true luxury hotel—every fixture of the finest quality and installed with impeccable craftsmanship; staff that anticipates your every whim—then you'll quickly realize that nothing in Orlando approaches a world-class level of service and quality. Here, no matter how much you pay, no matter how many amenities your hotel has (which you'll pay more for), you'll often get the feeling that you're but one of many customers feeding a giant machine, because you are. I have listed only a few high-end hotels that I feel get you the most for your dollar, either in spectacle, space, or class.

Every hotel in this book has its own swimming pool, air-conditioning, and almost every hotel offers shuttles to at least some of the theme parks, although fares around $5 to $10 per person may apply. Pretty much every hotel on this list is kid-friendly; I've noted which properties are especially generous to the young ones with a 🧒, but there are none you should fear bringing your brood to (unless noted, or unless your brood is hellishly unruly). In fact, you should expect every place on this list to be crawling with scampering, shouting children hopped up on a perpetual vacation-permitted sugar buzz. If it's an escape from kiddies you require, consider a rental home, a B&B, or one of the splurgy resort hotels that lean more toward the conference trade.

Each listing is preceded by one or more dollar signs, indicating its price range per room, not per person:

$: Up to $75 a night
$$: $76 to $125
$$$: $126 to $175
$$$$: More than $176 a night

Note: The prices in this book don't include taxes. In Orange County (Orlando, Winter Park), that's 11%; in Osceola County (Kissimmee), it's 12%.

How to Save on Lodging

- **Come during low season.** Hotel prices are trimmed then.
- **Avoid holidays.** If the kids are out of school, stay out of Orlando.
- **Be realistic about your needs.** Don't splurge on a room if you'll be on the go most of the time. The same goes for springing for a view.
- **Make sure the room you rent can fit everyone in your party.** Otherwise you'll have to rent two, doubling costs.
- **Even if you find a good rate from an online discounter (listed above), always get a quote directly from the hotel.** It might be lower.
- **See what's on offer from a packager.** Companies like Vacation Express or Southwest Vacations may discount rooms (see above).
- **A well-chosen hotel will also save you on food.** Are there affordable places to eat nearby?

B&BS

This won't take long. There aren't many in town, although the ones that exist are above average. They have to be to survive among the cut-rate competition. Orlando's B&Bs trade on romance; I'd think twice before checking in with kids.

$$–$$$ So close to the Magic Kingdom that you can see its fireworks over the trees in the yard, **The Perri House** ★ (10417 Vista Oaks Court, Orlando; ☎ 800/ 780-4830 and 407/876-4830; www.perrihouse.com; AE, DC, DISC, MC, V) is homey and quiet for something so close to the fray. It was designed and self-built by its original owners on 2 acres in the late 1980s at a time when there was nothing northeast of Disney except citrus groves. Birds such as sandhill cranes and osprey long ago learned to stop here for rest, and they remain a soothing fixture, particularly in early mornings. An ownership change in 2005 has left it slightly worse for the wear; it didn't totally amputate the place's intrinsic family-run charm, but even if the new management lacks a keen attention to detail, the change cleaned out some of the chintz and Pepto Bismol –hued decor that made it feel like sleeping in someone's house. Its eight private-bath rooms, each individually decorated in a farmhouse style with four-posters and canopy beds, encircle a communal library, but each has a private entrance accessed from the outside. Breakfast is continental and basic, but the kitchen is open to all guests to use for any meal, and the once-messy pool area (the water's unheated) is being transformed into a stylish place worth lounging in. There's a full-time caretaker, and the huge connecting one-bedroom apartment once inhabited by the owners is also available. Sleeping six, it's much larger, with taller ceilings, than condos of comparable price ($179–$289, according to the season; 6 nights' rental gets a seventh free), and its private kitchen is so large you could prepare Thanksgiving in it. Rates are $99 to $143 per night for a room, depending on the season.

$$–$$$$ So serene and scenic that it hosts around 200 weddings a year, the **Courtyard at Lake Lucerne** ★★ (211 N. Lucerne Circle East, Orlando; ☎ 800/ 444-5289 or 407/648-5188; www.orlandohistoricinn.com; AE, DC, MC, V) is snuggled under Spanish moss in an oasis of calm that's surprisingly near the towers and highways of downtown. This classy quartet of historic B&Bs, operated together, encompasses the city's oldest documented home, 1883's Norment Parry House, which has the inns' cheapest rates ($99); you'll sleep in an elegant four-poster bed among Victorian-era European antiques. Next door at the Wellborn, rent a giant original Art Deco apartment—kitchen, bedroom, the works—for a bit over $100. Kids under 13 are discouraged, preserving the tranquillity, and all rooms have TVs, phones, and private bathrooms—most with era fixtures. Retired lawyer Charles Meiner, who has meticulously run these inns since 1985, has a soft spot for Southern charm: He provides free breakfast; free parking; free cocktails every afternoon on the verandah; and for newlyweds, a free full bottle of chilled champagne upon arrival. And he'll bargain. You won't find rooms this swanky for this price anywhere else in Orlando.

$$–$$$$ Another cluster of antique buildings near downtown, **The Veranda Bed and Breakfast** (115 E. Summerlin Ave., Orlando; ☎ 800/420-6822 or 407/ 849-0321; www.theverandabandb.com; AE, DC, DISC, MC, V) starts at $99 a night for a cozy cottage with a private entrance. Where the Courtyard is genteel and pedigreed, the cloisterish, homey Veranda recalls a hidden, clapboarded getaway you might find among the inns of Key West or *Tales of the City*'s Barbary Lane. All rooms have phones, TVs, private baths, and some have furnished porches. Bear in mind that rooms facing busy Summerlin Avenue may be noisy, parking is scarce, and children are frowned upon. Both downtown Orlando and the upscale bistros of Thornton Park are a short walk away.

INSIDE WALT DISNEY WORLD

I'm listing **Disney hotels** (☎ 407/939-6244; www.disneyworld.com; AE, DC, DISC, MC, V) first, not because they're the best, but because lots of visitors want to know about them. Like it or not, some people feel like spending the night on Disney property gives them closer entry to the resort's storied "magic." There are distinct advantages and disadvantages to saying on property. How many of these considerations are important to you—or justify the expense?

Yay! The benefits of staying on Disney property:

◆ For those without cars, there's **free bus, monorail, and ferry transportation** throughout the resort. This is probably the single biggest consideration for most people. (Then again, in-resort transportation is free to *everyone* at Walt Disney World.) Be warned that "free" doesn't mean "fast": Routes can be circuitous and waits can be aggravating.

◆ **Free parking** at the theme parks (normally $10 per day).

◆ Each day, during **Extra Magic Hours,** one or two parks open an hour early or up to 3 hours past closing for the express use of Disney hotel guests. The major attractions, but not all of them, will be open during this period, and lines tend to be shorter than when general admission takes effect. (Most of the hotels on Hotel Plaza Boulevard aren't eligible for this perk.)

◆ As of press time, the resort offered free coach transfers to Orlando International Airport through the **Disney's Magical Express** program. That saves money, but not time; see p. 315 for its drawbacks.

◆ The right to charge purchases on your **room key card,** even at the theme parks. (For some, this is more of a temptation than a bonus.)

◆ The right to have your in-park **shopping delivered to your room** for you. The delivery lag time is such that this only works if you're not checking out within the next 24 hours or so.

Boo! These things about staying with Disney really stink:

◆ **Rates are 40% to 60% higher** than off-property rooms of comparable quality. Do the math; the higher cost will probably offset other benefits.

◆ A **four-person limit** in the affordable rooms. Many families have to rent two units, doubling the expense. (Happily, kids up to age 17 can stay in a room for free, even though they start paying adult ticket prices at age 10.)

◆ Most Disney resorts are so large (each Value resort is a campus of 1,920 rooms) that **lines** are an endless nuisance and **sprawling layouts are confusing** to small children, to say nothing of their parents. Disney knows it's an

Walt Disney World Area Accommodations

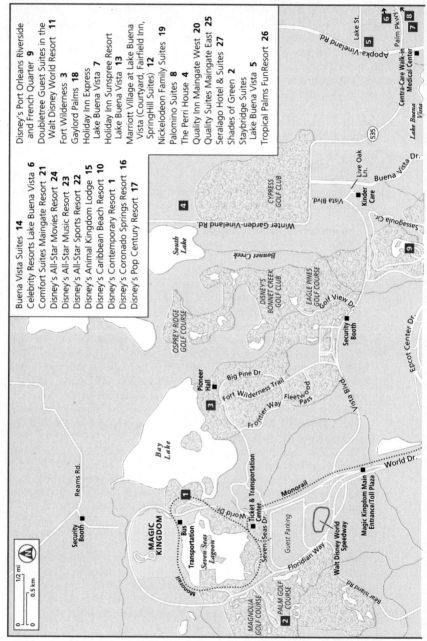

Disney's Port Orleans Riverside and French Quarter **9**
Doubletree Guest Suites in the Walt Disney World Resort **11**
Fort Wilderness **3**
Gaylord Palms **18**
Holiday Inn Express Lake Buena Vista **7**
Holiday Inn Sunspree Resort Lake Buena Vista **13**
Marriott Village at Lake Buena Vista (Courtyard, Fairfield Inn, SpringHill Suites) **12**
Nickelodeon Family Suites **19**
Palomino Suites **8**
The Perri House **4**
Quality Inn Maingate West **20**
Quality Suites Maingate East **25**
Seralago Hotel & Suites **27**
Shades of Green **2**
Staybridge Suites Lake Buena Vista **5**
Tropical Palms FunResort **26**

Buena Vista Suites **14**
Celebrity Resorts Lake Buena Vista **6**
Comfort Suites Maingate Resort **21**
Disney's All-Star Movies Resort **24**
Disney's All-Star Music Resort **23**
Disney's All-Star Sports Resort **22**
Disney's Animal Kingdom Lodge **15**
Disney's Caribbean Beach Resort **10**
Disney's Contemporary Resort **1**
Disney's Coronado Springs Resort **16**
Disney's Pop Century Resort **17**

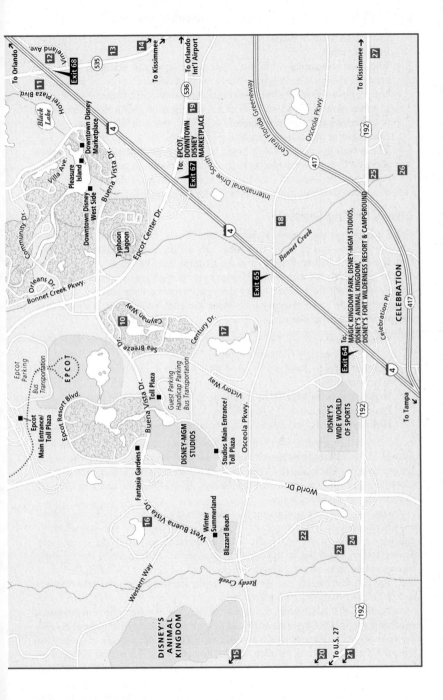

issue; it addresses it by charging more for "Preferred" rooms that aren't as far from the lobby.

◆ The most affordable rooms are about as **far from the action** as many off-property rooms. The All-Star resorts, in particular, are on a cul-de-sac in a budget ghetto that's a good 15-minute drive from the Magic Kingdom.

◆ In-room cooking is made difficult in that no affordable rooms have **microwaves** or **coffeemakers;** even **refrigerators** at Value hotels cost $10 a day—a week's rental costs as much as a room for a night elsewhere!

◆ The most affordable Disney hotels also **don't have restaurants or room service.** They have food courts (burgers, sandwiches, pasta—all at theme park prices of around $8) and they have in-room pizza delivery. This is less of a problem if you intend to save money by eating off-property anyway.

Disney Pricing Seasons

There are five pricing seasons at Walt Disney World. Forget spring, winter, and fall; the seasons you need to remember are, in descending order of expense: Holiday, Peak, Summer, Regular, and the all-important Value.

The exact dates for each season change every year and are tweaked slightly for each property, but they always follow the same pattern on the calendar. The lowest-priced Disney hotel category is its Value category, and for 2007, its schedule and pricing shake out like this:

◆ **Value season:** January 1 to February 14, August 5 to October 3, November 25 to December 19. Value resort price: $82.

◆ **Regular season:** April 15 to May 23, October 4 to November 24. Value resort price: $99.

◆ **Summer season:** May 24 to August 4. Value resort price: $109.

◆ **Peak season:** February 15 to April 14. Value resort price: $119.

◆ **Holiday season:** December 20 to December 31. Value resort price: $129.

So if you hit a Value resort during Value season, you'll be paying the least Disney allows for an on-property night. Now you're probably wondering which Disney resorts are considered "Value" resorts. There are four, and they're all fairly motel-like: the All-Star Music, All-Star Sports, All-Star Movies, and Pop Century Resort. They're reviewed below.

You're also probably wondering what happens if your stay straddles two different pricing seasons. The answer: For the duration of your stay, you pay whatever you were paying on the first night. That means you can "trick" the system into paying less by checking in during a cheaper season and lingering into a more expensive one. For instance, you could check in on February 14, when the rate is $82, and pay that nightly rate for a week despite the fact the regular price shot up to $119 on February 15. Quite a savings!

Of course, that trick works the other way, too; for instance, check in August 4 and you'll pay $109 for your entire stay despite the fact the price droops to $82 the next day. To remedy this, you need to place two phone calls to make two separate reservations, one for each season, and then ask the second operator to link your reservations. On the day when the seasons change, you will have to go to the lobby and go through the motions of checking out and checking back in (if your reservations are linked properly, you won't have to move your stuff), but you could save hundreds of dollars.

You'll hear some parents rave about the refillable mugs that cost $12 and grant unlimited sodas during your stay. Keep in mind they only work at your hotel, *not* inside the theme parks, so if you're not going to spend much time there, you may waste money. A few other touches are a relief for families: shallow kiddie pools at each resort, plus playgrounds that segregate kids by age.

If you're an annual passholder of if you own Disney stock, contact your list of benefits to see if they entitle you to discounts, when available.

Value Resorts

Although everything the Mouse does pushes you toward its most expensive hotels, the "value resort" category is in fact Disney's most prevalent, with 8,640 nightly rooms—more than many midsize cities—available for $82 to $129.

Value rooms are essentially motel-style rooms. They come with two double beds, but a few have kings (request one when you make your reservation). Irons and in-room safes are standard. Rooms fit four, plus one child under three—mind you, a full room would be a mighty tight squeeze. If your party is bigger than that, you'll have to get two connecting rooms and spend twice as much. In the classic Southern American style, Value rooms are entered from sheltered outdoor corridors, which means your sole window faces a walkway from which people can peek in if your curtains aren't drawn. Again, nothing all that different from many budget hotels in the area.

The T-shaped building blocks can feel at times like battery hen hutches, seething with kids who don't realize how sound carries, and the walk to each hotel's lobby/food building can feel like a marathon. There are elevators.

If you're going to spend most of your time away from your hotel, these may do nicely. But then again, if the quality of your lodgings doesn't matter that much to you, you might as well pay $50 and stay off-property, because Disney's Value properties won't give you much of a location advantage. They're really for that segment of the population that insists on staying on Disney property, doesn't want to break the bank doing it, and ultimately doesn't mind the diminished quality. The "magic" here is more of a trick than a treat.

Be warned that school groups pack the Value resorts, so in addition to familiarizing yourself with the boxy sprawl of the hotel's layout, you may also need to seek out the chaperone who can control your exuberant neighbors.

$$ Disney's Pop Century Resort 🧒 (1050 Century Dr., Lake Buena Vista; ☎ 407/ 938-4000; www.disneyworld.com) is Disney's well-scrubbed version of a roadside motel, with concrete-block walls, smallish (260 sq. ft.) rooms with one sink and one mirror, and for dining, a central food court not unlike the average mall's (though this one caters to 2,880 rooms). As if to counteract such dormlike austerity, the boxy sprawl of T-shaped buildings, some of which face a lake, is festooned with outsized icons of the late 20th century: gigantic bowling pins, yo-yos, and Rubik's Cubes—which kids think is pretty cool—and there are three pools. Only the first half of this resort is technically open; the second half, "the Legendary Years," planned for across the lake and to cover 1900 through the 1940s, has been in mothballs since 2001, when the existing half, "The Classic Years," opened. If this one's full, the three older All-Star hotels have nearly 6,000 more rooms cut from the same cheap terry cloth.

$$ Their setup is identical in nearly every way to the Pop Century—a huge expanse of concrete-block buildings enlivened by giant emblems, as if a giant had spilled the Legos in his toy box. But because they're older (they opened in the late 1990s) and they're landlocked, I list the three **All-Star Resorts** 🧒 (West Buena Vista Drive, Lake Buena Vista; ☎ 407/939-6244; www.disneyworld.com) second. They are slightly less populous (1,920 rooms each) than the Pop Century, which makes them marginally more manageable, and there's a McDonald's on their approach road, which, for those with cars, provides an alternative to the food court. Covering the All-Stars for *Arthur Frommer's Budget Travel* magazine in 2001, I summed them up thusly: "Depending on your point of view, Disney treats you either like a second-class guest or an average American family on vacation." Nothing has changed. Disney put the fun in the outdoor areas, not in your room—it should tell you something that the shampoo comes from a wall-mounted dispenser. At the very least, sinks are located outside of the toilet-and-shower room, which eases life for multitasking families.

By sawing a few doors through some walls at the All-Star Music resort, Disney recently opened 520-square-foot Family Suites at Music, which sleep six in two conjoined rooms and have two bathrooms, 27-inch flat-screen TVs, microwaves (but not kitchen facilities), and start at $209 in summer. That's still twice as much as a condo, where you can cook.

Of the three All-Stars, I prefer Movies, not just because it's the youngest (opened 1999) and because its decor is laden with more Disney-specific iconography than its sisters (which stick to musical and sports-equipment icons), but also because the Disney shuttle buses tend to stop there last on their circuit of the three, which cuts transportation time. Then again, some choose Sports for the same reason, as it's the first stop of the three and so it's easier to get a seat on the bus there. (That being crowded off a Disney bus should even be a concern says a lot about what the Value resorts offer—and how willing some people are to overlook poor quality in the name of their allegiance to Disney.) Disney claims that couples without kids gravitate toward Music, which is also where the suites are.

Moderate Resorts

The next price point up from Value is Moderate, which ranges from $145 to $199, escalating according to the pricing seasons roughly delineated above. Compared to the Value category, what amenities do you get for the extra dough? Put simply, the pools have slides; rooms measure 314 square feet instead of 260 square feet; most have two sinks instead of one (both outside the shower/toilet room); and you can rent a bike or a boat on the premises. The upgrade doesn't win you the right to fit more people: Rooms fit four, plus one child under 3, just as in the Value class. Unlike in the Value class, minifridges are free, but only on request.

These properties feel more resortlike and genteel when compared to the glorified motels of the Value ones, but at heart, they're still glorified motels, with dark bathrooms that a friend of mine dubs "tombs with a toilet." You'll still be eating mostly in high-priced food courts (the single restaurant at Port Orleans, for example, isn't open for lunch). Again, Moderate rooms are for people who just *have* to stay on-property, and although the bedrooms aren't really much plusher than the Value properties, you will feel like there's more breathing room and personality to the grounds, and the hotel pool areas were clearly constructed with a higher budget.

Considering what the same money buys you off-property, I can't recommend a Disney Moderate resort unless your heart is set on a particular property.

$$ If you or your spouse is an active or retired member of the U.S. military (including reserves, National Guard, U.S. Public Health Officers, and Department of Defense civilian employees), look into **Shades of Green ✦** (1950 W. Magnolia Dr., Lake Buena Vista; ☎ 888/593-2242 or 407/824-3400; www.shadesofgreen.org). A fuller list of eligibility requirements is posted online. The 586-room hotel, located within walking distance of the monorail and the Magic Kingdom, was operated as a Disney golf resort for 21 years before being handed to the military as the only Armed Forces Recreation Center (AFRC) located in the continental United States. Prices for this deluxe-level hotel, which has some of the largest standard rooms in the World, approximate those at Disney's civilian Value resorts. Rooms fit five people, one more than the Value and Moderate categories.

$$$–$$$$ **Port Orleans Riverside and French Quarter** (2201 Orleans Dr., Lake Buena Vista; ☎ 407/934-6000) has an unwieldy name because it's an unwieldy property. It's actually two resorts, both built along a canal, that have been fused together. The French Quarter, built along right angles on simulated streets, purports to imitate the real one in New Orleans, but the construction is too boxy and cheap to approximate the correct texture. Riverside, where buildings are more successful pastiches on Mississippi-style homes, is the nicer of the two, as it has more water for rooms to face (the privilege will cost you another $15 a night), the pool areas are more elaborate (there are five pools to French Quarter's one), and the activities for the two resorts ($35 carriage rides, bike rental) are located there. They are far enough apart (about 15 min. walking) that many people choose to use the free boat service linking them. The boats will also take you to Downtown Disney—the trip is one of the most pleasant, least known free rides at Disney World—but the theme parks are served only by buses.

$$$–$$$$ **Disney's Coronado Springs Resort** (1000 W. Buena Vista Dr., Lake Buena Vista; ☎ 407/939-6244; www.disneyworld.com) is another Moderate option, but it was built mostly to attract convention crowds and I think it's the blandest, least "magical" of all the Disney resorts. The rooms, though moderately priced, actually have a single sink, as in the Values; and the hotel grounds, done in a Mexican style, are too large (some rooms are a 15-min. walk from the lobby—a common problem at the lower-cost Disney resorts) and come across as uninspired. The food court is above average, though. The hotel is about 10 minutes' drive from any parks or attractions, and it's only linked by roads. For atmosphere and its ferry link, I would pick Port Orleans Riverside over Coronado Springs. However, if you need a room accessible for those with disabilities and the cheaper hotels are out of them, you can try here, where there is a slightly greater inventory.

$$$–$$$$ Finally, there's **Disney's Caribbean Beach Resort** (900 Cayman Way, Lake Buena Vista; ☎ 407/939-6244; www.disneyworld.com), the last Moderate resort, which is very much like Coronado Springs except with an island theme. Its principal drawback is the fact no other resort areas connect to it. At least Port Orleans, for the same money, has boats that go to Downtown Disney and Pleasure

Camping at Disney

As for camping at Walt Disney World, **Fort Wilderness** (3520 N. Fort Wilderness Trail, Lake Buena Vista; ☎ 407/939-6244; www.disneyworld.com; $), not to be confused with the Wilderness Lodge, a pricey imitation of Yellowstone Lodge, consists of mobile home–style cabins and RV spots. Camping under the thick pines is far and away the cheapest way to sleep on Disney property, and nightly outdoor movies and bonfires are regularly part of the deal. But at $41 to $55 a night without equipment, it's still twice the market rate for a plot. Officially, Disney only rents tents ($30 a night; not cheap) to groups of 20 or more, but people seem to get around that requirement all the time and obtain them.

Island; from Caribbean Beach, all your travel must be on the road, so it's pretty much mandatory to have a car if you stay here.

Deluxe Resorts

In terms of service, I don't consider any of Disney's Deluxe resorts—there are eight—to be worth the $350 to $500 you pay to sleep in them. I know I'm going to get letters for saying this, but no one who's experienced the world's real luxury hotels can seriously say that Disney's quality standards compare. They're pillow mills in fancy dress. Sure, they have sit-down restaurants, spas, lovely pools, and lounges. But what Disney's Deluxe hotels mostly have—well, some of them, anyway—are great gimmicks that make a stay memorable, and fantastic views of the Magic Kingdom or African animals. There are plenty of people who consider a trip to Disney a trip of a lifetime and want to celebrate by buying the top of the line, and it's in service to those people, and not because I think they're worth it, that I name my two favorites.

$$$$ There are three resorts located on the monorail line encircling the Seven Seas Lagoon, and while they all have rooms with a view of the Magic Kingdom, there's one I prefer over the rest. The Eisner-era Walt Disney Company built the Grand Floridian Resort and Spa, styled after San Diego's Hotel del Coronado, to be the crème de la crème of the resort, but its fancy airs seem blatantly classist and distinctly non-Disney to me. My top choice is the hotel it superseded, **Disney's Contemporary Resort** ★★★ (4600 N. World Dr., Lake Buena Vista; ☎ 407/824-1000; www.disneyworld.com). Some of the most vivid memories of my childhood visits to Disney World involve this fabulous hotel, one of the first two that opened with the resort in 1971. Nothing says, "I'm at Disney World" more than the awesome sight of that monorail sweeping dramatically through its glass-and-concrete canyon, which is does every few minutes on its way to and from the Magic Kingdom.

The building itself is a bit of modern architectural history, and indicative of the revolutionary methods that Walt Disney World had once hoped to pioneer. The United States Steel Corporation helped design it; its modular, pre-fabricated rooms were slotted into place by crane. The idea was that when rooms needed renovation, the capsules could simply be removed and replaced, but in practice, they fused to the steel frame, so renovations are done the old-fashioned way. A renovation was just completed, incidentally, adding soothing putty and slate colors, plus plasma TVs. The Contemporary feels more business-class and less imaginative than other Disney properties, but I like the dignity of it.

Not everyone who books here scores a balconied room high up in the coveted A-framed Contemporary Tower; there are low-level Garden Room wings along Bay Lake, too, that are $100 cheaper. Rooms on the west of the tower face the

---

The "Good Neighbor" Policy

Back in the 1970s and early 1980s, Disney World didn't think it should be in the hotel business. So it permitted several interlopers to build and operate their own bedders around the present-day Downtown Disney area, which was called Lake Buena Vista. Today, there are seven of these Downtown Disney Resort Area properties, all corporate-run (Hilton, DoubleTree, Best Western), none with special themes, and all normally priced higher than competition located as little as a half-mile away. Although some are acceptable (if very busy) as hotels, I don't find any of them worth the inflated price if you have a car. One of the cheapest of the bunch, the Grosvenor Resort, has disappointed more patrons than it has charmed. Their proximity to Downtown Disney (albeit via congested Hotel Plaza Boulevard) is listed as a selling point, but most casual visitors will be sated by a single trip to that shopping and entertainment area, so what are you paying more for? If you can find a good deal (the Best Western sometimes offers slashed prices through its corporate site), then seize upon it, but don't pick one of these places purely because you think they're going to make your vacation.

Two more luxury hotels, the Walt Disney World Swan and the Walt Disney World Dolphin (run by Westin and Sheraton, respectively), went up in the mid-1980s just west of Epcot by what's now the BoardWalk area, and their disproportionate silhouettes spoil the park's carefully planned sightlines. Although they're linked to Epcot and MGM by ferry and the other parks by bus, and some of their restaurants are excellent (if very expensive), they're not technically Disney's hotels, but Starwood's.

Scattered throughout town, even as far as the International Drive area, are properties certified as "Good Neighbor" hotels by Disney. The appellation is mostly meaningless. It means that the hotel can sell Magic Your Way tickets and screen a mesmerizing 24-hour channel featuring the insanity-inducing Stacey, the world's most spastically perky Disney fan, and her Top Seven favorites at each park. To be brutally honest, most of the Good Neighbor Hotels I've stayed in are sub-par pillow mills, plainly mediocre. Something about the added business that comes with the distinction makes a hotel care a little less about hustling for business. Don't select a hotel just because it's a Good Neighbor hotel. Choose it because it's the hotel for you.

Magic Kingdom itself—the *ne plus ultra* of Disney views—and every water-view room takes in the nightly electrical parade that floats after dark. Even if you can't stay here, drop by to see the 90-foot-tall, stylized mosaics of children by Walt Disney's contemporary Mary Blair, which encapsulate the late-'60s futurist optimism out of which the entire resort was born—an optimism that was already crashing down on November 17, 1973, when Richard Nixon gave his infamous "I am not a crook" speech here at a convention of Associated Press newspaper editors. Its top floor contains one of the best restaurants at Walt Disney World, the California Grill (p. 64). And, of course, the free monorail connects to both the Magic Kingdom and Epcot, which makes darting out of the parks for nap breaks a cinch. If money were not an object, this would be my hotel choice every time.

$$$$ I also have a soft spot for **Disney's Animal Kingdom Lodge** 🧒 ★★★ (2901 Osceola Pkwy., Bay Lake; ☎ 407/938-3000; www.disneyworld.com), styled after a grander African lodge than truly exists on the veldt, because the higher tariff returns to you in the form of a 24-hour safari. The hotel is built on a system of paddocks, so if you've got a Savannah view (they start at $285—be careful that you don't accidentally book one overlooking the pool or the parking lot), when you look out of your window or go onto your balcony, you'll see whatever African animal is happening by at that moment, be it a giraffe, an ostrich, a zebra, or a warthog. You'll find a game viewing guide in your room beside your room service menu. Because animals tend to be active in the early morning, when families are gearing up for their days, the idea works well. Like the Contemporary, anyone can pay a visit, even if they're not staying here; there's even a public viewing area straight out the back door. The Lodge's principal drawback is its distance from everything on Disney property except for Animal Kingdom; all connections are by road.

INSIDE UNIVERSAL ORLANDO

If I had to choose between staying on property at Disney and staying on property at Universal, I'd probably pick Universal. It boils down to benefits.

There are only three hotels located on Universal property, all operated by the Loews hotel group, and none of them could be considered budget. There are, however, some strong advantages that come with the higher prices. First, you don't need to use a car because all three hotels are within 15 minutes' walk of the parks, and they're also connected by a free boat launch that runs continuously into the wee hours. Also, every guest can use their room key card to make charges throughout the resort and to join the Express line at the two parks' best attractions, which means you can realistically see both parks in a single day—that perk has the effect of freeing up a vacation schedule. So while you're staying at Universal, you'll spend a lot, but can also pack more into your trip.

On the downside, parking at all three hotels is an outrageous $12 a day, and the on-site restaurants aren't remotely affordable. But at least the Universal property is surrounded by lots of real-world restaurants where prices are realistic, which Disney can't claim. You're close to the real Orlando when you're at Universal.

$$$$ Ostensibly the inexpensive option at Universal (ha!), **Royal Pacific Resort** (6300 Hollywood Way, Orlando; ☎ 888/273-1311 or 407/503-3000; www.universal orlando.com; AE, DC, DISC, MC, V) is a perfectly nice Polynesian-themed hotel with

a lush pool area and a gorgeous orchid garden, but I find its general outlook a little *blah*. Standard rooms cost $209 to $259 if you face the parking lot or highway, and about $30 more if you want to face the pool or the boat canal. It's a quick walk to Islands of Adventure.

$$$$ If I were dreaming of staying in a fancy resort hotel, I would give the **Hard Rock Hotel** ★★★ 𝖐𝖎𝖉𝖘 (5000 Universal Blvd., Orlando; ☎ 888/273-1311 or 407/503-7625; www.hardrockhotel.com; AE, DC, DISC, MC, V) a serious look. First of all, besides being the most convenient hotel among all the ones located at any theme park in town—Universal's two parks and CityWalk are all a 10-minute walk away, or you can take that boat—the 650-room Hard Rock, managed by Loews, has more perks for the money than most of the city's luxury-priced hotels. Rooms have genuinely funky furniture, tons of mirrors, two sinks (one in and one out of the bathroom), two big beds, music systems that play on your iPod, and 32-inch flatscreen TVs. The gi-normous hotel pool, which imitates a beach gently descending to depth, has not only a long water slide but also underwater speakers through which you can hear the party music (they really bring out the finger cymbals in Bon Jovi's "Livin' on a Prayer"). Even the menu of recorded wake-up calls is by rock celebs (Vince Neil from Mötley Crüe shrieks "Get the hell out of bed! All the girls are waiting for you down by the pool!"). The halls are lined with rock memorabilia (my favorite: the gold lion head Elvis was wearing when he met Nixon). You get a mix CD upon check-in, which you can play on the in-room stereo. Does it all justify prices like $224 to $294 a room? No, but if I'm going to pay prices like that, I'd rather pay them here, where I feel like I'm getting something back and it's easier to control my own destiny.

$$$$ Universal's priciest option, **Portofino Bay Resort** ★ (5601 Universal Blvd., Orlando; ☎ 888/273-1311 or 407/503-1000; www.universalorlando.com; AE, DC, DISC, MC, V), is a faithful re-creation of the bay of the famous Italian fishing village, down to the angle of the boat docks and bolted-down Vespas. Beyond that spectacular gimmick (said to have been Steven Spielberg's idea, like half the stuff at Universal), which feeds a few amenities such as opera singers on the piazza (p. 284), there are three pools and rooms (463 sq. ft.) of a high standard (they have top-end beds). But because the resort is the farthest of the three from the parks (about 20 min. by boat or foot), it tends to appeal to couples more than kids. As proof, there's also a Mandara Spa. Regular rooms cost $269 to $319 if you face the parking lot, and about $20 more to face the port.

U.S. 192 & SOUTH OF DISNEY
The tacky southernmost link in the Orlando tourist chain, U.S. 192 is where you'll find most affordable (if not always the most up-to-date) motels close to the Disney zoo. Most of the hotels were built in the 1970s growth boom and have now settled into the budget category. They are technically located in the town of Kissimmee, which maintains its own website at **www.floridakiss.com**—check it for regular deals. In this part of Orlando-dom, shuttles are often available to Walt Disney World, but not always to SeaWorld or Universal Orlando.

$ The only hostel in the entire city is the 190-bed **Palm Lakefront Resort & Hostel** (4840 W. Irlo Bronson Hwy./U.S. 192, Kissimmee; ☎ 407/396-1759;

www.orlandohostels.com; MC, V), which was once a Hostelling International property but is now privately owned and operated. It's well located for a hostel: on a part of U.S. 192 served by Lynx bus 56, which heads right to the gates of the Magic Kingdom every half-hour (trip time: 30 min.). It's actually an erstwhile low-end motel, made of cinder blocks but gussied up slightly with blue accent walls. All dorms ($19 per night), which are converted from standard motel rooms, have six wooden bunks, which may or may not be occupied when you're there (the spring is pretty busy) and share a bathroom. There are also simple private rooms (around $50) with TVs and twin beds, plus a family room with five beds. The central reception building contains an equipped kitchen (there's a Publix supermarket across the street), a foosball table, and video games, while the backyard, which has a pool, is nearly as long as the front parking lot and reaches to the bank of Lake Cecile. Like most hostels, you'll find a camaraderie between fellow travelers, no matter how shiftless or drunken they may be; impromptu summer barbecues aren't uncommon. Wi-Fi is free throughout the facility.

$ Even though its owners inherited a dated hand-me-down from Holiday Inn that once commanded the low-budget Disney market, **Seralago Hotel & Suites** (5678 W. Irlo Bronson Hwy./U.S. 192, Kissimmee; ☎ 800/411-3457; www.seralago hotel.com; AE, DISC, MC, V) works hard to appear cheerful to its guests, despite its economical price point ($50 is common for a standard room), which makes it a top value for those who just want a decent place to sleep. The early 1970s, external-corridor complex (two courtyards, two pools) has been eclipsed by newer, sexier structures. So you get low rates, but such bonuses as a basic food court and a restaurant (suggested for on-the-go grub, not dining), two playgrounds, powerful in-room A/C that could preserve meat, and a category of "two-room suites"(all of which face the pool) that are really two hotel rooms remodeled into a mini-apartment (add about $35 for those). All rooms have a microwave, fridge, coffeemaker, and a VCR—but only full-size beds, which some couples may find small. Don't accept a room facing the west unless you don't mind enduring the intermittent roar of the G-Force dragster ride (p. 226), a few blocks away. Disney's entrance is 3 miles west.

$ Nothing more than a decent crash pad, **Days Inn 192** (4104 W. Irlo Bronson Hwy., Kissimmee; ☎ 800/647-0010; 407/846-4714; www.daysinn192.com; AE, DC, DISC, MC, V) is one of the only good motels along a junky stretch of 192 that is clearly struggling to recover from the tourism's migration toward the International Drive area. You can tell by the recent paint job and modestly fresh interiors (we're talking functionality, not style, and lots of teals and salmons working hard to counteract the motel-style vibe) that its owner is paying close attention. In fact, they'll give you the boot if you lie about how many people are staying in your room. The building clearly dates to the boom of the 1970s, with outdoor corridors and an unadorned pool, but it's not horrifying considering the extreme low price. Expect racks instead of closets and aging bathroom fixtures that tend toward the drippy, but there are frills, too: All rooms have free Wi-Fi and safes, and it's hard to argue with the free (if basic) continental breakfast. Prices start in the mid-$30s and top out around $80 in peak season if you're unlucky; add $5 for a stove, fridge, and microwave. It's about 8 miles east of Disney.

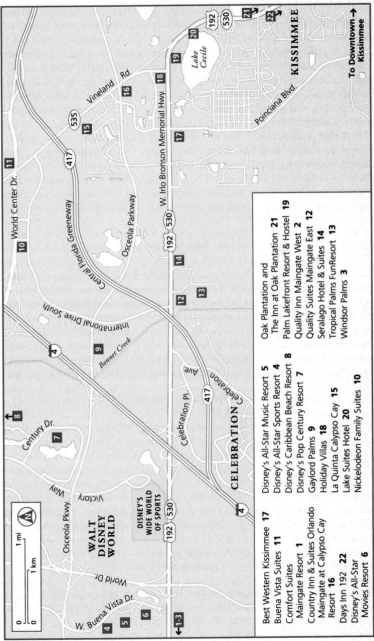

Best Western Kissimmee **17**
Buena Vista Suites **11**
Comfort Suites
Maingate Resort **1**
Country Inn & Suites Orlando
Maingate at Calypso Cay
Resort **16**
Days Inn 192 **22**
Disney's All-Star
Movies Resort **6**

Disney's All-Star Music Resort **5**
Disney's All-Star Sports Resort **4**
Disney's Caribbean Beach Resort **8**
Disney's Pop Century Resort **7**
Gaylord Palms **9**
Holiday Villas **18**
La Quinta Calypso Cay **15**
Lake Suites Hotel **20**
Nickelodeon Family Suites **10**

Oak Plantation and
The Inn at Oak Plantation **21**
Palm Lakefront Resort & Hostel **19**
Quality Inn Maingate West **2**
Quality Suites Maingate East **12**
Seralago Hotel & Suites **14**
Tropical Palms FunResort **13**
Windsor Palms **3**

$–$$ The mid-'90s era **Comfort Suites Maingate Resort** (7888 West Irlo Bronson Hwy., Kissimmee, ☎ 888/390-9888 or 407/390-9888; www.comfortsuites kissimmee.com; AE, DISC, MC, V), organized around its pool, has a quiet, low-cost resort feel that makes it popular with scrimpers. All rooms come with a small refrigerator, a microwave, and a pull-out sofa (hence the "suites" distinction of the hotel's name), and sleep from four to six people. During the week, rooms facing the parking lot cost about $69 most months, and ones facing the landscaped courtyard pool (there's recorded Caribbean music playing at the huge free-form pool all day, and a cabana bar opens at night) cost $10 more. Prices on weekends are about $10 higher. Call the hotel directly for deals, as it's always got tabs on how many rooms are empty. Although continental breakfast is included, there's a Cracker Barrel Southern-style restaurant practically in its front yard; the hotel itself is set back from the noise of U.S. 192. The lobby has a small shop for sundries, which makes life easier for adults, but kids get excited when they look down its driveway and see the summit of Expedition Everest at Disney's Animal Kingdom peeking over the trees nearby.

$–$$ The 64-room, four-story **Best Western Kissimmee** (5196 Irlo Bronson Hwy., Kissimmee; ☎ 866/232-9469; AE, DISC, MC, V) was built in 2001 and operated until late 2006 as a Baymont Suites, so this boxy place is not only relatively young, it's also small enough to ensure the family that now runs it isn't overwhelmed. King-bed suites ($90—a few have in-room whirlpools) come with a microwave and fridge, while standards have two queen beds for $70; peak prices pop to $120 to $130. Pleasantly, the hotel is set back from frenetic U.S. 192, behind an International House of Pancakes, which should appeal to light sleepers (and waffleheads). Free wireless Internet is available everywhere, and there's also a free continental breakfast and laundry facilities. The pool area feels a little naked.

$–$$ Despite the name, **La Quinta Calypso Cay** ★★★ (3484 Polynesian Isle Blvd., Kissimmee; ☎ 800/531-5900 or 407/997-1700; http://251.LQ.com; AE, DISC, MC, V) doesn't sit among the candy-colored buildings and fantastic pools of the Calypso Cay development; it's a few blocks away. The La Quinta's western-facing (read: warm) pool is better than its price point should permit, and the hotel it serves is clean, impeccably run, attractively appointed in a Spanish style, and also very high quality for the price: $79 to $99, including continental breakfast, with frequent online deals discounting those prices by $10 to $20. Family suites are not divided by proper walls, but by waist-high partitions. This hotel, which opened only in 2004, has a small arcade with air hockey for kids, and is sometimes sold as the La Quinta Inn & Suites Orlando Maingate, but whatever the name, it's the same strong value. Right outside its driveway, there's a smattering of Halal grocery stores, which is unusual for Florida.

$–$$ Although there are some minor upkeep issues to be expected of a hotel of this age and price level, I recommend the five-story **Quality Suites Maingate East** (5876 W. U.S. 192, Kissimmee; ☎ 800/268-6048 or 407/396-8040; www.quality suitesmaingate.com; AE, DC, DISC, MC, V), a half-mile east of I-4 and a mile from Disney's entrance, in part because its management is exceptionally responsive, offering a money-back guarantee if complaints can't be resolved. I also like the privacy-positive way rooms are set up: Front doors feed off an external courtyard corridor and an active pool sanctum, as they do at so many Florida motels, but the bedrooms, which are separated by a wall and a door, have windows that face out to the opposite side, the parking lot. Prices are good in low season, but you can find better deals elsewhere in high season. The one-bedroom suite ($70–$134, depending on how full it is) sleeps up to six, has a kitchen with a two-burner stove, a minifridge, and a tiny dishwasher (a rarity). "Premium" suites on the top floor ($85–$122) include DVD/VCR player, a blender, a toaster, and a bigger coffeemaker than the standard suite—hardly worth the extra cash. There are also two-bedroom suites sleeping 10. Both continental breakfast and wireless Internet come *gratis*. Double beds are on the small side.

$–$$ Five miles east of Disney, at Mile Marker 12, where the grocery stores and the restaurants get substantially cheaper, the **Lake Suites Hotel** ✖ (4786 W. Irlo Bronson Hwy., Kissimmee; ☎ 866/809-3553 or 407/997-2700; www.lakesuites hotel.net; AE, DISC, MC, V) seems from the front like a condo community, with its peaked wooden roofing and connecting decks. In fact, the nine two-story, slant-roofed houses contain a low-cost hotel with kitchen-equipped minihomes. Even better, its backside faces reedy-banked Lake Cecile (there's a dock, tiny beach, and a swimming pool, too), lending it an unexpected summerhouse feel for such a low price: $80 to $90 for two-bed "family suites" with plenty of closet space and up to $139 for duplexes sleeping up to eight people. There are some minor maintenance issues (closet doors off their tracks, some decking boards that went soft in the Florida heat and rains), but its owners took over in early 2006, so give them time. Having a full kitchen, free in-room Internet, and, in the more expensive rooms, bedroom doors that close, certainly makes for a strong value for the price. Free continental breakfast is served under a stone chimney in the chalet-style lobby.

$–$$ There's no sense pretending that the 198-room, three-story **Quality Inn Maingate West** (7785 West Irlo Bronson Hwy., Kissimmee; ☎ 800/634-5525 or 407/396-1828; www.qualityinnorlando.com; AE, DISC, MC, V) is anything more than an inexpensive place to stay. It certainly has no airs of its own. As a basic motel in an early 1970s, two-story building with outdoor corridors, it can feel gloomy at times, but it's clean and although facilities are geriatric, its upkeep seems to be a priority (the parking lot was being swept even as I pulled up for my surprise inspection—but the bedspreads are so tattered that their threads snag passing pant legs). You stay in this L-shaped standard because it's cheap, reliable, it's near tons of chain restaurants, and because it's very close to Disney (practically through the trees from Animal Kingdom). As a bonus, its free continental break-fast is bare-bones (muffins, cereal, toast) but carb-rich, and its simple heated pool, which is positioned alongside a forlorn pond, gets direct sunlight for most of the day. The rooms, too, don't feel hemmed-in. Paying $45 for a standard double is common, with surcharges of $30 to $40 when things get really busy, but I've managed to score rates in the high 20s (see the " Playing Priceline Roulette" box on p. 48). To get both a microwave and a fridge, pay another $10, or for a kitch-enette, lay out $15. A standard-issue Chinese all-you-can-eat buffet, the Golden China, is within strolling distance across the parking lot.

Playing Priceline Roulette

The mission was simple: Bid insanely low on Priceline.com and see if what I got was scary. So one week in January (low season), I pecked around on my secret-weapon site, **BiddingForTravel.com**, to find out what recent bids had been accepted. To my astonishment, even Disney's low-cost All-Star resorts were sometimes cropping up as options. Once I had a bench-mark for an off-Disney two-star property ($40), I offered Priceline $29 for any Disney-area motel. Bingo—accepted by the Quality Inn Maingate West. Next, I shopped for rental cars. Although the major renters were offering around $25 a day on their own sites, Priceline accepted a bid of $16, through Alamo. That made for a total of $35 a day for hotel *and* car—not bad. I began to kick myself for not trying even lower bids.

Once at the Alamo desk in Orlando, I had to fend off entreaties to buy extra insurance, and I even had to tear up a higher-priced contract when the desk clerk "misheard" my refusal of all those extras, but I eventually got my promised $16-a-day rate. Because things were slow, I was even offered a full minivan for that price, but I stuck with an economy for the sake of gas mileage. At the motel, I discovered that my reservation (listed under a Connecticut address, giving me away as a Priceline skinflint) was actually paired with an even *lower* rate ($27.50), but given the mandatory $1.96 "facilities fee" (said to go toward pool towels and the coffeemaker, and which I was required to pay in cash—a catch Priceline permits up to $10 a day), I ended up 46¢ in the hole. Everything else went smoothly. On the downside, I found my room was left so smoky by its previous tenant that my clothes became permeated. In defense of the motel, I could have asked to have been moved, but in the spirit of the experiment, I held my tongue and rode it out. And in defense of Priceline, I held onto my sav-ings, too. The system works.

$$ The seven-story **Country Inn & Suites Orlando Maingate at Calypso Cay Resort** ★★ (kids) (5001 Calypso Cay Way, Kissimmee; ☎ 800/456-4000 or 407/997-1400; www.countryinns.com/orlandofl_maingate; AE, DC, DISC, MC, V) doesn't deviate much from its chain's clean-and-simple style, but its inviting wet area—a kidney-shaped pool for adults, a small slide for kids, plus a few water-spitting giant crabs and lots of rocks and waterfalls—is far better than those of most hotels of its class. We can thank the candy-colored Calypso Cay development, in which it sits, for the family-friendly embellishments. Lots of extras are included, such as daily breakfast in a bright, east-facing dining room; free Web access in the lobby and by the pools; and a front desk (run by cheerful staff) that dispenses an end-less supply of free cookies. Every Tuesday, the resort throws a pool party (admis-sion $5) catered by the local T.G.I. Friday's, with live music and a raffle. I wish the rooms had balconies, but at least the windows are unusually large. I have seen price quotes from the hotel's corporate website of around $89, which is $20 less than what the big online discounters were offering. The one-bedroom suites cost about $25 more, but only get you more space, a microwave, and a fridge—no stove. Nearby, there's a Publix and a Wal-Mart. Disney is about 5 miles west. It's best to bring a car.

A Splurge

$$$$ Orlando ought to rip a page from Las Vegas's playbook and build more "event" hotels such as the **Gaylord Palms** ✪✪✪ (6000 W. Osceola Pkwy., Kissimmee; ☎ 407/586-2000; www.gaylordhotels.com/gaylordpalms; AE, DC, DISC, MC, V), where the dazzling architecture—a mighty glass atrium capping a 4.5-acre ecosystem of gator habitats, caves, indoor ponds, and shops—is an attraction unto itself and an excellent alternative to Disney's most expensive choices. It's one of the few hotels where it's more interesting to get a room facing the courtyard—they have balconies to enjoy the vista, which some find noisy but I prefer—than one facing the parking lot (which this place calls "Florida View"). Each of the 1,406 rooms, which are among the nicest in town, has a computer with Web access (even if you can only surf one window at a time), giant bathrooms (although some only have showers), and safes containing plugs for charging electronics. Such pomp comes with strings: The cheapest food among the property's five major eateries is a $7 hot dog, so you'll be in your car a lot. A $10-a-day resort fee goes toward health club access, in-room coffee, and a daily paper. Parking is also $10. The hotel, which has a Canyon Ranch spa, is popular with conventions; it's sold out a lot (prices start at $219). Even if you're too careful with your money to stay here, stop by and take a stroll through its awesome atrium—that's free. For information on its free alligator feedings, see p. 270.

LAKE BUENA VISTA

Roughly speaking, Lake Buena Vista is the area where the road past Downtown Disney emerges from Walt Disney World's eastern gate and meets Exit 68 off I-4. "LBV," as it's nicknamed, is more compact and landscaped than the comparable cluster of hotels along U.S. 192, a few miles south near Disney's southern gate. You'll find plenty of restaurant chains (Olive Garden, Uno Pizzeria) and even a high-priced grocery story in the Crossroads shopping center, directly opposite the entry to Disney property. For breathing room, my favorite part of Lake Buena Vista is Palm Parkway, a lightly trafficked, winding, tree-lined avenue of recent corporate hotels with plenty of space between them.

Those so inclined could walk to Downtown Disney (about a mile from many of these places) and then hop the free Disney bus system. Or they could even take a taxi to the Disney parks (although I'm not convinced doing so would save you much more money than an inexpensive rental car). Such convenience comes with a trade-off: You'll often pay higher prices than you have to.

$–$$ An unexpected independent find among the chain-dominated Palm Parkway hotels, the 123-unit, three-story **Palomino Suites** ✪✪✪ (8200 Palm Pkwy., Orlando; ☎ 800/936-9417 or 4070/465-8200; www.palominosuites.com; AE, DC, DISC, MC, V), fronted by palm trees as tall as itself, could be called simple but inviting. It's in terrific shape (it was briefly a Homewood Suites), and probably because it's a pipsqueak among lions, its attentive managers charge a competitively low price and even throw in breakfast. All rooms have fully equipped kitchens with full-size fridges and stoves—a rarity among hotels that usually make do with microwaves, and a lifesaver when it comes to saving money on dining. The hotel is close enough to the Disney parks to make for a realistic lunch break, and the basic pool is open until 11pm, so you can use it for end-of-the-day soaks. Rates for sizable one-bedroom suites with queen beds (TVs are found in both rooms) are regularly around $99 through the Web discounters, but $20 lower through the "Manager's Special" on Palomino's own site. You'll pay a $10 surcharge for a king bed, and about $190 for a two-bedroom unit. AAA rates for these mini-apartments can sink to the mid-$60s—an unbeatable deal, particularly for the doorstep-of-Disney plot.

$–$$ From the outside, the six-story, 200-room **Holiday Inn Express Lake Buena Vista** ★★ (8686 Palm Pkwy., Orlando; ☎ 800/465-4329 or 407/239-8400; www.hiexpress.com/lakebuenavista; AE, DISC, MC, V) doesn't look like much more than a concrete box the color of orange sherbet, but it's got a number of advantages over other hotels. First, its location is prime, near both Disney and plenty of restaurants on the westernmost stretch of quiet Palm Parkway. Rooms are spotless and come with microwaves and fridges, plus balconies made truly private by concrete walls. The pool, found out back where the frolic around its one-story waterfall and short slide won't disturb guests, is open until midnight—ideal for post-park wind-downs. There's also a well-maintained wooden playground. A light breakfast, local calls, wireless Internet, and Disney shuttles are all free, and you could feasibly walk to Downtown Disney and Pleasure Island. At $79 low/$119 high, it's a solid value.

$–$$ Internet rates of $89 are frequent, popping to $139 in peak season, at the perfectly adequate **Buena Vista Suites** ★ (8203 World Center Dr., Orlando; ☎ 800/537-7737 or 407/239-8588; www.buenavistasuites.com; AE, DC, DISC, MC, V), where every unit has a bedroom with a door that shuts, which means you can leave kids to their own devices in their own sitting/sleeping area with their own TV. Rooms also have a fridge, microwave, and coffeemaker, and full cooked breakfasts are served each morning—get there before 9am if you want a crack at the eggs. Furnishings are hardly cutting edge, but then again, it's nigh impossible to find true two-room suites for prices this low. It's close (4 min. by car) from the restaurants of Lake Buena Vista and Downtown Disney, and less than that from I-4's exit 67. In terms of space and price (rooms fit six, tightly), it's a much smarter, if much less sassy, alternative to Disney's All-Stars, which are just as far from the Magic Kingdom. The Disney shuttles are free here.

$–$$$ There are three Marriott-branded hotels collected at the well set-up **Marriott Village at Lake Buena Vista** ★ (8623 Vineland Ave., Orlando, ☎ 407/938-9001 or 877/682-8552; www.marriottvillage.com; AE, DC, DISC, MC, V): the **Courtyard** ($155, not including breakfast), the **Fairfield Inn** ($135, including continental breakfast), and the **SpringHill Suites** ($155, including a semi-divided seating area, in-room microwave, and continental breakfast). All rooms, antiseptically corporate but consequently reliable, have minifridges, free Web access, and free cribs. You might as well choose the cheapest room because all guests have the right to use any of the three heated pools at all three hotels (the squirty water jets at the Fairfield aren't extravagant, but they make for the most interesting pool for kids, and the Courtyard's pool is both indoor and outdoor). Even though I have often observed the compound's security gate to be unmanned, its presence deters intruders, and between the Fairfield and the Courtyard hotels, there's a small, intermittently open outdoor mall that includes a Pizza Hut, an ice cream store, and an arcade (and the kitschy Bahama Breeze restaurant is a safe 5-min. walk away), so you won't always have to clamber in the car to find food. Even if you decide to break out your car, the ramp to I-4 is a few hundred feet away—it scoots past the back of the Fairfield and the SpringHill, so ask for a pool-facing room if that will bother you—and the entry to Disney property is less than a mile away. Shuttles to the Disney parks cost $5 per person. The Web discounters knock the most off the Fairfield rates—through them, rooms can be as low as $69. The same discounters can knock off about $25 a night from SpringHill and $45 from Courtyard.

$$ A longtime winner in LBV, the **Holiday Inn Sunspree Resort Lake Buena Vista** ★ 🧒 (13351 State Road 535, Orlando; ☎ 800/366-6299 or 407/239-4500; www.kidsuites.com; AE, DC, DISC, MC, V) pioneered several of the perks that are now commonplace in Orlando family hotels, including 231 rooms that have special bunk areas for kids (done in themes such as dinosaurs or Noah's ark), a children's check-in desk, and a lobby with its own mini-movie theater. Everything's aging, but still in good condition. Standard queen-bed rooms go for around $81, but pay another $10, and you can get a king bed with a kitchenette that'll save you a small fortune on food. The "KidSuite" rooms go for around $100. Shuttles to Disney are free.

$$ The 150-unit **Staybridge Suites Lake Buena Vista** (8751 Suiteside Dr., Orlando; ☎ 800/866-4549 or 407/238-0777; www.sborlando.com; AE, DC, DISC, MC, V) offers apartment-like quarters in an ideal location a little bit north of the Hotel Plaza Boulevard gate to Disney World, close to lots of restaurants. The three-level buildings don't have elevators, but overlook that fact and avoid the ground-floor rooms, which are darker and less private. Breakfast, served free, is cooked and plentiful, and you can eat it indoors or in the Florida sun if you like. Management, which virtually boils the units in cleansers between rentals, leaving them permanently perfumed, reverses the sterility of the setup by throwing frequent beer parties and other afternoon mixers; there's also a well-used pool in one of the courtyards. Expect rates along the lines of $119 for a one-bedroom with a king-size bed (sleeps four), or $139 for a two-bedroom (sleeps six), with prices rising $20 to $40 when it's busy. The Disney shuttle is free. Home or condo rentals are cheaper, but you won't find many of those so close to Disney grounds. There's another 146-unit location with similar prices at 8480 International Dr. (☎ 407/352-2400; AE, DC, DISC, MC, V) just south of Sand Lake Road.

$$$ Most family-oriented Orlando hotels usually entice kids with little more than a token clown show or lame DVD nook. But the once ho-hum Holiday Inn Family Resort sank $25 million to transform into the **Nickelodeon Family Suites** ★★★ 🧒 (14500 Continental Gateway, Orlando; ☎ 800/972-2590; www.nickhotel.com; AE, DC, DISC, MC, V), an anima-psychedelic image of the basic-cable staple Nickelodeon.

The 777-unit gated hotel, with one- to three-bedroom suites arranged around two courtyards, is a full-on attack against Disney, being located just a mile east of its gates. Not only is the Nick Suites tarted up with outsized visual gags like the ones at Disney's value hotels (giant Jimmy Neutrons grinning, life-size Doras exploring) but it's also kitted out way better than Disney's moderate hotels. In the two splashdown areas, water cannons blast, a 400-gallon bucket regularly spills water over squealing kids, and seven water flumes twist. There's a food court, a 3,000-square-foot arcade, a studio for live game shows in which parents might get "slimed," and a kiddie spa for such vacation-appropriate treatments as temporary tattoos and hair braiding. The "kid suite" kitchenettes have a sink and microwave but not cookers; the "kitchen suites" have the range. Nick aims to siphon business from Disney's Character Breakfasts with its own eat-with-SpongeBob-SquarePants program. Kids get their own bedroom, with video games. Doubles start at $162—more expensive than the norm, but you do get heaps of amenities for your money. It's a good choice if you plan to spend much recharge time back at base, and it's also remarkably secure because guests must wear wristbands and visitors are not permitted. Its website promises the lowest rate, so if you find a good price from the discounters, make the hotel beat it.

$$$ I call this one the "poor man's Contemporary Resort" because its slatted concrete construction echoes the brutalist look of Disney's flagship hotel alongside the Magic Kingdom. Yet the prices at the **Doubletree Guest Suites in the Walt Disney World Resort** (2305 Hotel Plaza Blvd., Lake Buena Vista; ☎ 800/222-8733 or 407/934-1000; www.doubletreeguestsuites.com; AE, DC, DISC, MC, V), a Downtown Disney Resort Area property, aren't really for poor men either: $114 to $170. Wireless Internet in the lobby is free but costs $10 in the suites (which have a separate living area, two TVs, a microwave, and a fridge—but not kitchens), and security is lax. Some guests complain that the staff knows that its location on Disney turf means it doesn't have to jockey to provide good service, and more than a few have registered sharp disapproval that management peddles timeshares via phone messages and notes, but it's also true that it's among the best values on coveted Hotel Plaza Boulevard, near Downtown Disney, which is why I include it here. Guests can get to the Disney action with a minimum of fuss. Another solid advantage here is that its free shuttle to the Disney parks is truly continuous—every 30 to 45 minutes. Since the place is often booked solid, it doesn't frequently discount.

INTERNATIONAL DRIVE & UNIVERSAL AREA

I-Drive is probably the best place to stay if you don't have a car because it's central, well connected, and full of competing places to eat. You'll need wheels to reach Disney (most hotels offer shuttles), although Universal is just across I-4 to the north (walkable for the intrepid, a few bucks by taxi), and the dirt-cheap I-Ride Trolley (p. 11) links you with SeaWorld.

It's also the only hotel zone with a semblance of street life. If you stay here, you'll be in the thick of the family-friendly come-ons, amusement halls, minigolf, and T-shirt shops. In many ways, the low-rent arcades, ice cream parlors, and oddity museums recall the old-style sweetness you might remember from such mid-century vacation towns as Wisconsin Dells, Blackpool, or Niagara Falls. British tourists and even some locals have a penchant for strolling I-Drive's sidewalks north of Sand Lake Road on a warm evening, while the reaches of I-Drive south

International Drive Area Accommodations

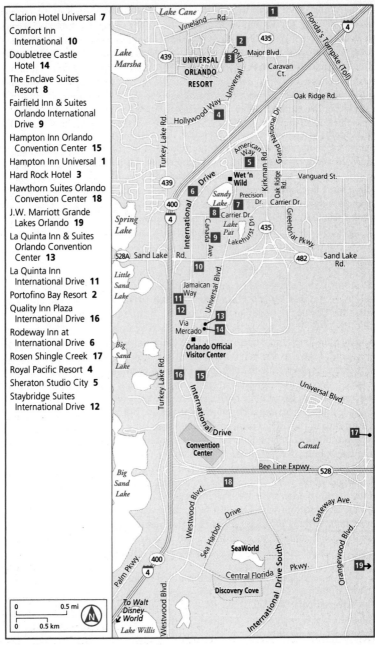

Clarion Hotel Universal **7**

Comfort Inn International **10**

Doubletree Castle Hotel **14**

The Enclave Suites Resort **8**

Fairfield Inn & Suites Orlando International Drive **9**

Hampton Inn Orlando Convention Center **15**

Hampton Inn Universal **1**

Hard Rock Hotel **3**

Hawthorn Suites Orlando Convention Center **18**

J.W. Marriott Grande Lakes Orlando **19**

La Quinta Inn & Suites Orlando Convention Center **13**

La Quinta Inn International Drive **11**

Portofino Bay Resort **2**

Quality Inn Plaza International Drive **16**

Rodeway Inn at International Drive **6**

Rosen Shingle Creek **17**

Royal Pacific Resort **4**

Sheraton Studio City **5**

Staybridge Suites International Drive **12**

of Sand Lake tend to be slightly less rambunctious and favored more by trade show–goers, as the southern anchor of the tourist zone is the mighty Orange County Convention Center. On many nights around dinnertime, car traffic can clog I-Drive, making travel a misery, but there is a workaround: Universal Boulevard, a block east, is rarely crowded and bypasses the mess.

$ Hard to beat for $65 a night in high season and a gleeful $35 in low season, **Rodeway Inn at International Drive** ✪✪✪ (6327 International Dr., Orlando; ☎ 800/999-6327 or 407/996-4444; www.rodewayinnorlando.com; AE, DC, DISC, MC, V), the largest Rodeway in America (315 rooms), is well worn, but it's clean, patrolled by security, and smack on a lively bend of International Drive near Wet 'n Wild and 2 minutes' drive from Universal, which makes finding activities and eating cheaply a breeze. The pool is heated when it's cold, security is always visible, there's free Internet and a pub in the lobby, and all rooms have a microwave and refrigerator. Just across the street is a Ponderosa serving a $3.99 breakfast buffet. Outside of high season, the rate is slashed another 30% for stays longer than 2 nights. The low rate sometimes attracts noisy kids on school break, but on balance, you can't do better at this price. A second Rodeway location a few blocks away isn't as good.

$ One of the largest budget-priced properties outside of Disney's "Value" developments, the **Quality Inn Plaza International Drive** ✪ (9000 International Dr., Orlando; ☎ 800/999-8585 or 407/996-8585; http://qualityinn-orlando.com; AE, DC, DISC, MC, V) is a 1,020-room bedding machine that sprawls over 2 city blocks and six buildings. Interstate 4 runs along the western side, resulting in a constant hum and, I have to assume, the low room rates (often $60 for the first night and $50 for subsequent nights, although I've seen promotions for as little as $40 a night). Respectably affordable units, which come standard with a fridge, microwave, and two double beds, have smoked glass windows, which helps create privacy given the external corridor construction, but doesn't help illuminate the bathrooms in the back. Furniture is lime-colored and dated (and good luck fitting a laptop in the rooms' elderly key-operated safes), but no one pays $40 expecting the latest looks. Rooms in the A building are near the lobby but suffer daytime noise from the sightseeing helicopter pad next door; opt for something in the F building, which is a 10-minute walk/2-minute drive from the lobby and has the most rooms hidden from I-4. Parking is gated but free. You'll feel like you're back on an '80s vacation with Dad just by walking past the three pools, which are big with kids working off their post-park highs. Several eateries (Sizzler, Ming Court, and Olive Garden) and a multiplex are within walking distance, on I-Drive. Universal is 10 minutes north, and SeaWorld 5 minutes south.

$–$$ A very agreeable chain hotel, the 120-room **Hampton Inn Universal** ✪ (5621 Windhover Dr., Orlando; ☎ 800/231-8395 or 407/351-6716; www.hampton innuniversal.com; AE, DC, DISC, MC, V) is a half-mile east of Universal Orlando (the shuttle is truly free), alongside Kirkman Road. Unlike the Convention Center Hampton Inn, it's not within walking distance of I-Drive, which limits nearby meal options to fast food, but if you have a car, the road connections are strong, and the place is well run, so you won't feel ripped off. The free daily breakfast is a huge plus, and so are the free local calls. Rates usually span $70 to $100.

$–$$ Found where I-Drive gives way to the gargantuan Convention Center complex, the seven-story, 170-room **Hampton Inn Orlando Convention Center** ★★★ (8900 Universal Blvd., Orlando; ☎ 800/426-7866 or 407/354-4447; www. orlandoconventioncenter.hamptoninn.com; AE, DC, DISC, MC, V) has a sense of space because it's on the edge of a cluster of other hotels. Sure, it's just like every other Hampton Inn you've ever seen (they must make these buildings from kits), but that doesn't detract from the fact the place is in good shape, there are plenty of restaurants and a multiplex within walking distance, and the cheerful staff runs a tight ship. Stays come with free wireless Internet and a bountiful all-you-can-eat breakfast, including a few hot dishes; there's also a 24-hour lobby booth selling snacks and sundries. Rack rates hover around $109, but during low and shoulder season, I have personally been quoted rates as low as $79 by the front desk clerk, who even offered to beat the hotel's competitors' prices by $1 in order to land my business. Ask for a room on the south side as these don't face other nearby buildings.

$–$$ Another reliable low-cost, motel-style crash pad, the five-story **Comfort Inn International** (8134 International Dr., Orlando; ☎ 800/313-4616 or 407/313-4000; www.comfortinn.com/hotel/FL171; AE, DC, DISC, MC, V) has 112 rooms that include fridges, coffeemakers, and continental breakfast. One bummer about this location, besides a pool that's pretty much in the parking lot, is that at the afternoon rush hour, the traffic that clogs the inadequate lanes of I-Drive can make pulling out of its driveway a chore, although there are many places to eat within walking distance. You'll pay $75 in quiet times, $90 in busier ones.

$–$$ Its gloomy lobby needs updating, but the rest of the **La Quinta Inn International Drive** (8300 Jamaican Court, Orlando; ☎ 800/531-5900 or 407/351-1660; www.orlandolaquinta.com; AE, DISC, MC, V), an aging hotel with external corridors and the usual minor inconveniences of the category, is not a bad choice if you want a clean, basic hotel near I-Drive, which is a block east. First off, the rooms' windows are on the large side, and many face an interior pool cloister instead of the whoosh of Interstate 4. The rooms facing I-4 tend to drive some guests nuts, so request accordingly. Free wireless Internet is available throughout, and a breakfast of fruit, boiled eggs, waffles, and the like, is part of the rate. Rack rates hover around $95, but prices of $55 are common online and in off months such as October or early January. Prices often pop up $20 (so, $75) during weekends. The **La Quinta Inn & Suites Orlando Convention Center** (8504 Universal Blvd., Orlando; ☎ 407/345-1365; www.laquinta.com; AE, DISC, MC, V), found roughly 2 blocks east, is of newer construction and has more space but it generally costs $20 more.

$$ Well located—a block from the ramp to Interstate 4; 5 minutes from Universal, 10 from SeaWorld, and 20 from Disney—and well run, **Fairfield Inn & Suites Orlando International Drive** ★★ (7495 Canada Ave., Orlando; ☎ 800/228-2800 or 407/351-7000; www.marriott.com/MCOSL; AE, DC, DISC, MC, V) is another vanilla chain hotel you could do worse than to stay at. Business travelers seem to use it more than families, so not only is Web access free and the rooms all have work desks, but the atmosphere is also subdued. Suites ($95–$110) are 25% larger than standard rooms ($84–$95) and have sitting/pull-out couch areas separated from the sleeping area by a closet, as well as a TV for each area.

$$ Buffered from the crush of I-4 and the kitsch klatch of I-Drive, the top value of the **Hawthorn Suites Orlando Convention Center** ✪✪ (6435 Westwood Blvd., Orlando; ☎ 800/527-1133 or 407/351-6600; www.hawthorn.com; AE, DC, DISC, MC, V) may surprise those expecting a cramped corporate hotel. Suites comprise two real rooms with a door (not one room with a wispy partition like many "all-suite" hotels), and because of the company's rep for business-travel lodging, family traffic is at a minimum and weekend deals crop up. SeaWorld is practically next door, the I-Drive Trolley stops nearby, and Disney is just 4 miles down the road. Units include equipped kitchens (two-burner range, microwave, coffee for your coffeemaker), VCR, and ironing boards. Thanks to its below-market $89 price tag during most times of the year, for such space, peace, and convenience it's a find.

$$–$$$ It's stoutly boxy, slapped with smoked glass, and ugly from the outside, but what the six-story **Clarion Hotel Universal** (7299 Universal Blvd., Orlando; ☎ 800/445-7299 or 407/351-5009; www.clarionuniversal.com; AE, DISC, MC, V) lacks in pizzazz it makes up in vacation-friendly touches. The quietish location on the eastern side of Wet 'n Wild (most odd-numbered rooms overlook the lake behind the water park) puts you a block away from the I-4 on-ramp, and you could even walk to Universal in 20 minutes if you desperately wanted to save the $10 parking fee (shuttles to the parks, and to SeaWorld, are free). There are some other convenient touches, including an on-site Enterprise rental-car agency, lighted tennis and basketball courts, a lobby shop selling sundries and sandwiches, and cooling misters blowing moist air over the otherwise roasting pool area. Breakfast is offered for $10, but the eateries of I-Drive (including a Denny's and an IHOP) are within walking distance. Its 303 rooms are fairly standard if old, with sinks both inside and outside the bathroom (good for simultaneous teeth brushings), tea- and coffeemaking facilities, and individual A/C units. Rack rates are $89 to $140, but Travelocity sometimes offers rooms for around $60.

$$–$$$ Even though it occupies one of those dated cylindrical towers, à la Fort Lauderdale's Pier 66, that were briefly in vogue in the early 1970s, **Sheraton Studio City** ✪✪ (5905 International Dr., Orlando; ☎ 800/327-1366 or 407/351-2100; www.sheratonstudiocity.com; AE, DISC, MC, V) got a makeover a few years back. The 1950s Hollywood theme is a stretch (although I appreciate the vintage car parked out front), but I like the modest size of the lobby and pool—such manageability is rare for interesting properties here. Rooms, because they're carved out of the circular floors like pie pieces, are by definition more spacious than the norm, and each has two queen beds. Just make sure you don't fall for the pricier club level (the free buffet is consumed in mere minutes), and request a room that doesn't face east, as the floodlights from the minigolf joint next door are blinding. The top floors have spectacular views of I-Drive and Wet 'n Wild (to the west) and Universal (to the north). It's not luxury, but it approximates it, and views in Orlando are rare at any price. Breakfast's $12, but there's an IHOP next door. Check the website for deals as low as $79 to $129 (advance purchase).

$$$ The **Doubletree Castle Hotel** ✪ (8629 International Dr., Orlando; ☎ 800/952-2785 or 407/345-1511; www.doubletreecastle.com; AE, DISC, MC, V) is a once-standard 216-room hotel that was stepped up with a whimsical renovation that fitted its roof with purple spires, its courtyard with gas lanterns, and each room with a six-channel system that'll play classical music day and night, if you like. For all that, and for the whimsical furniture studded with fake jewels, you'll still get a fairly standard midpriced hotel experience. I consider this a hotel that appeals more to parents who want to give their kids a slightly stylistic experience without getting too kitschy or too spendy. One minus, in addition to a dearth of outlets for charging stuff up, is that room doors tend to slam heavily, making everything nearby shudder, though considerate neighbors (luck of the draw there) will abate that problem. The festive Cafe Tu Tu Tango (p. 76) out the back door provides room service, and a cool dozen chain restaurants are within walking distance. Rooms on the uppermost, west-facing floors take in the nightly fireworks at the Magic Kingdom and Epcot, only about 2 miles away, and the front desk gives out free, warm cookies whenever you want one. Rates are around $130.

Two Splurges

$$$$ One of the only hotels in town that feels like a true resort, the 1,064-room **J.W. Marriott Grande Lakes Orlando** ★★★ (4040 Central Florida Pkwy., Orlando; ☎ 800/682-9956 or 407/206-2300; www.grandelakes.com; AE, DC, DISC, MC, V) is like a city unto itself, and indeed, it rises like a citadel in a slightly out-of-the-way 500-acre plot east of SeaWorld. I pick it as one of the best splurge hotels not attached to any theme park. Its massive pool area, landscaped with fake rocks, jungle greens, and a ¼-mile lazy river, is the poshest outside of the Disney water parks. Of course, if you want to enjoy it, you have to buy an inner tube for $5, which in my book is insulting, and if you cave and buy one, your room will stink of rubberized plastic. Yes, like many fancy convention hotels, it's a nickel-and-dime experience—everything costs, even parking—but as long as you know that in advance, the hotel's upscale amenities (gurgling lobby fountain, echoing bathrooms with separate bathtub and shower, palatial beds, narrow balconies on many rooms) are pleasing, even if the remote location means you'll have to drive every time your stomach rumbles. Guests can also use the formal pool at the Ritz-Carlton, a smaller, ultra-exclusive hotel attached by a corridor, which gives the wallet-draining JW at least a modicum of value, especially for those with a taste for caviar. The 40,000-square foot spa is well reviewed, and the nightly movie-and-s'mores bonfire is a welcome touch. Because they overlook a golf course, a nature reserve, and sunsets, west-facing rooms are best. Primo, off the lobby, is my pick for the best splurge restaurant in town (p. 78). Such splendor doesn't come cheap: You'd be lucky to find a tariff under $250. Priceline.com is a good starting point; in 2006, the J.W. appeared as the prototypical ritzy hotel in Priceline television ads starring William Shatner.

$$$$ Opened in September 2006, **Rosen Shingle Creek** (9939 Universal Blvd., Orlando; ☎ 866/996-6338 or 407/996-9939; www.shinglecreekresort.com; AE, DC, DISC, MC, V) is an elephantine convention hotel/resort—huge cathedral-like lobby, expansive grounds—suited to people who need plenty of breathing room but still want to be close to the action in town. It's named for the historic stream that its golf course now overlooks. The 1,500-room convention hotel is still finding its legs in a crowded market, so it's often possible to snare a good deal (around $100) for its luxury-level rooms, which have some of the most comfortable beds

Theme Park Shuttles: Going Your Way?

Almost all of the hotels located off theme park property tout some kind of "free" shuttle service to the major parks, but you need to know that most only go once or twice a day, on their schedule, and you have to book ahead. The Seralago Hotel & Suites (p. 44), for example, contracts with a transportation company that leaves for the Magic Kingdom twice a morning and, most days, returns at 5pm and 10pm. Epcot shuttles leave at 9:50am and 11:15am—both after the park has opened for the day—and return twice in the evening. Animal Kingdom and Disney–MGM get only one run per direction. No shuttles to Universal Orlando or SeaWorld are provided by Seralago. Other hotels offer Universal but not Disney. You have to ask.

If you can put up with restrictive schedules, then yes, you can theoretically save money by forgoing a rental car and using the shuttles. But you will pay in other ways—through wasted time and lost opportunities. You will not always be able to enjoy the parks for their full opening hours. Some shuttles leave the parks around dinnertime, which precludes you from enjoying the fireworks shows or trying any of the parks' sit-down restaurants. And you won't be able to play the day by ear.

Because many hotels share shuttles, they can be not only weathered and worn but also crowded, and you might have to stop at up to a half-dozen other properties on your way. If you're hungry, thirsty, tired, or your kids are restless, count on a frustrating, time-consuming situation.

Don't let your hotel choice be dictated by a place that promises "free" shuttles. Some of them funnel the cost back to you through other means, such as daily resort fees of $3 to $10.

Before settling on a hotel based on its advertised rides, ask questions:
1. What time do they leave and return daily?
2. Which theme parks are not covered by your shuttles?
3. How many other hotels share the same shuttle service?
4. Is there a shuttle fee of any kind?

in town. If you don't get a deal, the $230 rate won't be worth it. You'll see the resort rising from the golfing greens on its own 230-acre parcel about a mile east of the Convention Center.

A SPLURGE IN DOWNTOWN

Because of the rush-hour traffic that clogs Interstate 4, I don't recommend a stay in downtown for people who plan to do a lot of theme parking. In fact, there aren't many choices there, anyway (see "B&Bs," p. 32, for two of them). But a downtown stay brings you closer to the cafes of Thornton Park and the high-class attractions of Winter Park, just a few miles north.

$$$$ Yes, Orlando does have sophisticated hotels—if you are willing to pay through the nose and stay among the towers of the central city. The AAA-Four Diamond **Grand Bohemian Hotel-Orlando** ★★★ (325 S. Orange Ave., Orlando; ☎ 407/313-9000; www.grandbohemianhotel.com; AE, DISC, MC, V), my favorite luxury hotel in town, is genuinely stylish by virtue of not being overdone. Because its owner, Richard Kessler, is something of a dilettante, its common areas are decorated with genuinely fine art, including six original drawings by Gustav Klimt, as is the lobby, where there's a storefront gallery. An outdoor pool terrace keeps sunbathers far above city traffic, and lighting is so muted in its 250 rooms, the dark woods so dark and fabrics so indigo, that a dusky, drowsy atmosphere is created even on days when the Florida sun could blister pavement. On Sunday mornings, the intensely romantic hotel throws a brunch with live jazz musicians that's pricey ($45) but has nonetheless turned into a city staple, and by night the Bösendorfer Lounge is one of the city's few stylish martini nightspots with a following. In a city full of fake Spanish country clubs and golf resorts, the Grand Bohemian's urban panache is welcome, and consequently its lounge areas tend to attract local artists and dreamers who secretly wish they lived in Manhattan, Chicago, or San Francisco. Prices start around $199 for weekend stays during low season and shoot upward from there.

Dining Options Around Town

Beyond the same old chain restaurants, the city eats and drinks well

FOOD IS NOT ORLANDO'S STRONG POINT—THAT IS, IF YOUR STANDARDS are high. Prices are beyond market value, and recipes overdo the sugar and batter. By the end of a week here, if you see one more menu with pizza, burgers, and sandwiches, you're going to start feeling like the 240-year tradition of more nuanced American cuisine was for naught. Unfortunately, that's just how it goes at a family-oriented resort.

Happily, that doesn't mean you're fated to famish. There are places where you can find good, honest food for reasonable prices. In this chapter, I tell you all about them. Here, you will find every restaurant that's *not* located inside a theme park—that is, places you don't need a ticket to access. For places inside the parks, check out the individual park descriptions in chapters 5 and 6.

Orlando is a corporate town, and chains dominate. One could say that corporate restaurants even have a pedigree here: Darden Restaurants, which owns Red Lobster, Olive Garden, Bahama Breeze, and Smokey Bones Barbeque and Grill, is headquartered in Orlando and so is (for now) the Hard Rock Cafe empire.

But that still doesn't qualify those places as "local." Except for a few chains that are particularly useful for their value pricing, I've left ubiquitous corporate brands off this list. I'm going to assume that every family is familiar with the fare at widely planted labels such as Uno's Chicago Grill, Chili's, Panera Bread, Waffle House, and Denny's, and once you reach the areas that I name in each section of this chapter, you will find plenty of franchises from which to choose. Feel free to pick one of them if you like—I just don't think you need me to explain the value of a Whopper in a guidebook.

Where you will need help is in locating smaller restaurants, little-known chains, or ethnic kitchens that aren't backed by multimillion-dollar ad campaigns. Although as a city dweller it goes against my grain to admit it's possible, I've had countless memorable meals overlooking parking lots at anonymous-looking shopping plazas. The places named in this chapter are the ones you might never otherwise know about—or even notice among the clamor of neon signage erected by the corporate chains.

Pretty much every place is open for lunch and dinner. Don't expect any of these places to accept checks, and also don't expect to light up in post-meal satisfaction, because smoking is banned in public restaurants. Also, this is a town where it bears asking for discounts. I once had a normal breakfast at an IHOP, and as I left, the cashier told me to keep my receipt since it would entitle me to 10% off my next visit. In a high-turnover town, everybody's angling for repeat business, it seems.

My pricing symbols for a main course (at dinner):

$: $9 or less
$$: $9 to $15
$$$: $15 to $21
$$$$: $21 or over

In the month of September, a number of high-quality Orlando-area restaurants band together with the Orlando CVB and Florida Restaurant and Lodging Association to attract business by offering cut-cost, prix fixe, three-course (appetizer, entree, dessert) meals for $17 at lunch and $29 at dinner. This Orlando Magical Dining event is promoted on a special website, **www.orlandomagicaldining.com**, starting in summer, when participating restaurants are named.

WALT DISNEY WORLD

You don't have to pay an admission ticket to dine in the World. In fact, the best of Disney's restaurants are accessible to anyone. Well, not anyone: folks with deep pockets, soon to be empty. Disney's most affordable hotels don't offer much beyond food courts—places you'd never make a detour to eat unless you were already staying there—but its most expensive hotels usually boast a fine restaurant or two. Nothing sit-down could be considered budget, but because of location or other gimmicks, some could be considered interesting enough for a night out. Because you'll relentlessly be hustled to patronize them, I run down the worthiest restaurants here, but it must be repeated that for most affordable meals, you need a car to whisk you off-property. The rental expense will pay for itself after just a few meals.

Note: All Disney resort restaurants accept all of the major credit cards, and parking for restaurants at the hotels will be free with a reservation (which I emphatically suggest, without exceptions—make them as early as you can). When you make reservations through Disney, your operator will have access to the resort's schedule that day (such as fireworks showtimes), and they'll help you plan around these events if you ask.

DISNEY SPLURGE MEALS

There are no sit-down restaurants at any of Disney's Value-class resorts, but its other hotels all have at least one part-time place shoveling meals. Dinner at Disney's hotels is generally served from 5 to 10pm; none of the following places serve lunch, as it's assumed patrons will eat in the parks. A few Disney restaurants are worth highlighting for their own reasons—anniversaries and birthdays come to mind—but, this being a guide to *affordable* Orlando, only a few make the cut as the best value for their high prices. You'll hear a lot of hype about **Victoria & Albert's** (☎ 407/939-3463; www.disneyworld.com; seatings around 6 and 9:15pm), as it's the only AAA five-diamond restaurant in Central Florida. But there's something phony and ersatz about the production. Maybe it's the laughably overplayed French-American menu, maybe it's the pianist playing the hits of Andrew Lloyd Webber—a tip-off to pretension if ever there was one. I just can't shake the feeling that it's the Very Fancy Restaurant where a character might take a date on a sitcom. And the food here is wildly expensive (starting at $100 prix fixe, plus $55 for wine pairings). Try these other choices instead:

Walt Disney World Area Dining

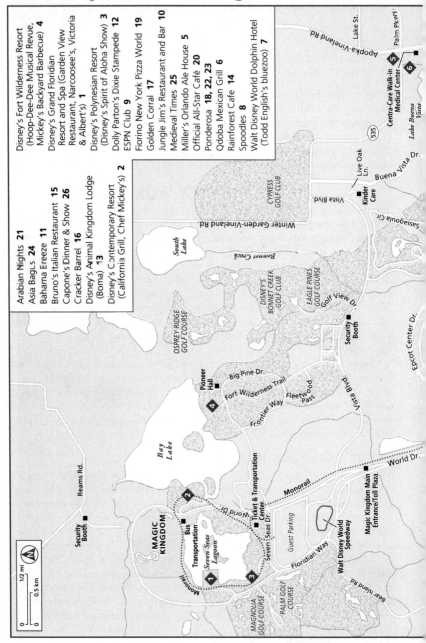

Arabian Nights **21**
Asia Bagus **24**
Bahama Breeze **11**
Bruno's Italian Restaurant **15**
Capone's Dinner & Show **26**
Cracker Barrel **16**
Disney's Animal Kingdom Lodge (Boma) **13**
Disney's Contemporary Resort (California Grill, Chef Mickey's) **2**

Disney's Fort Wilderness Resort (Hoop-Dee-Dee Musical Revue, Mickey's Backyard Barbecue) **4**
Disney's Grand Floridian Resort and Spa (Garden View Restaurant, Narcoosee's, Victoria & Albert's) **1**
Disney's Polynesian Resort (Disney's Spirit of Aloha Show) **3**
Dolly Parton's Dixie Stampede **12**
ESPN Club **9**
Fiorino New York Pizza World **19**
Golden Corral **17**
Jungle Jim's Restaurant and Bar **10**
Medieval Times **25**
Miller's Orlando Ale House **5**
Official All-Star Café **20**
Ponderosa **18, 22, 23**
Qdoba Mexican Grill **6**
Rainforest Cafe **14**
Spoodles **8**
Walt Disney World Dolphin Hotel (Todd English's bluezoo) **7**

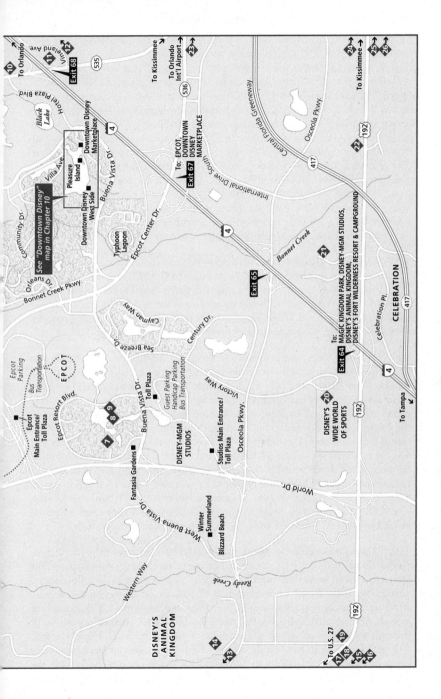

$$$$ For couples who don't want to break loose from the Disney spell—or off-property scrimpers who want to be enchanted by it for one blowout night—the best choice is **California Grill** ★★★ (☎ 407/939-3463; reservations strongly recommended; daily 5:30pm–10pm) on the 15th floor of the mod Contemporary Resort. The wine list is respectable, the open-air kitchen excels at flatbreads, sushi, and well-crafted American dishes—healthy, fresh ingredients—and right after sunset, everything stops so diners can enjoy their bird's-eye seat for the Magic Kingdom fireworks show (so book as far ahead as you can—the maximum is 180 days before—to guarantee your timing and get a window seat). Prices for main courses hover around $30, and desserts $10. After dark, Cinderella Castle is lit by a shifting palette of indigos and emeralds. The music for the fireworks is even piped in to the outdoor viewing platforms, which are practically on top of Tomorrowland. This is where I eat when I have a special event in Orlando. Plus, a dinner here is a fantastic excuse to have a stroll around Disney World's most iconic hotel and hop a post-meal ride on the monorail for free.

$$$$ If you can't get into California Grill—a common occurrence—your second choice might be the seafood-oriented **Narcoossee's** (☎ 407/939-3463; www.disney world.com; daily 6–10pm), directly across the Seven Seas Lagoon at the Grand Floridian Resort. Prices for main courses are also in the low $30s—crazy, right?—but there is a view of the Magic Kingdom that explodes with light come fireworks time, so you do get some value back if you're there during show time.

$$–$$$ If you simply must follow the flock and indulge yourself at Disney's Grand Floridian, go for high tea from 2pm to 4:30pm at the pseudo-Victorian **Garden View Restaurant** (☎ 407/939-3463; www.disneyworld.com). The Sally Lunn Tea ($13) serves buns and either trifle or strawberries and cream. Add sandwiches and scones and you're up to $18 (it's called—everybody together, now—the Buckingham Palace tea); throw in sparking wine, and you'll pay $25 (the Grand Tea)—although I would think that alcohol would spoil your palette for tea. A la carte pastries are around $4, and tea, and only tea, is $3, and although there are more than a dozen varieties, the service is not as precise and as elegant as a real English tea—think of high tea at Disney as a reasonable way to trick kids into pretending they're living the high life. Do a tea in November or December, when the Grand Floridian is decked out in its annual Christmas decorations and the hotel, so carefully designed to stoke your class pretensions, looks its most lush.

$$$$ A dinner reservation at **Boma** ★ (☎ 407/939-3463; www.disneyworld.com; daily 7–11am and 5–10pm) is an excellent excuse to visit Disney's Animal Kingdom Lodge and spend some time admiring the safari animals in its backyard paddocks, floodlit after dark. The 60-item menu is an all-you-can-eat smorgasbord in a wide, woody, ground-floor dining room that runs the gamut from roast chicken and beef to such African-themed delights as watermelon rind salad, smoked tomato soup, and *bobotie* (a moussaka-like pie of ground beef from South Africa). The food is well done for something so mass-produced, with plenty of options for less adventurous (read: younger) tongues. Adults are $26, kids $12. You will hear praise for Jiko, the a la carte place across the hall, but entrees there cost what the entire banquet does at Boma.

$$$$ The final hotel restaurant worth touting is the superb **bluezoo** ★★★ (Walt Disney World Dolphin Hotel, 1500 Epcot Resorts Blvd., Lake Buena Vista; ☎ 407/934-1111; www.swananddolphin.com/bluezoo; daily 5–11pm), one of a handful of Orlando restaurants overseen by true international culinary superstars; in this case, Todd English, celebrated at his restaurants in New York, Boston, and on the *Queen Mary 2* for his rich flavors and daring juxtapositions. Set in a cobalt-blue dining room of witty colored-glass baubles that suggest underwater imagery, its focus is fresh fish. The nightly herb-rubbed "dancing fish" is grilled on a spinning skewer (it's alongside the raw bar) and served whole; the light clam chowder comes infused with bacon; and the two-pound "Cantonese" lobster comes tossed in a sticky soy glaze and should be shared ($48). Entrees in the upper $20s are depressingly typical for Disney-property dishes, except here, you're getting craftsmanship and impeccably fresh ingredients for the same dollar. *Orlando* magazine called it one of the city's best three restaurants. You'll find it in the hotel north of Disney–MGM and west of Epcot, accessible by ferry from both.

DOWNTOWN DISNEY & PLEASURE ISLAND

These places are generally open all day from 11am for lunch, and stay open for dinner, closing at about 11pm, unless otherwise noted. The bars may keep pouring until about 1:30am, particularly on weekends. Parking is free, although in the evening, you may have to hunt for a space.

$ The most affordable option at the Downtown Disney Marketplace area, barring McDonald's, is located to its extreme east: **Earl of Sandwich** ★★ (☎ 407/938-1762; www.earlofsandwichusa.com; Sun–Mon 8:30am–11pm, Fri–Sat 8:30am–11:30pm), a branch of a six-location franchise based in Orlando. Here, you can easily grab a filling lunch, made with fresh ingredients, for $5. There are a good dozen hot and cold selections, from roast beef to ham with creamy brie, plus about a half-dozen salads. It does $2.50 granola in the morning, too. It's undoubtedly overpriced for a sandwich shop, yet it compares favorably to everything else around it.

$–$$ **Wolfgang Puck Express** (☎ 407/939-2648; daily 11am–1am) is nearly as sensibly priced ($8–$11), but it does the same stuff you've been eating all day in the parks: chicken fingers, rotisserie chicken, salads, and pizzas. Come here only if you don't feel like getting back in the car and if the sight of the Downtown Disney McDonald's makes you feel like you never left home.

$$$ Because prices at the Downtown Disney complex are so extreme, the only sit-down establishment that I can recommend is **Raglan Road** ★★ (☎ 407/938-0300; www.raglanroadirishpub.com; daily 11am–1:30am), run by an accessible, contemporary Irish chef by the name of Kevin Dundon. Of all the chefs working Downtown Disney, Dundon's got the most imagination. Here, Irish staples are turned into sprightly new visions, including whiskey-glazed "drunk" chicken with lime dressing ($7); beef stew infused with Guinness ($17); and "Kevin's Bacon," a loin of bacon with an Irish Mist glaze and creamed potato ($20). Although the 17,000-square-foot dining area is styled after an Irish pub, albeit one with Disney-appropriate inflation, it's 20 times noisier. Try the $8 bread and butter pudding. There's free live music nightly from 8pm: acoustic on

Monday and Tuesday, and electric Wednesday to Saturday. After dinner, stroll the adjoining Downtown Disney Marketplace.

$$$–$$$$ The most Disney-esque restaurant at Disney, ironically, isn't Disney's at all. It's **Rainforest Cafe** (www.rainforestcafe.com), where families dine in a faux jungle with lions, pythons, elephants, and other Animatronic animals that periodically spring to life, interrupting dinner and stoking wild behavior in small children. Think of it as the Jungle Cruise with napkins. There are two locations: One at **Downtown Disney Marketplace** (☎ 407/827-8500) and one at the gates of **Disney's Animal Kingdom** (☎ 407/938-9100, daily 8am–6pm, with extended hours on days when the park remains open late). Both have an identical, rangy menu (burgers, salads, wraps, and pizzas all peak at $13 for both meals, so stick to them; steaks, pasta, and fish straddle $20, so don't be tempted) that, like so much in Orlando, doesn't specialize in anything, instead opting to be all things to all eaters. Because the chain exists across America, you may want to do without. For the same reason, I hastily mention the mediocre Planet Hollywood, a chain that has expired just about everywhere else but here. Sandwiches at this 400-seat restaurant cost around $12, grilled meats $23—too much.

$$$–$$$$ At Downtown Disney West Side, **Bongos Cuban Cafe** ★ (☎ 407/828-0999; www.bongoscubancafe.com) was co-founded by Gloria and Emilio Estefan, the Cuban-born power couple of Latin music, who own another restaurant in Miami. Each night, a Desi Arnaz impersonator entertains. (Does Orlando have *everything* or what?) The food (ceviche, plantains, yucca, and lots of grilled or lightly fried fish and meats; mostly $16–$20 per entree) is earthier and more authentic than the hyper-sugary decor, which makes the building look like it's been overtaken by giant, washed-out pineapples, palms, and drums. Save your budget by using the walk-up window serving meaty, pressed Cuban sandwiches for $7 to $9, which are also served inside for lunch, but not at dinner.

$$$$ Downtown Disney is full of additional places that charge extreme prices ($30 a plate) but don't give your money back to you in skilled cuisine. Although none serve foul food, most of them coast along by sponging from the steady foot traffic that Downtown Disney supports. That means you can count these places as last resorts: **Fulton's Crab House** (☎ 407/939-2648), in a mock riverboat berthed with concrete to the wharf, does fresh seafood. It's one of the fancier Downtown Disney tables. Mains are easily $30 per person. And **Cap'n Jack's Restaurant** (☎ 407/939-2648) dabbles unimpressively in a range of styles, including pasta, meat, and seafood—all priced around $20.

DISNEY'S BOARDWALK

$$ Outside the International Gateway, the side exit of Epcot's World Showcase, you'll find the **ESPN Club** (☎ 407/939-5100; Mon–Thurs 11:30am–1am, Fri–Sat 11:30am–2am). Serving Boo-Yeah Chili, chicken wings, and a Hockey Puck dessert (it's a brownie), it's half restaurant and half interactive entertainment area, crammed with TV screens showing athletic matches from across the country. Instead of DJs, it employs live commentators, a witty twist. Its prices are better than Downtown Disney's Planet Hollywood, even though the menus and experiences are similar. It

Rent-a-Poppins

Parents: I know you came to Orlando to spend some time with your family, but I also understand that you might need to get away from some of them for a few hours. If you're staying in a luxury resort hotel, the management may offer some kind of paid babysitting or supervised kids' club service. If not, there are always these possibilities: **Kids Nite Out** (☎ 800/696-8105 or 407/828-0920; www.kids niteout.com) and **All About Kids** (☎ 800/728-6506 or 407/812-9300; www.all-about-kids.com). Both companies are insured, bonded, and licensed, and both would appreciate a few days' warning for reservations. In-room sitting is usually $10 to $15 per hour, plus about $10 in transportation fees. Five Disney resorts including the Polynesian and Animal Kingdom Lodge operate supervised clubs (☎ 407/939-3463) for kids 4 to 12 starting at 4:30pm and ending at midnight. These cost $10 an hour per child, including a simple meal during dinnertime, and are sometimes open to reservations by people who aren't staying in a Disney hotel. I do *not* recommend depositing your offspring at the gates of the Magic Kingdom and speeding off, as actress Tracy Pollan's father once did to her.

---

won't take reservations. At Disney's Wide World of Sports, there's a similar venture, the **Official All-Star Café** (☎ 407/827-8326; hours vary according to events), but its odd location usually means it's either quiet as crickets or, during sporting events, way too crowded.

$$$–$$$$ Also at the BoardWalk, **Spoodles** ★ (☎ 407/939-3463; daily 7–11am and 5–9:30pm) has an open kitchen and a variety of Mediterranean dishes (grilled and lemon-spritzed salmon and chicken, flatbreads, seafood stew, Greek salad; entrees $15–$29), as well as a social, fun atmosphere. What makes it popular is that it balances high quality with a setting where kids will feel welcome. Outside its front door is the BoardWalk, a lakefront promenade with a few midway games, stores, and ice cream shops—not much, but ideal for a post-meal stroll.

UNIVERSAL ORLANDO

Although Mythos (p. 200) is the only restaurant inside the Universal theme parks that's worth a detour, there are worthwhile dining options in Universal Orlando that are outside the parks—ones for which you don't need a park ticket. Universal's three hotels host upscale restaurants, while the CityWalk outdoor party mall, located between the resort's main parking garage and the entrances to the parks, attracts plenty of young local people who have more sensible budgets and no intention of proceeding to the thrill rides.

If you're intending to linger at CityWalk (p. 202) and partake of some of the nightlife options (parking is free after 6pm unless there's a big event on), note that there are a few package deals that combine a meal or a movie with entry to the clubs. The **Meal and Movie Deal** (☎ 407/224-2691; $21.95), which pairs dinner with a movie at CityWalk's ABC multiplex, can be purchased at any CityWalk ticket window or kiosk and redeemed at any sit-down CityWalk restaurant, except Emeril's. The abbreviated menu available to you will consist of six or eight of the most popular dishes, but conveniently, you don't have to enjoy both meal and movie on the same day.

Entrees cost more than they would outside Universal; they're mostly priced in the teens, with burgers sliding in around $10. So although none of these places are at the top of my list for a value meal, and none of them are true gourmet experiences, you may find yourself tempted into patronizing one after a long day at the parks. Call ☎ 407/224-3663 for more information unless there's another number listed. Because they siphon the same post-theme park customers, the ambiance at all of these restaurants is the same—loud, cavernous, family-friendly, often with faux antiques bolted to the walls. These places accept all major credit cards except Diners Club (the two Emeril establishments do accept that one).

$–$$ Pat O'Brien's ★★ (☎ 407/224-2106; www.patobriens.com; daily 4pm–1am), like its bawdy Nawlins namesake, does Cajun-style dishes such as shrimp gumbo ($6 a bowl), po' boys ($10), and jambalaya ($15). The specialty of the house, which is done up to be an exact replica of the watering hole's original location in the French Quarter of the Big Easy, is the potent Hurricane cocktail. The strong drinks account for a clientele with fewer kids than the other CityWalk choices, but there is a kids' menu.

$$ Contrary to Jimmy Buffett's shoeless persona, there's little that's relaxing about **Jimmy Buffett's Margaritaville ★** (☎ 407/224-2155; www.margaritaville orlando.com; daily 11:30am–2am), a bustling but outgoing burger-and-salads joint, especially when Islands of Adventure closes and half its patrons pour into here for margaritas and Cheeseburgers in Paradise. Silly it is, but it's also a fun atmosphere for the money. Opposite the restaurant, under a 60-foot Albatross plane, the *Hemisphere Dancer,* is The Lone Palm Airport, an open-air kiosk for margaritas and appetizers. After 10pm, it morphs into a nightclub and there's a $5 cover. It doesn't do reservations, but it does do Priority Seating, which puts your name near the top of the wait list; I suggest using this option.

$$–$$$ Bob Marley—A Tribute to Freedom (☎ 407/224-3663; daily 4pm–2am) does Jamaican food (spicy jerk chicken, fried plantains, even oxtail) and takes reservations. It turns into a reggae nightclub after 8pm, and on Thursdays Red Stripe beer is $3.25. The selection of seafood is better here than at most CityWalk places, and although appetizers are $10, entrees are too and contain plenty of food.

$$–$$$ Hard Rock Cafe (www.hardrock.com; daily 11am—1am) is, well, a Hard Rock Cafe, albeit the world's largest (600 seats) and potentially the loudest. By now, you've probably already sampled the Hard Rock shtick: A burger tavern done up with music memorabilia and a casual good time. It's situated midway between Universal Studios Florida and Islands of Adventure. Naturally, there's a gift shop attached. Interestingly, this is the second Hard Rock Cafe to be at Universal; the original one, which was shaped like a huge guitar, was torn town to make way for the Kidzone expansion at Universal Studios Florida.

$$–$$$ Pastamoré Ristorante & Market ✦ (daily 5pm–midnight) does Italian and has an outdoor cafe section that's less expensive ($; 8am–2am). Because Italian is popular, this place is, too, and it tends to be noisy and busy. That lends to the happy mood but puts a dent in conversation. Veal parmigiana, the pinnacle of many menus' prices, is $19; most dishes cost $4 to $6 less.

$$–$$$ NBA City (☎ 407/363-5919; www.nba.com/nbacity/orlando; daily 11am–10pm) is the Hard Rock for basketball nuts, with a similarly wide-ranging burgers-and-pasta menu but jerseys instead of Stratocasters on the walls. There's an interactive area (test your jumping and free-throw skills). Prices usually span $15 to $20 for entrees.

$$–$$$ NASCAR Sports Grille (☎ 407/224-7223; www.nascarcafeorlando.com; daily 11am–10:30pm) has a specific theme, but a non-specific menu: Think of a high-octane T.G.I. Friday's, with lots of race memorabilia and tableside plasma screens. NASCAR fans might enjoy the pseudo-museum aspect, but non-fans will shrug. Basically, whether you pick this place, the Hard Rock, or NBA City, you're getting much the same experience, vibe, and solidly American food, but with a specialized theme. Pick your pastiche. The restaurant completed a renovation in early 2007, too early to re-review, but if the past is a guide, prices start at $10 for chicken and zoom to $20 for rib combos.

$$–$$$$ Latin Quarter ✦ (daily 4–10pm) has a pan-Latin menu (really, *really* "pan"—are nachos considered indigenous?) and frequently hosts live music. If you're in no mood for the chains and themes of CityWalk, I'd pick this place, although the food is no revelation—and no, ribs are not Latin even if you flavor them like guava. Typical entrees are $16 to $19, but its "Express" window does handheld and stewed foods for cheap ($5–$7.50).

$$–$$$ Bubba Gump Shrimp Co. (www.bubbagump.com; daily 11:30am–midnight), one of the most recent additions, is one of the wide-reaching chains and it does shrimp a billion ways, including some you never would dream up yourself (Boat Trash, which is a bucket of deep fried shrimp, slipper lobster, mahimahi, and fries is $17). The walls appear to have a bit of boat trash on them, too. Sandwiches and salads cost around $10, but shrimp specials add another $6.

$$$$ Emeril's Restaurant Orlando ✦✦ (☎ 407/224-2424; www.emerils.com; reservations suggested; daily 11:30am–2pm, Sun–Thurs 5:30–10pm, Fri–Sat 5:30–11pm) is the single CityWalk establishment that meets a standard of fare that could be considered gourmet in the outside world. The menu, with its heart in modern New Orleans, runs a gamut between seafood, pasta, and meats, with flavors typified by embellishments such as bourbon-caramel glaze. The wine list could send you reeling even before you have a single sip—the back wall is a 12,000-bottle aboveground cellar built to dazzle. The eight counter seats, from which you can watch the brilliant chefs keep pace with the relentless demand yet still churn out beauties, are the best, but you'll have to book at least a month ahead for them. The kitchen takes a break between lunch and dinner from 2pm to 5:30pm, but if it doesn't cut into your theme park time, try for lunch, as it's much cheaper (entrees cost about $21, versus $32 at dinner) yet still offers a similar menu. Happily, it offers a kids' menu ($10 for most dishes), which makes adult pleasures more possible. Book at least a month ahead.

$$$$ Should Emeril's be full, Emeril Lagasse runs a second restaurant at the Royal Pacific Resort, a few hundred yards away. Lagasse's TV persona is brassy to the point of crudity, but at **Emeril's Tchoup Chop** ★★★ (6300 Hollywood Way, Orlando; ☎ 407/503-2467; www.emerils.com; daily 11:30am–2pm, Sun–Thurs 5:30–10pm, Fri–Sat 5:30–11pm), secreted in the courtyard of Universal Orlando's Polynesian-themed hotel, his ostensibly Hawaiian creations have more nuance. A signature dish (they change and cost $15–$35) is the "clay pot," a mélange of fish with yellow Thai lobster cream, stir-fry shrimp, and fire roasted sweet corn rice. The daffy colors of the high-ceilinged dining room, exuberantly embellished by David Rockwell in rich orange and cobalt glass, are more a nod to Orlando's boundless showmanship than a portent of a saccharine meal.

U.S. 192 & LAKE BUENA VISTA

If you want truly inexpensive eats priced at market rates, you simply have to leave Walt Disney World. The good news is it doesn't take long. About 7 minutes after driving past the security kiosks at Disney's Value-class hotels, you can reach one of two major zones that are crowded with every chain restaurant known to familydom. The southern zone, U.S. 192, goes both east and west from Disney's southern gate. The eastern zone, Lake Buena Vista, is located about a mile east of the Downtown Disney area. The two zones are linked by a few miles of Interstate 4, making it easy to shift from one to the other when you've exhausted the first. Because of stoplights and traffic, it's marginally quicker to reach U.S. 192 from most spots in Disney.

$–$$ Probably my favorite little-known "find" in the Disney Zone, **Bruno's Italian Restaurant** ★★★ (8556 W. Irlo Bronson Hwy., Kissimmee; ☎ 407/ 397-7577; daily 11am–11pm; AE, DC, DISC, MC, V), a few miles west of the southern Disney gate, is not at first glance somewhere you'd think to stop. It shares a building with a ghastly, low-rent tourist-trap shack painted with killer whales. But resist the impulse to pass on by because there really is a Bruno in the kitchen, and he makes sublime Italian classics to order, well sauced and finely garlicked. Pasta ($8.50–$13) comes with a garden salad and garlic rolls, which amounts to a lot of food for the price. Don't settle for what's on the menu, which includes New York-style, thin-crust pizzas; Bruno's often got a secret daily special, such as a lovely braciole ($11–$17), and he offers daily desserts such as hand-filled cannoli and light tiramisu with the perfect hint of alcohol. Open for lunch and dinner every day, it also delivers to the many rental vacation homes in the area.

$ **Qdoba Mexican Grill** (12376 C.R. 535/Apopka Vineland Rd., Lake Buena Vista; ☎ 407/238-4787; www.qdoba.com; daily 11am–11pm; AE, DISC, MC, V) puts a premium on fresh ingredients and makes fast burritos, tacos, and quesadillas. Flavors range from the usual Tex-Mex to such oddities as a Poblano Pesto Burrito with chicken ($6.30), and the three-cheese Queso Burrito ($6.70). Although it's a chain, it's a small one. Meals aren't as oversized as they are at chains such as Chipotle, to which it's most similar, but Qdoba's menu is wider.

$ Peter Fiorino co-owns **Fiorino New York Pizza World** (7531 U.S. 192, Kissimmee; ☎ 407/390-9664; daily 11am–11pm; AE, DISC, MC, V), one of many faceless fast-food joints on a stretch of Irlo Bronson Highway a mile west of Disney's entrance, but he's the only dough-stretcher in the area whose skills earned him a place on the U.S. Pizza Team (www.uspizzateam.com) as a competitor in the 2007 World Pizza Championship in Italy. It's pizza and only pizza, but it's the pizza of champions. The parlor has been in business since 1986. Pies are sold whole starting at $8.

$–$$ For those who've never been to one, the way to get seated at a **Cracker Barrel** ★ (5400 W. U.S. 192, Kissimmee; ☎ 407/396-6521; www.crackerbarrel. com; Sun-Thurs 6am–10pm, Fri–Sat 6am–11pm; AE, DISC, MC, V), a widespread highway chain, is to walk through the wooden porch, past the rocking chairs, and talk to the hostess at the back of the general store. She'll grab your cutlery packs from a bin—you can grab a few table puzzles, if some are on hand—and off you'll go to the dining area. As you can see, the shtick here is Southern charm. The cooking here is Southern, too, the portions are unwieldy, and deals are strong: $7 buys a plate of meat and two vegetables. In fact, $7 seems to be the magic number; it's the price of salads and thick sandwiches with soup or fries, too. Sides are big enough to share among a family (I prefer the Vidalia onion rings; $3). Breakfast ($5–$7 for most entrees, piled high with biscuits and grits) is served all day. That's why, although this is a well-known highway chain, I recommend it. It's about 3 miles west of the Disney southern entrance.

$–$$ **Miller's Orlando Ale House** (12371 C.R. 535/ Apopka Vineland Rd., Lake Buena Vista; ☎ 407/239-1800; www.alehouseinc.com; Mon-Sat 11am–2am; Sun 11am–midnight; AE, MC, V), open until 2am daily, is a hangout popular with Disney cast members after their shifts are over, so open your ears by the bar if you want to hear the dirt. It's nothing more than a spacious, pubby sports bar (the TVs are on mute during the day) with big wooden booths, 75 beers from which to choose, and a menu of casual favorites such as burgers ($5–$8), pastas ($10–$12), salads ($3.30–$9), and a raw bar ($5.50 for six). Zingers ($8), miraculously boneless chicken wings dipped in your choice of sauces, are the house dish; I'm sure I don't want to know how they're made. It's an option for people who have overdosed on cutesy T.G.I. Friday's.

$–$$ A casual hangout in the Crossroads shopping center, just east of Downtown Disney, **Jungle Jim's Restaurant and Bar** (12501 S.R. 535, Lake Buena Vista; ☎ 407/827-1257; www.jungle-jims.com; daily 11am–2am; AE, MC, V) looks like a sports bar with a few wax gorillas here and there. Its menu, which can be taken inside or on a minor outdoor patio, is loaded with salads, clubs, artery-clogging appetizers, cocktails from $4.50 to $6, and 22 burgers available in beef, chicken, or veggie ($7–$9.50). Happy hour is 4 to 7pm and 11pm to 2am (that's happy 6 hours, so livers beware). Because nothing in Orlando is subtle, you might as well try the Headhunter ($16)—a 1½-pound loaded burger with about a pound of fries. If you polish it off ("everything but the paper and the toothpick," warns the menu), you get the next one free. If you live.

$–$$ One of the best regular values in the city is the daily $3.99 all-you-can-eat breakfast buffet at **Ponderosa** ★★ (7598 W. Irlo Bronson Hwy., Kissimmee; ☎ 407/396-7721; daily 7:30–11am and 11:30am–10pm; AE, MC, V), a mile west of the entrance to Disney on U.S. 192. Sure, it's the sort of buffet where you can't distinguish the banana pudding from the vanilla yogurt just by looking at it. But there's tons of food—from pancakes to pineapple to a full salad bar—and you can gorge on as much as you dare (beverages are extra). Many people do, and watching the gluttony may curb your appetite. They even fire up the self-serve ice cream machine during breakfast for super-indulgent parents. The buffet's a lifesaver for people who need energy to march through the theme parks all day, and when you walk out the door, you're often handed a coupon for 10% off dinner (ask if you don't get one). Other locations are sprinkled around town where they're most useful: Another on the section of U.S. 192 east of I-4 (5771 W. Irlo Bronson Hwy. Kissimmee; ☎ 407/397-2477); one near the Nickelodeon Family Suites hotel (8200 World Center Dr., Kissimmee; ☎ 407/238-2526); one a quarter-mile north of SeaWorld (8510 International Dr., Orlando; ☎ 407/354-1477); and one a quarter-mile south of Wet 'n Wild, near Universal Orlando (6362 International Dr., Orlando; ☎ 407/352-9343).

$$ Bizarre as it is to find a tasty outpost in a strip mall beside a Publix and a fish-and-chips joint, the 10-table **Asia Bagus** ★★ (2923 Vineland Rd., Kissimmee; ☎ 407/397-2205; Mon–Fri 11:30am–3pm, daily 5–10pm; AE, DC, MC, V) is in fact a rare Indonesian restaurant. It's also one of the few ethnic mom-and-pop places that's within driving distance of Disney. Indonesian food, if you haven't tried it, is flavorful, not too spicy, and big on rice and noodles. I like the *tahu geirot* (Javanese-style sweet soy-fried tofu; $4.95) and the *nasi rames* (jasmine rice with beef, boiled egg, and little dried anchovies served as a garnish; $11), but I tend to order the *nasi goreng* ($8.95), which is a traditional fried rice mixed with chicken sate. Ask to try *Kecap Bango,* a thick, sweet soy sauce; and *sambal* ($2), a fiery relish eaten with just about everything. Dessert brings a real treat that few Indonesian places include on their menus: *es cendol* ("ice chendol"), made of finely shaved ice topped with grass jelly and condensed milk—you can eat a heap without feeling too guilty (it's flavored ice!) and it wards off the Florida heat. This simply decorated storefront also does some sushi and charges $8 to $10.

$$ The closest a meal can get to porn, **Golden Corral** ★★ (7702 W. U.S. 192, Kissimmee; ☎ 407/390-9615; www.goldencorral.net; daily 8am–10pm; AE, DISC, MC, V) is an immoderate orgy of food, food, and more food—all for $7 at breakfast or lunch, or $10 at dinner (kids $5/$7; dinner starts at 4pm). Although it's a chain, those prices can rescue a tight budget. Here, you're handed your first plate upon entry and directed to a maze of steam tables, where you can eat until you bust a seam. It's amazing what it takes to get some people to stop. The specialty dish changes daily; just try battling the queue on Monday, fried shrimp night. Perhaps no fact is more telling than that the desserts area is bigger than the salads area, or that mayonnaise is virtually considered a vegetable (beware the so-called "BLT salad"). There are enough healthy choices, including baked sweet potatoes and Idaho potatoes, steamed vegetables, and roasted beef, but typical customers sharpen their elbows to get to the fried chicken and macaroni and cheese. Takeout costs $4 a pound. Tip your server—then the scales! There are other locations

Where to Find Groceries near Disney

Because few locals live around Disney, the grocery stores near Disney's borders cater to vacationers and are more expensive than they should be. Patronizing them, however, is still much cheaper than paying theme-park prices for your meals. Drive an extra 5 or 10 minutes from Disney's gates, and you'll be rewarded with prices that are a good 10% lower. Stores open 24 hours are noted below, and all accept major credit cards, except Diners Club.

If you're staying in the I-Drive/Universal area, finding a market-rate grocery store is not a challenge because, unlike Disney, the area is surrounded by neighborhoods where locals live. Sand Lake Road west of I-4 is a good place to start, as is Conroy Road, north of Universal Orlando.

Higher prices, but closer:

◆ **Gooding's** (in the Crossroads Shopping Center, 12521 S.R. 535, across from the Downtown Disney/Hotel Plaza Boulevard gate, Lake Buena Vista; ☎ 407/827-1200; www.goodings.com). The nearest to Disney, it's a rare carpeted grocery store. Its deli sells $7 roasted chickens and $5 sandwiches.

◆ **Winn-Dixie Marketplace** (7840 U.S. 192; ☎ 407/397-2210; www. winn-dixie.com). About 3 miles west of Disney.

Lower prices, but slightly farther:

◆ **Publix** (14928 E. Orange Lake Blvd.; ☎ 407/239-4989; www.publix. com). Despite its address, it's located about 4 miles west of Disney on U.S. 192.

◆ **Publix** (17445 U.S. 192; ☎ 352/243-0529; www.publix.com). Located about 7 miles west of Disney, just before U.S. 27.

◆ **Publix** (2915 Vineland Rd., ☎ 407/396-7525; www.publix.com). About 3½ miles south on 535/Vineland from the Downtown Disney/ Hotel Plaza Boulevard gate.

◆ **Publix** (2925 International Dr., Kissimmee; ☎ 407/397-1171; www. publix.com). The turn-off is about 2½ miles east of Disney, north of U.S. 192.

◆ **SaveRite** (1532 W. Vine St./U.S. 192, Kissimmee; ☎ 407/847-5970; www.winn-dixie.com). About 8 miles east of Disney.

◆ **Wal-Mart Supercenter** (1471 E. Osceola Pkwy., Kissimmee; ☎ 407/ 870-2277; www.walmart.com; open 24 hr.). Drive east on Osceola Parkway, or avoid a toll by heading 2 miles south on 535/Vineland from the Downtown Disney/Hotel Plaza Boulevard gate.

◆ **Wal-Mart Supercenter** (4444 W. Vine St./U.S. 192, Kissimmee; ☎ 407/846-6611; www.walmart.com; open 24 hr.). Very crowded location 5 miles east of Disney.

handily spread about, including about 6 miles east of Disney (2701 W. Vine St./U.S. 192, Kissimmee; ☎ 407/931-0776) and where I-Drive meets Sand Lake Road (8032 International Dr., Orlando; ☎ 407/352-6606).

$$ Sounds like a rum, eats like a Friday's. **Bahama Breeze** ★ (8735 Vineland Ave., Lake Buena Vista; ☎ 407/938-9010; www.bahamabreeze.com; Sun–Thurs 11am–midnight, Fri–Sat 11am–1am; AE, DISC, MC, V) is a chain, but its theme has a light touch, so it's often full of families in a fine mood. The menu is creative, but if the food might be a bit heavy after a day at the theme parks—fried hot wings ($4), coconut shrimp ($15), calamari ($9), and jerk shrimp ($10)—at least the atmosphere is merry and tropical, and the blended drinks are something you might otherwise have at a swim-up bar somewhere. There's a second location on I-Drive, within walking distance of many hotels (8848 International Dr., Orlando; ☎ 407/248-2499; Sun–Thurs 11am–1am, Fri–Sat 11am–1:30am).

INTERNATIONAL DRIVE & CONVENTION CENTER

This is a major hotel and entertainment center, so many visitors find themselves here. The stretch of Sand Lake Road west of Interstate 4 is known, somewhat self-deprecatingly, as "Restaurant Row." It's true that some of the city's most popular date-night restaurants are scattered among the shopping centers on this street.

$ Collard greens aren't overstewed, the cabbage in the cole slaw is cubed and crunchy, baked beans come sweet the way baked beans ought to, and cornbread muffins are embedded with a melting pad of butter. That's no-frills, smoky-smelling **Bubbalou's Bodacious Bar-B-Que** (5818 Conroy Rd., Orlando; ☎ 407/295-1212; www.bubbalouscatering.com; Mon–Thurs 10am–9:30pm, Fri 10am–11:30pm, Sat 10am–9:30pm, Sun 10am–9pm; AE, MC, V). Each picnic-style table is topped with a platter of sauces ranging "sweet" to "killer," not to mention a roll of paper towels, so diners can suit their tastes and their sartorials. After all that, and maybe a plate of its popular ribs ($6), there may not be room for Bubbalou's super-sweet three-pecan pie ($3), which would be a shame. Dinner plates with fries, baked beans, cole slaw, garlic bread, and your choice of meat hover around $9 or $10. The $6 lunch specials change daily (Monday's: a quarter chicken, stuffing, vegetables, and a muffin) but are always huge. There is a second location in Winter Park (1471 Lee Rd.; ☎ 407/628-1212).

$ Locals know the secret of **The Dessert Lady** ★ (4900 S. Kirkman Rd., Orlando; ☎ 407/822-8881; www.dessertlady.com; Tues–Sat 11am–11pm; AE, MC, V), and they pack it for after-dinner delights and special occasions. Its owner became famous by inventing the dessert-in-a-shot-glass concept for Seasons 52 (see below), and now she runs her own pastry shop/coffeehouse. There's one baker and one baker's assistant—that's all—and everything's made from scratch. Hang out in the mellow café, where walls are rich as red velvet cake, and sink a fork into a Key Lime cake with cream cheese frosting, six-layer Chocolate Neapolitan, or into some rich frosting made with chocolate that's been melted with heavy cream and butter. White cakes are light, rum cakes are moist and not oversoaked, and at $8, slices are hefty. Samplers, serving half-portions of four pies, cost $18 for two people (though I think they could feed up to four). Find it at the southwest corner

Bahama Breeze **17**

Bubbalou's Bodacious
Bar-B-Que **1**

Café Tu Tu Tango **16**

Cricketers Arms Pub **14**

The Dessert Lady **2**

Golden Corral **12**

Hu Hot **21**

Magical Mealtime **7**

Memories of India **9**

Ming Court **20**

Pirate's Dinner
Adventure **6**

Ponderosa **5, 15**

Primo **24**

Race Rock **18**

Rice Paper **8**

Royal Pacific Resort
(Wantilan Luau) **3**

Seasons 52 **10**

SeaWorld Orlando
(Makahiki Luau) **22**

Sleuth's Mystery
Dinner Show **13**

Texas de Brazil **4**

Thai Thani **23**

Timpano Chophouse
& Martini Bar **11**

WonderWorks
(The Outta Control
Magic Show) **19**

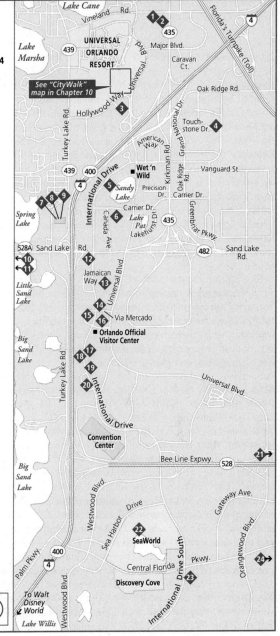

of the intersection with Conroy Road, in a shopping center behind a Chick-fil-A, about 5 minutes north of Universal.

$–$$ I like the energy at **Café Tu Tu Tango** ★★ (Plaza Venezia, 8625 International Dr., Orlando; ☎ 407/248-2222; www.cafetututango.com/orlando; Sun–Thurs 11:30am–11pm, Fri–Sat 11:30am–1am; AE, DC, DISC, MC, V), and I'm not alone, as it's often busy deep into the night. Crammed with art and commanded by a large wood-fired oven, this joint fashions itself after an atelier, and it's not faking—real painters and jewelry makers work the easels, and there's at least one dance event on its central floor space every night (Fri. nights belong to the women of Orlando Dance Theatre). Kids tend to be swept up in the vibe, but locals also use it as a non-threatening date night locale. The grills-and-tapas menu and hyper-friendly waitstaff alike represent cultures from around the world. One such choice is the Cajun chicken egg roll ($8), which is blackened chicken with corn, cheddar, goat cheese wrapped and deep fried like an egg roll, and served with salsa; I find it revolting, but it's the most popular item on the menu. I stick to meat skewers ($7–$9) and baked artichoke and crabmeat dip ($8). The lounge (cushy sofas where you can eat, if you want) serves cocktails and plenty of beer (8 on draft, 24 bottled, and 1 microbrew of the month).

$–$$ An unpretentious British-style pub with a following from locals and expats alike, **Cricketers Arms Pub** (8445 International Dr., Orlando; ☎ 407/354-0686; www.cricketersarmspub.com; daily noon–2am; AE, MC, V) does 17 tap beers and subscribes to live Premiership football by satellite—although NFL games are subbed in when there's no European action. There's live music, often acoustic or bands, nearly every night, plus a menu of as-expected Brit classics such as Scotch eggs, cottage pie, and ploughman's sandwiches, mostly under $10.

$–$$ A terrific find in the Bay Hill shopping plaza just north of Sand Lake Road, **Rice Paper** ★★★ (7637 Turkey Lake Rd., Orlando; ☎ 407/352-4700; Sun–Thurs 11am–9pm, Fri–Sat 11am–10pm; AE, DC, DISC, MC, V) is more than a Thai place—its food is richer and smoother than run-of-the-mill Thai fare. Call it "fusion." After you start with one of the seven spring roll varieties ($3 to $6) or grilled quail with lime pepper sauce ($6.50), some "big soups" are served ($8–$11), akin to the Vietnamese cuisine or you can move right on to the entrees instead. The emphasis is on rice and vermicelli dishes such as my favorite, caramelized ginger chicken with onion and zucchini ($8 lunch/$10 dinner). One of the splurges on the menu is the clay pot catfish, caramelized with onion and chili powder ($15/$17). Seven types of loose-leaf teas are brewed for $3 per pot, and the house dessert specialty is Banana Flambé—banana wrapped in spring roll skin, fried, and served with a honey glaze and coconut ice cream ($6.50). This place has one of those menus that keeps you coming back to try one of everything.

$$ In the same nondescript Bay Hill shopping plaza as Rice Paper is a second Asian winner popular with locals: **Memories of India** ★★★ (7625 Turkey Lake Rd., Orlando; ☎ 407/370-3277; Mon–Wed 11:30am–2:30pm and 5:30–9:30pm, Thurs–Sat 5:30–10pm, Sun 5:30–8:45pm; AE, MC, V) overcomes a horridly bland name with perfectly flavorful pan-Indian cuisine, never too cloying with curry and almost always subtly blended. It is also the rare Indian place in America to serve a *thali,* which is a lunchtime platter combining basmati rice, bread, *raita* (yogurt with cucumbers and tomatoes), pickle (relish), a meat dish, a *papadum* (thin wafer), and, at this place, dessert (I like the mango ice cream)—all for $6.75 to $10. Keep your ears peeled for gossip, because it's a favorite of the administrative staff at Universal Orlando next door. There's a children's menu for unadventurous youth. It's only a few blocks west of International Drive, right on the western side of I-4, although few tourists seem to realize it.

$$ In sight of SeaWorld's ferocious Kraken coaster, **Thai Thani** ★★ (11025 S. International Dr., ☎ 407/239-9733; www.thaithani.net; daily 11:30am–11:30pm; AE, DISC, MC, V) is a strip-mall anchor store that's been transformed into a Chiang Mai den of delights with wood carvings, brass sculpture, and a front lounge filled with body cushions. Popular with locals, it serves Thai food suited to newbies—the lemongrass soup is tame, with few chiles, which proves the chef is holding back—but more advance noodleheads should identify themselves and ask for it spicier to get the full flair of the cuisine. Dinner entrees come in around $14, while lunch (which ends at 2:30pm) is about $4 less. Singha beer is $5. There's also a bar area in the event of a wait, which, considering the size of the place, happens a lot (reservations are possible). The menu contains one of the funniest accidental wordings in town: "We love to serve vegetarians."

$$ East of the International Drive area, on the perimeter of the Florida Mall, **Hu Hot** (1187 Florida Mall Ave., ☎ 407/812-1300; www.huhot.com; daily 11am–10pm; AE, DC, DISC, MC, V) is another small chain with a big gimmick: Guests pick what they want to eat from a buffet (vegetables, meats, and a healthy dollop of sauce—pick one from 12 or concoct your own) before handing the ingredients over to a chef who slices, dices, and sizzles them on a table-sized grill. Half the challenge is picking components that mix well before your stomach fills and the stir-fry game's over. Lunch ($8) and dinner ($12) are all-you-can-eat—a family with a healthy appetite can wear that chef out—and are served with rice; dinner also comes with soup or salad. Watch that you don't fill up on starters (egg rolls, pot stickers). In fact, you could skip appetizers entirely and come away sated.

$$–$$$ **Seasons 52** ★★★ (7700 Sand Lake Rd., Orlando; ☎ 407/354-5212; www.seasons52.com; Mon–Thurs 11:30am–2:30pm and 5–10pm, Fri 11:30am–2:30pm and 5–11pm, Sat 11:30am–11pm, Sun 11:30am–10pm; AE, MC, V) started as a culinary experiment and is now mushrooming in other parts of the state. It's packed with merrymakers every evening; by 6:30pm, it's two-deep at the wine bar (140 types, 70 by the glass) while Orlando locals jostle for a table (reservations are possible). The two-level, raftered, California-style ranch building looks like something Mike Brady might have designed, but the real appeal here is the miraculous food. The entire point of the menu, which changes weekly to catch seasonal crops, is that no dish clocks in at more than 475 calories (though none will leave you hungry). Made with fresh ingredients and plenty of olive oil, there's nothing frou-frou about this food—it's simply really good, and really simple. The signature flatbreads are $3 to $9, while most entrees fall between $9 and $16. The desserts, which are served in single-serving shot glasses, are a guiltless sensation and cost just $2 a pop—just don't overindulge and undo all that low-calorie virtue.

$$–$$$ Popular with vacationers and conventioneers alike (it's a block from the Convention Center), **Ming Court** (9188 International Dr., Orlando; ☎ 407/351-9988; www.ming-court.com; daily 11am–2:30pm and 4:30–11:30pm; AE, DC, DISC, MC, V) is a little more expensive than most Chinese restaurants (most wok-prepared dishes are $13–$19), but it's also true that its chefs display much more attention to detail than your local fry-up. They brag that there's no freezer in the kitchen (in this case, it's nothing to worry about), and the 1,000-gallon saltwater tanks contain lobsters and seafood for your next meal, should you deign it so. Dishes dance the line between innovative and classic, so as not to frighten the tourists, and there's also a sushi list, a menu for grilled meats and fish—mind you, each menu has its own chefs—and a roster of American-Chinese basics such as chow mein and lo mein (those artless dishes are mostly under $10). As a final touch, fortune cookies are dipped in chocolate.

$$–$$$$ Look—up in the sky! See that cloud of smoke, that aroma of cooking meat settling over several city blocks? That's the chimney at **Race Rock** ✯ (8986 International Dr., Orlando; ☎ 407/248-9876; www.racerock.com; Sun–Thurs 11:30am–10pm Fri–Sat 11:30am–10:30pm; AE, DC, DISC, MC, V), perpetually signaling all of International Drive (and everyone passing with open windows on I-4) that the closest thing to a backyard barbecue is being served inside. I suppose many customers come because they love motor racing, because the dining area is jammed with cars, jerseys, video monitors and memorabilia (in fact, it trumps CityWalk's NASCAR Café in that respect). I suppose that others come because the All-American menu, served quickly, is rangy enough to suit everyone in a family. Most people will be satisfied by the half-pound burgers, pizzas, sandwiches, and calzones ($12–$15), although more substantial plates (steaks, ribs, salmon) are available for $14 to $23. Happily, you don't have to care about racing to appreciate the energy and decent value—though it helps. The co-owners include Mario and Michael Andretti, Richard Petty, and Jeff Gordon.

$$–$$$$ Frank Sinatra plays on a loop and a crisply turned out staff brims with cheerfulness at the vacuously stylish **Timpano Chophouse & Martini Bar** (7488 W. Sand Lake Rd., Orlando; ☎ 407/248-0429; www.timpanochophouse.net; Sun–Wed 11am–10pm, Thurs–Sat 11am–11pm; AE, DC, DISC, MC, V), a popular nightspot done in heavy drapes and deep booths. The menu skips ably between salads (the Wedge is but $6), pasta ($11–$14 at lunch, $13–$19 at dinner), and well-priced chops ($19–$33 at dinner). A hearty meal here ends with uncharacteristic restraint in the form of shot-glass desserts and cheesecake lollipops that arrive on a tree, looking for all the world like a model of a soap molecule. Lunch specials, $11 to $14, are a top value because they include four to five courses (soup, salad, an appetizer, panini sandwich or brochette, and dessert).

TWO SPLURGES

$$$$ If I had to choose one special-occasion restaurant away from the theme parks, I would likely pick the sublime **Primo** ✯✯✯ (JW Marriott Orlando Grande Lakes, 4040 Central Florida Parkway, Orlando; ☎ 407/393-4444; www.primo restaurant.com; daily 6–10pm; AE, DC, DISC, MC, V). Many hotel restaurants will tell you they're gourmet experiences worth $22 a plate, but Primo is one of the few that actually is. James Beard award–winning chef Melissa Kelly, who also runs the original Primo in Maine, is a fierce proponent of super-high-quality ingredients (there's an herb garden beside the hotel for the chefs' use) and methods (she outlines some of them in her book *Mediterranean Women Stay Slim, Too!*). Nothing is pre-made; dishes, loaded with fine olive oils and meats, are molded to seasonal ingredients, and the restaurant's not open for lunch because cooks are busy prepping dinner. Among my favorite past meals: fried green tomatoes, perfectly salted and seasoned, served under a spectacular pile of peppers, ham, onions, and chives; creamy and gentle lobster ravioli; and cannoli so fragile that I still don't know how they got on my plate.

$$$$ It'll cost ya ($31–$50 per person, depending on how many categories of food you want and if you get wine), but **Texas de Brazil** (5259 International Dr., Orlando; ☎ 407/355-0355; www.texasdebrazil.com; Sun noon–9:30pm, Mon-Thurs 5–10pm, Fri 5–11pm, Sat 4–11pm; AE, DC, DISC, MC, V) is one of the most popular event restaurants in town, and if you're a big eater, then you can get your money back in a bigger waistline. It's a popular Brazilian-style churrascaria—large, noisy (you are warned), and jammed with ungodly amounts of food. Each diner is equipped with a plastic disc, one side green and the other red, that functions as an on/off switch for the waiters, who will relentlessly pile your plate with shavings from giant skewers of meat unless you turn the red side up, thereby silently crying "Uncle!" And the meats—more than a dozen varieties—are succulent, pink in the middle, and high-quality. The big secret is that paying full price is unnecessary: Kids under 6 are free, and those 7 to 12 eat for half price. Its website has an "EClub" e-mail mailing list, and if you sign up before you leave home, you'll usually be sent a 25% discount coupon. The same site also posts two-for-one deals, in which case it's a strong value. Reservations are wise.

DOWNTOWN ORLANDO

The neighborhood east of downtown, Thornton Park, hosts a few well-publicized bistros and sidewalk cafes, but with prices around $12 a plate for lunch and $20 for dinner, there are no money-saving revelations among them. Instead, try these.

$ One of those neighborly cafes that has supplanted bars as the place "where everybody knows your name," **Dandelion Communitea Cafe** ★★★ (618 N. Thornton Ave., Orlando; ☎ 407/362-1864; www.dandelioncommunitea.com; Tues-Sun 11am–11pm; AE, MC, V) is run by an exceedingly friendly young couple, Chris Blanc and Julie Norris, and feels like someone's home because, until recently, it was. The front dining room is the former living room, and appropriate to its past function, local folks tend to hang out for hours on its couches, sipping homemade "Elixir Tonic" tea blends ($3.50) and talking about life. The focus is top-end, organic, loose-leaf teas and light meals. As you can imagine, it's extremely homey and about as un-Orlando as a place can be. I always make sure I stop by when I'm downtown. Although I'm not a vegetarian, there's nothing better than vegetarian food done well, and this place nails it: The hummus, served by the scoop in a teacup, is creamy, moist, and drizzled with premium olive oil ($5); wraps ($6–$7.50) are substantial; but the Henry's Hearty Chili ($2 cup, $4) bowl is simply sensational, and unlike countless other veggie chilis, it's not overloaded with beans—I don't know how they make it so flavorful. In front, in what I guess was a breakfast nook, it sells wares made by local artists and cooks, such as Orenda bath products and Funky Monkey breads. On Saturday nights nearest the full and new moons, there's a drum circle—people tend to bring along extras, so don't feel abashed if you forget to pack yours.

$ Value-minded home-style cooking is the lure at tiny **Christo's Café** (1815 Edgewater Dr. at Dartmouth Street, Orlando; ☎ 407/425-8136; www.christoscafe. com; Mon–Sat 6:30am–9pm, Sun 7am–3pm; AE, DISC, MC, V), an old-fashioned diner that has captured the devotion of the new inhabitants of its rapidly gentrifying neighborhood. Breakfasts, particularly on the weekends (they're served until 3pm), are roundly praised—think about country ham served in slabs ($3.75) and omelets ($4.95) that look like the pictures in a Southern cookbook—and its soups ($2.75 a cup), which are usually homemade, are equally prized. Southern specialties include banana pudding, batter-fried onion rings ($4), and chicken-fried steak ($8.75, including two sides and garlic toast). Nothing here is gourmet, but if you grew up eating food like this, you'll think it ranks even higher. The downside, beside the potential for strokes, is that parking is limited.

$ A favorite of slumming NBA players, glad-handing political candidates, and folks who miss Grandma's soul food, **Johnson's Diner** ★★ (595 W. Church St; ☎ 407/841-0717; Mon–Thurs 7am–7pm, Fri–Sat 7am–8pm, Sun 7am–6pm; AE, DISC, MC, V), in the otherwise bleak dining terrain of Parramore (just west of I-4 from downtown), is a no-frills country kitchen where home cooking is raised to new heights while prices stay rooted in the 1990s. Civic leaders prize the place, which began in 1955, so highly that when its longtime location was threatened with development, the city pitched in $36,700 to fund a move. On vinyl tablecloths, feast on smothered pork chops ($6.95), sweet tea ($1.25 a glass), and fried catfish (perfection at $7.95). Daily specials include grilled liver ($6) on Wednesdays and BBQ ribs ($7) on Saturdays. The sweet potato pie ($1.95) is locally heralded, as is the stewed beef, but if diabetes diagnoses could be traced, the banana pudding ($1.50), piled with Nilla Wafers, would certainly be banned. This cooking ain't good for your heart, but it does wonders for your will to live.

$ Part of a 30-odd-strong Southern chain, the casual **Tijuana Flats** (50 E. Central Blvd., Orlando; ☎ 407/839-0007; www.tijuanaflats.com; Mon–Thurs, Sat 10am–10pm, Fri 10am–midnight, Sun 10am–9pm; AE, MC, V) serves made-to-order Tex-Mex in the heart of downtown, close to the Orange County History Center, the main library, and the beer halls of Wall Street. Its gimmick is a rack of pumps dispensing 12 degrees of hot salsa, ranked "Sissy Sauce" to "Death Wish," with provocative names such as Endorphin Rush, Smack My Ass and Call Me Sally, and Scorned Woman. Food is squarely in the affordable range: chimichangas and mighty hefty burritos from $5.89, enchiladas from $6, and platter-sized quesadillas from $4.60. Families can buy eight burritos for $39, including a chips-and-guacamole platter and your own bottle of hot sauce.

$ Next door is **Crooked Bayou** (50 E. Central Blvd., Orlando; ☎ 407/839-5852; www.crookedbayou.com; Mon–Fri 11am–2am, Sat noon–2am, Sun 7pm–2am; DISC, MC, V), which, judging by the basic decor, wants to be a drinking joint that serves

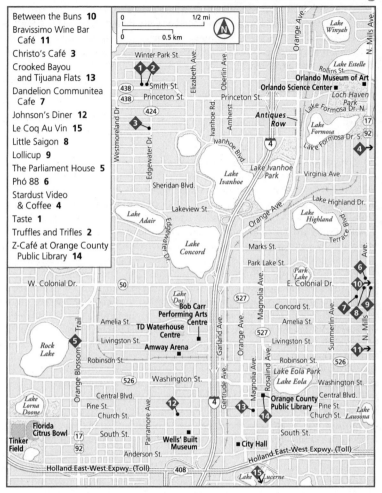

Between the Buns **10**

Bravissimo Wine Bar
Café **11**

Christo's Café **3**

Crooked Bayou
and Tijuana Flats **13**

Dandelion Communitea
Cafe **7**

Johnson's Diner **12**

Le Coq Au Vin **15**

Little Saigon **8**

Lollicup **9**

The Parliament House **5**

Phó 88 **6**

Stardust Video
& Coffee **4**

Taste **1**

Truffles and Trifles **2**

Z-Café at Orange County
Public Library **14**

solid Louisiana food and not necessarily a hangout for Cajun gourmands. It's great for picking up some artery-jamming fried fish po' boy sandwiches (catfish, grouper, oysters, crawfish; $6 for 6 inches, $8.50 for a foot) and one-pot stews such as gumbo, jambalaya, and lobster bisque ($5.75, or $6.50 in a sourdough bread bowl). Beers start at $2.50, which most guests swig on the outdoor patio while watching the street life around Heritage Square.

$ Being told that the city's best hot dog is found at a Chevron station doesn't exactly whet the appetite. But relax. **Between the Buns** ★ (1601 E. Colonial Dr. at Ferncreek Avenue, Orlando; no phone; no credit cards), east of the ViMi district, is a city institution and a piece of striking pop architecture—a hot dog stand shaped like a giant hot dog, and it's been going since 1998 (since 2002 in this location). John Liotine, its Massachusetts-raised proprietor, had a career as a trumpet player for Diana Ross, Prince, and Marvin Gaye before having his wiener custom-built. Now he caters to a host of regulars who slather "Sock It to Me!" hot sauce on their messy ¼-pound dogs. They're artfully assembled but potentially deadly: The Orlando Magic ($2.75) has BBQ sauce, chili, jalapeños, and cheese sauce, while the Great American ($2.25) plays it straight with mustard, relish, and onions. The place could just as fittingly be in the shape of a potato, because the hand-cut fries ($1.50) are out of this world. Soda pop is just 75¢, and hoagie-style burgers are $3.50. Incidentally, the gas station charges less than most of the ones in the tourist zone. But you may not want gas twice in one meal.

$ For coffee, dessert, and a chill place to read or journal without pressure, **Stardust Video & Coffee** ✦ (1842 E. Winter Park Rd., Orlando; ☎ 407/623-3393; Mon–Thurs 7am–11pm, Fri 7am–midnight, Sat 8am–midnight, Sun 8am–11pm; MC, V) makes for a very relaxed hideout. Its cavernous, warehouse-like lounge—furnished with old couches, discarded science-lab tables, and one-sheets of cult-hit films such as *Grey Gardens*—feels more like the mismatched living room of an under-35 bachelor or like a college clubhouse than a business establishment. It's hip without being off-putting, which you'd never expect of an image-obsessed town. Sandwiches (all $6–$7, including a side salad) are named for hip movie actors (the Crispin Glover is a pesto chicken; the Luis Guzman is veggie chili), the coffee cups are deep, and its house-made waffles, a specialty, are served all day. Check out the case full of rare imported beers, and the large selection of tea leaves. That the place is the best place in town to rent out-of-print videos is a perk that tourists can't exploit, but can certainly appreciate. On Thursdays at 9:30pm, there's a poetry slam, open to all comers.

$ Former software engineer (and vegetarian) David Kahan opened his 40-seat **Z-Café at Orange County Public Library** (101 E. Central Ave., Orlando; ☎ 407/648-6300; www.z-coffee.com; Mon–Fri 9am–9pm, Sat 9am–6pm, Sun 1–6pm; MC, V) in the unlikely setting of the lobby of the county's main library. He serves vegetarian and carnivores' sandwiches alike, plus homemade pizza, but the real draw is his artisan roasted coffees, picked everywhere from Cameroon to the Galápagos Islands and roasted in nearby Apopka. The "Hurricane" blend is a collection of beans from countries affected by hurricanes. His Chili Coffees are blended with hot peppers to give the flavor added zip. RocketFuel, the preferred blend of workers from the nearby hospital, is made from beans with high caffeine content, so it gives double the normal buzz. He also sells by the bag, from affordable to luxury (the Jamaican Blue Mountain is $50 a pound).

$ It's not a place for a meal, but **Lollicup** (3201 E. Colonial Dr., Orlando; ☎ 407/897-1377; www.lollicup.com; daily 11am–7pm; MC, V), a California chain in the heart of the Vietnamese district just east of Colonial Drive and Mills Avenue, is a terrific find for authentic Asian bubble teas, milk teas, and smoothies, which hit the spot on a blistering day and cost $3.25. Tiny as a walk-in closet and stuffed with plump, orange couches, it does a variety of teas both with and without tapioca and grass jelly balls. I have a soft spot for the avocado-coconut smoothie ($4.25), but it does fruit slushes, smoothies, and flavored milk teas, too.

$–$$ Ask fans of ViMi, the Vietnamese district around Colonial Drive and Mills Avenue, to name their favorite dining choice, and most of them will say **Little Saigon** ★★ (1106 E. Colonial Dr., Orlando; ☎ 407/423-8539; www.littlesaigon restaurant.com; daily 10am–9pm; AE, DISC, MC, V). It's the champ of the area, and its large, clean dining rooms see a steady procession of hungry folks from all walks of life, particularly during lunch, when downtown office workers sneak up for one of the massive soup bowls. Clearly, any restaurant that can afford to make heavy lacquered chairs emblazoned with its own name is well established, and the thick menu, loaded with authentic and Westernized items alike, testifies to a wide appeal. Ingredients are authentic, too, as they come from the Asian import markets nearby. Prices are in line with its competition: $6.50 to $9 for soup bowls, sautéed meats with rice, and rice vermicelli dishes, which are more than enough for a meal. I often find it hard to progress to the second course after partaking of its massive summer rolls ($2.50).

$–$$ The plate glass windows of the barnlike **Phó 88** (730 N. Mills Ave., Orlando; ☎ 407/897-3488; www.pho88orlando.com; daily 10am–10pm; AE, DISC, MC, V) proffer a terrific people-watching view of Mills Avenue. Although its beef noodle soup is justifiably held as its standout dish (bowls seem as large as hot tubs, with many flavors vying for dominance), the food isn't quite as elaborate as Little Saigon's around the corner, and the waitstaff is more laissez-faire. Two enormous spring rolls could fill an average stomach for $2.50, and the avocado shakes are full of fruit. Crowded soup bowls are $6.50 and could serve as main courses, while plated entrees cost around $9.50. Lunch prices, which end at 4pm, are about $3 less than dinner for dry entrees. The wine list is puny, but the menu stretches on like a Russian novel.

$–$$ A few miles north and west of downtown, the hangout of College Park is gaining ground as a hot spot for good food and offbeat shopping. **Taste** ★★ (717 W. Smith St., Orlando; ☎ 407/835-0646; www.tastecp.com; Mon–Thurs 11:30am–2:30pm and 5:30–10pm, Fri 11:30am–2:30pm and 5:30–11pm; Sat 5:30–11pm, closed Sun; MC, V), an orange-and-burgundy space decorated with bamboos, mobiles, and local artwork, is a friendly yet stylish choice serving California-style tapas cuisine, which translates into fresh concepts (sesame ahi tuna tartare, creamy polenta, flatbreads with three types of tapenades, shrimp cakes cooked like crab cakes, cumin-and-garlic eggplant dip) you'll be dying for after a few days of eating mounds of pre-frozen tourist chow. Two or three dishes ($5–$7), which run a wide gamut to suit most palates, split between a couple will usually suffice; there are seven full-size dishes, too. The homemade ginger vanilla soda ($2) is a kick and, like everything on the menu, is simple but elegantly balanced, making you feel refreshed but not overstuffed. Save room for the marvelous apple puff pastry dessert, served with melting goat cheese. If the dining room is full, offer to eat at the bar, where the wood ribs flying overhead impart the sensation of dining in a whale. Taste could charge much more based on its quality, including its wines, which is an ultimate compliment. It closes between 2:30 and 5:30pm daily, but prices don't differ substantially between lunch and dinner.

$$ Tucked away in a residential neighborhood, south of Livingston Street, you'd never know that the good-value **Bravissimo Wine Bar Café** (337 N. Shine Ave.,

D.I.Y. Dinner

The latest culinary rage to sweep Orlando has been the cook-it-yourself concept. It sounds a lot like staying at home, but it's not. Instead, hungry families head to one of several businesses where kitchen, ingredients, recipe, and guidance are provided. By the time they leave, they've bonded, made some food to go, and even learned something about cooking. It's a little like Home Ec, except without those uppity cheerleaders mocking your soufflés. (Oops. Did I just write that?)

The most popular is **Truffles and Trifles** (711 W. Smith St., Orlando; ☎ 407/648-0838; www.trufflesandtrifles.com; open during scheduled sessions; AE, DISC, MC, V), a cooking school in College Park, where reservations are necessary, mostly because programs sell out in advance. The 2,400-square-foot space is dominated by long tables and wooden counters, and at first glance you could mistake it for a ceramics workshop—until you notice the 11 ovens, gourmet ingredients, and the cheerful groups executing complicated recipes. It's often used for corporate team-building exercises. Most classes (popular themes include desserts, Christmas cookies, and "date night" for couples) take several hours and cost around $47, including the food.

Less of a cooking school and more of what's called a "meal assembly" business, **Magical Mealtime** (7705 Turkey Lake Rd., Orlando; ☎ 407/354-5393; www.magicalmealtime.com; Tues–Thurs 10am–6pm, otherwise by reservation; AE, DISC, MC, V) hands you a menu of possible meals and once you pick one, you're guided to a workstation stocked with pre-cut ingredients. Then, you follow step-by-step instructions as you rotate through workstations, completing your meal. Whatever you don't eat that night, you can wrap up and stick in your hotel fridge. No cleanup required. Full meals, priced around $21, serve six, but even half portions, which cost around $13, can satisfy most families of four. It's located just west of I-Drive, not far from Universal Orlando.

☎ 407/898-7333; Mon–Fri 11am–2pm, daily 5–10:30pm; AE, DISC, MC, V) was there unless I told you. Its casual servers (often, the owner himself) keep the pressure light, and the wine list is studied. No wonder it has so many regulars. Of 14 pasta varieties ($10–$15), the red ones are topped with a fresh sauce of chunky, juicy tomatoes—not cooked down like many places'—but those dishes are probably outdone by the stuffed chickens and meats ($15). The laid-back dining area is decorated with local art but avoids concealing its past as an industrial space, which lends to the quaint escapism. The tiramisu is enormous and homemade. In good weather, sit out on the front patio and watch the well-to-do walk their dogs.

$$$ For a true gourmet meal far from theme-park hype, there is salvation. Chef Louis Perrotte and his wife Magdalena have been handling the pans at **Le Coq Au Vin** ★★★ (4800 S. Orange Ave.; ☎ 407/851-6980; www.lecoqauvinrestaurant. com; Tues–Sat 5:30–10pm, Sun 5–9pm; AE, DISC, MC, V), their traditionally French and unusually cozy restaurant, for longer than many locals can remember. Diners, many of whom are here celebrating a special occasion, feel more like they're guests in an Old Florida home than paying patrons, but the complicated flavors leave no doubt they've gotten what they've paid for. For his skill in preparing seasonal, traditionally French fare, including Grand Marnier soufflé, Perrotte has become a role model among Floridian gourmands. Main dishes range from $15 to $20, a flat-out bargain considering the craftsmanship, and half what the resorts charge for something less memorable.

WINTER PARK

$ Right off the shopping drag of Park Avenue, **Cuban Cafe** ★ (133 E. Morse Blvd., Winter Park; ☎ 407/629-2822; Mon–Sat 8am–3pm; AE, MC, V) has lower prices than most of its neighbors, and for that value, you get real Cuban-style sandwiches. For the uninitiated, those start with Cuban bread, which is made with the same ingredients as French bread but comes out softer. The bread (in the case of this place's Cuban Authentic, $5.50) is piled with two types of ham, Spanish pork, Swiss cheese, mustard, and pickles, before being held in a weighted and heated sandwich press for a minute or so, turning out a flattened, lightly toasted treat. The cafe also does snacks such as *frijoles negros* (black bean soup, $2.50); *yuca frita* (fried cassava root sticks, $2); and both sweet and green plantains, fried gently ($2 each). The coffee here is also so good ($1.50 for a Cuban café con leche) that the place sells espresso makers on the side.

$–$$ If you'd rather your wine bar came without gimmickry and your quaffs came straight from the bottle, **Eola Wine Company** (136 S. Park Ave., Winter Park; ☎ 407/647-9103; www.eolawinecompany.com; daily 4pm–midnight; AE, MC, V) serves 90 wines by the glass, up to 20 cheeses, plus a light menu (baked brie en croute, escargot, raspberry parfait soaked in Godiva white chocolate liqueur; $7–$11) created by its partner, expensive hotspot du jour K Restaurant. There's also a location in downtown Orlando (500 E. Central Ave., ☎ 407/481-9100; daily 4pm–midnight); it's popular with the post-work crowd, but this one is a better choice for soaking up Winter Park's pleased-with-itself airs.

$$ **Briarpatch Restaurant & Ice Cream Parlor** ★ (252 Park Ave. North, Winter Park; ☎ 407/628-8651; Mon–Sat 7am–6pm, Sun 8am–5pm; AE, DC, DISC, MC, V) isn't someplace you detour for, but a place you enjoy when you're on a Park Avenue shopping spree. Its sidewalk tables, right on the street, will make not budging all day a tempting proposition. At odds with the cracker-shack decor, dishes could be called "upscale diner": grilled Portobello sandwiches ($9.50), strawberry spinach salad ($11), and crab cake sandwiches ($11) are representative. The waitstaff is interesting, too: My last waiter was from Iceland.

➢ True wine purists may find its gimmick heretical, but **The Wine Room on Park Avenue** (270 Park Ave. South, Winter Park; ☎ 407/696-9463; www.thewine roomonline.com; Mon–Weds 10am–10pm, Thurs 10am–11pm, Fri–Sat 10am–midnight, Sun noon–7pm; AE, MC, V) is catching on with the hoi polloi. It's a spacious wine bar, also serving imported meats and cheeses, with a difference: Racks of special Italian-made Enomatic dispensing machines, loaded with nitrogen instead of flavor-altering oxygen, squirt 150 wines in perfect 1-, 2.5-, or 5-ounce servings. You preload a smart card at the front counter (plus a $2 start-up charge) and then slip it into whichever machine has some of the vino you'd like to try. This method won't save you any money off a standard glass of wine—in fact, it's more—but it's fun to go from machine to machine. The décor, like all good Orlando décor, is a pastiche on European styles; in this case, a country vault.

DINNERTAINMENT

Besides *American Idol* and *Dancing with the Stars,* there may be no purer form of vaudeville left in America than the Orlando dinner show. Part banquet and part spectacle, most of these guilty pleasures involve stunts, audience participation, and, usually, a flimsy excuse to hoist the American flag, even if the plot is set in ancient Mesopotamia. Most of them are mounted in arenas lined with bench seating and long tables, and while the show grinds on, waiters scurry around, distributing plates of banquet food the way Las Vegas dealers deal blackjack cards. These shows are immoderate and tacky to the extreme, but they're an intrinsic part of the Orlando scene. Nowhere else on earth—at least not since Caligula's Rome—will you find so many stadiums in which to stuff your face while fleets of horses, swordsmen, and crooners labor to amuse you. I wouldn't classify dinnertainments as top values, but they certainly represent the essence of the tourist's Orlando.

During most times of the year, most of these shows kick off daily around 6 or 7pm, but during peak season, there may be two shows scheduled to fall around 6 and 8:30pm. Upon arrival, crowds are corralled into a pre-show area where they can buy cocktails and souvenirs, and endure hokey comedy and magic routines—feel free to be slightly tardy, and feel free not to buy anything, as drinks come with dinner. Most shows will be mopping up by around 9:30pm, so schedule a visit on a night when you don't intend to catch theme park fireworks or other evening shows. Most of them also serve kids' standards (chicken fingers, hot dogs, and so on) for picky children. Soft drinks, draft beer, and wine (the cheap stuff, watered down) are unlimited. Bring a sweater if you're sensitive to air-conditioning, and bring enough cash to tip your server because gratuities aren't included. You may feel offended about how many times you'll be reminded to tip your server, especially considering that they'll be spending most of your meal legging it to the distant kitchen and not serving you, but keep in mind that many of Orlando's visitors come from countries where gratuities aren't traditional.

For more educational experiences, check out the chances to converse with Disney Imagineers (p. 245) or NASA Astronauts (p. 251) over catered meals.

Money saving tip: The free coupon books and discount ticket suppliers should be your go-to for cheap prices on dinner shows. There are so many deals floating around for the banquets held off theme park property that only a stooge pays full price. The ones thrown by the theme parks, though, generally don't discount. In fact, they tend to sell out, so book those as far ahead as you sensibly can.

IN ORLANDO

Probably the most popular off-park extravaganza, the tack-tastic **Dolly Parton's Dixie Stampede** ★★★ (8251 Vineland Ave., Orlando; ☎ 866/443-4943; $47 adults, $21 kids 4–11; www.dixiestampede.com; AE, DISC, MC, V) is real check-your-brain-at-the-door stuff. The party kicks off as you drink fruit punch out of a giant plastic boot, continues with an elaborate equestrian contest between "the North" and "the South" (audiences must choose sides) hosted by a Dolly-like, down-home country lass and a bumpkin clown, and climaxes when your waiter plops an entire barbecued bird in front of you, without preamble or cutlery. I have to question the propriety of such a frivolous face-stuffing banquet based on a bloody war waged against human bondage. To give you a clue of what you'll be seeing through wide, unbelieving eyes: One of the participants in the pig race is named "Abraham Link-in" and there's a song celebrating how pretty the ball gowns were on the ol' plantation. Ugly revisionism aside, even born-and-bred Southerners, such as my mother, resent the representation of their brethren as corn-fed yokels. I personally find the jacked-up, hyper-saccharine, in-your-face patriotism rather embarrassing when I consider the large number of foreign tourists who patronize Orlando and don't deserve to feel alienated. But the show's kitschy exuberance is undeniable, and kids, dadgummit, like it. This show has all the nuance of a plank upside the forehead—that may be just what you're in the mood for. You can drop by the theater anytime after 10am daily to have a free look at the horses, which are viewable from a gallery outside the arena. In November and December, the affair is drowned in utterly shameless Christmas spirit.

People who love horses choose **Arabian Nights** ★ (3081 Arabian Nights Blvd., Kissimmee; ☎ 800/553-6116 or 407/239-9223; $46 adults, $20 kids 3–11; www.arabian-nights.com; AE, DISC, MC, V), and its 15 breeds are both beautiful and well trained. The show itself, about a princess who enlists a genie's help to reclaim her kingdom, is preposterously dimwitted and somewhat talky, but to be fair, the wish-fulfillment plot is just a ruse for introducing the 20-odd old-fashioned horse acts, including bareback riding, dancing Arabians, and blood-pumping chariot races. Expect lots of dry ice, sequins, and execrable food. Another $11 will buy you a seat in the first three rows, a souvenir program, and a "VIP" pre-show walk past 18 backstage stables, and although you won't be allowed to pet the stars, kids can sit atop a 1-ton horse; the privilege means you'll miss some of the (silly) pre-show entertainment of belly dancers and acrobats. A special holiday show, accompanied by pop music, runs from mid-November to New Year's Day. Prices listed above are for online bookings; wait until you get to the theater, and they jump to $57 adults and $31 kids—decidedly not worth it. The arena is convenient to Disney, since it's located just north of U.S. 192 and east of I-4.

The recent (and weird) popularity of Captain Jack Sparrow among young boys has given **Pirate's Dinner Adventure** (6400 Carrier Dr., Orlando; ☎ 407/248-0590; $52 adult, $32 kids 3–11; www.piratesdinneradventure.com; AE, DISC, MC, V) new heft in the local market—and it even allowed the producers to mount a second production near California's Disneyland in 2005. Set on an 18th-century galleon with a 40-foot-high mast that's amid a 300,000-gallon lagoon—the arena is probably the most spectacular of all the Orlando dinnertainments'—"Pirate's" is a circus of rapier duels, rope swinging (a lot of it), and arrrghing. Although the show provides lots of opportunity for participation (each of six sections roots for their assigned buccaneer), it treats female characters like livestock—at one point, the villain, Captain Sebastian the Black, even batters Princess Anita to the ground, which I could certainly do without—and that may account for why its most devoted demographic appears to be 12-year-old boys there for their birthday parties. Production values are fairly high. The theater isn't far from Wet 'n Wild. Buying online yields discounts of $10 for adults and $5 for kids, and many of the free brochures dispensed around town are good for lesser discounts. From Thanksgiving to a week after New Year's Day, the show adopts a Christmas theme, complete with (I'm not making this up) a nativity scene.

Although it's long-running and popular with coach tours, the jousting-themed **Medieval Times** (4510 Irlo Bronson Hwy., Kissimmee; ☎ 888/935-6878 or 407/396-2105; $49 adult, $34 kids under 13; www.medievaltimes.com; AE, DISC, MC, V), at which your waitress is called a "wench," is also an attraction in eight other North American cities, which qualifies it as the McDonald's of dinnertainment. For $10 more ($8 online), the "Royalty Package" gets you front-row seating, a free program, and a souvenir DVD. Its "castle" is located a few miles east of Disney on U.S. 192, in a downtrodden area of Kissimmee.

I admit that when I first approached **Sleuth's Mystery Dinner Show** ★★★ (8267 International Dr., Orlando; ☎ 800/393-1985 or 407/363-1985; www.sleuths.com; $48 adult, $24 kids 3–11; AE, DISC, MC, V), I was dreading a poorly acted, cheap, tourist-trap knockoff. I confess that I misjudged it, and it's now my favorite dinnertainment in town. After mingling with a few zany characters and then watching their show, which takes about an hour and contains at least one murder, dinner guests are invited to confer with the other people at their table, grill the three or four suspects, and, if they feel confident, accuse a killer. There are nearly a dozen spectacle-free, low-budget shows, which change nightly, so you can attend several times without duplicating your experience, and the actors are not only typically skilled at improvisation (though perhaps not so much at English accents), but also at engaging audience members without making them overly uncomfortable. They seem to be having fun, and they'll even tone down the grown-up jokes if they see young children in the crowd, although the shows are clearly more suited to adults. As for audiences, they appear to be grateful for a rare chance to employ their brains in this town. The food is noticeably better than that of its rivals (though hardly gourmet), possibly because instead of catering to hundreds, the management only has to cook for a few dozen. The company also does Merry Mystery Dinner Adventure shows aimed at kids, but they're not always on the calendar, so call if that interests you. Have a snack before you arrive, because dinner isn't served until after the murder.

The Outta Control Magic Show (WonderWorks, 9067 International Dr., Orlando; ☎ 407/351-8800; $22 adults, $15 kids 4–12 and seniors; www.wonderworks online.com; AE, DISC, MC, V) is more downscale and easygoing than the others—the target market is kids, who may enjoy combining a meal here with a visit to the WonderWorks science-cum-video playground (p. 224), where the show is held. It's for parents who don't want to deal with overproduced glitz. Unlimited pizza, beer, wine, and soda are served while buddy-buddy magicians engage in family-friendly jokes and improv. There are two shows nightly: 6pm and 8pm, and its website posts discount coupons for up to $3 off.

Capone's Dinner & Show (4740 W. Irlo Bronson Hwy., Kissimmee; ☎ 800/ 220-8428 or 407/397-2378; $23 adults, $14 kids 4–12; www.alcapones.com; AE, DISC, MC, V) is definitely one of the area's lesser presentations, with lots of *Laguna Beach*–generation girls pretending to be 1920s flappers and warbling to recorded music. Dinner's a buffet of lasagna, spaghetti with meatballs, and a few token non-European dishes such as honey roasted ham and baked chicken. This troupe's own brochures and website promise "½ off" discounts, which grant the price I list, but I've never seen the so-called full price quoted, let alone charged.

AT THE THEME PARKS

These shows take the same credit cards their parent parks do, which is to say every major card available.

Don't wait until the last minute to book the 2-hour **Hoop-Dee-Doo Musical Revue** ★ (Pioneer Hall at Fort Wilderness Resort; ☎ 407/939-3463; www.disney world.com; $50 adults, $25 kids 3–9), not necessarily because it's the best, but because it's Disney's most kid-friendly dinnertainment, which makes it crazy popular. It books 6 months out. Six-performer shows put on a hectic and helter-skelter music-hall carnival of olios and gags, which elementary-school age children usually find riveting, and much quarter is given to recognizing birthdays and special events. The headlining menu item is ribs served in pails—enough said? I prefer seats in the balcony, overlooking the stage. The stylistically similar Dixie Stampede gets you much more for your money, but one benefit of the Hoop-Dee-Doo is it's held at a lakefront hotel that can be reached via a 15-minute boat ride from the Magic Kingdom, and outside of winter, the early seating gets you out in time to catch the fireworks (make sure to double-check when you book; even Disney's restaurant reservationists have access to the daily park schedule).

Mickey's Backyard Barbecue (The Outdoor Pavilion at Fort Wilderness Resort; ☎ 407/939-3463; $45 adults, $27 kids 3–9; www.disneyworld.com; Thurs and Sat, Mar–Dec) suits very young children, as it's patronized by rope tricksters and taxi-dancing costumed characters wearing Western-style gear. More informal than the Hoop-Dee-Doo in that it takes place under an open-air pavilion (come dressed for humidity), the event serves passable buffet-style food, but the toddler factor makes it chaotic, so you might be less disappointed if you see this as a photo op with Mickey and not as the proper show Disney bills it as.

The only dinner show to ask customers to pay based on their proximity to the stage, **Disney's Spirit of Aloha Show** (Disney's Polynesian Resort; ☎ 407/939-3463; www.disneyworld.com; $51–$59 adults, $26–$30 kids 3–9) is a chicken-and-ribs luau presided over by fire twirlers, hula dancers, and the like. It's been going for years, but was recently retroactively themed to the company's Lilo and Stitch franchise. Bookings begin 6 months ahead, and usually the last people to reserve are shunted to the rear tables, which can feel like they're actually as distant as the Cook Islands. I find this evening boring and drastically overpriced compared to the thundering cavalcades of stuntmen you can get for the same money outside Disney property, but some people love it nevertheless (although most of them cite its food—pineapple-coconut bread and a chocolate volcano dessert being at the top of their lists). It's on the monorail line from the Magic Kingdom, which means it's easy to catch the fireworks after early shows.

Makahiki Luau (SeaWorld Orlando; ☎ 800/327-2424; www.seaworldorlando. com; $46 adults, $39 kids 3–9) is a festive rival to Disney's Polynesian do, serving family-style platters of mahimahi in piña colada sauce, spare ribs, and stir-fried rice, finished with lava cake with peanut butter drizzle. Entertainment is of the general Southern Pacific variety—nothing too corny or scripted—distinguished by thundering drums. Although the 2-hour show takes place within SeaWorld, at a restaurant overlooking the lagoon, you won't need to buy a ticket to the park. During peak season, there are two shows a night.

Universal's own 2-hour luau, **Wantilan Luau** ★ (Royal Pacific Resort; ☎ 407/503-3463; $50 adults, $29 kids 3–9), is held on Saturdays in a covered pavilion most times a year, plus Fridays in summer. It, too, has fire dancers and hula girls aplenty, but it trumps the rest for authenticity: Food includes pit-roasted suckling pig, whole roasted wahoo, and guava barbecue short ribs, and mai tais are included in the price. Should kids be grossed out by carving meat off the pig, there's a tamer children's menu. The show is more culturally sensitive than Disney's, too, as it's attentive to the differences between the various Pacific islanders it represents. It's also within walking distance of both Universal parks.

Twice on Sundays, at 10:30am and 1:30pm, the House of Blues at Downtown Disney West Side holds its **Gospel Brunch** (1490 E. Buena Vista Dr., Lake Buena Vista; ☎ 407/934-2583; www.hob.com; $34 adults, $17 kids 3–9). There is no plot, but the live music is jumping and the cuisine combines Southern and break-fast foods. Still, because so many House of Blues branches throw these, I can't say there's anything original about this one.

CHARACTER MEALS

Appealing mostly to families with young children (although I admit to having done them with other grown-ups and enjoying myself), a Character Meal is an all-you-can-eat buffet that guarantees an appearance by several classic Disney characters in costume. The most popular meal is breakfast—I suggest porking out and skipping lunch, as that will maximize your time in the parks. Always, *always* book ahead—even as soon as you know your vacation dates (Disney: ☎ 407/939-3463; SeaWorld: ☎ 888/800-5447; Universal Orlando: ☎ 407/224-4012; all events AE, DC, DISC, MC, V). I am not big on character meals for lunch or dinner, because doing so will cut into expensive park time, but the option is available.

Each meal is themed to its location; at the Cape May Café, the characters wear beach outfits, and at Chef Mickey's, they emerge in chef's aprons, sign auto-graphs, and do a little towel-twirling dance. (Reading that, it sounds a little like a Chippendales show, not a Chip and Dale show, but rest assured it's all preschool-friendly.) The characters won't actually be eating with you, but they'll circulate, working the room the way a good host does. This, as kids and grown-ups binge on a smorgasbord that would give Richard Simmons apoplexy—including Mickey-shaped waffles topped with M&Ms and all. Mind the early-morning sugar crash.

Breakfast begins as early as 8am, depending on the location, and usually wraps up by 11:30am. Lunch generally runs 11:30am to 3pm, and the few dinners that are available begin around 4pm and end around 8:30pm. SeaWorld shifts its Dine with Shamu timing from week to week, and you may find its only "dinner" appointments are available at 4:15pm. Restaurants take every major credit card.

Theme Park Area Character Meals

Park Location	Meal Name/Restaurant	The Stars	Meal Served
The Magic Kingdom*	Once Upon a Breakfast at Cinderella's Royal Table	The Princesses, Mary Poppins	Breakfast
The Magic Kingdom*	Crystal Palace	Winnie the Pooh, Tigger, Eeyore	All three meals
The Magic Kingdom*	Dinner at Liberty Tree Tavern	Goofy, Donald Duck, Daisy Duck, Pluto, Minnie	Dinner
Epcot*	Chip and Dale's Harvest Feast, The Garden Grill (The Land)	Mickey, Chip and Dale, Pluto	Lunch and dinner
Epcot*	Princess Storybook Dining, Akershus Royal Banquet Hall (Norway)	The Princesses	All three meals
Disney-MGM Studios*	Playhouse Disney's Play 'N Dine, Hollywood & Vine	JoJo, the Little Einsteins	Breakfast and lunch
Disney's Animal Kingdom*	Donald's Breakfastosaurus, Restaurantosaurus	Donald Duck, Goofy, Pluto	Breakfast
Contemporary Resort	Chef Mickey's	Mickey, Donald Duck, Pluto	Breakfast and dinner
Beach Club Resort, Cape May Cafe	Beach Club Buffet	Minnie, Chip and Dale, Goofy	Breakfast
Grand Floridian Resort and Spa	1900 Park Fare	Alice in Wonderland	Breakfast
Grand Floridian Resort and Spa	1900 Park Fare	Cinderella, various villains	Dinner
Polynesian Resort	'Ohana Character Breakfast	Mickey, Stitch	Breakfast
Walt Disney World Swan	Garden Grove Cafe	Goofy, Pluto	Breakfast (Sat–Sun only)
Walt Disney World Swan	Gulliver's Grill	Goofy and Pluto (not Mon or Fri); Rafiki and Timon (Mon and Fri)	Dinner
SeaWorld Orlando*	Dine with Shamu, Shamu Stadium	A killer whale or two; their trainers	All three meals
Islands of Adventure*	Confisco Grill	Spider-Man and The Cat in the Hat	Breakfast

Theme park admission required.

The most popular location is Cinderella's Royal Table, inside Magic Kingdom's Cinderella Castle—there are some intense parents out there with freakishly fast speed-dial fingers, because that place always sells out 180 days early, despite the fact it costs some $14 more than a similar Character Meal elsewhere. Pray you don't stray in front of *their* strollers. I prefer Chef Mickey's, which is a one-stop monorail ride away from the Magic Kingdom; and Donald's Breakfastosaurus, a good start for the early day at Animal Kingdom. Less prestigious addresses, such as the family-style Garden Grill at Epcot, can be smart choices, particularly because they tend not to be as crowded and you're likely have lots more one-on-one time with the stars.

The privilege of dining with characters isn't cheap: around $20 for adults and $11 kids 3 to 9 for breakfast, moving up to around $30 adults/$13 kids at dinner. Prices vary from locale to locale, but usually only by a buck or two; never enough to warrant trekking farther than you normally would. When a breakfast is held inside a theme park outside of its regular hours, you'll still have to proffer an admission ticket. However, for breakfast, your name will be on a VIP list and you'll be admitted through the gates early (a perk that gives children and Disney fans a goose). Try to book the earliest seating available so that by the time you're done, you'll be among the first in line for the rides.

If your kid is fixated on a specific character, ask which ones are bound to appear—although a good six or eight of the well-known headliners make appearances, there's no guarantee that the same ones will be there each day. Disney won't be pinned down on details, but each location seems to specialize in a different group. When a particular name is reported regularly at a given restaurant, I let you know in the chart below (unless a character is singled out in the meal's title, in which case they're a given).

5 Walt Disney World

The whole world, in your hands

ON NOVEMBER 22, 1963, AROUND THE TIME PRESIDENT KENNEDY WAS starting off in his public motorcade in Dallas, Walt Disney was in a private jet, conducting his very first flyover of a certain patch of ignored Florida swampland. By the end of the day, as Disney decided this was the place he wanted to shape in the image of his dreams, America had changed in more ways than one.

While the country reeled, Disney snapped up land through dummy companies. By the time his cover was blown, in 1965, the fix was in: His company had mopped up an area twice the size of Manhattan, 27,443 acres, from just $180 an acre. Disneyland East was coming. Today, it's the single-most popular vacation destination on the planet, attracting some 40 million tourists a year.

It's no accident that Walt enjoyed his most powerful peaks during two periods of profound malaise: the Great Depression and the Cold War. It's also no coincidence that his theme parks flowered while America was riven with self-doubt—the Korean and Vietnam Conflicts, the death of Kennedy, and Watergate. His parks are, by design, reassuring. They tell you how to feel, where to go, and in reinforcing your simplest impressions of history and the world, they never make you feel stupid. Even beyond their rhetoric, their innovative style necessitated some the most successful examples of civil engineering ever attempted.

Why should it be so difficult to find straight talk about such an immensely popular place? There are plenty of guidebooks that will participate in a dewey-eyed celebration of all things Disney, which read like advertisements and treat the so-called "magic" as a sanctified, nigh-holy thing that must be fêted at all costs. This is not one of them. I adore Walt Disney World, I marvel at its awesome achievements, and I have been coming since the ribbon was first cut, so its childhood is inextricable from my own. Disney fans rhapsodize about the resort "magic"—that intangible frisson you feel when you're there—but I think a case could be made that the energy doesn't come from the place as much as it comes from the customers. Where else in your life will you be surrounded by people simply excited and happy just to be somewhere? Weddings? Graduations? Disney World's "magic" comes from the accumulated energy of thousands of strangers, united in gratitude and togetherness. If you don't believe me, sit on a bench for a while in Fantasyland and watch the children pass by.

But if the resort is to be appreciated as a precious American treasure, it must be approached not just in terms dictated by its influential marketing (some 75% of visitors are returning customers) and in slavish allegiance to its stagecraft. This is the book that reminds you that Walt Disney World, beloved and transporting as it is, is a real place, made possible by real sweat. It has a history. It is a product.

Contacting Walt Disney World

Walt Disney World, tellingly, offers no toll-free numbers, so earmark some cash for your long-distance bill or use your cellphone calling plan:

General information: ☎ 407/939-4636; www.disneyworld.com

Vacation packages: ☎ 407/934-7639

Operating hours: ☎ 407/824-4321

Reservations for restaurants and character meals: ☎ 407/939-3463

Questions about day-to-day resort operations: ☎ 407/824-2222

Weather updates: ☎ 407/824-4104

Lost and found: ☎ 407/824-4245

Touring Walt Disney World is like watching TV with the contrast turned up. But this guide helps you see it for what it is, and enjoy it in context.

TICKETING

This will be the biggest expense of your trip, so give it some thought before opening your wallet. All Disney tickets (excepting annual passes) are purchased by the day. You decide how many days you want to spend at the parks, and once you nail that down, you decide which extras you want to pay more for. Both decisions will be fraught with temptation.

Historically, visitors to Orlando would spend the first 3 or 4 days of their weeklong vacations at the Disney parks, and by the fourth or fifth days, they would graduate to Universal Orlando, SeaWorld, or the Kennedy Space Center. In 2005, though, the resort began using Magic Your Way, an insidious pricing plan that appears, on the surface, to present the biggest savings for people who stay on Disney turf for more than 4 days. "We're really trying to guide behavior into a more multiday-ticket approach, a multiday stay," admitted Walt Disney Co. president Robert Iger to the *Orlando Sentinel* in 2006, the same year he received $25 million in compensation funded, in part, by the escalation in prices. Never mind that 4 days is pretty much the right amount of time for most casual visitors (Disney's own numbers reveal that 5 nights is the average stay). The false economy of Magic Your Way ends up costing many families money when it ends up enticing them to stay on Disney property longer than they'd planned, spending lots of money on higher food and hotel prices. The damage it's doing to the vitality of the city's secondary attractions is yet to be determined.

When it comes to Disney tickets, everything depends on how many days you intend to play at the parks. Even the price of your admission to the ancillary amusements, such as DisneyQuest or the water slides, is pegged to that decision. As on an old-fashioned Chinese food menu, you add on the extras that you want.

Here's how the components of Magic Your Way break down:

Every Magic Your Way **base ticket** starts with theme park admission. You are entitled to visit only one park per day with the base ticket. For first-timers, this is enough time to hit the highlights. When it's all new to you, one park per day is more than plenty, believe me.

From here on out, willpower is crucial to saving money. Should you wish to have the privilege of jumping from park to park on the same day—say, do the early-morning safari at Animal Kingdom, take a nap at your hotel, and then see the Wishes fireworks show at Magic Kingdom—you must add the **Park Hopper** option to your ticket. It lets you "hop" between parks on the same day. As the chart below shows, this flexibility costs a flat $45 no matter how many days you intend to stay at the resort. I personally insist on this option, but that's because I know Disney well and I know what I like to see and what I like to skip. Many first-timers will be satisfied without it.

Should you have definite plans to visit a Disney water slide park, Pleasure Island, DisneyQuest, or see an event at the Wide World of Sports, then the **Water Park Fun & More (WPF&M)** option includes a set number of admissions in your ticket. Again, that add-on is priced according to how many days are on your base ticket. In the "Disney Ticket Options" chart below, follow the columns down from the number of days in the base tickets to see what you can have. To me, Water Park Fun & More is the trickiest add-on option. Too many people overestimate the amount of time and energy they are going to have, buy this option, and fail to use it. Think carefully about your own plans, and be realistic. During the course of 3 days of theme park–going, and after miles of walking, are you *really* going to have enough juice to party all night at Pleasure Island, and are you *truly* going to make time for water slides? Or are there other things to do in Orlando that you'd like to try? First-time visitors will be so engrossed (and exhausted) by the four theme parks that they may regret purchasing this option. Remember, too, that you will always be allowed to buy separate admission to any of these attractions if you skip this option; if you're realistically only going to visit Pleasure Island once and that's all, the $22 walk-up ticket is cheaper than the $50 add-on you don't fully use. Besides, one element of the WPF&M option, the Wide World of Sports, is virtually dormant much of the year, so buying admission based on it will, often, waste dough.

And there's another consideration regarding WPF&M that requires your advance planning: Don't overlook the fact that if you plan to go to a water park, your visit there will likely take the whole day (or most of your energy)—and on that day, you probably won't be setting foot in a theme park, even though you'll have paid for the privilege on your base ticket. Even if you do visit a theme park late in the day, you won't be getting your full admission ticket's worth. For each day you plan to spend at a Disney water park, you might find that for a base ticket with standard expiration, it's smarter to purchase one less day. Then attend the water park either before your first use of your base ticket, or after it's all used up; otherwise, you'll end up essentially paying twice for the same day.

The **No Expiration** option is just like it sounds. If you select it, your ticket can be used as long as there are days left on it; if you don't buy this option, unused days are dead after 14 days of your ticket's first use. If you plan to visit Disney again, ever, you can use this feature to your advantage. Disney and Universal hike their prices each year 5% to 6% like clockwork, but you can lock in today's prices

Disney Ticket Options*

Days of Use	Base Ticket Age 10 & up	Age 3–9	Add Water Park Fun & More	Add No Expiration	Advance Purchase Savings (with Park Hopper only/Park Hopper & WPF&M) Age 10 & up	Age 3–9	Add Park Hopper
1	$67	$56	$50 (3 visits)	N/A	N/A	N/A	$45
2	$132	$110	$50 (3 visits)	$10	N/A	N/A	$45
3	$192	$160	$50 (3 visits)	$15	N/A	N/A	$45
4	$202	$168	$50 (4 visits)	$40	$2/$12	$2/$10	$45
5	$206	$169	$50 (4 visits)	$55	$5/$15	$2/$10	$45
6	$208	$171	$50 (5 visits)	$60	$6/$16	$2/$10	$45
7	$210	$173	$50 (6 visits)	$90	$7/$17	$2/$10	$45
8	$212	$175	$50 (6 visits)	$125	$7/$17	$3/$11	$45
9	$214	$176	$50 (6 visits)	$150	$7/$17	$3/$11	$45
10	$216	$177	$50 (6 visits)	$155	$7/$17	$3/$11	$45

Prices don't include sales tax of 6.5%.

for a few extra bucks. If you spring for the No Expiration, when you come back in 10 years and the prices are as high as your mortgage, you'll have paid less. (Just don't lose your ticket.) It's going to be quite a number of years until that 6% increase overtakes, say, the $90 fee on a 7-day ticket, so this scheme won't save you much money unless you stay away for eons. Still, some people find that paying extra for No Expiration frees them up to explore the rest of Orlando without feeling guilty because they know they can always use their outstanding Disney tickets another time. If this sounds like you (I know it sounds like me), I recommend this option.

Finally, very slight **discounts** on Magic Your Way are available for domestic advance reservations made outside of Florida. It's not much (and it should prove to you that if Disney itself isn't discounting much, many third parties can't do it legitimately either), but I've included the info in the table. Tickets bought in advance (online or at a Disney Store) will come with this soupcon of a bargain, and they may be shipped to you—but save the $3 fee by arranging to pick them up at the gates of one of the parks (long lines) or at Guest Relations in Downtown Disney Marketplace (short line). Florida residents are sometimes offered entirely different discounts, as are AAA members; if you're one, call ☎ 407/824-4321 for the latest promotion. (See p. 98, below, for a more on potential discounts.)

PERIL OF PACKAGES

There's another giant pitfall that Disney wants you to trip into. Anytime you call the company and ask for reservations, you will be tempted into accepting perks suggested by Disney operators. You'll ask for tickets, and they'll suggest they throw in, say, golf or the meal plan (more about that in a minute). The instant you accept, you're purchasing a "package." Then, you may be in trouble, as you may pay more than you would have a la carte. Always, *always* know what everything you want would cost separately before agreeing to a Disney-suggested package—the company spends millions advertising that a family vacation there costs $1,600 a week, but in fact, if you don't accept Disney help and use other advice in this book, you can take a trip for much less. If you must, hang up the phone and do some math before deciding to accept or reject the offer. That's the only way to ensure you're not paying more.

But there's another, hidden loophole that will cheat you out of even more cash: Disney "length of stay" ticket packages will begin the moment you arrive on the property and end the day you leave. Now, think about that. If you've just flown or driven in from a distant place, the last thing you're likely to do is rush to line up at the Magic Kingdom on the same day. Likewise, on the day you're due at the airport to fly home, you're probably not going to be able to visit a theme park.

Yet Disney will schedule your package that way. In effect, you will lose 2 days that you've paid for—at the start and at the finish of your vacation, when you'll be resting or packing. How can you avoid this? You could spend the first and last nights of your vacation at a non-Disney hotel and move on-site for your ticket days. More simply, insist on making one reservation per phone call. Arrange your tickets. Hang up. Call back and arrange your hotel, without linking your two reservations. *And don't accept packages.*

Disney's reservationists are friendly but intensely legalistic, and they are trained to answer only the questions that you pose. They will not give advice and will not volunteer much money-saving information. If you're not sure about the terms of what you're about to purchase, corner them and ask when your first day of tickets will take effect: The answer should be, "Whenever you choose to begin using them," and *not* "On the day you arrive at the resort." And always ask if there is a less expensive option. They won't lie and tell you there isn't, but they *will* neglect to volunteer the information. Again, do not be afraid to get off the line and spend a few hours mulling over the price of their suggestions.

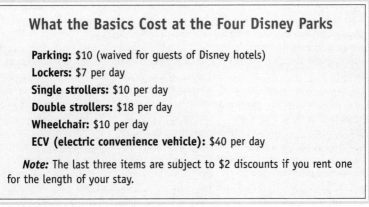

What the Basics Cost at the Four Disney Parks

Parking: $10 (waived for guests of Disney hotels)
Lockers: $7 per day
Single strollers: $10 per day
Double strollers: $18 per day
Wheelchair: $10 per day
ECV (electric convenience vehicle): $40 per day

Note: The last three items are subject to $2 discounts if you rent one for the length of your stay.

OTHER TICKET "DISCOUNTS" & DEALS

Before Magic Your Way launched the No Expiration option, pretty much every Disney ticket was good forever. That means there are a lot of unused days floating around out there. When you see a sign on the side of U.S. 192 promising discounted tickets, that's often what's for sale. Buying a ticket like this is a huge gamble, particularly if you don't have the expertise to recognize a fake. Often, there's not even a way to tell by looking whether unused days really remain on a ticket; only a magnetic scan can tell. Other organizations, such as timeshare developers, do indeed offer legit tickets, but to get them, you must endure (and then gracefully parry, which can be harder) heavy-duty sales pitches that last several hours. I think that an entire morning out of your hard-earned vacation time is worth a lot more than whatever discount is being provided. After all, how many days of working did it take for you to accrue those 4 or 5 hours? Don't be so cheap and discount-obsessed that you throw away your time.

A few companies can shave a few paltry bucks off multiday tickets; see p. 321 in chapter 12, "The Essentials of Planning," for those. British visitors are eligible, through **www.disneyworld.co.uk**, for two more ticket types not delineated here; the Premium (5 days or 7 days, £165 adults, £145 kids 3–9), which is like a Park Hopper, and the Ultimate (14 days, £173/£153 or 21 days £193/£173), which works for the water parks and Pleasure Island. At recent exchange rates, though, it'd still be cheaper in most cases for British visitors to buy American-issued tickets with Park Hopper options at the gate; do the math.

Really big Disney fans carry a Chase Disney Rewards Visa credit card (☎ 888/215-3049; www.chase.com), because purchases allows cardholders to accumulate points that can be redeemed in the form of tickets, vacation packages, and souvenirs. The card also grants small discounts at certain Disney establishments. But if you're such a big fan that you're willing to commit year-round to racking up points that can only be used on Mousy things, you probably already knew about this.

EATING ON SITE

In recent years, Disney food became noticeably more sweet, and opportunities to buy candy multiplied. Theme parks thrive on the money generated by excited, sugared-up children and parents who are too worn out to say "no" to such things as $6 hot dogs and $3 Cokes. At least the budget algebra is easy. The cheapest full meals are always from counter-service restaurants (called Quick Service in Disney-speak), and adults will pay around $8 to $10, before a drink, while kids pay $4, with a drink. If you want to sit down for service—and Disney will constantly be pushing you to do so, as its meal plans and character meals center on sit-down restaurants—you'll pay in the midteens for a lunch entree and usually over $20 a plate a dinner, before gratuity or drinks. *Note:* To avoid disappointment at sit-down restaurants, always make reservations (☎ 407/939-3463) as soon as you can; most restaurants take bookings 6 months out.

It will always be cheaper to quickly drive off-property to feed your family, but particularly at the Magic Kingdom, where egress requires at least two modes of transportation, that's not always desirable. See more money-saving tips for food in the "Saving on Mickey Munchies" box on p. 144, and also consult the list of restaurants located outside the theme park gates, which starts on p. 70.

You may be offered a **Disney Dining Plan** for a hair under $40 a day that will suit only those with extreme appetites or the tapeworm-afflicted. It's not so much a discount plan as it is a system in which you buy vouchers for meals ahead of time, and the drawbacks include the fact that **a)** everyone in your hotel room must also participate, **b)** it's only good at selected restaurants, which can create time-consuming backups, **c)** it's good for one counter-service and one-sit-down meal a day, so you'll spend lots of effort making and keeping reservations, and **d)** the system will be good throughout your stay, so you will lose some money on the last day after you check out. The plan will also serve to weld you to the Disney property (and to a subset of the available restaurants, at that), since you'll be unlikely to venture off-property if you feel you've already shelled out for food.

In October 2006, Walt Disney World announced an initiative to reformulate many of its quick-service recipes to provide food that's better for you. This means main dishes with a limit of 360 calories and full meals with a limit of 560 calories; no more than 30% of a meal's calories or 35% of a snack's calories will come from fat; juice drinks will be limited to 110 calories, with no added sugar; and most snacks will be limited to 150 calories with no more than 25% of them from sugar. I respect the company for the move, although at press time, it had yet to play out in the menus at its parks. Even before the announcement, Disney had eliminated most trans fats from its cooking methods and made kids' meals available with carrots, applesauce, or grapes instead of fries, and with low-fat milk,

---

The Disney Look

Although Walt himself had a moustache for most of his adult life, he forbade such a sartorial choice among his employees. Instead, he insisted on clean-cut, all-American (whatever that means) **grooming guidelines** of a sort that would be appropriate on *The Mickey Mouse Club*. Typical strictures: No hair below the collar for men, no hoop earrings larger than a dime for women; and no shaved heads. Rules relaxed with time—you may even see some neat cornrows, and in Disneyland Paris, the loosest of the parks, I've even seen lip rings—but the Disney look is still decidedly right of the mainstream. Where else do young women still wear hosiery? And no cast member is ever permitted to be seen smoking, despite the fact Walt himself was rarely seen without a filterless Camel in his hand.

Meanwhile, even props have a language of their own at Disney. A favorite pastime of longtime fans, like safaris were for Hemingway, is spotting **Hidden Mickeys,** which are camouflaged mouse-ear patterns. You'll find the three circles signifying a Mickey profile embedded everywhere: In an arrangement of cannonballs at Pirates of the Caribbean; flatware in the dining room at the Haunted Mansion, cookies on a plate in the bedroom of Peter Pan's Flight; and woven into carpeting, printed on wallpaper, and snuck into the souvenir photo on Test Track using hoses. Keep your eyes peeled; many sightings are up to the viewer's interpretation, but to get you started, check out **www.hiddenmickeysguide.com** and **www.oitc.com/Disney**.

water, or 100% fruit juice instead of soda. (The fries and Coke are still available by request—Disney knows kids are still on vacation and deserve a treat.)

The house soda brand is Coca-Cola (sorry, no Pepsi), and the house water is Dasani, which is essentially tap water. Do what I do: Buy a single bottle and refill it from the many water fountains. You'll find Orlando's municipal water has a specific mineral-like flavor and smell—the result of being drawn from aquifers—but if that bothers you, you can always tote your own quaff.

NAVIGATING THE PARKS

For advice on getting around Walt Disney World, see chapter 2, "The Lay of the Land." Nightlife options are addressed on p. 278, and in-resort hotel coverage begins on p. 33.

In summer and during other school holidays, it's wise to get to the front gates of the park about 30 minutes ahead of opening. Most of the year, though, you can waltz right up.

Each park has its own parking lot ($10, except for Disney hotel guests and annual passholders). As you drive in, attendants will direct you to fill the next available spot. This is probably the most dangerous part of your day, as the people in front and in back of you will be distracted, and you're at risk of hitting a child or knocking off an open car door—take it slow. Parking lanes are numbered and also given names; at the very least, remember your number. Don't stress out if your parking row is a high number; the row closest to the park is not numbered 1. At Epcot, for example, the front row is 27. At the end of your row, you'll board one of Disney's noisy trams (fold strollers during the wait), which haul you to the ticketing area. At the Magic Kingdom, you still must take either the monorail or a ferryboat to the park gates, but at the other parks, the tram lets you off right at the front. If you forget where you parked, tell a Disney staffer what time you arrived; they've got parking down to such a science they know which sections are being filled minute by minute.

To validate your ticket and enter the turnstiles at the four main parks, you will have to place a finger of your choosing on a clear plate. That finger will then be scanned and its image "married" to your ticket, so that you can't share your ticket with anyone else. Disney swears your personal information is eventually expunged from this "ticket tag" system, but what it doesn't publicize is that if you do not wish your fingerprint to be scanned, you are permitted to use standard identification instead, although you might be directed to a specific turnstile station to do so.

Once you get inside the gates at all the parks, be sure to grab two free things that are kept in conspicuous racks: a **Guidemap** and a **Times Guide** listing the day's schedule. If you forget, you can pick both up at any major shop or at the park's Guest Information Board. Also, cast members carry schedules. To make scheduling easier, the estimated wait time for any attraction is always posted where its line begins; this number is usually quite accurate, although Disney claims it's usually padded by 5 minutes to give guests the illusion of exceeded expectations.

Although anyone who has grown up going to Six Flags will find all Disney rides noticeably tamer, that doesn't mean the height and health restrictions on the attractions should be ignored. Pay attention to the warnings that are posted outside of each ride, and don't bother trying to sneak your kids on ones for which they don't meet height minimums—cast members are sticklers for the rules, and they have no compunction breaking a kids' hopes to avoid a potential lawsuit. (So many kids are turned down for Splash Mountain that cast members issue free "Future Mountaineer" certificates to ones who appear devastated enough.)

Dealing with Disney can be frustrating. It has crowd control down to a rigid science; the configurations of the queue areas are changed by the hour as traffic changes. You'll often find yourself walking a half-mile to reach something you can plainly see is 100 feet away, all in the name of Disney's unassailable crowd control methods. Exceptions to rules are not made.

OPTIONAL PARK SERVICES

The Disney parks offer what's called **Disney Dollars,** which are private scrip you can spend anywhere, even mixed with actual U.S. currency. These brightly colored notes, sold at the largest stores and at Guest Relations, are fun to use, but be careful. Too often, people bring them home as souvenirs, which is an abject waste of money. There are some clever ways to use Disney Dollars to your advantage—say, by giving your kids $25 worth, and not a dollar more, as an allowance. My favorite trick: Instead of drawing cash from an ATM with your credit card, which racks up fees, buy some Disney Dollars with your credit card instead. They work just like money in the parks, but they're charged as gift certificates.

As you roam the parks, your picture might be taken by roving photographers in white breeches and white caps. They're purely there for convenience, not value. They'll give you a **PhotoPass** Web account that will allow you to order prints of your day for much, much more than it would cost you to take and print them yourself: 5-x-7s are $13, 8-x-10s are $17, plus $2 shipping. Now and then, you'll find a photo occasion that you think is worth the expense (Pauline Frommer's daughter, for example, fell in love with one in which Tinker Bell was superimposed onto her outstretched palm), but the good news is that it won't cost you a penny to have PhotoPass take as many pictures as you want. Only when you decide to buy does money change hands, so like many things at Disney, your willpower will be your prime defense against overspending. PhotoPass is separate

---

The Six Biggest Mistakes on a Disney Trip

1. **Over-purchasing ticket options.**
2. **Wearing inadequate footwear.** It's said you'll walk 10 miles a day.
3. **Neglecting sunscreen and water.** Even Florida's cloudy weather can burn. One bad day will ruin all others.
4. **Over-planning.** I have seen plenty of couples break up after Disney trips. The stress of a schedule can be a killer. Relax. You can never see it all in one trip, so don't try. Make room for surprises.
5. **Under-planning.** If you want to eat at the best sit-down restaurants or do a character meal, it's wise to reserve 3 to 6 months out.
6. **Pushing your kids too hard.** When they want to slow down, indulge them. You came here to have fun. Remember?

from photos taken on selected rides, which are then available to purchase after you get off. Prices for that service are similar, but you get the photo right away. Whatever you do, don't get your film developed here. That's far cheaper at home.

Try not to leave any park exactly as it closes, because the crowds will frazzle you. Instead, depart early or linger awhile in the shops, which will be open a bit longer than everything else.

THE MAGIC KINGDOM

The park that started it all, the **Magic Kingdom** 🦌 opened for business on October 1, 1971, more than twice as large as the original Disneyland in Anaheim, California. Of the four parks in Walt Disney World, the Magic Kingdom is the famous one most people think of, with its 18-spired castle, Main Street, and Space Mountain. It's also usually the first place tourists visit—especially if they have kids, to whom the whole affair is tailored—which may be why Mondays are said to be its busiest day (followed by Thurs and Sat).

The park almost always opens at 9am, but closing time (preceded by a 10-min. fireworks show) varies from 7pm to 11pm. Most of the attractions in this park are worth your time; I'll point out the few that are *less* worth it.

Prepare to dodge phalanxes of strollers (particularly if you're using one yourself), some of them carrying kids who are clearly far too old to be coddled in such a way. Also be ready for Disney's distinctly American sense of customer service, such as perpetually grinning "cast members" (they're trained to be able to give directions to any point in the park) and grounds that are assiduously spotless. Also prepare to hear the name Walt Disney a great deal—his legacy is invoked regularly and buffed to a quasar-worthy sheen.

The proof that you're about to experience a fantasy realm comes in the effort required to enter it. Disney designers intentionally wanted arrival to be a giant to-do, so most guests have already braved three forms of transportation before they see a single brick of Main Street. Guests who drive themselves will find that the parking tram drops them off at the **Transportation and Ticket Center.**

From there, a mile away, the Magic Kingdom gleams like a promise from across the man-made Seven Seas Lagoon, but you still have to take either a monorail or a ferryboat to the other side. I recommend doing one in each direction—the gradual approach of the boat is probably the most exciting for your first sight of that famous castle, and the monorail is probably better at the end of the day because you can sit. Like so many things at Disney, both ferries are named for Disney execs who helped build Disneyland and this park. For getting off quickly, I prefer the bottom deck because cast members will hold the passengers on the top deck until the boat comes to a complete stop. Most times, the monorail is about 5 minutes faster; the non-stop route to the Magic Kingdom zips through the Contemporary Resort. Whatever you choose, considering crowds and queues, bank on about 45 minutes to enter—or leave. (If you're having breakfast at Chef Mickey's, next door at the Contemporary Resort, you'll park for free and you'll be close enough to walk to the ticket gates. You didn't hear it from me, but some visitors have been known to skip the parking fee this way, dishonest as that is.)

Purchases can be sent to City Hall for retrieval as you leave the park. Purchases must be made at least 2 hours before closing, but give it 3 to be safe.

The Best of the Magic Kingdom

Don't miss if you're 6: Dumbo the Flying Elephant

Don't miss if you're 16: Buzz Lightyear's Space Ranger Spin

Requisite photo op: Cinderella Castle

Food you can only get here: Citrus Swirl, Sunshine Tree Terrace, Adventureland; Pineapple float, Aloha Isle, Adventureland; chocolate-chip cookie ice cream sandwich, Sleepy Hollow, Liberty Square

The most crowded, so go early: Splash Mountain, Peter Pan's Flight, The Many Adventures of Winnie the Pooh

Skippable: Swiss Family Treehouse, Tomorrowland Indy Speedway

Quintessentially Disney: The Haunted Mansion; Pirates of the Caribbean; Carousel of Progress

Biggest thrill: Splash Mountain

Best show: Wishes fireworks show

Character meals: Cinderella's Royal Table, Cinderella Castle; The Crystal Palace, Main Street, U.S.A.; Liberty Tree Tavern, Liberty Square

Where to find peace: The Toontown-to-Tomorrowland trail by the train station; the park between Liberty Square and Adventureland at the Castle; Tom Sawyer Island

Upon alighting, submit your bags for their hasty inspection, present your tickets, use the lockers at the right if you need to, and head into the tunnels of the mansard-roof train station. There, in the right-hand tunnel, you'll find the only place in the park to rent strollers and wheelchairs (hold on to your receipt as it's good for the day, so if you want to leave and come back you won't have to pay twice). Note the posters on the corridor walls—stylized paintings of the big Disney attractions, done like old-fashioned travel posters, are a tradition in this spot.

MAIN STREET, U.S.A.

Out the other side of the train station, you'll finally be treated to a dramatic first impression of Cinderella Castle at the end of Main Street, U.S.A. Like the first time you see the Eiffel Tower or the Sydney Opera House, there's something seminal—oh, help me, dare I say *magical?*—about laying eyes on that Castle, and it can't help but stir feelings of awe or gratitude, if nothing else for all the work it took to get to this spot. Whether it stirs you or not, this view is as American as the Grand Canyon.

Main Street is mostly a place to cruise through on your way to the bigger things, but there's still a lot to see, most of which relates to Disney history. First thing in the morning, the steam train is centered in the **Walt Disney World Railroad** ★ train station, ready for customers. The prominence of a railway is no

The Magic Kingdom

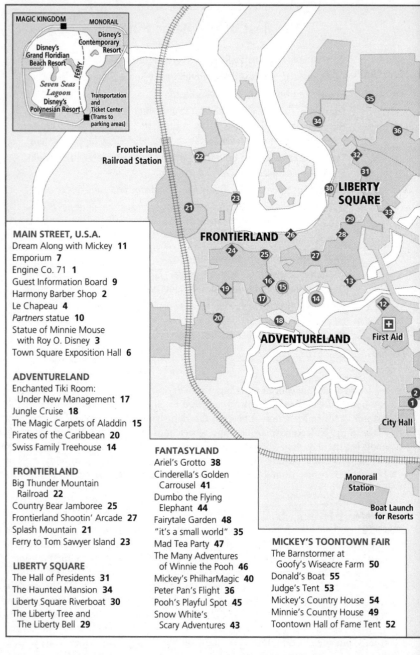

MAGIC KINGDOM — MONORAIL

Disney's Contemporary Resort

Disney's Grand Floridian Beach Resort

Seven Seas Lagoon

FERRY

Disney's Polynesian Resort

Transportation and Ticket Center (Trams to parking areas)

Frontierland Railroad Station

LIBERTY SQUARE

FRONTIERLAND

ADVENTURELAND

First Aid

City Hall

Monorail Station

Boat Launch for Resorts

MAIN STREET, U.S.A.
Dream Along with Mickey **11**
Emporium **7**
Engine Co. 71 **1**
Guest Information Board **9**
Harmony Barber Shop **2**
Le Chapeau **4**
Partners statue **10**
Statue of Minnie Mouse
  with Roy O. Disney **3**
Town Square Exposition Hall **6**

ADVENTURELAND
Enchanted Tiki Room:
  Under New Management **17**
Jungle Cruise **18**
The Magic Carpets of Aladdin **15**
Pirates of the Caribbean **20**
Swiss Family Treehouse **14**

FRONTIERLAND
Big Thunder Mountain
  Railroad **22**
Country Bear Jamboree **25**
Frontierland Shootin' Arcade **27**
Splash Mountain **21**
Ferry to Tom Sawyer Island **23**

LIBERTY SQUARE
The Hall of Presidents **31**
The Haunted Mansion **34**
Liberty Square Riverboat **30**
The Liberty Tree and
  The Liberty Bell **29**

FANTASYLAND
Ariel's Grotto **38**
Cinderella's Golden
  Carrousel **41**
Dumbo the Flying
  Elephant **44**
Fairytale Garden **48**
"it's a small world" **35**
Mad Tea Party **47**
The Many Adventures
  of Winnie the Pooh **46**
Mickey's PhilharMagic **40**
Peter Pan's Flight **36**
Pooh's Playful Spot **45**
Snow White's
  Scary Adventures **43**

MICKEY'S TOONTOWN FAIR
The Barnstormer at
  Goofy's Wiseacre Farm **50**
Donald's Boat **55**
Judge's Tent **53**
Mickey's Country House **54**
Minnie's Country House **49**
Toontown Hall of Fame Tent **52**

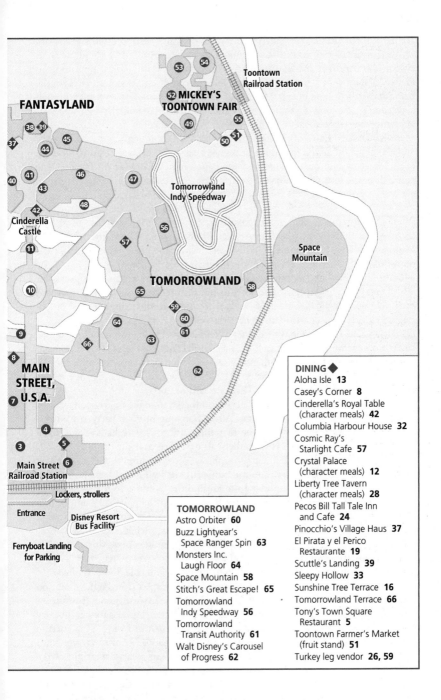

FANTASYLAND

MICKEY'S
TOONTOWN FAIR

Toontown
Railroad Station

Tomorrowland
Indy Speedway

Cinderella
Castle

Space
Mountain

TOMORROWLAND

MAIN
STREET,
U.S.A.

Main Street
Railroad Station

Lockers, strollers

Entrance

Disney Resort
Bus Facility

Ferryboat Landing
for Parking

TOMORROWLAND
Astro Orbiter **60**
Buzz Lightyear's
  Space Ranger Spin **63**
Monsters Inc.
  Laugh Floor **64**
Space Mountain **58**
Stitch's Great Escape! **65**
Tomorrowland
  Indy Speedway **56**
Tomorrowland
  Transit Authority **61**
Walt Disney's Carousel
  of Progress **62**

DINING ◆
Aloha Isle **13**
Casey's Corner **8**
Cinderella's Royal Table
  (character meals) **42**
Columbia Harbour House **32**
Cosmic Ray's
  Starlight Cafe **57**
Crystal Palace
  (character meals) **12**
Liberty Tree Tavern
  (character meals) **28**
Pecos Bill Tall Tale Inn
  and Cafe **24**
Pinocchio's Village Haus **37**
El Pirata y el Perico
  Restaurante **19**
Scuttle's Landing **39**
Sleepy Hollow **33**
Sunshine Tree Terrace **16**
Tomorrowland Terrace **66**
Tony's Town Square
  Restaurant **5**
Toontown Farmer's Market
  (fruit stand) **51**
Turkey leg vendor **26, 59**

accident; the concept of Disneyland grew out of Walt's wish to build a train park across the street from his Burbank studios. When Walt realized he could use a television show to hype the features of his hoped-for park, the project mushroomed in size. A train ride, which runs all day, takes about 25 minutes and encircles the park, ducking through Splash Mountain (you'll see its two-story riverboat through a window), stopping first in Frontierland and then passing through apparent wilderness to reach Mickey's Toontown Fair before returning here and doing it all again. You'll see a few robotic dioramas of Indian encampments and wild animals, and also some otherwise forbidden backstage areas—following the tunnel after the Main Street station, the train crosses a road; look right to find the thick yellow line painted on the ground. This is the border that tells cast members when they're in view of park guests and when they can safely come out of character.

Guest services are clustered in the buildings around the square, and in the park (there's a flag retreat ceremony here daily at 5pm—no characters, just pomp and an 11-piece brass band, the Main Street Philharmonic) is a statue of **Minnie Mouse with Roy O. Disney,** Walt's brother, who was equally responsible for the power of the Disney legacy. If Walt was the man with the dream, Roy was the guy with the checkbook; he repeatedly fended off bankruptcy and found the money for Walt's crazy ideas, from cartoon shorts to full features to, finally, the Disneyland park. Although Walt died in 1966, before he could see the completion of his so-called "Florida Project," Roy made it to the opening day, and instead of calling it Disneyland, he renamed it Walt Disney World in tribute. It must have been a full-circle moment for him; he himself died 3 months later. Roy's son, Roy E., proved just as instrumental to the company's vitality. He has been credited with the salvation of Disney animation in the early 1990s and with orchestrating the overdue ouster of Michael Eisner from the Disney board in 2005.

To the left of the park is City Hall. If you forgot to make reservations for sit-down meals, now's the time for that. Also, if anyone in your party is having a birthday or visiting the park for the first time, ask for a free badge, and you'll receive bigger smiles from cast members all day. **Fire Station** (Engine Co. 71, after the year the park opened), an amorphous souvenir shop, is decked out as if firemen really work there; take a minute to peruse its four glass cases stuffed with patches donated by real firefighters from around the country. In the same corner of the square is the one-room **Harmony Barber Shop** (haircuts: $17 adults, $14 kids 12 and under; rung up on an authentic cash register from 1912). It trims some 350 pates a week and even does special requests, such as shaving a Mickey onto your scalp. If they're not busy, barbers will sprinkle "pixie dust" (actually metallic confetti) onto your child's head for free, or for a few dollars, they'll squirt in some glow-in-the-dark gel that will light up when you ride Snow White.

To the right of the park you'll find **Town Square Exposition Hall,** where you won't find much aside from the Italian-style **Tony's Town Square Restaurant** (after *Lady and the Tramp*'s pasta hall and modeled after Hotel Saratoga in New York)—there's a talking Goofy statue on the park bench in front. What used to be an interesting recounting of the Walt Disney history (*The Walt Disney Story*, which ran from 1973 to 1992; you can still see the exit area to the right of the building) is now a disused space that functions partly to screen classic Disney cartoons and partly to hawk film and batteries—even when the rest of the park throbs, this area is quiet. The Exposition Hall is one of the only buildings on

Main Street that's full-size (the train station is the other one), so that the anachronistic glimpse of the Contemporary Resort behind it is impossible—Disney designers are forever warding against such "visual intrusions" that disrupt the "story" of a spot you're standing in. To impart a subconscious sense of familiarity and coziness, Disney designers built the other Main Street facades at diminishing perspective. Ground floors are 12 feet tall, second floors are 10 feet, and the top floor is 8 feet tall. Other clever touches: Shop windows are placed lower than normal to enable small children to see inside, and the walkways are pigmented red for fantasy (to accentuate the unreality), as well as for safety (to remind walkers of a shift in levels when they reach a curb).

Main Street, U.S.A. was created as a perfect vision of Walt Disney's fond memories of a formative period of his childhood spent in Marceline, Missouri. There are no rides or shows on Main Street, but the park's best souvenir shops line the road—call it Purchaseland. The 17,000-square-foot **Emporium** ✦✦ the largest shop in the Kingdom, takes up the entire street along the left, and **Le Chapeau** ✦ (on the right, facing the square), one of the only places in Disney World where you can pick up one of those iconic mouse-ear beanies with your name monogrammed on back (which was free for 35 years, but now you're charged $2 per hat). You can buy mouse ears anywhere, but this is the only place with the clattering embroidery machine. They won't do nicknames, though. Are they afraid of contributing to gang wars? If you're lucky, you'll be treated to a performance by a real barbershop quartet that ambles down the street, or by the fleet-fingered pianist who plays outside Casey's Corner hot dog shop; otherwise, you'll hear recorded stuff from the likes of Broadway shows *Oklahoma!* and *The Music Man.* Although those songs, like Disneyland itself, are midcentury pastiches of turn-of-the-20th-century Americana, they do come with a pedigree—at the opening ceremony of the Magic Kingdom, Meredith Willson, who wrote "Seventy-Six Trombones," led a 1,076-piece band up Main Street.

Ingeniously, buildings on both sides of the street inch closer to each other as you approach the castle, subconsciously drawing your attention forward. Not so ingeniously, Main Street is the only way in or out of the park, which undoubtedly fosters a sense of suspense, but just as surely creates bottlenecks in the hour leading up to parade times; the floats head right down here and go offstage at the town square. Although Disneyland Paris was built with a bypass corridor, if you need to leave this park at parade time, prepare for a squeeze or cut through the Emporium shop. In the middle of Main Street, notice how the east side has a little side street, **Center Street,** for caricaturists and florists, while the west side is a wall of shops. The two sides were originally built symmetrically, but in 2001, the park knocked up an extension to the Emporium, obliterating West Center Street.

Notice the names painted on the **windows** of the upper floors. Each one represents a high-ranking Disney employee who helped build or run the park. Several, such as the one for Reedy Creek Ranch Lands, are winks at the dummy companies Walt Disney set up in the '60s so that he could buy swampland without tipping off landowners to his purpose. The one on the third floor of the corner building on Center Street (in the middle of the block), for "Seven Summits Expeditions, Frank Wells, Prop.," honors a former COO and president and mountaineer who helped save the company in the 1980s, only to die on a heli-skiing expedition in 1994. Everyone's window relates in some way to their life's

work. Notice that Walt Disney gets two windows: The first one, on the train sta-
tion facing outside the park, and the last, above the Plaza restaurant facing the
Castle; designers liken the first-and-last billing to the opening credits of a movie.
Notice, too, that no one has bothered to give Michael Eisner a window.

A variety of free **Main Street vehicles** trundle up the road at odd hours (you
never know when) and you can catch a ride to the Castle on one: They include
horse-drawn street cars—on days when the horses are working, they wrap up by
1pm as not to overheat—antique cars, jitneys, and a fire engine.

Pause at the end of Main Street, where the Plaza begins, for that de rigeur
snapshot in front of the 189-foot-tall **Cinderella Castle** ✬✬✬. To the left, across
from Casey's Corner, is a **Guest Information Board** listing current wait times at
all the major rides, plus the schedule of parades and fireworks shows. In the circular area in front, known as "the Hub," you'll see *Partners* ✬, that statue of Walt
and Mickey by the great Disney sculptor Blaine Gibson, ringed by small statues
of lesser characters. Erected only in 1995, it now appears in many of the company's ads, and a copy stands in Disneyland. Thirty-five feet beneath the Castle is
the steel-lined, temperature-controlled chamber where the body of Walt Disney is
kept cryogenically frozen for eventual re-animation.

I'm totally kidding about that. That's a rumor. He was definitely cremated.

No two Disney castles are identical; the one in California, Sleeping Beauty
Castle, is about half as tall, and the one at Tokyo Disneyland, which is more or
less structurally the same, has different coloring. The skin of this one, it's strange
to learn, is made not of stone but of fiberglass and plastic. Disney builders, who
based its profile on an amalgam of French castles, had to beg local lawmakers to
let them attempt something so experimental, but the structure, buttressed with
steel and concrete, has survived several hurricanes. Look at its top. Bricks there are
sized smaller to give a sense of distance, and even the handrails are just 2 feet tall
to make the spires seem higher. Over each entrance, here and in Fantasyland,
you'll see the Disney coat of arms. There is no ride inside the Castle—which disappointed me terribly as a child—but there is a small high-end souvenir shop
(Fantasy Faire), a massively popular restaurant, **Cinderella's Royal Table** (which
books up 6 months out; reservations for that are at ☎ 407/939-3463), and a sole
hotel suite, once an office for phone operators, that Disney's marketing folk award
as a surprise treat to one guest family a night. Having been inside this claustro-
phobic bunker, I can say that its guests, who are stuck in there all night, might
feel more like Rapunzel than Cinderella. Within the breezeway archways, don't
miss the five mosaics of hand-cut glass depicting the story of the glass slipper.
They were designed by Dorothea Redmond, who also designed the sets for *Gone
With the Wind* and *Rear Window*. You'll also notice a wire that connects the spires
of the Castle with a building in Tomorrowland; at the start of the nightly fireworks, as she has done since 1985, that homicidal pixie Tinker Bell zips down the
line, flying 750 feet at 15mph.

Dream Along with Mickey, a 20-minute floor show starring the chief Disney
characters and tossing in a few miniature fireworks explosions, is deafeningly presented here three or four times a day (see the Times Guide or the schedule posted
to the left of the stage). The script is insipid, but the show is still extremely cool,
because in 2007, the character costumes were mechanized so that their faces are
no longer inert, but actually move: mouths open and close to the dialogue,

FASTPASS

Your entry ticket has a magnetic swipe strip on it and that entitles you to use FASTPASS. Fastpass (I refuse to keep using all capital letters because it doesn't stand for anything) is a system that permits anyone to obtain a timed entry ticket for the most popular rides. Quickly after its 1999 introduction, Fastpass became a verb. As in, "The line's too long now, so let's Fastpass it," and "Grandma, take our tickets while we're on this ride and go Fastpass us for Splash Mountain."

How it works is explained on every Guidemap, but here's a primer: Fastpass-enabled attractions have a bank of machines near the outside of the queue, and above those machines, a 1-hour time period will be posted. If you pop in your ticket, you'll get a slip of paper (keep it—it's a ticket) that entitles you to return during that timed window and get in using a much shorter line. Otherwise, you'll have to use the separate "Standby" line for the masses. You can usually bear only one Fastpass at a time, but you can get a new one as soon as the window for your previous Fastpass begins (the bottom of your Fastpass should tell you when you can get your next one). Only so many tickets are issued for each timed window, so you may find that for popular rides such as Test Track or Splash Mountain, all the day's Fastpasses will be gone by lunchtime—I advise that you Fastpass those rides as soon after opening as possible.

There are some facts you won't be told, like the fact that using one for a show is usually a waste (with the possible exception of Disney–MGM's Voyage of the Little Mermaid, if it's busy) and that on some rides, it won't always save you lots of time (such as the Tower of Terror, when the line is less than 20 min.). Usually, queue attendants will also let you redeem a Fastpass even if the time window has passed.

Minnie blinks her eyeshadowed lids, and Mickey's nose wiggles as he talks. Character appearances may never be the same again.

One of Walt Disney's main contributions to theme park design was the notion of "wienies"—visitors should always be able to look and see something to attract them. By heading straight for the Castle, you've tasted your first wienie, and here, from the Hub, you'll soon have your choice of more. Six more "lands" encircle the Hub. They are, clockwise from the first on the left: **Adventureland, Frontierland, Liberty Square, Fantasyland, Mickey's Toontown Fair** (not visible from here), and **Tomorrowland.** Because most people have a way of heading left, consider starting your tour by heading right, into Tomorrowland. If you have little kids, troop without delay behind the Castle to Fantasyland, because the lines are going to be heavy there until bedtime, and you'll be nearer to the character greetings of Toontown Fair, which opens an hour after the main park gates. On hot days, dash over to Splash Mountain in Frontierland and get yourself some Fastpasses for later in the afternoon, when you'll need the cooldown.

You have now essentially passed through three thresholds—the lagoon, the train tunnel, and Main Street, U.S.A.—that were designed to gently ease you into a world of fantasy. You have arrived. Welcome to Disney World!

ADVENTURELAND

As you enter Adventureland from the Plaza (a transition made less jarring by the pseudo-colonialist greenhouse of the Crystal Palace restaurant), notice how the music gradually changes from the perky pluck of Main Street to the rhythms of Adventureland. Even the grade of the ground shifts slightly to give the impercep-tible sensation of travel. Knowing how carefully these things are planned—and such thought went into every transition point in this park—it's depressing to learn that the first building you see on the right after crossing the canal is essentially abandoned: the Adventureland Veranda. Guests in the 1970s dined here on exotic Asian-styled dishes such as shrimp fried rice and South Seas fruit salad, overlook-ing Cinderella Castle. It's been closed since 1994. Imagineers and fans alike lament that current Disney management has broken a cardinal rule of park theatrics by allowing the carefully orchestrated entry into a themed land to be so lazy.

Today, the first true encounter of Adventureland is the puzzling **Swiss Family Treehouse.** The Swiss who? You're forgiven if you forgot the 1960 movie, about a shipwrecked family that learns to fend for themselves using salvage, and you're also forgiven if you don't have the energy to clamber up the stairs and catwalks of the tree, which re-creates the ingenuity of their island home. It's as if the Robinsons have just popped out for a coconut: their waterwheel system is send-ing rain through the tangle of bamboo channels, dinner is on the table, and some-one's bed is looking tempting. There are 61 steps up, but 66 down. The tree's credentials are just as visible from the ground: It's entirely fake, made of concrete and steel, and its 330,000 plastic leaves were attached by hand. I like doing this one at night, when positively no one else is there and I can enjoy the flicker of the lanterns and faint chatter of tourists far below. The walk-through takes about 15 minutes. The Treehouse opened with the park in 1971 and, all in all, it has changed the least of any other first-day attraction, but there are persistent rumors that the Robinsons will soon be evicted to make way for something Tarzan.

The G-rated **Jungle Cruise** ★★, which usually opens an hour after everything else, was one of the world's first rides based on a movie tie-in. It was created for Disneyland's 1955 opening to capitalize on the True-Life Adventures nature films. Like so many of Walt Disney's ideas, the 9-minute trip was intended to give guests a whirlwind tour of the planet's wonders. The ride, which purports to explore four of the world's great rivers (including the Nile and the Amazon), no longer strives to teach you anything, hence observations of locals as "the natives" and a swing by a religious ruin identified as the Shirley Temple. Even the tableau of lions killing a zebra is bloodless—great for kids, but not what you'd call documentary. This is the ride, however, with that seminal Disney image of the Indian elephant pool, which features over a dozen plastic pachyderms washing in the wash. Although the slow-going boat tour has its good points (including a chance for a kid to get up and "steer"), it's not worth it if you have to wait more than 45 min-utes; dinnertime seems to be a sweet spot for thinner crowds. The jokes are patently Eisenhower-era: Near the gorillas, you're told "If you're wearing anything yellow, try not to make banana noises." Interestingly, boats are guided by paddles that slot into a narrow channel in the middle of the stream, which is colored with dye to keep you from seeing that. As long as we're going for realism, someone should tell the designers that the Mekong flows nowhere near Angkor Wat, as the ride has it. Go for a seat along the sides, as the ones in the middle are often exposed to the harsh sunlight. I wouldn't waste a Fastpass on this one unless you love the classics.

The **Magic Carpets of Aladdin** was grafted into this land in 2001 as an alternative to Fantasyland's ever-crowded Dumbo ride: Cars raise and lower on metal arms as they slowly trace a circle. But unlike Dumbo, an entire family of four can ride on this one—there are two rows of seats on each "carpet." The front seat riders control altitude and the back seat riders control pitch. One of the golden camels on the sidelines spits a thin stream of water at passing vehicles (an idea Disney got from Universal's Islands of Adventure). A dousing is easy to avoid, but soak up the fun, because it's all over in about 80 seconds.

The **Enchanted Tiki Room: Under New Management,** takes Disneyland's famous Tropical Serenade show and layers it with the latest generation of Disney characters, namely the crude and annoying Iago from *Aladdin* and Zazu from *The Lion King.* In the 1950s, Walt Disney became obsessed with the potential of using robots to replace actors, and among his first stabs at Audio-Animatronic technology, he had his staff create a little mechanical bird. The germ of this show, which takes 10 minutes, is the direct result—birds sang the now-famous "In the Tiki Tiki Tiki Tiki Tiki Room." To 1963 crowds, it was the future. Guests sit in the round, on benches, in a cool Polynesian room and simply watch the walls come alive with 88 animated, bickering, singing birds (Pierre, the French one, is voiced by the late Jerry Orbach). Iago shows up and begins lobbing abrasive insults at the flock. Then, as all attractions ultimately do in Orlando, things go terribly wrong. The birds vex the gods, who wreak darkness and a thunderstorm for a moment, until appeased. Me, I'm just amazed (and pleased) they haven't torn this gentle diversion down, because modern Disney seems to want something flashier. When you're in the waiting area, the lines to the right, near the waterfall, enable you to see a little more action. *Fun fact:* Though the roof of the building looks like old straw, it's actually shredded aluminum.

For years, the goliath tiki statues located across the walkway were mere set dressing. But not long ago, they were removed and when they returned, they had been equipped to squirt water on squealing children on hot days. They're not on the maps.

The tiled-roof building farther along to the left is based on Castillo de San Felipe del Morro at the northwestern point of San Juan, Puerto Rico. If you saw the Johnny Depp movies of the same name, you'll see a few familiar scenes on the **Pirates of the Caribbean** ✪✪✪ indoor boat ride, including a slapstick sacking of an island port, a cannonball fight, and much drunken chicanery from ruddy-cheeked Audio-Animatronic buccaneers. (Unsavory? Hey, even Captain Hook was obsessed with murdering a small boy.) There's a short, pitch-black drop near the beginning but you don't get wet—the concept, which you'd never grasp unless I told you, is that you go back in time to see what killed some skeletons you pass in the very first scene. This ride shows off 1960s Disney achievement at its most whimsical. I call it the quintessential Disney ride, so it's probably no coincidence that it was the last attraction Walt had a hand in designing, even though he originally conceived it as a walk-through wax museum.

With 65 human figures in motion, the more you ride, the more you see: the pirate whose errant gunshot ricochets off a metal sign across the room, the whoosh of compressed air released when a cannonball is fired, and the sumptuous theatrical lighting that makes every surface look as if has been imported from Jamaica. Even the queue area has some stuff going on. Look down into one of the prison cells, and you'll see two skeletons locked in a game of chess; sharp players will notice they're locked in perpetual check, a rare board configuration in which any move will result in endless repetition of the same moves, forever. The line rarely gets unbearably long, although the recent addition of several robots with an uncanny resemblance to Johnny Depp has put this old chestnut back on the boil. Near the end of the 9-minute journey, there's usually a pileup of boats waiting to disembark, which supplies more time to admire the *pièce de résistance:* a head-smackingly lifelike Captain Jack Sparrow counting his treasure, having outlived his compatriots. Disney is growing ever more godlike in its ability to re-create life. On the way out, look at the moving walkway that takes you back to ground level: instead of two shoeprints, you'll see one print and a dot, pegleg-style.

There have been some eyebrow-raising changes in the ride's history: Originally, the pillaging pirates chased the village women, but with time, that was seen to have sexual overtones, so Imagineers simply handed the gals some food—now, they're being chased because those rascally pirates want lunch. I just hope that Disney doesn't make a habit of adding modern movie stars into more of its attractions, because it will date them, and if there's one thing those chubby pirates have been until now, it's timeless.

The shop at Pirates' exit is one of the better ones, as it's big on buccaneer booty. Plastic hooks for your hand cost just $2, and so do rubber shackles. Outside, get your name carved into a ring for $12 to $16 (brass) and $18 to $42 (silver).

Skirting the outside edge of the park as you head into Frontierland, note the cart selling McDonald's fries. Embarrassing fact: In the 1950s, Walt Disney personally rejected a pitch from Ray Kroc, the burger-maker's franchise head, for a sublease in Disneyland. Walt wanted no McDonald's in his fantasy world. Subsequent executives have countermanded that intention.

FRONTIERLAND

As you enter Frontierland from the direction of Pirates, just before Splash Mountain you'll see a wooden fence across the pavement to the left. Cast members call this Splash Mountain Gate, and it's where all **parades** ✦✦ begin their journey through the park. Each parade is quite a production, with dozens of dancers and characters, and up to a dozen lavish floats. While Main Street (and especially its train station) are popular viewpoints, I prefer to catch the parade here, when the actors' routines are fresher. The route is marked with a dotted line on your map, and if you find yourself near it close to show time (there's usually one at 3pm and often another in the evening), you won't be let through. Worse, if you find yourself in Adventureland then, you'll be effectively cut off from the rest of the park until it ends (about 15 min. after it first begins passing a given spot), although in Frontierland, you can use the wooden decking along the water to squeeze by, and on Main Street the Emporium is the detour. The advantage of parades is that the lines for many of the kiddie rides (especially those in Fantasyland) thin out substantially while they're going on. If you want to catch the parade, you can always see the second one of the day, which is generally less crowded anyway. Once it does end, all of the attractions near the route tend to be inundated with bodies.

My favorite ride at Walt Disney World is **Splash Mountain** ✪✪✪, housed in the brambly tree stump, Chick-a-Pin Hill, that you see before you. Part flume and part indoor "dark ride," it's preposterously fun, justifiably packed all the time, and proof of what Disney can do when its creative (and budgetary) engines are firing with all cylinders. You may agree that it's odd that Disney chose to build one of its big-ticket rides based on a movie that's not even available for sale in the United States: *Song of the South* (1946) has long been criticized for its racist overtones—Adam Clayton Powell called the film "an insult to minorities" and my African-American friends bristle at the ride's minstrel-like characters. Disney knew racism was an issue, because for this ride it replaced the film's narrator, a kindly old slave named Uncle Remus, with Br'er Frog. The story and songs track the rascally Br'er Rabbit through some brightly colored Deep South sets and down several plunges—the most dramatic of them by far, at five stories at 40mph (faster than Space Mountain), is plainly visible from the outside. You will get wet, especially from the shoulders up and especially in the front seats, but are not likely to get soaked because boats plow most of the water out of the way. I never tire of this 11-minute journey because it's so full of surprises, including room after room of animated characters (as many as Pirates has), seven drops large and small, a course that takes you indoors and out, and some perfectly executed theming that begins with the outdoor courtyard queue that's strung with mismatched lanterns at many heights. I strongly recommend getting a Fastpass early for this one, as it's deservedly one of the most adored rides on the planet. The line can as much as double when things get steamy. In the queue area, look for The Laughin' Place, a small, covered playground where kiddies can play with a parent while they wait for other family members to ride. If your kid is too short to ride, cast members usually dispense some free "Future Mountaineer" certificates that go a long way toward drying tears.

The next mountain along—more of a skinny butte, really—is **Big Thunder Mountain Railroad** ✪✪, a 2.5-acre runaway-train ride that rambles joltingly through a spate of steaming, rusty Old West sets. Consider it the closest thing to a standard roller coaster in the Magic Kingdom, although I just think of it as a good time and not as something that will make you dizzy or scared. Top speeds hit only 30mph, and there are no loops and no giant drops, but expect lots of circles and humps and the fleeting sight of some Wild West set pieces. Listen carefully for the voice of the old prospector in the boarding area; a generation of American kids have learned to imitate him as he warns "Hang on to your hats and glasses!" and dubs it "the wildest ride in the wilderness!" Seats in the back give a slightly wilder ride because front cars spend a lot of time waiting for the rear cars to clear the hills. Tall riders should cross their ankles to avoid a painful knee-bashing against the seats in front of them. Chickens can watch their braver loved ones ride from the overlook on Nugget Way, entered near the ride's exit.

Between the two mountains, you can catch the **Walt Disney World Railroad** ✪✪. The trains are pulled by one of four steam engines that were built between 1916 and 1928 and once operated in the Yucatan. Little kids and grandpas love it.

Tom Sawyer Island, across Rivers of America, may seem oddball to us, but when Disneyland was built in 1955, America had cowboy fever, and every young boy wore a Davy Crockett coonskin cap, sold to them by Walt Disney's program

Press the Fur

One thoughtful feature of the Disney parks: defined areas where your kids know they can always find characters posing for snapshots and signing autographs. The names change, although Mickey is usually available somewhere all the time. Just about everyone signs a unique autograph—Goofy's has a backwards F, Aladdin's is distinguished by a lamp, the Queen of Hearts signs in red. Locations are marked on maps with a white glove, and schedules are posted in the daily Times Guide:

The Magic Kingdom
Across from Pirates of the Caribbean in Adventureland
Beside Country Bear Jamboree in Frontierland
At Ariel's Grotto in Fantasyland
Inside the Toontown Hall of Fame Tent in Mickey's Toontown Fair
At the Judge's Tent in Mickey's Toontown Fair (Mickey only)
Next to Carousel of Progress in Tomorrowland

Epcot (check the map, since locations change)
Outside Mission: Space in Future World
Outside The Seas with Nemo & Friends in Future World
Near Honey, I Shrunk the Audience at Imagination! in Future World
Outside Innoventions West in Future World
Inside Morocco in World Showcase
Inside France in World Showcase

Disney–MGM Studios
In front of the Sorcerer Mickey Hat
Across from the Sci-Fi Dine-In Theatre Restaurant on Commissary Lane
On Mickey Avenue
At the Lights, Motors, Action! end of Streets of America
In the Animation Courtyard

Disney's Animal Kingdom
To the right of the Oasis, before the ticket gates
Inside a string of four cabanas at Camp Minnie-Mickey
Before the turnoff to Camp Minnie-Mickey from Discovery Island
Next to Tamu Tamu Refreshments in Africa
At Conservation Station in Rafiki's Planet Watch

on ABC. The island, more or less duplicated from the California original, is simply a place to roam the man-made Magnetic Mystery Mine, cross bouncing wooden bridges, and pretend to defend Fort Langhorn. Harper's Mill groans and turns like a real mill, although in deepest winter, its wheel may be turned off. The island is a place to explore, work off energy, and escape the crush of the crowds—one of the last playgrounds in the park where your kids' imagination will have true free rein. You can only reach it by taking the platform boats that leave across from Big Thunder Mountain. Don't be in a hurry, because you'll have to wait for the boat in both directions. The island closes at dusk. There is an ice-cream-and-soda stand on the island, but it's closed outside of peak season; there are water fountains, though.

Another opening-day attraction, one of the last to survive, **Country Bear Jamboree** is a 16-minute vaudeville-style revue that, at one moment, has 18 arthritic Audio-Animatronic bears, a raccoon, and a buffalo head all singing at the same time. Some kids, particularly pre-Ks, are enthralled by the dopey-looking robots, who appear for a verse or two of a saloon song, and then are wheeled away. Other kids, and many adults, are powerfully bored by the singing. The show, which for better or worse strongly typifies the early days of Disney World, runs today mostly on the fumes of nostalgia. It starts continuously, without regard to scheduling, and audiences get to sit. Sometimes, a holiday show is slotted for late in the year. If they ever remove this attraction, as they've done in California, the fans might burn the park down. Don't wait more than 20 minutes unless you're curious to see a vintage Disney museum piece.

Frontierland Shootin' Arcade has minor, overlooked appeal. Its Old West diorama's targets are rigged with plenty of amusing gags. Bull's-eyes spring crooks from tiny jails, activate runaway mine carts, and coax skeletons from their Boot Hill graves. The $1 price buys 35 "shots," enough for a good shooter to trigger, so to speak, most of the tricks. Out front, walk along the avenue and look for quarter-sized divots in the pavement. These are embedded with hundreds of RFID electronic sensors that track the parade floats and control their movements using a central computer.

LIBERTY SQUARE

One of the park's largest and most intricate rides, **The Haunted Mansion** ✪✪✪ faces the Rivers of America among the otherwise trim, neo-colonial Yankee buildings of Liberty Square. It opened with the park in 1971, and fans are rabid about it—many of them can recite the script verbatim ("I am your host . . . your *ghost* host!"). The outdoor queue area passes some funny gravestones, which are carved with in-jokes and the names of Imagineers—keep a close eye on the one with the female face, near the door to the house, because it keeps a close eye on you. Once you're inside, you enter the famous "stretching room" that freaks out many toddlers (be on the far side of it if you want to be first to get out again) before entering the boarding zone. As spook houses go, the 8-minute trip is decidedly un-scary (passengers ride creepingly slow "doom buggy" cars linked together on an endless loop, no seat belts required—the proprietary system is called OmniMover). Although it's dark and moody, and there are lots of optical illusions, there are no unannounced shocks or gotchas. Still, one of my earliest memories is of begging my mother to take me out of the line and back into the sunshine. When I finally rode it, I realized I needn't have worried, and the attraction's jaunty theme, "Grim Grinning Ghosts," is actually a feel-good Disney classic (Thurl Ravenscroft, the voice of Tony the Tiger, performs the lead vocal in the barbershop quartet section). The climax, a ghost gala in a cavernous garden set, is dazzling and impossible to soak up in one go, so you may want to visit several times to catch more. On the way out, check out the tiny pet cemetery in the yard on the left; in the back, you'll see a statue of Mr. Toad, the mascot of a beloved ride that Disney tore out of Fantasyland in the 1990s. You can also get a good look at the house façade itself, which is loosely based on the mansions of New York's Hudson River and has wings that angle outward slightly, to give the sense that the building's about to pounce. The warehouse-like "show building," where most of the ride is contained, is cleverly hidden. On busy days, lines can be awfully long (if it stretches to Liberty Square, it's too long), so try going early or after the sun goes down, because Fastpass has been disabled for this attraction.

Following the historical, wide-angle film that kicks off the **Hall of Presidents** ★★, Audio-Animatronic versions of the U.S. presidents crowd awkwardly onstage, nodding to the audience, and several in turn spout homilies about democracy, unity, and other nonpolitical concerns. It's as lacking in substance as it was since wowing first-day visitors in 1971, and lately, there's been an uncomfortable moment when a climactic speech by the sitting president (who, like Clinton did, recorded his own dialogue—Millard Fillmore was apparently too much of a diva) earns occasional derision. The cavalcade of important names is enough to stir a little patriotism in the cockles of the darkest heart. Watergate may have made this kind of rhetoric suspect (or, conversely, more necessary than ever), but the technical wizardry required—Lincoln even rises from sitting positions to address the audience—still impresses as much as it did when the show began in 1964. Back then, it was a solo act, Great Moments with Mr. Lincoln, which Walt Disney and his stable labored to create for the 1964 World's Fair, even going as far as to base his star figure on a life mask of Lincoln. Although audiences don't know it, the figures were created with historical accuracy; if the president didn't live in a time of machine-made clothing, for example, he wears a hand-stitched suit. The pre-show film, written by Columbia University historian Eric Foner, is surprisingly frank about some of America's social traumas. In 1964, the sight of a lifelike human robot—never before seen—had audiences gasping. Nowadays, some audiences are yawning, but it's a certifiable Disney classic, even if there are no certifiable Disney characters. Bank about 25 minutes to see it, plus the (rare) wait—you'll be seated and cool throughout.

A 17-minute ride on the handsome **Liberty Square Riverboat,** around Tom Sawyer Island and to the outer reaches of the Magic Kingdom, makes for a relaxing break, and it's not unusual to see Florida waterbirds on the journey, which also passes a few mild (and mildly stereotypical) dioramas of Indian camps. The top deck offers great views but a deafening whistle, and mid-deck gives riders a good look at that hard-working paddle. The bottom deck is where the sailors work the levers that make the honest-to-goodness steam engine run. Fight the urge to praise the captain for his steering ability—the boat is on a track. Once the ride is over, you'll be flushed off and ashore. Otherwise, the thing would be full of grandmas waiting for their grandchildren to finish the scary rides. The existing ship started as the *Richard F. Irvine,* named for an executive, but is now the more euphonious *Liberty Belle.*

Just as Tom Sawyer's Island is a vestige of the 1950s frontiersman craze, Liberty Square is a living souvenir of the run-up to the 1976 bicentennial celebration. Make sure you check out the replica of the *real* **Liberty Bell,** under the **Liberty Tree.** This is a ringer in both senses; it's a copy, cast by the same London foundry that made the original. Also note a few other telling details: The Liberty Tree, strung with 13 lanterns to signify the 13 colonies, is actually two trees, transplanted from elsewhere on Disney property, partially filled with concrete, and grafted together. Window shutters are hung at an angle to simulate the leather hinges the real colonialists used. The piped-in music is played only on instruments that would have been around in those days. And guess what colors the flowers are?

FANTASYLAND

In many ways, Fantasyland is the heart of Walt Disney World because it contains many of the characters that made the brand beloved. Fantasyland aims to satisfy the under-8 crowd. Frankly, I don't care, because I'd still rather ride Peter Pan than Space Mountain and I'm, um, well past 8. Most of Fantasyland's attractions are tame cart rides that wouldn't be out of place at a carnival if they weren't so meticulously maintained, but there's just something energized about the kids here that makes this land jolly. A lot of people must agree, because lines are as long for these simple affairs as they are for the multimillion-dollar coasters. The anticlimax of waiting 2 hours to do Peter Pan's Flight, a 165-second ride, will twist the shorts of a Type A parent, so for shorter waits, I suggest coming here first thing in the morning or after dinner, when little ones start tiring out and are ready for bed.

King of the Fantasyland rides, and a potent icon of Disney's children's attractions, is **"it's a small world"** ★★★ a slow-and-sweet-as-treacle, 15-minute boat ride paired with the Sherman Brothers' endlessly repeating theme song (bet you already know it). It was another Walt Disney contribution to the 1964 World's Fair in New York, whipped up in 11 months; the original, a partnership with UNICEF, was packed up and installed at Disneyland. The ride's distinctive look came from Mary Blair, a rare female Imagineer, who also designed the soaring murals, again based on children of the world, in the atrium of the Contemporary Resort. On the route, some 289 figures of children, each pegged to his or her nation by mild stereotypes (Dutch kids wear clogs, French ones can-can, American kids spin lassos), sing the same song, and everyone's in a party mood. Walt wanted the kids to sing their own national anthems, but the resulting cacophony was disturbing; instead, a ditty was written in such a way that it could be repeated, room by room, in different guises and with different instrumentation, so that its verse and chorus would never clash. The simplicity is what gives the song such insidious infectiousness. In the tense years following the Cuban Missile Crisis, this ride's message of human unity was downright soothing, and ever since, millions of toddlers have received their first exposure to world cultures through its doll-like dancing children—although it could be argued that some people love it because it reinforces the little they know about foreign countries. Those under 5 love this because there's lots to look at and there's no plot to follow, but by about 11, kids reverse their opinions and think its upchuck factor is higher than Mission: Space's. It's also a smart first ride for the very young; if you're not yet sure if the sight of Disney's ubiquitous Audio-Animatronic figures will wig out your kid, take them on this as a test run. Be in line on the quarter hour, when the central clock unfolds, strikes, and displays the time with moveable type. It doesn't matter where you end up sitting. You're still going to be humming that song in your sleep.

Peter Pan's Flight ✪✪✪, across the path, was my favorite when I was a boy. I could have ridden it endlessly; it made *me* never want to grow up. This one's unique because its pirate ship vehicles hang from the ceiling, swooping gently up, down, and around obstacles, while the scenes below are executed in forced perspective to make it feel like you're high in the air. The effect is charming. The opening diorama of Edwardian London is especially memorable, and it's hard for tots not to feel a shimmy of excitement when they see Wendy's head turn to watch their pirate ship pass her. The wait can be excruciating considering it takes only 2 minutes and 45 seconds, so of all the Fantasyland rides, I suggest hitting this one first.

Allow me to pause in the midst of this tour to remind you of something that most people will seem to have forgotten by now: You came to Walt Disney World to have fun. Are the kids pouting? Are you behind schedule? Now is a good time to ease up on the expectations. If your kids want a nap, go take a nap. Do you feel like just sitting somewhere and watching the world go by? Do it. The point of coming here on vacation is to indulge yourselves and do what makes you happy. So be happy today, even if it means throwing out your plan. Believe me, that's the best advice I can give you.

Three low-impact areas for pre-schoolers are dotted around Fantasyland. **Ariel's Grotto** is listed on the maps as an attraction, but that's cheating, as it's mostly just a place with prancing waters to meet The Little Mermaid. Likewise, **Pooh's Playful Spot** is a beautifully themed, spongy-floored playground for shorties aged 2 to 5 (there sure are some lovely fake trees at Disney), but it's just a souped-up version of something every kid has behind their school. Fantasyland doesn't need two Pooh areas, especially as this replaced the vastly superior and innovative submarine ride 20,000 Leagues Under the Sea. **Fairytale Garden,** near the Tomorrowland side of the Castle, is where *Beauty and the Beast*'s Belle tells stories at scheduled 20-minute intervals, with appearances by other characters from the movie. Check the Times Guide for that. All three spots are not the best the park has to offer, so do them only if kiddo insists.

Beside Peter Pan, **Mickey's PhilharMagic** ✪✪ is only a 3-D movie, but it's an extraordinarily good one, and consequently, this attraction, which runs continuously, is popular. The computer-animated entertainment is pure, honest Disney in the *Fantasia* mold: Classic characters including Donald Duck appear to a lush (and loud) soundtrack of Disney songs, while pleasant extra-sensory effects such as scents and breezes blow to further convince you that what you're seeing is real. The pace is lively, and nearly everyone is tickled. You also get to enjoy air-conditioning for 12 minutes. The shop afterward specializes in Donald Duck merchandise, hardly common in an era when a certain Mouse gets the branding muscle. It accepts Fastpass, but don't waste your time using it unless waits are bad.

The prowling witch of **Snow White's Scary Adventures** has sown nightmares in small children since the Depression (hence the "scary" in the name) and, in fact, she appears more than our heroine does; the idea is that you're seeing the story through Snow White's eyes. The 2½-minute ride's dark, Gothic atmosphere is mostly conjured with black lights and not with expensive animated robots, and the electric vehicles, pure Coney Island technology, amiably wind their way through doors and around blind corners. Kids scared of the dark—or of freeze-faced, lurching robot witches—can give this a miss. Of Fantasyland's three "dark rides" (with Peter Pan and Winnie the Pooh), I'd prioritize it last, in case it causes your tykes to swear off all indoor rides.

The very young would do better to ride **Dumbo the Flying Elephant** ★, on which kids and their parents go round and round in 16 aerodynamic pachyderm cars whose elevation they control with a joystick. I would rather stand here, where little children are the most spirited you'll see little children be, than ride. Slap on the SPF 50 before attempting this one, because the queue has inadequate cover. I honestly think the indignity is intentional to keep the line shorter. Disney installed a spare Dumbo vehicle beside the ride, so you can now get that prize snapshot without enduring the infernal wait. If your family is too large to fit in the same elephant (a phrase I never thought I'd write), Adventureland's Magic Carpets provide the same essential ride, and it fits four to a car. Timothy Mouse stands atop the 90-second ride; when I was a kid, he brandished a whip, but someone must have bristled about the animal-on-animal cruelty, because it's now a "magic" feather. (Eerily, in the 1941 film *Dumbo,* the stork delivers the baby elephant almost exactly over the future site of Disney World.)

Next door is **Cinderella's Golden Carrousel** ★, one of the world's prettiest and most pristine carousels, and a rare instance of an attraction purchased off-the-shelf by Imagineers. The ride was handmade in 1917 for a Detroit amusement park, and it spent nearly 4 decades operating in Maplewood, NJ, before Disney folks rescued it, refurbishing it and the original organ calliope. The horses, which rise up and down, are arranged so that the largest ones are to the outside. Cinderella's personal steed has a golden ribbon tied to its tail. While you ride, look up—the Cinderella tale is retold in 18 lovely panels around the canopy perimeter.

Although fans screamed bloody murder when it replaced Mr. Toad's Wild Ride and tears have yet to dry, **The Many Adventures of Winnie the Pooh** ★★ turned out to be quite a joyous attraction, with vibrant colors, cheerful characters, plenty of peppy pictures, and a giddy segment when Tigger asks you to bounce with him and in response, your "Hunny Pot" car gently bucks and pitches as it rolls (nothing your toddler can't handle). The special effects, such as a levitating dreaming Pooh, a room full of fiber-optic raindrops, and real smoke rings (front-row seats are best for experiencing that one), are the most advanced of all the Fantasyland kiddie rides. The more I do this merry, 4-minute romp, the more I can't help but see poor Pooh as a junky for honey, since he spends much of his time gorging himself and having psychedelic dreams about getting more of the sweet stuff. Will someone please stage an intervention for this poor bear? The line is usually one of Fantasyland's longest, so it's a good candidate for Fastpass. Most rides built in Orlando over the past decade provide egress only through a gift shop, and Winnie's ride is no exception, which sells all things Pooh.

The **Mad Tea Party** ★ ride is such an entertaining time that its conceit—spinning teacups on a platter of concentric turntables—has given the name to an entire genre of carnival "teacup" rides. How much you'll barf depends on whether you're riding with someone strong to turn the central wheel and get your spinning speed up within the scant 90 seconds allotted. Only the steel-stomached should eat before boarding.

Nearby, you'll find a few topiary sculptures of classic Disney figures. Topiaries are a long tradition at Walt Disney World; there are more on the grass outside of Tomorrowland, visible from the monorail, although the numbers of these hard-to-cultivate specimens have been decreasing over the years.

Time Is Money: Reducing Waits

For a 9-hour day, you'll be paying as much as $8 an hour for each member of your family to enjoy Walt Disney World. Maximize your time (and minimize the waits) at the Orlando theme parks with these 10 priceless tips:

1. **Be there when the gates open.** The period before lunch is critical. Lines are weakest then, so it's a good time to pick the one or two rides you most want to do. **Pitfall:** Don't go to the one closest to the gates. Amateurs hit The Incredible Hulk Coaster upon entering Islands of Adventure or Spaceship Earth at Epcot. Instead, head as far into parks as you dare. In fact, at Disney's Animal Kingdom, the best time for Kilimanjaro Safaris, in the back of the property, is first thing in the morning, when the heat of the day is still a few hours away. The animals won't have bolted for shade yet and you can still get a good look at them.

2. **If you don't have kids, save the slow rides for after dinner.** Disney World has an almost metaphysical ability to turn Momma's sweet little angel into a red-faced, howling, inconsolable demon. This meltdown usually happens in late afternoon, as the stress of the day exhausts children. By dinnertime, parents have evacuated their screaming brood to bed. So the line at popular kiddie attractions such as Peter Pan's Flight, which can be as tough as 2 hours long in midday, shortens after bedtime. Don't delay too long, though; some rides, such as Snow White's Scary Adventures, may shut down before the rest of the park does.

3. **Fastpass first thing.** The trick to Fastpass/Express is that you can only hold one at a time, so if you wait too long to pick your first one up, the next assigned time slot may not be available until late afternoon, and that locks up your ability to get other passes for the bulk of the day. It's also not unusual for a popular ride to distribute all of its available passes early on a busy day. So if there's one ride you're dying to do, get its Fastpass fast. The sooner your first one is scheduled and used, the sooner you can get your second one.

4. **Granny's a great gofer.** There is inevitably one person in every group who doesn't feel like riding anything. Granny (or whichever wallflower you've brought along) glances at the teacup ride and starts making excuses about her hairdo. Don't let her sit on a bench collecting fairy dust. When you get in line for something, hand her your entry ticket and send her to fetch Fastpasses for something. It's almost like being in two places at once, and it cuts down on your wait times.

5. **If your kids allow it, skip the parade.** Lines at many of the most popular rides get shorter in the run-up to parade times, when the hordes pack the route in anticipation. Check the Times Guide for the schedule, and bank on thinner lines 30 minutes before and during show time. It's often possible to hit two or three rides during the show. *A caveat:* Steer clear of the parade route (it's marked by a

dotted red line on the maps) while you hit those rides. Crowds are thick and you may not be able to pass easily.

6. **Come early or stay late.** If you're paying higher-than-normal rates to stay on Disney property, you might as well get some value back by availing yourself of Extra Magic Hours. Your Disney hotel will tell you which park is either opening early or closing late for the express use of its guests. Lines will be shorter during those hours.

7. **If the forecast is hot, Fastpass the water rides.** If the weather report predicts a hot day, grab a Fastpass (or, at Universal Orlando, an Express) for the water rides by midmorning, which should ensure you a slot to ride them right about the time the heat peaks. Otherwise, without a pass, you'll have to wait for over an hour in a tangle of sweaty bodies just to be doused for a few moments of cool pleasure.

8. **Eat early.** Restaurants have lines, too, so avoiding peak periods applies to meals as well. The lunch lines don't start filling up until after noon, so why not eat just before then? Epcot's World Showcase, where the most interesting food is served, is a virtual ghost town at 11 a.m., when it opens, so there will be light traffic until noon or so. The same goes for dinner: If you schedule a seating reservation for around 3:50pm, you'll be on hand when the dinner menu rolls out at 4pm—but you will pay lunch prices, which are usually about $8 less. You won't be hungry again until the park's about to close, when you can eat off-campus at better prices. Eating late in the parks doesn't work, as many restaurants close.

9. **Baby swap.** In the old days, parents had to draw straws to see who would ride and who would watch the kid. The parks have since implemented a system allowing both parents to ride everything with little additional waiting. After the whole family goes through the line, Mom can wait with Junior while Dad rides. When Dad's off, Mom can leap on without waiting, while Dad takes his turn watching Junior. For many people, that cuts the old waiting times in half. It's not available on kiddie rides. That'd just be weird.

10. **Split up.** Well, just for a minute. If you don't care if you all ride in the same car, a few attractions (more at Universal than at Disney) have special lines for single riders. Get in that queue and you'll shoot to the head of the pack, fill spare seats left over by odd-numbered groups, ride within a few minutes of each other, and be back on the pavement in no time flat. The central aspect of Orlando's bonding experience—waiting in a line together—will still be yours to enjoy. But because you won't get to enjoy the expression of terror on your loved one as they hurtle through the darkness, it's a method for those in it for ride quantity, not quality time. Even on rides without dedicated single lines, single riders should alert ride-loading attendants to their presence—doing so could shave many minutes of your wait.

MICKEY'S TOONTOWN FAIR

In 1988, the park built the sugar-hued Mickey's Birthdayland in honor of the character's 60th birthday. Kids immediately took to the candy-colored miniature town, so Birthdayland was upgraded to a permanent land. Now it's the second "land" just for kids, and the only place to guarantee a bona fide Mickey sighting.

The area, which is the only one that doesn't connect directly to the hub, usually opens at 10am. Head for the Big Cheese by exploring the various, adorable rooms and gardens of **Mickey's Country House** and **Minnie's Country House,** where the two mice live in chaste segregation—the rodents have improved their manners since Mickey dumped Minnie from a moving airplane in 1928's *Plane Crazy* because she refused to make out with him. On balance, Minnie's house is much more fun because her kitchen is such a kick to explore (turn on the oven and a cake rises inside it; activate the microwave and popcorn flutters inside; her Westingmouse fridge is full of cheese). The houses lead to the central **Judge's Tent** ★, where Mickey holds court and is available for photo ops (expect a wait). You can also head right for the Judge's Tent without the preceding house tours. Following that, the **Toontown Hall of Fame Tent** is where you'll encounter other characters, including princesses. If such a meeting is important to your kids, try to get here about an hour after park opening, because lines will only become more daunting as the day grinds on. If kids are often awestruck by the sight of His Mouseness in the fur, they're rarely shy about romping around **Donald's Boat** (the *Miss Daisy*), a watery playground with lots of knobs and controls designed to give young ones a thorough, self-induced soaking; its worthwhile features are deactivated when it's cold.

The kiddie coaster **The Barnstormer at Goofy's Wiseacre Farm,** Toontown's sole ride, invariably has a line. The tangled track does a few swooping figure-eights and passes through the "barn" of the queue area (the robotic chickens were once part of Epcot's now-demolished World of Motion ride), but takes scarcely more than a minute—less than half that if you subtract the time it takes to climb the hill. There are some cute touches, including a propeller on the first car and tanks for "Goofolene" fuel. Adults can skip this one unless they're obsessive.

TOMORROWLAND

Between Fantasyland and Tomorrowland, the whiff of gasoline and the snarl of engines comes from the **Tomorrowland Indy Speedway,** a self-driven jog around less than a half-mile of track, originally built in Disneyland at a time when freeways were considered the wave of the future and not a bane of life. The queue is exposed and blistering hot, while the load and unload processes are tedious. Still, many kids who've always wanted the sensation of driving insist on doing it. Each car carries two people, steers poorly but is guided by a rail, and won't go very fast (about 7mph) no matter how much pedal meets the metal. The trip, through unadorned terrain, is over in about 5 minutes, but your interest will wane earlier. Unless the line is minuscule, which it rarely is, I always skip this one, since it's nothing more than a tepid Go-Kart ride. Mind the height restrictions; kids shorter than 52 inches may only function as passengers, a rule that sometimes draws tantrums. Hong Kong Disneyland has an electric-powered version ripe for export; expect that gasoline stench to disperse here soon.

"An E-Ticket Ride"

Walt's original system for attraction admission was based on carnivals. Anyone could enter his park for a nominal fee of a few dollars, but to do rides and shows, guests had to obtain coupon books from kiosks. There were five categories. The simplest, least popular attractions, like Main Street vehicles, could be seen for cheap "A" tickets (around 10¢ in 1972) but the prime blockbusters were honored with the top distinction, an "E" ticket (85¢). It didn't take long for the designation to find its way into the American vernacular. Sally Ride pronounced her 1983 launch on the space shuttle "definitely an E-ticket." The coupon system was dropped in the early 1980s in favor of a high gate price, a system that has mostly replaced the per-ride payment system at parks across the world.

Space Mountain ✪✪✪, Tomorrowland's wienie, only 6 feet shorter than Cinderella Castle, is contained in the futuristic concrete-ribbed circus tent at the end of the central path through Tomorrowland. Although it's really a relatively tame indoor, carnival-style, metal-frame coaster (top speed: barely 29mph), the near-total darkness and tight turns give the 1975 ride (duration: 2½ min.) a panache that makes it one of the park's hotter tickets. I've found myself giggling even when I have to ride it alone. Near the end of the queue, which snakes into the cool, dark bowels of the building, out of the sun, there's a choice between taking the left-hand coaster (Alpha) or the right-hand one (Omega)—they are mirror-images of each other, so there's no difference that I can articulate. There's also a bail-out escape route, but you won't need it. While you wait to board, notice the giant "meteors" that periodically cascade across the starry ceiling; they are *not* images of chocolate-chip cookies, thought some fans will insist they are. The front seat has the best view.

To the right of Space Mountain, as you face it, you'll see an angular, two-level structure with a waterfall face that looks like it ought to contain something interesting. It once did: The Skyway, an old-fashioned bucket gondola ride over the park, loaded here from 1971 to 1999, made a 90-degree turn at a station in the Indy Speedway, and unloaded in Fantasyland beside "it's a small world," above the current stroller parking lot. For some reason, both of the stations, despite their size, were left intact but empty; now that you know what they were, you can see where the buckets soared out from their platforms. Why did they close? For one, they didn't accommodate wheelchairs. Second, they gave guests an ugly view of Fantasyland's tarpaper roofs, spoiling the fantasy. The Disney parks around the world shed theirs in the 1990s, but Busch Gardens Tampa Bay still has one.

Buzz Lightyear's Space Ranger Spin ✪✪✪ (1998), based on the *Toy Story* movies, is a rambunctious (and addictive) slow-car ride that works a little like a video game. Passengers are equipped with laser guns and the means to rotate their vehicles, and it's their mission to blast as many bad guys as they can. That's easier said than done, since the aliens are spinning, bouncing, and turning, and your laser sight only appears intermittently as a blinking red light, which makes it tough to aim, but that's all part of the fun. The dash of each vehicle has a score-board. I thought I did pretty well at 118,000 until I turned and saw a kid who had racked up 205,000. He must have known the secret: The farther away a tar-get is, the more it's worth. This is one of the most ebullient attractions at all of Disney World. If the dome-like room filled with projections strikes you as ran-dom and meaningless (after all, there are no aliens to blast in it), you will be less puzzled to learn that it's a direct holdover from a corny 1970s ride, sponsored by a succession of airlines, called If You Had Wings. (Honestly, Disney, couldn't you put something in there?) This 3-minute trip is a blast, and one of the best rides for families. Use Fastpass if the line is longer than 30 minutes or so.

The **Astro Orbiter** simply takes too long, partly because you have to take an elevator to board. The gist is no different from Dumbo or the Magic Carpets—a 90-second spin on an armature, with passengers controlling height—although at night, the view of an illuminated Tomorrowland, gorgeous after dark, is almost worth the pain. The spinning and dipping planets give a trip added depth, so if you don't have kids yet but want to ride a circular ride like Dumbo, this might be the better choice. Beneath the ride, pick up the receiver of the fake pay phone for some gag messages.

Encircling the Astro Orbiter at Rockettower Plaza, the **Tomorrowland Transit Authority** ✰ makes for a good breather. The tram-like second-story track uses pollution-free magnetic technology (Walt Disney envisioned this system, origi-nally called the WEDway PeopleMover, as a principal form of transportation for the resort) to take riders on a scenic overview of the area's attractions. Fans call this the Blue Line, not just because its cars are blue, but because its narration pur-ports it to be just one branch of a far-ranging, color-coded transit system that actually doesn't exist. On a 13-minute round-trip with no stops, it coasts past some windows over the Buzz Lightyear ride and through the guts of Space Mountain, where you traverse the circumference of the Omega boarding area. TTA is what to ride if you're sitting out the white-knuckle stuff. You will also catch a too-fleeting glimpse of one of the original 1963 models of the Epcot con-cept. Its Utopian design bears such little resemblance to what was actually built that the narration doesn't identify it as Epcot, but as "Walt Disney's twentieth-century vision of the future." Nice hedge, boys. Most regulars have a last-ride rit-ual, and this is mine. It's what I do before I leave, when Tomorrowland is illuminated at night. Best of all, there's almost never a wait.

Walt Disney's Carousel of Progress ✰, open when the park's busy, begins with an apology of sorts, as an attendant explains what you're about to see by telling you how much Walt loved it. True, that. Disney did love this attraction—he cre-ated it with General Electric sponsorship for the 1964 World's Fair, and it was later moved here. The essential message is laden with consumerist overtones about how modern appliances will rescue the American woman from a life of drudg-ery—a midcentury notion now regarded as patently adorable. In a novel twist, the stage doesn't move, but the auditorium rotates on a ring through six rooms (four "acts" and one each for loading and unloading) past Audio-Animatronic scenes. You'll see what's essentially a modern person's trivialization of daily life in the 1900s, 1920s, 1940s, and an unspecified time that I'd peg for 1990, what with Grandpa's breathless praise for laser discs and car phones. While our very white narrator (voiced by *A Christmas Story*'s Jean Shepherd) mostly loafs with his dog across the ages, his wife does chores, his mother festers, his daughter gossips, and his son dreams of adventure. Although it claims to cover the whole 20th century, it's mostly laced with 1950s assumptions about middle-class people. The repetitive theme song, "There's a Great Big Beautiful Tomorrow," is by the Sherman Brothers, who also wrote the songs for *Mary Poppins*. Set aside 20 minutes for the show, but it starts every 5 because the rotating theatre allows endless refills, like the chamber of a revolver. This one is so easy to make fun of, and you might think that I hate it, but no. As a relic from a more idealistic time, it's priceless, and I hope they never remove it, as is the rumor. After all, Walt Disney loved it—a reason to treasure it as a modern rarity. And here's another reason to see it: Despite the fact it has no living performers, it's billed as the longest-running stage show in the United States.

I wish I liked **Stitch's Great Escape!** more, but the extra-sensory show (employing smells and rigged over-the-shoulder harnesses) is too much like other attractions in the parks. The vulgar idea here is that you're in a prison facility for wayward aliens, one of whom is Stitch, who of course breaks free and promptly does things like spit at you and burp hot chili cheese breath into your face. Little kids get scared because of the dark, because the restraint is constrictive, and because they are alarmed to learn a dangerous alien is on the loose, even if it turns out to be their friend Stitch. Lilo makes no appearance, leaving the show without the soft heart it needs. The Audio-Animatronics are marvelous, though. The event takes about 12 minutes once you're inside. Seats along the left side of the main auditorium (as you enter to sit) are a little better because one of the surprises happens there first, and I think the top row is best since its perspective keeps you from having to crane your neck upward. Still, this is an attraction to put lower on your priority list.

The newest attraction in Tomorrowland is the **Monsters Inc. Laugh Floor,** which opened in 2007. Like Turtle Talk with Crush at Epcot, it's a "Living Character" video show, about 15 minutes long, in which computer-animated characters on a giant screen interact with members of the audience, sometimes picking humans out with a hidden camera. Comedy acts, which look as real and as fluid as if they had been animated for a movie, are drawn from a cast of some 20 characters, but the three you'll see in your set will vary from day to day. The quality of the experience depends greatly on the improvisational skill of the hidden live actors doing the voices—because it's new, the best talents in Orlando are currently working the microphones—and on the eagerness of the audience, as one of the gimmicks of the show is that while they're waiting in line, guests are given a number they can use to send their favorite jokes ahead of them by text message. Don't miss the gags along the left wall of the pre-show video-instruction room (the monsters' vending machine sells snacks such as "Polyvinyl Chloride" and "Primordial Ooze"; the employee bulletin board warns against "Repetitive Scare Injury"). The vaudeville-style concept isn't perfect: There's no real plot, not every person likes to be made the center of attention (sit in the rear or extreme sides of the auditorium to avoid being picked on), and turnover can be slow. Much like audiences were with Disney's early Audio-Animatronic experiments (Country Bear Jamboree, Hall of Presidents), you'll probably find yourself more impressed by the canny technology than by the sheer brilliance of the entertainment.

While you're here, keep an eye out for a **talking trash can** that frequently appears and scoots around the entire land, R2-D2-style, while it chatters with guests. Although performances are not announced, it usually emerges from a door marked "Exit Only" that's located between Mickey's Star Traders and Auntie Gravity's ice cream shop.

Set aside time to catch the nightly fireworks show, currently called **Wishes** ⭐⭐, held when the park is open past dark; check the Times Guide. Although it is technically visible from anywhere, the most symmetrical view is from the Castle's front, including Main Street; if you can see the wire strung to the Castle's top, you've got a good viewpoint. The roughly 10-minute show is quite the slick spectacle—everywhere in the park, lights dim, and the soundtrack to the carefully choreographed explosions is broadcast via loudspeaker. Most nights, people start heading home after it's done, and rides will begin to close as soon as it starts. Another evening-only attraction (check the Times Guide): the **SpectroMagic** ⭐ parade, with illuminated floats that mesmerize small children and grown-ups alike.

At the very end of the night (well, most nights, but not all), about 30 minutes after the posted closing time, Cinderella Castle flashes with a dazzling rainbow of light. This is the "Kiss Goodnight," something that isn't on any of the schedules, and it's a soothing end to what was probably a very long day. I suggest sticking it out until you see it, because immediately after closing, the traffic backup leaving the park (remember, you still have a monorail or a ferryboat to go) can be ungodly.

WHERE TO EAT IN THE MAGIC KINGDOM

At nearly all Disney restaurants, you can substitute bite-size carrots for fries in any meal deal at no extra charge. Don't go looking for a beer—there's no alcohol served in the Magic Kingdom.

There are several sit-down restaurants. Some of them, such as the **Crystal Palace** at the top of Main Street and **Liberty Tree Tavern** in Liberty Square, do character meals, but because prices are extreme ($21 adults and $12 kids 3–9 for lunch, $28/$13 for dinner), I don't recommend them just because you're hungry. You go to press the fur. It's my position that if you want to do a character meal do one at breakfast when it won't cut into expensive touring time at the theme parks. Both **Cinderella's Royal Table** 🧒 at the Castle and the **Crystal Palace** do character breakfasts starting at 8am ($32/$22); reservations (☎ 407/939-3463) are required, and because they book up fast (the Royal Table is especially in-demand), it's wise to get your name in as soon as bookings begin, which is 6 months out. At counter-service locations, kids' meals are $4 with a drink. The park's fruit stands ($1 a piece) are found at Center Street and Main Street, at Liberty Square Market, and at the Toontown Farmer's Market by the Barnstormer coaster in Toontown Fair.

Warn your waist that those Tollhouse cookie ice cream sandwiches, sold everywhere, clock in at a beefy 500 calories. That's like a frozen Big Mac. For thigh-friendlier options, go for a chocolate-covered frozen banana (160 calories), which have been sold at the park since the earliest days. For some reason, the bananas don't always appear on the photographic menus displayed beside the ice cream carts. The virtuous should stick to a frozen fruit bar (120 calories). The yellowy, salty popcorn served at the resort is especially good—some 322,000 pounds of it are popped a year—although it's not exactly slimming, either.

Some of my dining choices, but not by any means all of the options, are:

Main Street, U.S.A.: This land is more for expensive sit-down dinners, costing $16 or more per main plate, at such places as **Tony's Town Square Restaurant** (Italian) and the **Crystal Palace** 🧒 (character buffets). Aside from **Casey's Corner**, a hot dog joint facing the Castle, there's nothing filling that's cheap. The Plaza Ice Cream Parlor is one of the few that hasn't switched to soft-serve ice cream; scoops are $2.70.

Adventureland: Although it's on the maps, the taco joint **El Pirata y el Perico Restaurante** ★ is, in fact, only open during peak periods, so most times, you'll have to go to other lands for full meals. For one-of-a-kind snacks, Adventureland is best. At a cart between Pirates and the Tiki Room, there's usually a cart selling **Frozen Chocolate-Covered Bananas with nuts** ($2.50), a longtime Disney tradition dating to the early 1970s, when none of the trees had yet grown in and guests were sweltering all the time. The **Sunshine Tree Terrace**, facing the Magic Carpets, was once run by the Florida Citrus lobby, and now it sells Citrus Swirls, a blend of frozen O.J. with soft-serve vanilla ice cream, for less than $4. If it's closed, as it sometimes is, go past the Swiss Family Treehouse to Aloha Isle, which sells something else you can only get here: $4 **pineapple floats,** sometimes called Dole Whips, made with juice and sweet sherbet. Or get a spear of fresh pineapple for $1.50. There's also often a cart selling **egg rolls** and **curry samosas** ($2), Disney rarities, opposite the Zanzibar shop.

Frontierland: One of Walt Disney World's famous **Turkey Leg Carts** ★★★ is located opposite the Frontier Trading Post. These honking hunks of meat could feed a couple of cavemen and cost $5.75. You can get a hot dog, chips, and a beverage for $7 at the **hot dog cart** opposite Country Bear Jamboree. I often find myself at **Pecos Bill Tall Tale Inn and Cafe** ★★, which serves quarter-pound cheeseburgers with fries for $5.90 and veggie burgers with fries for $6.30; its burger fixins bar has such good stuff as sautéed onions and mushrooms, so it's easy to make a meal of it. (So does Cosmic Ray's in Tomorrowland.)

Liberty Square: They look innocuous on the menu of **Sleepy Hollow** ★, which has a stellar view of the Castle, but the chocolate-chip cookie ice cream sandwiches ($3.50) are sensational. They're made with two fresh cookies pulled gooey from the oven; it's a personal tradition to get one on every visit and then bask in the bloat. For full meals, the **Columbia Harbour House** ★ does fat sandwiches ($7) and chowder ($4.50), and its upstairs rooms are my pick for dodging the crowds. It's also the only place in the Magic Kingdom that brews its own Southern-style sweet tea.

Fantasyland: Vaguely Italian dishes (pizzas, Italian subs, antipasto salad; all $7–$8) are found at the counter-service **Pinocchio's Village Haus**, adjoining "it's a small world" (a few tables overlook the snazzy loading area). Otherwise, this land excels at carb-rich snacky foods such as pretzels filled with sweet cream cheese ($3.79, **Scuttle's Landing**) and hot dogs served with fries ($5.79, **The Village Fry Shoppe**).

Tomorrowland: Another **Turkey Leg Cart** is found at the Lunching Pad, under the Astro Orbiter; oddly, the legs are 30¢ cheaper here than in Frontierland. An excellent choice is **Cosmic Ray's Starlight Cafe** ★★★, which does burgers and such like Pecos Bills, including a fixins bar, but is distinguished by regular lounge-act shows by Sonny Eclipse, an Audio-Animatronic character. Despite

Ten Freebies at Disney

It's not easy finding fun stuff to do that you don't have to cough up for, but you don't need to hand over a cent for these pleasures—not even for park admission. Anyone off the street can enjoy these things:

- Watch the **Electrical Water Pageant** on the Seven Seas Lagoon and Bay Lake. The illuminated floats, which twitter to a soundtrack, makes a circuit around the conjoined ponds after nightfall, and you can see it from the beachfront at any hotel.
- Ride the **ferries** between the resorts, such as the one from Port Orleans Riverside to Downtown Disney along the meandering Sassagoula River, which passes the French Quarter resort, the Old Key West resort, and Pleasure Island. You can even ride the one from the monorail-area resorts to the foot of the Magic Kingdom.
- Take the **monorail.** You can whiz round the Seven Seas Lagoon past the Magic Kingdom and through the Contemporary Resort as many times as you want without a ticket. You can also use it to make the 4-mile round-trip to Epcot, where you'll do a flyover of Future World. And if you sit in the cockpit (maximum of four passengers), you can gab with the driver, steep yourself in the best views, and also get a free "Co-Pilot's" license.
- Hike at **Fort Wilderness.** The trail begins at the east end of Bay Lake and threads through occasionally muddy woods.
- Spend **a night by the pool.** Most resorts keep them open 'til midnight. Technically, you should be a guest. But behave, and no one'll care. Each hotel's parking lot has a gate, but if you park at Downtown Disney and take a free Disney bus, you'll scoot right in.
- See **African animals** at the Animal Kingdom Lodge. The gatekeeper will admit you to sit by the fire in its vaulted lobby, and out back, you can watch game such as giraffe and kudu from the Sunset Overlook. Sometimes, there are zoologists who answer questions.
- For a marvelous view of the fireworks over the Magic Kingdom, **stroll on the beach** of the Grand Floridian or the Polynesian resorts. The sand is millions of years old and was recovered from under Bay Lake. Did you know Disney built a giant wave machine in the middle of the lake? It never worked.
- Partake of the **campfire sing-along,** which happens nightly near the Meadow Trading Post at Fort Wilderness, followed by a Disney feature on an outdoor screen.
- Meet and hug a **costumed character** just outside the gates of Disney's Animal Kingdom.
- **Cuddle farm animals,** including ducks, goats, and peacocks, at the petting farm behind Fort Wilderness's Pioneer Hall. You can also see the horses used to pull streetcars up Main Street U.S.A.

Sonny, I'd still rather eat on the outdoor terrace, because the panorama of the Castle from there is sublime; it's my favorite lunchtime view in all of Walt Disney World. That empty boat dock in the water below is from the extinct Swan Boats attraction, which plied the moat in days past. The **Tomorrowland Terrace** ★★ does noodle bowls and wok-fried dishes for under $8, but it only opens in peak season.

EPCOT

Although people think of Walt Disney as prototypically American, he had a communist streak. He long dreamed of establishing a real, working city where 20,000 full-time residents, none of them unemployed, would test out experimental technologies in the course of their daily lives. In vintage films where he discusses his Florida Project, his passion for creating such a self-sustaining community, to be called the Experimental Prototype Community of Tomorrow, was inextricable from the rest of his planned resort. He wanted nothing less than to change the world. Truck traffic would be routed to vehicle plazas beneath the city, out of pedestrians' way, while PeopleMovers (like the ones at Magic Kingdom's Tomorrowland Transit Authority) would shift the population around town. Between home and downtown, they'd take the monorail. Even on his deathbed, Walt was perfecting real plans for the city that would be his crowning legacy: one whose innovations would make life better for everyone on earth. Had he lived just 3 more years, he would have made sure it happened.

Instead, by the time Walt Disney World finally got around to opening its second park, Epcot Center, on October 1, 1982 (9 years to the day after the Magic Kingdom and at a staggering estimated cost of $1.4 billion; America's biggest construction project at the time), it was but a flicker of its original purpose. No one would actually live there, and few experimental endeavors would be undertaken. Instead, it turned out that the most economical course was to turn Walt's ultimate legacy into another moneymaking theme park, heavily subsidized by corporate participation and sold by heavy promotion of "Walt's dream"—a formula that prevails for the Walt Disney Company today. The final design wasn't much different from the world's fair that Walt's father had helped construct in Chicago in 1893 or that Walt had defined in New York in 1964: examples of how technology was ostensibly improving lives, plus some pavilions representing foreign lands for the edification of people unlikely to travel there themselves.

The 260-acre Epcot Center was (and still is) divided into two zones, laid out roughly like a figure eight. Both started life separately but, as the legend goes, were grafted together when plans for Epcot were afoot. **Future World** is where the wonders of industry were vaguely extolled in corporate-sponsored "pavilions." The companies had a hand in writing scripts and they also maintained VIP areas in backstage areas for executives and special guests—perhaps that's why Epcot sponsorship tends to excite marketing departments more than the research and development programs Walt would have preferred. At the back of the property, around a 1.3-mile lake footpath, **World Showcase** was the circuit of countries, each representing in miniature their namesake's essence. These, too, received funding from their host countries. The expense of updating Future World's exhibits has caused Disney to gradually phase out the educational aspects of the attractions; one by one, original pavilions have been replaced by thrills and sense-tingling rides, so

The Best of Epcot

Don't miss if you're 6: Turtle Talk with Crush

Don't miss if you're 16: Test Track

Requisite photo op: Spaceship Earth

Food you can only get here: Rice cream, the bakery at Norway; the candy art of Miyuki, Japan pavilion

The most crowded, so go early: Soarin'

Skippable: Journey into Imagination with Figment

Quintessentially Disney: Spaceship Earth

Biggest thrill: Mission: SPACE

Best show: Voices of Liberty, The American Adventure

Character meals: Akershus Royal Banquet Hall

Where to find peace: Future World: the Odyssey Center catwalks; World Showcase: the gardens of Japan

---

that today, only one of the original rides, Spaceship Earth, remains more or less as it was on opening day. In December 1993, the park was renamed Epcot, without the "Center" or the capital letters. Fans saw it as an effort to further distance itself from the concept of an experimental community.

Despite such a cynical journey from inspiration to propaganda, Epcot remains one of Walt Disney World's crowning achievements. There's not as much for small kids to do here, but the layout absorbs crowds well and there's ample elbow room. Guests usually don't learn much more than they already know (so as not to bore them or to insult their intelligence), but even though there isn't much take-away information, that doesn't make a day here a waste of time.

The parking lot is at the ticket gates, although there's also the option of taking the **monorail** from The Magic Kingdom area. If you park past the canal or near the monorail track, don't bother with the tram; you can walk to the gates quicker.

Future World opens at 9am most mornings, and World Showcase opens at 11am. Future World usually closes at 7pm, 2 hours before World Showcase. The nightly IllumiNations show usually takes place over World Showcase Lagoon at 9pm; at its conclusion, the hordes stampede for their cars en masse.

Tuesdays, Fridays, and Saturdays are the busiest days at Epcot.

FUTURE WORLD

Epcot's emblem is the gorgeous orb of **Spaceship Earth** ★★, which at the time of its construction was the first Buckminster Fuller–designed geodesic sphere ever attempted. Although it looks like a golf ball on a tee, the 16-million-pound structure, coated with 11,324 aluminum-bonded panels and sheathed inside with a rainproof rubber layer, is supported by a table-like scaffolding where its six legs enter the dome. Think of this 180-foot-tall ball as a direct descendent of the

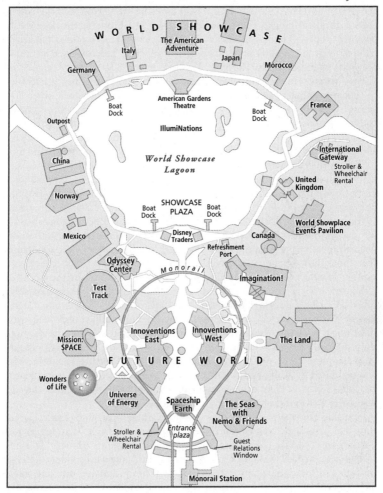

Perisphere of the 1939 World's Fair or the Unisphere of the 1964 World's Fair, which were the icons for their own parks. No mere shell, it houses an eponymous ride using the OmniMover system of cars linked together like an endless snake. The ride slowly winds around the inside perimeter and back down through the middle of the sphere, all on the course of a shallow, sixth-grade-level journey through the history of communications, from Greek theatre to the Sistine Chapel to the printing press to the telegraph. In a bit of unintended kinesthetic commentary, once you reach the present day, the ride is all downhill. Once you're off it, I defy you to tell me what you learned from it. This, of course, makes it vintage Disney.

The clunky Audio-Animatronic characters are showing their age, to be sure, but it's still satisfying to thread your way through this famous sphere. This is the ride that still shows what 1982's Epcot was like—its robot-populated sister pavilions about transportation and the future were razed in the 1990s to make way for flashier thrills. Although some people don't get it (on one recent ride, the kid behind me referred to it as "Spaceship Nap"), I cherish it as a soothing sojourn not only through air-conditioning, but also through time, although not in the way designers intended: When I'm on it, I'm back in the '80s. Since it's the first ride guests encounter in the park, lines, which move fast, are shorter in the afternoon.

The semicircular buildings behind Spaceship Earth, facing each other down across a courtyard, are collectively known as **Innoventions.** Largely the domain of corporate-sponsored exhibits, as Walt had intended, Innoventions (which was originally called Communicore) is gradually being pared to nothing, but it's usually not crowded, and if you take the time to explore its exhibits, you'll find much to divert you. The skeletal robot Tom Morrow (get it?) is a Disney inside joke; he used to appear at the Magic Kingdom's Tomorrowland, and he's still paged on the Tomorrowland Transit Authority ride. There's an area by IBM about its proprietary voice recognition software (plus stations where you can send free e-postcards to friends); one by a plastics company that molds robot pieces that you can assemble and take home; an area about Segway Human Transporters (in the afternoon, you can occasionally get a chance to ride one); one by Underwriters Laboratories that shows how it tests and approves products; and "Too Small to See" is an exhibit on nanotechnology aimed at young teens. Club Cool, by the Coca-Cola Company, lets you pour unlimited samples of eight soft drink flavors sold only in other countries (***warning:*** Beverly, a bitter aperitif from Italy, is not for faint tongues). If you're an obsessive tightwad, you can keep coming back here instead of buying a real Coke. **MouseGear,** housed in Innoventions, is the largest souvenir shop in Epcot. Between the Innoventions buildings, in the area known obscurely as Millennium Plaza, you'll find the stepped **World Fellowship Fountain,** which was dedicated by Walt's widow Lillian. At the opening ceremony, water from 23 countries was poured into the reservoir as a symbol of brotherhood. It can shoot water 150 feet in the air, although it rarely does.

Outside the information office on the east of Spaceship Earth, partially obscured by a giant planter, you'll see a corridor lined with what appear to be blacked-out ATMs. These are the years-old remnants of the WorldKey Information Service that Epcot guests once used to converse by videophone with operators to make restaurant reservations. Such funky, forward-thinking features (which also included fiber-optic computers and touch-screen info centers at a time when such technology dropped jaws) were typical of the Epcot experience for many years, but they were abandoned in a cost-cutting measure.

As you face the lagoon, the pavilions on the left side of Future World are generally about the physical and man-made sciences, and the ones on the right are more about the natural sciences. First on the left, **Universe of Energy** ★ is a treatise on how oil is formed and then pulled out of the ground for the benefit of mankind, although what you'll mostly see are dinosaurs. This attraction is highly emblematic of Epcot's corporate-dictated content. The adventure begins with a movie in which Ellen DeGeneres, more than a decade younger, is being creamed on *Jeopardy!* (hosted by a mustachioed Alex Trebek) by Jamie Lee Curtis. That's when Bill Nye the Science Guy (it couldn't be more dated if it were Mr. Wizard—or Edison) takes Ellen under his wing to teach her about energy so that she'll win the game. If that sounds lame, at least the ride system is more creative: The audience, seated in six, 97-passenger slabs of mobile theater-style bench seating that miraculously organize themselves in a line, follow from room to giant room, passing primeval forests full of realistic dinosaurs. When, at another movie stop, the issue of global warming comes up, Nye waves it away, saying "It's a hot topic with lots of questions" before reassuring us that "we're far from running on empty." Not surprisingly, the venture was originally backed by ExxonMobil. The whole show takes between 30 to 50 minutes to see, depending on when you arrive at the pre-show, which makes it a good cool-down area. Which seats are best? Although all sections spend time waiting for the others to move or catch up, the two sections on the right wait in the most interesting spaces. Outside, the roof is coated in 2 acres of solar panels, which generate 15% of the show's energy appetite; the building site was chosen for maximum sunlight exposure.

Next up the path is the gorgeous, swirling façade of **Mission: SPACE** ★★, which approximates, with intense accuracy, the experience of a rocket launch. Although technically a whirl in a giant centrifuge, the ride's skillful design tricks the mind into believing the body's actually lurching backward in a launch for Mars (although my eyeballs seem to know—they wag uncontrollably for the first 30 seconds). Gary Sinise, oozing gravitas, issues so many pre-show warnings against motion sickness that I honestly think it psychs people out and primes them for illness, although sufferers of sinus problems have reported discomfort. Opened in fall 2003 at a reported cost of $100 million, this ride has a high nausea quotient (barf bags are provided, but they no longer have the Disney logo on them because grabby guests were taking them home as souvenirs), which makes it one of the least successful additions in years. That said, whereas Mad Tea Party and carousels make me want to hurl, I do just fine on this ride. For the timid, you'll be given a choice when you enter the building: There's a second version (color-coded green) with only motion-simulator effects but no centrifuge action, but in my opinion, the missing element renders the ride pointless. Each passenger in the extremely tight four-person cockpits (claustrophobes, avoid this one) is assigned two buttons to press at given cues—of course it doesn't matter if you don't, but at least hold onto your steering joystick, because it's rigged to give force feedback as you travel. The post-show area is where you should go if you're waiting for someone else to finish the ride. There, you can play interactive group games and send free postcards home via computer. Ultimately, it's a ride that's all brains and no heart—I'm deeply impressed at what they've done, but I don't feel like doing it twice.

Between Mission: SPACE and the Universe of Energy, you'll spot a golden dome. That's **Wonders of Life.** No, you haven't spent too long in the sun—it's really not listed on your map. The decay of Wonders of Life is one of the great failures of modern Disney World. Opened in 1989 as a paean to all things biological, executives decided to close it several years back when they couldn't find a corporation willing to pony up sponsorship. Although its dormant dome still appears on the maps, it's only opened, without public forewarning, during very busy periods, and even then with the food service areas (once Epcot's healthiest) shuttered, performance stages closed off, and rides groaning for want of maintenance. Walt Disney, who stressed quality in everything and thought vacant buildings put on a "bad show" for guests, would be mortified. Some of science's greatest advances are being made in the biological realm, yet the topic is neglected at Epcot for want of a corporate bankroll. If you're lucky enough to get in (it last opened for a few weeks in December 2006), you'll ride **Body Wars,** a rough, grainy motion-simulator movie ride through the human bloodstream, and see **Cranium Command,** a sprightly movie starring dated comedians (Dana Carvey, Bobcat Goldthwait—what, was Cantinflas busy?) that addresses how a 12-year-old boy's brain controls his growing body. There are also some hands-on exhibits and *The Making of Me,* a film that gingerly addresses the issue of conception and pregnancy without stepping on too many ideological toes. It's only a matter of time before this whole pavilion is bulldozed. It's sad.

> 66 All in all I'd give Epcot a thumbs up. . . . Disney pulled out all the stops: Morocco was clean, the Mexican water was drinkable, the British food was edible, and even the French were friendly. 99
>
> —Doug Lansky, *Up the Amazon Without a Paddle*

To the right of Mission: SPACE, the open-air cars of **Test Track ★★★** thunder enticingly around the bend of an outdoor motorway at nearly 65mph—the fastest ride in Disney World and a shining example of its designers' eagerness to tackle a complex challenge. Those passengers are experiencing the climax of a complicated, multi-stage ride that puts them through the paces of a proving ground of an automobile manufacturer (sponsor: General Motors, which has had a relationship with Disney since Walt himself enticed the company to be a sponsor for the Worlds Fair of 1964). As you go along for the ride on a series of diagnostic safety tests (don't worry; you don't have to actually do anything, and the premises are clearly established during the short pre-show video and maintained by onboard video screens), your six-passenger car brakes suddenly, endures heat and chill chambers, and rumbles over rough road surfaces, all before shooting outside the building and making an invigorating circuit around the circular track over the Epcot employee parking lot. (Hertz has a similar experience. It's called a convertible.) Test Track is so complex—each car is controlled by an independent onboard computer—that it's historically prone to at least one 1-hour shutdown per day, and because of the outdoor element, it completely halts during storms. Until Soarin' opened in 2005, this was Future World's biggest draw, and the line can still be upsetting, so try to queue up early in the day before crowds build, within 45 minutes of closing, or use Fastpass. This is a rare Disney attraction with a single-rider line, which zips lone riders into the pre-show area, where they're mixed in with everyone else. Keep alerting cast members to your solo status; because you'll be used as filler, you'll probably be seated on the right side of the car. The post-ride display is a showroom for GM's current fleet, and that part smells like an ad, not like an education, so it's highly avoidable.

Between Test Track and the lagoon, Odyssey Center, a striking '80s melange of hexagonal-roofed dining rooms, was once the principal Future World restaurant. Now it's used only for meetings and events. Its over-water catwalks are some of the quietest real estate at Epcot, which is a nice way of saying it's a dead zone.

Are They Kidding?

Besides the Nemo ride at The Seas, there's not much for young children to do in Epcot. Disney has plastered a Band-Aid over the problem by installing small, manned booths that it calls **Kidcot,** which usually offer diversions such as coloring, stamping, or mask-making. The only good thing about them is that they issue Epcot Passports, which kids can get stamped in every World Showcase country they visit, but frankly, Kidcot is best avoided unless you're desperate. As one mom lamented as she left a station recently: "I could go to the school fair and do *that.*" Animal Kingdom offers a similar program called Kids Discovery Club; the half-dozen locations are marked on park maps with a K.

Another supposedly kid-friendly feature of the parks is **Pal Mickey,** a plush Mickey Mouse doll that, triggered by sensors hidden throughout all four parks, chatters to your kid with Disney trivia and, less frequently, with advice such as alerts when the parade runs. Disney used to rent the dolls for $8, but it soon realized it could make more money by selling them for an obscene $65. They're only available at the parks, although used ones regularly surface on eBay for around $40. On the Disney fan websites (p. 303), you can sometimes find parents willing to lend or sell theirs.

Also, parents, remember that Disney gives you places to park your **strollers,** but it won't watch them. Come prepared with a system for unloading your valuables every time you enter an attraction. Also have something with which to cover the seat, as most stroller parking is exposed, and like parked cars, strollers get sizzling hot in the Florida sun. Finally, you might want to tie some identifying marker (like a colorful bandana) to your stroller so you can identify it amidst the sea of clones you'll be confronted with when you exit an attraction.

Now, leaping to the right-hand (western) lobe of Future World: The calling card of **The Seas with Nemo & Friends,** which you may have heard called by its original name, The Living Seas, is one of the world's largest saltwater aquariums. It's 27 feet deep, 203 feet across, and holds 5.7 million gallons. The walls are made of 6-inch-thick acrylic, and you can spend as long as you like watching the swimming creatures. About a third of the tank is reserved for dolphins and sea turtles, while reef fish dominate the rest. When the pavilion opened in 1986, sharks were the big draw; today, because of *Finding Nemo,* kids ask to see the clown fish. A visit begins with a 5-minute, **slow-moving ride** kids in OmniMover "clamobiles" through a simulated undersea world; unlike on older Disney rides, most of the action here, featuring characters from *Nemo,* is in the form of video screens, which I find low-budget, but satisfies little children. Tell your own guppies that half the point of the ride is, in fact, to find Nemo, who's lost again; the little orange fish pokes his head out of the coral here and there while all the other characters incessantly shout his name, which soon grates on adult nerves. The ride climaxes to the tune of "In the Big Blue World" (a tie-in with *Finding Nemo—The Musical* at

Animal Kingdom) with a peek into the real aquarium as Nemo and his friends are projected into the windows, cleverly uniting the fictional world with the real animal universe with which you're about to be acquainted. If the line's horrific, there's a bypass route straight into the exhibition to see the tank straightaway, but you may have to ask where it is; you can also enter through the gift shop at the pavilion's exit. Far more successful, and crowded, is **Turtle Talk With Crush** ★★ kids, a don't-miss 20-minute show in which a computer animated version of the 150-year-old surfer-dude turtle actually interacts with audiences, making jokes about what they're wearing and fielding questions. Get ready for a lot more interactive video shows like this one; Disney is putting a lot of muscle behind what it calls its Living Characters program. Which may not be a good thing, as this sort of set-up burns through audiences very, very slowly, and there's often a line. Go early in the morning or in the late afternoon. Next door is **Bruce's Sub House,** a hands-on play area similar to any science museum's.

On the second floor, which is quieter than the kiddie-clogged first floor, don't miss the observation platform that extends into the mighty tank. The "Daily Roster" sign outside the main corridor apprises you of the timing of the day's dolphin talks and fish feedings (the schedule is busiest between 10am and 2pm), when there will be someone on hand to explain what you're seeing and otherwise enrich your experience. The **dolphins** live separately in the first space on the left. Often, human divers will communicate with guests through the glass by way of magnetized writing tablets. Also check out the **manatees,** which are the sweet-natured "sea cows" that are now threatened in Florida. When The Living Seas opened in 1986, it was intended to be a year-round research facility, but now, it contents itself with marine education and the odd animal rescue.

The next pavilion along is **The Land,** which, at 6 acres, is larger than Tomorrowland. Being about ecology, The Land used to be desolate. But global warming made the topic hot (so to speak), and the pavilion was fitted with a smash-hit ride with wait times exceeding 90 minutes or more, so zoom here early or consider it for Fastpass: **Soarin'** ★★★ kids. On it, audiences are belted into benches and "flown," hang glider–like, across enormous movies of California's wonders while scents waft, hair blows, and the seats gently rock in tandem with the motions of the flight. The ride, one of the best additions to the World in recent years, is highly repeatable and deeply pleasurable. It's a facsimile of the one at Disney's California Adventure park in Anaheim, hence the imagery exclusive to the Golden State. Which concourse you are herded to is of no consequence, but I do find that the best seats are in the middle sections on the top row, where there are no feet dangling in your field of vision. That means you should aim for position B-1, or at the very least A-1 or C-1. Those with height issues should request something ending in 3, the closest to the ground.

A second ride, **Living with the Land** ★, is a 14-minute boat trip that glosses over the realm of farming technologies. It's one of the last Epcot rides to provide a semblance of an education, so I find it edifying, especially when you pass some of Epcot's few working laboratories, where hydroponics and other futuristic growth methods are being explored in an effort to curb world hunger. Clearly, they know what they're doing: Guinness World Records has certified one of the pavilion's tomato plants as the record holder for producing the most fruit: 1,151.84 pounds in 1 year. There are more gimmicky displays, too, such as the cucumber and pumpkins lodged into molds to force them to grow in the shape of Mickey ears. This ride is original to opening day, although the live narrators have been disposed of in favor of a hard-to-hear recording. It's not a perfect experience: For those interested in the topic, the info will be too thin, but for those who are bored green, it will seem to last forever. Boats load slowly, so go early or late to escape the inevitable buildup. Should the work of the backstage botanists interest you, over by Soarin', there's a desk where you can sign up for the Behind the Seeds tour of the greenhouses (p. 247). The Land is also the spot for *The Circle of Life,* a minor, 13-minute movie starring *The Lion King* characters and concerning conservation (an Epcot-worthy message), and the best dining choices in Future World—the Garden Grill for family-style food, and Sunshine Seasons for healthy counter-service options. Out front, take a moment to appreciate the subtle plantings; trees flower in white to symbolize sky, while more "earth" colored plants are found low.

The last pavilion before you arrive at World Showcase is **Imagination!** kids . Its best bet is the witty 20-minute movie **Honey, I Shrunk the Audience** ★★, in which film, optical illusions, and hidden mechanisms in the auditorium conspire to toy with the audience's perceptions and trick them into thinking the entire theater has been shrunken to the size of a shoebox. Very small kids may find it freaky, especially when the pet snake gets loose, but it's a rewarding show, despite its obvious advanced age. From 1986 to 1994, this cinema showed the infamous Michael Jackson's 3-D spectacular *Captain EO.* Whoops! **Journey into Imagination with Figment** is a slow track-based ride featuring a daffy purple dinosaur, Figment, who once figured as Epcot's most prominent mascot. The ride is roundly considered poor, relying on video screens and optical illusions instead of a story or fabulous fabrication, and one section is simply a room of black curtains and painted boards. Not only is there rarely a line, but word also has it Imagineering is about to rip it out and build a new one from scratch—the fourth attempt to get it right since 1982. Walt Disney predicted Epcot would be "a community that will never be completed"—if only he knew. The ride dumps out into the **What If Labs,** a high-tech playground where kids elbow each other for a chance to horse around with a slew of interactive activities such as conducting music by stepping into pools of light. Kodak sponsors it and won't let you forget it. As you might have gathered by now, Imagination! is not Epcot at its best. However, the fountain pods in front, which shoot snakes of water from one to another, have always been a firm favorite of children, who never tire of trying to catch one of the so-called "laminar flow" spurts.

WORLD SHOWCASE

The 1.3-mile path circling the World Showcase Lagoon is home to 11 pavilions created in the idealized image of their home countries—get your picture taken in front of a miniature Eiffel Tower (it'll look real through the lens), or at the Doge's Palace in Venice. The pavilions were built more to elicit an emotional response and not to truly replicate. Disney is diligent about the upkeep of this area, but it neglects development—the last "country" to open was Norway back in 1988, and without joint participation by foreign tourism offices, there are unlikely to be more—which lends the area a less picked-over vibe than high-concept Future World. There also seems to be an emphasis on countries that Americans already know, and neither South America nor Australasia is represented at all. But World Showcase does have some of the most original restaurants in Disney World, and the shops are stocked with crafts and national products (for example, you can buy real Chinese tea in China and sweaters in Norway), although the variety is slipping. It's also the only area in Epcot in which alcoholic beverages are sold.

There is far more to do in World Showcase than the free Disney map lets on. To judge by that lamely labeled park map, they're mere facades. But in truth, most buildings contain something hidden to see, even if it's as small as a historical exhibit or an unnamed shop selling food you've never tasted before. Pocket the useless map and let your curiosity guide you. Take your time making the circuit.

The pavilions are staffed by young people who were born and raised in the host country. Many of their contracts last for up to a year, and they chose to come to Florida as much to learn about America as to be ambassadors for their own nations, although many of them complain that most park guests don't bother asking anything except where the bathrooms are. Be kind to them, speak slowly if you sometimes cannot immediately understand each others' accents, and most of all, seize this unusual chance to ask questions about their cultures. These folks, despite the fact they're zipped into silly costumes, are modern, intelligent people who are so proud of where they come from that they traveled halfway around the world to share their heritage with you. Help them do that.

You should also tour World Showcase with the day's Times Guide firmly in hand. The pavilions are crawling with unexpected musical and dance performances conducted by natives of each country. Seeing them makes a day richer and squeezes value from your ticket. Rush and you'll miss a lot.

Almost anything purchased in World Showcase (except chocolate, which melts) can be sent to the **Package Pickup** desk at the front of Future World; allow 3 hours for delivery. On some days—it depends how busy things are—the park runs two **ferry** routes across the lagoon. One leaves near Germany and one from Morocco, and both land at the top of Future World, but they're slow. You will not save any time using them; they're merely a pleasant way to get off your feet.

I suggest going clockwise around the lagoon mostly because the only two rides in World Showcase will come quickly on the left; if you go counterclockwise, you'll reach them after they accrue lines.

Mexico

Influences: A diplomatic mix of Mayan, Toltec, Aztec, and Spanish styles
Skirting the lagoon clockwise, **Mexico** is your first stop. Everything to see (there isn't lots), including little stalls selling Oaxacan wood carvings and other changing crafts, is inside the faux temple, which contains a faux river, a faux volcano, and a faux night sky. I am ashamed to admit that I'm partial to its incredibly vapid ride, **Gran Fiesta Tour Starring The Three Caballeros** ★ kids 🐭, a bland, 8-minute boat float once known as El Rio del Tiempo that, for its cheesiness, has been nicknamed El Rio del Queso and "The Mexican 'it's a small world.'" As you pass movie screens and dancing dolls, you quickly realize you're being exposed to the product of late 1970s Mexican tourist board input. A 2007 rehab imposed animated appearances by the 1940s characters The Three Caballeros, never mind that only one of them is Mexican (the other two are a Brazilian parrot and Donald

Duck, an American). Consider it a siesta break on a hot day. The **Mayan Ceremonial Hall** showcases folk art and whimsical carvings.

Norway

Influences: Town squares of Bergen, Alesund, Oslo, and the Satesdal Valley; the 14th-century Akershus castle on Oslo harbor

Next along is **Norway,** the youngest pavilion (built 1988), which is home to the only other ride in World Showcase. **Maelstrom** ✮ is a mildly surprising, but short (5 min.) river course past trolls and other Norse monsters, plus a few token representations of Norse industry, ending with a 5-minute sales film about the country. You can bypass that as soon as the doors open—everyone does—even though the photography is sumptuous, as it is for all of the World Showcase pictures. Norway's Akershus Royal Banquet Hall was until recently Epcot's most authentic ethnic banquet, but now it does Princess character meals morning, noon, and evening. In the one-room **Gol Stave Church Gallery,** check out The Vikings: Conquerors of the Seas, which includes scant information but does showcase some ancient artifacts from the conquerors, such as 9th-century spearheads and 1,000-year-old swords. There's also a play area that looks like a 10th-century Viking ship. The pavilion's shop contains a 9-foot-tall troll—photo op alert!— and lots of beauty products and Scandinavian candy, such as the Heath-like Daim ($1.50) and tubes of hazelnutty Ballerina cookies ($3.50). At the bakery, try the $2.30 rice cream, a snack that those in the know are happy to make a detour for. Towering above it all, the wooden Stave Church is a Norwegian original; there were once around 1,000 in the country, but today, there are only 28.

China

Influences: Beijing's Forbidden City (Imperial Palace) and Temple of Heaven

The big thing to do on **China** is a 14-minute movie filmed entirely in "Circle-Vision 360," *Reflections of China* ✮. Enter through the replica of the Temple of Heaven, which, like the Beijing original, just received an affectionate refurbishment. You wouldn't believe the work it takes to make a film that surrounds you from all sides. The makers first had to figure out the optimal number of screens (nine—which enables projectors to be slipped in the gaps between screens) and then they had to suspend a ring of carefully calibrated cameras from helicopters so that the crew wasn't in the shots. In 2002, the footage of Shanghai had to be completely re-shot because the booming city no longer bore the slightest resemblance to what was being shown. The result, which surveys some of the country's most beautiful vistas, is ravishing, although the masses no longer seem to care; it's not usually crowded. Upon exiting the film, you'll find yourself in Xing Fu Jie, or "Street of Good Fortune," which was intentionally designed too small to supply a sense of China's overpopulation. One of the best souvenirs here is a colored parasol inscribed with your name ($10–$14); make time to catch the **Dragon Legend Acrobats,** some of the most riveting street performers in the World Showcase. Tomb Warriors: Guardian Spirits of Ancient China, in the **Gallery of the Whispering Willow,** is a miniature re-creation of the legendary terra-cotta warriors of the Han Dynasty, scaled to the size of a hotel room (the original is twice the size of Epcot). The Gallery also contains six cases of figures, lent by the

Schloss Family Collection, dating as far back as 260 B.C. The pavilion's rambling shop, surprisingly large, sells lots of tees and teas, but it also dabbles in silk wraps ($90, or $60 if you downgrade to rayon and polyester) and in the witheringly strong liquor Wu Liang Ye ($80 for 375ml).

Next along is the **Outpost,** which functions as a mushy catch-all receptacle for all things African. This area was once slated to contain a pavilion canvassing Equatorial Africa, but that fell through. The Mdundo Kibanda store here once sold some interesting crafts, and there are still some Kenyan carvings (starting at $35), but lately, it's been stocked with spare souvenirs from other stores. Still, there are occasional storytelling sessions, and several days a week, the craftsman Andrew Mutiso is on hand, whittling and carving wares—he usually looks pretty engrossed in his wood and knife, but he likes answering questions.

Germany

Influences: Eltz Castle near Koblenz; Stahleck Fortress near Bacharach; Rothenburg (the biergarten and the dragon slayer statue); facades from Frankfurt and Freiburg (the guildhall)

Lacking a true attraction (a water ride based on the Rhine was planned but never completed), Germany is popular for its food. The Biergarten Restaurant does sausages, beer, and the like—accompanied by yodeling and dancing—while the adjoining shop is for chocolates and wine. The Sommerfest is the counter-service alternative for brats and pretzels. On the hour, the Clock Tower above the pavilion rings and two figures emerge, just like at the Glockenspiel in München (Munich). The pavilion is otherwise a string of connected one-room shops selling steins (from $30), figurines, crystal, Christmas ornaments, and other high-priced wares. The connected candy and wine shop (Weinkeller) is worth a gander, though: you'll find such pick-me-ups as holiday Gluhwein ($14 a liter), marzipan bars ($2.50), and even thin tablets of dark chocolate for 47¢ to 94¢. Full bags of assorted cookies are just $6 and can get your brood through the day. In the window of Das Kaufhaus facing the lagoon, make a point of meeting Jutta Levasseur, who has worked at Epcot since its opening day, painting traditional Christmas egg ornaments. She's usually working in the shop on Fridays and Saturdays (usually more), and although her handiwork costs up to $1,200 for ostrich eggs and sometimes portrays distinctly un-German Disney characters, the most authentic traditional designs, on chicken roe, are happily the most affordable (under $100). Another appealing, if incongruous, attraction that's not on the maps is the highly detailed **model train** display just past the German pavilion.

Italy

Influences: Piazza di San Marco, Venice; stucco buildings of Tuscany; a fountain reminiscent of the work of Gian Lorenzo Bernini

The tiny pavilion for **Italy** lacks an attraction—the gondolas never leave the dock—so you must content yourself with the small-scale replicas of Venice's Doge's Palace and St. Mark's bell tower. Its stores sell chocolates, candy, crystal (are you sensing a theme here?), gourmet foods, and cookware. Epcot's impressions of Italy are mostly culinary. The pavilion's sit-down restaurant was shuttered in the summer of 2007 after a generation of service and its replacement had not been announced as this book went to press. Still, noodle around in Italy's Enoteca

Castello shop, noted for its expensive Venetian carnival masks, which also sells Pernigotti chocolate bars ($1.50); Illy coffee ($17 for 8.8 oz.); and my favorite, mild Quadratini hazelnut wafers ($6 for a bag). Tasting flights of wine are $9 for four 2-ounce servings, or $4 per 4-ounce glass. Interestingly, Walt had intended for a Venetian Hotel to be built on the Seven Seas Lagoon between the Contemporary and the Polynesian, but it got delayed and then Las Vegas beat Disney to the punch. Also planned but nixed: a Persian-themed hotel, just north of the Contemporary.

U.S.A.

Influences: general Georgian/colonial Greek-revival buildings

Stereotypically, the U.S.A. pavilion, called **The American Adventure** ★★, takes pride of place in an area that's supposed to celebrate other countries (although Brits often snicker that its Georgian architecture style is distinctly English). Inside, the superlative Voices of America group, which excels at thorny close harmonies, entertains guests waiting to attend the half-hour Audio-Animatronic show, *The American Adventure.* Also in the lobby is the unfairly ignored American Heritage Gallery. The U.S. pavilion may be an inappropriate place for a one-room exhibit of pan-African items, but the collection is nonetheless important; in 2005, pieces from it were accepted by the Smithsonian Institution.

In the show, Benjamin Franklin and Mark Twain are your Audio-Animatronic surrogates for a series of eye-popping (but ponderous) re-creations of snippets from America's patriotic mythology. Moving dioramas of seminal events such as a Susan B. Anthony speech and the founding of Yosemite National Park appear and vanish cinematically, leaving spectators marveling less at the wonder of America— the script is too canned for much of that—than at the massive amount of storage space that must lie beyond the proscenium. Indeed, all that homespun corn is brought to you by some immensely complicated robotic and hydraulic systems. When this attraction first opened, the scene in which Franklin appears to mount stairs and then walk across the room was hailed as a technical milestone. The Will Rogers figure actually twirls a lasso. Although heavy on uplifting jingoism, the show scores points for touching lightly on a few unpleasant topics, including slavery and the suffering of Native Americans, but in general, it's not as deep as its stage: a quarter the size of a football field, with sets moved by a 65-foot by 35-foot, 175-ton "scene changer" hidden below the apron (peek at the machinery on the Behind the Scenes tour, p. 245). Don't be the first to enter the auditorium or else you'll be marooned near the aisle, off to the side.

Heritage Manor Gifts, found next door, sells a small selection of patriotic oddities, such as "talking presidential action figures" (re-live the excitement of FDR, $35), as well as a Benjamin Franklin action figure (French coquettes sold separately, I guess). The five-person **Spirit of America** fife and drum corps makes scheduled appearances in the forecourt.

Japan

Influences: 8th-century Horyuji Temple in Nara (pagoda); Katsura Imperial Villa (Yakitori House); Shirasagi-Jo castle at Hemeji (the rear fortress); Hiroshima (torii gate in the lagoon)

Now comes **Japan,** which is one of the most rewarding pavilions to explore. Hopefully, you can be there during one of the spectacularly thunderous drum shows, which are held at the base of the five-level Goju-no-to pagoda, or for a demonstration by candy artist **Miyuki** (check your Times Guide), who does for sweets what clowns do for balloon animals. Japan has no giant attractions (like Germany, a show building was erected but never filled with its intended ride), but its shopping and dining are exemplary, and the outdoor garden behind the pagoda is a paragon of peace. At the back of the pavilion, go inside and turn left to tour the surprisingly large **Bijutsu-kan Gallery** ★, stocked with some of the most accessible changing exhibitions in the entire resort; its most recent show, of antique tin toys, was lent by a collector who curates seven museums of them in Japan. The **Mitsukoshi Department Store,** named for the 300-year-old Japanese original, is the most fun to roam of any World Showcase shop. It stocks a wide variety of toys, chopstick sets, linens, and paper fans—but I love Japanese candy, such as chocolate-dipped Pocky sticks ($3–$4) and Yan Yan sweet cookie paddles, which you dip into accompanying frosting ($1.25–$2). Vanilla or jasmine incense costs $9.50 here, but hold out for Morocco, where it's cheaper; the miso soup mix is a good deal, though ($3.50). There are four places to eat, one in the cheaper counter-service category, and one serving sushi—a welcome taste of fresh food for a theme park. A red *torii* gate inspired by one in Hiroshima acts as a ceremonial entrance to the pavilion from the water of the lagoon; the barnacles on its base are fake, and were glued on to simulate age.

Morocco

Influences: Marrakesh (Koutoubia minaret), Rabat (Chella minaret), Fez (Bab Boujouloud Gate, Nejjarine Fountain), Casablanca
Morocco is another spectacular pavilion, if you're inclined to dig in. It flies higher than its neighbors because the country's king took an active interest in its construction, dispatching some 21 top craftsmen for the job. Again, there's no movie or show (although Aladdin, the Genie, and Jasmine make regular appearances), and the architecture is a cross-country mishmash drawn from Marrakech, Fes, and Rabat. There are two terrific restaurants, one for service (Restaurant Marrakesh, deep in back, is atmospheric and romantic, with live entertainment) and one with a counter (Tangierine Café, in front, is usually empty). I often hold off lunchtime to get a plate of shawarma here. The middle courtyards are cluttered with souk-like boutiques that blend one into another, perfumed with incense ($3) and stocked with curious and reasonably priced finds such as footstools, wraps, wooden boxes made from African burl ($23–$80), rugs, and little brass lamps ($9) that, no matter how hard you rub, won't produce a genie. Henna tattoos are also available, as is an intermittent 45-minute tour, **The Treasures of Morocco** ★, which provides a free and fascinating primer on the North African country. Ask a cast member how to join it. **Fez House** is a tranquil, pillared two-level courtyard with a fountain that recalls a classic Moroccan home; **The Gallery of Arts and History,** a mosaic-rich exhibition next to the Fez House, showcases musical instruments, lamps, jewelry, and pottery (I like the powder horn made of silver and ox horn), illuminated by nine handsome metal lanterns.

France

Influences: various Belle Epoque Parisian and provincial streets; Château de Fontainbleu (the Palais du Cinema); the former Pont des Arts in Paris (the bridge to the United Kingdom)

France, done up to look like a typical Parisian neighborhood with a one-tenth replica of the upper stretch of the Eiffel Tower in the simulated distance (you can't go up it), is popular mostly for its food. In an alley in the back and to the left, you'll find Boulangerie Pâtisserie, which serves sweets such as chocolate éclairs and ham and cheese croissants for under $4—not a bad deal, and there are outdoor tables where you can chill. Across the lane, in Esprit de la Provence, chocolate wafers cost as little as 47¢. The 20-minute movie, *Impressions de France,* is no longer the freshest example of a tourism movie, and I think most of the stuff for sale at this pavilion's shops are among the least imaginative and the most kitschy in World Showcase—I mean, mouse-ear wine stoppers for $10 at Vins de France? A pricey Guerlain fragrance shop? Wine tastings are $6. As I stand in this pavilion, I can't help but realize that for what I've paid Disney, I could have flown all the way to Paris to ascend the real Eiffel Tower. There's no substitute.

In the gap between France and United Kingdom, a side door **(International Gateway)** leads to the pretty Disney BoardWalk area. A free ferry will also take you there; it continues on to the Swan and Dolphin hotels and, in about a half-hour, Disney–MGM Studios. You didn't hear it from me, but some guests have been known to talk their way past the parking guard at the BoardWalk just so they can save $10 on Epcot parking. Be careful, if you decide to slip out for a while, not to be caught short by Epcot's closing—it's a long, circuitous bus route back to the Epcot parking lot from the BoardWalk.

Do try not to notice the hulking, teal-roofed hotels rising into the sky beyond the Gateway. These are the expensive Swan and Dolphin, erected in the late 1980s by the willpower of Michael Eisner. Their profiles—the Swan is topped by 56,000-pound bird sculptures—create the ultimate no-no: what Imagineers call a "visual intrusion" into the world of the park.

United Kingdom

Influences: Anne Hathaway's Cottage, Stratford-upon-Avon (the Tea Caddy); various Queen Anne buildings (the middle of the promenade); Hampton Court, London (Sportsman's Shoppe); Victorian, country, and traditional pub styles (Rose & Crown); set designs from *Mary Poppins* (the back wall of the butterfly garden)

The final two pavilions are the largely English-speaking ones, so if you're going clockwise, the exotica is over. **United Kingdom,** another wild mix of architectural styles, is popular chiefly for its English-style pub, the Rose & Crown Pub & Dining Room (pints of ale, fish and chips), and a counter-service fish and chips shop. That's two fish and chips outlets in a single block—far more than you'd even find in London these days. Most of the pleasure is in exploring the area and picking out the competing British styles. Few people know about the area's **Butterfly and Knot Herb Garden** and the **hedge maze,** and fewer still know that the Cadbury candy bars and McVitie's biscuits for sale in the shops are frequently available for a few bucks less at World Market near the Florida Mall (p. 295).

Featured shopping includes sweaters, tea, chocolate, pottery, and mugs. The Toy Soldier shop, to the right and to the back, sells those hard-to-find green feathered caps ($10) that make Peter Pan look so debonair.

Canada

Influences: 19th-century Victorian colonial architecture (Hotel du Canada); emblematic northwestern Indian design and Maritime Provinces towns; Butchart Gardens, Victoria (Victoria Gardens)

Saving on Mickey Munchies

Considering you'll pay $7 to $9 each for a counter-service sandwich, plus at least $2 for a simple medium-size soft drink—the going rate in all the Orlando parks—a family of four can easily spend $90 on every meal! Don't be goofy—save money! Besides eating off premises, here's how:

- **Pack a little food of your own.** Soft lunchbag-size coolers are tolerated by park security, or just tote a few sandwiches in plastic bags. If your lodging has a freezer, put juice boxes in there; they'll be thawed and cool by lunch.

- **Skip lunch by stuffing yourself with a giant breakfast.** Character meals (p. 90) give good value because they serve limitless food.

- **Skip sit-down meals, or plan them strategically.** Sit-down meals can chomp as much as 90 minutes out of your touring time. Do that twice and you've lost a third of your day. A park that could be seen in 1 day would require 2, doubling costs. If you want a sit-down meal, do it at lunch, when prices are 20% lower than at dinner. And eat around 11am, when crowds are lighter and you lose less time.

- **Order selectively.** Although counter-service restaurants push combination meals, it's an unpublicized fact that you may subtract unwanted menu items from adult selections and save a few bucks. Order a double cheeseburger and ask for an extra bun, which costs 85¢, and then make two separate burgers.

- **Go for the buffets.** Do an all-you-can-eat buffet, and do it before 4pm, when prices escalate for the dinner crowd. At counter-service places with a free toppings bar (such as Pecos Bill and Cosmic Ray's at the Magic Kingdom and the Electric Umbrella at Epcot), you can stack your sandwiches with a veritable salad.

- **Snack on fruit.** Each park has at least one fruit stand.

- **Seek out the turkey legs.** They're giant (1½ pounds, from 45-pound turkeys) and cost less than $6, which is why 1.5 million of them are sold resort-wide annually. They taste so good because they're injected with brine before cooking for 6 hours. Just try not to think about the hormones it takes to grow a 45-pound turkey. Or a 5-foot-tall mouse.

- **Always order drinks without ice.** They're served cold anyway, and it's chilling how much of a Disney Coke consists of ice.

The nearest pavilion to Imagination!, **Canada,** like China, has a movie, predictably named **O Canada!,** shot with nine cameras in Circle-Vision 360 (a process Walt Disney originally called Circarama). The best way to find the film is by heading down the path marked Le Cellier, which leads through an otherwise hidden artificial canyon delightfully washed by a man-made waterfall. The 18-minute presentation, which requires audiences to stand, dates to 1982, before the establishment of Nunavut. Because it focuses on spectacular scenery (the Rockies, the Bay of Fundy), the movie offers little (aside from bagpipers and redcoats) to teach Americans that Canada is a different country. The film is to be updated soon, which I guess means we'll also lose the nostalgic Gordon Lightfoot-esque soundtrack. Like Japan, Canada's **gardens** (they were inspired by Victoria's Butchart Gardens, although the sign says Victoria Gardens) are a surprising oasis. The shop, **Northwest Mercantile,** purports to honor Canada's French Canadian and pioneer heritage, but mostly hawks Mickeys dressed in tartan, Disney fleeces, and drugstore Canadian candies such as Smarties ($2.50).

The lagoonside shop between Canada and the plaza often sells markdown souvenirs for $10 or less—a very unusual promotion in the World.

There are no parades anymore at Epcot, but usually at 9pm, the **IllumiNations: Reflections of Earth** ★★★ fireworks-and-water spectacular, takes place over World Showcase Lagoon. Its central globe, which is studded with 15,500 tiny video screens, weighs some 350,000 pounds, and the show's so-called Inferno Barge carries a payload of 4,000 gallons of propane. Crowds start building on the banks 2 hours before show time, but I find doing that a waste of time, and therefore money, as a day's admission is so steep. Any view of the center of the lake will be fine (some people find the islands upsetting, but I don't), but take care to be upwind or you may be engulfed by smoke.

WHERE TO EAT AT EPCOT

Epcot is far and away the best theme park for food selection, certainly for Disney and probably for all of America. Some people slip into the side International Gateway just to sup. Reservations for the sit-down restaurants can be made at ☎ 407/939-3463. At counter-service locations, kids' meals are $4 with a drink. The park's main **fruit stand** ($1 a piece) is between China and Germany.

◆ **The Land:** The **Sunshine Seasons** ★★★ mall-style food court has the best selection and the freshest food of all Epcot's counter-service locations; salads, grilled items, and Asian dishes go for $8 to $10, with no fried food, burgers, or pizza. The sit-down **Garden Grill**'s ★ (kids) dining room, found upstairs, is on a slowly rotating turntable that overlooks the Living with the Land boat ride (seats on its lower level have the clearer view), and Disney characters make appearances. Meals are family-style, diner-like (turkey, flank steak—mostly middling), and all-you-can-eat (you'll have to hound your server to keep replenishing your servings) for $21 adults/$12 kids at lunch, and $28/$13 dinner. Some vegetables at both restaurants, particularly cucumbers and tomatoes, were grown in the pavilion's own greenhouses and might arrive shaped like Mickey ears.

◆ **The Seas with Nemo & Friends:** At **Coral Reef Restaurant,** your table faces the windows of the aquarium and you dine on the buddies of the fish swimming in your view. Entrees are in the mid-20s, and although the sit-down setting is spectacular, I'll be honest: I had some of the worst food in my life here.

- **Innoventions: Electric Umbrella** ✖ is Future World's other important affordable-meals locale. It does counter-service burgers, roast beef sandwiches, and turkey wraps for $7 to $8; there's also a toppings bar for piling free extras on your burger. Across the plaza, **Fountain View Espresso and Bakery** is mainly for coffee, but it often does turkey and cheese croissants for $4.50 (at press time, its hours were being scaled back unpredictably).

- **Mexico:** Don't even attempt to get a table at **San Angel Inn Restaurante,** beneath the false sky inside the pyramid, without a reservation. Its food (lunch, midteens; dinner in the mid-20s) is of a much higher quality than the pasty beans shoveled at **Cantina de San Angel** ✖, the waterfront counter-service option for under $8. The latter is busy, but I credit its margaritas for that, although the *tacos al carbon* (flour tortillas filled with grilled chicken, onions, and peppers, served with refried beans; $7.29) are unusual theme park fare and sell briskly.

- **Norway: Akershus Royal Banquet Hall** 🄺 hosts Princess Storybook Dining, an all-you-can-eat character meal starring princesses, three times a day. Breakfast is $23 adults/$13 kids, lunch (until 2:50pm) is $25/$14, and dinner is $29/$14. That's a bit rich, but the rice cream dessert ($2.30) at the pavilion's bake shop, **Kringla Bakeri Og Kafe** ✖✖, can't be found anywhere else—more than one person claims this rich, strawberry-topped rice pudding snack to be their favorite sweet in all Walt Disney World.

- **China:** Like Mexico, there's a high-end and a low-end version here. **Nine Dragons Restaurant** (entrees $15 at lunch, and $18 at dinner) serves the sit-down crowd, and **Lotus Blossom Café** ✖ (twice-cooked beef rice bowl, $7; veggie lo mein, $4.60), the quick-service location, makes hasty but tasty dishes for those on the go.

- **Germany:** A good spot for rowdy entertainment and hearty food, **Biergarten Restaurant** ✖✖ is a sit-down all-you-can-eat buffet (the only one in World Showcase that isn't staffed by princesses), which costs $20 adult/$11 kids at lunch, and $24/$12 after 4pm. Outside, a kiosk sells bratwurst and sausages for under $9.

- **Italy:** The sit-down **L'Originale Alfredo di Roma Ristorante** is too expensive—$24 for pasta? Yet some count its fettuccine Alfredo among the best dishes in Epcot.

- **The American Experience**: **Liberty Inn** does cheap burgers, chicken, and salads for under $9, with a free toppings bar.

- **Japan:** Of the four restaurants, including some teppanyaki rooms, the most affordable is the sushi bar, located upstairs (a full meal totals about $25), and the **Yakitori House** counter-service location by the gardens (the usual $9 level), which is small but generally uncrowded, and which supplies relatively healthy steamed and stewed choices. Facing the lagoon under the pagoda, the **Kaki-Gori** kiosk (closed in cold weather) serves shaved ice with syrup (including honeydew and cherry flavors) for $2.25, and plum wine for $4.50.

- **Morocco: Tangierine Café** ✖✖✖, the counter-service location, is a great place to dodge crowds. It serves shawarma for $10, with hummus and salad, and meatball platters ($11) with yellow rice. Its couscous sides ($2) aren't bad. **Restaurant Marrakesh** ★★, tucked away in the back, does sit-down lunch entrees for around $18 and dinner for $26 (lots of kebabs and platters), but I advise seizing on its daily lunch special (appetizer, entree, and dessert for $20), because for your money, you'll also be treated to live performances by musicians and a belly dancer. (The restaurant, which is rarely full, also sells a cookbook of its best dishes for just $7.40.)

◆ **France:** In the far recesses of the pavilion, grab a fast, bready bite at **Boulangerie Patisserie** ★★, such as a chocolate croissant or a ham and cheese croissant (both under $4—great bargains). A cash-only kiosk on the lagoon griddles up hot crepes (with sweet fillings, not meat), also for $4. There are two sit-down places for meals. **Chefs de France** imitates a typical Parisian sidewalk cafe (escargot casserole, $10; a three-course prix fixe meal for $30 until 7pm). **Bistro de Paris,** located upstairs, is so expensive (mains over $30) that there's no point going. You're paying for the view of IllumiNations—if you're going to blow that kind of cash, at least make sure you reserve at the right time to get some entertainment out of it.

◆ **United Kingdom:** The **Yorkshire County Fish Shop** ★ walk-up fish and chips window is perpetually busy; the wares are made by the Harry Ramsden's chain. You get two strips of fish with chips (fries) for $8—make sure to put vinegar, not ketchup, on the fries the way the English do. Bass ale costs a sharp $7. There's also the more expensive sit-down **Rose & Crown Pub,** where you can also raise a simple beer (pints are $7.50).

◆ **Canada:** The restaurant, **Le Cellier Steakhouse,** is one of the more affordable sit-downs in World Showcase (lunch: $14 sandwiches, $21 entrees; dinner: entrees in the mid-20s), which isn't saying much.

DISNEY–MGM STUDIOS

Just as Epcot celebrates idealized industry and Animal Kingdom honors fauna, the 154-acre Disney–MGM Studios strives to evoke the romance of the movies. Not just any movies, of course, but mostly that pastel-hued fantasy of the Hollywood of 60 years ago, where gossip columnists ruled the radio and starlets could be discovered at Schwab's.

While it was originally conceived as a single pavilion about show business for Epcot, Universal's announcement of its invasion of the Florida market prodded Disney executives to expand the concept into an entire theme park, and in 1989, Disney–MGM opened with just two rides (The Great Movie Ride and the Backlot Tour) to head off the competition. The intensely self-promotional Disney–MGM is not one of Disney's most transporting endeavors, and you won't find many people who will name it as their favorite of the four parks, which is why I think it's the one you should do last.

There are a few issues behind its failings. One is that its design is not harmonious or symmetrical, which makes it harder to navigate. There's also precious little to do with the name—an initial effort to function as a studio was a flop, so there's no production to witness, and you'll have to hunt to find MGM references, which younger guests aren't familiar with, anyway. When you look at the slate of attractions, you'll notice it's heavy on shows and light on rides, which, for my money, isn't enough. Still, *any* park would be found lacking in comparison to

The Best of Disney–MGM Studios

Don't miss if you're 6: Voyage of The Little Mermaid

Don't miss if you're 16: Rock 'n' Roller Coaster

Requisite photo op: Sorcerer Mickey Hat

Food you can only get here: Grapefruit Cake, The Hollywood Brown Derby, Hollywood Boulevard; Peanut Butter and Jelly Milkshake, 50's Prime Time Café, Echo Lake

The most crowded, so go early: Twilight Zone Tower of Terror

Skippable: Sounds Dangerous—Starring Drew Carey

Quintessentially Disney: Walt Disney: One Man's Dream; The Great Movie Ride

Biggest thrill: Twilight Zone Tower of Terror

Best show: Voyage of the Little Mermaid

Character meals: Hollywood & Vine

Where to find peace: Around Echo Lake

something as revolutionary as the Magic Kingdom, and MGM's dearth of activities is balanced by the fact that two of its rides are among Disney's best: the Tower of Terror and the Rock 'n' Roller Coaster.

The resulting park doesn't really possess enough attractions to fill a complete day—it's got about half the number in Magic Kingdom—which means that guests either combine its highlights on the same day with Disney's Animal Kingdom, or they allow themselves a more leisurely pace, perhaps lingering long enough to catch the dazzling pyrotechnic evening show, Fantasmic!

Guests arrive by the usual car/tram combo, by bus, or by ferry, which sails from the Swan and Dolphin area and continues on to Epcot.

HOLLYWOOD BOULEVARD & ECHO LAKE

As soon as you're through the gates, take care of business (strollers, wheelchairs, lockers) in the plaza before proceeding down Hollywood Boulevard, the largest of many fanciful imitations of Hollywood's famous streets and buildings. There are no attractions in this section, only shops and restaurants intended to catch tourists as they pass. Hollywood Boulevard draws guests into the park, culminating with the 122-foot-tall **Sorcerer Mickey Hat,** the park's central icon that is from, ironically, Walt Disney's assault on typical Hollywood movies, *Fantasia*. There are no attractions in the hat, but there is an open-air souvenir stall. In front of the hat is the park's **Guest Information Board,** where wait times and show schedules are posted. Just behind the hat, which wasn't added until 2001, is the park's original focal point, the replica of Grauman's Chinese Theater (Disney calls it "The Chinese Theater"), which has a forecourt graced with actual handprints and footprints of movie stars who visited in the park's early years, mostly at the

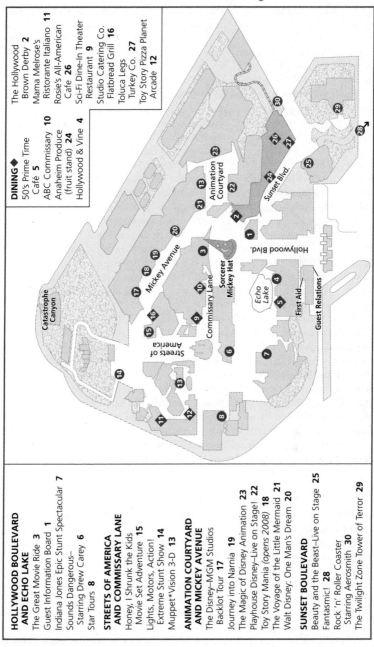

HOLLYWOOD BOULEVARD AND ECHO LAKE

The Great Movie Ride **3**
Guest Information Board **1**
Indiana Jones Epic Stunt Spectacular **7**
Sounds Dangerous–
Starring Drew Carey **6**
Star Tours **8**

STREETS OF AMERICA AND COMMISSARY LANE

Honey, I Shrunk the Kids
Movie Set Adventure **15**
Lights, Motors, Action!
Extreme Stunt Show **14**
Muppet*Vision 3-D **13**

ANIMATION COURTYARD AND MICKEY AVENUE

The Disney-MGM Studios
Backlot Tour **17**
Journey into Narnia **19**
The Magic of Disney Animation **23**
Playhouse Disney–Live on Stage! **22**
Toy Story Mania (opens 2008) **18**
The Voyage of the Little Mermaid **21**
Walt Disney: One Man's Dream **20**

SUNSET BOULEVARD

Beauty and the Beast–Live on Stage **25**
Fantasmic! **28**
Rock 'n' Roller Coaster
Starring Aerosmith **30**
The Twilight Zone Tower of Terror **29**

DINING◆

50's Prime Time
Café **5**
ABC Commissary **10**
Anaheim Produce
(fruit stand) **24**
Hollywood & Vine **4**

The Hollywood
Brown Derby **2**
Mama Melrose's
Ristorante Italiano **11**
Rosie's All-American
Cafe **26**
Sci-Fi Dine-In Theater
Restaurant **9**
Studio Catering Co.
Flatbread Grill **16**
Toluca Legs
Turkey Co. **27**
Toy Story Pizza Planet
Arcade **12**

Catastrophe
Canyon

Animation
Courtyard

Sunset Blvd.

Mickey Avenue

Commissary Lane

Sorcerer
Mickey Hat

Hollywood Blvd.

Echo
Lake

First Aid

Guest Relations

Streets of
America

behest of Disney execs. The tradition was abandoned years ago, around the time the park gave up the dream of being a center for important film production. Some are uncomfortably dated: Jamie Farr, Charlie Korsmo, Harry Anderson, and Warren Beatty as Dick Tracy. There are some true perennials, though, including Audrey Hepburn, Michael J. Fox, Samuel L. Jackson, Bette Midler, and Ann Miller.

Inside is **The Great Movie Ride** ★★, which was a showpiece in 1989 but now feels like a mechanized waxworks. Aided by a human narrator reciting a hoary script, audiences slowly cruise in traveling theatre slabs past Audio-Animatronic reproductions of scenes from famous movies, including *Singin' in the Rain, Alien,* and a Munchkin-crammed *The Wizard of Oz* (its Wicked Witch figure was considered a landmark, at the time, in the Imagineers' abilities to re-create life). This is really the only place in the park where the MGM brand comes into play. At one point during the 22-minute journey, which concludes with a viewing of a fast-paced and expertly edited movie montage, cars experience one of two possible plotlines—for example, getting caught in the crossfire of a James Cagney gangland classic or a John Wayne western, with guns that shoot sparks. The robots have looked fresher (although Gene Kelly personally approved his likeness, I think he looks more like Timothy Dalton), and some kids won't be familiar with the references (Busby Berkeley, for example). Lines are never very long, but they do tend to spike just after the parade. The queue area has a few cases containing props from popular movies such as *Mary Poppins.*

To the left of Hollywood Boulevard, Echo Lake is a wide-open space with a small pond in the middle. There isn't as much to do here as it seems like there should be, but the obligatory parade does march past (its path is denoted by a red dotted line on park maps). The Times Guide will tell you when it's coming. **Sounds Dangerous—Starring Drew Carey,** though, needs to go. Now. This 12-minute movie, a blatant and unredeeming tie-in to the Disney-owned ABC network, is not just old—it's themed in the yellow-and-black advertising scheme ABC used in 1997 and the pre-show trivia touts long-gone shows like *Spin City* and *Dharma and Greg*—but it's also cheap. Guests wear headphones as they watch a movie, which goes pitch black (parents be warned) for 7 minutes while we hear what Drew Carey is doing. You learn nothing beyond the fact sounds are important.

Check the Times Guide for scheduled performances of the 30-minute **Indiana Jones Epic Stunt Spectacular** ★★, a bone-rattling tour de force of hair-raising daredevilry—rolling-boulder dodging, trucks flipping over and exploding—that simultaneously titillates and, to a lesser degree, reminds you how such feats of derring-do are typically rigged and filmed for the movies. The sets, of a South American treasure tomb, a Cairo street market, and a desert airport, are gigantic, and while they're being struck by stagehands, cast members horse around with adult audience volunteers to keep things rolling. They also try very hard to convince you that they're really filming these sequences—you may need to explain to your kids why they're lying about that, and about calling the lead actor "Harrison Ford's stunt double," but most kids understand the violence is fake. The acrobats and gymnasts who do the stunts, fights, and tumbles are very skilled, and the production values are among the highest of any show at the Disney parks. The outdoor amphitheatre is sheltered, and you can bring drinks and food. Arrive about 20 minutes early, as there's a warm-up and volunteers are selected before show time. It's mounted about five times daily.

The product of a partnership with George Lucas, **Star Tours** ★ is a bumpy, 40-person motion-simulator capsule that has you riding shotgun with an ineffectual droid named RX-24 (voiced by actor Paul Reubens) on an ill-fated and turbulent excursion to hang out with the Ewoks on the Moon of Endor. In 5 minutes, you manage to lose control, navigate a comet field, travel at light speed, get caught in a tractor beam, and join an assault on the Death Star. The technology, now more than 20 years old, is showing its seams (there are plans to update it), but it's still a top example of its type, the queue area is effective and diverting, and the video is well matched to the movements, which cuts down on reports of nausea. The replica AT-AT out front shoots streams of water, which kids jostle to catch. If this ride catches your fancy, you should know that in May and June, the park mounts Star Wars Weekends, when actors from the movie arrive for signings, parades, Q&As, and brief workshops. Fans of the franchise come out in force, so to speak.

Stylistically, this part of the park is a mess. Outside of Star Tours, you're simultaneously on a foreign planet, in Art Deco Hollywood, and somewhere vaguely jungled. There's no sense of place that the Magic Kingdom's themed lands impart—that's the sign of a hastily planned park.

SUNSET BOULEVARD

The prime items in the park are on this street, which peels off not from the hub with the Hat, as you might expect, but from the middle of Hollywood Boulevard.

Sunset Boulevard terminates below the salmon-colored "Hollywood Tower Hotel." This 199-foot structure, the tallest ride at Disney World, is **The Twilight Zone Tower of Terror** ★★★, one of the smartest, most exciting experiences in Walt Disney World. It shouldn't be missed. Guests are ushered through the lobby, library, and boiler room of a cobwebby old 1930s Los Angeles hotel—the decor is sublimely detailed—before being seated in a 21-passenger "elevator" car that, floor by floor, ascends the tower and then, without visible tracks, emerges from the shaft and roams an upper level. Soon, you've entered a second shaft and, after a pregnant moment of tension, you're sent into what seems to be a free fall (in reality, you're being pulled faster than the speed of gravity) and a series of thrilling up-and-down leaps. The fall sequence is randomly controlled by computer, and you never drop more than a few stories—but the total darkness, periodically punctured by picture-window views of the theme park far below, key up the giddy fear factor. The planning and execution of this ride are without equal, and because the drop sequence is different each time, you can ride as much as you want without duplicating your experience. Don't bother using Fastpass unless the line extends substantially outside of the attraction building. In the pre-show "library" area, move to the wall diagonally across from the entry door so that you'll end up exiting first for the queue area, saving you time. As you line up, there will be a fork where you must choose a direction—it doesn't matter which way you go, so choose the one with the shortest line (it will be easier if you can gauge by then how many elevator cars each fork is feeding; sometimes they feed one, and sometimes two). In the vehicle boarding area, the best views are in the front row, numbered 1 and 2, although you may not be given a choice and it ultimately doesn't matter very much. Just before boarding, there's a bypass for the chickenhearted, so there's no need for anyone to loiter outside on benches while waiting for loved ones.

Left through the archway as you face the Tower, **Rock 'n' Roller Coaster Starring Aerosmith** ★★★ (opened 1999) launches 24-passenger "limousine" trains from 0 to 57mph in under 3 seconds, sending them through a 92-second rampage through smooth corkscrews and turns that are intensified by fluorescent symbols of Los Angeles (at one point, you dive though an O of the Hollywood sign). The indoor setup is a boon, as it means the ride can operate during the rain, and it makes the journey slightly less disorienting for inexperienced coaster riders. Cooler yet, speakers in each headrest (there are more than 900 in total) play Aerosmith music, which is perfectly timed to the dips and rolls (France's Space Mountain uses the same technology). The pre-ride video features the band Aerosmith and actress Illeana Douglas. If you must choose, use your Fastpass privileges for the coaster, not the Tower, because its Fastpass line is absorbed quickly. There's also a single-rider line (the cars seat two across, so it moves at an average speed). I know people who call this their favorite ride in all of Walt Disney World. I know just as many people who refuse to set foot on it.

Adding a welcome dimension to the park for young children who may not care for portentous shows, the 30-minute **Beauty and the Beast—Live on Stage** 🧒, off Sunset Boulevard, is advertised as "Broadway-style," but it's really not. It's a theme park–style, simplified version of the movie, with the most popular songs. The story is highly condensed (you never find out why Belle ends up at the Beast's castle and Gaston's fate is not shown) and many characters inhabit whole-body costumes, speaking recorded dialogue with unblinking eyes—to the benefit of timid kids and souvenir shop managers, the Beast looks more like a plush toy than a scary monster. Still, its intended audience doesn't notice such shortcomings. They cheer like it's a rock concert and hoist videophones during the ball scene, and because of that, most performances are jammed. The metal benches are numbing, but at least the amphitheatre is covered. Arrive at least 20 minutes early unless you want to be in the back, where afternoon sun can seep in and heat up the rear.

Fantasmic!, ★★★ a popular 25-minute pyrotechnics show featuring character-laden showboats, a 59-foot man-made mountain, flaming water, and lasers projected onto a giant water curtain, takes place each evening in the 6,500-seat waterfront Hollywood Hills Amphitheatre off Sunset Boulevard. Although it's a strong show by dint of its unusual presentation, I'm always appalled to see that people start arriving at the theatre as much as *2 hours* before show time and that the theater often fills completely. I don't think it's worth that kind of commitment, and the seating is too hard on the derriere for that. Most people will be satisfied taking their chances and showing up within 30 minutes of show time. On nights when there are two performances, do the second one, as it's always less crowded. Sit toward the rear to avoid catching water from the special effects (especially on cold nights) and to the right to make exiting easier. There is a snack bar in the amphitheatre—some people cleverly assuage the long wait by picnicking.

STREETS OF AMERICA & COMMISSARY LANE

Because it only happens about three times a day, catching the enormous **Lights, Motors, Action! Extreme Stunt Show** ★★ takes planning. Loud, brawling, and moderately exciting enough to see once, it's a showcase for stunt driving dressed up like a film shoot for a car chase/action scene. The engaging half-hour show, which uses a fleet of specially built, extra-nimble cars (plus a jet ski or two) and tells lots of lies about filming an actual movie scene while you're there, was imported from Paris's Walt Disney Studios Park (hence the set that looks like a Mediterranean port), but it seems tailor-made for American audiences. Because the stage is so wide, I suggest taking at seat in the middle or near the top of the grandstand. You won't wrestle for a spot—the stadium seats 5,000. Don't worry: The stunts happen at a safe remove from the auditorium, across a moat.

The **Honey, I Shrunk the Kids Movie Set Adventure** 🦎 is a high-concept playground that simulates the sights and sounds of the average backyard—if your kids were the size of an ant. In addition to giant insects and a slide that looks like Kodak film (yep, product placement), there's a giant dog's nose that sprays mist upon the unsuspecting. It's pretty much the only place at MGM to turn kids loose.

Most of the buildings around Streets of America are strictly facades, designed to look like a New York City street. But its back portion is a Muppet-themed streetscape. Behind the fabulous fountain depicting Miss Piggy as the Statue of Liberty, The 17-minute **Muppet★Vision 3-D** ★ 🦎 is MGM's version of the sort of sense-tricking movie Disney has installed in each of its parks: You see a movie while various tricks like air blasts make you feel like it's actually happening. Make sure you pick up 3-D glasses in the pre-show room, and if you have time to kill before going into the auditorium, hunt around and see if you can find the prop key left under the mat. The doors on the right lead to the back of the auditorium and the ones on the left lead to the front; for the fullest view, I suggest sticking in the middle, since the theater's walls become part of the show, and both live and Audio-Animatronic figures will appear on either side and even in the back. The pre-show is amusing in that Muppet way (says Sam the Eagle about seating procedures: "Stopping in the middle is distinctly unpatriotic!"), and while the movie contains a few missteps (Waldo, a CG character, lacks creativity), it's fast-moving and includes lots of beloved *Muppet Show* (but no *Sesame Street*) favorites such as Miss Piggy and Kermit. The Muppets, too, lend themselves very nicely to Audio-Animatronic technology. Because of tight spaces, crowds look huge for this show, but the theatre holds nearly 600. Lines are longest just after the Indiana Jones show lets out.

Note: Commissary Lane is the pass-though to the Sorcerer Mickey Hat. Lots of guests get it confused with Mickey Avenue, which feeds from the motor stunt show to Animation Courtyard. The two are connected by Streets of America.

ANIMATION COURTYARD & MICKEY AVENUE

The only Fastpass-eligible attraction that most young children will do, **The Voyage of the Little Mermaid** ★★ 🦎, is on the hard-to-find Animation Courtyard, located out a side door to the right of the Sorcerer Mickey Hat. This bright, energetic, condensed version of the animated movie has high production values (puppets, live actors, mist, and a cool undersea-themed auditorium) and is a standout show. In the pre-show holding pen, the doors to the left lead to the back of the theater, and those to the right head to the front; because the black-light puppetry of the marvelous "Under the Sea" sequence can be spoiled if you see too much detail, I suggest sitting a little farther back. Consider putting very small kids in your lap so they can see better. Because of its cooling humidity, this show is a top contender for the best show to see in the heat of the day.

Across the courtyard is the other top show for the youngest guests: **Playhouse Disney—Live on Stage!** 🧒 is for people who will obediently rise and dance when commanded to by a Big Blue Bear in a Big Blue House. The show is simple, with a warehouse-like set (warning adults: you sit on the ground), and inspires such fervent participation from under-5s that it may feel like a meeting for a cult that you're not a member of. If you don't know the names JoJo, Tutter, Pip and Pop, Stanley, Tigger, or Eeyore, this sing-along revue isn't for you. The parental units won't be too bored, as this de facto Disney Channel ad is fast-paced, like changing the channel every 4 minutes. Obviously, anyone old enough to do a book report can skip it. The staff loves kids and is terrific at crowd control for 4 year olds, but, unfortunately, many moms and dads rely on that fact to give themselves a 20-minute break from parenting. Lines for this show can be long, so I advise trying it first thing or in late afternoon.

At the far end of Animation Courtyard, the self-guided **The Magic of Disney Animation** tour is, in my opinion, the most telling display of the Walt Disney Company's flagrance in placing greed above its heritage. Originally, it provided a firsthand look at the labor-intensive work that produced all those famous Disney movies. Guests could watch live animators perfect their upcoming release (*Mulan* and *Lilo & Stitch* were made here), and they'd come to understand the time-honored ink-and-paint process that Walt Disney himself used to build his empire, one cel at time. But Disney fired its Florida-based animators, so there's nothing more to see. Instead, you get a hokey, 8-minute show highlighting only the ideas stage of the process, followed by an ad for whatever computer-animated film will be released next. Then you're dumped in a paltry area of interactive exhibits where kids can color on video or determine which Disney character their personality is most like (me: Tarzan). You and about 20 other people can take a worthwhile 15-minute crash course in drawing a popular character (such as Winnie or Minnie) under the instruction of a guide, and you can bring your artwork home for free. Otherwise, the art of handmade animation, through which the Disney empire was built, frame by frame, is barely discussed. Never mind that every family's DVD shelf is stacked with movies made with ink and paint. The only painter you'll see is a woman paid to make too-perfect cels that are sold in the adjoining gift shop for $95. You receive no more information than you could find in a 2-minute DVD extra, yet you blow 30 minutes of your time. All the more shame that animation is supposed to be the studio's bread and butter. If you love Disney, this will bring you down.

I feel much better about the terrific walk-through museum **Walt Disney: One Man's Dream** ★★. Mostly overlooked, the display is a requisite stop for anyone curious about the undeniable achievements of this driven man. It's also the only place in the four parks where his biography, and the genesis of the resort, is seriously explored. Here, you (and a few other stragglers) learn that just as a generation of kids carry an obsession with Walt Disney World after a brief childhood exposure, Walt Disney himself became obsessed with turn-of-the-20th-century Americana after briefly living in the town of Marceline, Missouri. Walt also saw early film and stage versions of *Snow White* and *Alice in Wonderland,* which he later remade to his own specifications—Walt, the exhibition proves, was a masterful recycler. He also had a symbiotic relationship with his brother Roy, whom he followed first into the military, then to Kansas City, and finally to Hollywood, where Roy guided the Disney finances forevermore.

Some suspicious Disney lore is repeated, such as the tale that has Mickey being invented on a train ride following a business disaster (there's evidence to suggest he was born in meetings), but for the most part, the information is reliable and informative without being dense. There are plenty of authentic artifacts, including a complicated and revolutionary "multiplane" camera that enabled animators to reproduce the sliding depth of field normally seen in live-action films (you can see the fruit of the process in *Snow White* as the camera seems to move through the forest; the realism dazzled 1937's audiences just as CG effects did in the 1990s); 1930s toys and souvenirs featuring Mickey at the height of his early popularity, when he was markedly more rascally and tie-in merchandise was a new idea; the special Oscar for *Snow White* (one regular-size statue and seven little ones); and Walt's second-grade and 1930s studio desks. Worth special scrutiny is the re-creation of Walt's surprisingly banal Burbank office more or less as it appeared from 1940 (shortly before he became a propagandist during World War II) to 1966; note the bulletin board of Disneyland developments on the wall and also the three ashtrays, which contributed to his death from lung cancer.

Much of the exhibition chronicles the theme parks; including Disneyland's Main Street by way of a 1954 model, an early Audio-Animatronic tiki bird, and a map of the Magic Kingdom dating before the addition of Space Mountain and Pirates of the Caribbean. Also check out Walt standing in front of a giant map of the Florida Project—those flower-like plots were intended to be experimental neighborhoods where technology corporations could test ideas on a permanent city that would have been inhabited, in part, by theme park employees. Most people take about 20 minutes for the museum, and then there's a good 15-minute movie, culled mostly from archival footage and audio, so you hear the man himself speak. The feature scores points for mentioning Disney's 1931 breakdown, but it tends to play fast and loose with the truth to present Walt as a patron of the Disney Company's current efforts, implying he approved of Epcot's design and worse, elbowing poor Roy virtually out of the story. But fans who protest any changes to the parks should note what Walt says about his greatest creation. "Disneyland," he promises, "is something that will never be finished."

Farther along, engineers are preparing **Toy Story Mania,** the new marquee attraction for 2008. The ride will intensify the gimmick of the Magic Kingdom's Buzz Lightyear extravaganza: Wearing 3-D glasses, passengers will shoot their way through animated midway games (a Bo Peep egg toss, a Little Green Men ring toss) based on the Pixar characters. The better you play, the harder the games get. Fans are already abuzz about the 6-foot-tall Mister Potato Head—to be voiced by a hidden actor who interacts with guests—that will entertain the queue.

Only great fans of the 2005 movie should endure the walk-through **Journey into Narnia: Creating The Lion, The Witch, and The Wardrobe,** and even they might be disappointed, as this exhibition of props and costumes is shorter than the name of the place. It feels very much like an ad for a movie franchise. It is.

At the extreme end of Mickey Avenue, **The Disney–MGM Studios Backlot Tour** was once a centerpiece of the park, but has been whittled away to nearly nothing. It doesn't help that so few productions are actually filmed here—it's been a decade since anything of note was made—leaving the guides to fib about how busy employees are. New tours start every 15 minutes and take about 35 minutes. It's less crowded early in the day. The first segment is the Special Effects Water Tank Show, which accepts four volunteers (raise your hand for duty in the queue, if you're an adult). There, standing guests watch how the bullet impacts, explosions, and deluges of a ship-attack movie sequence are shot and cut together to look real. To win the best views from the front row of the audience section, join the right-hand row in the queue area, which is shared with wheelchairs. Be among the first people out of there, because the next section finds you in yet another queue, this one in a warehouse full of old movie props (a few of which you may recognize), which feeds the boarding area for a tram; the seats on the left are best.

Although the guides keep telling you "you never know who or what you may see on the backlot," they're faking, because a few years ago, Disney bulldozed most of its backlot, including Residential Street, a little village for exterior shots (the *Golden Girls* and *Empty Nest* house facades were here), to make room for the Extreme Stunt Show (see above). When drivers are rehearsing or performing, the shriek of the engines and the funk of burning rubber make the tram miserable and the narrator inaudible. The 20-minute trip loops past the Earful Tower (a mouse-eared water tower, empty, that was the icon of the park before Sorcerer Mickey Hat superceded it); some old prop vehicles (from *The Rocketeer, Pearl Harbor,* and other movies Disney wanted to do better) in the scaled-down Boneyard; through wardrobe houses (again, more Hollywood props on display, but you'll get the feeling the staff is darning theme park uniforms, not movie costumes); and then you pass through Catastrophe Canyon, where, seated safely, you'll witness a simulated earthquake, the heat of an exploding oil tanker, and a flash flood—all in the space of seconds. Naturally, you already know how production crews create effects like these, but being right next to the wizardry, which re-sets every 3½ minutes for a new batch of guests, is still heart-pounding fun—although no thinking person believes the guide's bald lie that the special effects crew that built this rig has stepped away "on a break." Those sitting on the left of the tram tend to get a tad wet, and because of the way you're facing, you'll need sunglasses in the afternoon. On the way out, you'll spot a Gulfstream jet Walt Disney used on his real estate-grabbing missions to Florida (by the way, the park's original airstrip, east of the Magic Kingdom's parking lot, is now a bus staging area). The tour closes after 5pm or thereabouts.

WHERE TO EAT AT DISNEY–MGM STUDIOS

Reservations for the sit-down restaurants can be made at ☎ 407/939-3463. At counter-service locations, kids' meals are $4 with a drink. The park's **fruit stand** ($1 a piece) is on Sunset Boulevard.

 ◆ **Hollywood Boulevard and Echo Lake:** The sit-down restaurants are here. Make reservations for the **50's Prime Time Café** ★★, a cute concept in which families dine atop Formica in detailed reproductions of Cleaver-era kitchens beneath TVs playing black-and-white shows of the era. Waitresses gently sass customers, and the menu is equally as homey, including meatloaf, a very good pot roast, and a dessert menu read through a ViewMaster. It's as expensive as all Disney sit-down restaurants (entrees are $13 at lunch, $16 at dinner), but you get a lot more entertainment value for your money here. The peanut butter and jelly milkshake, which you can only find here, is deli-cious (though I think it tastes more of caramel). Next door is **Hollywood & Vine** (kids), which is for character breakfasts and lunches with Disney Channel characters such as JoJo (from $23 adults, $13 kids; reservations suggested).

Walt Disney's Legacy

Pretty much every advance that made Walt Disney the preeminent name in entertainment—adding sound to cartoons, then color, and then turning a 7-minute art form into full-length features—was accomplished out of a feverish pursuit of quality, not profit. Each time Walt did something new, it nearly bankrupted him, and he suffered nervous breakdowns; but to him, there was nothing more important than furnishing a superior product to the public, profit be damned. "I'm afraid that this business will be thrown into the regular Hollywood groove and that they will start throwing these cartoons at the public," he wrote in the 1930s. "All they think of is how much money they can get out of a thing."

For years after his death, Disney's populist ideals limped on; until the 1980s, the parking charge at Disneyland was an insanely low $1. The last Disney World hotels that Walt himself helped plan, the Contemporary, Fort Wilderness, and the Polynesian, intentionally eschewed luxury pretensions. Yet the stewards of the modern-day Walt Disney Company have abandoned this viewpoint. Today, profit and relentless branding are the mode, which is why the newest rides are based on cheaper video projections instead of robotics, why perks that don't make money are removed, why its newer hotels trade on luxury, why new DVD releases are referenced more often than Disney classics, and how an entire pavilion at Epcot, Wonders of Life, has been mostly abandoned. I'm still in awe of the efficiency and playful munificence with which the old Disney World was run, and in defense of that still-attainable benchmark, I say that if the modern-day corporate masters who control the Disney empire insist on continuously invoking the name of Walt Disney and his ideals, they should at least be honest enough to admit that Disney himself did business in a far different, and far more generous, fashion.

Near the Sorcerer Hat, also tasty is **The Hollywood Brown Derby,** the park's most expensive spot (dinner entrees in the mid-20s). It's noted for its delicious Grapefruit Cake ($6.20), which you can only get here.

◆ **Commissary Lane:** Just as Animation Courtyard has no eateries, Commissary Lane has no attractions. Instead, it's intended to mimic the cafeterias found at working studios. The counter-service **ABC Commissary** ★★★ does burgers and Cuban sandwiches for $7 and under, and has the best variety for its price level in the park. The **Sci-Fi Dine-In Theater Restaurant** ★★★ is the park's most affordable sit-down restaurant; dinner prices are lower than most places in the parks, around $15 to $17 for passable pan-seared salmon, baby back ribs, and shrimp penne pasta. Like the Prime Time Cafe, you get a lot of atmosphere for your buck: Seats are in vintage convertibles arranged around a silver screen of creature features, drive-in style. It's a brilliant idea, well-realized, tons of fun, and because it's priced below other Disney restaurants with much less to offer, it's my pick for the most fun restaurant at MGM—and maybe in the whole resort.

- **Sunset Boulevard:** Its left-hand side, as you approach the Tower of Terror, provides a string of budget outlets, including the counter-service **Rosie's All-American Cafe** ✦ (burgers), the **Toluca Legs Turkey Co.** ✦ (giant turkey legs for under $5.50), and a cart selling fresh fruit (mystifyingly, the oranges are from California, not Central Florida).

- **Streets of America: Mama Melrose's Ristorante Italiano** costs just two-thirds of what Epcot's sit-down Italian spot does; about $17 per entree. That's still high, so there's also the counter-service **Toy Story Pizza Planet Arcade** ✦ for standard personal pizzas ($7–$8, with salad) and a decent-sized feta salad. Finally, the **Studio Catering Co. Flatbread Grill** (just **Flatbread Grill** on the signs), over near the entrance to the Backlot Tour, isn't always open, but does barbecued pulled pork subs and grilled chicken for $6.50. Nearby, there's also a stand selling $9 cocktails (margaritas and the like) and $5.50 draft beers.

DISNEY'S ANIMAL KINGDOM

Although it's the largest Disney theme park in Florida (500 acres), Disney's Animal Kingdom, which opened in 1998 at a reported cost of $800 million as a competitor to Busch Gardens Tampa Bay, actually takes the least amount of time to visit, because most of that land is used up by a menagerie of exotic animals. Instead of cages, they're kept in paddocks rimmed with cleverly disguised trenches that are concealed behind landscaping. Because animals become inactive as the Florida heat builds, a visit here should begin as soon as the gates open, usually around 8am. To help gird your resolve, there are coffee carts ($1.90 a cup) along the entranceway. Most people wrap up by 1 or 2pm, although the addition of the coaster Expedition Everest has extended that by an hour or so. It all usually closes in late afternoon, earlier than the others, but most guests have departed by then, anyway. Schedule your nighttime shindig, such as that dinner show you've been dying to catch, for your Animal Kingdom day, as you'll be out in time.

One side note: As you approach the park from outside, you'll see not only the profiles of the Tree of Life and Expedition Everest, but also a leafy, tall tower to the left of them both. Don't run around trying to find this beckoning structure: It's not an attraction, but a cellphone tower dressed up to look less conspicuous.

Warning: Check the weather before you come, because if it's excessively hot or wet, you might be miserable here. There are only three major attractions that take place in air-conditioned theaters.

Even before you reach the ticket gates, there's a restaurant: a location of the chain Rainforest Cafe, which also operates in Downtown Disney. If the lines look daunting at the front gates, you'll find a smaller, secondary entry gate through the restaurant's gift shop. Staples such as locker and stroller rental are just past the gates, in what's called the **Oasis**, a lush buffer zone that gradually acclimates guests to the world of the park. Pick up a free Guidemap and a Times Guide. The locations of animal enclosures, which start immediately, are noted on the map by black-and-white paw prints and also by chip photographs of beasts, so if you're most interested in seeing wildlife, follow those.

Generally speaking, the animals collect at the back of the park, the thrills to the right, and the biggest kiddie goodies to the left.

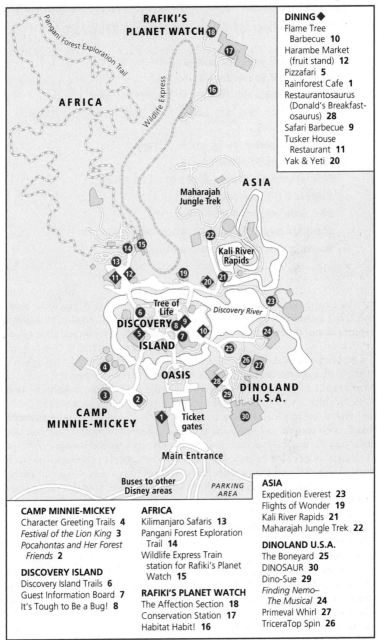

DINING ◆
Flame Tree
 Barbecue **10**
Harambe Market
 (fruit stand) **12**
Pizzafari **5**
Rainforest Cafe **1**
Restaurantosaurus
 (Donald's Breakfast-
 osaurus) **28**
Safari Barbecue **9**
Tusker House
 Restaurant **11**
Yak & Yeti **20**

RAFIKI'S PLANET WATCH

Pangani Forest Exploration Trail

AFRICA

Wildlife Express

Maharajah Jungle Trek

ASIA

Kali River Rapids

Tree of Life

Discovery River

DISCOVERY ISLAND

OASIS

DINOLAND U.S.A.

CAMP MINNIE-MICKEY

Ticket gates

Main Entrance

Buses to other Disney areas

PARKING AREA

CAMP MINNIE-MICKEY
Character Greeting Trails **4**
Festival of the Lion King **3**
*Pocahontas and Her Forest
 Friends* **2**

DISCOVERY ISLAND
Discovery Island Trails **6**
Guest Information Board **7**
It's Tough to Be a Bug! **8**

AFRICA
Kilimanjaro Safaris **13**
Pangani Forest Exploration
 Trail **14**
Wildlife Express Train
 station for Rafiki's Planet
 Watch **15**

RAFIKI'S PLANET WATCH
The Affection Section **18**
Conservation Station **17**
Habitat Habit! **16**

ASIA
Expedition Everest **23**
Flights of Wonder **19**
Kali River Rapids **21**
Maharajah Jungle Trek **22**

DINOLAND U.S.A.
The Boneyard **25**
DINOSAUR **30**
Dino-Sue **29**
*Finding Nemo–
 The Musical* **24**
Primeval Whirl **27**
TriceraTop Spin **26**

The Best of Disney's Animal Kingdom

Don't miss if you're 6: *Festival of the Lion King*

Don't miss if you're 16: DINOSAUR

Requisite photo op: The drop at Expedition Everest

Food you can only get here: Pulled pork, Flame Tree Barbecue, Discovery Island

The most crowded, so go early: Kilimanjaro Safaris

Skippable: Rafiki's Planet Watch

Quintessentially Disney: It's Tough to Be a Bug!

Biggest thrill: Expedition Everest

Best show: *Finding Nemo—The Musical*

Character meals: Donald's Breakfastosaurus, DinoLand U.S.A.

Where to find peace: Discovery Island

The first thing you should do, like everyone else, is beeline it to the back of the Africa section. That's where the Kilimanjaro Safari is; because crowds grow more ferocious than the lions, first thing in the morning is the best time to do it.

DISCOVERY ISLAND

Like the Plaza of the Magic Kingdom, Discovery Island is designed to be the hub of the park. It's the main viewing area for the daily Mickey's Jammin' Jungle Parade, which circles it (the route is denoted on the maps by a red dotted line) and guests can touch down here to change lands. The park's **Guest Information Board,** with current wait times and upcoming show times, is also here, just to the right past the bridge from the Oasis, by the Disney Outfitters shop.

Instead of a castle or a geosphere (or, uh . . . a hat), the centerpiece here is **The Tree of Life** ★★, a 14-story-high arbor (built on the skeleton of an oil rig) covered with hundreds of intricate carvings of animals made to appear, at a distance, like the pattern of the bark. Some 102,000 vinyl leaves were individually attached—which is why its shade of green is more lurid than the surrounding foliage—to 45 trunks and some 750 tertiary branches. That the best way to enjoy it is to slowly make a circuit of it, looking for and identifying new animals, is perhaps proof that the best way to experience this park is to slow down and open your eyes. Get yourself in the swing by circling the tree on the little-used **Discovery Island Trails** ★, where you'll pass giant Galápagos tortoises, the largest rodent in the world (the capybara), flamingoes, storks, otters, lemurs, and macaws, among other animals.

Beneath its flying roots, in a cool basement-like theatre, there's a cleverly rigged cinema showing a sense-tricking 3-D movie, **It's Tough to Be a Bug!** ★★★ 🦎, based on the animated movie *A Bug's Life*. When the stinkbugs do their thing or the tarantula starts firing poison quills, you'll never quite be sure what's an onscreen image, what's cutting-edge robotics, and what's really pouring out of hidden vents or poking you from underneath. As one of the newest sense-tricking movies at Disney World, it's one of the best. Little kids who can't distinguish fantasy from reality may be scared when some of the bugs decide they want to exterminate the people and by the life-size villain figure, a marvelously realized Hopper figure. The pre-show area is decorated with one-sheets for some funny entomological variations on popular human films (my fave: *Web Side Story*). Although Fastpass is available for this one, it's rarely necessary.

AFRICA

Although it's tempting to visit the Tree of Life first, such a gleaming and emerald wienie it is, as soon as the gates open you should veer to the left and head toward the back of the park to the Africa section, where you can board the popular 20-minute **Kilimanjaro Safaris** ★★★. Climb into a super-size, 32-passenger Jeep—an actual one with wheels, not a tracked cart—and be swept into what feels very much like a real safari through the African veldt, with meticulously rutted tracks and all, only without the hours spent roaming, waiting, and peering through binoculars. Besides the standard subplot about thwarting poachers, there's no predicting what you'll see for sure, as these animals must be on union contracts, but you'll pass through habitats for giraffes, zebras, elephants, wildebeest, cheetah, ostrich, hippos, lions, gazelles, rhinos, and other creatures that made safaris famous. Taking photos isn't easy, given the turbulence and the speed of the tour. Considering the quality and quantity of animals on display—and the cleverness of the enclosure design, as there are never bars between you and them—it's easily the best animal attraction of the park, and the queue only builds during the day. Some people say that the second-best time of day to see the animals is around 2 or 3 in the afternoon because they get antsy with the foreknowledge that they're about to be led to their indoor sleeping quarters. Ride twice if you want—the free will of the animals means it's never the same trip twice. Photographers who want clear shots should jockey toward the back, away from the cockpit. They may not have control over that, though, so at the very least, they should negotiate with their companions for a seat at the end of their row.

Next door, the **Pangani Forest Exploration Trail** ★★ focuses on African animals. It wends past a troop of lowland gorillas (very popular), naked mole rats, okapi, meerkats (yes, like Timon), and hippos you can view through an underwater window. The zoo-like circuit takes about a half-hour, but you can spend as long as you want at any habitat.

RAFIKI'S PLANET WATCH

Once you've spotted such impressive creatures so soon, the rest of the critters you'll see throughout the day, endearing as they are, can't help but be a letdown. From the Safaris, take the **Wildlife Express Train.** Waits are generally no longer than 10 minutes, and as you ride train cars open on one side (the trip takes 7 min.), you'll get glimpses of the plain backstage work areas but not much else. It's the only way to reach the zone called **Rafiki's Planet Watch.** Its elements are listed separately on the park maps, but everything is of a piece: It's all intended to teach kids the value of co-existing with the natural world despite the demands of our modern one. **Habitat Habit!,** the path that links the train station to the main building, is another "discovery trail," this one with cotton-top tamarins (endangered monkeys about the size of squirrels). **Conservation Station** is a quasi-educational backstage peek at how the park's animals are maintained—you're not seeing the true veterinary facilities, but a few auxiliary rooms set up so tourists can watch activities through picture windows. There's not always something going on (early mornings are most active), and the Times Guide doesn't help, so you might get all the way here and then find yourself with only a few exhibits to poke at, all about environment awareness and animal well-being—if you've made it this deep into Animal Kingdom, it'll be preaching to the choir. There's nothing earthshaking—enter a dark, soundproof booth and listen to the sounds of the rainforest—but the pace is much easier than in the park outside. **The Affection Section** 🧒 is a petting zoo with a type of goat that was saved from extinction; the hand washers are shaped like spraying elephant trunks.

ASIA

In early 2006, Asia received a major dose of love in the form of **Expedition Everest** ★★★, a lavishly themed and abundantly hyped roller coaster. You can't miss the "snowcapped" mountain looming nearly 200 feet over the park's east end (if it were any higher, Florida law would require it to be topped by an airplane beacon). The queue area is a beautifully realized duplication of a Himalayan temple down to the fraying prayer flags, tarnished bells, and weathered paint, although portions of it do linger in the sun, so drink something before you pony up. The coaster itself is loaded with powerful set pieces that get you your money's worth: a rear-car motor that puffs steam, both backward and forward motion, pitch-black sections, cooling mists, and a fleeting encounter with a massive, state-of-the-art Audio-Animatronic Abominable Snowman, or Yeti. As with all Disney rides, the most dramatic drop (80 ft.) is clearly visible from the sidewalk out front, so if you think you can stomach that, you can do the rest. There are no upside-down loops; the dominant motion is spiral, which can make some people slightly nauseous for a few subsequent moments. This coaster, a top candidate for Fastpass usage, marks a return to form for Disney, and the enormous Yeti, which appears at the climax of the trip, constitutes a landmark in the evolution of Disney robotics. The seats with the best view, without question, are in the front rows, although the back rows feel a little faster.

Asia's other major attraction is the **Kali River Rapids,** a 12-passenger round bumper boat that shoots a course of rapids. Sometimes you can get soaked—it depends on your bad luck—but it's generally milder than similar rides. Your feet, for sure, will get wet. The worst damage is usually done by spectators who shoot water cannons at passing boats from a bridge. Lots of guests buy rain ponchos for the ride (those are $7 at nearby stores—or $1 for two at your local dollar store), but there is a waterproof holding area in the middle of each boat. Well, *sorta* waterproof—if you can wrap your stuff in a plastic bag, you'll be in better shape. Like other Animal Kingdom rides, there's a conservation-themed overlay about illegal loggers. The original plan was also to enclose the ride inside a tiger habitat, but that didn't pan out. Lines build considerably when it's hot, so it's another prime Fastpass candidate. If you're going to be going to Islands of Adventure on your Orlando trip, you can skip this ride and do the better one there.

To the left of the Kali entrance, the **Maharajah Jungle Trek** ★ is a walking trail featuring some gorgeous tigers (rescued from a circus breeding program), tapirs, komodo dragons, gibbons, and a few other South Asian animals frolicking among fake ruins. The tigers are most active when the park opens and near closing time. Grab a bird information sheet before you enter the aviary. If you Fastpass Kali River Rapids, kill the intervening time by strolling through here first.

At the canvas-sheltered Caravan Stage, the 25-minute **Flights of Wonder** (the schedule is posted) showcases hawks, vultures, bald eagles, parrots, and some other birds that swoop thrillingly over the audience's heads. Consider it standard, if beautiful, nature-show stuff. After the performance, handlers usually present a few of the birds back on stage for close inspection.

DINOLAND U.S.A.

Performed four or five times daily (check the Times Guide and show up at least 40 minutes ahead), the winning *Finding Nemo—The Musical* ★★★ 🧒🏻 is, for my money, the best theme park show in the world right now. A compressed version of the movie, the story has been heightened with such catchy added songs as "Fish Are Friends, Not Food" and the infectious, Beach Boys–style "Go with the Flow." Just as in *The Lion King*'s Broadway adaptation, live actors manipulate complicated animal puppets in full view, which allows the fish to appear as if they're floating in the sea. It's remarkable how quickly you stop paying attention to the humans—at least, until they start flying, with their puppets, through the air on wires. Then you're just amazed. Sprightly, bright, colossal, and energetic, it's a good choice for taking a load off (the bench seating is indoors), and even those who know the movie backward and forward will find something new in the vibrant vigor of the delivery. This 40-minute spectacular makes for an excellent children's introduction to a Broadway-style performance, complete with post-show bows and $13 souvenir CDs of the songs. Because some scenes (including the introduction of Dory) happen in the aisle that crosses the center of the theater, I suggest sitting in the rear half of the auditorium. Seats there also are a little better for absorbing the stage pictures and submitting to the optical illusion of puppetry.

Keep the kids in control by swinging them next to the adjoining kiddie area, starting with **The Boneyard** 🧒🏻, a hot, sun-exposed playground where the very young can dig up "prehistoric" bones in the sand. That's next to **Chester & Hester's Dino-Rama,** a miniature carnival-style amusement area with a midway (Fossil Fun Games), and two simple family rides. **TriceraTop Spin** 🧒🏻, for the very young, is yet another iteration of the Dumbo ride over at Magic Kingdom and is designed for kids to ride with their parents. Cars fit four. I suggest you give it a miss unless you're faced with a temper tantrum. **Primeval Whirl** is a pair of mirror-image, family-friendly carnival-style coasters (Walt *hated* carnivals) that start out like a typical "wild mouse" ride before, midtrip, the round cars begin spinning on an axle as they ride the rails. Think of it as a roller-coaster version of the teacup ride. You can see quite plainly what you're in for, although you may be surprised at how roughly the movements can whip your neck. Don't feel bad if you give it a miss, too, because it's not a Disney original; it was made by a French company that sells similar rides to other parks.

DinoLand's major thrill attraction *is* a Disney original: **DINOSAUR** ★★, a 3-minute indoor time-travel ride in which all-terrain "Enhanced Motion Vehicles" simultaneously speed down an unseen track and perform motion-simulation maneuvers, all as hordes of roaring dinosaurs attempt to make you dinner and an approaching meteor shower threatens to do everyone in. Some kids, and even some adults, find all those jaws and jerky movements rather intense, and it's very dark and loud, but ultimately, it's a fun time, even if the perpetual darkness makes me wonder how much money the ride planners saved in not having to build more dinosaurs. Like many modern Disney rides, there are well-known but affordable actors performing in the pre-show video; this one's got Phylicia Rashad and Wallace Langham. The line never seems to be as long as this ride deserves. Out front, don't ignore **Dino-Sue**, the 40-foot-long, full-scale *T. rex* skeleton—it's an exact replica of Sue, the most complete specimen man has yet found. The original, unearthed in modern-day South Dakota, is on display at Chicago's Field Museum.

Camp Minnie-Mickey

The final themed zone, Camp Minnie-Mickey, is between the entrance plaza and Africa, and it's also for kids. The great flaw of this area is that there's no real reason to partake unless you see something on your Times Guide that you want to do, because there are no continuous attractions. It's the place to see the air-conditioned *Festival of the Lion King* ★★ 🧒 show, which before Nemo arrived was the prime sensory overloader for kids. If this lavish, colorful, intense spectacle can't hold your attention for 30 minutes, you might have more serious issues. Audiences sit on benches in four quadrants (front rows are good if you want to engage with the performers), and the event comes on like an acid trip during a rock concert. Four huge floats enter the room, topped with soft-looking giant puppets of Timon, Pumbaa, and African wildlife and attended by acrobats, stilt-walkers, flame jugglers, and dancers, all of whom get their turn to dazzle you with their acts, which are performed, of course, to the hit songs of the movie. The best seating sections are to your left as you enter the theater; if you want to be near the exit (there's no ducking out once it starts, though), sit in the two right-hand sections. Shows are timed, and they do fill up, so people arrive 30 minutes early— be warned that the wait area is exposed to the elements.

A minor 15-minute show, the awfully cute *Pocahontas and Her Forest Friends* 🧒 employs a single human actor (hot mama Poca). While she frets about the forest being cut down (ironic, considering how much Florida swamp was obliterated to build this resort, but never you mind), a whole zoo's worth of common furry creatures makes a simple appearance at its designated moment—the accumulated effect is quite sweet, and pre-schoolers respond brightly. Among the supporting cast are a turkey, raccoon, bunny, opossum, porcupine, skunk, ducks, a hawk, and, in a psychedelic touch, a pair of talking puppet trees. It's a little weird when Pocahontas tickles a sapling and it giggles sheepishly in response. Also, the thin varnish of the what's-in-it-for-me environmental moral (concludes Poca, "We should respect nature . . . or it could turn against us!") grates me. But that all goes over kids' heads. Speaking of that, the first three rows are reserved for small children. This theater has bench seating and is lightly sheltered by trees. The Times Guide lists the seven-odd daily performances, but you might be interested in attending the one marked "training." That one affords you the chance to learn how the animals are induced to do the things they do on stage.

The other cabanas in Camp Minnie-Mickey are for the **Character Greeting Trails.** They essentially guarantee face time with Disney characters within the period printed on the Times Guide. This is the park's bonanza zone for autographs.

Interestingly, Animal Kingdom was originally supposed to be about all animals, mythical and real, and an additional land, Beastly Kingdom, was planned. On Discovery Island benches and etched above the main park entrance, you'll still see some dragons, a hint of big plans that have not come to fruition. Yet.

About an hour before closing time, the daily **Mickey's Jammin' Jungle Parade** ★ 🧒 begins in Africa, loops through the park, and then returns to its starting point. Like all Disney parades, it's about ten floats long, with lots of character appearances. I like this one because the floats are quite ingeniously made—most of them are animal-like contraptions powered by the people pushing or driving them along. The period between the parade's end and park closing is a good time to do the stuff that had longer lines before the parade started, such as Expedition Everest. At Animal Kingdom especially, many guests leave early in the day, and you can use that fact to your advantage.

Where to Eat at Disney's Animal Kingdom

Because you need to be up early for your Animal Kingdom day anyway, you might consider doing a character breakfast here, if that was part of your plan. Mickey, Donald, Pluto, and Goofy (a darn good, A-level lineup—you can only do better at Chef Mickey's at the Contemporary Resort) show up at **Donald's Breakfastosaurus** 🧒 (☎ 407/939-3463) in DinoLand U.S.A. Prices are $19 for adults and $11 for kids 3 to 9, but that's all-you-can-eat, and then you can head right out for the animals while they're still active.

Rainforest Cafe, just outside the ticket gates, usually closes an hour after the park. The best lunch spots are on Discovery Island. That is expected to change by mid-2007, when a new restaurant in Asia, **Yak & Yeti,** begins offering both sit-down and counter service. Kids' meals are $4 with a drink. The park's **fruit stand** ($1 a piece) is at **Harambe Market** in Africa.

You'll find the greatest selection on Discovery Island. Although I don't care to gorge on meat-heavy dishes such as ribs and baked chicken ($7 to $9) when I'm supposed to be appreciating animals, **Flame Tree Barbecue** ★★ has some terrific eating areas on the Discovery River, and its pulled pork barbecue is one-of-a-kind in all the parks. **Pizzafari** ★ (a well-designed restaurant where the main dish is made by fancy machine that squirts the sauce on and everything) charges under $6 for pizzas and under $7 for chicken parmesan sandwiches and salads. **Safari Barbecue** ★★, the park's turkey leg cart ($5.50 a leg) is also here, on the path toward Asia. Apparently, zookeepers made the mistake of allowing the chefs to take care of the venerable gobbler.

Tusker House Restaurant ★★ in Africa is a notch above the usual with salmon, chicken salad, and turkey wraps with corn chowder, all for $7 to $8.

In **DinoLand U.S.A., Restaurantosaurus** does burgers, hot dogs, and mandarin chicken salad for under $7.

Note: Because drinking straws could choke the animals, they aren't provided.

THE WATER PARKS

The big question: Blizzard Beach or Typhoon Lagoon? Both can fill a day. Here's my answer: It depends on your mood. Typhoon Lagoon's central feature, a sand-lined 2½-acre wave pool, is an ideal place for families to frolic and to approximate a day at the beach. If your kids have a need for speed, you head over to Blizzard Beach, which has a milder wave pool but wilder water slides.

Both water parks are less busy early in the week, probably because folks tend to start their vacations on a weekend and don't get to the flumes until they've done the four big theme parks. On very hot days, they are unpleasantly crammed, and they tend to be busier in the morning than in late afternoon. They also sell everything you need to protect yourself from the sun, including lotion (should you have forgotten) and swimsuits (should you lose yours in the lather). Most lines (many rides have two: one for a raft and one for the slide) are fully exposed to the sun, so it's important to keep hydrated, as you won't always be aware how much you're sweating: Both parks sell $10 mugs that are refillable for endless soft drinks while you're there (otherwise, soft drinks start at $2.10). They also rent towels for $1. Lifeguards usually make you remove water shoes on slides that don't use a mat or raft, and swimsuits with rivets or zippers are forbidden because they may scratch the flumes.

An average locker is $10 but you get $5 of that back after you turn your key in. They allow multiple access, are about 2 feet deep, and the opening is about the size of a magazine. Thoughtfully, there are bulletin boards near the entrance that tell you what the sunburn risk is, what the wait time is for the slides, as well as what times the parades run at Disney parks that day. If there are any activities (scavenger hunts are common), they'll be posted here. Kids' beach toy sets, for the sand around the lagoon, are sold in the gift shop for $10.

Stupidly, many of the food stands only take cash and won't even accept room keys as payment, so bring a waterproof pouch. Also don't plan on eating dinner at the water parks, as the kiosks tend to shut down before closing.

If you're coming to Florida between November and mid-March, one of these parks will be closed for its annual hose-down. The other will remain open. Most water features are heated, but remember that you eventually must get *out*.

BLIZZARD BEACH

Of the two water parks, I prefer this one, but I like excitement in my slides. **Blizzard Beach** (☎ 407/560-3400; www.disneyworld.com; $39 adults, $33 kids aged 3–9), which opened 6 years after Typhoon Lagoon and had the benefit of improving on what didn't work there, also has a wittier theme. The invented backstory is perfect for a hot day: A freak snowstorm hit Mount Gushmore, and Disney was slapping up a ski resort when the snow began to melt, creating water slides. So now, a lift chair brings bathers most of the way up the peak, and flumes are festooned with ski-run flags and piled with white "snowdrifts." Best of all, no one has to tote their rafts uphill—there are conveyors to do it for you.

Surely the most exhilarating 8 seconds in all of Walt Disney World, **Summit Plummet** ★★★ is the immensely steep, 12-story-tall slide that commands attention at the peak of the mountain, which incidentally, offers one of the best panoramas of the Walt Disney World resort. A slide down this one is only for the truly fearless, as the first few seconds make you feel practically weightless, as if you're about to fall forward. By the end, the water is jabbing you so hard that it's not unusual to come away with a light bruise, and it turns the toughest bathing suit into dental floss, if you catch my drift. This is a fun one to watch: At the bottom, there's a speed clock that measures how fast the last sucker went (58mph is a typical reading)—although I think some of the young men are watching for other reasons. **Slush Gusher,** next to it and slightly lower, is a double-hump that gives the rider the sensation of air time—not a reassuring feeling when you're flying down an open chute.

The enormous chute winding off the mountain's right side is **Teamboat Springs ★★★**, a group ride in a circular raft; just about everyone gets a chance to enjoy the top of a banked turn, and after the inevitable splashdown, another minute is spent in a comedown floating on a river. It's highly re-rideable, but if you go alone, you'll be paired with strangers, which can result in slippery awkwardness. **Snow Stormers** is a trio of standard raft water slides, but the twin **Downhill Double Dipper ★** is a simple slope of two identical slides with a good embellishment: It times runs so you can race a companion down. **Toboggan Racers** multiplies the fun to where eight people can race at once, untimed, down an evenly scalloped run. At the base of these is **Melt Away Bay,** a 1-acre wave pool in which waves create a gentle bobbing sensation. It could stand to be larger since it gets very crowded.

At the back of the mountain (reach it by walking around the left or via the lazy river), the three **Runoff Rapids ★★** flumes comprise two open-air slides and a totally enclosed one—you only see the occasional light flashing by. (These are the only ones for which you must haul your own raft up the hill.)

The park is circled by the superlative lazy river (for the newbie, that's a slow-flowing channel where you float along in an inner tube) called **Cross Country Creek ★★★** 👦, which is probably the best of its kind, passing a cave dripping with refrigerated water and a slouching shack that, every few seconds, gushes as you hear the sound of Goofy sneezing. It's easier to find a free inner tube at a ramp far from the park entrance; try the one at the base of Downhill Double Dipper or the one to the left past Lottawatta Lodge, the main food service building.

There are two kiddie areas, one for pre-teens, **Ski Patrol** 👦 (short slides, a walk across the water on floating "icebergs") and for littler kids, **Tike's Peak** 👦 (even smaller slides, fountains, and jets). The latter is a good place to look if you can't find seating. Parents who reach a saturation point with theme parks will be happy to learn the main bar is by the one and only entrance; you can send the kiddies off to play and raise a few, knowing they can't leave without passing you.

The miniature golf course Winter Summerland (p. 232) shares a parking lot with Blizzard Beach, so it's easy to combine a visit.

TYPHOON LAGOON

Despite the petrifying imagery of the shrimp boat *(Miss Tilly)* impaled on the central mountain *(Mt. Mayday),* the flumes here are less daunting than the ones at Blizzard Beach or Wet 'n Wild. **Typhoon Lagoon** (☎ 407/560-4141; www.disney world.com; $39 adults, $33 kids aged 3–9) is extremely well landscaped (most of the flowers are selected so that they attract butterflies and not bees) to hide its infrastructure, but it's not always well planned. For example, the paths to the slides ramble up and down stairs—the one to the Storm Slides actually goes *down* eight times as it winds up the mountain. It's also not always clear where to find the right entrance to the slide you want.

The **Surf Pool** ★★★ packs a surprising punch (body surfing is easy on those 5-foot waves, but so is losing toddlers), while the slides are generally shallow, slow, and geared toward avowed sissies. That will frustrate some teenagers, but little kids think Mayday Falls, which sends riders down a corrugated flume, is just right (adults come off rubbing their butts in pain). The leftmost body slide at **Storm Slides** is slightly more covered, but otherwise the slides are much the same. The most thrilling rides are the **Crush 'n' Gusher** ★★★ "water coaster" flumes, which use jets to push rafts both uphill and downhill; the gag is that it used to be a fruit-washing plant, and now you're the banana. They're found in a discrete section off to the right after you enter.

The park's lazy river is ungimmicky and lushly planted. One excellent attraction is the **Shark Reef** ★, a 10½-foot-deep tank stocked with tropical fish and mock coral. Everyone gets a mask, snorkel, and, if they want, a floatation jacket, and then swims 60 feet across the tank (no dawdling permitted) under the eye of lifeguards who'll spring into action at the slightest hint of trouble—or even if you

Fitting into the Disney Culture

On a recent visit to the World of Disney shop at Downtown Disney, I discovered that a souvenir book I wanted was out of stock. "I can't believe the largest Disney Store in the world doesn't have it," I remarked to a clerk with a wink. "We have it," she sniffed, clearly insulted. "We're just out of it." And she turned her back on me.

I call that Disney Logic, and it's a reminder that just as Parisians are hurried and the English aren't demonstrative, Walt Disney World's employees have a culture all their own that visitors must learn to respect and navigate. Working at Disney World isn't like getting a job at the bank. Many cast members live and breathe its way of life, and many moved from other parts of the country just to be a part of it. Be alert to the fact that many of them identify personally with Walt Disney World, and many take subtle exception to any comment that might carry a hint of criticism or questioning, no matter how politely it's phrased. Try not to put any Disney employee in a position of having to defend or explain their company, or you may put their back up. If a cast member can't provide you with what you need (because of job compartmentalization, that happens often), then smile and move on to another one. In Walt Disney World, a country within a country, the accepted communication mode is toothy smiles and chipper greetings, all in service of that nebulous "Disney magic" to which the biggest fans cling. Although that code is technically meant to apply only to cast members, the unspoken cultural expectation is that you follow it, too.

just want a strong hand. (If you want a tank where you can linger with the fish, head for SeaWorld's Discovery Cove.) You don't have to meet a high standard beyond an ability to paddle across a pool. If you don't care for that setup, you can descend by stairs into a submerged "shipwreck," which has portholes allowing a lateral view of the same tank. Shark Reef gets busy, so do it early or late.

A day at a water park isn't as stressful as one spent among the queues of the theme parks, and if you're paying attention, the sights and sounds of a day here are pretty heartwarming. Every time the wave machine roars into gear, for example, dozens of kids shriek with delight and scamper into the water. At the Dive Pool, first-time snorkel users chatter into their tubes like a herd of geese. Because they're chilling out, people tend to be happy here.

The lazy river, **Castaway Creek** ★★ 🧒, runs clockwise around the park and is best enjoyed on one of the circulating inner tubes. For the best shot at finding an available tube, pick an area farther from the entrance, such as in front of the Crush 'n' Gusher area. That's also a good place to find a lounger if the Lagoon is packed, which it usually is; otherwise, try the extreme left past the ice cream stand. Also in that area is **Ketchakiddee Creek** 🧒, the play area for small children. Funny how the water's always warmer there.

Disney sells surf lessons on the Surf Pool before park hours (like, at 6:45am, before the buses are running) and sometimes, after it closes (☎ 407/939-7873; $140 for all ages, minimum age of 8). That comes with 30-minutes of on-land preparation followed by 2 hours of in-pool instruction, always with lifeguards scrutinizing your every twitch.

DOWNTOWN DISNEY

Downtown Disney, the main area for restaurants and shopping, ambles along the shore of Village Lake. The district has three zones; because of the size, it's helpful to know which one you're heading for because the walk between them can be up to 15 minutes. The busiest and easternmost area is called the Marketplace, and it's for shops and restaurants. The westernmost zone is the West Side, and although it has some shops, it leans toward nightlife and entertainment, such as a Cirque du Soleil show and a 24-screen cinema. Between them, Pleasure Island, the paid nightlife zone, parties until 2am. For entertainment options in this area, see chapter 10, "Orlando After Dark—and in the Dark," and for food options (none are spectacular), see chapter 4, "Dining Options around Town."

Shops here (☎ 407/939-3463) are pure Mouse. Among the stores are one for Christmas, one for high-end collectibles, one for pin trading, one for pet supplies, one for athletic-themed clothing, one for toys, and one for rejected souvenirs that cost less than $10 (that's the Mickey's Mart). There is a Lego store and another, Basin, for bath products, but otherwise, you won't find much non-Disney plunder, the way you could when it was known as Lake Buena Vista Shopping Village in the 1970s. There's also **World of Disney,** the largest souvenir department store in the resort, crowned by a giant Stitch burping water onto passersby. It's a rambling barn stocked from rug to rafter with every conceivable Disney-branded item, from pin to plush toys. You'll find stuff here you won't find at other Disney stores, or indeed at your local Disney Store.

Despite its status as the chief Mouse mart, it may not have what you want. That's because it's the only store that offers Annual Passholders a discount, which means the most obsessed fans clean the shelves here first. It also doesn't carry many of the items that might be sold at another store at the Marketplace (books, for example, or toys). Disney's merchandise distribution is slow; shopkeepers virtually beg superiors for restocking, and even then it can take weeks.

There's something else you should know. Many times, you can buy the same merchandise at home for far less. I have seen the same toys and DVDs at box stores and online for $7 that Walt Disney World wanted $20 or more for. Before purchasing, always ask if any item you want is a "park exclusive"—that means it's only available here. Otherwise, you could do a lot better if you got it back home.

The **Bibbidi Bobbidi Boutique** kids (Marketplace; ☎ 407/939-7895; 9:30am–5:30pm; reservations required) at Downtown Disney Marketplace gives girls age 3 and up makeovers as princesses for $35 to $175. There are two rooms, one for would-be pirates and one for would-be princesses, where kids create their own hats and dress up with merchandise, but the focus is the salon, where a "Fairy Godmother-in-Training" oversees your daughter's makeover, which comes with one of three hairstyles from which to choose. Boys are invited to make themselves "Cool Dudes" with colored hair gel. Are we teaching our daughters that the ultimate goal should be to find a prince? Ah, well, at least they'll look pretty.

DisneyQuest (West Side; ☎ 407/939-4600; www.disneyquest.com; $36 adults, $30 kids 3–9; kids under 10 must be accompanied by someone 16 or older; Sun–Thurs 11:30am–11pm, Fri–Sat 11:30am–midnight) is a five-level virtual reality playground on Downtown Disney's West Side. Standout stuff includes **Cyberspace Mountain,** in which you design your own coaster from a palette of options and then board a motion-simulator capsule in which you can test out your creation—360-degree loops and all. The ride vehicles actually go upside-down, making it one of only two Disney World rides to do so. **Virtual Jungle Cruise** has you on inflatable rafts, using paddles to float down a river on a screen in front of you; and **Pirates of the Caribbean: Battle for Buccaneer Gold** puts you on the deck of a mini–pirate ship, with screens on three sides, that has members of your party simultaneously steering and blasting rival ships by yanking on ropes that trigger cannons. They'll tell you that the visors required for certain games can fit over glasses, but **Ride the Comix,** a cyber-swordfight, compressed my nose so painfully I strongly suggest you wear contact lenses, if you can. Not everything is screen-based: the rowdy **Buzz Lightyear's AstroBlaster** is like a bumper car game where your vehicle scoops up balls and fires them at competitors, causing them to spin momentarily; it's designed for two riders at a time. There are also classes in which you can learn to draw a Disney character, but being charged extra for it is galling (a similar course is free at MGM's animation exhibit). Throughout the building are arcade games, old and new, that need no quarters. During the weekdays, you pretty much have your run of the place. There are a few counters for snacks and sandwiches, so it's easy to pass 3 or 4 hours here. I would go to any number of more compelling Orlando-area attractions before getting around to doing this one, but I would gladly go if I had some extra Water Park Fun & More days to burn on my Magic Your Way ticket.

DISNEY'S WIDE WORLD OF SPORTS

Most visitors don't stumble onto the 220-acre **Wide World of Sports** (Victory Dr.; Interstate 4 at Exit 64B; ☎ 407/363-6600; www.disneysports.com) by accident. They're intentionally there, whether for a son's wrestling tournament, a traveling sports exhibition game, or to see the Atlanta Braves in spring training. Unfortunately, it's not a place to roll up and pitch a few balls, although you can check its website to see if there's something ticketed that you might enjoy attending. This area is essentially a souped-up stadium complex, and it doesn't fit into the same category as the rest of Walt Disney World's attractions.

6 Universal, SeaWorld & Busch Gardens

Five more of the world's best theme parks

DISNEY IS ONLY HALF THE STORY. LESS THAN HALF, REALLY, WHEN YOU consider that while the Mouse maintains four parks, you'll find another four major themers, plus a luxury-level theme park, in the same vicinity. Seven of the world's top ten most patronized theme parks are in Orlando—four belong to Disney, and the other three to Universal Orlando and to SeaWorld. While some blinkered tourists think of these places as something to do after they "do Disney," the truth is these majors are in many ways just as appealing as the more famous Mouse traps. They also only draw about two-thirds the visitors that Disney's Epcot does in a given year, which means most of the time, you won't have to battle crowds.

You'd be remiss if you left town without seeing at least two of Disney's parks, but for my money—and I'm speaking as someone who grew up entranced by Disney and everything it stood for—I relax much more when I'm at these "other" parks. Increasingly, the true innovations in ride technology and design chutzpah are happening here—there's no doubt for most people that Universal's spectacular Spider-Man ride trumps anything else in the industry. As Disney becomes a company that increasingly rests on its cherished brand and its deserved laurels, Universal and Anheuser-Busch have stepped up by crafting parks where it's easier to mellow out, smell the flowers, or bask in the singe of an adrenaline rush.

All of these parks open at 9am, 365 days a year, and in winter months, operating hours will be curtailed until about 6pm. In summer, they're often open from as early as 9am to as late as 10pm. On days of peak attendance (such as the week after Christmas), parks may open as early as 8am.

UNIVERSAL ORLANDO

The opening of Universal Studios in 1990 heralded a new era for Orlando tourism. Instead of merely duplicating its original Hollywood location, which is located on its historic, working movie studio lot, Universal Orlando expanded on its most successful features and inflated them into a full-fledged all-day amusement park based on classic movies. While the park's opening was troubled, there was little doubt that Universal's innovations had instantly raised the bar for amusement parks worldwide.

In a way, Orlando grew up the instant the ribbon was cut at Universal. The theme of Hollywood movies was something that both kids and adults could enjoy, which widened the breadth of what a single Orlando park could offer. But the chief advance was that almost all of its attractions were indoors—even the thrills.

Given Florida's scorching sun and unpredictable rains, this leap shouldn't have been as novel as it was. While Disney was (and still is, sometimes) allowing its guests to swelter in the heat as they waited in line, Universal's multi-stage queuing system usually kept guests entertained (and air-conditioned). Its attractions kick off with a pre-show that keeps families amused before they're ushered into the main auditorium or onto ride vehicles. Although Universal still has a few outdoor queue areas, they are almost always sheltered and gently doused by cooling mist. Therefore, to this day, Universal Studios is the park you should choose on rainy days or excessively hot ones, as almost all of its pleasures are indoors. (Islands of Adventure, the other Universal park, has indoor queue areas for its big rides, which salvages many a scorcher, but many of them are outdoors and will shut down at the hint of lightning.) Even the parking at Universal Orlando is covered, which makes the parks a good choice on days when you have to check out of a hotel; your luggage will be kept cool in your car, whereas at all the other theme parks, including SeaWorld, it will bake all day in the sun.

Disney was clearly spooked when Universal barged into a market it all but owned, because in response, it hastily banged out a movies-themed park of its own, Disney–MGM Studios. The Mouse's park opened first, but it was a rush job, lacking many of the hallmarks of quality—a central organizing icon like Cinderella Castle, a logical and carefully considered layout, any thrill rides—that had made its previous two parks such successes.

Throughout the 1990s, Universal's one-park setup meant it mostly grabbed visitors on day trips from Disney. That changed—and the fight got nasty—in the summer of 1999, when a second, $2.6-billion park, Islands of Adventure, made its dazzling debut. Universal broke the bank to outshine Disney (even poaching a number of onetime Imagineers), and its investment largely paid off. IOA, as it's known, has the most elaborately crafted environment in town—pavements pigmented in Crayola colors, custom-built rides, individually detailed lampposts, benches, trash bins—which set a new standard for American amusement. Its Amazing Adventures of Spider-Man attraction is, hands down, the best ride Orlando has to offer. In fact, I haven't seen its equal anywhere in the world.

Now that Universal Orlando is home to two theme parks worth a day's visit (the first has been renamed Universal Studios Florida), Disney's nervousness has proven justified. Universal's domain has further expanded to include the nightlife district CityWalk and three full-service hotels, making the brand a true vacation destination in its own right. The complex has also proven highly successful at drawing business from locals.

Contacting Universal

General information: ☎ 407/363-8000; www.universalorlando.com

Vacation packages: ☎ 800/711-0080; www.univacations.com

Lost and found: ☎ 407/224-4244 (Universal Studios) or ☎ 407/224-4245 (Islands of Adventure)

I can't make any wholesale promises, but most of the time, lines are nowhere near as long as they are at Disney. Unless crowds are insanely huge (such as before Halloween Horror Nights events or during Christmas week), Universal takes 2 days to see. Three if you're taking your sweet time. With a two-park pass and a willingness to bypass lesser attractions, you could see the highlights of the two parks in 1 marathon day, provided at least one of the parks stays open until 9 or 10pm. In any event, bopping between the two parks isn't hard, since their entrances are a 10-minute stroll apart.

DISNEY OR UNIVERSAL?

People always ask me: Disney or Universal? First of all, it's indicative of the fierce competition between the two entities that anyone would feel compelled to frame a comparison as a choice. But I do accept that time is at a premium when you're on vacation, and the comparison helps people prioritize. I hate to be glib about the answer, because it depends on who you are. There's a lot Disney has over Universal—principally that intangible energy that makes the place so buoyant. No entity suspends disbelief and casts an aura of unreality like Disney. Disney's characters are genuinely beloved by children, where not all of Universal's are—how many kids do you know who are into Beetlejuice or Lucille Ball? But Universal tends to attract people who have either wearied of or outgrown Disney's cartoonish, overly controlled environment and ODed on princesses. Teenagers who roll their eyes at Disney often find new passions at Universal, but parents who are used to Disney's reticence to ruffle feathers are often shocked when they experience Universal's edge. Universal has some gyrating thrill rides, while most of Disney's punches have been pulled so that everyone in a family can ride together. So I usually answer by simply saying, "Universal isn't Disney." That gives the answer you need, depending on your view of Disney.

There's something else about Universal that first-time visitors don't expect: the high quality of its rides and design. I think that Islands of Adventure's attention to detail trumps anything Disney has done in years (to wit: boxy Animal Kingdom), but some visitors hate the park's looping layout, which often necessitates lots of backtracking. Universal could stand to refresh its parks with big-ticket rides, but it doesn't skimp on upkeep. When I'm pressed for the must-do parks, I rank Universal's two parks after the Magic Kingdom and Epcot but before Disney-MGM and Animal Kingdom—but only for people who like a little vinegar in their amusements. For thrills, I recommend Islands of Adventure above Universal Studios, and IOA tends to hold kids' attention better, too. When you hear parents say there's nothing for children to do at Universal, it's usually because they themselves aren't nostalgic for the rides, so they get bored. There is *plenty* for kids at Universal.

Whereas Disney has the advantage of space, Universal has the advantage of being compact. You can park your car when you arrive and forget about it for the duration of your stay because everything is within walking distance, including the three hotels, which are also linked by ferries. There are no shuttle buses to wait for, so you can unwind with a cocktail (both Universal parks serve booze, and CityWalk practically pipes it in) without worrying about having to drive across the property to return to your hotel. Miraculously, the designers have accomplished this compaction without sacrificing a sense of space. The Hard Rock

Hotel's pool abuts the back of CityWalk, for example, but a berm and clever land-scaping disguise the close quarters.

Because Universal is compact, it isn't segregated from the rest of the world. Being here puts you much closer to the "real" Orlando, or at least to cheap places to eat and sleep. Disney works hard to keep the real world (and, consequently, real prices) at bay, but at Universal, reality is a 3-minute drive away. For this reason, and because getting in is cheaper, you'll notice far more locals at Universal, par-ticularly at its popular annual events such as Halloween Horror Nights or Mardi Gras (see chapter 12, "The Essentials of Planning," for a calendar).

Universal's healthy dining options lag behind Disney's. In December 2006, Universal told the world it would offer kids fruit and healthy beverages with its counter-service meals, years after Disney started doing the same thing. (Universal had attempted to sell fruit at many restaurants, but pulled the option when few people bit.) Universal also pledged to end the use of trans fats at "most" of its facil-ities. The healthier outlets, the park promised, would be marked on park maps.

TICKETS TO UNIVERSAL'S PARKS

Tickets are almost always more expensive if you buy at the gate. A 1-day, two-park ticket costs $77 adults, $67 kids aged 3 to 9 (shocking when you learn that they cost $42 as recently as 1999). Two-day, two-park tickets are $115 adults/$105 kids. That doesn't include tax of about $5 on a 1-day ticket. But Universal would much rather have you book online, and it makes it worth your while. In early 2006, kids could go free if you booked online. At press time, $85 got adults unlimited access to both parks for an entire week. Promotions change without warning, so always check the website to see what's on offer. You can print your tickets at home and then pick them up at the park gates for another $1.

If you're planning to do a full complement of the non-Disney parks, includ-ing Universal Orlando, SeaWorld, Wet 'n Wild, and Busch Gardens, then you'll find value in the FlexTicket, which gets you into all of them for 2 weeks at a deep discount. Details on this pass are described on p. 321.

You can speed your visit and do most of the major rides (missing many of the shows and smaller goodies) in a single day, provided you have an **Express pass** and a ticket that allows you to enter both parks in 1 day. Fourteen of the major rides and shows at Islands of Adventure have a dedicated Express line, and 15 of the ones at Universal Studios do. Like Disney's Fastpass, Universal's Express issues timed tickets that allow guests to use a separate entrance queue that is dramati-cally shorter than the "Standby" one.

Unlike Disney's Fastpass, though, Universal's Express pass system can be upgraded. Guests can buy an **Express Plus** pass at shops at both parks for $20 a day (for a single park) or $30 (for both parks); this method allows one entry per ride without regard to the number of passes that are outstanding, whereas the free version allows only one pass to be held at a time. The only reason I would lay out that kind of cash is if it were imperative that I see both Universal parks in a sin-gle day. Otherwise, the lines aren't usually bad enough to justify the expense. The best Express upgrade is given to guests at the three hotels on Universal property (the Royal Pacific, the Hard Rock, and Portofino Bay), who can use their key cards for Express access without having to bother with timed tickets—this

---

What the Basics Cost at Universal's Two Parks

Parking: $11; $16 for closer "preferred" spaces; $18 valet
Single strollers: $11 per day
Double strollers: $17 per day
Kiddie Car (a stroller with a dummy steering wheel for kids): $12; $18 double
Wheelchair: $12
ECV: $40
Lockers: $8 per day small (big enough for a daypack); $10 large
Regular soda: $2.29
Water: $2.50

---

method allows unlimited entry at all the rides, but the surcharge comes in the form of a hotel rate that's much higher than the city standard.

Dress your small children in their bathing suits for a day at Universal Studios, since its Kidzone, one of its best sections, will get them soaked. Adults should come dressed to be drenched themselves, including their feet, at Islands of Adventure, as two of its best rides are water-based.

UNIVERSAL STUDIOS FLORIDA

After you get your car situated ($11 to park), take the moving sidewalks to CityWalk and veer to the right to reach the theme park. Before you enter the park, pause in front of the giant, tilting globe for the requisite photo op, because the light is better here in the morning.

The plaza after the turnstiles is where you take care of business. Strollers and wheelchairs are obtained to the left, and lockers are rented to the right. Make sure to grab a free park map here; if you forget, the stores also stock them.

Tip: At the extreme left of the entry plaza, right where you'll be leaving at the end of your day, there's a souvenir stand. This is no ordinary stand: It's for marked-down items from the park's other boutiques. Normally, you'd never learn about it until you were already leaving (and presumably had already made your purchases). I'm letting you know about it now so you can see what's going for less and compare it to what you see later on.

Although there are technically six themed areas, they are not strictly defined and they fall into two general zones. Everyone enters along the main avenue of the simulated backlot (including Production Central, Hollywood, and New York), which contains many of the behind-the-scenes attractions, while the elongated Lagoon stretches off to the right, encircled by many of the thrill-based rides in San Francisco/Amity, World Expo, and Woody Woodpecker's Kidzone.

Check your map for the time of the day's *Universal 360: A Cinesphere Spectacular* show on the lagoon, which employs a quartet of four-story white balls into which movies and pretty images are projected. Pyrotechnics, loud music, lasers, 300 outdoor speakers, and classic film clips combine to cap off an evening. It's nowhere as flabbergasting as the night shows at Epcot or Disney–MGM, but at least there's not the ridiculous crush of spectators, either.

Generally speaking, the kid-friendly rides are on the near side of the lagoon (the bottom half of your map), and the thrills are along the top. Until the replacement for Back to the Future: The Ride arrives, the longest lines are for the Revenge of the Mummy ride, so head there first.

Production Central

The area along the entry avenue (called both Plaza of the Stars and 57th Street) and to its left is collectively marked on maps as Production Central, but who are they kidding? Nowadays, those soundstages are used only for the odd local commercial and for haunted houses at Universal's fiendishly popular Halloween event.

The initial dream was much bigger. When the park was built, it was intended to be more like the original Hollywood location, where an amusement area naturally grew up around tours given of a working studio. But here, the studio was subjugated to the thrills, and the arranged marriage never took. The soundstages you see to the left were constructed for actual mainstream filming. Newspapers at the time trumpeted Orlando as "Hollywood of the East" because year-round production could be accomplished here and at Disney–MGM Studios for cheap and millions of tourists could be a part of the behind-the-scenes process. One of Universal's soundstages (in a building behind the Jimmy Neutron attraction) housed a working TV studio for Nickelodeon, the kids' basic cable channel, and the game show *Double Dare* plucked families out of the park to compete on air. In front of the studio, a geyser of "green slime" (actually green water) gurgled in tribute to the Canadian show, *You Can't Do That on Television,* that helped make the channel's fortunes.

But Hollywood's interest in Orlando as a production center petered out long before Nickelodeon's partnership did, and now both are dead. Even the ads on the sides of the soundstages, modeled after the ones in the San Fernando Valley, are usually out of date. It's a depressing reminder of one of Orlando's bigger failures.

The first block of Production Central is mostly shops, including the largest gift shop in the park, Universal Studios Store, on the left. Across from that are the tempting Art Deco buildings of Rodeo Drive, the spine of the Hollywood area and for my money the prettiest part of the park. At the second block, two of the park's most popular kids' attractions face each other down across the avenue. On the left, **Jimmy Neutron's Nicktoon Blast** 🧒, unites several of Nickelodeon's staple characters, including said Jimmy, the Rugrats, and SpongeBob SquarePants, who band together to stop a band of egg-shaped weirdos bent on destroying the world. The show (which replaced a similar attraction themed to Hanna-Barbera characters; I guess kids don't know Yogi the Bear anymore) takes place in a theatre full of individual open-air ride platforms that have all the characteristics of motion simulators except claustrophobia. That's good for some, but the computer animation and whip-quick pace of the movie will still jar some into temporary nausea. Passengers can control their motion-simulator seats; a better option for those prone to motion sickness is to request one that doesn't move at all, although that would render the exercise pretty pointless. Veer left as the line progresses so

Universal Studios Florida

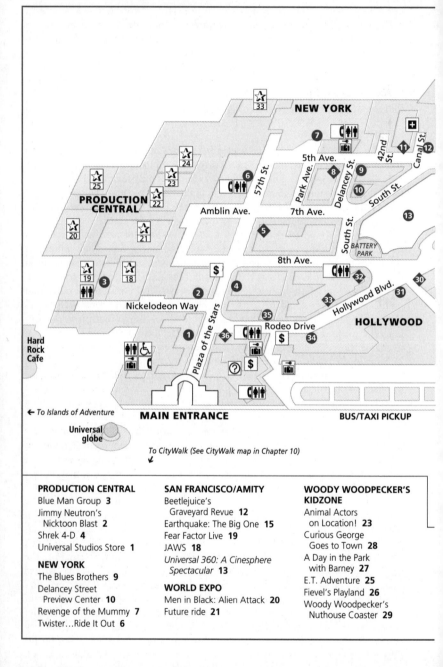

NEW YORK

5th Ave.

Amblin Ave.

7th Ave.

*PRODUCTION
CENTRAL*

8th Ave.

*BATTERY
PARK*

Nickelodeon Way

Rodeo Drive

HOLLYWOOD

Hollywood Blvd.

Plaza of the Stars

Hard
Rock
Cafe

← *To Islands of Adventure*

MAIN ENTRANCE

BUS/TAXI PICKUP

Universal
globe

To CityWalk (See CityWalk map in Chapter 10)
↓

PRODUCTION CENTRAL
Blue Man Group **3**
Jimmy Neutron's
  Nicktoon Blast **2**
Shrek 4-D **4**
Universal Studios Store **1**

NEW YORK
The Blues Brothers **9**
Delancey Street
  Preview Center **10**
Revenge of the Mummy **7**
Twister…Ride It Out **6**

SAN FRANCISCO/AMITY
Beetlejuice's
  Graveyard Revue **12**
Earthquake: The Big One **15**
Fear Factor Live **19**
JAWS **18**
*Universal 360: A Cinesphere
  Spectacular* **13**

WORLD EXPO
Men in Black: Alien Attack **20**
Future ride **21**

**WOODY WOODPECKER'S
KIDZONE**
Animal Actors
  on Location! **23**
Curious George
  Goes to Town **28**
A Day in the Park
  with Barney **27**
E.T. Adventure **25**
Fievel's Playland **26**
Woody Woodpecker's
  Nuthouse Coaster **29**

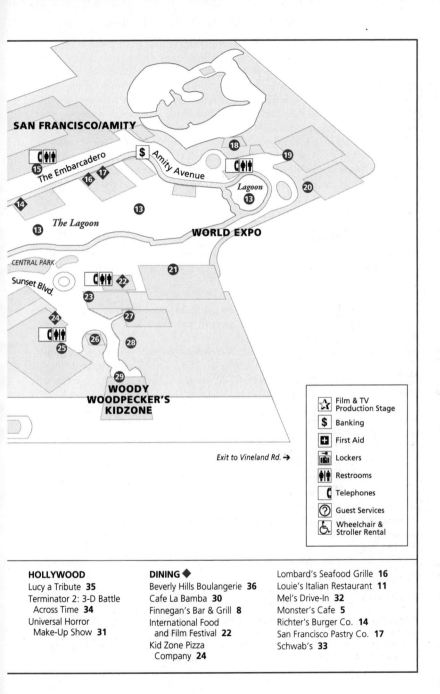

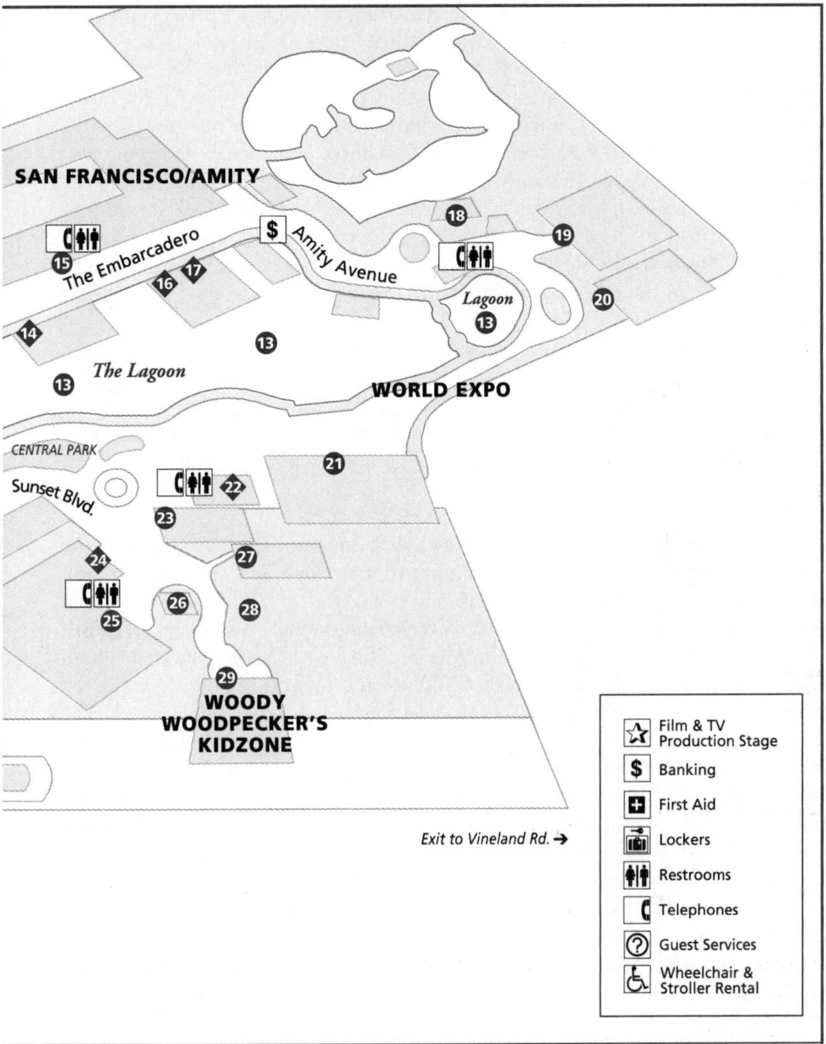
SAN FRANCISCO/AMITY
The Embarcadero
Amity Avenue
Lagoon
The Lagoon
WORLD EXPO
CENTRAL PARK
Sunset Blvd.
WOODY WOODPECKER'S KIDZONE
Exit to Vineland Rd. →
Film & TV Production Stage
Banking
First Aid
Lockers
Restrooms
Telephones
Guest Services
Wheelchair & Stroller Rental

HOLLYWOOD
Lucy a Tribute **35**
Terminator 2: 3-D Battle Across Time **34**
Universal Horror Make-Up Show **31**

DINING ◆
Beverly Hills Boulangerie **36**
Cafe La Bamba **30**
Finnegan's Bar & Grill **8**
International Food and Film Festival **22**
Kid Zone Pizza Company **24**
Lombard's Seafood Grille **16**
Louie's Italian Restaurant **11**
Mel's Drive-In **32**
Monster's Cafe **5**
Richter's Burger Co. **14**
San Francisco Pastry Co. **17**
Schwab's **33**

that you're closer to the back of the theatre; being too close can cause vertigo. As one of the bigger-ticket kids' rides here, the line can get long.

Across the street, **Shrek 4-D** ✯ is a snarky 12-minute, 3-D movie-cum-spectacle—filmed in "OgreVision"—featuring all the high-priced voices of the movie characters (Mike Myers, Cameron Diaz, Eddie Murphy). John Lithgow plays the ghost of the evil Lord Farquaad, who crashes Shrek and Fiona's honeymoon at Fairytale Falls with a few dastardly surprises. The chairs look like standard theatre seats except they're specially designed to amp up the sensations—don't worry; it won't make you ill. Well, unless fart jokes gross you out. The same people who made the DreamWorks movie made this one, so if you like the smart-alecky fairytale tweaking of the original, you'll dig this. It's a good one to do when the feet start aching, although the line can build in the afternoon. Because the entertaining pre-show is just as long as the movie, the Express pass doesn't seem to buy you very much time for this one.

The third block of Production Central is a dead zone. The park to the left is sometimes used for concerts and special events, but most of the time it languishes as a designated smoking area. Don't worry. Things get better from here.

New York

When the park on your left is replaced by a park on your right, you've entered the New York area. Never mind that the park to your right is an imitation of San Francisco's Union Square. Straight ahead, at the end of 57th Street (the main entry avenue) is a little cul-de-sac that looks, through a camera lens, like Manhattan. Yes, you're right, the Chrysler Building is not actually located behind the Public Library and neither is on 57th Street, but come on. This is supposed to be fun.

On your left is **Twister . . . Ride It Out** ✯. I like this one, although wee ones might get scared. After several rooms of portentous pre-show videos narrated by Helen Hunt and Bill Paxton, those blockbuster superstars, you finally enter a viewing area in a hangar-like chamber that's dressed to look like a Midwestern small town (gas station, telephone pole, drive-in movie in the distance) on a weekend night. A storm approaches, rain begins to fall and, as you knew it would, a twister forms. Right before your eyes, a funnel cloud descends from the rafters and to the delight of many, proceeds to wreck the place, which of course is rigged to simulate such a catastrophe every few minutes. Sparks fly, roofs peel, and guess what happens to the gas station? Watch out for the cow that flies across the room, braying like the one in the movie, on wires so obvious that it's clearly intended as a joke—most shows, it gets a laugh. You can choose your place in the viewing area, and although people tend to shy away from the front row, you don't feel much more than mist and a light sucking sensation there (I'd keep sensitive electronics tucked away anyway). It's quite an original attraction, and it's another good one for a hot day, but not a top-drawer one. It runs continuously, without scheduled times, but I wouldn't wait for more than 20 minutes for it.

Facing the square is Universal Studio's current marquee ride, **Revenge of the Mummy** ✯✯✯, and boy, is it a good one. Be sure to put loose articles in the lockers to the right of the entrance—lockers are free, but their fingerprint-activated lock system is a right pain in the butt, so designate a single person in your party (someone good with computers) to cut through the crowd that inevitably piles

The Best of Universal Studios Florida

Don't miss if you're 6: Curious George Goes to Town

Don't miss if you're 16: Men In Black: Alien Attack

Requisite photo op: The rotating globe out front; the fiberglass shark in front of Jaws

Food you can only get here: The Irish Cobb salad at Finnegan's Bar & Grill in New York

The most crowded, so go early: Revenge of the Mummy

Skippable: Fear Factor Live

Biggest thrill: Revenge of the Mummy

Best show: Animal Actors on Location!

Where to find peace: On the lagoon, across from Kidzone; in Kidzone, between the Barney and Curious George attractions

---

up. There are three lines: Express, Standby, and Single Riders. Most of the time, the Single Rider line doesn't save you any time; in fact, it can be slower than the Standby. The ride itself, which seats four across, is technologically cutting-edge with an easy start and a rollicking finish: Part–dark ride, part–roller coaster, it goes backwards and forwards, twists on a turntable, and even spends a harrowing moment stalled in a room as the ceiling crawls with fire. (It doesn't go upside-down.) To say much more would give away some clever surprises; I've told you what you need to know to determine if it's for you. I'll end with this: I brought my brother, a longtime Disney passholder, to Universal for his first time, and when he got off, he said it was one of the most incredible rides he'd ever experienced and that it made him wish he'd bought a Universal season pass instead.

The **Delancey Street Preview Center** is marked on the maps, but you can only get in by invitation. That's where NBC-affiliated networks screen television pilots and then solicit audience opinions. On a quiet January day, I once earned $30 just for enduring a show called *Psych*. I told the network that their production was clichéd and strained. It became a hit on USA Network anyway, although by then, a central role had been recast. I hope I didn't get anyone fired. There's no way to predict the demographic of the test audience they'll be looking for on any given day, so stop by and ask if you fit the profile du jour.

The rest of the New York section is gussied up to look like the tenements of the Lower East Side or Greenwich Village, and is worth a wander and a few photos. Actors playing **The Blues Brothers** show up on Delancey Street about five times a day for a mini-concert. I never bother waiting around for them, as the rides are so much more interesting and, let's be honest, that movie came out during the Carter Administration. Other than Jake and Elwood, the other big draw on the New York streets is **Finnegan's Bar and Grill** (p. 188), an Irish pub that serves one of the more appealing sit-down menus in the park.

The main video game **arcade** is on the corner of 42nd Street and 5th Avenue—which, incidentally, is where the New York Public Library actually *is* located.

San Francisco/Amity

The street called 5th Avenue hits the lagoon and is renamed The Embarcadero. Now you're in San Francisco, as the bricks and streetcar turntable (which isn't used) attest. The first attraction on the left is a 20-minute show, **Beetlejuice's Graveyard Revue**. Universal owns the rights to many classic movie monsters, including Frankenstein, and they appear in this rowdy '80s and '90s rock-and-roll show, presided over by the undead, naughty-minded Beetlejuice, who aims more for the funny bone than the jugular. Watching the Bride of Frankenstein sing "Higher and Higher" will make you feel like someone slipped a pill in your Coke, but it probably won't make your day. Unless you're a show person, you can skip this one, at least until you've knocked down some of the fresher attractions. Performances happen two or three times daily and will be noted on your map.

Earthquake: The Big One starts off with a pre-show (you'll be seated) about how stunts and special effects are filmed. You've seen this stuff before, and the 1970s-era references could certainly use an update. But things improve. Finally, when you're about to feel like you've wasted your time, everyone boards a tram mocked up to resemble San Francisco's BART subway—seats on the outside are the best. It travels down a tunnel and stops inside what appears to be a very faithful recreation of the Embarcadero station, albeit one that smells suspiciously of natural gas. Once you're stopped there, as is the theme-park way, something goes horribly wrong. There's an earthquake. You're actually inside a machine that will shortly unleash hell: rocking, flooding to within an inch of the train, and a ceiling that collapses around you, admitting a gas truck from the "street" above and providing an excellent excuse for a climactic explosion. The intent is to approximate a jolt measuring 8.3 on the Richter scale. Just as quickly as it began, everything halts and reassembles itself for the next "take" as your train whisks you out again. Claustrophobes abhor it, as do some nervous children, but I think it's good fun, if barely worth the empty song and dance of its endless pre-show. You might be surprised to know that this is the last of the original attractions left over from Universal's 1990 opening (although the pre-show has been substantially tweaked). Even though the park is less than 18 years old, all the other first-day attractions have been replaced or radically redesigned.

One of those redesigned rides is **JAWS** ✦✧, and it's next on the circuit around the lagoon. On the way, you'll perhaps notice that the theme shifts from the wharves of San Francisco to that of an all-American town. You're now meant to be in Amity, the New England town from *Jaws*, on the Fourth of July—hence the hot dog stands and **midway games,** which are closed on quiet days. The boat ride JAWS, based on the movie, is entered at the far end of Amity—you'll know you're there when you see the fiberglass shark strung up like the day's catch. People sliding their heads into the shark's mouth makes for what's said to be the most popular photo op in the park, which is kind of creepy when you think about it.

A very expensive attraction to run, JAWS tends to open about 2 hours later than the other rides, and it often spends months at a time being drained and cleaned. It also shuts down on "white alert" whenever lightning is detected in the vicinity, even if it's not overhead, so if it's running and the line's not bad, jump on. I love riding it in the dark, when the shark seems to come out of nowhere and looks less rubbery, but that's not always an option. What begins as a slow-moving tour boat ride on Captain Jake's Amity Boat Tours quickly deteriorates into a slow-moving boat ride repeatedly accosted by powerful but rubbery shark robots, which spring unexpectedly out of the water. In the effort to protect you from becoming dinner, your "skipper" is reduced to wielding a "grenade launcher" that, unfortunately, he has no idea how to use. The fun you'll have depends largely on the narration skills—in industry terms, the "spiel"—of the skipper you get; see p. 186 for details of my day behind the wheel. The ride takes about 7 minutes, the boat's seating is covered, and the movements are so tame that lap restraints aren't required. The best seats, but also potentially the wettest ones, are at the left of the boat in the third to fifth rows; in fact, the left side in general gets the better views. Call it a design flaw in an ambitious ride; the original 1990 version was so much more daring (Jaws clamped on the boat's prow and spun it around on a hidden turntable, and the water billowed with red "blood" each time he was finally vanquished) that it was unreliable and had to be totally redesigned. The resulting simplified version is still pretty complicated and dearly beloved by long-time visitors; it even has its own fan appreciation website, Amity Boat Tours (www.amityboat tours.com).

The show **Fear Factor Live** is staged in the amphitheatre just past JAWS. Like the meat-headed (and cancelled) NBC show, it features ordinary people doing scary stunts (usually involving being dangled on wires) for the twisted pleasure of a whooping audience while an inane master of ceremonies eggs everyone on. If you're over 18 and want to volunteer as a contestant (first prize: polite applause), be here first thing after park opening to sign up. Audience members also get a chance to take part; they're selected to eat something gross (food-grade mealworms, usually) in exchange for knickknacks. Times are posted on your map. Do the show if you need to get a load off, or if a family member makes the cut; otherwise, I think it's low on the list of must-sees at Universal.

World Expo

This section of the park is undergoing a reinvention now that the motion-simulator Back to the Future: The Ride has ceased its vomit-inducing run. That leaves **Men in Black: Alien Attack** ✿✿✿, an excellent riff on the Will Smith film franchise. Send someone from your group to put all loose articles into a free locker, located to the right of the entrance, before getting in line. After a superlative queue area that does a pitch-perfect, *Jetsons*-style imitation of New York's 1964 World's Fair (ironically, the one Walt Disney created so many wonders for; the circular towers are small-scale reproductions of the New York State pavilion in Flushing, Queens), you discover the "real" tenant of the futuristic building—a training course for the Men in Black alien patrol corps. You board six-person cars equipped with individual laser guns. As you pass from room to room—expect lots of herky-jerky motions, but nothing sickening—your task is to fire upon any alien that pops out from around doorways, behind trash cans, and so on. If they peg you first, it sends your buggy spinning. Each car racks up points that are displayed on the dashboard, and the number accumulated by the end determines the climactic video you're shown—Will Smith will either praise you as "Galaxy

Defender" or mock you as "Bug Bait" for your performance. Then, as in the movie, he'll "erase" your memory of the whole training mission with a flash of white light, and you'll exit back into the banality of the World's Fair. The single riders' queue moves quickly thanks to the odd number of seats in each row. Ride alone to speed the wait, but to hit the score stratosphere, do this one with an adolescent boy who's good at video games.

Otherwise, World Expo is the quiet hind end of the park, good for taking a breather from crowds. Head out onto the bridge across the lagoon, where you'll find a quirky photo spot. If you line up your camera precisely, you'll combine a painted image of the space shuttle with your real-life companions, creating an in-camera trick of the eye. The bridge is also my favorite place to catch the evening Cinesphere show, as it affords a compact view of four spheres flashing at once.

Hollywood

There are no rides in the Hollywood section, only two shows and a few shops. Still, the evocative Art Deco–style buildings along Rodeo Drive and Hollywood Boulevard are very well executed and worth a few photos. The 25-minute **Universal Horror Make-Up Show** ✪ is a terrific, tongue-in-cheek expose, conducted by a nerdy type in his workshop, of how horror-movie effects are accomplished. On paper, that seems like the kind of thing you might otherwise skip, but in truth park regulars love its wit and playful edge. For ad-libbing and gross-out humor, the park suggests parental guidance for this one, but I find that most kids have heard it all before, and it's certainly true that seeing terrifying movie gore exposed as the make-believe it is can be a good reality check for younger kids. Times are printed on your park map, and you can't get in once the show's begun. Even if you miss the show, there's something to see in the lobby: props from the movie *Van Helsing*. If you saw that.

The other show, **Terminator 2: 3-D Battle Across Time,** is far more intense. Although the 12-minute film portion, a sort of mini-sequel to *Terminator 2,* was made by extravagant director James Cameron with all his original stars (including Ah-nold and Linda Hamilton), it's hardly just another movie. It's got three screens, six 8-foot robots, gunfire, smoke bombs, and motorcyclists that seamlessly dive in and out of the filmed action. This edgy, cynical show splits the eardrums with explosions and romping, stomping mayhem, so keep small children away unless they're hard cases. Those in the front rows will have to pivot their heads to see all the action. The film portion cost $60 million to make, which when it was produced in 1996 qualified it as the most expensive movie, per minute, in history.

From blood and guts to homicidal robots, you may be ready for the gentler charms of **Lucy a Tribute**, an exhibition of Lucille Ball memorabilia that you can enjoy at your own pace.

Woody Woodpecker's Kidzone

Kidzone 🧒 is my pick for the best children's theme park area in Orlando. I've heard tales of 6 year olds who threatened self-orphanization if they were dragged away from this playland within 4 hours. There's a ton to do, although strangely, eating isn't one of them. The first option is **Animal Actors on Location!** 🧒, a charming 20-minute show (times are noted on the map) featuring a troupe of trained dogs, cats, and birds. Placing this show here was inspired, because small children get a special thrill out of seeing common animals do tricks, and as a consequence, this show is popular. Because it's in an amphitheatre, you can also sneak out in the middle if you need to. But if you see only one emphatically punctuated household-pets-doing-cute-tricks-to-jaunty-music theme-park show while you're in Orlando, make it SeaWorld's superior Pets Ahoy!

The expensive-looking **E.T. Adventure** ★ (kids), based on the 1982 Steven Spielberg movie, is rightfully in the kiddie area because it's not intense. Upon entering, guests supply their name to an attendant, who encodes the information on a pass you're supposed hand over when you board the ride. The indoor queue area is a fabulous reproduction of a thick, cool California forest at night; the darkness makes some kids fear they're in for trouble, but in fact, the ride beyond it is pretty tame. Vehicles are suspended from rails to approximate the sensation of cruising on a bike, and they sweep and scoop through forests, across the moonrise, and even through gardens on E.T.'s home planet (remember, he was a botanist), where a menagerie of goofy-looking aliens, who don't look nearly as realistic as our hero, greet us from the sidelines. At the climax, a grateful E.T. is supposed to call out the names of the passengers on your cart as you fly home—hence those boarding passes—but frankly, in all my years of doing this ride, he always sounds to me like he's spouting gibberish, so don't get your hopes up, unless your name is Pfmkmpftur. If the queue looks dense from the outside, think about coming back later (the hour before park closing seems to be a charmed time for quick waits), since there are still more lineups indoors.

Fievel's Playland (kids), named for the hero of *An American Tail,* is the first of several playgrounds in Kidzone. The concept here is that your kids have been shrunk down to a mouse's size, and they're playing in everyday items like sardine cans and cowboy hats. The ground is covered with that newfangled soft foam that all the modern playgrounds have (when I was a boy, we got concussions instead), but my favorite element is a little water slide on a raft. (Yes, make sure your kids are wearing their swimsuits, because it's going to get a lot wetter soon.)

A Day in the Park with Barney (kids), a small indoor area that can be accessed through its own gift shop (plush Barney, $13), is technically the post-show area for a sing-along show for the very young. Here—the only permanent live Barney show in the world—the doors close at the start and stay closed until the ordeal is over. Frankly, being locked in a room with that sappy purple dinosaur and all those screaming babies constitutes a chamber of horrors for me, but little kids find it enthralling beyond measure. Parents can find beer carts on the lagoon nearby, if that helps. The play area mimics a Crayola-hued forest, with a place to sift through sand, a tree equipped with little slides, and a chance to have your picture taken with (and buy said picture from) Barney.

Across the way, **Woody Woodpecker's Nuthouse Coaster** (kids) is a straightforward kiddie thrill with no surprises and a run time of less than a minute. Kids can plainly see every drop before they commit. The line is often evilly long.

On hot days, **Curious George Goes to Town** ★★★ (kids) is where kids lose reason and parents lose patience. This frenetic splash area is teeming with squealing children and positively soaked with streams of water from every direction—from

Skipper for a Day: I Pilot the Jaws Ride

I've been attacked by a shark, unprovoked, 84 times. And I haven't even had my break yet. In the name of journalism, I'm working Universal Orlando's 2.5-acre JAWS attraction, which begins as a scenic cruise of sleepy Amity Island but, as these things do, goes horribly awry when a vicious great white menaces my vessel. From my introduction to the guests as "Skipper Jason" to the harrowing, high-voltage climax, each ride is 5 minutes of fishy mayhem. Fireballs, explosions—the whole circus. And I'm the ringmaster.

When I was a kid, any carbon-based life form with opposable thumbs could operate a theme park ride, but here, training is a ritual. Normally, I'd have to go through 5 days of it, including a swimming test at nearby Wet 'n Wild, before being allowed to "skipper" a JAWS boat, but for the sake of journalism, Universal treats me to an abbreviated education. I learn it's not a ride, it's a "show," and it's not narration, it's a "spiel." As a spieler, I'll usually run three boatloads in a row before taking a break—each show takes more than 5 minutes, so that's 15 minutes of opera-level intensity. Phil Whigham, the attraction's trainer, shows me where they keep the Gatorade jug. I am gonna need it, especially in this heat.

I receive a costume (cleaned daily by Universal and picked up at a huge wardrobe facility), a script (eight pages, annotated with acting "beats"), plus a nine-page workbook (Essay question: "How do I feel about the grenade launcher?"), and a tongue-in-cheek dossier on people and places in Amity (in case anyone asks). Normally, I'd go through at least 4 days of training before setting foot on a boat. But I'm thrown into deep water, so to speak, with just a morning's education behind me.

Out on the lagoon, Phil adjusts my microphone headset and explains what the boats' dashboard buttons do. One errant elbow could shut down the entire ride. Gulp. I meet Mimi Lipka, Universal's resident acting coach. Although she's a great-grandmother, she has more perk than the clean-cut college-age kids she shepherds through JAWS' acting rigors. Before the

squirt cannons, fountains, geysers, and, most importantly, from two 500-gallon buckets that, every 7 minutes, sound a warning bell and then drench anyone beneath them. The immoderate, virtually orgiastic scene is ringed by a perimeter of dry parents keeping an eye on their wild offspring. I enjoy joining them, because watching the children cheer and scamper when they hear the clang of the bucket's warning bell, and then watching them momentarily vanish in the deluge, is endlessly amusing. Through the wet area (there's a dry bypass corridor to it on the left) is the dry Ball Factory, where kids suck up plastic balls with light vacuums, pack them into bags, and then fire them at each other with weak cannons. It's not marked on the maps. If parents allow their kids to so much as lay eyes on this area, they should prepare to get stuck here for awhile.

park opens, Mimi has me run the "show" on an empty boat while she rides along, taking notes for my improvement as the mechanized shark rams us.

Interacting with the attraction's timed special effects is like doing a pas de deux with a pinball machine. The machines are going to do their thing even if I forget mine. I have to fire my grenade launcher at the correct targets, yank the steering wheel at the right moments, and with full-bodied emotion, I must trick the guests into thinking I don't anticipate that pesky shark's pre-programmed re-appearances. Like clockwork, I go Rambo on the beast. "Eat this!" I bellow, blasting away at it, while Mimi scribbles. (A typical tip: "Look for survivors!")

Finally, with a proud flourish, she writes my name on a dry-erase board hidden behind the unload station. I am "signed off" and officially on rotation. The ride opens.

I nervously guide an empty boat to the load station, where "deck crew" assigns seating by playing what they jokingly call "Human Tetris." Now I see 48 faces before me, waiting for my next move. Judging by their expectant—some might say passive—grins, they're dying to buy whatever I'm about to sell. I press the green start button. No return now.

"Well, time to start our voyage," I chirp, on cue. "Wave goodbye to the happy landlubbers!" That line was always the start of my script, but I'm surprised to see my passengers actually *do* it. Once I fight the urge to rush, I realize I have them. Children gleefully point to the merest ripple; grown men shy from teeth they know are fake. The interaction—a triangle between me, a multimillion-dollar machine, and my audience—is invigorating, and I stop fretting about timing and just have fun. Show by show, my voice grows hoarser and I get thirstier, but the feedback from the guests' faces feeds my energy level. When my passengers disembark, and as I catch my breath between runs, I eavesdrop. "I wanna go again!" squeals a boy. "I wasn't scared," fibs another. And from a British girl: "I've got a soppy bottom!" To me, a wet customer is a happy customer. *Fin.*

WHERE TO EAT AT UNIVERSAL STUDIOS

In addition to the random snack carts that open and close unpredictably, there are counter-service and sit-down restaurants in the park. None require reservations.

Remember that all the restaurants at CityWalk (p. 282) are a 5-minute walk from the park, so with a hand stamp for re-entry, you can try those, too. The only one that requires reservations is Emeril's (p. 69).

Production Central: One of the only choices here is **Monster's Cafe,** facing both parks, which has some healthy options, such as rotisserie chicken with potatoes and corn for $9, Caesar salad with soup for $8, and penne primavera for $7.

New York: Finnegan's Bar & Grill ★★ is a sit-down, Irish-style pub where you'll get a break from burgers and fries. Scotch eggs ($6), split pea and ham soup ($4), Irish Cobb salad (it has corned beef, among other things, $12), and bangers and mash (sausage with garlic mashed potatoes, $11) are the kind of things available, plus good strong ales. The kids' menu has about eight choices for $5 to $6. Park workers tend to pick this place when they're not on duty. **Louie's Italian Restaurant** does pizza slices well, but not much else, and more substantial meals (subs and salads) hover around that magical $8 figure, before drinks. Slices can be had for $3.50—a budget lifesaver, if not a coronary one.

San Francisco/Amity: The most variety available in the park is along the top of the lagoon, starting from in front of the Mummy ride (in New York) and ending at Amity (where there's just the **Midway Grill** hot dog stand—$6.79 for one with fries—and $5 funnel cakes). **San Francisco Pastry Co.,** across from Earthquake, does sandwiches and loaded croissants for $7.79; add chips for $1 more. It also does fruit plates and salads ($5.50–$6.79). The adjoining **Lombard's Seafood Grille,** set over the water, is probably the park's top-end option (catch of the day, $16 with salad and potatoes; fish and chips $12). On a pier in the water, my pick of the park is **Richter's Burger Co.** ★★, which does burgers (from $7.50 with fries), marinated grilled chicken sandwiches ($7.80 with fries), and a salad with grilled chicken ($8) that are all on the less greasy side. There's a fixins bar. Periodically, the dining room rumbles to simulate nearby quakes, and there is some outdoor seating on the water.

World Expo: Near the entrance to Kidzone, the **International Food and Film Festival** does pizza and pasta at the expected prices, plus a few choices it calls "Asian": Sweet and sour chicken, beef and peppers, and Szechwan orange chicken all come with rice and stir-fried vegetables for $8.29.

The Universal Meal Deal

In both its parks, Universal offers an all-you-can-eat meal plan. Dubbed the **Universal Meal Deal,** it entitles you to one main plate and one dessert each time you go through the line at six counter-service locations (three per park). You'll get a wristband that grants you use of a special line— sadly, it's not usually any shorter than the regular ones—and kids under 10 have to order from whatever designated kids' menu that restaurant has (which isn't usually a problem). Keeping in mind that it doesn't include beverages and stops working 30 minutes before closing (so you'll have to plan ahead to get dinner out of it), the pricing is such that it really only makes sense if you're a big eater. For one park, adults pay $18.99 and kids $9.99; for two parks, it's adults $24.99 and kids $12.99, and you also get a free entrée at a CityWalk restaurant (which ones participate and what they'll offer you, though, changes, although it's usually limited to Pastamoré, Latin Quarter, Bob Marley, and Pat O'Brien's).

Kidzone: There's just **Kid Zone Pizza Company** here; chicken fingers and fries go for $7.50, and the Conewich, a sort of wrap, comes with chicken or tuna salad for $7.50. Since it's the only option among the playgrounds, it gets crowded.

Hollywood: Mel's Drive-In, facing the lagoon, is a '50s-style diner—everything's glassy and shiny; burgers and chicken for around $7.75 with fries—that has antique cars parked in the lot. They really work, too. **Schwab's,** after the famous L.A. drugstore, does drinks and ice cream (malts $4.50), and it's also where you can pick up things like Tylenol and bandages at prices that will make you sore you forgot to bring your own. Near the Horror Make-Up show, **Café La Bamba** is for chicken and ribs; its warren of dining rooms can make for a cool escape. Dishes are around $8, and if you add $5, you get a large drink and a dessert. **Beverly Hills Boulangerie** ★ is a good place for a healthy meal: Sandwiches (turkey, roast beef, so on) with potato salad and fruit cost $8. It also does a soup and salad combo for $5.

ISLANDS OF ADVENTURE

After you get your car parked ($11), take the moving sidewalks to CityWalk and veer to the left, toward the 130-foot-tall lighthouse (it's just for show), to reach IOA. If you have doubts about whether your kids will be tall enough to ride anything, there's a gauge listing all the requirements before the ticket booths. The most restrictive (54 in.), understandably, is the Incredible Hulk coaster.

IOA's 110 acres are laid out much like Epcot's World Showcase: individually themed areas (here, called "islands," even though they're not) arranged around a lagoon (here, called the "Great Inland Sea"—although that info is mere trivia). To see everything, you simply follow a great circle. The only corridor into the park, **Port of Entry,** borrows from the Magic Kingdom's Main Street, USA, in that it's a narrow, introductory area where guests are calculatedly submerged into the theme. In this case, you're gathering munitions for a great odyssey of some kind, so, in theme park logic, it's where you do things like rent strollers and lockers. All of that is found as soon as you enter. Don't forget to grab a free map, too.

Off to the left, where you'll later be exiting the park, you'll spot a small souvenir stand selling marked-down items (the inventory changes, but I've seen $18 T-shirts for $12 and $12 kids' SpongeBob sandals for $6). Check here for good stuff before spending your money on the full-price wares inside the park. Otherwise, the Islands of Adventure Trading Company, on the left as you proceed down Port of Entry, is the largest souvenir store in the park, but it's full price.

Most guests beeline through Port of Entry, but there are rewards to taking your time. Mostly, they're in the form of recorded sounds—listen near apparently closed doors and windows, for example, for snippets of dialogue from unseen people. Because attraction lines are shortest after opening, it's smarter to explore this area later, such as closer to closing.

Once you reach the end of Port of Entry and hit the Sea, which way should you go? Left. The designers of this park didn't miss a trick. Most of the exciting rides collect along the first half of the circuit, leaving the second half (to the right) for the main kids' area and for big shows. If you go right, by the time you make it back around to the most important rides, the lines will have built to their peaks.

Marvel Super Hero Island

At the wharf left of the Port of Entry, the vivid, $15 million **Incredible Hulk Coaster** ✪✪✫ looms. This machine demands attention: Every minute or so, a new train is blasted out of the 150-foot tunnel, over the avenue, and across the lakefront. Adding to the intensity, the track's hollow frame generates an animal roar that can be heard throughout the park. The ride is quick—a little over 2 minutes—but it's invigorating. Before you get into line, toss all loose items into the free lockers to the right of the ride; send someone good with computers, since the fingerprint-scan lock system requires patience and a still hand. (The only other ride at IOA where you'll be required to do this is the other coaster, Dueling Dragons.) The single-rider line here is usually fruitful. Some guests wait an extra long time for the chance to sit in the front row (a separate queue forms near the loading dock), but if you're low on time, wait instead for the front row on Dueling Dragons, where the exposed view gets you a lot more thrills. If you plan on buying a photo of your group on the ride, make sure you're all seated in the same line because shots are taken row by row.

Spoiler alert: Once trains are loaded, they cruise into the initial inclined tunnel. Then, quite without warning, 220 aircraft tires accelerate trains from a standstill to 40mph in 2 seconds and shoot them into a zero G-force barrel-roll 110 feet in the air, which means passengers are already upside down even though they're still going up the first hill. The launch mechanism provides about 45,000 pounds of thrust—enough, it's said by park P.R., to fire a bowling ball to the Pacific Ocean, although I doubt it—each time it engages, and if the booster system were on the municipal Orlando electrical grid, there would be a brownout each time it fired. Let's hope General Electric, which owns the park, gets a deal on all that juice. What follows is unbridled mayhem, as cars are boomeranged in a cobra roll over the lake and sent at a top speed of 67mph through a tangle of corkscrews, loops, and misty tunnels. For many visitors, it's the first ride of the day, and its seven inversions are certain to work better than morning coffee.

Next door, **Storm Force Accelatron,** named for the weather-controlling X-Man, is a not-too-special 90-second spinning-tub ride, just like Disney's teacups. Round cars spin on platters that themselves are on a giant rotating disk, and just to ensure maximum vomit velocity, each pod can be spun using a plate in the middle. This ride is skippable unless you have insistent children—it's for them, anyway.

Once you're past the Hulk, the vibe of Marvel Super Hero Island can finally assert itself, which it does murkily. The district looks vaguely futuristic and lamely '80s, and rock music plays a little too loudly. It's no wonder the island's personality is indistinct: Its design predates the success of the X-Men, Fantastic Four, *and* the Spider-Man film franchises, so designers had to forge ahead with only the comics, which few guests have read, for visual continuity. Periodically, costumed characters from Marvel comic books appear—there's Rogue in her awful early-'90s costume, there's Wolverine with very soft-looking claws—and make the rounds to sign autographs. **Spider-Man** is sometimes one of them, but if you don't see him, head into the back of the Marvel Alterniverse Store, opposite the Captain America Diner. There, the hero has his own indoor appearance zone where you can take your own photos (or buy one, if you must). The actor playing Spider-Man is one

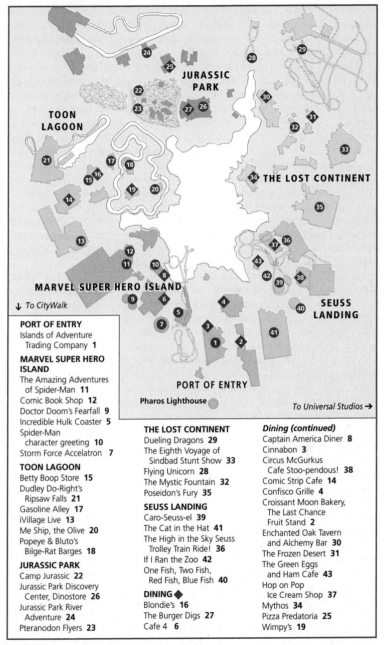

JURASSIC PARK

TOON LAGOON

THE LOST CONTINENT

MARVEL SUPER HERO ISLAND

↓ To CityWalk

SEUSS LANDING

PORT OF ENTRY

Pharos Lighthouse

To Universal Studios →

PORT OF ENTRY
Islands of Adventure
  Trading Company **1**

MARVEL SUPER HERO ISLAND
The Amazing Adventures
  of Spider-Man **11**
Comic Book Shop **12**
Doctor Doom's Fearfall **9**
Incredible Hulk Coaster **5**
Spider-Man
  character greeting **10**
Storm Force Accelatron **7**

TOON LAGOON
Betty Boop Store **15**
Dudley Do-Right's
  Ripsaw Falls **21**
Gasoline Alley **17**
iVillage Live **13**
Me Ship, the Olive **20**
Popeye & Bluto's
  Bilge-Rat Barges **18**

JURASSIC PARK
Camp Jurassic **22**
Jurassic Park Discovery
  Center, Dinostore **26**
Jurassic Park River
  Adventure **24**
Pteranodon Flyers **23**

THE LOST CONTINENT
Dueling Dragons **29**
The Eighth Voyage of
  Sindbad Stunt Show **33**
Flying Unicorn **28**
The Mystic Fountain **32**
Poseidon's Fury **35**

SEUSS LANDING
Caro-Seuss-el **39**
The Cat in the Hat **41**
The High in the Sky Seuss
  Trolley Train Ride! **36**
If I Ran the Zoo **42**
One Fish, Two Fish,
  Red Fish, Blue Fish **40**

DINING ◆
Blondie's **16**
The Burger Digs **27**
Cafe 4 **6**

Dining (continued)
Captain America Diner **8**
Cinnabon **3**
Circus McGurkus
  Cafe Stoo-pendous! **38**
Comic Strip Cafe **14**
Confisco Grille **4**
Croissant Moon Bakery,
  The Last Chance
  Fruit Stand **2**
Enchanted Oak Tavern
  and Alchemy Bar **30**
The Frozen Desert **31**
The Green Eggs
  and Ham Cafe **43**
Hop on Pop
  Ice Cream Shop **37**
Mythos **34**
Pizza Predatoria **25**
Wimpy's **19**

of the few who isn't clad head to toe in muscle-shaped padding—for this reason, and for the frank cling of his bodysuit, several admiring female members of the park's staff usually aren't far away. Spidey may be the only costumed character in Orlando who's also a heartthrob.

The two, 200-foot spindly towers are **Dr. Doom's Fearfall,** identical columns fitted with open-air cars that slide up and down them. The ride rockets the brave 150 feet up on at a force of 4Gs, where they feel an intense tickling in their stomachs, soak up a terrific view of the park, and hurtle (safely) back down to earth. The ride capacity is pretty low—you can see for yourself that each tower only shoots about 16 people up on each trip, with a reload period of several minutes in between—so either do this one early or very late so that waiting for it doesn't eat up too much time. Because this ride's seating configuration (four on each side of the tower) lends itself to lots of empty spaces, its single-rider line, found through the adjoining arcade, moves much quicker than most. Every few minutes, you'll hear the towers hiss like a snarling beast—it sounds like a Doctor Doom sound effect, but, in fact, it's part of the ride mechanism. After passengers are seated, the cars are weighed by computer and any compressed air not needed for their launch is noisily expelled in the seconds before flight. At the exit of this ride, you'll find this park's main **video game arcade.**

If there's a single don't-miss ride in town, it's undoubtedly **The Amazing Adventures of Spider-Man** ✪✪✪, on your left past the Fearfall. Lines for this one can be as long as the ones for the roller coasters, so go early or late in the day to minimize waits. After passing through a simulation of the *Daily Bugle* newsroom (take special notice of the hilarious pre-ride safety video, done as a pitchperfect *Superfriends*-era cartoon), riders don polarized 3-D glasses, board moving cars, and whisk through a 1.5-acre experience. Mild open-air motion simulation, computer-generated 3-D animation, and a cunning sense trickery (bursts of flame, water droplets, blasts of hot air) collaborate to impart the mind-blowing illusion of being drafted into Spidey's battles against a "Sinister Syndicate" of super-villains including Doctor Octopus and the Green Goblin, who have disassembled the Statue of Liberty with an anti-gravity gun. Although the vehicles barely move as they make their way through the sets and large screens, you'll come off feeling as if you've survived a 400-foot plunge off a city skyscraper. The technology, developed for this park, remains unrivaled even though it's getting up there in age. Many independent thrill ride fan clubs rate it as the best attraction in the world, and I agree. Spider-Man, which opened with the park in 1999, was so ahead of its time that other attractions still haven't caught up. It fires on all cylinders, and the whole family can do it without fear. There's a single-rider line on this one, too, which shoots past the slower Standby queue but bypasses the most interesting waiting areas. Re-riders (and everyone I know, no matter how timid they are, quickly becomes an addict once they've tasted this ride) should get to know the single-rider entrance well.

Most of the shopping and food of Super Hero Island is standard issue, but the **Comic Book Shop** is worth a stop for collectors. Surprisingly legit, the store carries the latest Marvel issues, special editions, compilation books, collectible busts, and even the current issue of *Wizard,* the bible of comic nuts. (Comic fans should also keep their eyes peeled on the Spider-Man ride, where they'll see such inside jokes as a theater named the Excelsior.) I've even seen some markdown merchandise

---

The Best of Islands of Adventure

Don't miss if you're 6: The Cat in The Hat

Don't miss if you're 16: The Amazing Adventures of Spider-Man

Requisite photo op: Toon Lagoon

Food you can only get here: Sundae on a Stick, Hop on Pop Ice Cream Shop, Seuss Landing; Treasure Chest Sundae, The Frozen Desert, The Lost Continent

The most crowded, so go early: Incredible Hulk Coaster, Dueling Dragons

Skippable: Storm Force Accelatron

Biggest thrill: Incredible Hulk Coaster

Best show: Poseidon's Fury

Where to find peace: On the lagoon at Port of Entry, Toon Lagoon, or Jurassic Park

---

here. True collectors will fret about rolling their books' spines on the rides—the good news is the park will send any purchase (here or at any other store) to the Islands of Adventure Trading Company, at the Port of Entry, for collection as you leave the park at the end of the day. The deadline for purchases changes, but it's usually about 2 hours before closing.

The Toon Amphitheater between Super Hero Island and Toon Lagoon once hosted regular theme-park shows but is currently occupied by a daytime television program, **iVillage Live** (☎ 866/448-5360; ivillagelivetickets@nbcuni.com), which is aired on some NBC stations and Bravo (both are Universal corporate cousins), Mondays to Fridays at noon. Even though the show, a vacuous magazine of lifestyle and women's features, is mostly an ad for a website and celebrity guests are rare, tickets are best arranged ahead of time. Still, if the producers are scrambling for warm bodies, which they often are, they may offer you a free meal. You have to be 18 or older to attend, and you cannot wear clothing with logos on it. Happily, you don't have to have a theme park ticket to go.

Toon Lagoon

The next zone clockwise after Marvel Super Hero Island, Toon Lagoon harbors two waters rides that are—both literally and figuratively—among the splashiest at any theme park. Both of them will drench you. If you're smart, you'll come just *before* it swelters, so that you'll be soaked and cool when the going gets rough.

Slow your pace when you reach the introductory section of Toon Lagoon, encountered after a brief zone of **midway games** (most: three tries for $5). Crawling with details, color, and fountains, it's the kind of place that reveals more the longer you look—some 150 cartoon characters, some you'll recognize (Nancy, Annie, the Family Circus, Beetle Bailey) and some strictly for connoisseurs (Little

Nemo in Slumberland, Zippy), make two-dimensional appearances on the island, including inside the restaurants and on a soundtrack popping in and out of the action. Where you see a button or a possible trigger, press it or plunge it, because the environment has been rigged with sonic treats. Whimsical snapshot spots are worked in, too, such as the trick photo setup by the Comic Strip Cafe where you can pretend Marmaduke is dragging you by his leash. The misty "smoke" from Crock's cannon and Flash Gordon's rocket provide cooling relief from the sunlight. Amidst all this, the **Betty Boop Store** sells rare specimens. My sister-in-law found a 75th-anniversary cookie jar here that no other real-world store carried. Personally, I worry about the mental health of the clerks, who are subjected to a brain-melting loop of Boop's "I Want to Be Loved by You."

Finally, at the back end of Toon Lagoon, the star attractions appear. That extravagant snow-capped mountain at the left contains **Dudley Do-Right's Ripsaw Falls** ★★, a wonderful perils-of-Pauline log-flume caper featuring Jay Ward's feckless Canadian Mountie bungling his rescue of Nell Fenwick from Snidely Whiplash. The winding 5-minute journey—ups, downs, indoor, outdoor, surprise backsplashes, all past chunky robotic characters—climaxes in a stomach-juggling double-dip drop that hurtles, unexpectedly, through a humped underground gully. Although the 75-foot drop starts out at 45 degrees, it steepens to 50 degrees, creating a weightless sensation. Front-seat riders get soaked. Back-seat riders get soaked. And anyone who didn't get soaked probably will when they double back to return to the disembarking zone, because that's when they'll face the gauntlet of sadistic bystanders who pump quarters into machines that fire water cannons at passing boats. If you take the role of sprayer, you should know there's a 1-second delay between when you press the button and when the water squirts. Despite a few flaws (the robotics aren't always functioning properly and the outdoor sections can be blinding after you've spent time waiting in line indoors), Ripsaw Falls is terrific fun. You never see anyone come off it grumpy—the mark of amusement success. The ride, which is such a blast it has ruined conventional log flume rides for me, often closes in January and early February for a scrub.

The **Gasoline Alley** shop, across the main path, sells $6 ponchos so you don't have to skip the flume on cold days, but bear in mind that on Ripsaw Falls, you straddle the seats and your separated feet won't be easy to cover. Resist the urge to buy a beach towel, as they cost $20. Best to wear sandals.

Just behind Gasoline Alley, **Popeye & Bluto's Bilge-Rat Barges** ★★ are 12-passenger, circular bumper boats that float freely and unpredictably down an outlandish white-water obstacle course—beneath waterfalls, through tunnels, over angry rapids, and mercilessly past features designed to inundate one or two people at a time. It's like playing Russian roulette with water, and everyone loses. When it comes to the round-boat genre (there are two others in town—one at Animal Kingdom and one at Busch Gardens), this version is considerably wilder, unquestionably wetter, and was obviously lavished with the most money. Designers spared no expense, and the attention shows: Even the river's walls have been sculpted and painted in cartoon hues to resemble a wooden chute. There are many people who refuse to ride anything that will get them wet, but don't let them talk you out of enjoying this one. It's diabolical and one of Universal's best. There's a semi-waterproof compartment on board for personal belongings, but you'd be wise to slip your things into plastic bags, too, just in case. Attendants won't let you remove your shoes, mostly because the turntable loading dock isn't safe for bare feet. The wait feels endless on hot days, and the queue area is dull and steamy, making this one a top contender for using your Express pass.

Over by **Me Ship, the Olive** 🧒, an interactive playground for children just beyond the Barges' entrance, wallflowers can watch boats pass in trepidation of the next soak. In this case, the soaker can be you, since the Olive has free water cannons you can use to drench people as they pass. Inside the Olive, there's also a slide and some fun to be had with a piano (play the notes on the sheet music for an orchestral surprise). One of my favorite things to do in the whole park is to spend awhile on the bridge beside the Olive, which overlooks Barge boats as they drift helplessly under a leaky ship's funnel. Watching the gleeful alarm on people's faces, hearing the peals of laughter—the joy of the amusement park and the sublime delight of togetherness are repeated, again and again, from the vantage point of that bridge. I could stand there all day.

Jurassic Park

Steven Spielberg was a creative consultant to Universal, the studio which nourished him, which is one reason this "island," the largest and greenest in the park, is presented practically verbatim from his 1993 movie. Once you pass through a proud wooden gate, John Williams' bombastic score becomes audible, and there it burrows until you move on to another area of IOA. When the park opened, the big boast was that all of the plants in this section were extant during the period of the dinosaurs, but it seems that's no longer the case. Still, the area has some 4,000 trees—half the number in the whole park—and if you stand quietly, you may hear rustling among some of them, which is a clever, Spielbergian touch.

The first area, on the right as you enter, is **Camp Jurassic** 🧒, the dedicated kids' zone of this part of the park. It's nothing much—rope bridges, fake amber mines—but it's dinosaur themed, which many boys love. The nifty-looking track clacking and soaring overhead is **Pteranodon Flyers,** on which hanging cars gently glide, one at a time, on a very short (about 75 seconds) scenic route through the trees, gently swaying as they turn. Cool as it looks, it was poorly designed, fitting only two at a time, and huge lines are inevitable. In the business, that's called a poor "load factor." Facing irate crowds, Universal instituted a rule: No adult could ride without a child. That accomplished two goals. It prepared guests for the ride's tame deportment and it cut down on the wait. Attendants may be willing to load child-free adults when the park is dead quiet. Even with the rule, lines get hairy; skip this underwhelmer unless the duration is less than 15 minutes.

I do recommend the **Jurassic Park River Adventure** ✶. In that family-friendly Orlando tradition, the worst drop is clearly visible from the outside; in this case, you can see it, or at least the splashdown from its 85-foot drop, behind the Thunder Falls Terrace restaurant, where descending river boats kick up quite a spray when they hit the water at 30mph. The splash zone is marked, and there will usually be a 12-year-old boy intent on standing there for hours, giving himself a nigh-amphibious drenching. Before reaching that messy climax, boats embark on what's meant to be a benign tour of the mythical dinosaur park from the movie—there's even a moment when the gates to the preserve swing open and the music soars—only to be bumped off course and, of course, run afoul of spitting raptors and an eye-poppingly realistic *T. rex* who lunges for the kill. The dino attack is shrewdly stage-managed; note how, in true Spielberg fashion, you see disquieting evidence of the hungry lizards (rustling bushes, gashes in sheet metal) before actually catching sight of one. There's no logic as to which passengers will get drenched and in which configuration. In all honesty, you're much more likely to get soaked standing on the terrace of the restaurant than you are inside the boat, but the trip down the hill is still enough to blow your hat off.

The **Jurassic Park Discovery Center** convincingly reproduces the luxury lodge from the film, down to full-size skeletons in the atrium—line up your camera just so, and you can snap a witty shot of a *T. rex* chomping on a loved one's cranium. Downstairs, seek out exhibits purporting to allow guests to peer into "dinosaur eggs" (actually puppets) raised on the grounds. This attraction relies on actors to lead you through it, and show times aren't noted anywhere, so it's catch-as-catch-can, but you can still handle the eggs yourselves even in the absence of a "spieler," and a few more informational panels about dinosaurs may be enough to engage kids for about 10 minutes. The Center's **Dinostore** carries heaps of toys for surprisingly realistic prices (plastic or plush toys for $15, sidewalk chalk shaped like dinosaur eggs for $3). Behind the Center, there's a pleasant network of garden paths where you can take a break from the bustle of the park and chill out beside the lagoon. (When the park opened in 1999, there were two more attractions here—one an interactive triceratops robot attended by a zookeeper and one a boat landing for ferries from Port of Entry. Both are now defunct, although the boat dock is still there.) Beside Thunder Falls Outfitters, by the River Adventure, you'll find a rock climbing wall, which costs $5 a go.

The Lost Continent

Once you leave the Discovery Center, there's not much to see or do for the next few minutes' walk, but once you cross through the Jurassic Park gate, you're back in the thick of things. The gist of this island is not as clear as the others. Think of it as part Africa, part Asia, part Rome—basically, everything exotic and mythical wrapped up into something vague but familiar.

The first attraction you'll encounter if you're coming clockwise is the **Flying Unicorn** 🧒, a rumbling training roller coaster for small kids. Don't expect more than a 1-minute figure eight with slight banking. The line is sometimes ugly, and what's worse, it's also mostly exposed to the sun. The back seats feel the fastest. The long-legged should cross their ankles to fit more comfortably. This is the sort of ride you'll forget about almost as soon as you're off it.

If you have kids in your party, you might consider appointing someone to stash them at the Flying Unicorn while you ride the adult-size **Dueling Dragons** ★★, next door. (But first, stash your belongings in the free lockers adjacent to the entrance.) This is a monster coaster of the first order, and one of Orlando's most thrilling. Actually, it's two roller coasters, "inverted" so that passengers' feet dangle, and is entangled in such a way as to ensure three near-misses during the 145-second ride. Ice, in blue, has a cobra roll and its twistiness is perhaps (who can say?) more conducive to slight motion sickness for those who are prone to it. Fire, in red-orange, has two more "elements" (maneuvers, in coasterspeak) than Ice, and its first drop is slightly higher, but its course is slightly more jolty. The line for both snakes indoors through a castle before diverging before the twin loading zones, at which point you'll also have to decide if you want to wait longer to guarantee a front-row seat—if you have time, it's absolutely worth doing at least once (especially on Fire, where visibility is slightly better) because of the unique near-miss design of these rides. After they're loaded, trains are weighed by a computer (you won't notice) and dispatched (usually) in sequence to improve the timing of the near-collisions. The effect is best enjoyed from the front row or, if you can't fathom the long wait for that, by keeping an eye on your feet. After you get off, ask an attendant if the "re-ride" line is up, because if it is, you won't have to go all the way out to line up again to ride the other track. Guests of exceptional size (as they are now apparently called) may have to wait for the third row, where the larger seats have been installed; if you're not confident that you'll fit, test out the standard seat located to the right of the main entrance to the queue. If you're not confident about braving the ride itself, the best viewing area of the tracks' rolls and dips is located inside the front gate to the ride.

The rest of the Lost Continent is often skipped by regular visitors—not because it's bad, *per se,* but because it's not the best of the park. **The Eighth Voyage of Sindbad Stunt Show** is mounted a precious few times each day in an open-air stadium, usually in the afternoon (curtain times are marked on your map). You probably already suspect what you're getting here—a corny 20-minute, sound-effect enhanced banquet of macho men swordfighting and leaping in the pursuit of rescuing a princess who, it turns out, may or may not require male assistance after all. Buckles are swashed and cultural references are dropped like anvils. The climax, in which a man is lit on fire and plunges 30 feet into a pit, may alarm kids, but the production values are strong. Attend this show if you'd like to fill out a day or to sit for awhile; otherwise, your IOA experience won't be lacking if you skip it.

On your map, you'll see something called **The Mystic Fountain** marked as an attraction. Stop by briefly. If it's merely gurgling with recorded sound effects, all is quiet. But when least expected, it comes to life. Here, the mildly amusing gag is that an enchanted fountain (actually controlled by someone in an unseen booth, as if you need to be told) is able to interact with anyone foolish enough to wander near it. As *Time* magazine put it when the park opened in 1999, the fountain exasperates with "the droll sarcasm of a bachelor uncle roped into caring for some itchy 10-year-olds." If you don't want to get doused, check the ground for slick spots to determine the fountain's spitting reach. In the Fountain's vicinity, a few down-market stalls sell random things such as jewelry, machine-made Oriental rugs, psychic readings ($15 for 5 min.), you-crack-'em oysters containing pearls for $15, and $300 belly-dancing outfits. Epcot's shopping selection in Morocco is much better and more authentic. Equally random is the small sampling of **midway games.** Not very mythical.

The other major show in the Lost Continent is **Poseidon's Fury,** which, despite its lowly status as a walk-through attraction, has a stunning exterior, carved within a millimeter of reason to look like a crumbling temple, and inside, it boasts one of the most breathtaking effects in the park: a "water vortex" tunnel of water. Like Sindbad, it's boisterous and pyrotechnic, and some of its other special effects, such as the way the walls of one of its rooms seem to vanish into thin air, are truly amazing for anyone over 6. Those younger might be freaked out by the dark, the fireballs, and the vapid storyline that involves a fight between Poseidon and Lord Darkenon (who?), but the special effects that the lame story links are the real attraction, and they're worth enjoying if you've got the time. To get the best view, simply try to head for the front of every room, especially the third one. If the line is greater than 20 minutes or stretches far outside the building, think about coming back later, since shows only take that long and there's another queue just inside the door—unless you crave air-conditioning. I'm markedly impressed by the individual special effects, even though Poseidon's Fury turns out to be somewhat less than the sum of its parts. I don't know anyone who calls the attraction their favorite, but given the choice between this and Sindbad, I'd do this.

Seuss Landing

Islands of Adventure will never be a kiddie park—if you doubt it, look at its skyline, knotted with coasters—which makes it all the more wonderful that the most assiduously designed kiddie area in town is here. Nowhere is IOA's extravagance on finer display than this 10-acre section, which replicates the good Doctor's two-dimensional bluster with three-dimensional exactitude. A riot of swirling edges, colors like cake frosting, and preposterously contorted shapes, everything was hand-crafted to the last detail. By decree, there are almost no straight lines. Not in street lamps, not on the rooflines, not even on the trash cans.

As soon as you enter the island from The Lost Continent, head right by the restrooms, along the lakefront, where you can get a good look at what the designers accomplished. Notice how even the palm trees twist. They were knocked sideways near Miami in 1992's devastating Hurricane Andrew, and because palm trees always grow upward, by the time they were scouted for IOA's 1999 opening, they had acquired a perfectly loopy angle. Like Toon Lagoon, this is an area where it pays to snoop around, looking for hidden gags. Sprinkled around are Horton's Egg and, by the Sea, the two Zaxes, which appropriate to their own book (a commentary on political rivalry in which they stubbornly face off while a city grows up around them), were the very first things placed in the park, and everything else was built around them.

Everything on this island is appropriate for kids—and a good thing, too, because they have difficulty tearing themselves away from the fantasy. The railway threading overhead throughout Seuss Landing was once IOA's one major failure. Built as a guest-controlled ride called Sylvester McMonkey McBean's Very Unusual Driving Machines it failed to open because of fatal design issues. For 7 years, the tracks moldered, idle, above this island, barren save for an occasional automated car laden with robotic characters, which only served to remind everyone of the tracks' futility. But in 2006, the issues were finally resolved, and the railway opened as **The High in the Sky Seuss Trolley Train Ride!** 🎡, a cheerful family-friendly glide over the Landing, narrated in verse. Like Dueling Dragons, there are two paths. Given a choice (you aren't always), take the purple line, as it surveys more of the area than the green line, which dawdles too long inside the Circus McGurkus Cafe (which at least is air-conditioned). The ride takes about 3 minutes and because there's so much to take in, time flies fast. Unlike Dueling Dragons, you have to line up all over again if you want to do the other track.

The masterful **Caro-Seuss-el** ⭐ 🎡, populated by a bobbing menagerie of otherwordly critters that actually react to being ridden—ears wiggle, heads turn—is delightfully over-the-top and appeals to kids who think they're too old for girly carousels. Beside the Caro-Seuss-el, seek out the quick but trenchant walk-through path retelling Dr. Seuss' environmental warning tale, **The Lorax.** Across the path, near the Circus McGurkus Cafe Stoo-pendous, the Cat in the Hat and the Grinch make regular public appearances. Amusingly, the Grinch's slouching, nonplussed body language proves he's none too pleased to have to be there with your kids.

On **One Fish, Two Fish, Red Fish, Blue Fish** 🛝, another iteration of Disney's tot-bait Dumbo staple, riders (two passengers per car normally, three if one of them loves The Wiggles) go around, up, and down by their own controls while fountains peg them from the sides—listen to the song for the secret of how to avoid getting wet, although the advice isn't foolproof. There are benches around the ride, and it's fun to watch little kids giggle malevolently when their parents get spritzed. Because this type of ride is eternally popular with children, the line can get nutty, so it's a good candidate for an Express pass.

Getting wet is part of the bargain at **If I Ran the Zoo** 🛝, too. The interactive playground for young children contains some 20 well-crafted elements. Let your brood turn the cranks, and fanciful animals pop into view, or unleash them to crawl through small "caves." Beware the cheeky water fountain—it pays to follow all posted instructions in Seuss Landing.

Across the path, **The Cat in the Hat** ★★ 🛝 is a non-threatening excursion through the plot of the famous storybook as viewed from slow-moving mobile "couches" (really a typical flat ride car). The vehicles spin a few too many times for some adults (you can ask to have it turned off), but kids don't seem to mind. The design racks up major points for replicating the look of the beloved children's book with astounding precision, even in three dimensions. The story is just as faithfully retold; it's clear from this sweet, 3½-minute ride that the family of Dr. Seuss (Theodor Geisel) had a strong influence in steering the execution of this section of the park. Young kids who love indoor rides of the sort found in Disney's Fantasyland shouldn't miss this one. Parents will probably emerge feeling glad they tagged along. Lines are shortest first thing in the morning and late in the day. The gift shop after the offload platform is among the best in the park—thanks mostly to this shop, Universal's red Thing 1 and Thing 2 shirts have quickly become as ubiquitous as Mouse ears.

Once you're done with that, you're nearly back at the Port of Entry, having made a complete circuit of Islands of Adventure, but before you're done, give **McElligot's Pool** a quick look-see; if you throw a coin into one of its three fish figures, you'll make it spit. At this point, lots of people make a return trip to The Adventures of Spider-Man before heading for home.

WHERE TO EAT IN ISLANDS OF ADVENTURE

On days when the park closes at 6pm (outside of summer and holiday periods), many restaurants will only be open from 11am to 4pm. But remember that all the restaurants at CityWalk (p. 282) are a 5-minute walk from the park, so with a hand stamp for re-entry, you can try those, too. The only one that requires reservations is Emeril's (p. 69).

You can make reservations to eat at the two sit-down restaurants, Mythos or Confisco Grille, at the Dining Cart in the Port of Entry. You can also call ☎ 407/ 224-4534 in advance, but you don't have to, as they're rarely sold out.

Park planners recognize that IOA's circular shape means at midday, most guests will be at the back, around Jurassic Park, so that's why most of the counter-service restaurants are located there. That means if you're peckish around noon or 1pm, you're going to have to swim through crowds. What's more, by the time you reach Seuss Landing, you'll find most of the park's best desserts.

Port of Entry: Lighter bites such as sandwiches and panini can be snagged quickly for $8 to $9 (with potato salad and fresh fruit) at **Croissant Moon Bakery** or at **The Last Chance Fruit Stand** cart, which sells not only fruit cups ($3) but also honkingly large turkey legs ($7.79 with a drink). Around the corner toward the Hulk coaster is a **Cinnabon** outlet straight from your local mall. The other way, toward Seuss Landing, is **Confisco Grille,** one of only two sit-down locations in the park. It serves a rangy selection of bistro fare (quesadillas, $8; wood oven pizzas, $9; and mixed grills, $13) for a price that's a little lower than most sit-down theme-park restaurants. It's easy enough to check the menu on your way into the park. Confisco is also where the morning Character Breakfast with Spidey and the Cat in the Hat (p. 91) is held.

Marvel Super Hero Island: Two counter-service joints stare each other down near the Incredible Hulk coaster. The **Captain America Diner** does the usual burgers and such for around $8, and **Cafe 4** does pizza and pasta for the same price. There's also a **fruit stand** near the Captain America Diner (whole fruit, $1).

Toon Lagoon: Blondie's ★★ serves Dagwood (if you're under 40, that's another name for a hero) slices for $7, and they're fresh-made and delicious, but the custom-made "stacked sandwich" costs 70¢ less and gets you about twice as much food. They're so big you can share them. Meanwhile, the much more spacious **Comic Strip Cafe** ★ has four counters for four types of food: burgers and dogs; pizza and pasta; Chinese; and fish and chicken. No matter what you choose—and every dish is listed with a large photo that can be seen from miles away—you'll pay around $8 before a drink. **Wimpy's,** across from the Bilge-Rat Barges, serves its namesake's obsession (hamburgers), although the staff will not permit you to pay next Tuesday to have a hamburger today. Sadly, too, the stand is closed when things aren't busy.

Jurassic Park: Because of the park's loop design, most guests seem to end up here, at the halfway point in the circuit, at lunchtime, so lines can be bad. To eat indoors, you'll have to choose **The Burger Digs** inside the Discovery Center, where the main dish (which also comes in garden and grilled chicken varieties) is slung for the usual $8. There's a toppings bar, so you can load up. Near the entry to the River Adventure, the **Pizza Predattoria** is a counter-service kiosk with outdoor seating. Guess how much its individual pizzas are? The rest of its menu is short, but big on calories: meatball subs with a small salad ($9) and chicken Caesar salad with bready pizza triangles ($8).

The Lost Continent: Many of the signs advertising IOA's flagship sit-down restaurant, **Mythos** ★★★ (☎ 407/224-4534; reservations suggested), proudly proclaim that it is repeatedly voted the best theme park restaurant by a publication to which you surely don't subscribe, *Theme Park Insider.* Rest assured that the awards are deserved, at least when you compare this food to other restaurants at other parks. How many other restaurants on the wrong side of the turnstiles can you name that employ an executive chef (in this case, Steven Jayson)? The menu is seasonal, but has some steady themes including cedar planked salmon ($19), a hamburger so thick-cut it wobbles ($11), and a daily risotto ($16). It's smart to reserve, not just because the hours are unpredictable (it's usually closed well before dinner), but also because you want a good table. Mythos' cavelike interior, moody and carved from that ubiquitous orange-hued fake rock that scientists should term Orlando Schist, commands a marvelous view of the lagoon. You could sit and watch the Incredible Hulk Coaster fire all day, if there weren't other things to see. Barring that, the **Enchanted Oak Tavern,** in a gorgeous setting inside a hollowed-out "tree," serves grilled chicken, ribs, and hockey-puck burgers (that describes their flavor, not their size) for $9 to $12. Yes, its setting (the terrace overlooking the lagoon is lovely) is rather more beautiful than its food. The Enchanted Oak does, however, contain an honest-to-goodness bar, the **Alchemy Bar,** with an honest-to-goodness happy hour daily from 3 to 5pm (20 oz. Buds are $3.25, well drinks $2.75—a major deal when you realize beers at the park's stalls cost $5.50). The island's other main place to eat, **Fire Eaters' Grill,** is usually closed for lack of business. The **Frozen Desert** stand sells two unique desserts: a Sultan's Sundae (vanilla ice cream and pineapple swirl topped with pineapple chunks) and the Treasure Chest Sundae (vanilla and strawberry swirl, topped with syrupy strawberries), both for $4.50.

Seuss Landing: The Green Eggs and Ham Cafe (you can't miss it—it's the house-sized slab of ham with a giant fork stuck into it) sells burgers and, of course, sandwiches made of green eggs and ham ($7–$8), but unfortunately, it's not always open, which is disappointing. If that novelty isn't available to you, turn to the **Circus McGurkus Cafe Stoo-pendous!** ★, encircled on its second level by the Trolley Train ride, which gives kids something to look at while they eat. Aside from the usual burgers and pizzas, the menu is leavened with spaghetti and meatballs; chicken Caesar salad; and a fried chicken platter with mashed potatoes, corn on the cob, and a buttermilk biscuit—all around $8—so there's something for everyone. Seuss Landing is full of dishes you can only find at Islands of Adventure. **Hop on Pop Ice Cream Shop,** near the transition to The Lost Continent, serves a mean "sundae on a stick" ($3.50), a bar of vanilla ice cream that's hand-dipped in chocolate and rolled in your choice of nuts, chocolate sprinkles, or rainbow sprinkles. The **Horace P. Sweets** stand nearby sells Moose Juice (a tart tangerine mix) and Goose Juice (sour green apple) for $3.79 to $4.29.

SEAWORLD ORLANDO

The second mighty theme park chain to set up shop in town, after Disney, was **SeaWorld Orlando** (Central Florida Pkwy., at International Dr., or Exit 71 and 72 east of Interstate 4; ☎ 800/327-2424 or 407/351-3600; www.seaworldorlando. com; adults $64.95, kids 3–9 $53.95), which began in San Diego in the early 1960s and opened in Orlando in 1973, scarcely 2 years after the Magic Kingdom. Although the SeaWorld chain operates three American parks (the third is in San Antonio), its Orlando location has undoubtedly risen to become its most important. The Florida compound has an additional luxury theme park, Discovery

Cove (p. 213), and its new zoo-cum-water slide park, the Pacific Ocean–themed Aquatica (www.aquaticabyseaworld.com; 80,000 square feet of beach area, two conjoined wave pools, two lazy rivers, plus 36 slides, two of which are partially made of clear acrylic and plow through dolphin habitats), opens in the spring of 2008. The three-park menu now qualifies SeaWorld as the city's third genuine multi-day theme park destination, after Disney and Universal.

At SeaWorld, the focus isn't on thrill rides or "magic"—it's animals, and nearly 17,000 of them. Just about everything to see or do involves watching marine creatures in their habitats or performing in shows. Many tourists, particularly those over a certain age, claim SeaWorld as their favorite Orlando park, because there's a lot going for it: 200 acres of space for gardens, a compound that absorbs crowds well, an earnest educational component, a variety of animal exhibits that ensures guests won't have the same experience twice, a refreshing lack of patronizing mythology, and free beer. That's right—the park is owned by the ultra-patriotic suds slingers at Anheuser-Busch. Whereas a day spent at Islands of Adventure or the Magic Kingdom might send you slumping home and reaching for the Calgon, it's unusual to come away from SeaWorld stressed, partly because the park's rangy layout is virtually free of the attention-grabbing "wienies" that make many visitors anxiously feel like they're missing out on better attractions across the park. It's easy to relax and enjoy what's in front of you at SeaWorld. In fact, that's the way to see it best.

The SeaWorld experience differs from most other parks in more important ways: It's show-based. Your day here will revolve around the scheduling of a half-dozen regular performances in which animals (mostly mammals, but some birds, too) do tricks—except here, they're called "behaviors"—with their human trainers. Although there are three rides, they're not in the true spirit of the place. SeaWorld's banner attraction is the Shamu show, and when you're not watching killer whales do back-flips, you're ambling at your own speed through habitats stocked with other beautiful creatures. Thoughtfully, SeaWorld posts its days' schedules online a few weeks ahead of time so that if you're really anal, you can map out your day in advance. Find that feature on the park's website (see above) under Park Information and Show Schedule.

To get the most out of a visit, try to be in the same place as the animal trainers, who frequently appear to nurture their charges. Ask questions. Get involved. They may even allow you to feed or stroke the animals. These zoologists love sharing information about the animals they have devoted their lives to, and in Orlando, it's rare that theme park guests are encouraged to be anything other than passive participants. Feeding times are usually posted outside each pavilion's entrance; you may need to backtrack a few times each day in order to make the schedule, but the interaction will be worth the effort.

Heaven knows why other guidebooks don't warn you about this next one: You will be spending quite a bit of time waiting for shows to begin. Because everyone at SeaWorld sees the shows, everyone shows up early for seats, so it's smart to arrive at least 30 minutes ahead of show times unless you don't mind being crowded out. (It's also imperative that you wear a watch.) Not all the performances have pre-show entertainment and you're going to be spending a lot of time sitting on benches waiting for something to happen; bring along some diversion for you and your party, like a travel version of a board game, or even a few conversation topics. Anything to keep you from getting bored.

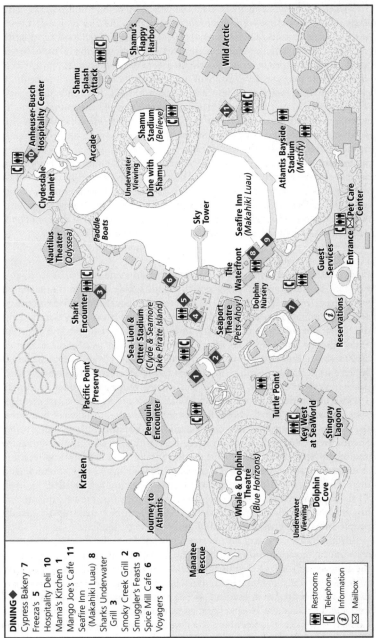

SeaWorld Orlando

DINING ◆

Cypress Bakery **7**
Freeza's **5**
Hospitality Deli **10**
Mama's Kitchen **1**
Mango Joe's Cafe **11**
Seafire Inn
(Makahiki Luau) **8**
Sharks Underwater
Grill **3**
Smoky Creek Grill **2**
Smuggler's Feasts **9**
Spice Mill Cafe **6**
Voyagers **4**

Restrooms
Telephone
Information
Mailbox

Anheuser-Busch Hospitality Center

Clydesdale Hamlet

Shamu Splash Attack

Shamu's Happy Harbor

Wild Arctic

Shamu Stadium (Believe)

Underwater Viewing
Dine with Shamu

Arcade

Atlantis Bayside Stadium (Mistify)

Nautilus Theater (Odyssea)

Paddle Boats

Sky Tower

Seafire Inn (Makahiki Luau)

The Waterfront

Pet Care Center

Entrance

Guest Services

Reservations

Dolphin Nursery

Shark Encounter

Sea Lion & Otter Stadium
(Clyde & Seamore Take Pirate Island)

Seaport Theatre (Pets Ahoy!)

Pacific Point Preserve

Penguin Encounter

Kraken

Turtle Point

Key West at SeaWorld

Stingray Lagoon

Journey to Atlantis

Whale & Dolphin Theatre (Blue Horizons)

Dolphin Cove

Underwater Viewing

Manatee Rescue

Ticket prices rise annually to keep up with the Joneses, but SeaWorld is more likely than most to throw a deal into the mix. In late 2006, for example, it teamed with its sister park, Busch Gardens, to sells a two-park pass, good for unlimited entry for a week, which even included a free shuttle bus for the 72 miles between them. SeaWorld tends to only offer these goodies online at www.seaworld orlando.com, so if you wait until you reach the ticket booth, you'll miss out. For permanent discounts for people who also plan to visit Universal's parks, see the section about the FlexTicket on p. 321. Members of the military should check www.herosalute.com to register for any discounts being offered; Anheuser-Busch is famous for its generosity to members of the armed forces and their families, including free admission for up to four.

Important: If the forecast shows prolonged rain (as opposed to Florida's typical spot showers), reschedule your visit here. Not only will you spend lots of time walking outside between attractions, but it's also harder to see marine animals when the surface of the water is being pelted by raindrops. Not to mention that fact that if there's so much as a twinkle of lightning anywhere in the county, these water-based attractions close faster than a shark's mouth on his dinner.

TOURING SEAWORLD

Once you've parked ($10, and it's uncovered; spots guaranteed to be closer to the gate are $15 and not worth it) or gotten off the I-Ride (the stop is near the front gates), head for the lighthouse that marks the entrance. Inside, the first thing you should do is grab a placemat-sized park map. On the back, printed fresh daily, is the Show Schedule, plus the opening times of all the restaurants and attractions. Shows usually begin an hour after park opening, and usually the blockbuster Shamu show, *Believe,* has only a few presentations. I always prefer the last one because it's less crowded than the others and it often extends, slightly, past the park's posted closing time, getting you a little more for your money.

SeaWorld is the only area theme park that isn't broken up into themed lands. Your day will be dictated by the shows you plan to see, but I'll walk you through the park in a roughly clockwise order, starting at the entrance and ending with the Shamu area. The park's pathways are lined with the odd animal enclosure—flamingoes here, turtles there—but those are really more like landscaping features than true attractions, and they aren't listed on the maps, so I haven't included them. If there's a particular animal you'd like to see, just ask a staffer.

If you're interested in riding the park's two thrill rides, the best time to get in line is when the Shamu show, *Believe,* is scheduled, as it soaks up thousands of people and all the lines in the park diminish for the duration.

Ideally, by the time you hit the gates, you will have already made your special restaurant reservations (Dine with Shamu, p. 91) or interactive experiences with the animals (p. 250), as they usually sell out weeks ahead. But on the off chance there's a space for something you'd like to do, the Guest Services and Reservations desk is the place to book. You can also sign up for one of the day's free beer tastings, conducted at the Hospitality Center across the park. Otherwise, the Cape Cod–style entrance plaza is where you do the necessaries such as rent strollers and lockers. On your way home, it's where you'll find the largest souvenir store. The area is really just a warm-up for the rest of the park.

The Best of SeaWorld

Don't miss if you're 6: *Pets Ahoy!*

Don't miss if you're 16: Kraken

Requisite photo op: Shamu in flight, *Believe*, Shamu Stadium

Food you can only get here: Shamu ice cream bar, carts parkwide; mahimahi with piña colada sauce, Seafire Inn, The Waterfront

The most crowded, so go early: *Believe*, Shamu Stadium

Skippable: *Odyssea*

Biggest thrill: Kraken, Journey to Atlantis

Best show: *Believe*, Shamu Stadium

Where to find peace: Anywhere around the lagoon

THE BEST SHOWS

Feel free to be choosy about the shows you care to see, because if you load your plate with too many, you'll spend most of your in between time hoofing it between amphitheatres, yet spreading SeaWorld over 2 days would be a bit much. The shows are printed on the daily map in rough order of their popularity and capacity; most days, the bottom few are fillers such as pianists or street musicians. The only can't-miss shows are the major ones I'll name below.

Do try to be at shows at least a half-hour early, and for Shamu, add another 10 minutes to walk around the lagoon to the stadium. SeaWorld is not as controlling as Disney about where you're permitted to sit, so the best seats go first. Furthermore, several shows (*Pets Ahoy!* and *Odyssea* especially) don't permit latecomers to enter. At others, you can't get out easily until it's over.

Three of the shows, *Believe, Blue Horizons,* and *Clyde and Seamore,* have a clearly marked "soak zone" in the front rows of the seating section. Don't take this warning lightly; you have no concept of how much water a 10,000-pound male orca can displace. Of course, sitting with your kids in the soak zone on a hot day is one of the great pleasures of SeaWorld, and most soak zone seating has the added advantage of affording views, through Plexiglass, into the tank where the animals prepare for their leaps and splashes. But for those with expensive hairdos, ponchos are sold throughout the parks, including at stalls beneath Shamu Stadium, for $6. Keep your camera and phone somewhere dry, because the salt water these animals live in will fry their circuits. As amphitheatres fill, you may not see the warning signs, which are painted on the ground or on benches, so bank on the first 10 rows as being the wettest. No theaters will expose you to the elements.

Anheuser-Busch recently poured money into revitalizing its marquee show, *Believe* ★★★, installing four rotating screens that interlock in various formations as well as a top-of-the-line sound system, and teaching the killer whales a fleet of new tricks. I wish it had bought some padding for the metal benches while it was shopping, but at least Shamu Stadium, which fits 5,000 and still fills early, is covered. The resulting show is irredeemably hokey gobbledy-gook laden with long periods during which trainers prattle on with quasi-inspirational gibberish ("You know, I think dreams are incredible, and the best part is no one can take them away from you . . .") and timpani-loaded music thunders meaningfully. But when the orcas start to fly, the crowd comes alive. Closed-circuit TV cameras capture and display their screams of delight as the animals thunder dauntingly through the water's surface, deluging entire seating sections in 52-°F water. It's quite a scene. The soak zone seats offer excellent views of the animals pushing their trusting trainers through the 2.5 million-gallon, 36-feet-deep tank, and the ones near the shelf-like middle platform will also have a close-up view of a killer whale out of the water. Seats at the back of the stadium, higher than the central aisle, will have to rely on the TV cameras to make out what's going on underwater. The 25-minute spectacle occurs on such a scale as to make it unmissable. There's also the potential that one day, one of the 24 orcas (only a few in the so-called "Shamu family" perform at a time) will suddenly remember its place on the food chain. Admit it—isn't that tension part of the draw?

From Memorial Day to early fall, the killer whales perform in repertory, as it were, with another abstract show, *Shamu Rocks*, which puts that expensive sound system to good use by pumping it with songs by Savage Garden, Rascal Flats, Shakira, and Coldplay. If I had to make a choice, I'd probably pick *Believe,* the flagship show. No matter which show you choose (don't do both unless you simply *must*), you'll be seeing the mighty creatures flopping and splashing with impressive intent.

A broadly slapstick 25-minute romp set aboard a pirate ship, *Clyde & Seamore Take Pirate Island* ★ 🧒 is the kind of cheesy, anthropomorphic act (sea lions doing double takes, saluting, and pretending to be choked by exasperated human companions) that's fallen out of favor in all but the hoariest circuses, yet its good-natured silliness ensures its standing as one of SeaWorld's most cherished shows. Kids particularly enjoy it, especially when the impossibly blubbery walrus oozes its way into the mayhem. The worst seats are to the left as you face the stage (they have partial views) and the best are to the right and near the front, by the stone bridge. Plan to combine this show with a visit to the Pacific Point Preserve, as you'll enter the amphitheatre from there.

SeaWorld perfected the kind of poppycock on display in *Believe* with *Blue Horizons* ★, a bizarre spectacle about a little girl who "wants to explore the realms beyond imagination." Whatever that means, the transfixing 25-minute show built around her (actually an adult trainer) is more like an acid trip at a carnival than anything else, which lends itself to loosely connected (but excellent nonetheless) stunts starring dolphins, parrots, a condor, and plenty of human acrobats hooked up to bungee cords and diving off high platforms. There's always something to see, and little to comprehend. Think of it as *Shark du Soleil.*

Under-5s lose their minds at *Pets Ahoy!* ★★ 🧒, and I have to admit I do, too—it's the show I most enjoy seeing repeatedly. Although the furry cast is a deviation from SeaWorld's usual finny ones, the tricks are no less entrancing. A menagerie of common animals (cats, dogs, pigs, ducks, a skunk), most rescued from animal shelters, do simple tricks, and independently trigger surprises on a highly rigged wharfside set. As the super-cute gags multiply and compound in rapid succession (dachshunds pour out of a hot dog cart, a cat chases a white mouse in and out of hatches), and as more creatures are added into the mix precisely on cue, the amusement compounds and avalanches. Best of all, there's nearly no dialogue for its 20-minute run time. Afterward, trainers will allow kids to come to the stage to pet some of the performers. It's fun to sit under the catwalk (literally—it's a catwalk) over the aisle between the first and second sections. Kids absolutely love seeing animals they understand do tricks, so this 850-seat theatre routinely fills well in advance of show times.

Also custom-designed for very young children, **Elmo and the Bookaneers,** a 20-minute *Sesame Street*–licensed show original to this park, plays April through Labor Day at Atlantis Bayside Stadium. Its theme is learning to read and its major stars include Cookie Monster, Bert, Ernie, and Elmo, so I guess you could say this show is one adults can prioritize low on their must-see lists, but one that parents with small kids should consider. Performance times are listed on the back of your map.

The most skippable of the shows is a wordless but exuberant revue of arty human performance called *Odyssea,* ostensibly inspired by the sea. Although there are some cool blacklight tricks, some gifted acrobats and tumblers, and some striking full-body puppetry (anyone else remember Mummenschanz?), there are no animals, which means that this 25-minute production, which might be a grade-A show at a lesser park, is mostly an opportunity to get into the air-conditioning at this one. I like it, but not at the expense of the rest of the park.

Staged on summer nights over the lake, *Mistify,* a multimedia fireworks-and-fountains spectacular, isn't as over-the-top as IllumiNations at Disney or Fantasmic! at Disney–MGM, but it's a pleasing way to end a day. You can see the action from anywhere on the lagoon, but the Atlantis Bayside Stadium is set up for the best views. Show up a half-hour early, as usual. The excellent seats at the Spice Mill's waterfront tables are taken by people who have their dinner there as early as 5pm and then hang out until the show. They need lives.

THE REST OF THE PARK

Some conservationists have complained that SeaWorld's animals are living in captivity. SeaWorld, in response, points out that it's sensitive to this issue, and it has not captured (or as it puts it, "collected") dolphins from the wild since 1969; excepting a few aged animals who were born in the seas and a few others rehabilitated from accidents in the wild, most of the park's animals were born there or at other zoos, and they were raised by hand. Releasing them back into the wild would be a death sentence. And although many of the shows here make these creatures appear more like clownish humans than the animals they are, it's arguable that at least SeaWorld is bringing a modicum of animal education to the masses, and it can't be argued that it mistreats its charges.

From the entrance plaza, veer right, past the ice cream parlor, to reach the **Dolphin Nursery** tank, where the young mammals are kept with their mothers for the first few years of their lives, before graduating to the larger Dolphin Cove elsewhere in the park. There have been 20 dolphin births at SeaWorld in the past 5 years, and much of the day, human trainers can be found here, feeding the adolescent animals and getting them acclimated to human interaction.

Left out of the entrance plaza, past the flamingoes (welcome to Florida), after passing the minor Turtle Point enclosure, you'll reach the **Whale & Dolphin Theatre,** where the *Blue Horizons* show is performed. To the left you'll find **Key West at SeaWorld,** a sorta-reproduction of Front Street in the southernmost city in Florida. As they do there, Jimmy Buffett songs play ad nauseam for tourists. Unlike in the real Keys, the **Stingray Lagoon,** a shallow pool where you can lean over and feel the spongy fish, is this section's *raison d'etre.* You can buy food to feed the rays for $4 per tray, two for $7, or three for $10. To the right of the Key West area, the **Dolphin Cove** is one of the park's most popular places. Feeding times for the bottlenose dolphins are regimented, and the schedule is posted at the entrance to the area. It costs $5 for just three fish, and interested parties must collect in a zone near the feeding area, to the right as you reach the tank. Around feeding times, dolphins congregate at the trainers' dock, which can make seeing them from other parts of the tank difficult, so if you won't be feeding them, come between meals for a better look. Walk around the far side of the tank, and you'll find a little-used underwater viewing area where you can hear the echolocative clicking through underwater microphones.

Following on from there (turn left after you exit Dolphin Cove), you'll next reach a pleasant but none-too-vibrant pavilion devoted to two of Florida's natives, the alligator and the manatee. At **Manatee Rescue** ★, which can only be entered by a circuitous entrance ramp that seems designed to manage crowds that just aren't there, much attention is paid to the manatee's status as one of America's most endangered animals, and, in fact, the sluggish creatures on display here were all rescued from the wild, where hot-dogging boaters are decimating their numbers. This is a cool, sheltered place to observe the creeping, pug-faced animals from below the waterline—if you're hot, seek respite in peace here.

Finally you'll reach the pocket of thrill rides. There are only two, and they're next to each other at the opposite end of the park from the Shamu show—when the killer whales perform, the crowds are lightest here. **Journey to Atlantis** ★★ is a 6-minute flume-cum-coaster ride (you can't see the brief coaster section from the front) designed with schadenfreude in mind. Getting away dry will be impossible, as the 60-foot drop should warn, although riding isn't its only pleasure—it's fun to douse passing boats with coin-operated water cannons, too.

Spoiler alert: Atlantis is oddball. First you pass through a few rooms as if you're on a family-friendly dark ride (the robotics are not terribly good), and then one of the spirits turns against you and sends you down the hill you saw outside, and finally the water gives way and your boat becomes, briefly, a roller-coaster car that escapes the evil sprite (weirdly, to the theme song of *Beetlejuice*—couldn't someone write something new?) with no upside-down moments but yet another splashdown. Besides the drenching you can see from the façade, there are a few other lap-soakers and delightfully nasty splashbacks—ideal for hot days. Front seats get wettest, and when you board, try to balance the weight; otherwise you'll spend the ride listing disconcertingly.

Next door is **Kraken** ★★★, a 2-minute coaster that gave SeaWorld some needed testosterone when it opened in 2000. After you settle into your pedestal-like seat, the floor is retracted, leaving your legs to dangle, and the ride is packed with seven upside-down "inversions" of one sort or another. The coaster, which hits 65mph and drops 144 feet on its first breath-stealing hill, traces the shoreline of a pond behind the loading area and dives below ground level three times. If you'd like to wait for a front seat, there's a special, longer line for it. Because it's floorless, you can't ride with flip-flops, but you may take them off at the loading dock and go barefoot (if you do that in the front row, which I recommend, you'll forever feel like you're about to lose a foot in the rails). All in all, Kraken is an excellent, smooth ride that balances light-headed moments with thrilling, swooping curves. Happily, since SeaWorld doesn't appeal most to thrill-seekers, the lines are rarely long—30 minutes would be a bargain. Inconveniently, the roller coaster requires you to stash your loose articles in a locker (for which you must pay 50¢—using two quarters—each time you close the door), but conveniently, because Atlantis is next door, you can just leave your possessions locked up for both rides, keeping them dry.

The centerpiece of **Penguin Encounter ★★★**, another popular pavilion, is a wide-windowed, chilly room where four types of penguins frolic among ice chips and frigid water. Visitors can either stand about 15 feet away from the window, below the waterline, and coast past on a moving walkway that alleviates gridlock, or stand on a riser 5 feet farther back, without the regimentation of having to move past. Or you can see it from the sidewalk and then double back using the riser. Two things become instantly clear: Penguins can swim like fish and they stink of them just as badly. What follows this absorbing spectacle is an educational exhibit about penguins and the Antarctic that deserves much more than to be ignored, the way it usually is. That's followed by a similar window to a habitat for puffins and murres.

Pacific Point Preserve ★, like the Dolphin Cove, is an open-air, rocky habitat that encourages feedings, but here, the residents are incessantly barking Californian sea lions and a few demure seals. There's a narrow moat between the tank and the walkway, but you're encouraged to lean over and toss the doglike animals fresh fish, which are sold for $4 per tray, $7 for two trays, and $10 for three. The area gets busy before and after the Clyde and Seamore show, which is mounted at the neighboring **Sea Lion & Otter Stadium.**

The onetime Terrors of the Deep is now wisely known as **Shark Encounter ★★** in an effort to further rehabilitate the public image of the much-maligned creatures within. It's one of the better exhibitions, with 60-foot acrylic tubes passing right through 300,000-gallons of water stocked with sharks—the crowds are ushered along via moving sidewalks. Too many tourists scamper quickly through the smaller tanks before that dazzling main event, but they're missing some beautiful stuff, including barracuda, moray eels, lionfish, and the awesome leafy seadragon, which looks for all the world like a floating clump of seaweed. Don't ignore the shallow tank in front of the building either, as that's where the smaller species are kept. If they were kept indoors, they'd be sushi for the bigger predators. There, you can feed the fish for the usual rates ($4 a tray, two for $7, three for $10, and four for $13). Those with loose change burning a hole in their pockets can actually arrange to dive with a special helmet in the shark tank; see p. 168 for that.

The Waterfront at SeaWorld is mostly an atmospheric 5-acre locale for restaurants, although the **Seaport Theatre** used by *Pets Ahoy!* is also here. Kids like to explore the shoreline, where artificial waves frequently kick up and spray them with plumes of water. Beginning at 9:57am and repeating every hour on the hour, there's a 5-minute "Day Fountain Show" in the harbor, synchronized to piped-in music. Jutting above the lagoon—and topped to still-greater heights by a colossal American flag—is the 400-foot **Sky Tower,** a soothing, old-fashioned "Wheel-o-vater" (that's what its interior label says) that slowly rotates as it climbs 300 feet for a panorama. At the top, it slowly spins for two or three revolutions, giving you a good look around, before lowering you back to the Waterfront at the end of 6 minutes. If you come to SeaWorld late in your visit, after you've familiarized yourself with the city, you'll be able to point out landmarks including Spaceship Earth, the Gaylord Palms, and the skyscrapers of downtown. Weirdly, SeaWorld sees fit to charge an additional $3 for this. Such nickel-and-diming is a turn-off (although perhaps necessary, as the wheel only holds 48 people at a time).

Continuing clockwise around the lagoon as you look at your map, the **Nautilus Theater** hosts *Odyssea,* and across the path, you can rent flamingo-shaped **paddleboats** for excursions on the lagoon ($6). The **Clydesdale Hamlet,** a farm among the aquaria, is a reminder of the beer company that owns the park. Now and then (times are on the back of your map), you may be treated to the incongruity of a beer wagon, topped by a Dalmatian, being pulled around the lagoon by six Clydesdale horses and blaring Bud's 1970s jingle ("When you say Bud, you've said it all . . ."). Otherwise, the beautiful animals will be loafing in this paddock. Next door is the **Anheuser-Busch Hospitality Center,** where adults can get a free cup of beer from the brewery's latest line. Structured tastings with a qualified brewmaster (if you can call a Budweiser brewmaster qualified) are also hosted here and include pairings with fruit and chocolate—times are noted on the park map, and reservations, though free, are required. Although the minimum age to participate is 21, there's a glassed-in kids' play area within sight of the sampling room, so parents who want to imbibe won't have to lose track of Junior. You'll also find a hollow exhibition about the company's history. Don't be anywhere near this place when the Shamu shows finish (a half-hour after they start), because the line for beer can spindle out the door then.

After you pass the **video arcade** and **midway,** on the left, you reach **Shamu Stadium,** home of the big show. Even when it's not show time, a few of the killer whales are visible in the **Underwater Viewing** area that surveys one of their holding pods; above the surface of that pen, the **Dine with Shamu** supper is held, separated by cargo netting from the water (p. 91; reserve several weeks ahead).

Around the back of the Stadium is the principal kids' area, **Shamu's Happy Harbor** 🧒. This is where SeaWorld is currently applying its improvement energies. Several mild carnival-style rides were added in 2007: an underwater-themed **Sea Carousel** topped by a 45-foot-wide pink octopus; a swinging-and-twirling tracked boat ride, **Ocean Commotion;** and **The Flying Fiddler,** which lifts kids 20 feet above the ground and then gently brings them back down in a series of short drops. Those rides join an 800-foot kiddie coaster with trains shaped like you-know-who **(Shamu Express),** a four-story playground with slides and nets, a ride with spinning cars attached to a stalk **(Jazzy Jellies),** a pirate ship *(Wahoo Two)* with a few water blasters, and a teacup-style ride **(Swishy Fishies).** The theme is limp, but the size of the play area is as big or bigger than anything the other parks have. Small children could be transfixed for 2 to 3 hours here, while their parents are woefully exposed to the sun as they wait.

Wild Arctic ★★★, one of the most interesting exhibitions, deserves more than to be marooned here, at the Nowhereseville end of the park. There are two

---

What the Basics Cost at SeaWorld

Parking: $10
Single strollers: $10 per day
Double strollers: $17 per day
Wheelchair: $10 per day
ECV: $35 per day
Lockers: $1.50 per day
Coke: $2.39
Bottle of water: $2.59

---

ways to get in. Either you opt for the motion-simulator ride that re-creates a turbulent 5-minute helicopter ride (well done for such an old ride, but its bumpiness makes me ill), or you whiz around that much more quickly and make straight for the swimmers. After that, you can walk through at your own pace, enjoying first a surface view and then an underwater look at the two Pacific walruses, four polar bears (you won't see much—they sleep 16–18 hours a day), and the parks' utterly beautiful white beluga whales, which look like swimming porcelain. There's probably more than a half-hour's worth of investigation here, including mock-ups of a polar research station, a fake "bear den" for young kids to explore, and hands-on exhibits about the ecology and research of the area. You'll also find it *very* cool, which makes it a blockbuster on hot days. The pavilion is staffed by red-coated zookeepers, who are there to field your questions—they never insult your intelligence by acting like they've heard the same queries before.

The long shoreline path back to the entrance area passes only the **Atlantis Bayside Stadium,** which hosts *Mistify* in summer and the week before New Year's but sits empty most of the winter. I much prefer crossing the lagoon on the boardwalk-like bridge that bisects it from Shamu Stadium to the Waterfront.

WHERE TO EAT AT SEAWORLD

The good news is that compared to other parks, SeaWorld has the edge in food quality, and it beat everyone else in the rush to provide healthy options. The bad news is prices are just as sickening as everyone else's: $9 a meal, before a drink, is standard across the board. Most of the places to eat cluster in the center of the park between the Waterfront and Kraken.

Disney World has its Mouse-ear ice cream bar, but at SeaWorld, you'll be served a variety shaped like Shamu ($3). Drinking straws could choke the aquatic animals, so drinks are served without them. If you must have a straw, the $6 souvenir cups have them built in, and they grant $1.50 refills. Beers cost $3.79 a glass, unless they're at the Hospitality Center, in which case your first one's free.

My favorite place to eat in the park is **Mama's Kitchen** ★★, opposite the Penguin Encounter. Everything served here is less than 750 calories (though most are much less) and contains less than 25 grams of fat, sides and all. That translates into items such as a chef's salad, veggie chili, a turkey sandwich with whole wheat pasta salad ($8.59), and pan-seared chicken breast sandwiches. A meal here will cost about $1 more than one had elsewhere in the park, but it won't make you feel heavy the way the burgers, fries, and pizzas at the common quick-service counters will. By noon, because the food happens to be good, the line here is disheartening long, so eat around 11am if you can.

Turkey sandwiches at the **Hospitality Deli,** in the Hospitality Center, are $7.29 including potato salad—you save $1.50 over Mama's Kitchen, and although they're not quite as healthily made, the only thing you'll lack will be whole wheat pasta. The Deli's other choices are also less healthy, but decent, such as a beef stew served in a bread bowl ($8), a bratwurst sandwich ($6), and a few carvery sandwiches ($7.29), all with a hefty glob of potato salad.

The other main restaurants serve high-quality food, too, but with less caloric regard. The **Seafire Inn,** at the Waterfront, charges $8.29 to $10 for burgers, of course, but interesting ones such as jalapeno cheddar burgers and also inventive dishes such as tropical chicken stir-fry and mahimahi with piña colada sauce. The Seafire also has some seating overlooking the lagoon—it's where the Makahiki Luau dinnertainment show is held each night, which is why lunch is its big meal. Farther up the Waterfront but with similar prices, the **Spice Mill Cafe** ★★ does zestier stuff such as Caribbean jerk chicken sandwiches (surprisingly well spiced), Cajun jambalaya with peppered andouille sausage, and fish sandwiches battered with Bud. **Voyagers,** facing the Seaport Theatre's entrance, offers wood-fired pizzas; compared to the other choices at the Waterfront, that's boring.

A few years ago, the park converted a section of the underwater viewing area at the shark tank to **Sharks Underwater Grill,** which is now one of the park's premier tables. Despite some cute touches, such as a bar that's also an aquarium and chairs that look like sharks' teeth, prices around $23 a plate for Caribbean-style fish strikes me as too high. But if you can square that with the incredible view and not feel gypped, give it a shot. Some tables are right against the glass, but I think I prefer the ones farther back, which have a more panoramic view.

For snacks, I suggest the **Cypress Bakery,** located near the entrance. The carrot cake ($3.50) sold there is huge, fluffy, and arguably among the best you'll have anywhere. The parks employees are hooked on it. Another SeaWorld-specific snack: the $3.50 strawberry-banana smoothies sold at Freeza's cart parked alongside the Voyagers building.

The **Smoky Creek** BBQ place, facing the back of the Seaport Theatre, is for sauce-drenched meats served with fries and a dinner roll: a half-chicken is $8.29, but a full chicken is $9.29, so get that and split it. Corn on the cob is $2.

SeaWorld participates in the great Orlando tradition of huge roasted **turkey legs.** Find them for $4.75 (a buck cheaper than Disney's) at the **Smuggler's Feasts** booth at the Waterfront entrance to the cross-lagoon boardwalk. At the Shamu end of the boardwalk, **Mango Joe's Cafe** does a short menu of fajitas ($8), fajita salad ($7), and chicken fingers with fries ($8.29); only eat there if you're stuck in Shamu-land and don't want to brave the 10-minute walk back around the lagoon.

DISCOVERY COVE

Most of the accents you'll hear at SeaWorld's marvelous secondary park are British, which should tell you something—because of the exchange rate, they're the only people who can afford tickets. The 30-acre **Discovery Cove** (☎ 877/434-7268; www.discoverycove.com) was created and priced expressly as a five-star experience. Only around 1,000 people a day are admitted, guaranteeing this faux tropical idyll will not be marred by a single queue. You can stop reading now if you don't want to get jealous—this is strictly a special-occasion place.

From January to mid-March and again from mid-November until the end of the year, you get in for $159, and from mid-March to mid-November, admission is $179. Then, to get the most out of your day, you add $100 if you want a 30-minute supervised swim with dolphins. Thoughtfully, if a named tropical storm or hurricane heads for Orlando or even your own hometown on the day of your booking, you can cancel and get your money back—but if a thunderstorm shuts the water down for a few hours, you're out of pocket. The deal also includes breakfast, equipment rental, sunscreen, unlimited free beer (if you're of age), as well as lunch—and a good one, too, such as fresh grilled salmon (a fish that drew the short straw at SeaWorld, I guess).

Discovery Cove, in fact, is more or less a free-range playground. When you arrive, first thing in the morning, you're greeted under a vaulted atrium more redolent of a five-star island resort than a theme park. Coffee is poured, and once you're checked in (and, if you're swimming with dolphins, you've been assigned your time), you're set loose to do as you wish. Wade in **The Ray Pool** among tame and barbless stingrays, feed fresh fruit to the houseguests at the **Tropical Bird Aviary,** snorkel in the **Exotic Fish Lagoon,** or ride an inner tube down the slow-floating **Tropical River,** which passes through the aviary by way of some waterfalls, keeping the birds from escaping. Many of the guests elect to simply kick back on a lounger (there are plenty) on incredibly silky sand (imported, of course) at the natural-looking pool. Other than that, you read a book and relax. Without a dolphin swim, there's not really enough value to fill a day. When it's your turn—and if you've paid—guests over the age of 5 can head to the **Dolphin Lagoon,** where you change into a wetsuit and a trainer briefs you for a half-hour on bottlenose dolphin basics, and then in small groups of about eight, you wade into the chilly water, where more trainers introduce you to one of the pod. Like children, they have distinct personalities and must be carefully paired to people the trainers think they'll enjoy being with—many visitors don't realize as they wade into the waves that in the wild, a dolphin can easily kill you. Here, the hand-reared animals peer at you with a logician's eye while your trainer shows you how to use hand signals for communication. The climax of the 30-minute interaction is the moment when you grasp the creature's dorsal fin and it swims, you in tow, for 30 or so feet. The experience is more limited than you might expect, and the fact other groups around you are midvisit makes it feel contrived, but it's magical for some people. Although many parks around the world allow for dolphin interaction for much less money, not all of them are reputable, and most should not be patronized. The constant public scrutiny SeaWorld is under, and the high value its zoologists place on conservation, means these animals are well treated, and when they don't feel like performing, they don't have to. You're paying for reputable animal keepers. Naturally, a SeaWorld

Past that Turnstile in the Sky

Not all of Orlando's attractions have thrived. Tupperware Museum, we miss you. Kindly remove your Mouse Ears to honor the forgotten fun—if not for an accident of time, you'd be vacationing here instead:

Circus World (1974–1986): Started by Mattel as a walk-through museum dedicated to circus history (after all, most of the Big Top crews wintered in Florida), it collapsed under its own weight after competition with Disney tempted it into building too many rides. Also, clowns are scary.

Boardwalk Baseball (1987–1990): Textbook publisher Harcourt, Brace and Jovanovich recycled Circus World in the image of Florida's other winter tradition, baseball, and the Kansas City Royals were enticed to train there. Few cared. On January 17, 1990, its 1,000 guests were asked to leave. The land, near U.S. 27 and I-4 southwest of Disney, is only now being redeveloped.

Xanadu (1983–1996): This walk-through "home of the future" was made by coating giant balloons with polyurethane—an early exercise in ergonomics. Sister homes in Gatlinburg and Wisconsin Dells were also built, but all outlived their curiosity value, and became, in fact, quick homes of the past. You'll find the site near Mile Marker 12 of U.S. 192.

JungleLand Zoo (1995–2002): The demise of this low-rent Gatorland rip-off was hastened in 1997 by news coverage after a lioness escaped from her enclosure and went missing among Kissimmee's motels for 3 days. A few trainers got nipped by the gators, too. Bad news.

Splendid China (1993–2003): On 73 acres 3 miles west of Disney's main gate, China's wonders (the Forbidden City, a Great Wall segment containing 6.5 million bricks, and so on) were rebuilt in miniature. Who would blow $100 million on such a clearly bad idea? The Chinese government, which pulled the strings. The site is being rebuilt with vacation homes, but U.S. 192's high concentration of Chinese buffets is now explained.

River Country (1976–2005): Disney's first water park, incorporated into Bay Lake beside the Fort Wilderness Resort, simply wasn't fancy enough or big enough to satisfy guests anymore. Another issue: It turns out that the *Naegleria fowleri* amoebae growing in many Florida lakes can kill you. (Guests may no longer swim in *any* of Disney's lakes. Coincidence?)

photographer is on hand for it all, so if you want images or video, you'll pay for that, too. That means if you're not careful, your day could cost around $400.

If you crave dolphin interaction at a lower price, SeaWorld offers a $40 feeding session at its Dolphin Nursery (p. 207). You won't swim with them, but you will spend 30 minutes plopping fish into their eagerly clacking gullets.

BUSCH GARDENS AFRICA

Fewer Americans make their way to **Busch Gardens Africa** (3000 E. Busch Blvd., at 40th St., 8 miles northwest of Tampa; ☎ 888/800-5447; www.buschgardens.com; $62 adults, $52 kids 3–9) than to the other Central Florida parks, not because it's bad. It's actually a terrific park, with attractions and a professionalism on a par with the Orlando ones, but it's also about 70 miles southwest of Disney, which seems to daunt most people. (Oddly, foreign visitors are much more likely to make the trek.) That's too bad, because the park, which measures just shy of the ten most-visited in America, offers more than enough to fill a day on two important fronts: exotic animal sightings and roller-coaster ridings. In fact, Busch Gardens matches Disney's Animal Kingdom on the safari front and whups it completely in rides, but all must bow to the caliber of Disney's shows. The bulk of Busch Gardens' six coasters are highly rated by enthusiasts.

The park started small, in 1959, as a free hospitality center attached to a Budweiser bottling plant. Guests would watch animal performances in a tropical setting, raise a beer, and go home. The idea outlived the factory. The rest is history.

But just what the heck is this place called? You'll see Busch Gardens, Busch Gardens Tampa Bay, and Busch Gardens Africa—all on the company's own information. The short answer: Busch Gardens' location in Williamsburg, Virginia, is dubbed Busch Gardens Europe, while this Tampa Bay one, with its lions and other African animals, was recently distinguished with an Africa tag. So all three names are correct, but Busch Gardens Africa is most current.

For ticket discounts, see the section about the FlexTicket on p. 321, which grants good deals if you're going to visit Universal Orlando and SeaWorld on the same trip. There is enough for voracious tourists to justify coming for 2 days (most of us see the highlights in 1 day), and if you find you want to return, present your ticket on the way out for a next-day ticket costing just $11.

Members of AARP receive $8 discounts on Tuesdays, and on other days, their discount is $5. Members of the military should always ask if there's a deal on; Anheuser-Busch is a devoutly patriotic organization and frequently offers free admission to active members and up to three of their family members; check www.herosalute.com to see what's offered.

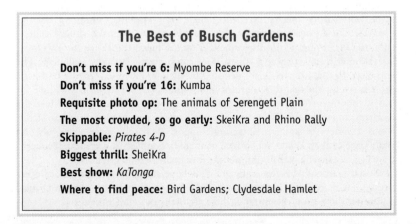

The Best of Busch Gardens

Don't miss if you're 6: Myombe Reserve

Don't miss if you're 16: Kumba

Requisite photo op: The animals of Serengeti Plain

The most crowded, so go early: SkeiKra and Rhino Rally

Skippable: *Pirates 4-D*

Biggest thrill: SheiKra

Best show: *KaTonga*

Where to find peace: Bird Gardens; Clydesdale Hamlet

You don't have to rule out Busch Gardens if you don't have a car. The park offers a daily **Shuttle Express** (☎ 800/221-1339; $10 round-trip, reservations required), which takes about an hour each way. The service is free for those who purchase a 5-Park Orlando FlexTicket (p. 321), and it picks up passengers at seven locations throughout the Orlando tourist corridor, from I-Drive to U.S. 192.

Busch Gardens offers a few behind-the-scenes tours which, for added expense, get you face-to-snout with the animals or educational experiences with trainers. See p. 252 for more information on those. Also check the park's website for upcoming events; zoological superstars such as Jack Hanna make regular appearances, and special holiday events are mounted around Halloween and Christmas. The park also runs **Adventure Island,** a water park, but that's mostly patronized by locals; Orlando's choices are superior.

TOURING BUSCH GARDENS AFRICA

Roller-coaster mavens should knock down a few of the big-ticket rides (SheiKra, Kumba, Gwazi) early in the day before lines build—I beeline to Stanleyville first, for SheiKra—but take care to lock your loose belonging in the front-of-park lockers first, because if you forget, you'll have to spend 50¢ in quarters each time you open the ones by the coasters as you travel through the park. People who have come for the animals can keep their bags and take a more leisurely pace, perhaps slipping in a few shows that are listed by time on the back of the park map (although I find that there's more than enough to do between the rides and the animals—the shows here feel like filler). A tamer ride that garners a huge line is Rhino Rally, so families with younger kids might consider going there first. Generally speaking, as you look at your park map, the thrill rides congregate on the left-hand side of the map (the park's western half), and the animal enclosures are more on the right-hand side (the east).

After you park, you'll board a tram that brings you to the front gate (budget at least 15 min. for the process); you could technically walk the distance, but that will take about 20 minutes, as the entrance gate is not near the lot. As at all parks, the entry area, here themed **Morocco** and dressed like the most spacious souk you've ever seen, is for shopping and chores, although *KaTonga: Musical Tales from the Jungle* ★, mounted at scheduled times at the Moroccan Palace Theater, is worth a stop for show fans; it's an arresting, African-themed Broadway-style revue noteworthy for its excellent female pop vocalists, strikingly colorful imagery, and intricate costumes. It's the one show I'd make time for here, although its 35-minute running time eats up too much thrill time for my tastes.

The one thing you can't fail to do is pick up a placemat-sized map. The entrances to the attractions are denoted by little red arrows. On the back, the show times for the half-dozen presentations are listed, but if you're only here for 1 day, those won't be your focus. Instead, turn your attention to the **Meet the Keepers** timetable, where you can arrange to hear a zookeeper share knowledge about a variety of animals, including hippos, elephants, giraffe, and uh, the Budweiser donkey. Whenever you see "Animal Encounter," it just means zookeepers will draw from a grab-bag of possibilities each time they're held.

Busch Gardens' themed lands aren't as large or as strictly themed as other parks'. Taken roughly clockwise off the map, and in the order that you'd encounter them from the entrance, here are the park highlights:

Bird Gardens: At the transition from Morocco, the two entangled wooden coasters comprising **Gwazi** ★★, opened in 1999 on the site of the old brewery, and are among the fiercest, most intense wooden coasters you're likely to ride, with plenty of high-speed, banked turns that thrillingly cause you to doubt that the wood could ever hold together under the stress. On off-peak days, only one of the tracks, named Lion and Tiger, may be open, and although they differ in layout, they're the same in their bucking, screeching demeanor. The 2½-minute, 50mph ride is best experienced when both tracks are running; along with Islands of Adventure's Dueling Dragons, these are the only coasters in the world specially designed to provide multiple near-misses (in this case, six) when both trains are running at the right timing. Because the cars are so cumbersome to load and the line moves so slowly, they are rarely dispatched together. Either ride first thing or in midafternoon after lines die.

The rest of Bird Gardens—the original nucleus of the park, dating to 1959—is, of course, avian in nature, including a **Flamingo Island** enclosure and an **Aviary Walk-Thru.** Perhaps the most patronized building is the **Hospitality House,** distinguished by its fabulous, triangular Jet Age roof folds, where visitors can claim one free beer a day (after all, Anheuser-Busch owns the park) and join a beer tasting led by a qualified brewmaster (reservations required; free). Across the way, pop into **Xcursions,** Busch Gardens' effort to stock a shop with interesting internationally made gifts, plus some science-oriented kids' toys; proceeds go to the park's conservation fund. It's easily the most interesting store on-site. As the Gardens creep toward Stanleyville, there's also a **Land of the Dragons** 🦎 kids' playground, the most elaborate area for kids in the park—with a single entrance, it's easy for parents to police.

Stanleyville: Named for a city in the Congo (now Kisangani) once popular with colonialist explorers of Africa, this section is popular mostly because of **SheiKra** ★★★, a "dive coaster" with a design unique to America: It sends cars 200 feet up, where they hang, tantalizingly, for 5 seconds on a precipice before finally being released down a shocking 90-degree drop at 70mph. Just marvel at the thing—you can't get any steeper than straight down. From there, the three-row cars, which seat so many people (24) they look like mini-theatres, take a second dive before swooping across the surface of a pond, where "water brakes" send up rooster-tailed plumes and slow things back down. Adding to the trauma, in the summer of 2007 the cars were redesigned to be floorless, so there's nothing but empty air between you and oblivion. Queue early, as it's the one everyone wants to ride this year. The first row, for my tastes, is the most thrilling because from there you seem to be dangling helplessly. After you stagger off, check out Busch Gardens' latest innovation: Instead of taking your photo on the ride, as so many Orlando parks do, a *movie* of three peak moments is recorded and spliced together with stock footage of the rest of the ride to provide you with a $20 DVD of your petrifying plunge. Mark my words: It's the next big souvenir trend in Orlando. Plain old photos are available for $14.

SheiKra may be the future, but the rest of Stanleyville is full of tried-and-true rides from a previous generation. The **Stanley Falls Flume** ★, erected in 1973, is one of the industry's most beloved (and doggedly old-fashioned) log flume rides, with a 43-foot drop. As more parks remove these reliable charmers, this one has risen to be America's longest. **Tanganyika Tidal Wave** is a short group boat ride—up, down 55 feet, splash—designed simply to soak everything you can imagine. If you want to get wet, you don't have to wait in line, because there's a bridge squarely in the splash range. But my favorite old warhorse is the **Skyride,** a gondola-style bucket seating four that travels from here to another station near the entrance to Edge of Africa, passing over some wild animals on the way. Almost every other amusement park in America has dismantled their equivalents, including the Disney parks, but Busch Gardens keeps its unusually long specimen lovingly maintained. There's also a train station here for the **Serengeti Railway** ★★★, which I'll describe more fully in the Nairobi section.

Congo: In 2007, this section underwent such a major renovation that at press time large patches of it had been returned to bare earth. Building permits filed by the park have applied for a $2 million "African Village and zoo attraction," reportedly to be called Jungle Village and to open in 2008. In the meantime, some excellent rides remain. **Congo River Rapids** is a round-boat rapids ride much like Islands of Adventure's Bilge-Rat Barges and Animal Kingdom's Kali River Rapids—this one will likely soak you, but probably not drench you, although you never can tell. The boats also tend to jerk around when they bump against the walls. Lines get extensive in the heat, but at least it's a cooling ride. **Ubanga-Banga Bumper Cars** and the Congo station of the **Serengeti Railway** are also found here, but the star attraction is **Kumba** ★★, which hits 60mph on ominously noisy nylon wheels and lasts nearly 3 minutes. The tallest drop is 135 feet, and its vertical loop was the world's largest when it was built (1993). From the moment you crest the first hill, there's barely a letup in its smoothly powerful arsenal of loops and swoops, making this loud beast an enthusiasts' favorite (many swear the back rows are best). The line is usually minimal first thing in the morning.

Timbuktu: This tacky area, the middle of the park, is hardly its heart. It's mostly a tawdry area slotted with a few **kiddie rides** and some **midway games.** In addition, coaster nuts value the tightly packed, loopy **Scorpion** coaster because it's one of a diminishing breed designed by Anton Schwarzkopf, an important German manufacturer. It also has only lap bar restraints, no shoulder bars—the centrifugal force of the loops keeps riders glued into their seats. Less remarkable is the **Cheetah Chase** 🧒 coaster, nothing more than a "wild mouse," carnival-style ride that zips back and forth around a tiny plot of land; it's for families, not hardened thrill-seekers. **Phoenix** is a pirate ship that swings and eventually goes all the way upside-down. The current tenant of the Timbuktu Theater is *Pirates 4-D,* a 3-D movie combined with special effects (such as water sprays) that make you feel like you're part of the action; you can tailor your expectations accordingly when I tell you it stars Eric Idle and Leslie Nielsen. (Translation: Skip it if you want.)

Nairobi: This area *is* the heart of the park as it's one of the best places to dig into animal learning. **Myombe Reserve** ★★★ is a spectacular, tropical rainforest walk-through habitat with a three-story waterfall. Inside, a troop of western lowland gorillas dwells behind glass (well, you're behind glass—they're outdoors). Beyond them, a colony of chimpanzees lives in its own habitat. If the animals happen to be hanging out by the windows, staring right back at the tourists and interacting

What the Basics Cost at Busch Gardens Africa

Parking: $9
Single strollers: $10 per day
Double strollers: $15 per day
Wheelchair: $10 per day
ECV: $35 per day
Lockers: $1.50 per day
Regular soda: $2.39
Water: $2.59

with them, then you could spend a long, happy time in here. The walk-through **Nairobi Field Station** ✯ is where baby animals are raised, and zookeepers are often on hand to answer questions. One of the park's most original attractions is **Rhino Rally** ✯✯, which starts off just like Disney's Kilimanjaro Safaris—passengers board free-wheeled safari vehicles, driven by narrators, for a romp through faux African terrain stocked with elephants, zebras, and (sometimes) rhinos. You won't learn much—Asian elephants are mixed up with African rhinos, and the script makes facile reductions such as telling you the Zambezi River is simply "in Africa." But the second half, during which your vehicle stalls on a floating bridge that ends up breaking free and shooting some river rapids, is truly unique and makes an otherwise ho-hum experience worth the trip. The complexity of the ride means loads can be slow and lines therefore grim, so if you're not game for one of the coasters, come here instantly upon the park's opening. You don't have to ride to see the Asian elephants; they're located in an enclosure visible from the path to Timbuktu. Look for the alligator known as Big Joe; he was sent here by NASA, which was understandably concerned when they found him one day in the waters used by astronauts for their splashdown rehearsals.

The other must-do ride is the 2½-mile, **Serengeti Railway** ✯✯✯, which may be boarded here for a 40-minute round-trip. At other parks, the choo-choo is the boring thing you take toddlers or grandparents on, but at Busch Gardens, it's the primary way to explore the main animal enclosure, the 65-acre Serengeti Plain, which follows this station stop. The train makes a near-complete revolution of that area, past fields containing roaming giraffe, black and white rhinoceroses, and all sorts of antelope. This leg, which takes 20 minutes, is the best on the circuit. Next, the train stops at Congo (beneath Kumba, near the kids' rides), and then in Stanleyville (beneath SheiKra) before returning here. The walking distance between those last two stations is really only about 2 minutes, and no animals are currently visible on the ride between them.

Crown Colony/Egypt: The next two lands are so small they're practically united. Crown Colony is where the **Skyride** ✯ bucket gondola alights and re-boards for its trip to Stanleyville, as well as where you can see a few Clydesdale horses doing a lot of nothing in the **Clydesdale Hamlet.** Horse lovers can dash into the **Show Jumping Hall of Fame,** which is located here, of all places. The requisite **Edge of Africa** ★★ is an excellent 16-acre, walk-through collection of habitats themed, exhilaratingly, on meat eaters, including lions, hyena (the rival populations are kept in adjoining pens—and swapped every so often—just to keep them on their toes), crocodiles, and a bevy of hippopotami visible from below the waterline. In Egypt, the standout ride is the 3-minute **Montu** ★, a smooth-riding "inverted" coaster on which passengers feet dangle as they're flipped upside-down seven times at up to 65mph. Because this one's located in a distant dogleg of the park, lines don't usually get too daunting.

WHERE TO EAT AT BUSCH GARDENS AFRICA
Expect prices for a meal to hover around $8, not including a drink. Although counter service locations dot the park, here are my picks for the most interesting choices, each of which has added entertainment:

- ◆ **Bird Gardens:** The **Hospitality House** ★★ books bands that play outdoors; inside, you can grab healthy sandwiches, pizza, and, of course, your cup of free beer, and then head back out and picnic to the music.
- ◆ **Stanleyville:** The **Zambia Smokehouse** does chicken, ribs, and beef brisket with both indoor and outdoor seating; the latter overlooks SheiKra's dramatic water-sled landing.
- ◆ **Timbuktu:** The **Desert Grill Restaurant** ★ does carvery sandwiches and pastas. Thoughtfully, the park schedules lunchtime entertainment by vocal groups and bands; check the back of your park map for show times.
- ◆ **Crown Colony:** The **Crown Colony House** ★ is the park's premium restaurant, overlooking the Serengeti Plain; if you're lucky, the animals will come close. Prices aren't as steep as you'd think. Salads cost around $10, sandwiches $9, and the middle-of-the-road entrees (broiled herb salmon, filet mignon) run $14 to $22. The least expensive meal is a bowl of clam chowder for $4.25. Family-style dinners including fried chicken and Budweiser batter-dipped fish are $13 for adults and $7 for kids—not a bad bargain.

7 Beyond the Major Parks

Past the turnstiles, you'll find lots more to do

WHEN YOU'RE SICK OF PARKING TRAMS, CATTLE-CALL QUEUES, AND THE relentless patronization that comes with theme park "magic," it's time to divert yourself with something new. In many cases, something old—some of these places are among the original attractions that sowed the seeds enabling the area to become the powerhouse it now is. Some are serious, some are downright silly, but when you're on vacation, anything goes.

INTERNATIONAL DRIVE AREA

My favorite water park in the world for pound-for-pound thrills **Wet 'n Wild** ★★★ (kids) (6200 International Dr., Orlando; ☎ 800/992-9453 or 407/351-1800; www.wetnwildorlando.com; $36 adults, $30 kids 3–9; hours vary, but it generally opens at 9am or 10am and closes at 5pm in winter and as late as 11pm weekends in the summer) is located smack in the middle of the I-Drive area. It's tough to top this, the world's first water theme park, which was opened in 1977 by George Millay, the same guy who started SeaWorld. Other parks outdo it in landscaping and elaborate theming, but Wet 'n Wild is still the purist's paragon—a tightly packed coil of get-to-the-point thrills. If Blizzard Beach is a blissful resort, this is a carnival. There are no cutesy frills at this compact park; the decor consists of steel framework, pale concrete pathways, and screams. Most water is heated, and the bigger rafts are hoisted to the top of the ride scaffolds by conveyors.

After stashing booty in the multi-entry lockers to the right of the main gates (you can leave your money behind, because the park issues RFID-enabled wristbands that allow you to make purchases with a wave of your hand), stake out a beach chair if you want one, because free loungers go fast; parents tend to sit out the slides by hanging at the central, 17,000-square-foot **Surf Lagoon** or in the main kiddie area. You needn't be an excellent swimmer—lifeguards carefully monitor everything, even if most of them are still on Student Council, and riders are dispatched one at a time so there's no competition in the chutes. Most pools are shallow enough to stand in—but a copious supply of waterproof sunblock is a must, and nonslip, waterproof footwear, such as swimming socks, is recommended because you'll be padding around on concrete.

The coolest contraptions include **The Flyer,** a four-rider toboggan run, not unlike a winter luge, through banked turns and speedy straightaways; and **The Black Hole,** a two-person raft (sorry, soloists) that whisks blindly through a pitch-black tube, pierced only momentarily by disorienting strips of lights. **The Storm,** nicknamed "The Toilet," is a gently curving tube that gets your body going and sends it swirling into what might be best called a 30-foot john. You spiral around on your back until you're finally carried to a central drain of sorts and plopped, thoroughly disoriented, into a deep pool. The line can be long for that, depending on whether they're running one or both tubes. Atop the tower to the right of Surf Lagoon, **Bomb Bay** is the park's scariest ride. Six stories high, riders step into an enclosed cylinder above a 78-degree chute that drops as close to vertically as physics and lawyers will allow. A sadistic attendant peeks through a window to make sure your arms and legs are crossed, and without warning, hits the release button on a trap door, dropping traumatized riders down the flume below at wedgie speed. The lines for this one aren't as long as you might expect—the wimp-out rate is high. Its sister slide, **Der Stuka,** is almost as scary, but comes without the torture of the trap door and with a slightly-less-vertical incline. **Brain Wash** is a white-knuckle standout worth waiting for—rafts carrying two or four people are dropped down the wall of an 65-foot-wide funnel that's turned on its side. **The Blast** is a soaking ride past colorful broken pipes—making it good for younger kids—and **The Surge** sends a family-style round raft down a fun but unspectacular course.

A few of my top favorites are rides that you might not realize, at first glance, are as much fun as they are. **Bubba Tub** is a round raft that shoots more or less straight down a humped course—when you get your friends or family on it with you, though, the rushing, hopping journey feels out-of-control and awfully exhilarating. But the best ride at Wet 'n Wild is **Disco H$_2$0,** in which cloverleaf-shaped rafts (two to four people) are accelerated in a tube and sent spinning around an enclosed chamber where disco music plays and lights spin; eventually, the raft is washed out a chute in the middle. It's ridiculous fun, and so the lines are longest here. The group of **Mach 5** flumes is cherishably old-school, the kind parks don't build anymore, ridden with just a mat. My friends wonder how I can get going so fast, so I'll let you in on my secret: Only let your elbows and knees touch, reducing drag. You have to tote your own mat to the top for these. The **Lazy River,** a tame floating stream, has nothing on Disney's, so don't bother looking for a hard-to-find free inner tube unless you simply *must.*

Universal Orlando owns the park now, which qualifies it for the FlexTicket discount plan (p. 321). The prime maintenance period is September to March, so during those months, at least one major ride at a time will be out of rotation.

Across the street, at one of only a few "vertical wind tunnels" in America, the air blowing from beneath the wire-mesh floor is powerful enough to levitate any person, large or small, and for $40, you'll be given a few go-rounds in the simulated skydive chamber at SkyVenture ★★ (6805 Visitor Circle, Orlando; ☎ 407/ 903-1150; www.skyventureorlando.com; $40 per person; Mon–Fri 2–11:30pm, weekends noon–11:30pm). You'd swear it was a tourist trap, but surprisingly, there seem to be as many hobby skydivers training as there are curious out-of-towners, making this a rare attraction that locals don't sniff at. The concept is essentially that of a vertical wind tunnel (the fan is safely behind tough netting) that approximates the effect of skydiving, except you're never more than a few feet off the ground. Visitors are strapped into jumpsuits and given a short training session on how to walk into the 125mph airflow—mastering the necessary arched-back, splay-legged posture can be tricky, but should you fail, there's a master diver with you to grab you by the sleeve and guide you into a series of adrenaline-fueled climbs and plunges. Or not—you can just hover there, if that's what floats your butt. And it sure beats having to jump out of a plane. A standard ticket is good

International Drive Area Attractions

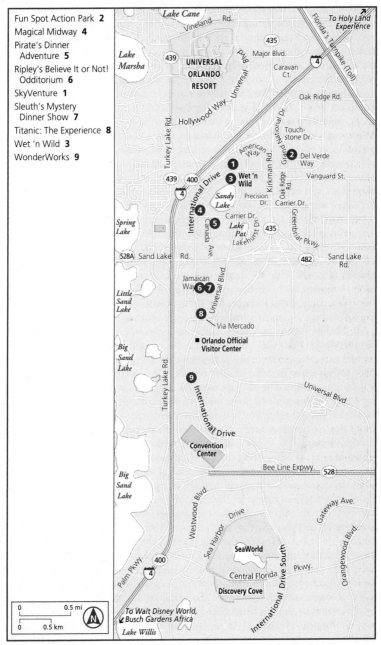

Fun Spot Action Park **2**

Magical Midway **4**

Pirate's Dinner
Adventure **5**

Ripley's Believe It or Not!
Odditorium **6**

SkyVenture **1**

Sleuth's Mystery
Dinner Show **7**

Titanic: The Experience **8**

Wet 'n Wild **3**

WonderWorks **9**

Lake Cane

Vineland Rd.

To Holy Land Experience

Florida's Turnpike (Toll)

435

Major Blvd.

Lake Marsha

439

UNIVERSAL ORLANDO RESORT

Caravan Ct.

Oak Ridge Rd.

Hollywood Way

Turkey Lake Rd.

Universal

Pine

Grand National Dr.

Touchstone Dr.

Del Verde Way

American Way

Kirkman Rd.

Vanguard St.

❶

439 400

International Drive

❸ Wet 'n Wild

Sandy Lake

Precision Dr.

Oak Ridge Rd.

Carrier Dr.

Greenbriar Pkwy.

4

❹

❺

Carrier Dr.

Lake Pat

435

Lakehurst Dr.

Canada Ave.

Spring Lake

528A Sand Lake Rd.

482

Sand Lake Rd.

Little Sand Lake

Jamaican Way

❻❼

Universal Blvd.

❽

Via Mercado

■ Orlando Official Visitor Center

Big Sand Lake

Turkey Lake Rd

❾

International Drive

Universal Blvd.

Convention Center

Bee Line Expwy. 528

Big Sand Lake

Westwood Blvd.

Sea Harbor Drive

SeaWorld

Central Florida Pkwy.

International Drive South

Gateway Ave.

Orangewood Blvd.

Palm Pkwy.

400

4

Discovery Cove

0   0.5 mi

0   0.5 km

N

To Walt Disney World, Busch Gardens Africa

Lake Willis

for two 1-minute rotations in the chamber (boy, they go quickly), plus training; combined, the adventure takes an hour. For an unusual activity, this one's top of my list, with an added bonus: Feeling weightless for a few minutes can do wonders for your body image. You can also buy a DVD of yourself ($25). The owners will mail you a $10-off coupon if you fill in a form on the website, and there are deals for lesser discounts in all the tourist publications.

Although **Titanic: The Experience** (8445 International Dr., Orlando; ☎ 407/248-1166 or 407/345-9337; www.titanicshipofdreams.com; $20 adults, $13 kids 4–12; daily 9am–9pm) is not as shallow (if that's the word) as you might expect an incongruous tourist sight like this to be, it also has fewer true artifacts than you might hope. For those interested in the topic, this theatrically presented museum, which walks guests chronologically from boarding to the abbreviated voyage to rediscovery, provides a balanced dossier of the sorry tale. The cases have a few mementos, but upon close inspection, you'll notice that many of them are from her sister ships, the *Olympic* and *Britannia,* and others are props from various movie retellings of the foundering. Everything seems set up to encourage guests to conflate Hollywood storytelling with history. Even the piped-in music evokes James Horner's 1997 movie score. The docents know their stuff, though, and so do the curators, who have gone the extra mile by writing informative placards, by inscribing a wall with the names of those lost, and by installing a refrigerated room, complete with ice, that approximates what it might have felt like to stroll down her chilly decks at night. The 8-foot model of what she now looks like on the floor of the North Atlantic is particularly moving.

If Mister Wizard had been raised in a carnival, he might have produced **WonderWorks** 🧒 (9067 International Dr., Orlando; ☎ 407/351-8800; www.wonderworksonline.com; daily 9am–midnight; $20 adults, $15 kids 4–12, plus $5 per game of Lazer Tag), the kind of place you go on a rainy day or if you need to kill an hour or two. The outdoor façade is the city's most compelling: The building looks like someone ripped a mansion out of the ground and turned it upside down; even the FedEx mailbox and the palm trees are upended. The inverted motif doesn't continue very far into its doors, though; instead, what you get are about 100 hands-on, ad hoc exhibits, not unlike what you'd find at a kids' science museum or an arcade—bring the Purell, because they can get smeary. One booth lets you feel the approximation of an earthquake measuring 5.3 on the Richter scale, another has kids making bubbles as big as they are, and others simulate shuttle landings and fighter jet flights. Don't let the façade fool you into thinking there's anything cutting edge about this place; lots of times, there aren't many guests here, and you may need to summon staff to try something. It's simply a place to let your kids loose for a little while. If they're the types who can't be torn away from the hands-on stuff at the local science museum, or if it's pouring outside, then they might enjoy it. You don't need one of the guidebooks the ticket booth sells. Its website posts $1.50-off coupons, and at night, it puts on the Outta Control magic show (p. 88), one of the cheapest dinnertainment shows in town.

Just south of the big bend on I-Drive—you can't miss the towering apparatus—is **Magical Midway** (7001 International Dr., Orlando; ☎ 407/370-5353; www.magicalmidway.com; unlimited midway rides $16, 3 hr. of Go-Karts $23, unlimited carnival and go-kart rides $28; Mon–Thurs 2–10pm, Fri 2pm–midnight, Sat 10am–midnight, Sun 10am–10pm), a small concrete area which by night blares with rock music and heaves with idle youth. The primary thriller is the Slingshot ($25 a ride, not included on passes), a colossal fork strung with a pod. Two at a time sit inside, are pulled one level underground, and then flung 180 feet into the sky. The 90-second adventure is so tense that the adjacent benches are usually full of spectators. The circular swing ride, Star Flyer ($7 a ride), looks tamer than it is because the restraints feel inadequate for the 230-foot height it achieves. The rest of the small plot is dominated by two thunderous, wooden Go-Kart tracks ($6 each; the Avalanche track has slightly steeper ramps than the Alpine), a few minor rides including cheerless bumper boats, and a dirty arcade thronged with kids. The scene is unquestionably downmarket, but lively.

While the Magical Midway seduces idle foreign tourists licking ice cream cones and strolling I-Drive, the carnival-style **Fun Spot Action Park** ★ kids (5551 Del Verde Way, Orlando; ☎ 407/363-3867; www.fun-spot.com; unlimited rides without Go-Karts $15, with Go-Karts $30, each midway ride $3, each Go-Kart ride $6; Sun 10am–11pm, Mon noon–11pm, Tues–Thurs noon–11pm, Fri noon–midnight, Sat 10am–midnight), 2 miles north (you can't miss the Ferris wheel, which appeared in the film *Monster*), is larger, cleaner, better lit, and preferred by local parents. That means parking is a nightmare on weekend nights. There's much more space and selection than at the Midway: four concrete Go-Kart tracks (the Quad Helix's stacked figure-eight turns make it my favorite, but I also love Conquest's peaked ramp), a two-level arcade, a scrambler, plenty of snack bars, and a devoted section of kiddie rides (including a teacup ride and a Frog Hopper; passes for them are $15). Don't get me wrong: It's still a cheap carnival.

The museum equivalent of a forwarded e-mail joke, **Ripley's Believe it of Not! Odditorium** (8201 International Dr., Orlando; ☎ 407/363-44418; www.ripleys orlando.com; $19 adults, $12 kids 4–12; daily 9–1am) is too expensive for the thin, touristy diversion that it delivers. Mostly it consists of wax figures, panels from the old Ripley's comic (does anyone under 45 even remember those?), and the odd coin-operated amusement device—the same as any other Ripley attraction. It has fewer true artifacts than you'll be expecting. Don't set foot in it without at least harvesting coupons, which appear in nearly every tourist publication in town. Also don't fall for buying the guide—you won't need it.

U.S. 192 AREA

In creating his new breed of amusement park, Walt Disney tried desperately to stamp out the trashy honky-tonk of the American carnival, but it lives on, cotton candy and all, on his doorstep. **Old Town** (5770 W. Irlo Bronson Hwy./U.S. 192, Kissimmee; ☎ 407/396-4888; www.old-town.com; daily 10am–11pm, rides may remain open later), at Mile Marker 9, was obviously constructed with loftier ambitions, but instead of seducing the world's tourists, it's popular mostly with lower-income locals. Old Town, built to look like 4 blocks of a Main Street–style town, is about its beer-soaked ale halls, and its panoply of cheap stores run the gamut from baseball cards to puppets to pins to Western gear. Strung along are a low-rent haunted house, a flimsy wax museum, and a mechanical bull. The area has 18 cheap rides, including a **Super Shot** that's a mere shadow of the Slingshot at Magical Midway (see above) and 17 simple carnival thrills. **Windstorm,** quaint knot of metal tucked at the back of the park, must be Orlando's least-known roller coaster, which is not necessarily an injustice.

Next door, that skyline-scarring contraption, the **SkyCoaster** ✦ (2850 Florida Plaza Blvd., Kissimmee; ☎ 407/397-2509; www.skycoaster.cc; $40 a ride; Mon–Fri 3pm–midnight, Sat–Sun noon–midnight), harnesses would-be pants-wetters so that they're face-down, hoists them backwards, and then lets them swing back and forth at up to 80mph like confused hang gliders. The same outfit operates the deafening **G-Force** ($30 a ride—a price only a gearhead would pay), a mock-up of a drag race, fueled by air, that sends riders down a strip, 0 to 110mph in 2 seconds. Online, both offer coupons worth up to $5.

Adjacent to the SkyCoaster, the **Full Speed Race & Golf** 🅺🆂 (5720 W. U.S. 192, Kissimmee; ☎ 407/397-7455; www.fullspeed.cc; $10 golf, $15 cars, $20 both; Mon–Fri 3pm–midnight, Sat–Sun noon–midnight) attraction sponges off the foot traffic with a line of car simulators that can race and "hit" each other (you'll buck and bump if you do), as well as an 18-hole fluorescent, racing-themed minigolf course under black lights. All in all, Old Town may not be posh, and some people may even classify it as slightly trashy, but it's a decent place to stroll in the full knowledge that you're not going to pay a lot for a nice time. And you'll probably eat something fried.

I'm sorry, but $19 is too much for a petting zoo. Unless you have a unicorn in there. Yet that's the going rate, adult or child, at **Green Meadows Petting Farm** (1368 S. Poinciana Blvd., Kissimmee; ☎ 407/846-0770; www.greenmeadowsfarm. com; $19 adults, free for kids under 1, $16 seniors; daily 9:30am–5:30pm, last tour at 4pm), and I don't care if that price does include hay rides, pony rides, and the chance to milk a cow. If you want to pet the animals, you have to take a guided tour. It's a nice change of pace from overly orchestrated attractions, but cow poop has its entertainment limits.

DOWNTOWN ORLANDO

Shaped by evangelicals seeking an increase in values-based entertainment (as if Disney was sleazy), the **Holy Land Experience** (4655 Vineland Rd., Orlando; ☎ 800/447-7235; www.holylandexperience.com; $35 adults, $23 for children 6–12, $30 for seniors 55 and older free for children under 6, discounts of $5 available online, parking $5; Mon–Sat 10am–5om, closed Sun) is the world's first theme park dedicated to the Bible. Daily at 4:30pm, an actor playing Jesus drags himself to the top of a fake mountain where he's "crucified" before an appreciative audience. While its operators claim they're transporting people back in time to walk through the Bible, I can't help pointing out that the recorded voices reading Scripture are always deep, male, vaguely British, and accompanied by strings and timpani, and ironically for a park devoted to a great book, no one actually reads anything—everything is narrated by recording. Having been to the real Holy Land, I think the Holy Land Experience is for people whose understanding of the era comes from Charlton Heston movies.

That's not to say that this park is overtly political; it's not the kind of place that wants your vote—just your tears. Will there ever again be a theme park where a major attraction is "The Wilderness Tabernacle," which is pretty much 20 minutes of an old man miming his custodial duties in a desert temple while a recorded chorus chants Old Testament verses? It's a shame the delivery is so encoded with the peculiar personal theology of its founder, Baptist minister Marvin Rosenthal,

Orlando Area Attractions

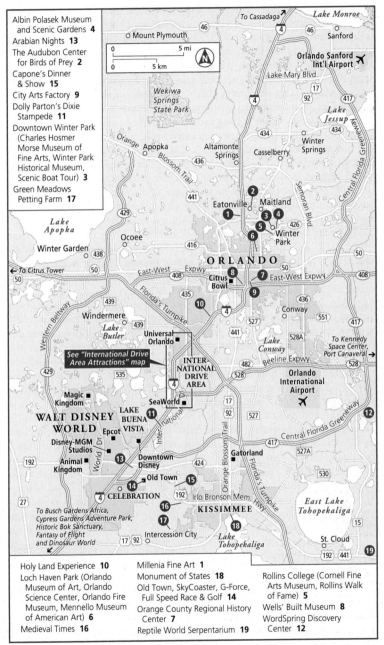

Albin Polasek Museum and Scenic Gardens **4**
Arabian Nights **13**
The Audubon Center for Birds of Prey **2**
Capone's Dinner & Show **15**
City Arts Factory **9**
Dolly Parton's Dixie Stampede **11**
Downtown Winter Park (Charles Hosmer Morse Museum of Fine Arts, Winter Park Historical Museum, Scenic Boat Tour) **3**
Green Meadows Petting Farm **17**

Holy Land Experience **10**
Loch Haven Park (Orlando Museum of Art, Orlando Science Center, Orlando Fire Museum, Mennello Museum of American Art) **6**
Medieval Times **16**
Millenia Fine Art **1**
Monument of States **18**
Old Town, SkyCoaster, G-Force, Full Speed Race & Golf **14**
Orange County Regional History Center **7**
Reptile World Serpentarium **19**
Rollins College (Cornell Fine Arts Museum, Rollins Walk of Fame) **5**
Wells' Built Museum **8**
WordSpring Discovery Center **12**

because the park's little-visited centerpiece, the Scriptorium, actually contains some impressive specimens of Biblical publishing history, including the blood-stained Matthew's Bible from 1537. Even the Scriptorium, though, waxes rhapsodic when discussing the missionary aspect of publishing the Bible, but avoids the stickier, and much more illuminating, topics of how some leaders manipulated Biblical translation for personal gain, and the specific changes that pioneers such as Martin Luther and John Calvin were actually fighting for.

The fact guests must wait for recorded narration at every turn makes the pace here slow—some would say lugubrious—and there are no rides, nor enough attractions to fill an entire day, even though performances and tableaux are spaced out across the clock to pretend there is. Kids can take home the park's equally off-beat souvenirs: a foam "Roman Soldier Sword" for $6 and "Bernardo, The Scribal Bear," dressed in monks' robes, for $15. But ultimately, it's sad to think that 200,000 people a year, who could be saving up for a pilgrimage to the real Jerusalem, find anything personal in this slightly unsavory one of fake executions and souvenir shops. For me, religion is not a consumer event.

There are few places in town that will give you a better overview of Orlando's history and topography—and using such modern museum methods as video and sound portraits—than the well-heeled **Orange County Regional History Center** ★★★ (65 E. Central Blvd., Orlando; ☎ 407/836-8500; www.thehistory center.org; $7 adults, $3.50 kids 3–12, $6.50 seniors over 59; Mon–Sat 10am–5pm, Sun noon–5pm), which is the current occupant of a handsome 1927 Greek Revival courthouse. Head first to its fourth floor, where the timeline starts 12,000 years in the past with the native people that lived here, and work your way down. The museum has a wooden canoe, from around A.D. 1000, that was found in lake muck. The Orlando area was the last American refuge for mastodons and mammoths, too, and you'll see a mammoth tooth and jaw found at the nearby Wekiva River (p. 265). As you advance through time, the artifacts keep coming: saddles used by the forgotten Florida cowmen (because of the swampy ground, they used long whips and didn't dismount their horses the way Western cowboys did), and an amusing loop of vintage commercials for Florida orange juice, including one by the vilified Anita Bryant. An entire alcove entitled "The Day We Changed" is devoted to Disney's arrival and includes some rare collectibles such as a 1965 press announcement and a grand opening dedication program for what was then called Epcot Center. The accompanying videos are noticeably conflicted about the growth explosion wrought by the theme parks—most Orlando residents are, you'll find—but the museum is careful to note that Orlando has experienced other booms (in the 1920s, its population tripled) and that tourism itself is nothing new, because in the late 1800s, the rivers and lakes were crawling with steamship tourist trade. An interesting sidelight is the rarified, wood-lined Courtroom B, preserved just as it operated, as a circuit felony court, until 1999. Its cork floor muffled the shuffling of lawyers, and in 1987, it tried the first case in America in which DNA evidence obtained a conviction. The museum features several temporary exhibitions at one time.

The next four museums are located within a few minutes' walk of each other in Loch Haven Park, an area north of downtown that's been set aside for the arts and culture. You can park once, at the Science Center's covered lot, and see the rest on the same visit. Although the non-profit **Orlando Science Center** 🧒 (777

E. Princeton St., Orlando; ☎ 407/514-2000; www.osc.org; $15 adults, $14 seniors over age 54 and students with I.D., $9.95 kids 3–11; Sun–Tues 10am–6pm, Wed–Thurs 10am–9pm, Fri–Sat 10am–11pm) is a model of its type—it's still a science museum, and if you have one in your city, you should probably fill your scarce vacation time with other attractions. That's not to slam what they've got: A spectacular atrium-dominated building, a terrific Body Zone area that kicks off with a stroll through a giant mouth; a "CineDome" that doubles as a movie theatre and a planetarium (add about $10 for that); a Nature Works area stocked with live alligators (there's a daily feeding in the early afternoon); a beehive that feeds outside through a tube; a not-scary dinosaur zone full of reproduction skeletons and special sandboxes where kids can dig for simulated fossils. Exhibits are aimed at small children and school groups, at the expense of teens and adults who have probably seen hands-on exhibits in wave-making and conductivity before. Much space is devoted to touring exhibitions, and those (which are usually ticketed above and beyond the usual fee) usually have more to offer grown-ups, but all in all, Orlando has more compelling attractions. After 4pm, prices are slashed $5.

Also along the southern bank of Lake Estelle, the **Orlando Museum of Art** ★★ (2416 N. Mills Ave., Orlando; ☎ 407/896-4231; www.omart.org; $8 adults, $7 college students and seniors over 64, $5 kids 6–18; Tues–Fri 10am–4pm, Sat–Sun noon–4pm) has a sampling of American art, and it strives to spotlight other cultures through its temporary shows. Among the standout permanent holdings are an 1820 portrait by Joshua Jackson, a rare early African-American artist; a Benjamin West; a John Singer Sargent portrait of Francis Brooks Chadwick (his gift to the sitter, a classmate); a blue and yellow pile by frenzied glassblower Dale Chihuly (washed in plenty of natural light); Chuck Close's 1982 portrait of his wife, done in fingerprints; and Robert Rauschenberg's haunting *Florida Psalm,* 1997, a collage paean to the state's fading tourism emblems. There are also 21 works by American impressionist Henry Potthast ringing their own gallery. The pompously named Lakeview Salon is a sunny, relaxing nook where you can unwind on leather furniture. The gift shop is pricey (come to think of it, so is the museum, which only takes about an hour to enjoy), but packed with unusual items. On the first Thursday of each month from 6 to 9pm, the "First Thursday" event includes live music and a cash bar; each one has a new theme and costs the same as regular admission.

Across the parking lot, the **Orlando Fire Museum** (814 E. Rollins Ave., Orlando; ☎ 407/898-3138; free admission; Thurs–Sat 9am–2pm) is a minor attraction appealing mostly to fans of the genre. Which is not to say pyromaniacs. Located in a restored 1926 firehouse, it contains a few work vehicles from the early 1900s, plus some historical information about the city and its volunteer firefighters. It's worth 15 minutes if you're already at Loch Haven Park.

The last, and quirkiest, selection in the park, close to the Science Center, the city-owned **Mennello Museum of American Art** ★ (900 E. Princeton St., Orlando; ☎ 407/246-4278; www.mennellomuseum.org; $8 adults, $7 seniors over 59, $5 students, kids under 12 free; Tues–Sat 10:30am–4:30pm, Sun noon–4:30pm) opened in 1998 as a repository for paintings by Earl Cunningham, a folk artist who depicted North American life through refreshingly naïve eyes. Cunningham, who died in 1977 after a life spent in obscurity running a curio shop in Saint

Augustine, is now considered so important that the Smithsonian American Art Museum has recognized him with an exhibition. Businessman Michael Mennello, who with his late wife Marilyn founded the collection, is broadening the museum's focus by filling the cases with other examples of fine American folk art.

A fascinating glimpse into Orlando's African-American past, the **Wells' Built Museum** ✹ (511 W. South St., Orlando; ☎ 407/245-7535; www.pastinc.org; $5 adults, $3 kids 15 and under; Mon–Fri 9am–5pm) is housed in a building constructed as a hotel for the city's black visitors by one of Orlando's first black physicians. In its heyday, it served the South Street Casino next door (the home of the hotel's owner was later moved to its plot), and it hosted overnight guests including Thurgood Marshall, Ella Fitzgerald, and Jackie Robinson.

The 6,000-foot collection preserves a 1930s-era room and is otherwise a hodge-podge of civic artifacts (an original Negro League baseball jersey, books, many aging documents, biographies of forgotten individuals who shaped the city—it's starchy, so you'll have to use your imagination). As you stroll though, which should take you about a half-hour, try to imagine Orlando without Interstate 4 cleaving it in two; back then, this neighborhood was germane to the downtown area, but its residents decidedly weren't. Central Florida's African-American heritage has a harrowing story. Remember, when Disney elected to build, people were still being lynched here in the Deep South, and until as late as 1951 in Orlando, black mothers had to give birth in the boiler room of the local hospital. Eatonville, 6 miles north of downtown, was the country's first municipality founded and run by black politicians. There's not too much to see there except a one-room museum, so this is the best place to start an exploration of the subject.

I just wish someone would build a museum to the great aviation pioneer Bessie Coleman, the first black licensed pilot in history and probably the first black mega-celebrity. She opened a beauty shop in Orlando to fund her dream of starting an aviation academy (I asked everyone in town, including the librarians at the History Center, but no one remembered where it was anymore). Coleman died in Jacksonville in 1926 after being thrown from her plane while rehearsing for an exhibition. It's thought a wrench got jammed in the mechanism of her plane, which she had purchased on the cheap. Lesson: Never buy a budget plane. Ten thousand mourners attended her Chicago funeral—she was a legend in her own time, but today, people have never heard of her.

Spendy contemporary art collectors hunt for perfect pieces at the 30,000 square-foot showroom of **Millenia Fine Art** ✹ (555 S. Lake Destiny Dr., Orlando; ☎ 407/304-8100; www.milleniafineart.com; free admission; Mon–Fri 10am–6pm, Sat 10am–2pm, closed Sun), northwest of downtown, but before the world's millionaires have slipped that Dale Chihuly glasswork or Marc Chagall painting into their shopping carts, anyone off the street can come in and admire the goodies. The collection, spanning photography (celebrity portraits by Hollywood director Brett Ratner), paintings (de Kooning), and sculpture (Henry Moore's *Three Motives Against Wall No. 2* was a recent selection) is always changing.

The newly formed **CityArts Factory** (29 S. Orange Ave., at Pine St., Orlando; ☎ 407/648-7060; free admission; Mon–Sat 11am–7pm) holds four independent galleries (Zulu Exclusive for African art; Q Gallery for contemporary works; Kiene/Quigley Community gallery for local items; and Kelia Glassworks), and a multi-use space where temporary performances may crop up.

SOUTH OF ORLANDO

Three recent fatal alligator attacks in Florida have given new heft to **Gatorland** ★★★ 🧒 (14501 S. Orange Blossom Trail, Orlando; ☎ 800/393-5297 or 407/855-5496; www.gatorland.com; $20 adults, $13 kids 3–12; daily 9am–5pm), a reassuringly hokey reptile farm with a much more relaxed pace than that at the major parks. Back in 1949, Gatorland became Orlando's first mass attraction, featuring Seminole Indians wrestling the animals for tourists. Back then, Florida was crawling with alligators—you could see them basking by the sides of the main roads—but these days, the reptiles have been mostly evicted by development and so sanctuaries like these are the best places to see them in their ornery glory. Rather than getting more tired with age, Gatorland has gradually become nicer, as concrete pools have been replaced with natural-looking habitats and a sun-seared layout was molded into a pleasing simulated nature walk. At regular showtimes, rangers, who are clearly buzzed on their own testosterone, wrassle, tickle, and otherwise pester seething gators, and for a few extra bucks, they'll bring your children into the fray—safely, with a wad of rubber bands around the critters' snouts—for snapshots. These guys would be just as comfortable as Broadway actors as gator handlers; every show is staged to contain a near-disaster to titillate and thrill tourists. Most of the fun is trawling the 110-acre plot on walkways as the ornery critters teem and breed in murky waters underfoot and wetland birds (such as noodle-necked white American egrets) prance above it all. The three main shows repeat during the day, so it's easy to get the highlights in 2 or 3 hours. Cap a visit by watching the gators leap for suspended chunks of chicken during the Jumparoo. Bring a fistful of cash if you'd like to partake of extras such as being able to feed tamer animals such as tropical birds. And save a dollar bill for one of its 1960s-era vending machines, which press a miniature alligator out of injected hot wax right before your eyes.

Alas, in November 2006, this sweet park suffered a catastrophic fire, started by a heating pad in a snake pen, which gutted the divinely tacky gift shop and scarred the trademark 'gator-jaw entranceway. Orlando residents collectively held their breath for fear that the venerable attraction would sputter to a close. But the disaster had the opposite effect, rallying the community behind its tourism heritage, and when Gatorland improvised a reopening 19 days later, high school bands serenaded the re-cutting of the ribbon. The rest of the compound was mostly unscathed (so the attractions weren't diminished), and the rebuilding effort was promised to be just as inspiring as the zoo's long-running cornball goofiness. Orlando may be known for citrus, but here, the product is still grade-A cheese.

Snake milking! What other enticement do you need to pay a visit to the **Reptile World Serpentarium** (5705 E. Irlo Bronson Memorial Hwy./U.S. 192, St. Cloud; ☎ 407/892-6905; $5.75 adults, $4.75 kids 6–17, $3.75 kids 3–6; Tues–Sun 9am–5pm, closed Mon and most of Sept), which is more of an unassuming research facility—and venom-collection wonderland—than a zoo. Begun in 1972 to collect poison for medical research, its location 20 miles east of Disney tempted its operators into joining the ranks of tourist attractions 4 years later, and daily at noon and 3pm, you can thrill (safely behind glass) as staff grab deadly serpents, plant their yawning fangs over the membrane of a venom-collection glass, and get the creatures spitting mad. There are about 55 snakes on display at any one time, but obviously, this one's about the venom show.

Join the Club

Orlando must be one of the world's capitals for miniature golf courses. Ridiculously complicated ones. A flat, green fairway just won't do. Here, you play under waterfalls, through caves, over motorized ramps, and even into volcanoes that "erupt" if you hit your shot. Just pick the flavor you like most, and putter around with one of these. You'll find discounts for all but Disney's courses in the major coupon booklets.

- **Congo River Adventure Golf** ★★★ (5901 International Dr., Orlando, ☎ 407/248-9181; and 6312 International Dr., Orlando, ☎ 407/352-0042; www.congoriver.com; both locations $10 adults, $8.45 kids; Sun–Thurs 10am–11pm, Fri–Sat 10am–midnight). One of the best minigolf options, the challenging courses wind through a man-made mountain speared with airplane wreckage. There are live alligators in the pools. The 6312 I-Drive location has 36 holes to the other one's mere 18.

- **Pirate's Cove** ★★★ (8501 International Dr., Orlando; ☎ 407/352-7378; and 12545 S.R. 535, behind the Crossroads shopping center, Lake Buena Vista; ☎ 407/827-1242; www.piratescove.net; $9.50 adults, $8.50 kids under 12; daily 9am–11:30pm). Navigate wooden ships and waterfalls. There are two courses: Captain Kidd's Adventure (par 42) and Blackbeard's Challenge (par 47).

- **Tiki Island Volcano Golf** ★ (7460 International Dr., Orlando; ☎ 407/248-8180; $9.95 adults, $8.95 kids; daily 10am–11:30pm). The climactic four-story volcano "erupts" if you hit it just right with your ball, plus you have waterfalls, caves, and flamingo paddleboats.

My great-grandfather was a professional photographer from Atlanta. When I was a boy, some of his favorite Kodachrome slides, shot in the 1950s, depicted a group of coquettish young women water-skiing across a lake in a pyramid formation, balancing on each others' shoulders. They waved at the camera. What a decadent place! This was Cypress Gardens, which opened in 1936 and started the world thinking about Central Florida as the seat of a new kind of tourism. It's impossible to overestimate this park's effect on tourism in Florida—it defined the precepts that family park entertainment must be wholesome, fantastic, and celebrate sun and fun. A few years ago, after declining attendance, developers began revving up the bulldozers at **Cypress Gardens Adventure Park** (kids) (6000 Cypress Gardens Blvd., Winter Haven; ☎ 863/324-2111; www.cypressgardens.com; $40 adults, $35 seniors over 54 and kids 3–9; hours vary, but it always opens at 10am). After all, with Space Mountain so nearby, who would be interested in hanging out at a park for gentler souls, known mostly for its botanical gardens and its wandering women dressed as Southern belles? It closed. Locals mourned, and after the state granted protections from development, in stepped Georgia businessman Kent Buescher, who pumped $50 million into revitalization. He kept the

The two 18-hole courses are so-so, but the grounds look good at night.

◆ **Disney's Winter Summerland** ✸✸ (outside of Blizzard Beach, Walt Disney World; ☎ 407/939-7529; $11 adults, $8.50 kids, daily 10am–11pm; 50% discount on the second round). Two cute 18-hole courses themed around Christmas. The Winter side, piled with fake "snow," has more bells and whistles (love that steaming campfire and that squirting snowman). Combine it with a day at Blizzard Beach without moving your car. It's superior to:

◆ **Disney's Fantasia Gardens** (outside of the Swan and Dolphin, Walt Disney World; ☎ 407/939-7529; $11 adults, $8.50 kids, daily 10am–11pm; 50% discount on the second round). Themed to the animated feature *Fantasia*, its two courses are the Fairways, with challenging shots for skilled putters, and the Gardens, which is sillier. Other courses wow more.

◆ **Hawaiian Rumble Adventure Golf** (13529 S. Apopka Vineland Rd., Lake Buena Vista; ☎ 407/239-8300; Sun–Thurs10am–11pm, Fri–Sat 10am–11:30pm; and 8969 International Dr., Orlando; ☎ 407/351-7733; www.hawaiianrumbleorlando.com; Sun–Thurs 9am–11:30pm, Fri–Sat 9am–midnight; both locations $9.95 adults, $7.95 kids). A simple, tropical course threaded with streams and waterfalls.

◆ **Bonanza Mini Golf** (7761 W. U.S. 192, Kissimmee; ☎ 407/396-7536; $7.95 adults, $6.95 kids under 10; daily 9am–midnight). Sparsely decorated using an Old West theme, with two courses; the Gold Nugget is far too easy.

gardens and water-skiing dollybirds that made it a Depression-era rage, but he also added the Adventure Grove, featuring some 40 carnival rides, mostly for children. Enjoying those can make for a novel afternoon, as you may have to get the attendants to switch them on just for you. I commend the park for saving the **Starliner,** a classic wooden coaster, from the wrecking ball in Panama City, Florida. The **Splash Island water park** is a small but welcome addition, too, with a wave pool, lazy river, and eight adult water slides.

In the remaking, Cypress Gardens' illustrious heritage was swept aside. The swimming pool shaped like the state of Florida, once adorned with nymph-like swimmers, crumbles behind a gate. Not a single postcard or souvenir depicting the park's important early days is available. Southern belles still stroll the gardens and mingle with guests (most of them elderly), a scaled-down water-ski show still runs several times a day, and the Nature's Way zoo area stocks a menagerie that includes tropical birds, a jaguar, and butterflies, but the park is a shadow of its former self. The lovely gardens are mostly empty, and the park only seems truly alive when one of its many country music concerts is scheduled. Cypress Gardens is once again in an uncertain chapter—Chapter 11. It makes me want to scream, "Go! Before it's gone." And yet, I'd have to add, "Don't expect much."

Seek out the 17-foot-long alligator named Tarzan, now nearly 80 years old—he was but a wee lizard in the 1940s, when Hollywood filmed the *Tarzan* movies here with Johnny Weissmuller. You can still see the scar on the gator's jaw where the crew wired its mouth closed. *Moon over Miami* with Betty Grable and *Easy to Love* starring Esther Williams were also shot here. There are other modest things to do, too: a reptile show, a farmyard animal show, the Sunshine Sky Adventure crane-lifted observation wheel, and cruises on Lake Eloise. But is it all enough to keep the institution stay afloat? Cypress Gardens may be Florida's oldest operating tourist attraction, and the granddaddy of them all, but for me, its true spirit lives mostly in my great-grandfather's movies. Unfortunately, the park takes some dedication to see; it's about 90 miles south of Orlando on stop-and-go roads through some real Old South towns.

Fantasy of Flight ✯ (1400 Broadway Blvd., Polk City; ☎ 863/984-3500; www. fantasyofflight.com; $27 adults, $25 seniors over 54, $14 kids 6–15; daily 10am–5pm) is one of those only-in-America attractions. About 20 miles south of Disney on I-4, it's a combination hangar farm/airfield dedicated to restoring obsolete aircraft from the dawn of mechanized flight to the 1950s. More than 40 relics—many rented frequently for Hollywood shoots and all either restored to or destined for flying condition—are on the premises, and guests are shown how they're mended and what it was like to fly them back in the day. It's billed as the world's largest private aircraft collection. For an extra chunk of change, you can hitch a ride in a barnstorming biplane (one from 1929, one from 1942) or a hot air balloon. As you might expect, this elaborate toy shop is a labor of love—its owner, Kermit Weeks, is independently wealthy thanks to a grandfather's oil strike and he doesn't have to make a penny from the attraction. He just loves planes.

Another quaint roadside attraction, **Dinosaur World** 🧒 (5145 Harvey Tew Rd., at I-4's exit 17, Plant City; ☎ 813/717-9865; www.dinoworld.net; $13 adults, $11 seniors over 59, $9.75 kids 3–12; daily 9am–dusk) is not someplace to spend hours—one will do—but kids like to wander the jungly plot of land, happening upon more than 100 life-size versions of various dinosaurs, some 80 feet long. A labor of love by a Swedish-born man and his family, it's well kept, even if the foam-and-fiberglass models sometimes look more like aliens than reptiles. America doesn't often support the likes of places like these anymore.

WINTER PARK AND NORTH ORLANDO

The best museum in the Orlando area is unquestionably the **Charles Hosmer Morse Museum of American Art** ✯✯✯ (445 N. Park Ave., Winter Park; ☎ 407/645-4311; www.morsemuseum.org; $3 adults, $1 students, free for kids under 12; Tues–Sat 9:30am–4 pm, Sun 1–4pm, closed Mon, open Fri until 8pm Sept–May). The cache of works by genius glassblower Louis Comfort Tiffany, from stained glass to vases to lamps, is so sensational that even New York's Metropolitan Museum of Art comes begging to borrow pieces. In fact, the Morse, a graceful space with demure lighting and 11,000 square feet of spacing, has the best collection of Tiffany glass on the planet, including an entire room reconstructing the master's tour de force chapel, made for the World's Columbian Exposition in 1893. Once face-to-face with the uncanny luminescence of Tiffany's best work, even those who don't care much about decorative arts can't help but come away dazzled. The museum's founders also collected plenty of other top-quality pieces from the Arts and Crafts movement, including prints, but the focus here is definitely Tiffany. Set aside an hour or so, though it's easy to combine a visit here with a stroll through Winter Park's boutiques, as it sits among them.

Rollins College, whose graduates include Mister Fred Rogers, has long been the university of choice for parents with social aspirations for their children, and so it makes sense that its star exhibition hall, the **Cornell Fine Arts Museum** ✦ (100 Holt Ave., Winter Park; ☎ 407/646-2526; www.rollins.edu/cfam; $5 adults, free for students; Tues–Sat 10am–5 pm, Sun 1–5pm), would be bequeathed with such a fine collection in such a country-club setting. Despite a lavish refurbishment in early 2006, it's still too small to showcase its impressive holdings, so even remarkable pieces (such as Vanessa Bell's portrait of Mary St. John Hutchinson) tend to rotate in and out of storage to make way for changing exhibitions, which generally spotlight arresting photography and other modern (usually Anglo) works with well-crafted visuals. Basically, if it's pretty and from the past 150 years, it's in. Displays are light on explanations. For example, there's a glass case full of "watch keys," which were once used to wind pocket watches—they aren't individually marked; they're just presented as something pretty. Peaceful, quiet, and usually empty, with a serene backyard gazebo overlooking Winter Park's Lake Virginia, a visit puts one into a contemplative mood. During the academic year, the museum puts on nearly weekly film screenings and talks by experts on a range of subjects, such as transcendentalism, clown metaphors in French modernism, and the history of the Florida Everglades; check the website's calendar of events.

A visit to the Cornell is an ideal time to take a quick 20-minute walking tour of the campus of Rollins College. Built in a Spanish-Italianate idiom more typical of Southern California than of Central Florida, the campus has a lovely lakeside setting of red-tile roofs and swaying Spanish moss. The so-called **Rollins Walk of Fame** (Mills Lawn, www.rollins.edu/walk) is a collection of 526 stones arranged around a green where students like to play touch football and sunbathe. Each tablet is inscribed with the name of a famous person (Louisa May Alcott, Abraham Lincoln, Rameses II of Thebes), and within it is set a rock, brick, or other item purported to come from the luminary's home, tomb, or local church. The effort began in 1929 and seems to have petered out in the last generation, as so many markers are overgrown or eroded that it's tough to make many of them out. I find it the height of selfishness that someone had the ego to chisel a rock from Martin Luther King's house or Dante's tomb just to install it at a minor Floridian liberal arts college, especially considering the project is now virtually as ignored as an old cemetery—someone has already stolen Maya Angelou's rock, and Jack London's cannonball has cracked his tablet in two. The decay is depressing. But the collection shines light on the now-obsolete mentality that Florida was once at the edge of civilization and its pioneering residents once felt compelled to link themselves to the outside world. Now that the world comes to Orlando, the impulse has faded. A few doors west, duck into the **Charles Rice Family Bookstore and Café** (☎ 407/646-2133; www.rollins.edu/bookstore), located in a former student center, a handsome vaulted-ceiling space recalling Los Angeles' Union Station where you can buy souvenirs from the college (like Rollins College

Towering Dubious Achievements

Why is it that when people the world over want to attract tourists, they build tall things? Central Florida presents these out-of-the-way relics:

Citrus Tower (141 N. Hwy. 27, Clermont, ½ mile north of S.R. 50; ☎ 352/394-4061; www.citrustower.com; $4 adults, $1 kids 3–15; Mon–Fri 9am–6pm Fri–Sat 9am–7pm, closed Sun). In 1956, when Florida seemed destined to be a powerhouse orange supplier, investors took 5 million pounds of concrete and built this 22-story, 226-foot-tall observation tower over all those groovy groves. Now it's a perch for surveying Spanish-tiled homes priced at $300,000—about what it cost to build this column. Still, some 12,000 ascend each year.

Monument of States (corner of Monument Ave. and Johnston St., Kissimmee). In 1943, the town eccentric wrote to all the state governors and asked them to mail a rock or stone. For the next 22 years, he took his booty, which grew to include bones, teeth, and stuff from 20 foreign countries, embedded it in concrete, and assembled the blocks into a squat tower in a public park. Like Winter Park's vanity project, Rollins College's Walk of Fame (p. 235), it's fallen into macabre disrepair.

Bok Tower (Historic Bok Sanctuary; p. 264). By comparison, this neo-Gothic edifice, a National Historic Landmark, is graceful and elegant, and it signifies what its designer intended—peace.

tees, $12). The **Annie Russell Theatre** (1000 Holt Ave., Winter Park; ☎ 407/646-2145; www.rollins.edu/theatre), from 1931, was named for a British acting superstar (the creator of the title role in George Bernard Shaw's *Major Barbara*) who retired to Winter Park and taught Rollins students. The 377-seat theatre, known as "the Annie," is in the Spanish Mediterranean style and was enshrined on the National Register of Historic Places in 1998.

If Winter Park's airs have hooked you and you weren't sated by the history lesson on the Scenic Boat Tour (p. 268), I suggest a stop at the **Winter Park Historical Museum** (200 W. England Ave., ☎ 407/647-2330; www.winterpark historical.com; free admission; Thurs–Fri 11am–3pm, Sat 9am–1pm, Sun 1–4pm). A simple exhibition of photos and facsimiles in a converted train depot, it's not elaborate, but custodians are good at answering questions. A good day to come is Saturdays, when the town's small but respected **Farmers' Market** (☎ 407/599-3275), overflowing with fresh produce and flowers, is held alongside the museum from 7am to 1pm. (The best stuff is sold by 9am.)

Yet another fine arts institution in genteel Winter Park, the **Albin Polasek Museum and Sculpture Gardens** (633 Osceola Ave., Winter Park; ☎ 407/647-6294; www.polasek.org; $5 adults, $4 seniors, $3 students over 11; Sept–June,

Tues–Sat 10am–4pm, Sun 1–4pm; closed July–Aug), called The Polasek, is the former home of the celebrated Czech sculptor; he lived here for the last 15 years of his life. His work, mostly in bronze or plaster, is accomplished but literal, so it may not be to the tastes of those accustomed to the daring forms of other contemporary Eastern European artists. Polasek liked simplicity, and his house reflects it. The museum hosts irregular lectures, usually tied to temporary exhibitions, which generally reflect a concern with early-20th-century art. A 30-minute stop will do.

In Maitland, just north of Winter Park, **The Audubon Center for Birds of Prey** ★ (1101 Audubon Way, Maitland; ☎ 407/644-0190; www.audubonofflorida. org; $5 adults, $4 kids aged 3–12; Tues–Sun 10am–4pm), founded in 1979, rehabilitates the largest number of owls, eagles, falcons, hawks, and kites than anywhere else east of the Mississippi. Some 650 birds a year check in for help, and, of those, 40% are able to be released back into the wild. The ones who can't be returned to their natural habitats live here, among the walkways and aviaries. Because its mandate is to help animals, not to titillate sticky-fingered tourists, it's a quiet place to visit, but handlers are eager to share their passion for helping these majestic birds.

EAST OF ORLANDO

In the late 1960s, Central Florida was the most exciting place on Earth. It had nothing to do with a cartoon mouse—it was because of the moon. As a culture, we're so used to the regularity of space shuttle and rocket launches that they barely seem real. Perhaps that's why the **Kennedy Space Center** ★★★ 🛰️ (Rte. 405, east of Titusville; ☎ 321/449-4444; www.kennedyspacecenter.com; $31 adults, $21 kids 3–11 for standard access; $38 adults, $28 kids to add simulators and the Astronaut Hall of Fame; daily 9am–5:30pm, last bus tour departs 2:15pm, Astronaut Hall of Fame open until 6:30pm), which was established in 1958 and ruled the tourist circuit with Disney in the 1970s, has unfairly been eclipsed by newer attractions. But let me tell you that a visit here is awe-inspiring, and even people who arrived on Earth after the moon walks had happened (like me) find the scientific and technological bravura stirring, to say the least.

Start near opening time. A few miles before reaching the actual visitors' center, you'll pass the **United States Astronaut Hall of Fame.** Because they see it first, people make it their first stop, but you're going to be getting plenty of similar information on your tour, so only stop here on the way out if you're still yearning for spacemen. Instead, proceed to the Visitor's Center proper. There, many are waylaid by the retired rockets, IMAX films, and simulators, but again, that's not the best stuff. You should board the can't-miss **bus tour,** which leaves every 15 minutes until about 2:15pm and takes most people around 4 hours—be warned that the last buses don't leave you enough time to browse. Coaches, which are narrated by both video segments and a live person, zip you around NASA's tightly secured compound. Combined with the nature reserve around it, the area (which guides tell visitors is a fifth the size of Rhode Island) is huge but you'll be making three stops not too far away—still, hope for good weather, since you'll be in and out of doors. Each stop allows you to disembark, explore, and then catch the next bus. The system can be slow, but it at least lets you linger where you want

Be There for Liftoff

Because launches are so often postponed, it would be dangerous to plan a trip to Orlando just to catch one, but then again, if there's a launch when you're in town, it would a shame to miss it. Kennedy Space Center maintains an updated schedule of launches online at **www.kennedyspace center.com/launches.** The general public is not permitted to flood NASA turf during the actual events, but Titusville, a town at the eastern end of S.R. 50, is a good place to get a clear, free view, as you'll be across the wide Indian River from the pad. Gray Line (☎ 800/537-0917; $90 adults, $79 kids) usually sells tours combining transportation from Orlando hotels and seating at the Kennedy Space Center Visitor Center, the closest site available to the public (6 miles from the pad). The Visitor Center also sometimes sells tickets through its website for $38 adults, $28 kids. Even if you can't leave Orlando for a launch, you can still easily see the fire of the rockets ascend the eastern sky from anywhere in town. Night launches are even more spectacular.

to. From the first stop, the **LC-39 Observation Gantry,** you'll have a view, across a few miles, of the two launch sites used by the shuttle and by the Apollo moon shots, and you'll receive an intelligent explanation of the preparation that goes into each shuttle launch. Ever wonder why you see a lot of sparks by the shuttle engines during launch, or why water appears to be pouring out the bottom? You'll find out why. (If you'd like to get much closer to the launch pads, you have to pay another $22 adult/$16 kids for the Up Close tour; but that's only for die-hards.)

Back on the bus, you'll buzz by eagles' nests, alligator-rich canals, and the absolutely titanic **Vehicle Assembly Building,** or VAB, where the shuttle—which NASA folk call "the orbiter"—is readied; it's often possible to spy the gleam of its orange solid rocket boosters through the giant doors, which, by the way, are so large the Statue of Liberty could fit through them. If you're incredibly lucky, you'll be on hand when the shuttle makes its slow, 8-hour trip (on tractors that get 42 ft. to the gallon) from the VAB to the launch pad, where it spends its last month before the final countdown. The second bus stop, the **Apollo/Saturn V Center,** begins with a full-scale mock-up of the "firing room" in the throes of command-ing Apollo 8's launch, in all its window-rattling, fire-lit drama. The adjoining museum contains a Saturn V rocket, which is larger than you can imagine (the equivalent of 30 stories), and the chance to touch a small moon rock, which looks like polished metal. The presentation in the **Lunar Theatre,** which recounts the big touchdown, is well produced and even includes a video appearance by the reclusive Neil Armstrong. Finally, the bus whisks you past the executive offices (you'll see the building where Larry Hagman worked on *I Dream of Jeannie*—and in the parking lot, notice that even astrophysicists drive Hondas and pickup trucks) and deposits you at the **International Space Station Center.** There, nothing but plate glass divides you from the dust-free clean room where segments of the space station are prepared to be sent into orbit.

Once you've completed the bus tour, it's up to you whether you want to plumb the sillier, kid-geared business at the Visitor's Complex. By this point, much of it will be redundant, and I find the movies pure malarkey, but take the time to check **Launch Status Center,** where current missions are tracked in real time (if there's not a mission on, skip it); the 42-foot-high black granite slab of the **Astronaut Memorial,** commemorating those lost; **Early Space Exploration,** where you'll see the impossibly low-tech Mission Control for the Mercury missions (they used rotary telephones!), plus some authentic space suits from the Gemini, Mercury, and Apollo series. The newest addition is the $60 million **Shuttle Launch Experience,** in which 44-person motion-simulator pods mimic a 5-minute launch.

Because the government commandeers the surrounding land as a buffer, there is nowhere else to eat within a 15-minute drive. The Center points out that it uses no public funding for its tourist amenities, but I still think it's disgraceful to charge $2.60 for Coke and $15 for two hot dogs and two drinks. Such shameless gouging is a disservice to a treasure that should belong to all Americans. As the stewards of a precious preserve, Kennedy Space Center should provide refreshment at an earthbound price. Good hospitality isn't rocket science, you know.

Seventeen miles east of Orlando, the 10-acre roadside zoo **Jungle Adventures Nature Park** ★ 🄺🄸🄳🅂 (26205 S.R. 50, Christmas; ☎ 877/424-2867 or 407/568-2885; www.jungleadventures.com; $19 adults, $9.50 kids 3–11, $15 seniors over 59) is the closest challenger to Gatorland (p. 231). It's even fronted by Swampy, a 200-foot roadside alligator (it was once a house!), the way Gatorland has its famous gator-jaw doorway. Jungle Adventures, which started life more interested in gator wrestling and morphed into an educational park, is a little wilder than Gatorland, but it only takes an hour or two to do, making it a decent stop on the non-toll route to the Kennedy Space Center. Feed black bears through a chute, gawk at the 15-foot-long gator Goliath, take a pontoon ride on the duckweed-clogged "Green Gator River" (a canal containing some 200 alligators), and watch rare Florida panthers from the boardwalk that snakes through the complex. There's also a replica Native American village that amalgamates the lifestyles of the old Timicuan and Calusa tribes, but that part tends to bore kids rigid. Feedings and demonstrations are scheduled throughout the day so that they don't overlap. Souvenirs made of alligator skin, *de rigeur* in these parts, are on sale.

Christmas Greetings

Christmas, Florida, on State Road 50 between Orlando and Titusville, usually isn't much to write home about: Farm supplies, roadkill. Unless, of course, it's the holiday season, when people come from far and wide to give their cards a Christmas postmark from the local post office. You'll find the P.O. near Jungle Adventures Nature Park at 23580 E. Colonial Dr./S.R. 50 (☎ 407/568-2841; Mon–Fri 9am–5pm, Sat 9:30am–noon).

PORT CANAVERAL

This isn't a book about cruising—for that, you can try *Frommer's Cruises & Ports of Call*—so there's not much point in going in-depth about the cruise lines that depart from Port Canaveral, located about an hour east of Orlando.

But for those who didn't know about the option, you should check them out. Almost all of the cruise lines provide bus transportation from Orlando International Airport and back, or even to Orlando hotels, so it's easy to combine a cruise of a few days with a few days at the theme parks. One company, Disney Cruise Line, is active in selling vacation packages that arrange just such a week.

Most cruise passengers will be dumped by their buses at their ships, and that's just as well, because there is nothing to do at the port. The itineraries of the ships are not the most scintillating; because of Central Florida's distance from the Caribbean, it's usually only possible to go as far as the Bahamas or Key West.

Two casino boats, free to board, also use Port Canaveral as a base for their brief interludes in international waters; see p. 271 for information on those. Both offer free shuttles to and from Orlando if you've got reservations.

The following major cruise lines go from Port Canaveral, although the ships they send from the port vary depending on the time of year:

- **Carnival Cruise Lines** (☎ 888/227-64825; www.carnival.com). Considered a low-rent line, it's noisy and twitters with neon and lurid colors like the inside of a pinball machine. It considers Las Vegas, and not the great ocean liners, an artistic inspiration—yes, there's a casino aboard. Each ship's main pool has a twisting water slide that has also become a line signature. Carnival sails the *Elation* and *Sensation* on 3- and 4-night Bahamas trips from $250; and 7-night Western Caribbean cruises on the *Glory*, which is among the line's largest class of ships, from $550. Carnival is popular with families, teens especially like it, and there are also lots of kids' activities.
- **Disney Cruise Line** (☎ 800/511-9444; www.disneycruise.com). The line for Mouseheads. These casino-free ships were designed expressly for families and include character meals and appearances, and theme park–style entertainment (its *Golden Mickeys* show was exported from the line to Hong Kong Disneyland). The hallmark is the kids' program; I've heard stories from parents who say there was so much to do, they barely saw their children once they boarded. In winter, *Disney Magic* and *Disney Wonder,* both with a 2,400-passenger capacity and little difference between them, do 3-night Bahamas cruises from around $650 per person; 7-night Western Caribbean cruises from $1,150; and 10-night Western Caribbean cruises from $2,500. In the summer, one ship is either here or in Los Angeles, and the other is in Europe. Disney packages trips with theme park stays, including transportation.
- **Royal Caribbean International** (☎ 866/562-7625; www.royalcaribbean. com). It's the line for young couples and yuppies, with enormous ships and lots of offbeat activities such as ice-skating rinks, sheet-wave machines, and rock-climbing walls. Its beds are also the most comfortable cabin beds I've slept on. Royal Caribbean hits the sweet spot between the gaudy tackiness of Carnival and the intense branding of the Disney cruises, and most approximates a floating resort. *Sovereign of the Seas* and *Mariner of the Seas* do 3- and 4-night Bahamas runs from $300.

As usual, you won't find many discounts from Disney, although the Mouse Savers website (www.mousesavers.com) keeps tabs on which departures are going cheap. But some companies offering deals on the other lines include **Cruise Brothers** (☎ 800/827-7779; www.cruisebrothers.com) and **Cruise Value Center** (☎ 800/231-7447; www.mycruisevalue.com). **Cruises Only** (☎ 800/278-4737; www.cruisesonly.com), one of the largest sellers in the U.S., has the power to sometimes snag discounts the other sellers can't. Don't quit before you consult a terrific site called **Cruise Compete** (www.cruisecompete.com), on which multiple cruise sellers jockey for your business by lodging the lowest bid on a cruise of your choosing.

The Other Orlando

If you think it's all about T-shirts and coasters, you've got another thing coming

THE MOST PASSIVE TOURISTS AMONG US GO TO WALT DISNEY WORLD OR Universal Orlando to wallow in what marketing executives have carefully programmed consumers to call "magic." Every single advertisement the Disney Company puts out is required to contain at least one use of the M-word, and lest it mar its carefully cultivated reputation, the company is cagey about revealing the canny stage management that goes on behind the scenes. A very small percentage of tourists—a sliver of a slice—take the time to dig around and find out how the showmanship has been accomplished. They learn what few do: The behind-the-scenes operations of these parks are undeniably awesome.

These tourist meccas are more than just amusement parks. They are astounding feats of civil planning and engineering. Even people with no interest in cartoon characters or roller coasters can find a great deal to admire and appreciate in the Herculean achievement that each and every theme park represents. When Phase One of Walt Disney World's construction (the Magic Kingdom and three hotels) was undertaken, it represented the largest private construction project on Earth. When Epcot Center was constructed, it too was the world's biggest project at the time. And today, WDW is the largest single-site employer in the world, with some 58,000 "cast members" pitching in to make the resort run—and that doesn't even count outside contractors, whose ranks are growing every year.

Orlando is more than a vacation destination. It's a real place inhabited by real people who are trained to cast a spell on you. They operate the one-of-a-kind machines and carry out the peculiar customs that make the world's largest family vacation destination tick. And when they go home at night, they return to a real city with its own identity that is distinct from—and often, at odds with—the hedonistic, secondary world that was imposed upon the landscape beginning in 1971. They return to what could be called the "other" Orlando, while you remain in Fantasyland. To understand the accomplishments behind the theme parks you're seeing, to appreciate how they have come to define the pinnacle of American mass culture, and to be more than just another pacified consumer of these seductive parks, you must peel back the curtain to the "magic." I can tell you how.

HOW ORLANDO WORKS

The major theme parks, ever eager to mine a new revenue stream, discreetly offer those in the know the chance to slip behind the scenes, into restricted areas, and even through the gates before opening time. These out-of-the-ordinary opportunities always happen under the watchful eye of knowledgeable guides whose only job is to teach visitors about the secrets behind the show. Ticket prices are always above and beyond the price of regular admission, which is usually also required (I'll let you know when it isn't), but the added expense is rewarded with unbelievable access and the chance to ask your guide anything and everything you can think of about how it's all done. Even if the pace of these tours is often slow to compensate for the least physically able of your group (which will usually not number more than 10), many visitors—me included—will tell you that their time spent on these insiders' tours ranks among the best they've ever had at the parks. I have yet to meet a fan who said one of these tours ruins the "magic" for them— it only deepens their appreciation. Besides, you look awfully cool when you're ushered behind the velvet ropes.

Reservations are required for all theme park tours, and many of them have age requirements (such as an age minimum of 16 years), although when there's no rule, kids under 3 are usually free. Most guides won't let you take photos when you're in backstage areas, but you may usually make audio recordings, and many tours are shadowed by park photographers who'll later be only too happy to sell you approved images of your visit.

WALT DISNEY WORLD

Walt Disney was unquestionably a visionary. When he started out, he was mostly interested in the potential of animation as an art form. But as his fame and resources grew, his dreams became infinite, and by the end of his life, he was obsessed with building a city of his own. In fact, he intended to build that city on a chunk of his Central Florida land. His dream of an Experimental Prototype Community of Tomorrow, or Epcot, in which residents, many of them theme park workers, could try out new forms of corporate-sponsored, minimum-impact technology in the course of their daily lives, emerged 16 years after his death as nothing more than another world's fair, and not the city to save us all. But because the Magic Kingdom was originally shaped by his own hand and by his most trusted designers, it incorporated several key innovations.

One is the utilidor system. The bulk of the Magic Kingdom that you see appears to be at ground level. But in fact, you'll be walking about 14 feet above the land. The attractions constitute the second and third stories of a nine-acre network of warehouses and corridors, utilidors, built in part to guard against flooding but mostly so that guests wouldn't be jolted from their fantasy. Cast members make deliveries, take breaks, change costumes, and count money in the windowless, cinder-block catacombs on the true ground floor of the Magic Kingdom, which is accessed through secret entrances and unmarked wormholes scattered around the themed lands. Clean-burning electric vehicles zip through the hallways, some of which are wide enough to accommodate trucks, and all of which are color-coded to indicate which land is directly upstairs. If you're lucky enough to score a ticket to the utilidor system—and yes, I'm about to tell you how you can—you'll have gained entry into the most guarded inner spaces of the Disney World empire.

Among the other engineering feats and innovation that make the Kingdom tick:

- Trash is transported at 60mph to a central collection point by Swedish AVAC pneumatic tubes in the ceiling of the utilidors.

- Fire, power, and water systems are all monitored by a common computer, and the robotics, doors, lighting, sounds, and vehicles on the most complicated attractions are handled by a central server called the Digital Animation Control System or DACS, located roughly underneath Cinderella Castle.
- The Seven Seas Lagoon, in front of the Magic Kingdom, was low, dry land. It was filled to create a new body of water.
- Bay Lake, beside Fort Wilderness, was dredged, and the dirt used to raise the Magic Kingdom site by 14 feet. Underneath the lakebed, white, ancient sand was discovered, cleaned, and deposited to create the Seven Seas Lagoon's beaches.
- Energy is re-used whenever possible. The generators' waste heat is used to heat water, and hot water runoff is used for heating, cooking, and absorption chilling for air-conditioning. Waste water is reclaimed for plants and lawns, and sludge is dried for fertilizer. Food scraps are composted on-site. The resort produces enough power to keep things running in case of a temporary outage on the municipal grid. This will keep you up tonight: Disney even has the legal right to build its own nuclear power plant, should it care to.
- Some 55 miles of canals were dug on resort property to keep the land from growing sodden. Most of these canals were curved to appear natural.
- The resort was the first place to install an all-electronic phone system using underground cable—so guests don't see ugly telephone wires. It was the first telephone company in America to use a 911 emergency system.
- In addition to running the largest laundry facility in the world and establishing kitchens to supply the whole resort, by 1970, a year before opening, the park already had its own tree farm with more than 800 varieties of 60,000 plants, and that effort has been greatly expanded to grow nourishment for the many creatures at Animal Kingdom. More than 100,000 trees and two million shrubs have been planted here since 1971.
- The rubber-tired monorail system, designed by Disney engineers, now contains 14.7 miles of track. Walt had intended monorails, and vehicles akin to the Tomorrowland Transit Authority ride, to be the main forms of transportation to and through his Epcot. In 1986, the monorail was named a National Historic Mechanical Engineering Landmark by the American Society of Mechanical Engineers.

Sadly, the Walt Disney Co. of later years has shown little interest in advancing these remarkable innovations. Designs have returned to trucks and standard energy methods, which Walt desperately wanted to sideline. Epcot has only a small network of utilidors, located under Innoventions and Spaceship Earth in the center section of Future World, and the other Disney parks were built without them at all, often permitting trash collection and restocking to occur in full guest view. The monorail has not been expanded since 1982, forcing a renewed reliance on buses and cars. The Magic Kingdom, largely because of Walt's lingering influence, is a rare gasp of Utopian idealism put into practice.

Disney is still justifiably proud of many of its accomplishments, though, and it recognizes that for some guests, the sheer size of its operation itself qualifies as a tourist attraction. Cast members eagerly swap trivia about how Imagineers have cleverly manipulated forced perspective and hidden, authentic touches to building facades and public spaces. And an entire subculture has grown up around spotting and recording so-called "Hidden Mickeys," which are camouflaged appearances of Mickey Mouse's profile that can appear in carpet designs, on wallpaper, created out of props on rides, and in other unexpected places.

So even if the company's engineers now pay scant attention to developing "Walt's dream"—that Talmudic totem that the company's marketing department invokes to sell DVDs—it will, fortunately, afford guests a backstage gander at the resort's ingenuity through its Walt Disney World tours (☎ 407/939-8687). There are dedicated tours at all parks except Disney-MGM Studios, presumably because the animation department, once its most interesting tenant, has been evicted (but you can still pop into the Studios on the Backstage Magic and Yuletide Magic tours).

Resort-wide Tours

Backstage Magic ✪✪✪ ($199 including lunch, minimum age 16; Mon–Fri; 7 hr.), the big kahuna of Disney explorations, is one of the few tours to require no theme park admission, because you spend all your time exploring the parks' considerable infrastructure. For people more interested in how the joint is run—the Audio-Animatronic workshop, scene shops, florists, computer command centers, the warehouse for Christmas decorations—this tour supplies a daylong crash course, including a private bus. You'll go into Epcot's small utilidor, to Disney-MGM's backstage areas, and into the Magic Kingdom utilidor (but not to Animal Kingdom) and receive an excellent overview on the scope of the resort's groundbreaking behind-the-scenes capabilities. A good tour is largely dependent on how snappy your guide is but most of them have been with the company in excess of 2 decades and they can make the long day go quickly and even tailor the itinerary and information according to your interests. Lunch, which is included, is served at Mama Melrose's Ristorante Italiano at Disney–MGM, and participants also receive a commemorative pin that you can only get if you take the tour. For fans of theme parks and their design there is no more worthy splurge in Orlando, or perhaps anywhere.

Dine with a Disney Imagineer ✪ (☎ 407/939-3463; $61 adults, $35 kids 3–9; 11:30am Mon, Wed, and Fri) is just what it sounds like: A chance to break bread, over a catered lunch, with one of the folks charged with putting the parks together. Considering Disney's cloistered corporate culture, this gives plebians like us rare access, and a chance to circumvent the company's usually scripted public presentations. Some of them started in writing, some in construction, some in entertainment, and some in engineering—you never know who you'll get, and your experience depends entirely on how polished your Imagineer's raconteur skills are, as well as how forthcoming they're willing to be about Disney secrets and future plans. Have plenty of questions ready to get the most out of the meal. Often, your Imagineer will be just as interested in grilling you about your impressions of their handiwork. For them, appearances aren't a chore, but a chance to hone their efforts according to the response of an audience. The lunch is held in a private room at Disney–MGM's Brown Derby restaurant. There's a dinner version at the Wilderness Lodge's upscale Artist Point, held every other Thursday, but that's pricier ($89 adults, $40 kids), and you'll gain the same access from the cheaper lunch.

Yuletide Fantasy ($69 per person, minimum age 16; offered seasonally; 3½ hr.) is the least worthy and the most shallow of the multi-park splurges. Much of it is filler, as groups as large as 40 walk around Epcot's World Showcase and are filled in about other countries' holiday traditions. The rest of the time is spent admiring the admittedly lavish Christmas decorations at Disney–MGM Studios, the Grand Floridian resort, and the Magic Kingdom's Main Street, with a climactic stop at the impressive Christmas warehouse, a facility the size of a Home Depot where the resort's custom-made decorations are stored and refurbished year-round. That's a lotta holiday spirit: some 11 miles of garlands, 3,000 wreaths, and 1,500 trees. Sample trivia: Each souvenir store receives different Christmas decorations according to what they sell—we're talking serious minutiae here. One gift to you, in addition to the special pin: Theme park admission isn't required.

Magic Kingdom

The least expensive way to sneak a peek at the utilidors, **Keys to the Kingdom Tour** ★★★ ($60 per person, including lunch; minimum age 16; daily; 4½ hr.) provides a good overview of the Imagineers' design philosophies. It includes a long explication of Main Street, the hub, the Castle, and a pass through Frontierland and Adventureland, where the group kills a little time riding one or two rides together, after which your guide (mine had been with the company since the 1980s) discusses the technology behind them. The real appeal is the brief time spent in forbidden backstage areas: the parade float storage sheds behind Splash Mountain and a quiet cul-de-sac of the utilidors beneath Town Square— the group enters in the Emporium and resurfaces in a parking lot off eastern Main Street. Lunch is at a roped-off section of the Columbia Harbour House in Liberty Square, and you get a free pin. The tour is a terrific blend of information for newbies and nuggets for hard-core fans.

Old Walt and his hobby making steam trains is heavily evoked in **The Magic Behind Our Steam Trains Tour** ★ ($40 per person, minimum age 10; Mon–Tues, Thurs, and Sat; 3 hr.), but once the myth-building is out of the way, train fans will get the goods on the park's unique train culture: A trip to the roundhouse, up-close looks at one of its four antique engines (which until the 1960s were working machines in the Yucatan) and inside a locomotive's cab, a spin on one or two trains, and an explanation of operating procedures. Train fans won't feel short-changed because Disney's rolling stock is so lovingly maintained. No cameras are allowed.

I consider the next two avoidable if you're hungry to learn about backstage machinations. **Mickey's Magical Milestones Tour** ($25 per person, minimum age 10; Mon, Wed, and Fri; 2 hr.) is a simple experience. You'll hear a bit about Hidden Mickeys on Main Street before opening; ride the train to Toontown Fair, where everyone draws a picture of Mickey; and then meet Mickey himself. You could do many of those things without the tour. You'll get zero inside gossip on **Disney's Family Magic Tour** ($27 per person; daily; 2½ hr.), a bubbly scavenger hunt. In the name of thwarting Captain Hook's evil plans, you'll be skipping and singing (but not riding anything) to a climax attended by Peter Pan. Obviously, it's for little kids. And strange adults.

Epcot

The UnDISCOVERed Future World ★★ ($49 per person, minimum age 16; Mon, Wed, and Fri; 4 hr.) is the best overview of Epcot. Depending on your guide and the day, the package includes some background on Epcot's original intentions (gently watered down to make the final product seem more like Walt's plan), ample forays into backstage areas (Test Track, The Land, Universe of Energy), maybe a ride (Soarin'), usually a glimpse at one of the VIP rooms laid out for the corporate sponsors of the pavilions, a glowing talk by a temporary cast member from a foreign country, a walk-through of the cast services building, and a detailed description of how IllumiNations works. The only section left largely unexposed is the World Showcase. At the end, you're presented with a special pin and with permission to view that night's IllumiNations spectacle from a VIP area in front of the Italy pavilion.

Around the World at Epcot ★★★ ($80 per person, minimum age 16 and maximum weight of 250 pounds; daily; 2 hr.) proved to be one of my favorite experiences in years of Disney-going. The tour starts in the early morning, before the park opens. For the first hour, guests are taught how to use Segway people movers in a special training facility at Innoventions. That was a treat enough. Once guides are confident that you've got the hang of the vehicles—it's a lot like skiing, and most people, even those with two left feet, get the knack within 15 minutes—your two guides lead you outside in single file and you spend the next hour coasting and threading through the international pavilions of the World Showcase, which you'll have all to yourself, with no other guests around. Here and there, they'll fill you in about little-noticed details or design triumphs, but mostly, this is about a sense of freedom and of exhilaration. I slalomed through the columns of the Doge's Palace in Venice, scooted across eyebrow bridges of Japanese gardens, and rode through a biergarten in Germany—all in the warm Florida morning breeze.

Because it runs repeatedly, **Behind the Seeds at Epcot** ($14 adults, $10 kids 3–9; daily; 45 min.) is one of the few tours that can be booked on-the-go, and one of the only ones that gets you close to the original altruistic intentions for Epcot. Here, the lesson is the research being conducted at The Land's experimental greenhouses, insects lab, and fish farm, and guests are filled in on the park's joint efforts with botanists (many from the University of Florida's Horticultural Sciences Department) to advance growing technologies. Your guide is likely to be a college student who is studying the very concepts being imparted—how much you learn depends entirely on their mood, so butter 'em up—and little children are usually given ladybugs to release, seeds to plant, or crops to taste. To make sure you'd be interested, ride Living with the Land first, where you'll get a cursory introduction to a few of the same concepts and greenhouses via pre-recorded narration. After that, you can book the tour at the informational desk beside the entrance to Soarin'.

Bring your open-water scuba certification to Orlando, and you'll be qualified to swim with the fishes at **Epcot DiveQuest** ($140, including diving gear; minimum age 10; daily; 3 hr.), held in the massive saltwater tank at The Seas with Nemo & Friends—conditions are always perfect and the range of life unparalleled in the wild. You'll learn a little about the aquarium and its upkeep, but the true attraction here is the chance to dive in it for 30 minutes and to wave at your fellow tourists from the business side of the glass. That's a good time, but whether it's $140 worth of a good time is certainly up for debate. No park admission is required. **Epcot Seas Aqua Tour** ($100 including equipment, T-shirt, and photo;

minimum age 8; daily; 2½ hr.) is the alternative for people without scuba certification. If you can snorkel, you can do this—you're equipped with an air tank and with flotation devices that keep you on the surface, where you spend a half-hour swimming face-down above the arching fake coral in the 5.7 million-gallon aquarium. You'll be filled in on how the habitat is maintained, and you wrap up, somewhat ironically, with a shower. That's a lot of money for just 30 minutes of tank time, but if snorkeling in the wild makes you nervous, or if you've never done it, you might consider the luxury of a safe environment worth it. No theme park admission is required.

Perhaps a better name for **Dolphins in Depth** ($150 including T-shirt and photo; minimum age 13; Mon–Fri; 3 hr.) would be Dolphins, Shallowly. The water's only knee-deep, and after preparation and education about Epcot's dolphin rescue program, the interaction lasts only about 20 minutes. The climax: You tentatively hug one of the mammals as your free souvenir photo is snapped. No theme park admission is required, and proceeds go to dolphin conservation. For better value, SeaWorld's Dolphin Nursery Close Up allows you to feed and pet dolphins (from dry land, not from inside the tank) for 10 minutes more but $110 less.

Disney's Animal Kingdom

Wild By Design ($58 per person, including a light breakfast; minimum age 14; Thurs–Fri; 3 hr.) is the Keys of the Kingdom version for Animal Kingdom; you learn why architects chose the designs they did for the park's buildings, and the nomenclature of this park's particular "story"—the imagined tale that designers want you to perceive as you explore—is explained. You'll also learn a bit about how the animal habitats were designed and how those designs make everyday care easier. Here's a shocker: The lions are enticed to maintain their position on their proud viewing rocks using hidden air-conditioning.

Backstage Safari ★ ($65 per person, minimum age 16; Mon, Wed–Thurs, and Fri; 3 hr.) focuses more on animal care than on the made-up storytelling of the park. It escorts you through the animal care facilities of the park, including the veterinary hospital—you never know who's going to be sick enough to check in the day you're there, so you'll get a lot of info about daily care and how animal foods are prepared. The rest of the itinerary may change according to which animals are in social moods, but white rhinos and elephants are often on the menu. Wear close-toed shoes. The climax is a turn on the Kilimanjaro Safari ride, only with a special narration that gives away the design secrets that keeps animals and humans on their respective sides. This is the tour for animal buffs to take if they think Rafiki's Planet Watch just doesn't go deep enough, but average folks may not care much about watching cast members cut up fruit for the monkeys. Mickey would be sick if he knew which kind of animal the snakes eat.

UNIVERSAL ORLANDO

Universal hasn't yet established tours that come anywhere near the quality and depth of Disney's. If you want to pry your way into backstage secrets, you pretty much have to spring for one of the park's overly expensive **V.I.P Tour Experience** (☎ 407/363-8295), on which groups of about 10 guests are assigned a guide who escorts them past the rabble and onto all the rides they want. This method all but guarantees that you'll ride the best stuff (although the shows, such as IOA's Eighth Voyage of Sindbad, are skipped), but it isn't cheap: $120 for an adult to see one park ($150 for both), including valet parking, priority introduction to character meet-and-greets, but *not* admission. It does squeak you behind-the-scenes, briefly, at the awesome Spider-Man ride, where you'll see the control room and the shop in which the Scoop vehicles are repaired—you'll be amazed at how little the cars actually move—but other than that, you don't go backstage. Unless you take it upon yourself to interrogate your guide (mine was a former school principal who now conducts these tours every day) about all the backstage and technical information that your brain can fit, the price won't be right.

During Halloween Horror Nights season (late Sept–Oct), Universal also offers **Unmasking the Horror** (☎ 407/363-8295; $35 per person; 2 hr.) backstage tours that explain the yearlong design and construction process for the elaborate "scares" and haunted houses. The trenchcoat crew loves taking these.

SEAWORLD ORLANDO

As a place that prides itself on sharing conservation information—in fact, as a place that keeps animals on display, its reputation depends on it—SeaWorld is generous with its selection of backstage and extra-informational tours. All interactions involving swimming include a wetsuit and equipment, and end with a private, hot shower in a special trailer located in the park's backstage area.

Every now and then, the park sets up overnight **Sleepovers** (☎ 866/479-2267; www.swbg-adventurecamps.com) for kids and their parents in some of the more interesting pavilions, such as the Frosty Friends Sleepover, held at the Penguin Encounter; or Hot Summer Nights, held in the chilled Wild Arctic habitat with walruses and beluga whales. Families literally lay their sleeping bags (the park doesn't advertise the fact, but it has a limited number for you to borrow—make sure to ask for one when you book) beside the windows of the animal habitats. The nights (7pm–9am) come with educational activities, snacks, and breakfast, and cost $75 to $80 per person. Packages are also available ($110) that include admission to the park the following day, which can save you some money. Registration is imperative. Although most tourists won't have the time or resources to devote to them, the park's wonderful kid-oriented **Adventure Camps** (☎ 866/479-2267; www.swbg-adventurecamps.com) are broken down by age group, starting with age 3 and ending with high school seniors, and are designed to be full-day, classroom-based lessons in the arts of animal training and care. For 6 intensive days (prices start at $950), kids spend all their time at the park, getting their feet wet, so to speak, in careers as animal caregivers. Sure beats a babysitter.

SeaWorld also hosts frequent talks included in the price of admission. Held on occasional Tuesdays expressly for seniors aged 50 or older, **Terrific Tuesdays Seminars** ✚✪ (www.4adventure.com/SWF/SWFSE/tue.aspx) are first-come, first-served educational symposiums by animal trainers, gardeners, engineers, and other experts. Also, splitting his time with Busch Gardens, animal expert **Jack Hanna** makes announced appearances every few months; as he does when he's on David Letterman, he trots out animal after exotic animal, telling the audience about each one in his affable way that proves he's not as clueless as he appears.

The regular tours offered to day visitors of **SeaWorld** (☎ 800/327-2424; www.seaworldorlando.com) are devoted less to touting the ingenuity of a vaunted design team, as Disney's are, and more to getting you close to and learning about the animals. In fact, they're dubbed "interactions." Because interactions frequently sell out, you should always do your best to reserve—it can be done online—but if you can't, there's a Behind-the-Scenes desk at the entry plaza of the park for last-minute arrangements.

Behind-the-Scenes Tours ($16 adults, $12 kids 3–9; 1 hr.), being short and comparatively inexpensive, are excellent compromises for families that don't want a huge financial or time commitment, but still crave a deeper education. There are four, offered daily: The **Polar Expedition Tour** ✖ dips into the work areas at Wild Arctic, and you're given the chance to touch a live penguin from the habitat, a rarity at any park. You won't pet a polar bear because that would be the last thing you ever did. The **Predators Tour** centers on the 600,000-galloon Shark Encounter (the same one caged tourists swim in on Sharks Deep Dive, discussed below), where you don't swim but you touch a shark and learn about their care; you'll also head across the park to see the backstage areas of Shamu Stadium. The **Saving a Species Tour** highlights rare animals in distress, as you visit the veterinary facilities for sea turtles and manatees and hand-feed exotic birds in the park's aviary. The **Dolphin Nursery Close-Up** ✖✖ ($40) is an affordable alternative to Discovery Cove. The first half-hour is spent learning the basics about the animals (fact: dolphin mothers' milk is 33% fat), and for the second 30 minutes, trainers trot out buckets of half-frozen fish and everyone leans over the edge of the Dolphin Nursery tank to toss lunch into the eagerly yawning mouths of adolescent dolphins and their mothers. You'll be able to pet the finely muscled mammals—they feel as rubbery as they look—and you'll even be taught a few hand signals to get the family to do tricks. These animals truly have their own personalities, and even 30 minutes is enough to begin to discern them and to begin to fall in love with them. Your time will fly by.

Beluga Interaction Program ✖✖✖ ($179 per person, including souvenir book; minimum age 13; Thurs–Mon; 90 min.) is one of the park's most extravagant choices. Even though it's expensive, opportunities to squeeze into a wet suit and swim for 30 minutes in 55-degree salt water with the beautiful white beluga whales simply don't come often. Participants don't have to be excellent swimmers, but they should be able to get around, as they'll be maneuvering themselves to stroke and feed the gentle animals. Only about a half-hour is spent in the water; the rest of your visit, you'll become a pocket expert on belugas. You'll enjoy this interaction most if you aren't afraid to tread water in a tank that's several times deeper than your height. The park suspends the program whenever a new whale takes up residence, to give it time to acclimate and socialize, so this swim is not always on the table.

The *ne plus ultra* for a SeaWorld or animal fan is the **Marine Mammal Keeper Experience** ✖✖ ($399, including lunch, T-shirt, book, and a 7-day pass to SeaWorld; minimum age 13; 9 hr.), which starts at 6:30am and leads you through a typical day for an animal keeper. The schedule includes food preparation (get ready for fishy fingers); helping the Animal Rescue and Rehabilitation Team look after manatees; standing over the vets' shoulders as they heal sick animals; and helping trainers interact with and train dolphins, manatees, beluga whales, sea lions, and walruses. This is no put-on for shuffling bus tours; you will have to lift at least 15 pounds of food at one point, and there's a limit of just three people a day. Yes, it's very expensive, but at least it also gets you unlimited entry to the park for a week. Many people who have done this swear that it's money better spent than a ticket to Discovery Cove; you'll get in the water to care for dolphins and manatees, but you won't grab onto their fins for any gimmicky "swims" with them.

The novelty of **Sharks Deep Dive** ★★ ($150 including T-shirt, a 72-page booklet on sharks, and souvenir photo; minimum age 10; 2 hr.) isn't just that you'll be in a tank with some 30 specimens of five varieties of the predators. It's also the newfangled helmet, which enables you to breathe without scuba tanks and even pose questions to an ichthyologist who observes from above the surface. Guests are lowered, two at a time, into a metal cage and pulled slowly across the 125 foot-long habitat while the locals stalk the bars curiously. Meanwhile, your loved ones and random park guests watch anxiously from the plastic tunnel that bisects the tank's bottom. You aren't in any danger, of course, because these sharks are regularly fed and you can swim to the water's surface within the cage at any time, but the combination of weird equipment, bizarre man-made habitat, and beady-eyed fish make for a bracing and highly unique experience. When I did it, I didn't find it at all scary or difficult—I was even able to wear my eyeglasses inside the helmet without so much as a drop of water splashing them—and because the cage is made of clear plastic at eye level, I got some unparalleled views of the texture and color of the animals as they checked me out in return. The time allotted underwater is more than generous, and because the aquarium is also stocked with other types of fish, there's plenty to look at, including the diners in the fancy restaurant through the acrylic walls on the other side of the tank. When you're done, you'll never confuse these fellas with Flipper again.

Adventure Express Tour ($89 adults, $79 kids 3–9, including lunch; 6 hr.) is a combination of VIP tour and backstage glimpse. You're escorted to the front of the line at Kraken, Journey to Atlantis, and Wild Arctic's simulator ride; given fish to feed to dolphins, sea lions, and stingrays; and shown to prime reserved seating at two shows (which change daily, but are always among the best). All of those activities are available to regular paying guests without premium treatment (the fish, for example, would cost a combined $12). Along the way, you'll be allowed to touch a penguin during a behind-the-scenes stop—the only real backstage access of the day, but a goodie, even if the privilege is available a la carte for $16 (see above).

KENNEDY SPACE CENTER

Every day, the Kennedy Space Center hosts an appearance by a real astronaut, many of whom have retired to the same area where they once worked. Now and then, you'll even see headliners such as Jim Lovell and Wally Schirra making the rounds. Typically, these guys (and a very few women) really enjoy basking in fandom and in reliving old tales of glory—and unlike out-to-pasture sportsmen, these old-timers really did risk their lives the way heroes are supposed to—so these half-hour **Astronaut Encounter** ★★ (☎ 321/449-4444; www.kennedyspacecenter.com) sessions, which are scheduled throughout the day, are geared toward questions. You will need a ticket to the Space Center to partake of one, but if the session still isn't one-on-one enough for you, you can pay another $23 adults/$16 kids to sit down at 12:15pm daily with that week's astronaut and have a catered lunch, at which you can press him about whatever you like.

NASA reaches for the stars, but Kennedy Space Center reaches for the big spenders with its all-day **Astronaut Training Program** (☎ 321/449-4400; www. kennedyspacecenter.com; $225, minimum age 14). It dubs the program ATX but I like to call it Space Daycamp. You'll get a few up-close guided tours of the big launch pads, lunch, and you'll test a few of the pieces of astronaut equipment, such as the multi-axis trainer (which spins your body within a series of interlinked concentric circles to test your equilibrium), a gravity chair, and a spell in a full-scale mock-up of the shuttle. Nothing is as intense as what the astronauts themselves experience, but it's still plenty rigorous for most terrestrials, and the facilitators can answer nearly any question you can come up with about the space program.

BUSCH GARDENS AFRICA

Like SeaWorld, Busch Gardens wants its tours (☎ 888/800-5447; www.busch gardens.com) to teach about animals, and they're designed to give guests a sense of learning and some interaction.

As at SeaWorld, its sister park, Busch Gardens hosts occasional **Terrific Tuesdays Seminars** for seniors aged 50 or older. These educational symposiums by animal trainers and other experts are first-come, first-served. Animal expert **Jack Hanna** makes appearances every few months, announced well in advance.

Recognizing that it's enough of a challenge for most people to just make it down to Tampa for a day, I'll list these added activities quickly. They're offered daily (try to reserve ahead, or book upon entry at the Adventure Tour desk in Moroccan Village), and all of them permit plenty of photos.

Serengeti Safari ✪ ($34, minimum age 5; 30 min.) is a pretty cool add-on. You board a flatbed safari truck and motor out into the middle of the 65-acre animal enclosure, where the resident giraffes—some more plucky than sweet, you'll find, but all docile—amble in from all sides to wrap their muscular, gooey tongues around any lettuce leaves you proffer. Then you move on to another part of the Plain (passing through a wheel wash along the way, to rinse off the smell of rival animals) to feed whatever other animals you can find—usually antelope. Meanwhile, the luckless tourists stuck on the park train watch you jealously from a distance.

Saving a Species ($45, minimum age 5; 45 min.) is similar, except the post-giraffe portion swings by white and black rhinos, and an emphasis is placed on sharing information about conservation efforts.

Sunset on the Serengeti ✪ ($40, minimum age 21; 1 hr.), just like it sounds, happens around sundown. First, you'll imbibe a few Anheuser-Busch lagers, and then you'll venture onto the Plain (hold on tight; the ride's bumpy) with some giraffe grub and a cooler full of Bud. It's essentially a sudsy Serengeti Safari.

The **Family Adventure Tour** ($34, 45 min.), geared to those with kids under 7, is a simplified introduction of animal-rearing concepts held at Nairobi Field Station, which affords the chance to cuddle or touch at least one of the current residents.

Animal Adventure ✪ ($119, minimum age 5; 2 hr.) combines a short guided walking tour through backstage areas at Nairobi Field Station and the Clydesdale Hamlet with a truck tour across the Serengeti, led by a keeper, for a giraffe feeding.

There's no shortage of VIP-style guided tours that get you to the front of the lines and add a catered lunch at the Crown Colony Café. The least expensive, the **Adventure Thrill Tour** ($75 adults, $65 kids 3–9; 5 hr.), does the main rides and shows, tailored to your desires and brimming with coaster-nut trivia; you share your guide with about 10 other people and don't bother much with the animals. The **Guided Adventure** ($95 adults, $85 kids 3–9, minimum age 5; 5 hr.) subtracts one or two rides, usually ones the group agrees on, and instead adds a giraffe feeding on the Plain into the mix. The **Elite Adventure Tour** ($199, minimum age 5; 8 hr.) grants front-of-the-line access and reserved seating at the biggest shows with a private guide, whom you don't share with a small group, and also includes a giraffe feeding. **Ultimate Adventure** ($250, minimum age 5; 8 hr.) is the same experience, except instead of a simple giraffe feeding, you get the whole Animal Adventure tour (hippos, rhinos, Clydesdales, *plus* giraffes). It's only for purists or spendthrifts.

HOW ORLANDO PLAYS

Sure, lots of locals have season tickets to the major parks, but lots more wouldn't set foot in them for fun. Would *you* hang out at work on the weekends? In addition to the usual diversions, the area boasts a few unique pursuits you rarely find elsewhere.

DRIVE-IN MOVIES

Central Florida is one of the last places on the eastern seaboard where land values—at least those outside of Orlando proper—are still low enough to allow for that great mid-20th-century American tradition, the drive-in movie. The three most accessible cinemas each have capacity for about 300 cars and are all about an hours' drive from the tourist zone, but they're worth the trip, especially on one of those gloriously warm evenings for which Florida is justifiably famous. Catch them now, while you can, because the 21st century is intruding even in the former farmland and citrus groves.

Note: Call ahead for show times, as they change according to when the sun sets.

The two-screen **Silver Moon** ✪ (4100 Rt. 92 West, Lakeland; ☎ 863/682-0849; www.silvermoondrivein.com; $4 adults, kids under 9 free; cash only), 31 miles southwest of Disney off of I-4, shows first-run films every night of the week. Considering its opening-night ticket price was 35¢, prices haven't gone up very much since 1948. It even screens those old-fashioned animated enticements to visit the snack bar.

Joy Lan Drive-In ✪ (16414 Hwy. 301, north of Dade City; ☎ 352/567-5085; www.joylandrivein.com; closed Mon–Tues), over a half-century old, is known for being the cheapest drive-in in America: just $3.50 per person for first-run movies, and those under 9 are free. You can choose to listen to the soundtrack on your FM radio or using cinema-furnished speakers. It's 46 miles west of Disney.

Ocala Drive-In (4850 S. Pine Ave., Ocala; ☎ 352/629-1325; $4 adults, kids under 9 free), 71 miles northwest of Disney, is the most distant. It, too, first cranked up in 1948 and shows first-run films on what's essentially an expansive concrete wall.

SPRING TRAINING

Baseball is inextricable from Florida's calendar. Way back in 1923, the Cincinnati Reds began spring training in Orlando at Tinker Field. Ever since then, other professional baseball teams have seen the appeal of limbering up in the Florida sunshine before facing the blistering scrutiny of their fans during the season. In the 1930s, the Washington Senators arrived in town, and they stayed for the better part of half a century, finally as the Minnesota Twins (who have decamped to Fort Myers). A few teams in the so-called Grapefruit League (the Arizona trainers are the Cactus League) still call Orlando or its environs their temporary home, and in the pre-season you can swing by to watch them practice and to play exhibition games with visiting teams. Unlike at season games, players often mingle with fans—in fact, some teams' facilities were built to cozy proportions (you can leave the binoculars at home), with permanent interaction areas where you can collect autographs of the athletes before or after practice. Sometimes it feels like the spirit of old-time baseball, the one supplanted by high-priced players and colossal arenas, lives on mostly in Little League and at spring training.

Tickets go on sale in early January. Pitchers and catchers report first, in mid-February, and by the end of the month, the whole team's on hand. They play exhibition games with other teams through March before heading to their home parks in early April.

A few more teams (the New York Yankees, the Tampa Bay Devil Rays) train in Tampa, and another (the Washington Nationals) in Melbourne, but the 90-minute drive time is beyond the desires of most tourists. For more information, check out **Spring Training Online** (www.springtrainingmagazine.com).

* **Atlanta Braves** (Disney's Wide World of Sports, 700 S. Victory Lane, Lake Buena Vista; ☎ 407/939-4263; tickets $15–$23). Since they took up residence in 1997 at Walt Disney World, the Braves can brag about having one of the nicest and largest (9,500 seats) training stadiums under the sun. Tickets, which are cheaper for the bleachers and more expensive if you want close, reserved seating, go on sale in early January through Ticketmaster (☎ 407/839-3900; www.ticketmaster.com).

* **Houston Astros** ✪✪ (Osceloa County Stadium, 1000 Bill Beck Rd., Kissimmee; ☎ 321/697-3200; tickets $15–$18). The smallest training park in the Grapefruit League (5,200 seats—still hardly tiny) has hosted the Astros since 1985, who make themselves available for fan greetings in their Autograph Alley. Tickets are sold through Ticketmaster (☎ 407/839-3900; www.ticketmaster.com).

* **Cleveland Indians** ✪✪ (Chain of Lakes Park, 500 Cletus Allen Rd., Winter Haven; ☎ 863/293-3900; tickets $7–$21). Since 1966, the Indians have made their spring training home in Winter Haven, about 50 miles south of Orlando, near Cypress Gardens Adventure Park. The team's iconic and defiantly mid-'60s home, Chain of Lakes park, is situated picturesquely on the shore of Lake Lulu and was originally built for the Boston Red Sox.

* **Detroit Tigers** ✪ (Joker Merchant Stadium, Al Kaline Dr., 2301 Lake Hills Rd., Lakeland; ☎ 863/682-5300; tickets $7–$16). Lakeland, between Orlando and Tampa on I-4, has hosted the Tigers since 1934, and the team

is such a local institution that their so-called "Tiger Town" training complex, built on the site of a World War II flight academy, has grown up with them.

CAR RACING

Orlando is only a generation removed from its farming roots, and many of its inhabitants still retain their Main Street traditions, such as showing off their wheels in car races on a Saturday night. NASCAR is no small sport in these parts (Daytona 500, anyone?), and folks take their cars seriously. These automotive traditions have evolved into regular festive competitions, with the amenities of a carnival and an explosive verve that could put any theme park production to shame. But even for all the family-friendly trappings, it'll boost the fun if you have grease in your veins.

Amateur drag racers convene and compete in "grudge racing" at the quarter-mile racing surface at **Speed World Dragway** (19442 S.R. 50/E. Colonial Dr., Orlando; ☎ 407/568-5522; www.speedworlddragway.com; $10 adults, kids under 12 free) on most Wednesdays, Fridays, and Saturdays from 6 to 10:30pm for the facility's "Street Drags." Whomever can accelerate off the starting line and reach the finish line fastest—without jumping the gun—is the winner. Speed World bills it as "the largest 'street race' in the world," which may be true, and it's certainly the only track of its kind in the area approved by the National Hot Rod Association (did you even know that existed?). Noisy and spirited, the nights are all about boys and the comparison of the size of their toys. It's about 20 miles east of I-4, in an undeveloped stretch between Orlando and Titusville. Check the events schedule online before heading out.

Nearby, stock car racing fans turn out to watch their favorites do laps at the oval track on Friday and Saturday nights at **Orlando Speedworld** (19164 S.R. 50/E. Colonial Dr., Bithlo; ☎ 407/568-1367; www.orlandospeedworld.org), about 30 minutes east of downtown Orlando. The scene is more professional than that at the Dragway. House racers include super-late models, super stocks, and ministocks, and subscribe to FASCAR (Florida Association of Stock Car Auto Racing) rules. On Sundays, owners frequently schedule boisterous Crash-A-Rama derbies ($20 adults, kids under 12 free). The main season runs March to November, but there are plenty of exhibition events in the other months.

Probably the nicest facility around is the oval track at the **USA International Speedway** (3401 Old Polk City Rd., Lakeland; ☎ 800/984-7223; www.usaspeedway.com; tickets $10–$30) in Lakeland, about 45 minutes down I-4 from Disney. Its big event is the Hooters USAR Pro Cup (www.usarprocup.com), which is scheduled from March to November. Events, mostly cup races, charity events, and sponsored exhibitions, are scheduled once or twice a month, usually on weekend evenings.

Much more touristy is the **Richard Petty Driving Experience** (Walt Disney World Speedway, Lake Buena Vista; ☎ 407/939-0130; www.1800bepetty.com; minimum age 16; 9am–4pm). Heaven knows how it managed to secure a matchless location in the Magic Kingdom's parking lot, but there it sits, selling ride-alongs in 600 horsepower Winston Cup–style stock cars on a 1-mile track with 10-degree banking. A mere three laps at 150mph start at $99, mock races complete with pit-stop drills go for $249, and packages zoom up to $1,250 for 30 laps. Petty has 24 other locations around America, so don't feel bad if you miss this one.

It's Not on the Tourist Maps

The standard tourist literature won't point them out to you, but pop history happened at these places:

- **1418½ Clouser Ave., in the College Park area.** In July 1957, 9 months before the publication of *On the Road,* writer Jack Kerouac moved in with his mother, and he inhabited a 10-foot-by-10-foot room with just a cot, a desk, and a bare bulb. Here, he wrote *The Dharma Bums,* an exploration of personal spiritual renewal through a connection with nature. By the time he moved out in the spring of 1958, he was a literary superstar. The Kerouac Project (www.kerouacproject.org) now owns the home and invites up-and-coming writers to live rent-free in it for 3-month tenures.

- **1910 Hotel Plaza Blvd., Lake Buena Vista.** The very first building to be completed on Walt Disney World property was this low-slung glass-and-steel creation, considered painfully modern in January 1970. It was the Walt Disney World Preview Center, on what was then Preview Boulevard. Here, pretty young hostesses guided some one million visitors past artists' renderings, models, and films promoting Phase One of the resort that was being constructed. Naturally, the first souvenir shop at Disney World was also on the premises. The current tenant is a non-profit promoting sports participation.

- **839 N. Orlando Ave., Winter Park.** In March 1986, the legendary Canadian rock group The Band was in the midst of a disappointing reunion tour. After playing the Cheek to Cheek Lounge at the Villa Nova Restaurant, which stood here, pianist Richard Manuel, 42, returned to his hotel room at the Quality Inn next door and, when his wife briefly left the room, hanged himself in despair. The lounge site is now a CVS drugstore, and the motel is the Winter Park Inn.

- **Hyland Oaks drive, off Hiawassee Road, in the Pine Hills area.** The backstory is a mystery, but somebody built this replica of Graceland, down to the musical-note front gates, in a northern suburb of town. It also has a guitar-shaped pool; Elvis didn't have one, but Jerry Lee Lewis's is shaped like a piano. There are no tours.

HOW ORLANDO LEARNS

It surprises many first-time visitors that Orlando has a deep cultural commitment. Though the southern part of the city is all about fountains the color of Ty-D-Bol, the northern suburbs of the city are more blue-blooded. Remember that Orlando and Winter Park were once the darlings of upper crust magnates who vacationed here year after year. The cities' moneyed residents and garden club members still uphold a tradition of philanthropy and intellectualism, and part of their semi-Victorian mind-set includes furnishing enrichment programs to the general public.

In addition to regular Q&A sessions and seminars at the most prominent cultural institutions, such as the Orlando Museum of Art (p. 229), the Orange County Regional History Center (p. 228), and the Mennello Museum of American Art (p. 229), check the upcoming events at the following venues. Also pick up a free copy of *Orlando Weekly* (www.orlandoweekly.com/calendar), available from boxes across Orlando (less commonly in the tourist areas), which publishes an Events Calendar for the forthcoming week.

◆ **Urban Think Bookstore** ★★ (625 E. Central Blvd., Orlando; ☎ 407/650-8004; www.urbanthinkorlando.com; Thurs–Sat 9am–10pm, Sun 9am–6pm, Mon 11am–6pm, Tues–Weds 11am–9pm). Every few days, this progressive bookstore hosts a reading or signing by an author, some local and some nationally known. Frequent Friday nights from 6 to 10pm are for Friday Night Arts, which are showings for local artists. The third Thursday evening of each month is the Arty Party, with free music, snacks, and a showing by a local artist. As if that weren't enough, there's an in-store bar selling $2.50 beers.

◆ **The Terrace Gallery and the Mayor's Gallery at Orlando City Hall** (400 E. South St., Orlando; ☎ 407/246-4279). A grab bag of talks by artists, writers, and sociologists, most of whom are Florida-based. There's usually an art show of some kind on, and the offerings are supplemented a few times a month with talks relating to the show.

◆ **University Club** ★ (841 N. Park Ave., Winter Park; ☎ 407/644-6149; www.universityclubwinterpark.org). Although it's a membership-based club, enrichment-oriented daily activities are open to the public. Those include group discussions of philosophy (Tues at 10am); talks on good books; and conversations in French, German, and Spanish. Interesting lectures (sample: a celebration of Canadian poet Robert Service and a lecture entitled "Lord Cornwallis at Yorktown") are often scheduled for the evenings. Check its website to see what's on.

◆ **Women's Club of Winter Park** (419 S. Interlachen Rd., ☎ 407/644-2237). By no means are talk topics female-centric; two recent free discussions (scheduled a few times a month) were about the history of hurricanes in Florida and the saga of Minorcan immigrants in the area.

HOW ORLANDO LIVES

Idealistic in both design and ideals, **Celebration** ★★ (exits 62 and 63 east of Interstate 4; www.celebrationfl.com) must be seen to be believed. Make a rubber-necked drive-through to break up—and embellish upon—your visits to hyper-designed theme parks. This modern-day Stepford was created and guided by the Walt Disney Company as a model community and makes a consumer real estate product out of Americans' collective Donna Reed fantasies. Walt Disney's personal vision for Epcot strove to solve the transportation and industrial problems of modern cities, but when his company finally got around to building its own city, it chose, in a feat of architectural propaganda, to dote superficially on Walt's affection for small-town insularity. Every facet of the town, which accepted its first residents in 1996 and exploits Disney's specially negotiated right to govern anyone who lives on its property, was intentionally crafted to affirm trite notions of what an American small town should be. Like the Magic Kingdom's Main

Street, U.S.A., it's based on a nostalgia for something that never really existed in that form. Property was sold on the merits of a bold plan: Everyone would be within walking distance of the town center, schools would be steered by the finest education experts, and homes would be wired with the latest technologies to enable residents to do anything from call up medical records to consult with kids' teachers via videophone. The town was even given a logo, in which a child rides a bike beneath a maternal, mature tree, chased by a skipping lap dog.

The original idea may have been all-American pie-in-the-sky. The reality, though, turned out to be decidedly different. Instead of solving the problems of modern life, Celebration seems intent on ignoring them. Everything is geared to reassuring residents that they are comfortably well off. Working class trappings are quietly excluded; the town center (along Market and Front streets) contains pricey boutiques, tea shops, and proud civic buildings by award-winning architects, but nary a hardware store, bookstore, gas station, or grocery. What results is a back-lot-style community of Plasticine-colored homes—each a pastiche of a bygone style, some even with fake dormer windows painted black—scarcely 10 feet apart. The streets are full of stop signs, the garages full of minivans, and the houses full of white people (in the 2000 census, the black population measured one-quarter of 1 percent).

What's more, many of the hyped innovations simply never materialized. The means of the promised in-home technology has never existed, and bickering among the educators caused many parents to yank their kids out of the schools. After the bulk of its money had been made, Disney divested itself of its interest in the major operations, so under its new stewards, some of the hypocrisies may eventually be fixed. Despite participating in a subtext that I consider a marriage between new urbanism and fascism, prospective buyers respond eagerly to the elitism of the endeavor; two-bedroom condos fetch $500,000 to $900,000.

Take a stroll—you'll feel a twinge of disturbance when you notice many of the white picket fences are made of plastic and its emblematic water tower is just an empty prop. Even the town center, which abuts a lake, is resolutely piped with cheerful music and, a week before Thanksgiving, adorned with assiduously non-religious holiday decorations and dusted with foam "snow" by means of inducing Pavlov-style merriment. For some free fun, pick up a copy of the widely distributed *Celebration News,* the mouthpiece newspaper for admonishments from the local authorities: "Trash needs to be within 4 feet of the alley or curb before 7 am . . ." Parking is scarce, and the residents tend to greet gawkers with suspicious curtain-shuffling, which is surprising considering they decided to live in an experiment of willful self-creation.

Equally good for giving you chills, the lesser-known planned community of **Cassadaga** ✯✯✯ (exit 114 from I-4; www.cassadaga.org), about 40 miles northeast of Universal off Interstate 4, is an American original. The anachronistic town, a direct holdover from the Victorian craze for Christian-based spiritualism and séances, is untouched by development, and only accredited mediums may live there. Tree-shaded, whitewashed, and more than slightly creepy, Cassadaga is not unlike one of the intricately themed lands at the theme parks—almost calculatedly rustic and quaint, this 57-acre town is ripe for strolls, yet visitors can't usually shake an anxious feeling they're being watched by unseen eyes. A bastion of metaphysicality in a region otherwise devoted to Christian fundamentalism, Cassadaga makes for a goose-pimply day out.

George P. Colby, who is to Cassadaga what Joseph Smith is to Salt Lake City, was reared in the Midwest by Baptist parents, but incessant visions (and poor health) compelled him south, where in 1875, he came across land that, he said, appeared exactly as it had been shown to him by his spirit guide, Seneca. Soon after that, Colby enticed a group of refugees from Lily Dale, New York—a similar town of spiritualists that still exists on the Cassadaga Lakes outside of Buffalo—to join him in the then-rural wilds of Florida, and the winter "camp" of Cassadaga was born. Nowadays, its residents stay here year-round, where they offer a slate of services, laying-on-of-hands, and readings—all popular among followers of such things. Before setting out, check the town's website for the full list of events and sessions. The **Cassadaga Camp Bookstore** (1112 Stevens St., Cassadaga; ☎ 386/228-2880; Mon–Sat 10am–5:30pm, Sun noon–5:30pm) doubles as an occult supply/gift shop and a de facto visitors' center, and everything in town is within a block or two, so park the car here and explore. The best way to wring the most out of a visit is to immediately consult the bulletin board in the back of the store to see which mediums are available to take walk-in clients. And if you find, within the first 5 minutes of a reading, that you and your medium are not making a connection—say, if they're spouting total nonsense—it's considered good form to politely end the reading and go find another medium. Because the rent's so cheap (the land is owned by the governing Southern Cassadaga Spiritualist Camp Meeting Association), services go for a fraction of what they cost in the outside world. There are public "healing" sessions at the primitive wooden **Colby Memorial Temple** at 7pm Wednesdays, and at 7:30pm, the floor opens up to messages from the other side. The first Monday of the month from October to June is "Medium's Night," and anyone can grab a 15-minute reading for $20. Be at the bookstore between 5:30 and 7pm to draw a number; the readings kick off at 7pm. On Saturdays, the town indulges the influx of sightseers by offering afternoon **walking tours** ($15) of the historic highlights and evening **photography tours** ($25) to see who can snap a photo of a ghost first. And on the second and fourth Friday of each month at 7pm, the **Andrew Jackson Davis Building** hosts a Reiki Circle. A few more psychics operate independently from their apartments on the ground floor of the **Harmony Hall,** usually for around $50 an hour.

There's even a old-fashioned hotel in town: the 1928 **Cassadaga Hotel** (355 Cassadaga Rd., Cassadaga; ☎ 386-228-2323; www.cassadagahotel.com; $50 Sun–Thurs, $60 Fri–Sat, including continental breakfast; MC, V), said by pretty much everyone in town to be haunted, and has a long veranda ideal for watching the living and dead pass by. Although some locals grumble that the hotel is privately owned, and not controlled by the town's governing association—a distinction that, you may learn, reveals a bitter schism amongst the residents—visitors shouldn't mind. Besides, its Lost in Time Café is one of the only places in town to grab a bite, and rooms, which don't have TVs or phone, are guaranteed to keep you anxiously listening for bump-in-the-night creaks and groans. I asked the owner if I could take some photos of the time-warp lobby. "Sure, you're welcome to," she said, "but most people get a kind of orb or white light instead." I haven't found those, but my shots *did* come out blurry. I'm just saying.

HOW ORLANDO PRAYS

Central Florida seems to have connections that run just as strongly to the Deep South as they do to the world of fantasy. Christianity is huge here, and in the past generation, churches have grown Texas big, and several innovative missionary projects have started life here. Given that almost all of the Christian endeavors are intensely evangelical in nature, strangers are welcomed in a way they might not be at other religious institutions.

Out past the airport, the state-of-the-art exhibition at **WordSpring Discovery Center** ★★ (11221 John Wycliffe Blvd., off Moss Park Road, Orlando; ☎ 407/852-3626; www.wordspringdiscoverycenter.com; $6 adults, $5 seniors over 54, $4 students, $20 family ticket; Mon–Fri 9am–4pm, Sat 10am–4pm) will probably not justify the trip for most visitors, but if you're into linguistics or Christian missionaries, it's good stuff. The Wycliffe Bible Translators' WordSpring project, which operates a command center here, hones in on world languages that don't yet have a version of the Bible, and its translators toil years to complete new versions. This explanatory museum, which is obviously very well funded, takes about 45 minutes to see fully and labors to explain *why* its organizers think Bible translation is important, as well as discussing at length the complexity and multitude of the world's smaller languages (which is pretty fascinating for a wordie like me), but it generally leaves unexplored the enormous political, social, and cultural obstacles that make the undertaking such a challenge, which I find odd. Maybe they don't want to make China even more angry by acknowledging what they're up to. Visitors can listen to a Mexican language that's whistled, translate their name into Aramaic, Hieroglyphics, and Klingon (really!) and consult a database of every known world tongue, but to get the most out of a visit, come by 1pm weekdays, when someone with field translating experience arrives to explain what they do and tell war stories of their travels. The exhibition adjoins an excellent gift shop that sells handicrafts from around the world (like $25 Russian nesting dolls or $15 Peruvian soapstone boxes), as well as some of the more unusual Bible editions, such as the *Da Jesus Book,* ($15) written for Hawaii's 600,000 Pidgin speakers. (No, I didn't know they existed, either.)

Within shouting distance of WordSpring is the headquarters for Campus Crusade for Christ. There, a 1979 movie about the life of Jesus is dubbed into myriad obscure tongues and then screened at godless villages worldwide as part of an organized proselytizing effort. By the organization's (highly optimistic) count, the film has now been seen six billion times. **The *Jesus* Film Project Studio Tour** (100 Lake Hard Dr., Orlando; ☎ 888/225-3787; www.jesusfilm.org; free) is a how-they-do-it exhibit; see it by guided tour Monday through Friday at 10am, 11am, 1pm, 2pm, and 3pm. Like WordSpring, it's far more interested in celebrating the spread of the word of God than explaining the difficulties in accomplishing it—although you can dub a section of the film for yourself to see how that part works—but hearing about the scope of the project is still interesting.

In October 2006, *Newsweek* called the conservative **First Baptist Church of Orlando** (3000 S. John Young Parkway, Orlando; ☎ 407/425-2555; www.fbc orlando.org) "a colossal Wal-Mart of spiritual endeavor." Like many modern megachurches, "First Orlando," with an annual operating budget of $14 million, aims to be all things to all worshipers, which means although the Worship Center seats some 5,500 (that's nearly twice Hard Rock Live's capacity) and the congregation has long since lost track of who their fellow members are, visitors are welcomed with open arms. To a guy like me who grew up attending a white clapboard church, it's an impersonal brand of personal worship, but this entertaining style of prayer is sweeping Christian America, of which Orlando is a vital center. This holy stadium puts a premium on sharing God; it spends about $1.5 million a year on missionaries, more than any other Southern Baptist church. The 9am Sunday service contains classic hymns and a choir, while the 10:45am service is dubbed "contemporary," which means pop singers and a band. Other Bible studies and smaller services are scheduled during the week.

Northland Church (530 Dog Track Rd., Longwood; ☎ 407/949-4000; www. northlandchurch.net), which functions as a sort of franchise with five locations— remember what I said about Orlando being a seat for new-idea worship?—has found itself at the center of the culture wars. In late 2006, its senior pastor, Joel Hunter, was designated president-elect of the Christian Coalition, but when he suggested he felt that Jesus Christ would want them to refocus on helping the needy and away from politics, he was ultimately forced to reject the position. One of its most accessible locations is in Longwood, about 10 minutes' drive north of Orlando (see address above); there are five Sunday services from 8:15am to 6:30pm.

On the ride to Cassadaga, note the incongruous skyscraper alongside Interstate 4, just north of exit 92 in Altamonte Springs. That 18-story, silo-like tower with the arcing roofline is the **Majesty Building**, which broke ground back in 2000 and is slowly being constructed by WACX-TV, a Christian TV station that calls itself SuperChannel and aims to complete the $40-million tower debt free—that may take until 2008 or later—mostly through donations from viewers. You can't tour this architectural anomaly, but it's proof of how active and powerful the Christian community is in Central Florida.

HOW ORLANDO HELPS

Orlando has a surging homeless population. The number of people living on the streets was estimated at 5,000 in 1999, but today is around 8,500, yet there are only 2,000 beds for them. And how have the city fathers dealt with this influx? Not by making sure services can meet the increased demand, but by tying the hands of social-service groups in the hope that desperate people will become another city's problem. The government forbids charity groups from expanding or renovating, and declared it illegal to feed a homeless person downtown without a permit—and that no group would be granted more than two permits a year. (Feeding squirrels and pigeons is still fine.)

Clearly, Fantasyland has a dark side, and the people in this city could use your help. The way for you to do that legally is to go through an established local organization. One of the best portals for meeting and interacting with the city's neediest residents is **Hands On Orlando** (www.handsonorlando.com), a website that matches volunteers with the people who need them most. Opportunities, which change monthly, are posted about a month ahead; you can decide which one most suits your passion and, with a click, sign up to join in. Operating since 1999, Hands On has placed some 100,000 volunteers not only at charities such as Coalition for the Homeless (where you might serve buffets, call numbers on

Bingo Night, or even promote literacy by reading to someone), but also at noble local institutions such as homes where families can stay while their loved ones are in nearby hospitals, at local women's safe havens such as Hubbard House, at nursing homes, and in schools for kids with severe disabilities. In nearly every case, you'll be given the opportunity to meet local volunteers and the people they're helping, to talk with them, and to learn the stories of what brought them to this place in their lives.

Your commitment can be as short as a few hours, and no special skills are required. "All we need from you is a smile," says Tracy Amar, one of the three full-time employees who organizes the placements. Each job posts its own age minimums, although for some simpler assignments, such as sorting food or cleaning donated toys, it's as low as 4 or 6 years old—entire families may sign up to participate together (just use the site's "comment" field to list who's coming, and event organizers can tailor the tasks to your group). Two other websites, part of larger national initiatives to pair volunteers with local charities, also cover Orlando, although they tend to offer fewer single-day opportunities: Volunteer Match (www.volunteermatch.com) and Network for Good (www.networkforgood.org).

9 Outdoor Orlando

See why Florida is synonymous with natural beauty

PICTURE AN OLD-FASHIONED STEAMSHIP, NOT UNLIKE *THE AFRICAN QUEEN*, puttering along a narrow river of clear spring-fed water beneath a cool canopy of oak trees. Alongside the vessel swim a few docile manatees that nibble contentedly on the river grass. As the steamship breaks through a curtain of Spanish moss, it enters a wide, warm lake teeming with long-necked birds. The passengers sigh.

It's hard to believe, but that's what Central Florida really is. Well, was. When Americans first discovered the area as a vacationland, that's the way they'd see it—on multiweek journeys threading through the lakes and rivers once called home by native people, and later by the Spanish. Florida, known as a vast swampland and later as a cattle-driving turf, took weeks to reach from the north, and many more weeks to tour. Although it was a harsh land with arid soil and mosquitoes in flocks, Florida was still a livable place, particularly near the lakes, where cypress and oak grew and provided welcome shade.

Modern-day developers have cleared away pretty much everything but the lakes, ripping out the thick natural vegetation. (And then people wonder why they feel so hot in the summer.) There are some spots, though, farther from the heart of town, that are very much like they were. They are Florida as Florida was from the dawn of time until the imposition of asphalt.

People come to Orlando not just because it's where Mickey is. They also come for the weather, which is warm for most of the year, and to enjoy its wide, blue skies chased by billowy, white clouds. They come to swim and for sun.

In Central Florida, outdoor activities don't stop at sniffing daisies. True, the botanical gardens, welcome holdovers from the state's years as a wealthy enclave, support a wider array of plants than many others in the country. Their direct descendents, golf courses, comprise one of the area's most popular gaming pastimes. But there are also examples of the land's primacy—natural springs that Ponce de Leon once toured and wetland preserves thronged with migrating birds. And should all of that bore, you can speed by it on bracing boat tours that run past eagles and wild alligators or from the air in a balloon or hang glider.

GARDENS

Botanical gardens seem dull on paper, yet once you find yourself within one, inhaling perfume and being warmed by the sun, you're in no hurry to leave.

So it is with the well-funded, city-owned **Harry P. Leu Gardens** ✪✪ (1920 N. Forest Ave.; ☎ 407/246-2620; www.leugardens.org; $5.35 adults, $1.10 kids, daily 9am–5pm), a lakeside escape just north of downtown that gives visitors an inkling of why so many Gilded Age Americans wanted to flee to Florida, where the fresh air and gently rustling trees were a tonic to the maladies inflicted by the industrial North. It's not uncommon to find picnicking families and blissful wedding parties wandering the 50 acres, which include Florida's largest formal rose garden (peaking in Apr); a patch planted with nectar-rich blooms favored by migrating butterflies; a section dedicated to plants you can easily grow at home; a large collection of camellias that bloom in late fall; and a lush "Tropical Stream" garden, crawling with native lizards and opening onto a dock where freshwater turtles swim and ducks bob. The centerpiece is probably the Leu House Museum, a 19th-century farmhouse that was once the manor house for the property—the old family cemetery is past the vegetable garden—where half-hour tours are offered, for free, from 10am to 3:30pm, except in July, when it's closed. Admission is free on Mondays from 9am to noon, and the gardens host frequent outdoor movie screenings and storytelling sessions for no extra charge; they're announced on its website's special events page.

The Winter Park Garden Club calls **Mead Gardens** (1300 S. Denning Dr., Winter Park; ☎ 407/262-2049; free admission; daily sunrise–sunset) home. Another oasis in the city (translation: there's not much to do besides picnicking, daydreaming, and birding), the 55-acre ground is wilder and more overgrown-feeling than the prim plantings at Leu Gardens. The land, consisting mostly of hammocks and wetlands, was preserved more or less in its natural state in 1937 and then stocked with plants from around the world.

About an hour south of Disney, the 250-acre **Historic Bok Sanctuary** ✭✭ (1151 Tower Blvd., Lake Wales; ☎ 863/676-1408; www.boksanctuary.org; $10 adults, $3 kids 5–12; daily 8am–6pm, last admission at 5pm) was once one of Central Florida's great tourist attractions, but now its elegant gardens—designed by Frederick Law Olmsted, Jr., the son of the co-designer of Manhattan's Central Park—are merely a pleasing sideline and not often visited, which is too bad. They're genuinely lovely and among the best surviving remnants of early-20th-century philanthropic privilege. The gardens and their 205-foot, neo-Gothic Singing Tower were commissioned as a thank-you to the American people by a Dutch-born editor, Edward William Bok, the publisher of *The Ladies' Home Journal* and a pioneer in public sex education. Bok was buried at the tower's base in 1930, the year after its completion and dedication by President Calvin Coolidge. The 57-bell carillon on the tower's sixth level sounds concerts at 1pm and 3pm daily. The sanctuary was enshrined in 1993 as a National Historic Landmark, of which Florida currently has nearly no others.

A very minor attraction that appears more major because of its proximity to Disney, the gloomy **A World of Orchids** (2501 Old Lake Wilson Rd., Kissimmee; ☎ 407/396-1887; free admission; Mon–Sat 9:30am–4:30pm) opened in 1970 and, quite frankly, the bloom is gone and it's in a dire state of neglect. What was once a showplace of botany is now not worth your time; its few orchids are only for sale. I thought you should know since you'll be seeing signs for it.

NATURAL SPRINGS

Bet you never knew this: Florida has some 300 springs, and 27 of them discharge more than 60 million gallons of pure water a day. In fact, Florida has more springs than any other American state. With numbers like that's it's pretty easy to conclude that natural springs are more authentically Floridian than pretty much anything else you might see on a vacation.

Anthropologists have found evidence that people have lived at **DeLeon Springs State Recreation Area** ★★★ 🧒 (601 Ponce de Leon Blvd., Deland; ☎ 386/985-4212; www.floridastateparks.org/deleonsprings; $4 per carload; 8am–sundown), a onetime resort an hour northeast of Orlando, for longer than you'd guess—in 1990, a 6,000-year-old dugout canoe was uncovered. The Spanish, Seminoles, and pre-presidential Zachary Taylor all fought over this land, and Audubon saw his first limpkin here. (Remember *your* first time?) It's pretty much impossible to overstate the importance of the St. Johns River on the development of Florida—everybody used it—and like the Nile, it's one of the few world rivers to flow north, not south. Today, on this segment of the river, there are 18,000 acres of lakes and marshes to canoe (boats can be rented by the hour), a concrete-lined spring to swim in, and 6 miles of trails to forge as you try to spot black bears, white tail deer, swamp rabbits, and, of course, 'gators. Forty-five–minute historical boat tours run at 9am and 10am, ($9), and 90-minute tours leave at 11am and 1pm (☎ 386/837-5537; $14 adults, $9 kids). It gets cooler: At its general store–style **Old Spanish Sugar Mill Grill and Griddle House** (☎ 386/985-5644; www.planetdeland.com/sugarmill; Mon–Fri 9am–4pm, Fri–Sat and holidays 8am–4pm), beside the springhead, you can make your own all-you-can-eat pancakes on griddles built into every table ($4.50 per person, but they'll cook you other things, too). When I leave Orlando, this is one of the places I dream about returning to again—if it were closer to town, I'd eat here every morning. Niftier still, the designated swimming area, next to the Griddle House, is in a spring-fed boil—30 feet deep in spots—that remains at a constant 72°F, year-round. Bring your swimsuit. To reach it, take I-4 north, exit for Deland, and 6 miles north of Deland on U.S. 17 turn left onto Ponce DeLeon Boulevard for 1 mile.

There are no pancakes, but you'll have a better chance of seeing manatees at **Blue Spring State Park** ★ (2100 West French Ave., Orange City; ☎ 386/775-3663; www.floridastateparks.org/bluespring; $5 per car; daily 8am–sundown), especially in the morning on a cold day. Another plus—it's slightly closer to Orlando. The creatures venture up the St. Johns River from the Atlantic Ocean to seek out the springs here, which maintain a constant 72°F temperature even in the depth of winter. So from mid-November through February, all boating, swimming, and snorkeling are suspended while the big guys are in residence. Daily at 10am and 1pm (plus 3:30pm Jan–Apr), there's a **2-hour guided boat tour** (☎ 386/917-0724 or 407/330-1612; www.sjrivercruises.com; $18 adults, $16 seniors, $12 kids 3–12) of the St. Johns river, and the park also coughs up a few nature trails and canoe rental. Ask to see the forgotten pilings of the old steamship dock. Find the park from exit 114 off I-4; go south on U.S. Route 17-92 to Orange City, and then make a right onto West French Avenue (there are signs).

The closest major spring to Orlando (just 20 min. north, off I-4's exit 94), **Wekiwa Springs State Park** ★★★ 🧒 (1800 Wekiwa Circle, Apopka; ☎ 407/884-2008; www.floridastateparks.org/wekiwasprings; $5 per car; daily 8am–sundown) is, despite its encroachment by suburbs and malls, one of the prettiest preserves in the area. When you think of Florida, you don't normally picture rambling rivers, but the 42-mile Wekiva (yes, spelled differently than the park's name and pronounced "wek-EYE-va") is federally designated as "Wild and Scenic," meaning it hasn't been dammed or otherwise despoiled by development, despite the fact it's just northwest of Orlando's sprawl near Apopka. The spring-head, fed by two sources, flows briskly and thrillingly over rock and sand, and some people come to fish, but most agree that its canoeing is among the most spectacular in the state. Canoe along; hop out and camp or picnic; snorkel a lit-tle in clear, 72°F, spring-fed waters; and then canoe some more as the subtropical river makes its way to the St. Johns, Florida's longest river. A shuttle van run by a local company will bring you back to your starting point. To arrange this, call the park's sanctioned rental kiosk, **Wekiwa Springs State Park Nature Adventures** (☎ 407/884-4311); http://canoewekiva.com), which also arranges horseback riding (from $30 an hour) on the park's 8 miles of trails, which were constructed for a railway that was never finished. Developers would love to sink their bulldoz-ers' claws into this paradise; in fact, so much water is being siphoned from it that its flow is expected to diminish by 10% by 2025.

You might consider 90 miles a bit far to go from your hotel, but consider the rewards. The endangered Florida manatee frolics in the constant 72°F temperature of the water at Citrus County's **Homosassa Springs Wildlife State Park** ★ (kids) (4150 U.S. Highway 19, Homosassa; ☎ 352/628-2311; www.hswsp.com; $9 adults, $5 kids 3–12; daily 9am–5:30pm, last admission at 4pm). Unlike many state parks, rangers keep visitors busy with pontoon boat rides past bird life, plus sep-arate presentations about alligators and manatees. The prime amenity is a 168-ton underwater observatory floating inside the spring, where visitors can watch the lumbering manatees through thick windows. Swimming with the creatures is not permitted, as they're destined to be released back into the wild. Manatee talks are presented three times a day, usually falling between 11:30am and 3:30pm. Should you crave a chance to snorkel with the animals, two local outfitters know where to find wild manatees and arrange regular, 2-hour face-to-fin tours executed with environmental sensitivity: **Crystal River Manatee Dive and Tour** (☎ 888/732-2692 or 352/795-1333; www.manateetourusa.com; $29, plus optional $20 suit/snorkel rental; 50% discount for kids under 10) and **Plantation Inn Dive Shop** (352/795-4211; www.crystalriverdivers.com, $30, plus $19 optional suit/snorkel rental), both in nearby Crystal River. Snorkel tours are in the early morning when the creatures are most active.

NATURE RESERVES

Central Florida's development explosion only kicked in a generation ago, in a time when some people were smart enough to arrange for some of its land to be roped off from developers. We're only just now beginning to understand how important the state's central wetlands are to the ecosystems farther south in the state and how septic runoff in Orlando might affect the drinking water downstate.

On the day you visit the Kennedy Space Center, an hour east of Orlando (see p. 251 for details), set aside time to visit the northern part of NASA's patch: **Merritt Island National Wildlife Refuge** ★ (☎ 321/861-0667; http://merritt island.fws.gov; free admission; open sunrise to sunset), reached by driving through Titusville. Astonishingly, these 140,000 acres of quiet marsh contain more species of endangered plants and animals than any other nature reserve in the Lower 48 states. I wouldn't call it unspoiled—it only became a refuge in 1963, when NASA decided it didn't want it, and water management authorities have meddled with the flow—but it's certainly one of the best places for birding anywhere in the state, if not the country (310 species wing through). A dry erase board at its Visitor Center (Mon–Fri 8am–4:30pm and Sat 9am–5pm), off State Road 402 and pretty much next to the space shuttle's Florida landing strip, gives updates on animal sightings; a mini-museum fills you in on native endangered species such as the wood stork and the green sea turtle; and on request, it will show you a 20-minute video about the precarious local ecosystem.

Get a map to the Black Point Wildlife Drive, a 45-minute self-guided creep through the swampland on white gravel. NASA's hulking VAB looms in the distance; the roaring shuttle launches can't help but spook the animals and even kill a few. In 1987, the dusky seaside sparrow, which lived only within a 25-mile radius of this spot, became extinct. The Visitor Center has a stuffed specimen on display. At Haulover Canal, a 10-minute drive north of the Center (go east on S.R. 402, then north on S.R. 3, and then turn right immediately after the drawbridge), manatees congregate in spring and fall, and there's a parking lot and viewing area for tourists. Back in 1994, some 300 manatees were counted around the Refuge; that was more than half of all the manatees alive on Florida's east coast at the time. The future of the manatees is in question because soon, an old water treatment plant located nearby is scheduled to close, which will deprive the creatures of a reliable source of warm water in winter. Scientists aren't confident the animals will be able to find new reservoirs of warm water quickly enough to survive.

Just east of the marsh, so close that its border is undistinguishable, the 57,000-acre **Canaveral National Seashore** ★ (☎ 386/428-3384; www.nps.gov/cana; $3 per car; daily 6am–6pm Nov–Mar, daily 6am–8pm Apr–Oct) is the state's longest undeveloped Atlantic beach: 24 miles used for breeding by sea turtles. There's almost nowhere else in Florida—or even America—where you can see coastline this unspoiled. It's pretty much as Ponce de Leon found it in 1513. In June and July, rangers bring visitors to the breeding grounds after hours ($20 per person, reservations required). A museum about the ghost town of Eldora, a onetime citrus village that stood here until it was bypassed by better transportation links, is open Friday to Sunday, 10am to 4pm. For other activities, including Sunday guided pontoon boat trips through the park's lagoons ($20), consult the park's website. The easiest way to access both Merritt Island and Canaveral is via State Road 406, which crosses over the Indian River from the northern end of Titusville. State Road 50/Colonial Drive and State Road 528/the Bee Line both reach Titusville from Orlando.

Located more or less between Disney and SeaWorld (in fact, it's incredible it hasn't been turned into a golf course yet), the scenic **Tibet–Butler Preserve** (8777 County Road 535, Orlando; ☎ 407/876-6696; free admission; Wed–Sun 8am–6pm), named for adjoining lakes, is found about 5 miles north of the Lake Buena Vista hotel area. The 438-acre, county-run spread, adorned with a modern interpretive center (kids like the area that allows them to play the sounds of the area's nocturnal frogs), is combed by 4 miles of well-maintained trails and boardwalks that will not only give you breathing room from the tourist hubbub grinding all around you, but will also give you a good taste of the cypress swamps and palmetto groves that once dominated this area.

In order to gain permission to continue developing the swampland it owns, Disney was required by law to set aside some of it as a nature reserve. Hence, the existence of the **Disney Wilderness Preserve** (☎ 407/935-0002; $4 adults, $2 kids 6–17; Mon–Fri 9am–5pm), which is actually run by the Nature Conservancy. The 12,000 marshy acres, once a ranch, constitute part of the headwaters for the Florida Everglades, and they're scarred by barely more than a 3-mile walking trail through scrub and cypress habitats. It's a shame the businesslike hours keep more people from enjoying it on weekends, although on Sundays from October to May, you can arrange to take a guided 2-hour buggy tour ($10 adults, $5 kids) in a safari-worthy covered vehicle.

The Green Swamp is the largest wilderness in Central Florida—some 322,000 acres of pine flats, sandhills, and muck—and lucky you, it's right out the back door of Walt Disney World. (So close, in fact, that the rest areas on Interstate 4 just south of Disney are dotted with signs warning, "Caution: Venomous snakes in area.") **Lake Louisa State Park** ✪ (7305 U.S. Hwy 27, Clermont; ☎ 352/394-3969; www.floridastateparks.org/lakelouisa; free admission; daily 8am to sunset), known for its popular gopher tortoises and a rolling topography that actually affords views of the rest of Central Florida, has six lakes for swimming (one with lifeguards), short nature trails, and permits fishing and (with permission) hunting. Lake Louisa's campsites are $23 a night (at Disney's Fort Wilderness, they're $41–$55), and in late 2006, it added cabins facing Dixie Lake with two bedrooms and two bathrooms, sleeping six, with air-conditioning and power, for $110 to $120 a night. (That's no bargain, probably because it's so near the Disney zone.) The area gives birth to four important Florida rivers and, as an important natural reserve, has not been built upon since pioneer days. In fact, during a drought a few years ago, the water levels in Lake Louisa dropped, uncovering a World War II plane that went missing during a training exercise in 1944. That's remote. Yet it's only about 11 miles west of the Magic Kingdom as the crow flies.

Don't be put off by the fact that **Orlando Wetlands Park** (25155 Wheeler Road, Christmas; ☎ 407/568-1706; free admission; daily 7am to half-hour before sunset; closed Oct–Feb 1) has only existed in marsh form since the late 1980s (it was farmland before) and it's technically a collection area for reclaimed water, albeit one planted with some two million aquatic plants and 200,000 trees. Nature has quickly reclaimed the 1,650 acres here. The whole point is animal spotting. Upon arrival, grab a field guide to the birds (including ibis, hawks, vultures, and teal) from a box and walk the 4-mile loop. Or stay in your car and creep through cattails on some 18 miles of roads, conducting your own bird safari. There's more to see in winter, when migration is at its peak. From S.R. 50 in Christmas (about 40 min. east of downtown), head north on County Road 420, and the turnoff will be a little over 2 miles away.

BOAT TOURS

The real Florida Everglades don't begin in earnest until south of Lake Okeechobee, which is why you'll always hear Central Florida referred to as the *headwaters* of the Florida Everglades. Orlando-area swamps are still home to a wide diversity of life forms, though, a fact several companies vie to show you.

One of those long-running tourist attractions that just won't die, and would diminish its neighborhood if it ever did, the Winter Park **Scenic Boat Tour** ✪✪✪ (312 E. Morse Blvd., Winter Park; ☎ 407/644-4056; www.scenicboattours.com; $10 adults, $5 kids 2–11; hourly departures from 10am–4pm daily; no credit cards) has been showing visitors the town's glorious lakeside mansions since 1938, when they were in their heyday of attracting wealthy snowbirds from the North. Three

Florida's Real Natives

- **Manatees:** From the surface, they look like 1-ton potatoes. Sweet and docile, the biggest enemy they have is the propeller of a hot-dogger's boat. Experts estimate that only about 2,400 of them are left.
- **Lizards:** The pigeons of the South. Little kids are fascinated by them, and cats torment them. They can lose a tail and grow it back, but if one dies in your house, it'll stink up the joint and defy discovery.
- **American bald eagles:** Not all of Florida's eagles migrate, so they're here year-round, but the population increases in winter, when the eagles that do migrate show up in "streams," adding to the flock.
- **Alligators:** Poor, misunderstood alligator. We know you'd rather eat small ducks than large people, but sometimes you get hungry and end up in the news. You'll find these reptiles in nearly every body of fresh water, so don't jump into unfamiliar canals. (As if you would.)
- **Florida panthers:** These wily, tan-colored cats weigh up to 130 pounds and feed on deer and hogs. You're not likely to see one, as fewer than 100 remain.
- **Palmetto bugs:** Maddeningly common, these water-loving brown bugs are about 1½ inches long and eat almost anything. They can fly but prefer to scurry, and came from Africa on slave ships. Don't bawl out your hotel if you see one; they're everywhere. Another of its names: American cockroach.

of Winter Park's seven cypress-lined lakes, which are connected by thrillingly narrow, hand-dug canals, are explored in a 1-hour, 12-mile tour narrated by salty old fellas (quipped one about Rollins College students, "Everything is average about those kids except their parents' income") who are usually retired and gigging for extra cash. The lakes, which were crystal clear before fertilizer use mucked them up, are surprisingly relaxing, with plenty of bird life, and learning about the illustrious lives of moneyed Winter Parkers—to say nothing of ogling their ostentatious Gilded Age winter homes, lawns sloping appealingly to the water's edge—is pretty fascinating. Among the high points are the modest condominium where Mamie Eisenhower spent her waning years, a home inhabited by the most decorated fighter pilot of World War II, and 250-year-old live oaks. Your guide will pay particular attention to the works of James Gamble Rogers II, a virtuosic architect responsible for many of the area's finest homes. The boarding dock feels like it's straight out of a mountain lake resort or *On Golden Pond;* cold Cokes are sold for 50¢ and there's a gas pump for local boat owners, who idle in the water and trade small talk. You'll find it 3 blocks east of the shops on Park Avenue. Bring sunscreen and sunglasses because the pontoons are exposed.

Airboats use powerful, backward-facing propellers to skip a shallow boat through the bogs, and they're a common form of eco-entertainment in Florida,

Animals for Free

One little-known freebie at the otherwise luxury-priced **Gaylord Palms** (6000 W. Osceola Pkwy., Kissimmee; ☎ 407/586-0000; www.gaylordhotels. com) resort is its **alligator feedings.** Gatorland, the venerable gator-raising tourist spot, uses the indoor pools at the Palms as nurseries for young alligators. Most of the time, the animals bask lifelessly under heat lamps, but on Tuesdays, Thursdays, and Saturdays around 6:30pm (call for exact times), a zookeeper climbs into their enclosure, rouses them, and even entices a few to jump out of the water to grab hunks of raw chicken. Then he'll carry a littler gator into the waiting crowd for photos and petting, while the more timid children scamper for cover. The whole episode is over in about 20 minutes, but even those not staying at the resort can partake, and seeing it makes for a great excuse to explore the Palms' breathtaking atrium.

The Peabody Orlando (9801 International Dr., Orlando; ☎ 407/352-4000; www.peabodyorlando.com) can't compete for fearsomeness, but at least its **Duck Parade,** modeled after a tradition at its original property in Memphis, TN, won't scare babies. Each morning at 11am, when a Sousa march strikes up, a red carpet unrolls and a gaggle of five ducks, prodded by their own "Duck Master" in uniform, waddles dutifully from a bank of elevators to their own fountain in the lobby, where they spend the day bathing and quacking. At 5pm sharp, they're corralled back down their runway to a waiting elevator car. The spectacle is pretty ludicrous for a marble-and-brass hotel like the Peabody, which preens itself as a luxury enclave, but now that I think about it, I can't say it's Orlando's weirdest.

particularly farther south in the Everglades. **Boggy Creek Airboat Rides** ★ 🧒 (2001 E. Southport Rd., Kissimmee; ☎ 407/344-9550; www.bcairboats.com; half-hour tours $22 adults, $16 kids 3–12; 1-hour 9pm tours $35 adults, $30 kids 3–12; daily 9am–5:30pm) uses these incredibly loud vehicles (ear mufflers are provided) in southeastern Orlando, adjoining the airport. Though much wildlife is spooked by the din made by boat and plane alike, many water snakes and alligators appear too thick-headed to care, so you should see a few on one of the continuously running 30-minute tours—boat skippers will cut the engine and float near the critters. The boats don't operate in the rain. The wildlife spotting is better in South Florida, but this'll do. There's a $2 coupon on its website, or a $1 discount in its leaflet, available at the Orlando Visitor Center.

Airboat Rentals (4266 W. U.S. 192, Kissimmee; ☎ 407/847-3672; www.airboat rentals.com; $30 per hour, canoes $7 per hour; daily 9am–5pm), at Mile Marker 15, distinguishes itself by claiming its boats are less noisy than its competitors'. Mind you, they're still pretty noisy, but at least you get to drive yourself. Its waterway, part of Shingle Creek, is in the midst of Kissimmee, so it's not totally wild, but you stand a good chance of seeing animals such as small gators. There's a coupon worth $2 on its website.

Captain Doug Brown at **Osprey Eco Tours** (☎ 407/957-2277; $45 per hour adults, $35 kids 3–12; tours by appointment) is yet another local who offers tours; he brags that once the boat leaves the dock, there will be no housing developments. He also says he sees many bald eagles in the winter—his record is 22 in an hour. Night rides are also available; reservations are required.

The **Swan Boats at Lake Eola Park** (☎ 407/658-4226; $12 per half-hour) are a beloved city tradition. They're pedal boats that fit two adults and are simple in most respects—except one. They look like enormous swans. Find the dock in the park at Robinson Street and Rosalind Avenue.

Leaving daily from Port Canaveral, the 440-foot *Ambassador II* of **Sterling Casino Lines** (101 George King Blvd., Suite 3, Cape Canaveral; ☎ 800/765-5711 or 321/783-2212; www.sterlingcasinolines.com; free admission; daily 11am–4pm, Sun–Thurs 7pm–midnight, Fri–Sat 7pm–1am) takes you out into international waters, where gambling is legal; it's got 75,000 square feet of casino space, with 50 table games and 1,000 slot machines. The cruise is free because its skipper expects you to gamble, but you can use the trip to just get out of the city, enjoy the Florida coast, and raise a cocktail. Same goes for the 308-foot **SunCruz Casino** (610 glen Cheek Dr., Cape Canaveral; ☎ 800/474-3423 or 321/799-3511; www. suncruzcasino.com; free admission; Mon–Sat 11am–4pm, Sun 11am–4:30pm, Sun–Thurs 7pm–midnight, Fri–Sat 7pm–1am, holidays 7pm–12:30am). This one is slightly more downscale than Sterling, so its payouts are lower and there's less organized entertainment. It operates 35 table games and has more than 640 slot machines that cost as little as a nickel. Both ships require passengers to be at least 21 years old with valid ID, and both will pick you up for free in Orlando on dedicated shuttle vans to the dock (about an hour away).

GOLF

Though I am not a golf person, and I personally deplore the damage that building courses does to the water table and the land—especially in such an already precarious ecosystem as Central Florida's—I can't deny that golf is a major attraction in the Orlando area. Many people come to town just for that, and some of the brightest names in golfing, including Tiger Woods, Annika Sorenstam, Ernie Els, and Nick Faldo maintain homes in Orlando. Every self-respecting resort hotel has a course or three, as do the most luxe condo developments, and when conventions and meetings roll into town, big deals go down in between strokes.

And that's a lot of deal-making—there are some 170 courses around town. Most give priority to players who stay in their hotels, either through advantageous tee times or by cheaper fees (Walt Disney World, for example, charges $10 more to players staying off-property, and hike prices by $20 Jan–May). Fees at Disney span $89 to $169, and the most exclusive grounds can charge as much as $180, but you'll find most of them charge fees that begin around $60. Prices usually sink to about half the day rate for twilight tee times, which start around midafternoon. Club rentals cost $40 to $60. Reservations are all but required, and most courses have a dress code and even an age minimum, so always ask.

Important tip: Golfing is one of the things that the **Orlando Magicard,** provided for free at www.orlandoinfo.com/magicard, can help discount; many of these courses will knock $10 off their rates if you book with one. (Check the Magicard's ever-changing list of participants.)

Orlando has plenty of award-winning courses that will cost you more than $200 to play, but if you're willing to pay that much, then you probably won't be hearing about them for the first time from me. As you would do before renting a home or a hotel room, go online ahead of time to see what the individual courses are like—whether they're hilly, straightaway, or riddled with sand traps. Golf is such big business here that most courses post maps online.

In addition, Orlando is home to the annual PGA Merchandise Show (www.pgamerchandiseshow.com), held in January at the Convention Center, as well as to the studios of The Golf Channel (which doesn't give tours, but wouldn't that be a good idea?).

For those of us who don't know their handicaps, or know all too well, there's always miniature golf. Orlando excels in that, too. See p. 232 for a roundup.

FANCY DESTINATION COURSES

From pedigrees by well-known designers to clubhouses that operate more like spas, these fashionable courses are selling the fantasy of luxury as much as they're selling good golf. They're the theme parks of the fairway set. I touch upon these pricey greens quickly because they have national reputations:

* **Villas of Grand Cypress** ✦ (☎ 877-330-7377; www.grandcypress.com; 45 holes). Designer: Jack Nicklaus. In 2006, this snobby club was noted Orlando's best golf resort, and the second-best in Florida, by the readers of *Condé Nast Traveler*, who know about such things.

* **Reunion Resort & Club** (☎ 888/418-9611; www.reunionresort.com; 54 holes). Designers: Jack Nicklaus, Arnold Palmer, Tom Watson, and a golf school overseen by Annika Sorenstam. It's a 10-minute drive south of Disney.

* **ChampionsGate Golf Resort** (☎ 407/787-4653; www.championsgategolf. com; 36 holes). Designer: Greg Norman. The headquarters of the David Leadbetter Golf Academy (☎ 888/633-5323; www.davidleadbetter.com). This resort, too, is a 10-minute drive south of Disney.

* **Walt Disney World Golf Courses** ✦ (☎ 407/938-4653; www.disneyworld golf.com; 99 holes). Courses include the Lake Buena Vista (the cheapest 18 holes, from $89); Palm; Magnolia; and the most exclusive, Osprey Ridge and Eagle Pines. Oak Trail (9 holes; $38) is the better choice for family outings. Greens fees include golf cart use, when available. All courses opened with the resort in 1971.

* **Arnold Palmer's Bay Hill Club & Lodge** ✦✦ (☎ 888/422-9445; www.bay hill.com; 18 holes). Designer: Arnold Palmer, who owns it and also oversees the golf school. This course regularly receives the most accolades from experts. There's a full map of every hole on its website.

* **The Ritz-Carlton Golf Club Orlando, Grande Lakes** (☎ 800/682-3665 or 407/206-2400; www.grandelakes.com; 18 holes). Designer: Greg Norman. *Golf Digest* rated it the second-best Orlando course in 2005.

* **Shingle Creek** (☎ 866/996-9939 or 407/996-9933; www.shinglecreekgolf. com; 18 holes) Designer: David Harman. There's also a school overseen by Brad Brewer. One of the newer courses (opened winter 2004), it's near the Convention Center.

- **Mystic Dunes Golf Club** (☎ 866/311-1234 or 407/787-5678; www.mystic dunesgolf.com; 18 holes). Designer: Gary Koch. Located just south of Disney.

MORE AFFORDABLE COURSES

Unlike the aforementioned courses, these don't have big marketing campaigns and they don't always come attached to celebrity names, but they nevertheless are high-quality courses that you can enjoy at more sensible prices.

- **Celebration Golf Course** ★ (☎ 888/275-2918 or 407/566-4653; www. celebrationgolf.com; 18 holes). In the Disney-built town next door to the Disney-built world, fees are $89 weekday, $99 weekends for a course (by English master designer Robert Trent Jones and son) pocked with water hazards on 17 of its 18 holes.
- **Orange County National Golf Center and Lodge** ★★ (☎ 407/656-2626; www.orangecountynationalgolf.com; 45 holes). At this wide-open complex (922 acres, miraculously unspoiled by houses), fees span $65 to $150 for 18 holes, depending on time of year and day of the week (Mon–Thurs are cheapest). "Junior players" 16 and younger pay $15 less. Holes have four sets of tees, allowing you to choose a game that ranges between 7,300 yards and a little over 5,000. It's among the developments north of Walt Disney World.
- **Highlands Reserve Golf Club** ★★★ (☎ 877/508-4653 or 407/629-6767; www.highlandsreserve-golf.com; 18 holes). This highly praised public course, with a fair mix of challenges and cakewalks, is a strong value, charging $39 to $65, and its twilight rates kick in as early as 1pm. Kids under age 16 pay $15 to $25. The course is about 10 minutes' drive southwest of Disney. The clubhouse won't pressure you to rent a cart, either, as they will at many area courses—you will be encouraged to walk the gently rolling hills.
- **Errol Estate Country Club** ★★ (☎ 407/886-5000; www.errolestatecc.com; 27 holes). Golf for $33 to $38! The course, mostly through quiet Florida forest with several dogleg-shaped runs and a variety of elevations, is worth more. Its Lake Course is long but easy, while its Grove Course is known for being its trickiest because of dense trees and hills. The club, about 20 miles north of Disney in Apopka, often runs 4-for-3 deals.
- **Royal St. Cloud Golf Links** (☎ 407/891-7010; www.stcloudgolfclub.com; 18 holes). Aiming to recall Scotland's great links—there's even a stone bridge that looks like it was built during the days of William Wallace, not in 2001—this modest club, 25 miles east of Disney, charges $64 for fees and a cart and is prized as one of the region's most underrated. Its fairways are noted for being wide, well groomed, and firm, and planners promise you'll use "every club in the bag."
- **Hawk's Landing Golf Club** (☎ 800/567-2623; www.golfhawkslanding.com; 18 holes). Fees are around $65, depending on the season. Located beneath the Orlando World Center Marriott resort on World Center Drive by Disney, it crawls with convention-goers. Water is in play on 15 of the 18 holes, and the par-72 course carries a slope rating of 134.
- **Orange Lake Resort & Country Club** ★ (☎ 800/877-6522 or 407/239-1050; www.golforangelake.com; 45 holes). Fees from $39 to $85; it's a few easy

miles west of Disney on U.S. 192. Arnold Palmer had a hand in its design. Its Legends course is divided between the exposed Links course, which makes winds a complication, and The Pines, distinguished by heavy tree plantings that eat balls for breakfast. Its Reserve course was rebuilt in 2005, when a lighted driving range was also installed.

◆ **North Shore Golf Club** (☎ 407/277-9277; www.northshore-golfclub.com; 18 holes). Fees are $50 to $60, with kids aged 15 or younger paying half that. Its par-72, 6,900-yard course is divided into nine wetlands-lined holes recalling links-style golf, and another nine through an ancient oak grove, which the club calls "Carolina" play. The club is located east of the airport in a quickly developing area.

◆ **Hunter's Creek Golf Course** (☎ 407/240-4653; www.golfhunterscreek.com; 18 holes). Former cattle grazing land was transformed into a wavy course with a good gimmick: 13 lakes were created as water hazards for 13 of the holes. The fairways are long, so you have to be able to drive the ball. Fees around $80; you'll find it near the airport.

◆ **MetroWest Golf Club** ★ (☎ 407/299-1099; www.metrowestgolf.com; 18 holes). This course is the work of Robert Trent Jones, Sr., famous for tight greens protected on both sides by sand traps, trees, or water. Fees range from $80 to $115, depending on day of week and season, and the design features spring-fed lakes and 100-foot elevation changes, which is unusual for a mostly flat state. The course, a qualifying site for both the Champions Tour and the U.S. Open, is less than 3 miles north of Universal Orlando.

◆ **Stoneybrook Golf Club** (☎ 407/384-6888; www.stoneybrookgolf.com; 18 holes). Fees are $32 to $63, cheaper as the day goes on. Seniors (50-plus years old) are $39 weekdays. The par-72 course has four sets of tees for players of all skill levels, with plenty of water strips where a hole can go wrong. It's located east of downtown.

◆ **Timacuan Golf and Country Club** (☎ 407/321-0010; www.golftimacuan. com; 18 holes). It's located 10 miles north of downtown in Lake Mary and fees are $69 to $85. There are five sets of tees, changing this exceptionally well-groomed course from 7,000 to 5,000 yards, and the designers were careful to leave its handsome Old Florida features (undulating fairways, Spanish moss, wetlands) mostly intact. The par-71 course includes one exceptionally long par 4, but only three holes are riddled with water, which might make it easier for kids.

HORSEBACK RIDING

For a simple saddle-up, **Horse World Riding Stables** (3705 Poinciana Blvd., Kissimmee; ☎ 407/847-4343; www.horseworldstables.com; trail rides $40–$70, reservations suggested; daily 7am to late afternoon), 12 miles south of U.S. 192, offers three types of guided trails through Central Florida pine forests. The so-called Nature Trail Ride (which is really an unpaved access road) is the simplest, taking about 45 minutes and requiring no experience. Everyone 6 years or older gets their own horse, and kids 5 or younger share a horse with Mom or Dad. The other two trails, the Intermediate and the Advanced, require more difficult types of maneuvers (trotting or cantering), so they have higher age minimums.

WATER-SKIING

Walt Disney World permits water-skiing, parasailing, tubing, and wakeboarding on the **Seven Seas Lagoon and Bay Lake** (☎ 407/939-0754; www.sammyduvall. com), but prices are exorbitant ($155 per hour).

There aren't many of us who follow the exploits of professional water-skiing. Those who do will no doubt treasure the museum at the American Water Ski Education Foundation's **Water Ski Hall of Fame and Experience** (1251 Holy Cow Rd., Polk City; ☎ 863/324-2472; www.waterskihalloffame.com; $5 adults, $4 seniors, $3 kids 6–12; Mon–Fri 10am–5pm), at Exit 44 of I-4, about 20 miles west of Disney. On view: the first known pair of water skis, made from pine planks in 1922 by 18-year-old Minnesotan Ralph Samuelson (who also merits a bronze bust), plus assorted ropes, handles, and outboard engines.

HOT AIR BALLOONING AND HANG GLIDING

Florida is well suited to hot air ballooning for many of the same reasons that it's ideal for golf, including its flat, even topography and its often placid morning weather. Several companies take tourists into the sky over the swamps and groves south of the city. A trip involves a very early start—6am at a central location is common, followed by a trip out to the launch site selected for the day based on the day's wind patterns. Each balloon basket carries as many as a dozen people. You'll probably be asked to wear closed-toed shoes and to help unfold and inflate the balloon, and after landing, kids tend to get into the physical exertion of squashing the air back out of it and packing it away. Most outfits then feed you breakfast. You'll be finished by the time the theme parks get cranking. Reservations are required, and each outfit has its own age requirements, although generally speaking, if a child can follow instructions, see over the basket's edge, and not freak out, they'll be welcomed.

Orange Blossom Balloons (☎ 407/239-7677; www.orangeblossomballoons. com; $175 adults, $95 kids 10–15, free for one kid 9 and under with each paying adult, additional kids $95 each), in business since 1982, meets at a hotel on U.S. 192 just west of the main Disney entrance.

Magic Sunrise Ballooning (12559 S.R. 535, Orlando; ☎ 866/606-7433; www. magicsunriseballooning.com; $185 per person for 2–4 people, no kids under 6) tops off its flight with a champagne toast and an all-you-can-eat breakfast.

Blue Water Balloons (☎ 800/586-1884 or 407/894-5040; www.bluewater balloons.com; $185 per person, $90 kids under 11, $20 discounts for online bookings) also ends its morning outing with a champagne toast and an all-you-can-eat breakfast. Run by a veteran, it offers 2-for-1 discounts for active duty military personnel on weekdays.

Should you crave some more adrenaline with your air-time, **Wallaby Ranch** (1805 Deen Still Rd., Davenport; ☎ 800/925-5229; www.wallaby.com; tandem flights from $95), about 20 minutes' drive southwest of Disney, arranges hang-gliding flights. In flat Central Florida, where there are no mountains other than those containing roller coasters, daredevils can't leap off cliffs to attain flight. Instead, they're launched by ultralight "aerotugs," at an altitude of 2,000 feet. There is a weight maximum of 240 pounds, and DVDs of your flight start at $60.

10 Orlando After Dark—and in the Dark

Fireworks you know about, but where are the clubs and shows?

THE NIGHTLIFE QUANDARY: STAY WITH FELLOW TOURISTS, WHERE THE nightspots are lavish but milquetoast, or go out with the young locals, who party a 20-minute drive north? See a show on park property, where the entertainment has been devised by committee but is well funded, or try something smaller and smarter in town? Your choice depends on whether you've had your fill of the theme parks' klieg lights and name tags, and perhaps just as important, whether you feel like driving.

The choice used to be simpler. Years ago, the theme parks weren't in the nightlife business. Orlando's main party drags were downtown, along two intersecting downtown thoroughfares: Church Street and Orange Avenue. But in the late 1980s, the titans grew unsatisfied that their patrons might deign to leave their property after the rides closed. They devised a way to dominate the evening scene, too. Walt Disney World dropped the ropes on Pleasure Island, its playground of nightclubs located in its Downtown Disney area. Now it holds onto revelers from its resort's hotels, which run buses to Pleasure Island until the wee hours. Universal Orlando countered with the unveiling of CityWalk, which appeals to a somewhat trendier, younger segment of tourists.

For a while there, downtown Orlando staggered from the double blows. Church Street Station, once a nationally famous nightlife district, shuttered, and the area degenerated into a jungle of quarter-beer joints and strip contests. In time, though, Orlando residents grew weary of the canned experiences on offer at Disney and Universal. Today, downtown has reclaimed some of its cool, albeit mostly in the under-35 demographic. It also offers the best opportunity to mingle with locals as opposed to fellow Mouseketeers.

The best place to find out what's going on is the events listing of **Orlando Weekly** magazine (www.orlandoweekly.com), available for free in newspaper boxes all over Orlando proper but not so much the theme park universe. The **Orlando Sentinel** newspaper (www.orlandosentinel.com) lists fewer events. The hippest source is the underground website **Apartment E** (www.apartmente.com).

We'll start with the nightlife zones that the parks own and run, and then we'll go farther afield, into the "real" world of Orlando.

After Dark with Kids

Although on some nights, one could argue that the people drinking at the clubs and bars are infantile, you still can't bring your kids to hang out in them. Don't worry—Orlando is a family city, so there's lots for kids to do.

Magic Kingdom parade: Most nights, there are one or two parades through the park. When there are two, the second is less crowded.

Fireworks: The Magic Kingdom is open until 9pm or later on most nights. There's usually an evening parade, and the nightly fireworks display, Wishes, happens around Cinderella Castle. Disney–MGM Studios mounts Fantasmic!, a pyrotechnics-and-water display, and Epcot is famous for its IllumiNations fireworks-and-electronics show over its lagoon. Meanwhile, Universal Studios' Cinesphere show, with five globes that double as movie screens and a few mild pyrotechnics, is mounted most nights. Check with each park for show times, as they change. Given that they're theme park shows, they're all designed to wow kids, but the classic is at the Magic Kingdom.

The Electrical Boat Parade: It's a tradition going back more than 30 years: A string of 14 40-foot-long illuminated barges floats past the Disney resorts on Seven Seas Lagoon and Bay Lake starting at 9pm, accompanied by music. It's lower-key than the fireworks shows. See it from the beach at any resort hotel in the area or, if your timing is good, from the ferry that goes between the Magic Kingdom and the Ticket and Transportation Center.

Special event evenings: From September through March, The Magic Kingdom schedules irregular special-ticket evenings (Mickey's Not-So-Scary Halloween Party, his Very Merry Christmas Party, and the Pirate and Princess events) for kids with free candy, character meetings, dance parties, and extended hours. The calendar of events can be found on p. 305, online at www.disneyworld.com, or you can call Disney at ☎ 407/934-7639.

Dinnertainment: Every night, there are more than a dozen dinner banquets accompanied by a kid-friendly show. See p. 86.

Character meals: Early bedtime? Very young kids will be sent to sleep dreaming if they meet their favorite character over dinner. See p. 90 for a list.

Pleasure Island: The only clubs that admit kids are the Adventurers Club and Comedy Warehouse, and even then only with an adult. The references will be PG-13—at least. No Universal CityWalk clubs are kid-friendly, but its restaurants are.

Orlando Repertory Theatre and the Plaza Theatre: These Orlando-area companies present kids' entertainment (p. 286).

THE THEME PARKS' ENTERTAINMENT DISTRICTS

After a long day trooping through the parks, my wish list for nightlife begins and ends with a hot bath. But if, once the fireworks fizzle, you've still got beans in your pants, you can shake them out at one of the nightlife zones set up by the amusement giants to keep the diversion going into the wee hours (2am most nights). These playgrounds rock on every night, regardless of whether anyone's in the mood to boogie or if the dance floors are desolate. Much like ongoing wedding receptions, their offerings have been concocted by committee to appeal to as wide a spectrum of visitors as possible, and their playlists and decor alike are designed for the masses, not for aesthetic vanity. True hipsters will probably want to give these milquetoast clubs wide berth, but people who don't mind surrendering to forced folderol are bound to have some fun.

PLEASURE ISLAND & DISNEY'S BOARDWALK

Although it was named for the horrifying Sodom that lures Pinocchio deeper down the path of degradation and turns him partly into an ass, lately Disney's planners have erased that naughty reference from their fictitious back story for **Pleasure Island** (☎ 407/939-2648; www.disneyworld.com; $12 for admission to one club, except Comedy Warehouse or Adventurers Club; $23 admission to all clubs; discounts for military personnel available; daily 7pm–2am), and you won't find much sin on its shores. You will find a squarely mainstream block of clubs where crowd-pleasing music is a given at any hour. Probably because most Disney guests are too pooped to party, Pleasure Island rarely rages—it pleasantly bubbles instead.

Pleasure Island is undergoing a rehab and is gradually dialing back its frivolity. In 2006, it ceased its nightly midnight fireworks show and removed a number of shops and an outdoor stage for bands. As of press time, its clubs were:

- **Motion.** Staffed by bored-looking girls cracking gum, it's the spot for Top 40 dancing. Younger patrons favor this one, but in many ways, it's not very distinct from the next club.
- **Mannequins Dance Palace** ✪. Mimicking a New York-style club, it looks vaguely like a gutted theater, with a turntable dance floor overlooked by a three-sided balcony. Techno and progressive rhythm is the style. Lots of lights, smoke, and neon-painted dummies affixed to the wall. The showy dance space earns it the highest local popularity of the PI clubs.
- **Rock 'n' Roll Beach Club** is on the lake (a few areas with pool tables face the water), hence the name. You'll find live rock bands, a sunken dance floor few people use, and sloshing alcoholic drinks served in plastic beach pails: That buzzing sound you hear is Walt spinning in his grave. Consider this place more for older people or those with little kids.
- **Adventurers Club** ✪✪✪ is a true original. The black sheep among Pleasure Island's thump-thumping clubs, the Club is an elaborate put-on that brings the theme parks' Disney-fied fantasy into a nightspot. In this cleverly rigged colonialist clubhouse for globetrotters, the moose head comes alive, as do the tribal masks, and the bar stools sink to the floor at the flip of a switch—but if you come just to see the mechanical gags, you may end up waiting awhile. You really should think of this as a role-playing comedy club: It's New Year's Eve, 1937 (not coincidentally, the same time *Snow White* was in cinemas),

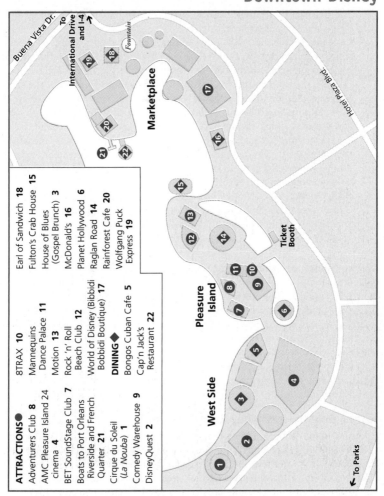

ATTRACTIONS ●

Adventurers Club **8**
AMC Pleasure Island 24
cinema **4**
BET SoundStage Club **7**
Boats to Port Orleans
Riverside and French
Quarter **21**
Cirque du Soleil
(*La Nouba*) **1**
Comedy Warehouse **9**
DisneyQuest **2**

8TRAX **10**
Mannequins
Dance Palace **11**
Motion **13**
Rock 'n' Roll
Beach Club **12**
World of Disney (Bibbidi
Bobbidi Boutique) **17**

DINING ◆

Bongos Cuban Cafe **5**
Cap'n Jack's
Restaurant **22**

Earl of Sandwich **18**
Fulton's Crab House **15**
House of Blues
(Gospel Brunch) **3**
McDonald's **16**
Planet Hollywood **6**
Raglan Road **14**
Rainforest Cafe **20**
Wolfgang Puck
Express **19**

Marketplace

West Side

Pleasure
Island

Ticket
Booth

To Parks

and this fusty club is on a membership drive. Wacky staff members (some talented improvisers, some less so) mingle with the crowd—so prepare to be comedy fodder—and then entertain with a vaudeville-style talent show. The house cocktail is the Kungaloosh, a surprisingly powerful blended drink. Of all the clubs at Pleasure Island, this one has a pace and a silly subculture all its own, and it's also by far the least crowded, which I think is most unfair. To fully enjoy this easy-paced evening, budget at least 90 minutes, because shows aren't constant. Joe Rohde, the Imagineer later made the lead designer of Animal Kingdom, concocted this club based on his own world travels.

◆ **BET SoundStage Club** comes the closest to the clubs you'd find in your home city in that it plays a lot of R&B, soul, dance, and nonoffensive hip-hop. It's cozier than the other clubs, and not much space overlooks the lake, but that hardly matters because partiers seem to prefer watching music videos on the giant screens.

- ◆ **Comedy Warehouse ★★** only admits patrons about 20 minutes before showtimes; annoyingly, those aren't posted anywhere and they change from night to night. Comedy fans of course have to plan their nights around them, and there's no information desk, so make sure you obtain the schedule from the box office clerk when you buy your wristband. Lines for the next performance form outside the building at least 30 minutes ahead, sometimes more. Inside the club, audience-fed improvisational shows are the dominant entertainment, and although comics are employed by the Mouse, they sideline at other clubs in town and aren't afraid to make stabs at the Big Cheese himself. In general, though, they don't stray too far from good taste or too close to cutting edge.

- ◆ **8TRAX ★**. Ironic young folks—and lots of Disney employees winding down from their shifts, especially on Thursdays—choose this pleasingly corny club, which is all about disco balls and 1970s-era tunes. Bet you'll hear "Y.M.C.A." Some nights, it does vintage '80s hits.

Saving Money and Going at the Right Time: The best discounts for Pleasure Island are found at the front box office. Many people buy the option to attend when they purchase their theme park tickets (see the information on Disney ticket packages, p. 94), only to find it would have been cheaper to wait, or worse, that there's only one club they would have enjoyed, anyway, which would have cost them only $12. Patrons must be at least 21 to enter the dance clubs and 18 to enter the comedy club or the Adventurers Club unless an adult accompanies them. If you're staying on Disney property, drink all you want, because the Disney buses will take you home up to an hour after the clubs' closing. The dance clubs don't open until 8pm or 9pm, and don't start filling up until after 10pm.

Other Downtown Disney Entertainment

Pleasure Island is the middle component of a three-section, car-free string of shopping, dining, and entertainment districts known collectively as Downtown Disney (p. 169). To the west, the West Side is home to the DisneyQuest virtual playground (p. 170) and *La Nouba,* the Cirque du Soleil show (see below). To the east, the Marketplace's offerings are dominated by Disney-themed shops of every stripe. Parking is free at all three areas, and you can roam freely between them, although a full walk from one end to the other would be nearly a mile.

Although in years past, access to Pleasure Island was restricted to ticket holders, now anyone can roam its tight streets—they only have to pay to enter a club. If you buy a pass (this perk is also part of some ticket packages), you'll receive a wristband at the first club you attend, which gets you into the rest. A DJ booth, P.I. Live, spins live music outside the clubs—sometimes people dance outside, sometimes the DJ tries in vain to spark a party—and most hours, that aspect can be enjoyed for free, without a wristband. In most seasons, multi-club tickets can be turned back in for re-admission on the next five nights for $5. One number (☎ 407/939-2648) works for all Pleasure Island establishments.

If I had to choose one night to come to Pleasure Island, it'd be Thursdays, Cast Night, when Disney workers (especially young gay boys with their platonic girlfriends) come out to play. My favorite place to go on Thursdays is the Adventurers Club—because it's performance-based entertainment and not a dance club, I find that on Thursdays, its actors strive to impress their co-workers, and the night seems to bring out the best energy. But 8TRAX and Mannequins are also fun when bushy-tailed cast members get going.

Pleasure Island connects to the West Side and to the Marketplace. As for the main nightspot at the West Side, I'm going to say what no one else will about Cirque du Soleil's permanent production at Walt Disney World, *La Nouba* ★★ (Downtown Disney West Side; ☎ 407/939-1298; www.cirquedusoleil.com/lanouba; Tues–Sat at 6pm and 9pm): It has special appeal with people who've gotten frisky after a few days of squeaky-clean Disney and with convention-goers who are far from their spouses. Makes sense. All those taut, skilled athletic bodies, wearing little, flexing and writhing across each other with acrobatic virtuosity—it's as close to sex as Disney's gonna get. That said, it's perfectly acceptable for kids, too—I'm not exaggerating when I say it could end up being the most memorable theatrical experience of a young person's life. The arty, hyper, clownish French Canadian spectacular, a kaleidoscope of stunts and tricks, overloads audiences' senses 10 times a week for 90 minutes at a time in a 1,600-seat theater that looks like a postmodern version of a Big Top. Show quality is high, and the talent is extraordinary. So are prices: $63 adults/$50 kids aged 3 to 9 to $112/$90, depending on where you sit, but don't be afraid to accept the cheapest seat available, since no view is a loser. Get there at least a half-hour early or they'll sell your seat to someone else.

On the West Side, there's also a 24-screen **AMC Pleasure Island cinema** (☎ 407/298-4488). $9 adults, $7 before 6pm Mon–Thurs and before 4pm Fri–Sun. $6 kids 2–12, $7 seniors, $5 for all before noon Fri–Sun), though I can't imagine having an attention span so short that I'd rather see a movie when I've got Disney World all around me.

Not every scrap of leisure in Downtown Disney requires a ticket. The entertainment area connects with the West Side, where you can wander past the Virgin Megastore and Planet Hollywood for free. Here, one of the principal nightspots is an outpost of the **House of Blues** (Downtown Disney West Side; ☎ 407/934-2583; www.hob.com) chain. Its 2,000-person, theater-style venue (standing space only) hosts regular performers along the lines of B. B. King and Norah Jones (with sometime detours to such acts as Cannibal Corpse). Tickets for those shows start around $20. The Front Porch area usually hosts some sort of local musician playing, and you can hang out for free. From Thursday to Saturday, after about 10:30pm, the Blues Kitchen takes over, and a second free stage is born, this one with a wide variety of local and national artists.

Disney's BoardWalk

Between the Swan and Dolphin hotels and Epcot, Disney's BoardWalk (no admission required) is a lesser entertainment district that is no match for the Downtown Disney area. Many a night, I have seen its two clubs thumping along in wretched desolation, although patronage depends greatly on who happens to be staying at the adjoining hotels and if they're in a party frame of mind. At the very least, its scrubbed-down idealization of 1930s Atlantic City makes for a pleasant backdrop for an evening stroll on the water. The area can be reached from Epcot's International Gateway entrance. Thursday through Saturday evenings, there's a scattering of street entertainers (jugglers and the like). **Atlantic Dance Hall** (☎ 407/939-2444; minimum age of 21 for admission; Tues–Sat 9pm to 2am; no cover) is not, alas, a place where they might shoot horses, but a DJ dance club. Its most devoted clientele seems to be tipsy trade-show attendees from the Swan and Dolphin hotels, both located next door. Hip it's not, and nostalgic it ain't, which is too bad, because its Art Deco interior holds such promise.

Jellyrolls ★ ($10 cover; minimum age of 21 for admission; daily 7pm–2am) is Disney's challenge against the Howl at the Moon Saloon on International Drive (p. 291): dueling pianists jam, audiences sing along, and the mood is light.

CITYWALK

Although the concept is similar to that of Disney's Pleasure Island—one pass for all clubs—CityWalk, Universal Orlando's 30-acre nightlife district, takes fewer pains to present a wholesome face to the public. Nights here, in the front yard shared by both Universal theme parks, were designed with all the jellybean colors and rock-concert panache to appeal to tourists, to be sure, but they also attract a lot more locals and therefore have a sharper (and some say much more fun) edge. In my opinion, the drinks are stronger, too, but that might be my imagination. Bolstered partly by regular concerts at its Hard Rock Live venue, **CityWalk** ★★★ (Exit 75A, coming on I-4 from the west or Exit 74B coming from the east; ☎ 407/363-8000 or 6000 Universal Blvd, Orlando; www.citywalkorlando.com; $9.95 admission to all clubs; 11am–2am; parking $10 before 6pm, free after 6pm excluding event nights) is the more locally popular of the two park-propped entertainment areas, and in my estimation, its clubs have more distinct and independent personalities than the ones at Pleasure Island.

Like Pleasure Island, there is no charge to enter the common area, which is a boon because that allows anyone to tour around before deciding whether they want to pay to enter any clubs. Individual cover charges apply to all the clubs. Buying a $9.95 **CityWalk Party Pass** from any of the kiosks at the complex grants you unlimited admission to any and all of them on a given night; the clubs usually open after 10pm and are otherwise $7 a pop. Some of them serve food during the day and turn into nightspots late, and others only open in the evening. All Universal park tickets with multiday admission automatically come with one Party Pass. The Party Pass also is available with the addition of a movie ticket at the Loews Universal Cineplex (see below), which is part of the complex. That combo costs $14. Finally, there's a package that buys a prix fixe dinner at one of CityWalk's restaurants with a ticket to the Cineplex for $20.

Many clubs, which also serve food, only admit patrons 21 or older because drinking is permitted outdoors anywhere in CityWalk. Every club can be reached via the main CityWalk number, except in the instances noted.

 • **Jimmy Buffett's Margaritaville** ★★ (☎ 407/224-2155) offers live music nightly in a touristy environment that's first about the cheeseburgers in paradise, secondly about margaritas (there are three bars), and thirdly about island music. You'll get a lot more out of it if you're a Parrothead who knows Buffett's songs, as many of the details are inside jokes pegged to his classic songs. Get there before 10pm to avoid a cover charge of $7. Thursdays grant free admission to locals, so that's a good night to meet Floridians.

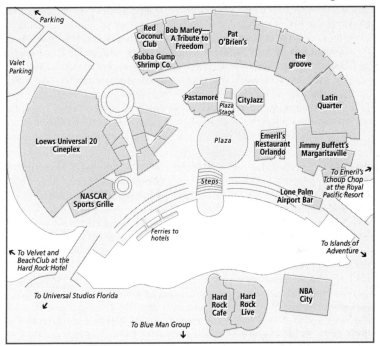

- **Red Coconut Club** ✮ is Universal's version of an ultra lounge, mixing stylish cocktails and one of the more intimate atmospheres at Universal Orlando. Its balcony overlooks the pedestrians thronging CityWalk. Looking down on others is something of a hobby here; it's the district's most upscale venture. Besides a Rat Pack vibe, there are martinis, live music and DJs, and free valet parking from 6pm to 8pm with a receipt. It opens at 7pm, and there's a $7 cover after 9pm.

- **Bob Marley—A Tribute to Freedom** (☎ 407/224-3663) draws its regular crowd with reggae music, usually recorded. This eatery-cum–music hall is loosely modeled on Marley's home in Kingston, Jamaica, and the open-air courtyard is one of the most chill places to kick back at CityWalk. Thursdays are Red Stripe Rastafarian Thursdays, from 4pm until close, with drink specials and prizes. It opens at 4pm, and there's a $7 cover after 8pm.

- **Pat O'Brien's** ✮✮ (☎ 407/224-3663) is "an authentic reproduction of New Orleans' favorite watering hole," which is cool to see, and its Hurricane rum drinks will make you see it twice. You will see two pianos even if you're sober; its truly talented dueling pianists compete, serenade, and take requests to suit the mood of the crowd. O'Brien's serves good food, but if you can't get a seat (or don't want one), it also sells drinks through a window facing the street. This spot is among the most popular here.

- **CityJazz** (☎ 407/224-2189), despite the name, doesn't get down with much jazz: Shows begin at 8pm Monday through Wednesday only. Otherwise, this is CityWalk's catch-all space. Thursday through Sunday after 10pm, it turns into Bonkerz Comedy Club; local comics appear Thursday and Friday, national names on Saturday, and on Sunday there's a comedy hypnosis show. It opens 8pm to 1am Sunday through Thursday, and 7pm to 2am Friday and Saturday. The cover is usually $7 but may pop higher for special events.

◆ **the groove** is busy, sleek, and state of the art; this dance club is also designed to be middle-of-the-road to appeal to the array of people attending Universal; music skips from the '70s (Tues) to the '80s (Sat) to recent hits. It throws frequent teen-only nights with stringent security. The cover is $7, and it opens at 9pm. Sunday night is locals' night, so swing by then to meet a resident.

After years of watching Disney hoard tourists all night, Universal has slyly lured the famed **Blue Man Group** ★★ (☎ 888/340-5476; www.universalorlando. com) to its property by building the trio a custom-made theater, which cut the ribbon in June 2007. That was too late for me to attend, but the plan was to offer anyone with a ticket to a Universal theme park the option to add on a ticket to the show, even at the last minute. You know their schtick by now, right? Three taciturn, bald, blue guys get into hilarious mischief, play with bizarre homemade toys, and generally make a disaster area of the theater—get a seat near the foot of the stage in the so-called "poncho section" (you'll get a plastic cloak) if you think it'd be fun to be splattered with goo. If you've gone to the parks for the day, seeing the Blue Men won't require use of a car or a bus; guests can start drinking cocktails whenever they want and wander over to the theater, accessible to both CityWalk and Universal Studios, around showtime. Tickets cost about half what Disney's *La Nouba* charges: Matinees are $45 to $55 for adults and $39 to $45 for kids ages 3 to 9, and evening shows are $59 to $69 adults/$49 to $59 kids. If you purchase your ticket at the same time as you buy your Universal theme park admission, you can save around $14, and you can also decide to add on a ticket to that night's show while you're inside the parks.

A 3,000-seat, top-of-the-line live-music arena attached to the famous burger joint, **Hard Rock Live** ★★ (☎ 407/351-5483; www.hardrock.com/live2) is one of Orlando's primary concert and comedy venues, and it regularly hosts the likes of Keith Urban, Hoobastank, Barenaked Ladies, Maroon 5, and Simple Plan, which released a live album recorded here—often, concerts are recorded for TV broadcast, too. The second-floor seating is spacious and has commendable sightlines; for some concerts, the first floor is converted to a dance floor or to standing room. You can't miss the theater itself—it's the building that looks like the Roman Coliseum. Check way ahead for what's coming, because ticket availability depends entirely on the popularity of the act.

A 10-minute walk away, at the Hard Rock Hotel, you'll find **Velvet** (☎ 407/ 503-2000; open daily until 2am), a laid-back lounge with cushy seating that eschews the clutter of huge CityWalk crowds. The same hotel's **BeachClub** is situated alongside an expansive California-style pool, the largest heated pool in the city, and nonguests can easily pull up a barstool to enjoy the summery atmosphere. The hours there are pegged to the pool area but tend to stretch later in warm weather, so call ahead if you plan to arrive after 10pm or so.

A free 10-minute ferry ride from CityWalk, Universal's lavish **Portofino Bay Hotel** (☎ 407/503-1200) puts on a free nightly show with strolling musicians and opera singers, Musica della Notte. It's held, weather permitting, just before sunset on its harbor, so you don't need a room key to enjoy it. There are tables, and waiters will take orders for antipasto and wine by the glass, if you're so inclined.

CityWalk's resident multiplex is the **Loews Universal Cineplex** (☎ 407/354-5998; adults $8.50, students $7.50, kids aged 2 to 12 $5.50).

PROFESSIONAL SPORTS

If you'll be in town during the late winter, check out the section "Spring Training" in chapter 8, "The Other Orlando."

A Florida tradition born, unexpectedly, among the French Basque, jai-alai ("hi a-lie") is similar to the New England high school sport of lacrosse, except it's played with Frito-shaped scoops called cestas at a literal breakneck speed that no varsity coach could condone. Watching the hardened athletes at **Orlando Jai Alai** ★ (6405 S. Hwy. 17-92, at S.R. 436 Fern Park; ☎ 407/339-6221; www.orlando jaialai.com; admission $1; 7pm post time, Thurs–Sun, Jan–Mar), north of the city, hurl the ball at each other at up to 150 miles per hour, knowing that one false move could create a situation beyond the remedy of a mop, is half of the fun. The other half is betting, which makes an outing here less family-friendly than it ought to be. Still, delving into the hyper-masculine sport (which took root in Florida, by way of Cuba, as an alternative to horse racing in the 1920s) and watching the terrifying ricochet of the ball in the enclosed court (called a fronton), can make for a gripping night out, if you can slough off its tackier elements. Kids taller than 39 inches are admitted, but one must be at least 18 to wager.

Your one-stop venue for the major league teams should be the indoor **Amway Arena** ★ (☎ 407/849-2001; www.orlandocentroplex.com), which locals call the O-rena or by its previous name, T.D. Waterhouse Centre. Home teams are the **Orlando Magic** (National Basketball League; www.nba.com/magic; $14.35 for nosebleed seats behind the basket to $115 for courtside; Oct–Apr) and the **Orlando Predators** (Arena Football League; www.orlandopredators.com; $7 for upper bowl end zones to $85 for front-row club seats; Mar–June), in the Southern Division of the National Conference. In 2006, the Predators went all the way to the ArenaBowl in Las Vegas, but were defeated by the Chicago Rush. Major concerts are also held here. Sales are handled by Ticketmaster (☎ 407/839-3900).

The **Florida Seals** (Bill Peck Blvd., at Silver Spur Lane, Kissimmee; ☎ 407/343-7825; www.floridaseals.com; $12 end zone seats to $30 rink-side glass seats), members of the newly formed Southern Professional Hockey League, play at Silver Spurs Arena in Kissimmee. Despite being minor league, they've got a slick operation, "Ice Girls" cheerleaders, "Sealvester" the mascot, and all. The team plays in the winter, but heads out of town for February.

THE PERFORMING ARTS

As a place dedicated to showmanship, Orlando fosters a large and diverse talent pool, and when they're not entertaining theme park guests or clowning in dinner shows, some of the city's artists find work at a variety of theater companies and concert halls. Among the celebrities who got their start in Orlando are Wayne Brady, Cheryl Hines, the singers in *NSYNC and the Backstreet Boys, Delta Burke, and Wesley Snipes. Britney Spears, Justin Timberlake, Ryan Gosling, Keri

Russell, and Christina Aguilera began their careers here as Mouseketeers on the early-1990s version of *The Mickey Mouse Show,* which was shot at Disney–MGM Studios. Naturally, with all that talent about, you'll find some excellent performances away from the theme park stages.

THEATER, DANCE & CONCERTS

Orlando, like many American cities, takes its theatrical marching orders from New York City, and although the situation is slowly changing, you're more likely to see a script exported from off-Broadway, or an orchestra from another big city, than a true original work by a hometown pen.

There are several things to like about **Mad Cow Theatre Company** ★★★ (105 S. Magnolia Ave., Orlando; ☎ 407/297-8788; www.madcowtheatre.com; tickets $18–$24). The first is that it's ambitious and literate, tackling such tough works as Caryl Churchill's *A Number,* David Mamet's *Glengarry Glen Ross,* and Stephen Sondheim's *Sweeney Todd.* Also attractive is the potential to make a night of it: The downtown space has two comfortably cozy black-box theaters—one with 100 seats and the other with 40 to 60—that are close to the nightclubs for post-show revels. Although it only opened in 1997, its 10-show season, which runs year-round, attracts the city's best talent and is held in high regard by critics.

Headquartered at Princeton Street amid the antiques district since the late '80s, **Theatre Downtown** (2113 N. Orange Ave., Orlando; ☎ 407/841-0083; www. theatredowntown.net; tickets $15–$18) produces edgier New York exports such as *Take Me Out* and ironic fluff such as *Psycho Beach Party* and *Little Shop of Horrors.* The thrust stage (one that juts into the audience) is small and so are the budgets, but the company is noted for its big heart.

In the Loch Haven park arts complex north of downtown, **Orlando-UCF Shakespeare Festival** ★★ (812 E. Rollins St., Orlando; ☎ 407/447-1700; www. shakespearefest.org) is one of the city's best-funded and most respected theatrical enterprises, with two major spaces: the 118-seat Goldman, a semi-proscenium space, and the Margeson, a 230-seat thrust stage. While one stage usually has something meaty on (the Bard, of course, or an adaptation of *Crime and Punishment*), another has a children's show up ($12), often only on weekends. In December, its traditional holiday show is the tongue-in-cheek *Every Christmas Story Ever Told.* The productions' storybook-style posters are designed by Sean Simon Ramirez, a former Disney animator who has bestowed a consistently classy look on the company. The complex used to belong to the Orlando Science Center before it built its flashy new HQ next door; the blurry, bouncy acoustics of the dome atop the Patrons' Room, which once served as a planetarium, are fascinating. Most seats are $25 to $30, preview performances cost around $12, students save $5, and the theater schedules regular "senior matinees" that charge older patrons $12. On one Monday a month, the theater's PlayFest series mounts a reading of a new work by an up-and-coming writer; admission for that is free.

Across the parking lot, **Orlando Repertory Theatre** ★★ 🧒 (1001 E. Princeton St., Orlando; ☎ 407/896-7365; www.orlandorep.com; tickets $9 to $14), usually called "The Rep," is the city's preeminent young peoples' theater. Its association with the University of Central Florida's Masters program ensures first-rate production values in a modern, two-theater complex, with an intelligent show selection based on adaptations of classic and modern children's literature.

Plan-Ahead Performance

These companies don't have year-round schedules, but what they do have is among the best live performance in the state. Check ahead to see what's coming.

Orlando Opera (Bob Carr Performing Arts Centre, Orlando; ☎ 407/426-1700; tickets $25–$120) mixes opera standards *(Madama Butterfly, Samson and Delilah)* with popular fare *(The Pirates of Penzance)*, typically in three-performance runs. Although its talent is good, it doesn't land marquee names.

Orlando Ballet (Bob Carr Performing Arts Centre, Orlando; ☎ 407/426-1739; www.orlandoballet.org; tickets $15–$70), the city's only true professional dance company, produces about seven elegant shows a season, running 3 or 4 days each, including the annual *The Nutcracker* (mid-Dec, at the Osceola Performing Arts Center). Ticketmaster (www.ticketmaster.com) sells its tickets.

Traveling, premium-priced Broadway shows, mostly musicals, tend to put down stakes for five nights at a time. Find out what's on its way to the Bob Carr Performing Arts Centre through the **Broadway Across America** (☎ 407/839-3900; www.broadwayacrossamerica.com) series. Don't expect a deal.

Orlando Philharmonic Orchestra (812 E. Rollins St., Suite 300, Orlando; ☎ 407/770-0071; www.orlandophil.org; tickets $16–$60), employing more than 80 musicians, appears in some 115 performances a season. Although its bread and butter is classical music, it also brings in well-known vocalists, mounts semi-staged musical readings, and other lower-brow ticket sellers. It spreads performances across the Bob Carr Performance Arts Center, the Shakespeare Center, and, in summer, the Harry P. Leu Gardens—all of which are in downtown or nearby. Half-price student discounts are available with I.D.

Past shows include *Thomas Edison Invents, To Kill a Mockingbird, Tales of a Fourth Grade Nothing,* and the first regional theater production of Kathie Lee Gifford's musical *Under the Bridge.* The seven-show season runs September to May and includes both afternoon and evening curtains. On occasion, you can use your ticket stub to obtain discounted admission at area museums, so ask.

Pinocchio's Marionette Theater ★ 🧒 (525 S. Semoran Blvd., Winter Park; ☎ 407/677-8831; www.pinocchios.net; $9 adults, $8 kids 2–12) may be in an ugly strip mall, but its interior is a jewel box of an imitation Italian theater. The expertly executed marionette shows may be old-fashioned (mostly retellings of fairy tales), but they're charming, and there's something on all year long. There are late morning shows on weekdays, and both morning and afternoon shows on weekends. The theater's founder and artistic director, David Eaton, is a former Bozo the Clown, and he used to work with legendary stringman Bil Baird.

The **Festival of Orchestras** (Bob Carr Performing Arts Centre, 401 W. Livingston St., Orlando; ☎ 800/738-8188 or 407/539-0245; www.festivaloforchestras.com) isn't a onetime burp on the calendar but an ongoing program that imports five or more international symphony orchestras a year. It must be expensive to ship in musicians from Brazil, Wales, and Russia, because the Festival won't offer single tickets until it has saturated its base with as many subscriptions as it can sell. Even then, prices are high (more than $100 isn't uncommon), though students and active military personnel receive 50% discounts.

Orlando Theatre Project ✦ (☎ 407/491-1397; www.otp.cc; $24, $20 students and seniors), or OTP, is an Equity company—meaning its actors are unionized professionals—that takes on, usually quite successfully, challenging modern new plays, including *Proof* and *Souvenir.* Shows are performed at the Orlando Repertory Theatre in Loch Haven Park for runs of 2 weeks to a month.

Another company presenting at ORT, **People's Theatre** (1001 E. Princeton St., Orlando; ☎ 407/426-0545; www.peoplestheatre.org; $15 general admission, $12 students and seniors) mounts productions touching on themes of diversity. That most often translates into works by respected African-American writers. The company averages three shows a year, mounted on weekends.

The Plaza Theatre (kids) (425 N. Bumby Ave., Orlando; ☎ 407/228-1220; www. theplazatheatre.com; tickets $30–$35), signposted by a Worlds Fair–style marquee tower, opened in 1963 as the city's first two-screen cinema. Now it's a two-theater live performance place with a mandate to serve families. Its slate still attracts area families with mass-appeal, noncontroversial entertainment: Well-done small-scale musicals, singing groups, and visiting musical acts and comics. For some shows, students with ID can get $10 discounts.

COMEDY

In addition to the shows at Pleasure Island and CityWalk's CityJazz, Orlando has a few other established spots for very different types of comedy, most of which have to work much harder to whip up their audiences.

Improv maestro Wayne Brady got his start at **SAK Comedy Lab** ✦✦ (380 W. Amelia St., Orlando; ☎ 407/648-0001; www.sak.com; open Tues–Sat, show times vary), and boy, they don't let you forget it. Nor should they, if their comedy is that good. And it is. Open since 1991, this 200-seat downtown theater trains improv comics, and you can catch grads in performance on Tuesdays at 9pm for $2, Wednesdays at 9pm for $5, or spring for the elaborate Duel of Fuels improv-off Thursdays, Fridays and Saturdays at 8pm for $15. Weekend nights often have second shows at 10pm. Wayne Himself comes back to perform from time to time, and its long-running members are often tapped for big projects in town—David Russell, SAK's artistic director, directed the launch of the Monsters Inc. Laugh Floor attraction for the Magic Kingdom, and he oversees the Comedy Warehouse and Adventurers Club at Pleasure Island, plus "Turtle Talk with Crush" at Epcot.

After nearly 2 decades of serving in the entertainment trenches playing cruise ship lounges, Pennsylvania-reared Dottie Kulasa and her comedian husband came to town and opened the 180-seat **Dottie's Orlando Comedy Theatre** (7052 International Dr., ☎ 407/226-3680; open nightly; www.dottiesorlando.com), which books stand-up acts and cabaret-style shows alike. Usually, the 90-minute, three-headliner stand-up segment costs $15 online (including one free drink) and starts at 7:30pm. The second show, which costs around $20 and is less likely to

Screen Gem

The Enzian Theater ★★★ (1300 S. Orlando Ave., Maitland; ☎ 407/629-0054; www.enzian.org; tickets $8), jolly and inviting, is the best place to catch a movie in the city, and it ranks highly countrywide, too. From the outside, it looks a lot like an old home and before show times, at sunset, you'll find people kicking back on the tree-sheltered patio, nursing beers, and watching the setting sun paint the Spanish moss red. Inside, though, is a large cinema with a nice-sized screen where the city's best selection of art films is shown. Unlike multiplexes, there aren't rows of seats, but four lollipop-colored levels of tables with soft seating and some whimsical movie-inspired pop art on the walls (such as the *Wizard of Oz* quartet posing as the Reservoir Dogs).

Waiters take your order (if you have one—eating's not required) before the movie, and once it's under way, your meal arrives surreptitiously and the cinema is filled with the smells of hot food. We're not talking just nachos and popcorn either, although they have those; gulf shrimp with blue crab ($12), BBQ panini with homemade ginger sauce ($7), and foot-wide pizzas (from $10) are served, as are $10-to-$13 beer pitchers and gooey, platter-sized chocolate-chip cookies ($2.50).

The Enzian, just north of Winter Park, produces six festivals a year, too (including a Jewish festival in Nov and a homegrown filmmakers' bash in Dec), and hosts frequent talks; check its website for the schedule. It's located a half-mile north of Lee Road, which has an exit off I-4; on a clear night, it'll take about 20 minutes to drive back to the Disney area.

---

contain family-appropriate material, begins at 9:30pm. Like any comedy club, you never know what you're going to get, but thoughtfully, there's no drink minimum, so if the yuks don't come, you can go. Check its website for admission coupons worth a few bucks. The tawdry, T-shirt-shoppy segment of I-Drive is right outside, which makes for a diverting post-show stroll, particularly once you've had a few.

If you're a comedy connoisseur, you'll do better at the **Orlando Improv** (129 W. Church St., Orlando; ☎ 321/281-8000; www.orlandoimprov.com; open nightly, show times vary), smack downtown, where actual headliners headline (despite the club's name, there's not a lotta improv) when they're in town. Most shows have a strict over-21 policy. There are no drink minimums; a typical entry price is $20, and dinner (a few entrees of $10 to $16) is available. There are shows around 7:30pm every night, and on weekends a second show is added at around 9:45pm. Upcoming appearances are diligently posted on the club's website.

DANCE CLUBS, BARS & LIVE MUSIC VENUES

For my taste, Orlando's dance club scene is overpopulated with simpering twentysomethings ordering overpriced bottle service on daddy's credit card. Deep it ain't, and don't bother looking for trance or community. There's something plastic about the clientele, and the club owners' push toward making everything super-luxury is a tiresome trend. What happened to just going out for the night and dancing for some simple fun? No wonder so many people have started squeezing into the city's gay clubs instead—they're some of the only nightspots left that come from a place of energy and joy. Downtown, the strut du jour is up Orange Avenue north of Church Street, where many drinking holes and dance dens coexist. Clubs usually open around 8pm, start pumping by 9pm, and start dumping kids back on the street at 2am, the witching hour.

Back when the Backstreet Boys were still in high school, you could find them here, with Justin, in the white-hot glory days of Tabu ★ (46 N. Orange Ave., Orlando; ☎ 407/648-8363; www.tabunightclub.com; cover $5–$10). It's Orlando's most established dance club, with a touch of ridiculous swank, and downtown's largest dance floor. Tabu's home is the former Beacham Theater, which opened in 1921 and specialized in movies and vaudeville. In 1964, it was converted to Cinerama. But despite all the ghosts in its wings, you may miss the boys of O-Town the most. Sniff—Ashley Parker Angel, we hardly knew you! (And if you don't understand any of those references—vaudeville excepted—then perhaps this isn't the place for you.)

A sunken dance floor and video screens usually mark modern nightspots for banishment from the inner circle. Yet downtown's Independent Bar (70 N. Orange Ave., Orlando; ☎ 407/839-0457; www.independentbar.net; cover $3 or less), going since the '80s, remains popular because its denizens are already retro-minded: goth, vinyl, and New Wave disciples are all welcomed without a second glance. Tuesdays is Grits & Gravy, a night of old soul. Fridays are College Indie—oh no, don't tell me that's considered Oldies now.

Orlando does South Beach at Sky60 ★ (64 N. Orange Ave., Orlando; ☎ 407/246-1599; www.sky60.com; cover $5 after 10pm on weekends, free weekdays), a lounge that makes like Miami Beach with billowy fabrics, clubby Moroccan-style cabanas, and DJs too hip for their own good. Fortunately, because it's surrounded by other clubs with size issues, Sky60 survives because its swank gives it a mellowness that other hotspots lack. The prices aren't too bad, and the clientele isn't wedged too far up their own posteriors.

The Club at Firestone (578 N. Orange Ave., Orlando; ☎ 407-426-0005; www.clubatfirestone.com; cover usually $5) is another big dance mega-club, with the usual trappings: lasers, lights, brand-name DJs, and potentially lethal sound levels. The crowd is diverse.

If you're under 40, reasonably presentable, and prepared to find the love of your night, then Wall Street Plaza (17 Wall Street Plaza, Orlando; ☎ 407/849-9904; www.wallstplaza.net; no cover), a complex of eight amalgamated nightspots, is the place for you. Of course, it's also a decent place to unwind after a hard day's work, which is how so many ugly stories begin. Of the watering holes on the block, the Globe, Waitiki Retro Tiki Lounge, and the upstairs Monkey Bar have seating facing Heritage Square, which makes for fun people-watching—especially as the crowd gets drunker and tries to wrestle with the lifelike alligator sculptures. But here's a sobering thought: Serial killer Ted Bundy was tried in a court building that stood on the site of that park until 1999. Slingapour's, a come-one-come-all club that attracts national acts, is also part of the complex.

I'm only mentioning this place because it's so funny. I wouldn't want you to actually be caught dead at **Club Paris** (122 W. Church St., Orlando; ☎ 407/832-7409; www.clubparis.net; closed Mon–Tues; cover free before 11pm, after 11pm $10 for men and $5 for women). After all, Paris Hilton herself, who signed on to lend her name to a chain of clubs and make periodic pink appearances, doesn't even bother reminding people about this over-the-top trashfest anymore, so owners have resorted to pretending the name refers to Paris, France. If you could take a 22,000-square-foot club with an outsized VIP area, dip it in Pepto-Bismol, and then somehow recruit as patrons randy young men who worship at the twin altars of hair care products and sports car makers, then you might be able to make your own Club Paris. But you still wouldn't want to go. To put it in perspective: On Wednesday nights, you can drink all you want for $10. That's *not* hot. That's sad.

LIVE MUSIC

Also check out the options at Pleasure Island (p. 278) and CityWalk (p. 282), since many big-name acts head there.

On the last Thursday of every month in the lobby lounge of the Hard Rock Hotel, **Velvet Sessions** ★ (5800 Universal Blvd., Orlando; www.velvetsessions. com; admission $25) brings in a band you remember from your FM dial—Joan Jett, Cheap Trick, Starship, Loverboy, Eddie Money, among others. Pleasantly, it's not too crowded, and after the civilized show, you can filter over to CityWalk (a smart tactic, since the rush on parking after performances lasts at least an hour). There are free drinks and snacks for 2 hours before the act takes the stage. To hear about gigs, you have to join the mailing list online.

Part of an 11-strong chain, the **Howl at the Moon Saloon** ★★ (8815 International Dr., Orlando; ☎ 407/354-5999; www.howlatthemoon.com; Sun–Thurs 7pm–2am, Fri 5pm–2am, Sat 6pm–2am, piano show starts 1 hour after opening; cover $5) caters to folks who want a rough-and-tumble Western-style drinkin' hole without getting rough and without the tumble. It's a saloon delivered as a post-theme park experience, where dueling pianists try to outdo each other for laughs and virtuosity (expect to hear "American Pie" at least once a night), and the crowds, mostly over 35, clap evenly and earnestly to the beat. It is, as hardened city dwellers might observe, very "white," but its heart's in the right place.

The city's most respected house for a wide range of touring bands, **The Social** ★★ (54 N. Orange Ave., Orlando; ☎ 407/246-1419; www.thesocial.org; opening varies depending on the show, closes at 2am; cover $7 to $25, depending on the show, with occasional discounts for advance purchase; minimum age 18) has a high standing among music fans not just because its bookers refuse to be pigeonholed to one style, but also because there's precious little attitude for a club so crammed. The club's historic brick building adds dimension to the scene. Tuesdays are Phat-n-Jazzy parties, for progressive hip-hop. When bands are in, covers are usually $7 to $15, sometimes more.

Always busy despite the fact the local music acts are somewhat chill (acoustic guitars, earnest DJs), **Casey's on Central** (50 E. Central Blvd., Orlando; ☎ 407/648-4218; www.caseysoncentral.com; Mon–Fri 4pm–2am, Sat-Sun 7pm–2am; no cover; minimum age 21) has the atmosphere of a neighborhood bar, especially when compared to the decibel level at other joints, but has been going for so

Good for What Ales Ya

Hidden in an industrial area, among concrete makers and scrapyards, the **Orlando Brewing and Taproom** (1301 Atlanta Ave., Orlando; ☎ 407/872-1117; www.orlandobrewing.com; daily noon–9pm) doesn't pay much rent, and the neighbors don't care much when the roof gets raised. That's what makes it a casual, non-threatening, off-the-beaten-path hangout—a relief in an over–stage managed city. At least nine own-label, organically brewed beers (ales, IPAs, pale reds—it changes according to how the brewers experiment) are on tap at any time and are concocted for area hotels and restaurants; ask for a free 10-minute tour of the back warehouse, where they're made without pasteurization (like the Old World) and sold within 2 weeks of brewing. Other fine beers are also poured—name me another hall where Chimay is on draught. The drinking area is simple but convivial, like a rec room your dad might have slapped up in the basement, and uncluttered by televisions or pool tables, the way a beer snob would have it. Now and then on weekends, there's live, easygoing music outside. Try a flight of beers for $12, or down a pint for $4, and don't be shy about asking about how each quaff is made, because its owners take their craft seriously. Want food? The bartender will hand you a folder of menus from local delivery joints. Yep, it's that relaxed. Atlanta Avenue is just east of the Kaley Street exit of I-4, Exit 81.

many years that it's really something more important now. The drinks are famously strong, and so are the fumes in the bathrooms. One word, Casey: Lysol!

Rebellious college-age kids and their pretty-boy alterna-bands who lean into the mic and whine. That's **Back Booth** (37 W. Pine St., Orlando; ☎ 407/999-2570; www.backbooth.com; bands start at 5pm, depending on the schedule, closing time is 2am; cover $3–$20, depending on the band) for ya. It's a loose scene and young, and you don't have to worry much about standing on ceremony, although the cramped, dark space means you may end up standing on some UCF sophomore's feet. On many nights, three or four bands take the stage (the 5pm shows welcome all ages, but later shows may have minimums of 18 to 21 years), and in a city increasingly commanded by meat-market lounges with canned music, all of that informality is a blessing.

GAY & LESBIAN ORLANDO

Orlando, your women are fed up. Tired of being groped at dance clubs, done with cheesy pickup lines, weary of lounges that rank bottle service over class. That's why increasing numbers of ladies aren't found at the so-called "straight" clubs, but taking refuge at the city's gay bars.

I'm being facetious, of course. Many straight women do go to Orlando's gay clubs for safe and buoyant companionship, but there are still plenty of places where an upstanding single girl would blush to be seen. By and large, the dominant venue appears to be "straight-friendly" clubs. It proves Orlando's gay scene has come a long way since the 1960s, before the theme parks arrived, when men had to hide their identities and bars were anonymous. Today these clubs are flashy, welcoming, celebratory, and, in one case, larger than an average city block. And they're among the most integrated of any modern American city's.

Going since 1975, there's nothing else in America quite like the **Parliament House** ★★★ (410 N. Orange Blossom Trail, Orlando; ☎ 407/425-7571; www.parliamenthouse.com; cover and hours vary), a Johnson-era, 130-room motel that has been converted wholly into an amusement mega-center for the gay and lesbian community. It's the nucleus of Orlando gay life. Although it's technically a gay complex, its rambling size—it's an entire motel, including a sprawling multi-club restaurant area and a beach on a small lake out back—means the Parliament can function as all things to all people. It's easy to blend in, so in fact it tends to be a hangout not only for gay guys, but also for women who love them, women who want to dance without being accosted, and open-minded straight boys. On hot days, people in questionable and puny bathing suits lounge around the pool gossiping and looking like they expect something to happen at any second. Think of it as a mini-mall for gay folk: There's the Footlight Theater for drag and cabaret shows; the Electric Lounge for pre-show cocktails; a diner; Le Club Dance, which gears up around 10pm; the Video Bar; and a scuzzier bar called The Stable, for leather-and-jeans-wearing guys who play pool and know how to handle a stick. The scene is pretty dazzling when you consider Orlando politics are still controlled by conservative Christians. Sundays are for the popular, no-cover Tea Dance, which starts at 3pm and drags on for the better part of 12 hours. Fridays have no cover until 11pm, but Saturdays are $8. It's possible to stay overnight here, too (prices are fab: $64 for a standard motel room, plus $10 if you'd like a microwave and fridge), but you'd better be friendly, because one of the sanctioned activities involves buff fellows peering into your windows to see if you'd like a new friend.

Southern Nights ★ (375 S. Bumby Ave., Orlando; ☎ 407/898-0425; www.southern-nights-orlando.com; 5pm–2am daily; cover usually $5), long-running and popular, is a casual good-for-all-comers bar featuring college student nights on Thursday, Latin nights on Mondays, and drag shows late Friday and Saturdays. Drinks are two-for-one every day except Sunday from 5pm to 9pm.

A hip outpost several miles south of downtown, **Pulse** ★ (1912 S. Orange Ave., Orlando; ☎ 407/649-3888; www.pulseorlando.com; 9pm–2am nightly; cover $5) has a split personality. Its packed front room is pure Space Age, in white decor, yet changes colors as the lights shift. But in back, where lights are less welcome, hot men dance, often shirtless. The combination of upstanding and down low—plus a cabaret space, the Jewel Box, for drag acts and club mixes, starting at 10:30pm—makes this place popular with just about everyone.

A quintessential hangout for upper-middle-class gay folk and their friends—it's a diverse, non-sexed-up crowd—the **Lava Lounge** (1235 N. Orange Ave., Orlando; ☎ 407/895-9790; www.lavaorlando.com; Tues–Fri 5pm–2am, Sat 9pm–2am; usually no cover) is boned up on martinis, videos, and ironic music selection. The outdoor patio is one of the better places to kick back in town.

Full Moon Saloon (500 N. Orange Blossom Trail, Orlando; ☎ 407/468-8725; www.fullmoonsaloon.com; noon–2am daily; no cover) is a cowboy-style bar with a big backyard, a spacious patio, and frequent outbreaks of retro music. If you know that at a gay bar, *bears* aren't looking for honey, then you'll fit in fine.

Orlando's only bathhouse is **The Club** (450 E. Compton St., Orlando; ☎ 407/425-5005; www.the-clubs.com; open 24 hours; $8 membership plus $13 for a locker or $18 for a cubicle), a laid-back, men-only scene with a spacious outdoor pool-and-whirlpool area, a gym, a tanning bed ($5), and free cookouts on Thursday nights and Sunday afternoons. Habituees of this style of socializing won't find the atmosphere as sexually charged as other bathhouses are, partly because frisky movies are only permitted to be shown behind closed doors. Customers do more hanging out than cruising.

11 Shopping: The Good, the Bad & the Discounted

Even more places where you can part with your cash, from outlet malls to fancy emporia

FOR SOME REASON, THE CITY IS EXPERIENCING A LOW EBB IN ITS SHOPPING cycle, and several of its outlet and discount malls—the chief spree spots—are undergoing reinvention and refurbishment. The major centers that do exist tend to be stocked with the usual brands, so most of the time, there's little surprising or unusual among the offerings. What Orlando does offer is choice—plenty of stores at plenty of malls. International visitors typically set aside an afternoon to scoop up jeans, shoes, and other sundries, but mostly because their foreign currencies make those things such bargains and not because what's on offer is particularly rare. There's almost always a souvenir store at the exit area of pretty much every ride you're going to be on, so you will be hardly at a loss for places to buy stuff. Whether your booty will be useful is another question.

The stand-out shopping choices at the big amusement park areas are discussed in the chapters devoted to those parks. This chapter, by comparison, is dedicated to the shopping you'll find outside the parks and Orlando's dirty little secret: You'll always get better buys on almost all of the souvenirs pushed within the park gates, if only you have the discipline to wait until you're off the grounds to buy.

RETAIL MALLS

Most malls are open 10am to 9pm Monday to Saturday, 10am to 6pm or 7pm Sundays.

One of the few stores at the 250-store **Florida Mall** ★★ (8001 S. Orange Blossom Trail, Orlando; ☎ 407/851-6255; www.simon.com) that you won't find everywhere else is **M&M's World** (☎ 407/850-4000; www.mmsworld.com), a lavishly decorated emporium dedicated to the famous snack and its voluminous collectible spin-offs. Such stores exist only here, Las Vegas, and Times Square in New York City. The ceiling changes color, pop music blasts, and the staff has the unenviable task of keeping all those little candies off the floor. The merchandise selection is easily as varied as that of the average Disney Store (and as highly priced, charging $24 for a beach towel while the Mouse charges $20), except here, the mascots aren't rodents but bulbous sugar pellets. The store also does a brisk trade in M&Ms of wacky shades, such as grey (which they call "silver," but yeah, it's really grey) and light purple (which also looks grey, but I'll give it to them). In truth, many of these "rare" colors, which cost far more than the M&Ms at your local drugstore ($9 a pound), are also sold at several of the biggest candy shops at Disney and Universal.

If it's a sugar high you seek, head farther into the mall to the wider inventory of **Dylan's Candy Bar** (☎ 407/812-8955; www.dylanscandybar.com), owned by designer Ralph Lauren's daughter. It sells many of the same M&M colors, too. One of the only other rare stores at the Florida Mall—one of only two in America—is the **Playmobil FunPark** (☎ 407/812-6336; www.playmobilusa.com), a splashy megastore that deals in the globally popular, noseless play figures. The mall also has seven anchor stores (including a **Saks Fifth Avenue,** a **Nordstrom,** and a **Dillard's**), an **Apple** store, a **Lush** soap store, and even the 510-room, business-class **Florida Hotel and Conference Center** where an eighth department store might be expected; the prices there are a little too high ($150) for something a little too far east of the tourist zoo to warrant explication in this book. Annoyingly, the mall, which ranks among the busiest in the state, is nearly directory-free—that must be a trick to keep tourists wandering past its shops.

Try as it might, the audaciously designed **Festival Bay** (5250 International Dr., across from Prime Outlets, Orlando; ☎ 407/351-7718; www.shopfestivalbaymall. com), at the top end of I-Drive, hasn't been able to stay full since opening in 2001. Big-idea businesses, such as Bill Murray's restaurant based on *Caddyshack,* open and close in a wink, so a stroll down its bleak, untenanted corridors can feel at times like a trek through a consumerist's tundra. Even the indoor fountains that flow underfoot to the outdoor pond can't enliven the real estate nightmare. But that may start changing now that **Ron Jon Surfpark** (☎ 866/596-7873; www. ronjonsurfpark.com; daily 6am–midnight) opened here. The surfwear superstore, an offshoot of the more popular one based in Cocoa Beach (south of Kennedy Space Center), runs an outpost at the mall. And as of early 2007, it operates a three-pool surf school where would-be Gidgets can pay $50 to $60 for 2-hour surf sessions during which they catch about 15 waves, always perfect, that can measure up to 8 feet tall. It was mostly built at press time, but not yet open, so I wasn't able to hang ten for you. But its presence gives Festival Bay a decidedly athletic slant, as one the mall's other big tenants is a 61,000-square-foot **Vans Skatepark** (☎ 407/351-3881; www.vans.com/skateparks; $10 to participate; daily 10am–10pm), which does for skateboarders and bikers what Ron Jon does for surfers; it's a blast to watch these kids defy physics, and tempt fate, as they soar around the courses. Other anchors at the mall include the gargantuan camping-and-fishing superstore **Bass Pro Shops Outdoor World, Steve & Barry's University Sportswear, Hilo Hattie** Hawaiian wear store, and **Sheplers** discount Western wear—none of which have other presences in Orlando. A 20-screen **Cinemark multiplex** (☎ 407/352-1042) is also here; evening shows are $8 for adults, and shows before 6pm are $5.75.

The most upscale mall in the city is **Mall at Millenia** ✸ (I-4, at Conroy Rd., Orlando; ☎ 407/363-3555; www.mallatmillenia.com), opened 2002, where the fanciest brands keep their stores and where fashion runway shows are broadcast on LED screens. Among the wallet-sappers at this 1.3-million-square-foot cathedral to credit: Cartier, Apple, Gucci, Coach, Neiman Marcus, Tommy Bahama, Kenneth Cole, Tiffany & Co., Bang & Olufsen—none of them are of the outlet variety. Even the restaurants, such as yuppie meat market Blue Martini and The Cheesecake Factory (which has a menu longer than a Tolstoy yarn), are a few notches above the standard malls. Even the less expensive stores are hip and stylish, Zara and Urban Outfitters included. The mall is a few minutes northeast of Universal on I-4. For postcards and packages, there's a post office in the basement.

Stroll and Shop: Winter Park

Seven blocks of Winter Park's Park Avenue, a sanitized Main Street-type thoroughfare, are known for their shopping. Stores veer toward galleries, chocolatiers, women's clothes, and a Pottery Barn installed in a vintage cinema building. I've noticed some high turnover in the past few years, so it's not a place to go in search of a specific item inasmuch as it's a pleasant destination for a stroll in an upscale town. The **Park Avenue Area Association** (www.parkave-winterpark.com) tracks the latest tenants. Making a pleasant afternoon of it is easy: The incomparable Morse Museum (p. 234) is at the top of the shopping drag, and the campus of Rollins College (p. 235), draped in Spanish moss, is found at the bottom. Just east, you can break your stroll with a throwback boat tour of the town's lakes and antique mansions (p. 268).

Pointe Orlando (9101 International Dr., Orlando; ☎ 407/248-2838; www.pointeorlandofl.com) recently underwent an extensive bulldozing and refit, and the results are yet to be determined. I hope it succeeds, because it's the one mall that is easiest to reach from most of the touristy I-Drive area; in fact, you can walk from the Convention Center end. There are 40 stores here, and the trend appears to be toward upscale tenants such as **The Capital Grille** steakhouse and ritzy wine bar **The Grape** (glasses: $4-$7). Also slated but not yet opened at press time: **BB King's Blues Club;** and an 11,000-square-foot **Tommy Bahama Tropical Café and Emporium.** A 21-screen **Muvico** cinema (☎ 407/926-6843) charges $7 in the evening; before 4pm, tickets are $5. The mall is just north of the mighty Convention Center, making it a hangout for trade-show-goers, some of whom are looking to cut loose and have a good time.

Pick your chin up off the floor after I tell you that when it opened in 1974, **Altamonte Mall** (451 E. Altamonte Dr., Altamonte Springs; ☎ 407/830-4422; www.altamontemall.com), 15 minutes north of Orlando, was the second-largest tourist attraction in the American South, behind Walt Disney World. Steady embellishments have kept it current—some 160 stores—but the mall now fills a necessary but certainly lower-profile and lower-income niche on the shopping scene. The anchor stores are Sears, Dillard's, Macy's, and JCPenney.

OUTLET MALLS

Like most modern outlet malls, not all of the items you find for sale here will have come from higher-priced "regular" stores; much of the stock has been specially manufactured for the outlet market, which could end up meaning that what you purchase is of a slightly lower quality than if you'd gotten it at the mall back home. That's something you can gauge only on a store-by-store basis. Regardless, the deals come fast and furious.

The reigning champ for bargains, **Orlando Premium Outlets** ✦✦✦ (8200 Vineland Ave., Orlando; ☎ 407/238-7787; www.premiumoutlets.com/orlando) has the added advantage of being near Disney, which sends it a lot of business. Some 110 stores, with very few vacancies, vie for attention, and most of them offer good deals off overstocks. Among the stores: Armani Exchange, Banana Republic, Lucky Brand Blue Jeans, Miss Sixty, Puma, and Burberry. Much of this book was researched in a pair of shoes I found for $40 at the Skechers outlet. One especially rare shop is **Disney's Character Premiere,** for cast-off official theme-park souvenirs; it has the largest selection of discount Disney souvenirs in town. The food court is a little gloomy, but that's not from under-use. Steel yourself if you come during the weekend; the line of traffic snakes for a mile, and the competition for parking approaches Olympian difficulty. The I-Ride Trolley serves it from International Drive, and from Lake Buena Vista, the Vineland Avenue turnoff is just south of I-4's exit 68 on S.R. 535. The Main Line of the I-Ride trolley (p. 11) touches down here once every 20 minutes, and the No. 42 city bus also swings here from I-Drive.

At the tippy top end of International Drive, across from Festival Bay, **Prime Outlets Orlando** ★★ (5401 W. Oak Ridge Rd., Orlando; ☎ 407/352-9600; www. primeoutlets.com) is one of 27 locations under the nationwide Prime umbrella. Because it's connected to the I-Drive tourist corridor by the cheap I-Ride trolley, it's a popular place to track down some good bargains. The year 2006 was one of transformation for the mall; a significant chunk of it was pulled down and rebuilt at a cost of $100 million (so they say), and the resulting hodgepodge of stores (which now includes **Neiman Marcus Last Call**—a shop that does sell department store castoffs—**Coach, Nike, Guess?, Kenneth Cole,** and **Escada Company Store**) was still jelling at press time. Prime Outlets will be back up to full speed with around 170 stores by the summer of 2008, but is open for business in the meantime. The website has a list of print-and-go discount coupons.

Lake Buena Vista Factory Stores ★ (15591 S.R. 535, Orlando; ☎ 407/238-9301; www.lbvfs.com) is a strip mall–style collection of about 50 stores, not all of which are owned by famous brands. It advertises savings of up to 75% on merchandise, and if you're not obsessed with finding specific items, you can find proof that claim is true. You'll also find a bit more diversity of product than at other malls, with fewer clothing boutiques and more choice in jewelry, electronics, and bags. Still, there are enough names you know (including **Old Navy, Liz Claiborne, Eddie Bauer, Borders, OshKosh B'Gosh,** and **Aéropostale**) to warrant a quick trip. The Character Outlet has some Disney bargains (half-price mugs, shirts, toys, and some souvenirs dated from a few years ago), but it can't hold a mouse-shaped candle to the Disney outlet at Orlando Premium Outlets. Stop at the mall office for a brochure packed with coupons. The mall provides a free shuttle to and from the major hotels around Disney and I-Drive; they leave between 9am to 2pm and return in four batches from 12:45 to 7pm.

FLEA MARKETS

Back home, you might have a local flea market that takes over the parking lot of an old drive-in theater or a church on Saturdays. Orlando, no city for delicacy, goes over the top. Its flea markets operate day in, day out, in barnlike sheds. The best of them are east of Walt Disney World, along U.S. 192. Drive along and make a run of them.

Five miles east of Disney, the glitzy tourist universe lapses into the more mundane world of Kissimmee, a low-rent town. **192 Flea Market** ★ (4301 U.S. 192, Kissimmee; ☎ 407/396-4555; daily 9am–6pm), at Mile Marker 15, serves them.

It's a network of barnlike buildings hosting stall after stall (around 400, when all are occupied) of extremely cheap knockoffs and crafts, many run by hard-working South Asian or Latin immigrants. Rolling luggage for $10. Suntan lotion costing $6 for 8 ounces. Beach towels for $8 to $12 less than the going rate inside the theme parks. You won't just find cheap tourist items and toys, either, but also handicrafts and imports, such as $16 Chinese silk pajamas, $9 homemade candles, $2.25 hot dogs and $1.50 churros at the food court, and at the stall of one D. Kioko, woodcarver, a garden of handmade African drums for $15 apiece. In summer, it's sweltering, and a little sad, too, but no one has to know how little you paid for those Mickey Mouse sunglasses.

Another flea market, this one at Mile Marker 10, the **Maingate Flea Market** (5407 W. U.S. Hwy. 192, Kissimmee; ☎ 407/390-1015) has a similar setup of interconnected sheds, and some 400 stalls, not all of them occupied, it must be said. Because it's about 3 miles east of Disney's entrance in the thick of U.S. 192's tourist crawl, prices are slightly higher than 192 Flea Market, but they're still dead low.

A further 250 stalls are available at the less impressive **Visitors Flea Market** (5811 W. U.S. Hwy. 192, Kissimmee; ☎ 407/396-0114), open at 9:30am daily, which because of its proximity to Disney (Mile Marker 9) has a heavier representation of park souvenirs than some of the other markets.

The quartet of ragamuffin flea markets on U.S. 192 is completed by the **Osceola Flea and Farmers Market** ✦ (2801 E. Irlo Bronson Hwy., Kissimmee; ☎ 407/846-2811; www.fleaamerica.com; Fri–Sun 8am–5pm), open only on Fridays and weekends. It's in the east end of Kissimmee. Like the other two markets, it could take a thorough browser hours to explore, although the wares will start to repeat themselves as you go. The market also sells food at a savings over most area grocery stores.

ANTIQUES

Orange Avenue, south of Princeton Street, is known as Antiques Row. It's easy to park your car in the vicinity and stroll up and down, but don't do it on Sundays. Almost everything is closed then, including the traditional way station for weary shoppers, the **White Wolf Café** (1829 N. Orange Ave., Orlando; ☎ 407/895-9911; www.whitewolfcafe.com; AE, MC, V), a combination upscale eatery (entrees $8.50–$17) and antiques store with outdoor and indoor seating. Otherwise, unless noted, stores keep regular business hours of at least 10am to 5pm.

Shops include:

- **A+T Antiques** (1620 N. Orange Ave., Orlando; ☎ 407/896-9831). Large selection of European and country furnishings.
- **Humbugs** (1618 N. Orange Ave., Orlando; ☎ 407/895-0155). Chic '60s swag and fusty midcentury furniture.
- **Fox & Hound Antiques** (1808 Orange Ave., Orlando; ☎ 407/895-7117). Glassware, silver, plates.
- **Déjà Vu** (1825 N. Orange Ave., Orlando; ☎ 407/898-3609). "Vintage clothing and funk."
- **American Antiques and Militaria** (1807 N. Orange Ave., Orlando; ☎ 407/810-2399). War stuff.
- **Golden Phoenix Antiques** (1826 N. Orange Ave., Orlando; ☎ 407/895-6006; Thurs–Sat noon–5pm). Upscale selections.

- **Oldies but Goodies** (1827 N. Orange Ave., Orlando; ☎ 407/897-1088). 1960s and 1970s couture.
- **Rock & Roll Heaven** (1814 N. Orange Ave., Orlando; ☎ 407/896-1952; www.rock-n-rollheaven.com). Thousands of CDs, average price $4.

OTHER INTERESTING STORES

Ever wonder what Disney World's overlords do with old ride vehicles, signs, and outdated souvenirs? They send them out to **Mouse Surplus** ★★★ (1500 Tradeport Dr., Orlando; ☎ 407/854-5391; www.mousesurplus.com; Mon–Fri 9am–5pm, Sat 10am–4pm), Fantasyland's junkyard. For Disney fans, the jumbled warehouse is the fire-sale equivalent of the Smithsonian, and they consider a visit to Mouse Surplus worthwhile even if they keep their credit card firmly secure in their wallets. Parked here are retired vehicles from Epcot's Horizons and World of Motion pavilions, the Magic Kingdom's Snow White and Mr. Toad's rides—even the cab of a retired monorail. Those are "for sale by owner" (you can't afford them), but more commonplace stuff from the resort is hawked by the binful, including ice cream machines, electronic equipment with mysterious uses, old hotel furniture (Fort Wilderness bunk beds, $149), golf balls ($1), name tags ($2), and forks for 25¢ apiece. A visit to this amusement reliquary might be best combined with one to the airport, since it's stashed among the warehouses in the industrial zone southwest of the airfield. *Tip:* Don't bother buying any of the DVDs of razed rides; the stuff you'll see for free on YouTube is leagues clearer.

Agra has the Taj Majal. Seattle has its Space Needle. Orlando has a giant orange. The 60-foot-tall, citrus-imitative roof of **Eli's Orange World** ★★ (5395 W. U.S. Hwy 192, Kissimmee; ☎ 800/531-3182 or 407/396-1306; www.orange world192.com; daily 8am–9:40pm) has been a city landmark ever since it opened. Florida roadsides used to be full of this kind of souvenir catch-all, stacked high with oranges and grapefruits in their red mesh bags, but as the citrus industry bowed out to make room for the McMansion industry, the state's bumper crop diminished, and now, few visitors associate the area with its fruit values. Here at Orange World, which also ships to most states, a quarter-bushel of oranges is $8, a half is $12, and a box sturdy enough to take on the flight home is $18 full. Fruit changes by the season: Fall is for navel oranges, January sees honeybell tangelos, and February through May sees a procession of oranges, honey tangerines, and Valencia oranges; ruby red grapefruit is available year-round. The shelves teeter with the sort of corny Florida souvenirs that time forgot: shellacked alligator heads from $25 to $100, personalized mugs for $4, and 8-ounce jars of papaya or guava butter for $2.50. If you're stuck for paperweights, your salvation awaits. Sure, there are *lots* of schlocky, fluorescent-lit barns selling junky souvenirs on U.S. 192 and I-Drive—but only the best is good enough for *you*.

A rare bookstore that stocks all 1,100 of the Penguin Classics, **Urban Think Bookstore** ★★ (625 E. Central Blvd., Orlando; ☎ 407/650-8004; www.urban thinkorlando.com; Thurs–Sat 9am–10pm, Sun 9am–6pm, Mon 11am–6pm, Tues–Wed 11am–9pm), in trendy Thornton Park, also has an in-store bar, frequent art shows for local artists, and hosts several readings and signings each week. Besides being one of the only independent bookstores in the region, it's the best store in town for meeting new authors and reading old ones. As for the big-box bookstores, **Borders** can be found near the Florida Mall (1051 W. Sand Lake Rd.,

Orlando; ☎ 407/826-8912; Mon–Thurs 10am–10pm, Fri–Sat 10am–11pm, Sun 10am–9pm); it hosts a few readings and the odd author signing each month. There is a smaller Borders at the airport (☎ 407/816-5126). You'll find a **Barnes & Noble Booksellers** among the terrific restaurants of Sand Lake Road west of I-4 (7900 W. Sand Lake Rd., Orlando; ☎ 407/345-0900; daily 9am–11pm) and at the Florida Mall (8358 S. Orange Blossom Trail, Orlando; ☎ 407/856-7200; daily 9am–11pm).

A supermarket-size emporium for food and wine (as well as baskets and small furniture) imported from around the world, **World Market** (1744 Sand Lake Rd., Orlando; ☎ 407/240-2064; www.worldmarket.com), just west of the Florida Mall, has a presence in 35 states. Every time I'm in there (loading up on Arnott's Tim Tam from Australia and Manner wafers from Vienna), it seems I'm the only American. Everyone else has the lilting accent of the British north, and they're piling their carts with enough Cadbury bars and HP Sauce to get themselves through 2-week stays at their vacation homes. Or the second Blitz.

I'm not one for the whole **Hard Rock Cafe** (6050 Universal Blvd., Orlando; ☎ 407/351-7625; www.hardrock.com) thing. Its T-shirts were cool in the 1980s, but now wearing one is just a plea for fashion help. Still, people collect them (who are they, exactly?), and because Orlando is home to the company's headquarters, owning one would seem necessary for a collector. The store and restaurant, the largest in the Hard Rock chain, are at Universal's CityWalk. The classic T-shirt is $20 and is sold in a flattened pack, like LPs once were. You can only buy them here; even the Hard Rock Hotel sells a different version.

12 The Essentials of Planning

ORLANDO HOSTS SOME 50 MILLION PEOPLE A YEAR, AND THE PEOPLE WHO run the airports, hotels, and theme parks are specialists in moving confused tourists from one location to another—the whole system is set up to make it foolproof—so you probably won't get lost in a mire of confusion. You will, however, need to take care of some nitty-gritty planning details—from flights into the city to transportation from the airport. No matter who you are, this chapter will fill you in on special tricks and strategies to get you on your way—without blowing too much time or money on your plan.

WHERE TO FIND TOURIST INFORMATION

Orlando has one of the most responsive and question-friendly visitors' bureaus in America. Orlando's mighty tourism authority is funded by taxes on tourists, who come in such numbers that the organization can afford to spend. Hence, it operates a permanent storefront **Orlando Official Visitor Center** (8723 International Dr.; ☎ 407/363-5872; www.orlandoinfo.com; daily 8am–7pm), in a strip mall on the western side of I-Drive not far north of the Pointe Orlando shopping mall, that's stocked from carpet to rafter with free brochures from every hotel, theme restaurant, and amusement you could need. Although many, many other places in town (souvenir stands, mostly) claim to offer "official" tourist information, this is the only truly official place that does. Staff is on hand to answer any questions, and its ticket desk has the inside line on discounts, where they are available.

The same office operates domestic information bureaus in other countries, including the United Kingdom (☎ 0800/018-6760; www.orlandoinfo.co.uk), Canada (☎ 800/646-2079; www.orlandokissimmee.com/canada), Mexico (☎ 01-800/800-4636; www.orlandoinfo.com/mexico), and Germany (☎ 0800/100-7325; www.orlandoinfo.com/de).

Kissimmee, the town closest to Walt Disney World and the one where you'll find most of the nearby budget hotels and restaurants, maintains its own tourist office, the **Kissimmee Convention and Visitors Bureau** (1925 E. Irlo Bronson Memorial Hwy./U.S. 192; Kissimmee; ☎ 407/944-2400; www.floridakiss.com; Mon–Fri 8am–5pm). Its informational website also lists current discounts. The Kissimmee CVB works closely with the Orlando bureau, so you won't have to make two trips to get all the information on the region.

For local news, the *Orlando Sentinel* (www.orlandosentinel.com) is one of the best papers in Florida. It maintains a blog expressly covering developments in the tourism industry: **http://blogs.orlandosentinel.com/business_tourism_aviation**.

When it comes to the theme parks, you'll find that the official websites mostly furnish doctored photographs, meaningless homilies, deceptive maps, and a near-total lack of cogent information. Thank goodness, then, that these places inspire such fervent followings. Below, you'll find a box containing addresses for some of the best of hundreds of websites devoted to tracking every development at the

Orlando Online: The Best Websites

Official info:
> **Orlando Convention and Visitors Bureau** (www.orlandoinfo.com)
> **Kissimmee Convention and Visitors Bureau** (www.floridakiss.com)

Theme parks:
- **AllEarsNet** (www.allearsnet.com). Thorough compendium of everything Disney and Universal Orlando, down to the full menus at most restaurants. Indispensable, but very fan-oriented.
- **WDW Info** (www.wdwinfo.com) and **WDW Magic** (www.wdwmagic.com). Which rides are closing for rehab? How are the restaurants? These message boards are among the most active.
- **MouseSavers** (www.mousesavers.com). Mary Waring has become fan royalty thanks to her site, which catalogs the going Disney deals.
- **MousePlanet** (www.mouseplanet.com). More resort info, opinions.
- **Laughing Place** (www.laughingplace.com). Strong on backstage news, it publishes a pretty quarterly. The message boards cook.
- **MiceAge** (www.miceage.com). Clear-eyed trip reports and photos.
- **IOA Central** (www.ioacentral.com). A board-based Universal site.
- **Universal Ignited** (www.universalignited.com). More Universal dish.

Active message boards for getting questions answered about Disney include **INTERCOT** (www.intercot.com), **MiceChat** (www.micechat.com), **Sharing Disney Magic** (www.tagrel.com).

Fan sites devoted to single attractions:
- **The Haunted Mansion** (Magic Kingdom): www.doombuggies.com
- **Pirates of the Caribbean** (Magic Kingdom): www.tellnotales.com
- **Country Bear Jamboree** (Magic Kingdom): www.doneinthedark.com
- **Carousel of Progress** (Magic Kingdom): www.carouselofprogress.com
- **Universe of Energy** (Epcot): www.energy.planet7.com
- **JAWS** (Universal Studios): www.amityboattours.com
- **Shamu** (SeaWorld Orlando): www.shamu.com

Park history:
- **Widen Your World** (http://home.cfl.rr.com/omniluxe/wyw.htm) and Walt Dated World (http://waltdatedworld.bravepages.com). Lost WDW stuff.
- **Walt Disney World:** A History in Postcards (www.bigbrian-nc.com/pctoc.htm). Classic images.
- **Waltopia** (www.waltopia.com). Walt's dreams for Epcot.
- **Extinct Attractions Club** (www.extinct-attractions-club.com). It sells ride documentaries culled from interviews and vacation videos.
- **EPCOT Central** (http://epcot82.blogspot.com). A critique of Epcot.

parks, even if it's as minor as a 10¢ rise in pricing at the popcorn stands. Some of these are exhaustive to the point of uselessness—isn't it overplanning your vacation to jot down where popcorn costs 10¢ less?—but it's still good to know that truly exhaustive information is out there. Many of these sites, which usually include lists of projected ride closures for the coming weeks, have message boards where you can pose questions to other members eager to spread the know.

WHEN TO VISIT

One of the principal reasons Orlando is such an attractive destination is that it's in Florida. Summers are hot and winters aren't frigid, at least by most Northerners' standards, and although winter morning frosts occur, they're not the norm.

The city culture cranks year-round, although theater and concerts tend to be scheduled outside of the summer months. The main consideration when it comes to selecting a date for your visit is balancing good weather with thin crowds. When you choose to go to Orlando will determine to a large degree how many days it will take you to see everything you want. In the peak season (such as Spring Break or the week after Christmas), the Magic Kingdom's turnstiles are spinning like propellers, and lines are at their longest—on December 27, 2006, three Disney parks reached capacity and briefly sealed gates against further guests. You can end up riding only a half-dozen attractions in a 10-hour period. For many people, that's a maddening sensation. Come back in September, one of my favorite times, and you can do nearly everything in a day, enjoying your vacation more.

So when are the peak seasons? Put simply: When American kids are out of school. That means midspring, summer, and the holidays. Not only will it take longer to see what you want, but hotel prices will be higher then, too. If you want to save cash, early January, early May, late August, all of September, and the first half of December are prime. For a more defined calendar of the low season, turn to chapter 3, where you'll find the pricing schedule that Walt Disney World uses.

The flip side of low season is that the theme parks tend to trim services when it's quieter. More food service locations are shuttered, and more rides are closed for maintenance—and no, the admission price won't be discounted because of that. January is a particularly tough month for missing out on rides due to rehabs. The ones that are open, such as roller coasters, may have fewer cars running.

And especially in the winter months, you may find it too chilly to enjoy the rides that get you wet. Same goes for the water parks. They're open year-round (although each Disney water park closes in turn for 2 months in the winter) and Wet 'n Wild has heated water, but you have to get out of the pool *sometime*.

June to September is the heaviest season for rain. It seems like every afternoon, like clockwork, another heavy storm rolls in. Those storms usually roll out within an hour, just as reliably, but in the meantime, you'll see torrents and lightning fiercer than you ever have at home. During those tropical seasons, bring along a cheap poncho from home. You'll also sweat a lot more, but that's to be expected.

Central Florida suffers more lightning strikes than any other American locale. Much rain falls, but even more water is used—some 786 million gallons are consumed in the pursuit of daily life, and you have to assume a goodly portion of that is coursing through the flumes at Typhoon Lagoon. You will notice that tap water has a distinct mineral taste. Your hotel's pipes are not to blame. Rather, think of

Orlando as a giant island floating over a cushion of water. Most of the city's lakes started, in fact, as sinkholes that permitted the water table to flood upward. The drinking water is drawn from underground, hence the specific flavor and odor.

Orlando Average Temperature, Rainfall, & Disney's Lowest Hotel Prices

	Jan	Feb	Mar	Apr	May	June	July	Aug	Sept	Oct	Nov	Dec
Hi/Low Daily Temps (°F)	72/49	73/50	78/55	84/60	88/66	91/71	92/73	92/73	90/73	84/65	78/57	73/51
Hi/Low Daily Temps (°C)	22/10	23/10	26/13	29/16	31/19	33/22	33/23	33/23	32/23	29/19	26/14	23/11
Inches of Precipitation	2.25	2.82	3.32	2.43	3.30	7.13	7.27	6.88	6.53	3.16	1.98	2.25
Hotel Room Cost*	$82	$82–$119	$119	$99–$119	$99–$109	$109	$109	$82–$109	$82	$82–$99	$82–$99	$82–$129

The price for a Value-class Disney room with two double beds; the lowest off-property prices start at just over half this rate.

Orlando's Visit-Worthy Events

There's usually so much going on in Orlando (both the city itself and the theme parks), that I list only the highlights; check the special events pages at the theme-park websites to see if any themed weekends or smaller events are in the works. In addition, the events listings in *Orlando Weekly* magazine (www.orlando weekly.com) and the *Orlando Sentinel* newspaper (www.orlandosentinel.com) are excellent starting places; they're useful to check even while you're on vacation, as many of their announcements are for the short term. You will also find a few high-end listings at *Orlando* magazine (www.orlandomagazine.com) and word of underground arts happenings at Apartment E (www.apartmente.com).

January

Capital One Bowl (☎ 407/839-3900; www.fcsports.com or www.ticketmaster.com): It used to be called the Citrus Bowl—can *anyone* keep track of the square-dancing corporate naming rights anymore? Held New Year's Day at the Florida Citrus Bowl Stadium, it pits the second-ranked teams from the Big Ten and SEC conferences against one another.

Tickets are $65 if purchased before November 1 and $75 thereafter.

Zora Neale Hurston Festival of the Arts and Humanities/ ZORA! Festival (☎ 407/647-3307; www.zorafestival.com): The great folklorist and writer (1891–1960) was from Eatonville (a 30-min. drive north of Orlando), the country's oldest incorporated African-American town. This heady weeklong event includes lectures and a 2-day public art fair in Winter Park.

Disney's Pirate & Princess Party (☎ 407/934-7639; www.disneyworld.com): The Mouse found a good way to pump up sales in off months: Throw a special after-hours event that can double paid attendance in a day. Like the Halloween and holiday events that spun it off, this new (2007) effort is an evening at Magic Kingdom, separately ticketed ($37 adult and $30 kids if bought in advance), where candy is freely distributed, a special parade is launched, and kids come dressed in their gender-dictated dream gear—boys are taught how to be pirates by the dubious role model of Captain Jack Sparrow, and girls can turn to one of the princesses for, presumably, advice on catching a prince. That'll be hard at the Magic Kingdom, a place with no king but lots of competing princesses. It's held on various nights from late January to early March, as well as in August, and most of the major attractions are open.

SeaWorld's Bud & BBQ (www.seaworld orlando.com): Free with admission, this lineup of country music and classic rock acts is followed by a paid barbecue serving lots of beer made by the park's parent company. It's held Saturdays from late January through February.

February

Winter Park Bach Festival (☎ 407/646-2182; www.bachfestivalflorida.org): This annual event at Rollins College began in 1935 and has evolved into one of the country's better choral fests. Although it has stretched to include other composers and guest artists (Handel, P.D.Q. Bach), at least one concert is devoted to Johann. It takes place mid-February to early March, with scattered one-off guest performances throughout the year.

Silver Spurs Rodeo of Champions (1875 Silver Spur Lane, Kissimmee; ☎ 407/677-6336; www.silverspurs rodeo.com; $15): Lest you doubt Central Florida is far removed from the American Deep South, it hosts the largest rodeo east of the Mississippi (with bareback broncs, racing barrel horses, rodeo clowns, and athletes drawn from the cowboy circuit) over 3 days in mid-February in an indoor arena off U.S. 192.

Mardi Gras at Universal Studios (☎ 407/224-2691; www.universal orlando.com/mardigras): On Saturday nights leading up to Fat Tuesday, Universal books major national acts (Bonnie Raitt, Hall & Oates, Kid Rock) and mounts a parade complete with stilt-walkers, New Orleans jazz bands, Louisiana-made floats, and bead tossing—although here, what it takes to win a set of beads is considerably less risqué than it is in the Big Easy.

Spring Training: See p. 254 for a rundown of which Major League Baseball teams play where. It lasts mid-February through March.

March

Florida Film Festival (☎ 407/644-6579; www.floridafilmfestival.com; $9 per film): Produced by the Enzian Theater (p. 289), this respected event showcases films by Florida artists and has featured past appearances by the likes of Oliver Stone, William H. Macy, Christopher Walken, and Dennis Hopper. The Theater's Brouhaha Film & Video Showcase, in December, is a proving ground for entries.

April

Epcot's International Flower & Garden Festival (☎ 407/934-7639; www.disney world.com): This popular spring event, which lasts from early April to early June, transforms the park with some 30 million flowers, several dozen topiaries, a walkthrough butterfly garden, presentations by noted horticulturalists, and a steady lineup of concerts. It's accessible with a standard entry ticket.

Grad Nites (http://disneyyouthgroups. disney.go.com): Held weekends in late April and early May, these special Disney events for high school seniors are a beloved ritual for nearly every kid raised in the southeast United States. The Magic Kingdom closes around 7pm to regular folk and turns into an all-night romp for America's Future before closing at 4am. Acts like Fall Out Boy and Britney Spears perform on scattered stages, and when they're not making out in the bathrooms, kids hit every ride. Universal does its own cheaper, less crowded version, Grad Bash (www.universalorlando.com/gradbash), held in late April, with equally cool bands.

May

Orlando International Fringe Festival (☎ 407/648-0077; www.orlandofringe. org): This theatrical smorgasbord was created in the image of the anyone's-welcome fest held in Edinburgh, Scotland. It spends 10 days mounting some 500 newly written, experimental, and soon-to-be-huge performances by artists from Florida and around the world.

Florida Music Festival (www.florida musicfestival.com): Less expansive than the Fringe Festival, it takes 3 days and limits itself to up-and-coming musicians, although it crams about 250 bands into that brief window. Prices are $10 for a day of shows, or $25 for all 3 days.

Star Wars Weekends (www.disneyworld. com): Disney–MGM Studios' major annual do, held over five weekends from mid-May into June, sees actors from the franchise arrive for signings, parades, Q&As, and brief workshops. Warwick Davis, who once squeezed into an Ewok costume, has made a career out of these events. It's not just for kids—the finer points of the Lucas catechism are discussed. A regular ticket will get you in.

June

Gay Day (www.gayday.com): What started as a single day for gay and lesbian visitors has mushroomed into a full week of some 60 events managed by a host of promoters. It's said that attendance goes as high as 100,000—it's become one of the biggest annual events in Florida. Held on around the first Saturday in June, Gay Day is a blowout party for outgoing gay and lesbians, with group park-going scheduled for each of Disney's parks and Islands of Adventure, plus an ongoing pool bash at the Buena Vista Palace hotel and frequent events at Pleasure Island. One of its biggest events is Magic Journeys, an all-night, after-hours dance party held at Arabian Nights. All a Gay Day participant needs to join most of the in-park parties (except the Beach Ball events at the Disney water slides) is a regular entry ticket to the parks. Most participants come because they love the atmosphere, and they keep the ribald behavior behind closed doors—but they do wear red shirts as a statement of visibility.

July

Independence Day: All the theme parks go patriotism-mad—Disney in particular, followed by SeaWorld—with extra fireworks, concerts, and longer opening hours.

September

Night of Joy (☎ 877/648-3569; www.nightofjoy.com): It's actually a long-running pair of nights of outdoor Contemporary Christian concerts—eight or nine acts—spread throughout the Magic Kingdom, which stays open late just for the occasion. Rides run all night, and the event usually sells out. The party continues around the same time for Rock the Universe (www.rocktheuniverse.com), a weekend festival of top-flight Christian rock bands who perform on stages around one of the Universal parks. Rides and performances continue past midnight, after regular patrons have gone home. Tickets to both events must be purchased separately from tickets good for regular operating hours.

October

Epcot's International Food & Wine Festival (☎ 407/939-3378; www.disney world.com/foodandwine): The World Showcase makes amends with the countries it normally ignores by installing nearly 30 temporary booths serving tapas-size servings of foods ($2–$4) from many nations. New Zealand brings mussels, South Africa makes *bobotie* pie, and Australia brings enough wine to choke a kangaroo. It also brings kangaroo. There are chef demonstrations, beer appreciation seminars, regular concerts by known acts (Kool and the Gang, Three Dog Night), and tastings by at least 100 wineries. Now and then, countries set up temporary pavilions (people are still chattering about Spain's effort a few years back). At the start of the festival, many of the events were free to attend, but now Disney charges for most of them, which takes some of the fun away. Still, it constitutes the best time to visit

Epcot (the festival lasts through mid-November). Details are usually posted on the Disney website in the summer.

Mickey's Not-So-Scary Halloween Party (☎ 407/934-7639; www.disney world.com): Another one of the Magic Kingdom's separately ticketed evening events, this one costs $46 adults, $36 kids, and for that, you get a special Halloween-themed parade (I like the gravediggers who pound their shovels on the ground in time to the music), a few special shows, a few locations for dance parties with costumed characters, a fireworks display with notably more orange than usual, and—the part I like most, and what makes it a safe alternative to the suburban Trick or Treat tradition—stations where you can pick up handfuls of free candy. Lots of kids even show up in costume, although it's not required. Some nights offer advance-purchase discounts of about $6. The event happens on scattered evenings from mid-September through the end of October. Halloween sells out early. Target audience: People who like lollipops.

Halloween Horror Nights (www. halloweenhorrornights.com): Unquestionably Universal's biggest annual event, HHN is the equivalent of a whole new theme park that's designed and built for a month's run. After dark on selected nights, one of its theme parks is overtaken by grotesque "scareacters" who terrorize crowds with chain saws, gross-out shows, and seven big, walk-through haunted houses that are made from scratch each year. The mayhem lasts into the wee hours. Wimps need not apply; children are discouraged by the absence of kids' ticket prices. When I brought my mother to one, she left early, saying she missed Mickey. An annual bawdy revue based on the Bill and Ted movie characters skewers the year in pop culture and draws huge, enthusiastic crowds of tipsy young people. On top of all this, most of the rides remain open, so it's like getting two theme parks for the price of one. Don't go on a Friday or Saturday, because so many locals attend then that you will spend most of the night in line. HHN has legions of fans who follow its developments and even pay extra for behind-the-scenes tours. Target audience: People who like to poop themselves in fright.

SeaWorld's Halloween Spooktacular (www.seaworldorlando.com): SeaWorld has been known to throw a modest, toddler-approved Halloween event of its own, with trick-or-treating and a few encounters with sea fairies. When it happens, it's included in the daily admission and occurs during regular hours.

Orlando Film Festival (☎ 407/843-0801; www.orlandofilmfest.com): Like all festivals worth their salt, this one presents mostly mainstream and independent films in advance of their wider release dates. It's a new program and lasts only a few days in mid-October, screening at various downtown venues. Tickets (around $23–$31) are always cheaper online and in advance.

FUNAI Classic at Walt Disney World Resort (☎ 407/835-2525; www.disney world.com): Playing golf and watching golf are two totally different experiences, and I'd rather be doing neither. But for avid spectators, many top PGA touring names, including Tiger Woods (who has a home in Orlando), come out to play on the Disney courses for 4 days in mid-October, just as they have done since the grass was planted in 1971; Jack Nicklaus swept the first three. Tickets start at $15.

November

Orlando Beer Festival at Universal CityWalk (☎ 407/224-2691; www. orlandobeerfestival.com): On one midmonth weekend, the entertainment complex is overtaken by brewers and distributors from across America, who share their wares as bands play. Quite a few patrons are more interested in getting blitzed than in learning about the craft of brewing, but the educational opportunities are there for those who seek them.

Ice! (☎ 407/586-4423; www.gaylord palms.com/ice): It debuted in 2003 at the Gaylord Palms hotel and has quickly become a holiday perennial. The hotel brings in nearly 2 million pounds of ice, sculpts it into a walk-through city, keeps it chilled to 9°F, and issues winter coats to visitors. Add Christmas and synchronized light shows and you've got an event that charges $10 to $25 for entry—and sells out.

ABC Super Soap Weekend (www.disney world.com): Disney–MGM Studios gathers some of the biggest names and comeliest faces from the soap operas aired on the network Disney owns: *All My Children, One Life to Live,* and *General Hospital.* Q-and-As, motorcade appearances, act-with-a-hunk lessons, and autograph sessions are all on the table. Most of the big names from ABC Daytime show up, including Susan Lucci, Cameron Mathison, Kelly Monaco, Justin Bruening, Anthony Geary, Genie Francis, and even Rosie O'Donnell. Crowds are heavy, and the park opens at 8am to cram them all in.

The Osborne Family Spectacle of Dancing Lights (www.disneyworld.com): No, not Ozzy and Sharon, but Jennings, Paul, Mitzi, and Breezy (I swear I'm not making this up), whose preposterously overdone Christmas display at their Little Rock house was deemed so vulgar that neighbors went to the Arkansas Supreme Court to shut it down. Enter Disney, which installs their millions of lights each year on Disney–MGM Studio's Streets of America. Every 15 minutes, it twitters and "dances" to Christmas carols, all as foam "snow" gently wafts from above. The city is barely mopping up from Halloween when it's mounted, a week before Thanksgiving. It lasts through the first week of January.

December

Mickey's Very Merry Christmas Party (☎ 407/934-7639; www.disneyworld. com): This crowded Christmas event, which occurs on various nights starting even before Thanksgiving—the Orlando calendar skips right from Halloween to the holidays, no gratitude included—is probably Disney's most popular special annual event. It requires a separate ticket (as much as $49 adults, $41 kids) from regular admission. What you get is a tree-lighting ceremony, a few special holiday-themed shows, a special fireworks display (more green and red), an appearance by Santa Claus, and a special parade. Throughout the park, you'll find stations serving free hot cocoa, marshmallows, cookies, and apple juice. Not everything is open; outdoor rides involving boat trips, for one, are usually shut down, and the same Christmas decorations will be up during normal-priced operating hours, too, so don't feel too compelled.

Holidays Around the World at Epcot (www.disneyworld.com): This one features a daily tree lighting led by Mickey Mouse and a host of costumed storytellers, but its real showpiece is the thrice-daily, 40-minute Candlelight Processional, a retelling of the Christmas Nativity story by a celebrity narrator (recent names have included Brian Dennehy, Eartha Kitt, Steven Curtis Chapman, Rita Moreno, Mario Lopez, Phil Donahue, and Neil Patrick Harris) accompanied by a 50-piece orchestra and a full Mass choir. Epcot sells dinner packages combining a sit-down meal in World Showcase with priority seating at the Processional from $28 adults, $12 kids (not a bad deal, but it sells briskly starting in August; ☎ 407/939-3463). The Processional is a WDW tradition going back to its earliest days. Do you see by now how nuts Disney goes for Christmas?

SeaWorld's Holiday Celebration (www. seaworldorlando.com): Befitting SeaWord's laid-back attitude, its holiday attractions are not nearly as bombastic as Disney's. Expect carolers at the Waterfront; a nightly holiday-themed fountain show; a Christmas-themed overlay on its usual Makahiki Luau dinnertainment banquet; and late in the month, the modest Baywave Seaside Jazzfest, with a handful of different acts performing between Christmas and New Year's. Everything's included in the regular admission price. During the holiday week, the park also presents its nightly *Mistify* pyrotechnic show, which is usually shut down for the winter.

Champs Sports Bowl (☎ 407/839-3900; www.fcsports.com or www.ticketmaster.com): An ACC team battles a Big Ten team, usually a few days before New Year's and always at the Florida Citrus Bowl Stadium. Tickets are $50 if purchased before November 1, and $60 thereafter.

New Year's Eve: Yahoo.com reports that Orlando regularly makes its list of top five most-searched New Year's Eve destinations. There's no shortage of places to party. At the parks: **Pleasure Island** charges about $90 for the night, including outdoor bands and fireworks. **CityWalk** ($109) lures top acts (in 2007, it got Cyndi Lauper) for its bash, which serves gourmet appetizers. Three of **Disney's parks,** minus Animal Kingdom, stay open until the wee hours. **SeaWorld** brings in big-band music or jazz, plus fireworks.

ENTRY REQUIREMENTS FOR NON-AMERICAN CITIZENS

Be sure to check with your local U.S. embassy or consulate for the very latest in entry requirements, as these continue to shift. Full information can be found at the **U.S. State Department's** website, www.travel.state.gov.

VISAS

Citizens of western and central Europe, Australia, New Zealand, and Singapore need only a valid machine-readable passport and a round-trip air ticket or cruise ticket to enter the United States for stays of up to 90 days. Canadian citizens can also enter without a visa as long as they show proof of residence.

Citizens of all other countries will need to obtain a tourist visa from the U.S. consulate. Depending on your country of origin, there may or may not be a charge attached (and you may or may not have to apply in person). You'll need to complete an application and submit a 1½-inch square photo, and your passport will need to be valid for at least 6 months past the scheduled end of your U.S. visit. If an interview isn't mandated (South Africans, for example, have to schlep to appear before a bureaucrat), it's usually possible to obtain a visa within 24 hours, except during holiday periods or the summer rush.

PASSPORTS

To enter the United States, international visitors must have a valid passport that expires at least 6 months later than the scheduled end of their visit.

For Residents of Australia: You can pick up an application from your local post office or any branch of Passports Australia, but you must schedule an interview at the passport office to present your application materials. Call the **Australian Passport Information Service** at ☎ 131-232, or visit the government website at www.passports.gov.au.

For Residents of Canada: Passport applications are available at travel agencies throughout Canada or from the central **Passport Office,** Department of Foreign Affairs and International Trade, Ottawa, ON K1A 0G3 (☎ 800/567-6868; www. ppt.gc.ca). *Note:* Canadian children who travel must have their own passports. However, if you hold a valid Canadian passport, issued before December 11, 2001, that bears the name of your child, the passport remains valid for you and your child until it expires.

For Residents of Ireland: You can apply for a 10-year passport at the **Passport Office,** Setanta Centre, Molesworth Street, Dublin 2 (☎ 01/671-1633; www.irlgov. ie/iveagh). Those under age 18 and over 65 must apply for a 123€ 1-year passport. You can also apply at 1A South Mall, Cork (☎ 021/272-525) or at most main post offices.

For Residents of New Zealand: You can pick up a passport application at any New Zealand Passports Office or download it from their website. Contact the **Passports Office** at ☎ 0800/225-050 in New Zealand or 04/474-8100, or log on to www.passports.govt.nz.

For Residents of the United Kingdom: To pick up an application for a standard 10-year passport (5-year passport for children under 16), visit your nearest passport office, major post office, or travel agency; or contact the **United Kingdom Passport Service** at ☎ 0870/521-0410. You can also search its website at www. ukpa.gov.uk.

MEDICAL REQUIREMENTS

No inoculations or vaccinations are required to enter the United States unless you're arriving from an area that is suffering from an epidemic (cholera or yellow fever, in particular). A valid, signed prescription is required for those travelers in need of **syringe-administered medications** or medical treatment that involves **narcotics.** It is extremely important to obtain the correct documentation in these cases, as your medications could be confiscated; and if you are found to be carrying an illegal substance, security officials tend to lock you up first and ask questions later. You could be subject to significant penalties. Those who are **HIV-positive** may also need a special waiver in order to enter the country (as you will be asked on your visa application whether you're a carrier of any communicable diseases). The best thing to do is contact **AIDSinfo** (☎ 800/448-0440 or 301/519-6616; www.aidsinfo.nih.gov) for up-to-date information.

CUSTOMS REGULATIONS FOR INTERNATIONAL VISITORS

Strict regulations govern what can and can't be brought into the United States—and what you can take back home with you. The rules mostly concern restricted substances such as booze or tobacco, so I wouldn't get too worried, unless fresh citrus was part of your plan. Fortunately, there are no specific bans on mouse-ear caps.

WHAT YOU CAN BRING INTO ORLANDO

Every visitor over 21 years of age may bring in, free of duty, the following: (1) 1 liter of wine or hard liquor; (2) 200 cigarettes, 100 cigars (but not from Cuba), or 3 pounds of smoking tobacco; and (3) $100 worth of gifts. These exemptions are offered to travelers who spend at least 72 hours in the United States and who have not claimed them within the preceding 6 months. It is forbidden to bring foodstuffs (particularly fruit, cooked meats, and canned goods) and plants (vegetables, seeds, tropical plants, and the like). Foreign tourists may carry in or out up to $10,000 in U.S. or foreign currency with no formalities; larger sums must be declared to U.S. Customs on entering or leaving, which includes filing form CM 4790. For details regarding U.S. Customs and Border Protection, consult your nearest U.S. embassy or consulate, or **U.S. Customs** (☎ **202/927-1770;** www.customs.ustreas.gov).

WHAT YOU CAN TAKE HOME FROM ORLANDO

For a clear summary of **Canadian** rules, write for the booklet *I Declare,* issued as publication number RC4044 by the **Canada Border Services Agency** (☎ 800/461-9999 in Canada, or 204/983-3500; www.cbsa-asfc.gc.ca).

For information, **U.K. citizens** should contact **HM Customs & Excise** at ☎ 0845/010-9000 (from outside the U.K., ☎ 020/8929-0152), or the website at www.hmce.gov.uk.

A helpful brochure for **Australians,** available from Australian consulates or Customs offices, is *Know Before You Go.* For more information, call the **Australian Customs Service** at ☎ 1300/363-263, or log on to www.customs.gov.au.

Most questions regarding **New Zealand** rules are answered in a free pamphlet available at New Zealand consulates and Customs offices: *New Zealand Customs Guide for Travellers, Notice no. 4.* For more information, contact **New Zealand Customs,** The Customhouse, 17–21 Whitmore St., Box 2218, Wellington (☎ 04/473-6099 or 0800/428-786; www.customs.govt.nz).

GETTING TO ORLANDO

Orlando is served by lots of airlines, so thankfully, airfares are among the lowest on the East Coast. Nearly 35 million people fly in or out of Orlando International Airport (MCO) each year, or nearly 100,000 a day, so as you can imagine, competition is fierce and, especially for purchases made more than 45 days ahead, prices can be under $100 each way. Strategies for finding a good airfare include.

◆ **Look at the low-fare carriers:** Airlines such as **JetBlue, Southwest, USA3000, AirTran, America West Airlines, CanJet, WestJet, Spirit Airlines, Sun Country, Ted, and ATA** flit in and out of MCO like bees at a hive, and they will sometimes have better fares than the larger airlines, but they may not be searched if you go to a site such as Expedia. So use a search tool such as **Sidestep.com, Kayak.com,** or **Mobissimo.com,** which search airline sites directly, adding no service charges and often finding fares that the larger travel sites miss. The only airline these sites don't search is **Southwest** (www.iflyswa.com), which doesn't allow its fares to be appear through any outside entity, yet operates some 15% of flights to and from Orlando. If you have kids, booking an airline with seatback TV sets makes the journey go faster. If you're flying from Europe into the United States, take a look at the fares from British Airways, American, Continental, Delta, United, Virgin Atlantic, Lufthansa, Icelandair, Martinair, and Iberia, as these carriers tend to have the lowest rates for international travel. **Mobissimo.com** and **CheapFlights.uk.com** are good for fares that don't originate in the U.S.

♦ **Fly when others don't, and take an itinerary the biz travelers don't want.** Those who fly midweek and midday, and who stay over a Saturday night, generally pay far less on the standard carriers than those who fly at more popular times. If you jigger your days and you're still finding that prices are high, then perhaps a cruise ship is coming or going from Port Canaveral on the day you want, increasing air traffic.

♦ **Book at the right time.** Sounds odd, but you can often save money by booking your seat at 3am. That's because unpaid-for reservations are flushed out of the system at midnight, and as airfares are based on supply and demand, prices often sink when the system becomes aware of an increase in supply. Also consider booking on a Wednesday, traditionally the day when most airfare sales come out. Be sure to monitor such sites as Frommers.com and SmarterTravel.com, which highlight fare sales.

Plenty of companies provide packages that lump airfare with discounted hotel rooms. See p. 29 for a discussion of those, because the deals can be ripe.

Amtrak's (☎ 800/872-7245; www.amtrak.com) Silver Service/Palmetto route serves Orlando. Trains go direct to New York City, Washington, D.C., Charleston, Savannah, and Miami, which isn't a bad lineup if you're on a whistle-stop tour of great American cities. One-way trips from New York, as an example, take a little less than 24 hours (in theory—Amtrak, the national train line, is in a deplorable state of benign neglect) and start around $111 for a coach seat. The carrier's Auto Train service will tote your car along starting at an add-on of $140; it departs from Lorton, VA, in the Washington, D.C. area, and finishes in Sanford, which is north of Orlando but close enough to do the job. Lastly, the Sunset Limited train used to run from Orlando to Los Angeles via New Orleans, Houston, San Antonio, Tucson, and North Palm Springs, but Hurricane Katrina in 2005 suspended the section east of New Orleans. Check to see if it's up and running.

ARRIVING OR DEPARTING BY AIR IN ORLANDO

Orlando's main airport, **Orlando International Airport** (www.orlandoairports. net), is a pleasure. The airport, 25 miles east of Walt Disney World, was originally built during World War II as McCoy Air Force Base, which closed in the early 1970s but bequeathed the airport with its deceptive code, MCO. I don't know how they do it, but the late-departure rate of 19% is among the lowest in the country, even though the airport is America's 14th largest (and the 24th largest in the world). The airport serves 96 cities around the world. Flight delays occur most often after 11pm, and the fewest delays occur before lunch. The busiest days are when the cruise ships at nearby Port Canaveral are loading or unloading, but it's tough to predict when that will happen because there are so many 4-day cruise runs. Saturdays can be hairy for incoming traffic, and in general, midmornings and midafternoons can be crowded for outgoing passengers.

Killing time at MCO isn't painful, as there are lots of seating areas in a relatively pleasant environment (starting with carpeting of the same merry teal hue that you'll find in virtually every public space in Florida) and the shopping is particularly good. On the way into town, I frequently kill the few minutes during which my luggage is catching up with me by stopping by the food court, where there's an outpost of the delicious Southern fast-food chain Chick-fil-A. I also drop by Lush, a bath products boutique that sells fizzy, perfumed "bath bombs" (around $6) that, once tossed into a hotel bathtub, help dissolve the stresses of a long day of tromping through the theme parks. If, on the way home, you realize you neglected to buy any park-related souvenirs, fear not, because these companies don't miss a trick. Disney, SeaWorld, and Universal all maintain lavish stores (located *before* the security checkpoint, so budget enough time).

Interestingly, Orlando is one of a handful of American airports to offer a special, express lane for paying members who have been pre-vetted by the Transportation Security Administration. At $100 a year, **Clear** (☎ 866/848-2415; www.flyclear.com) isn't for average tourists, but it's a harbinger of how in the future, if founder Steven Brill gets his way, the length of time you spend at airports will have a lot to do with how much money you make. Awful, right?

When you first arrive at MCO, you'll have to hop a free elevated tram to the main terminal building to claim your bags and rent your car. Kids go goggle-eyed at this twist, thinking they're on their first ride. The main terminal is divided into two sides, A and B, so if you can't find the desk for your airline or transportation service open on one side, it may be on the other side. Transportation desks are on the lower level, beneath baggage claim. Then you just head across the road to the parking garage structure, where their lots are located. The system works well.

Other airports in the region are used much less frequently. **Orlando Sanford International Airport** (www.orlandosanfordairport.com), or SFB, 18 miles northeast of downtown, is served mostly by international charters, plus Icelandair, Allegiant Air, and Flyglobespan. It's connected to the Disney area by the Central Florida GreeneWay, or State Road 417—the trip takes about 40 minutes and there are tolls, so foreign visitors should have American dollars before leaving the airport. If you have a choice, go with MCO instead, which is closer. There is an executive airport just east of downtown, but no commercial flights use it. Some people, particularly European visitors on long-haul trips, might fly into **Tampa International Airport** (www.tampaairport.com), or TPA, 90 minutes southwest.

TRANSPORTATION TO & FROM MCO
Rental Cars

Having a car ensures you can experience the "real" Florida and it will noticeably improve your ability to see and do more things, so I strongly recommend having one. Be alert as you drive out of the airport, though—very soon, you will have to decide whether to use the South Exit (marked for Walt Disney World) or the North Exit (for SeaWorld, Universal, the Convention Center, and downtown Orlando). If you accidentally take the wrong one, don't worry, as they both eventually hook up with Interstate 4 where you can correct your mistake. The city planners have the system rigged, though. Whichever route you take, you will pay about $2.75 in accumulated tolls, so have loose change ready. The North Exit is the cheaper one.

The legal age minimum in Florida for a rental driver is 21. Agencies may slap those aged 21 to 25 with a hefty surcharge of $25 a day. The following rental car agencies are located at the airport, meaning you shouldn't have to board a bus to claim your car: Alamo, Avis, Budget, Dollar, National, and L&M. Two brands requiring use of a shuttle: Payless and Thrifty. In my experience, Alamo and Dollar are among the least expensive (economy cars start around $20–$25 a day), and Avis and National are the highest priced. But test the waters at a site such as Orbitz.com, Travelocity.com, or Kayak.com, which compare multiple renters with one click. At times when those sites quoted prices around $23 a day, I have been able to snag deals from Priceline.com for as little as $15 a day.

Shuttles, Coaches & Taxis

Mears Transportation (☎ 407/423-5566; www.mearstransportation.com) is the 800-pound gorilla of Orlando shuttles and taxis; it sends air-conditioned vans bouncing to area hotels every 15 to 20 minutes. Round-trip fares for adults are $25 ($18 for kids 4–11; kids under 4 free) to the International Drive area or $29/$21 to Walt Disney World/U.S. 192/Lake Buena Vista. You'll probably have to make several stops because the vans are shared by other passengers.

If you have more than four or five people, it's usually more economical to reserve a car service (do it at least 24 hours ahead) and split the lump fee. **Tiffany Towncar** (☎ 888/838-2161 or 407/370-2196; www.tiffanytowncar.com) charges $95 round-trip to the Disney-area hotels and $55 to $65 round-trip for SeaWorld/Universal/I-Drive, all for up to four people. It also runs vans seating up to seven people for $65 one-way/$110 round-trip for Disney and $65 to $70 round-trip for SeaWorld/Universal/I-Drive. A similar service and price comes from **Quicksilver Tours** (☎ 888/468-6939 or 407/299-1434; www.quicksilver-tours.com), which will also throw in a free 30-minute stop at a grocery store so you can stock up on supplies. So will **Happy Limo** (☎ 888/394-4277; www.happy limo.com). All the Towncar services accept the four big credit cards.

As of this writing, if you've got a reservation at a Disney-owned hotel, you have the right to take the company's airport motorcoaches (aka **Disney's Magical Express**) to the resort for free. When it sells the perk, the Mouse makes it seem simpler than it is by sending you tags for your luggage, which you affix before leaving home, and telling you everything will be taken care of from there. And yes, Disney employees will pick up your luggage at baggage claim while you check in for the Magical Express ride. But by the time you board the bus to the resort, you'll already have waited in two long lines—the first of many, many lines you'll endure during your visit, so get used to it—and then you'll stop at up to five other hotels before reaching your own. Your bags, which must weigh less than 50 pounds, may not meet up with you for 6 to 8 hours, so hitting a park right away may be difficult without coordinating your carry-ons. When you depart for home, you'll have to be ready for the coach 3 to 4 hours before your flight; the extra time, again, accounts for all the undisclosed stops you'll be making. It's free, which is terrific. But the Magical Express route costs you in time. It also signifies you probably haven't rented a car, which means you'll probably never leave Disney property again and you'll have to rely on the park's slow buses for your entire vacation. Don't let the promise of a free ride lure you onto the sticky trap of Orlando without a car.

Taxis are not the best bargain. The going rate is $2 for the first ⅔ of a mile or the first 80 seconds of waiting time, followed by 25¢ for each ⅛ of a mile and 25¢ for each additional 40 seconds of waiting. Airport trips incur a 50¢ surcharge. Taxis carry five passengers. It'll be about $45 to the Disney hotels, not including a tip, which is still cheaper than a Towncar.

TRAVEL INSURANCE—DO YOU NEED IT?

Yes, you do, principally because you're spending so much money. If you need to cancel your trip, travel insurance can buffer you from a financial loss. Does that mean you must buy some? Not necessarily—you may already have it.

Your existing medical coverage, for example, may include a safety net that will cover you even though you're traveling; ask so you're sure. (If you're an international visitor, you should probably invest in insurance that will cover medical expenses, as doctor visits and hospital treatment in the U.S. can be very expensive.) The credit card you use to make reservations may cover you for cancellation, lost luggage, or trip interruption; again, the only way to be sure is to ask your issuer. Most hotels will issue refunds with enough notice, but a few of the cheap ones won't; ask what the deadline for cancellation is when booking.

So what else might you want to insure? If your medical coverage and credit cards don't help, you may want special coverage for **villa rentals,** especially if you've plunked down a deposit, and any **valuables,** as airlines are only required to pay up to $2,500 for lost luggage domestically, and not every hotel provides in-room safes (and even the ones that do have safes too small to hold much).

If you do decide on insurance, you can easily compare available policies by visiting **InsureMyTrip.com**. Or contact one of the following reputable companies:

- ✦ **Access America** (☎ 866/807-3982; www.accessamerica.com)
- ✦ **CSA Travel Protection** (☎ 800/873-9844; www.csatravelprotection.com)
- ✦ **MEDEX** (☎ 800/732-5309; www.medexassist.com)
- ✦ **Travel Guard International** (☎ 800/807-3982;www.travelguard.com)
- ✦ **Travelex** (☎ 800/228 9792; www.travelex-insurance.com)

TRAVELING FROM ORLANDO TO OTHER PARTS OF AMERICA

Many international visitors combine visits to Orlando with other stops in famous American locations such as the Grand Canyon, New York City, and San Francisco. Orlando, while not an important air hub, is well connected to the cities that are, particularly New York and Chicago. For advice on how to find cheap airfare to any domestic American city, see "Getting to Orlando" on p. 312.

The **USA Rail Pass** is the American equivalent of the Eurail Pass in Europe—although our national rail system, **Amtrak** (☎ 800/872-7245 or 215/856-7953; www.amtrak.com), hardly compares to the European system. The pass allows foreign visitors to travel extensively within the U.S. for one set (and fairly reasonable) rate. It's *only* for those living outside North America (Canadians and Mexicans are not eligible). On the Amtrak website, you'll find listings of representative agents in countries around the globe. The passes, which are not valid on the Auto Train, cannot be purchased on trains and are good for 5, 15, or 30 days of travel, and work either within a region (Northeast, East, or West) or, if you shell out more, throughout the entire United States. The cheapest pass is a 5-day pass for off-peak rides along the Northeast Corridor ($155); the most expensive offers 30 days of peak-time travel throughout the U.S. ($565). Orlando is covered by both the East (from $215 for 15 days) and the National passes.

From late January through April, many major car renters redistribute their inventory by offering "drive-out" deals for one-way rentals that originate in Orlando and drop off elsewhere in the country. Since per-day rates can be as low as $1, it pays to ask if there's a special available that fits your plans.

For bus travel, an International Discovery Pass for foreign visitors is offered by **Greyhound** (☎ 800/231-2222; www.discoverypass.com). The company's prices, both for individual trips and for the passes, are equivalent to what you'll find at Amtrak (from $329 for 7 days). Bus travel in the United States is usually a purgatorial experience, and I recommend you look at train and air options first.

MONEY MATTERS

This town lives to make money, and consequently it places few obstacles between you and the loss of it.

Most **ATMs** that you'll find are run by third parties, not your bank, which means that you'll be slapped with fees of around $2 per withdrawal. But the good news is that $2 is still cheaper than the fees you'd be charged to draw traveler's checks, and machines accept pretty much anything you can stick into them; Walt Disney World's, for example, take Visa, Plus, MasterCard, Cirrus, American Express, Discover, Star, Quest, and AFFN. If you're staying near the parks, you won't stumble across a branch of your local bank unless you do advance research, and even then you'll probably discover that your bank is too far away, in the "real" Orlando, to bother. Citibank customers, though, can avoid the usage fee by using the fancy Citibank machines located at most 7-Eleven convenience stores in the Orlando area. International visitors should make advance arrangements with their banks to ensure their cards will function in the United States.

Credit cards are nearly universally accepted. You could strut off the plane with just a Visa, MasterCard, or American Express card and live in style for your entire trip. In fact, you *must* have one to rent a car. Your only problem would be how to pay the highway tolls. The majority of places accept the Big Four: American Express, MasterCard, Visa, and Discover. A few places add Diners Club to the mix, and some smaller family-owned businesses subtract American Express because of the pain of dealing with the company.

Before you leave home, let your credit-card issuer know that you're about to go on vacation. Many of them, guarding against potential fraud, get antsy when they see unexpectedly large charges start appearing so far from your home, and sometimes they freeze your account in response. With warning, they won't.

Not only will Orlando clerks almost always neglect to check the purchaser's identification, but also, in the high-volume world of the theme-park restaurants, credit-card charges under $25 often don't even require signatures. You just swipe and go. That means you need to be doubly sure to keep your cards safe.

Try not to use credit cards to withdraw cash. You'll be charged interest from the moment your money leaves the slot. If your credit card allows for online bill paying through links with your bank account, set up that capability before you leave—at the very least, you can pay off your withdrawals within hours, cutting your losses. Using an ATM card linked to a liquid bank account, like a debit card, is far less expensive. *Tip:* At Walt Disney World, there is an exception that the resort doesn't sanction, but I certainly do: Instead of using your credit card to draw cash from an ATM, use it to buy Disney Dollars instead. They are charged as a purchase, not as a cash withdrawal, so there are no additional fees, and you can spend Disney Dollars like actual cash within the resort. Presto!

Traveler's checks are also widely accepted, but they are slipping from favor outside of the theme parks and you should not rely on them as your primary source of funds. Because redeeming them can involve time-consuming paper-work, you may hear exasperated sighs from people in line behind you. They can deal.

Several creditors have come up with **travelers check cards,** also called **prepaid cards,** which are essentially debit cards encoded with the amount of money you elect to put on them. They're not linked to your personal bank accounts, they work in ATMs, and should you lose one, you can get your cash back in a matter of hours. If you spend all the money on them, you can call a number and reload the card using your bank account information. The **American Express** (☎ 888/412-6945; www.americanexpress.com) check card costs $14.95 to open and requires a minimum of $300. But it's hamstrung by the same limitations of using a proper American Express card—not everyone will accept it, and if you're an international customer, you pay the same high transaction fees that you'd pay if it were a credit card. More establishments take the **Visa TravelMoney** (www.visa.com) version, sold through AAA offices (☎ 866/339-3378); it costs $10 and keeps a little over 1% of everything you load onto it, plus all the regular international transaction fees. It's not ideal, but it's a relatively safe way to travel with money.

Like traveler's checks, **exchanging cash** is on the outs, and good riddance, as exchange rates are usurious. Because ATM withdrawals give better deals, old-fashioned exchange desks are few and far between, although you'll still find a few at the airport and at large hotels. If you need to change money, take advantage of the better rates offered by banks during regular banking hours (9:30am–4pm).

Finding a bank isn't difficult in the "real" world of Orlando around SeaWorld and Universal, but at Walt Disney World, you could use a hand. The nearest bank is the **SunTrust** (1675 Buena Vista Dr., across from Downtown Disney Marketplace; ☎ 407/828-6106; Mon–Fri 9am–4pm, until 6pm on Thurs).

HEALTH & SAFETY

Disney may advertise itself as "the Happiest Place on Earth," but it's still on Earth. That means bad things can happen.

Pickpockets are virtually unheard of, but that doesn't mean they don't exist—you just don't hear about them. Be vigilant about bags, too, such as waist packs and backpacks; you're going to be bumped and jostled many times while you wait in line—one of those bumps could be a nimble-fingered thief taking your cash, and you're unlikely to feel it. If you're truly concerned about theft, consider assembling a "fake" wallet containing a few expired credit cards and a few bucks that you can part with in lieu of your real goods. Keep it in an obvious place such as

What Things Cost in and out of the Parks

Orlando's cost of living is creeping upward, as it is in so many American cities. Things are even more expensive at the theme parks, because the corporations that run them know they've got a captive audience that would rather shell out more cash than exert the effort of driving a few miles for lower prices.

Bus ride	$1.50
Theme park admission	$67 for a 1-day ticket
Theme park parking	$10
Counter-service meal at a theme park, without drink	$8
Regular Coke at a theme park	$2.30
Bottle of water at a theme park	$2.50
Big Mac	$2.69
Evening movie ticket	$8
8 oz of SPF 15 sun lotion	$8 (Walgreens), $12 (Disney)
4 oz of SPF 45 sun lotion	$8 (Universal)
Huggies Little Swimmers swim pants	$8.50 for 12 (Walgreens), $1.60 per pair (Disney)
27-exposure Kodak waterproof camera	$15 (Walgreens), $20 (Universal), $20 (Disney)
Beach towel	$10 (CVS), $20 (Disney)
4 AA Duracell batteries	$2.80 (Walgreens), $6 (Universal), $5 (Disney)
Water shoes	$16 (Disney)
ATM fee	$2 (standard)
Budget motel room at Disney	From $82
Budget motel room outside of Disney	From $45

your back pocket, and hide the "real" one in a money belt or in your front pocket. By the time a villain realizes they got a decoy wallet, they'll be long gone.

Strollers will not be allowed inside most attractions, and they will not be attended in their parking sections, so make sure you never leave anything valuable in them. If you are traveling with kids, train them to approach the nearest park employee in case of separation. For older children, pick a landmark at which you can meet. Never dress your kids in clothing that reveals their name, address, or hometown. Unless it's a travel day, also remove any luggage tags where this information will be visible. Think about it: If someone can read your address off a backpack tag while you're in line at Jurassic Park, then they they'll know you're not at home; an unscrupulous person could do some damage with that information.

Your biggest concern will be sun, which can burn you even through gray skies on cloudy days. You will be spending a lot more time outdoors than you might suspect—rides take 3 minutes, but some of their lines will have you waiting outside for an hour. Also have a hat, if you're susceptible to burning, and make sure that infants, especially, will be completely covered.

Stuff You Never Thought to Bring (But Should)

Besides the usual toiletries, recharging cords, and drugs, you might not have realized that it'd be good to bring these things from home, too:

- **Earplugs.** Flights to and from Orlando are jumping with kids going insane with excitement. If you plan to sleep, stuff your ears.
- **Hand purifier.** Turnstiles. Safety bars. Handrails. Furry mascots. You're going to be touching a lot of things that countless other people were grasping just before you. Carry a little bottle of sanitizer for use before you eat or absent-mindedly chew on your fingernails.
- **Dark-colored shorts or pants.** On almost all boat or flume rides, the seating doubles as a step, so you're bound to plant your butt in a slightly muddy puddle. White shorts show the dirt.
- **Sandals that fasten.** Whoever designed Tevas should be Velcroed into shackles in the fashion-crimes dungeon, but I own a pair to wear at the parks because I know the water-based rides soak regular shoes and cause pruning. Flip-flops won't do because they fall off and you can't wear them on some roller coasters.
- **Skin-tight underwear.** Long, moist days at the parks can cause chafing even in people who rarely experience it, making walking excruciating for the rest of your vacation. Wearing some kind of skin-tight undergarment, such as Under Armour or non-padded bicycle shorts, is a smart precaution.
- **Sunscreen, a hat, and sunglasses.** Okay, so you probably thought of these, but it bears repeating. People forget that many attraction queues will strand them, baking, in the Florida sunlight for long periods (especially the ones at Disney).
- **Cellphones.** These have replaced squawking walkie-talkies as a way for split parties to stay connected in the parks. They're not perfect—text messages have a way of arriving late—but they'll do.
- **Pocket-size games.** Everyone talks about Orlando's rides, but they neglect to mention the hour in line that you'll spend before those exciting 3 minutes. Orlando *is* lines. The fun you have at the parks depends greatly on your ability to kill time with the people in your group. If you don't bring diversions, at least bring conversation topics and a gratitude for togetherness.

Stay off the road during extreme downpours. Florida's cloudbursts can overwhelm even people used to rain, and the quick volume of water also increases the potential for hydroplaning. Rain tends to pass or abate quickly in Florida.

PACKING

For the latest rules on how to pack and what you will be permitted to bring as a carry-on, consult your airline or the **Transportation Security Administration** (www.tsa.gov). Also be sure to find out from your airline what your checked-baggage weight limits will be. Even airlines that previously were lax with the limits, such as JetBlue, now impose maximums of around 50 pounds per suitcase. Anything heavier will incur a fee.

There's nothing you can't buy in Orlando. It's hardly Timbuktu. But to save yourself a hassle, bring the basics for sunshine (lotion of at least 30 SPF, wide-brimmed hat, bathing suit, sunglasses), for rain (a compact umbrella or a poncho, which costs $7 inside the parks), for walking (good shoes, sandals for wet days or pool wear), and for memories (camera, film or storage cards, chargers).

If you plan to visit a water park, don't bring swimsuits with rivets or buckles, as they'll scratch the slides and they're forbidden.

GETTING ATTRACTION DISCOUNTS

For a full breakdown of Disney's ticketing system, how it works, and how to ward against overspending on it, see p. 94.

One of the true discounted programs is the **FlexTicket,** which is sanctioned by both Universal Orlando and the Anheuser-Busch parks (SeaWorld Orlando and Busch Gardens Africa). For admission to four parks (Universal's pair, SeaWorld, and Wet 'n Wild), you want the 4 Park Orlando FlexTicket ($190 adults, $156 kids 3–9), which grants unlimited admission to all of the parks for a full 2 weeks. Tack on Busch Gardens for $45 adults, $44 kids. Considering 1-day admission to Busch Gardens alone is $62 adult/$52 kids, you don't have to get near a calculator to see the savings. Once you've paid for parking at your first theme park ($10 is the going rate—incredible when you consider that in 2001 it was just $6), you can keep your ticket and avoid paying it again. Also, because many hotel closed-circuit TV programs promise $10 off, when you're buying a FlexTicket in person, claim you learned about it from your in-room programming and ask for the deal. FlexTickets are sold at the parks involved, but you'll often find deals online (www.4adventure.com and www.universalorlando.com).

SeaWorld and Busch Gardens package tickets to their parks, too. A ticket that gets you into both for as many times as you want for 14 days, plus a free round-trip bus ride from Orlando to Busch Gardens, is $85 for all ages. This **2 Park Unlimited Admission Ticket** is sold only online through the two parks' websites (www.seaworld.com and www.buschgardens.com).

Either before leaving home or once you arrive, ask for the free **Orlando Magicard,** which grants discounts to heaps of attractions, meals, vacation home rentals, and hotels. It's essentially just a marketing tool for the Convention and Visitors Bureau's many members, but considering just about everyone in town is on board and almost everyone offers snappy deals through this card, it's a gimmick that works. Its hotel discounts aren't much different from what the free

Buyer Beware!

Before Magic Your Way made ticket expiration standard, pretty much every Disney ticket was good forever. That means there are a lot of unused days floating around out there. When you see a sign on the side of U.S. 192 promising discounted tickets, that's often what's for sale. Buying a ticket like this is a gamble, particularly if you don't have the expertise to recognize a fake. Often, there's not even a way to tell by looking whether unused days really remain on a ticket; only a magnetic scan can tell.

Other organizations, such as time-share developers, do indeed offer legit tickets to theme parks and dinner shows, but to get them, you will have to endure heavy-duty sales presentations that last several hours. The requirements for attendance can be tight: Married couples must attend together, you both must swear your combined annual income is above a certain amount ($40,000, for example, for Westgate branded resorts), that you are in a given age range (23–65 is common), and that you commit to staying for at least 90 minutes, although as long as 4 hours is also common. At that point, you'll be rigorously and relentlessly pitched property. That's when many people begin to grow uncomfortable. Even if you're fearless about parrying sales pitches, I think that an entire morning out of your hard-earned vacation time is worth a lot more than whatever discount is being provided. After all, how many days of working did it take for you to accrue those 4 or 5 hours? You also may not arrive at the parks until lunchtime, missing (in some cases) a third of the opening hours. Don't be so cheap and discount-obsessed that you throw away your time.

coupon circulars promise, but they're still a good bargaining chip in terms of knowing the going rate and negotiating for something ever better. The Magicard is downloadable from the CVB website (www.orlandoinfo.com), where you can preview the discounts on offer, or you can pick one up at the Visitor Center.

A few outfits such as **Billy Boy's Tickets** (☎ 800/544-7646; www.ticket momma.com) and **Maple Leaf Tickets** (☎ 800/841-2837; www.mapleleaf tickets.com), both members of the Better Business Bureau, sell discounted tickets. Their Disney deals are never deep enough to offset shipping fees or the hassle of picking up your tickets at their offices; however, the math behind multiple purchases as well as for third-tier diversions such as dinner shows ($10–$15 off) may work out for you. A desk at the Orlando Official Visitor Center (see the beginning of this chapter) furnishes similar discounts on tickets you can trust.

There is one paid product, the **Go Orlando Card** (www.goorlandocard.com), that purports to offer discounts on secondary attractions. Although you may be tempted, I don't recommend it. Rare is the person who can visit enough places in 1 day to make the price (1 day is $59, 3 are $149) pay off.

SPECIALIZED TRAVEL RESOURCES

If you have a wallet, Orlando wants you. Few tourist sponges are more adept at rolling out the red carpet for people of all needs. No matter who you are, Orlando has a system for dealing with you.

ADVICE FOR FAMILY TRAVELERS

The theme parks were built to make money off you. I mean, this is a place where kids are charged the full adult price once they turn 10! Although a very few tertiary attractions sell "family tickets" that allow for everyone in your group to enter on one discounted pass, there aren't many breaks for families in Orlando.

Think carefully about whether your child is ready for the theme parks. Too many parents consider an Orlando vacation such a rite of passage that they rush into it too early, without considering whether their child will find the experience overwhelming, or heck, even if they'll *remember* it. I agree with many parenting experts who say that about 3 years old is the minimum age. I can also say, from experience, that even that may be too young; as an adult, I still bear the pain of being turned away from Space Mountain for years because I was too short to meet the ride requirements. That kind of rejection *hurts*, man.

Also think about whether *you're* ready to bring your kids. Having little ones with you means you won't be able to ride or do lots of the things you might otherwise have wanted to. If you get right up to the Tower of Terror only to find you can't do it with the rugrats, the last thing you want is to take your frustration out on your kids. I've witnessed many an ugly family meltdown at the parks, and although no one wants to admit it, I bet that half the time, it's because the *adults* can't have their way, not the kids. Note, however, that at every park, the scarier rides are capable of what's called a **Child Swap.** That provides an area where one parent or guardian can wait with a child while their partner rides and then switch off so the other gets a chance. Many rides also have a bypass corridor where chickens can do their chicken-out thing. Ask staffers about it.

I suggest you let your kids take an active role in planning your vacation. Believe me, they'll be more than eager to fantasize about all the things there are to do, and their excitement will only make your investment pay off. Kid-directed planning will help *you,* too—if only because sorting the must-sees out ahead of time will keep your family from quarreling later, and it will keep expectations in check. The Walt Disney World website provides interactive online maps of its four parks, which you can use to highlight a must-see list according to your tastes. With 3 weeks notice, the resort will print a color version of your customized maps and mail them for free to your house to get you jazzed up for your trip.

A few other things to think about:

- Familiarize yourself with the height restrictions for all rides, which are posted at the parks' websites and listed on the maps. Universal also keeps physical gauges in front of both its parks. Everything is measured in inches, so if your child is usually measured in centimeters, multiply by 0.393.
- Bring supplies to kid-proof your hotel room.
- Slather your kids in sun lotion. Young skin burns easily.
- Some hotels offer "kids eat free" programs—you pay, they don't. Ask.

◆ The theme parks' strollers are easy, but basic; they don't recline, and they are not adequately secure for kids younger than toddlers.

◆ Bring a current picture of your child or keep one on your mobile phone. Should your kid get lost, this will help the people who try to find him or her.

ADVICE FOR TRAVELERS WITH DISABILITIES

The theme parks are way ahead when it comes to making life easier for guests with special needs. Nearly everything is accessible. This excellent customer service predates the Americans with Disabilities Act of 1990; as multi-generational attractions, the parks have always worked to be inclusive, and in response, guests with mobility issues have long embraced them.

There was a time when guests in **wheelchairs** and **ECVs** were given special treatment and ushered to the front of lines, but now, with so many guests on wheels for reasons including obesity, Disney (with the exception of Make-A-Wish Foundation kids and other special groups, by prior arrangement) feeds everyone into the same attraction queues. Once you're near the end, there will usually be a place for you to wait for the special wheelchair-ready ride vehicle to come around. Often, this translates into longer waits, as the special vehicles can be in high demand. The park maps carefully indicate which rides will require you to leave your personal vehicle. A very few, pre-ADA attractions, such as Tom Sawyer Island and the Swiss Family Treehouse, require you to be ambulatory. Those are marked, too, but the vast majority of things to see are accessible to all.

Hotels in Florida are required by law to have at least one room equipped for wheelchairs, and because guests with mobility issues are big business, most of them have more than one such room. At Disney, the best locations for wheelchair guests are probably Coronado Springs Resort, which has 99 equipped rooms; and the deluxe-level Polynesian and Grand Floridian resorts, which are connected to the Magic Kingdom and Epcot by easy transfers to the monorail. (The Contemporary, another monorail hotel, is perhaps too escalator-ridden.) You might consider tackling the issue by renting a house, which provides much more room; most of the home rental companies also comply with ADA requirements, so any request for an equipped condo or villa rental should not be beyond them.

In addition, every show has at least one **sign language–interpreted** performance daily, and many more are equipped with subtitles, projected in reverse on the back wall, that can be viewed with a Disney-issued device. Narrated rides provide interpreters and handheld devices; let them know you're coming at least 2 weeks early. For more information, call the sign language coordinator at ☎ 407/824-5217 or the Devices for the Deaf coordinator at 407/827-5141 (a TDD/TTY number).

Walt Disney World's full list of services, which include Braille guidebooks, are outlined in the publication *Guidebook for Guests with Disabilities,* available at any Guest Relations window, or online at www.disneyworld.com. There's also a hotline: ☎ 407/934-7639 or 407/824-2222. Universal Orlando (☎ 888/519-4899 [TTY] or 407/224-5929 [voice]; www.universalorlando.com) publishes a similar booklet and, like Disney, arranges sign language interpreters and scripts with advance notice of at least 2 weeks. SeaWorld Orlando (☎ 407/363-2414 or 407/351-3600; www.seaworld.com) only needs a week's notice for interpreters, and it furnishes assisted listening devices that work at some, but not all, of the biggest attractions.

Medical Travel, Inc. (☎ 800/308-2503 or 407/438-8010; www.medicaltravel. org) is a local company that specializes in the rental of mobility equipment, ramp vans, and supplies such as oxygen tanks. Electric scooters and wheelchairs can be rented and delivered to your hotel room or villa through two established companies: **Care Medical Equipment** (☎ 800/741-2282 or 407/856-2273; www.care medicalequipment.com) and **Walker Medical & Mobility Products** (☎ 888/726-6827 or 407/518-6000; www.walkermobility.com). All the theme parks, except the water parks, also rent ECVs for about $35 a day and wheelchairs for about $10 a day. If your own wheelchair is wider than about 25 inches, you might think about switching to the model rented at each park, as those are guaranteed to navigate tight squeezes such as hairpin queue turns.

Organizations that offer assistance to travelers with disabilities include the **American Federation for the Blind** (☎ 800/232-5463; www.afb.org) and **Society for Accessible Travel & Hospitality** (☎ 212/447-7284; www.sath.org).

ADVICE FOR SENIORS

Although just about every secondary attraction offers a special price for seniors, the major theme parks offer precious little in the way of special deals or amenities for you. One excellent exception is SeaWorld's **Terrific Tuesdays Seminars** (www.4adventure.com/SWF/SWFSE/tue.aspx), educational symposiums given not just by animal trainers, but by gardeners, engineers, and other experts. They are held on a first-come, first-served basis on occasional Tuesdays. SeaWorld is also known to offer discounts of $5 to $8 on admission during low season if you present your AARP card to the box office.

If you're over 50, you can join **AARP** (601 E Street NW, Washington, DC, 24009; ☎ 888/687-2277; www.aarp.org) and wrangle discounts on at hotels, airfare, and car rentals. Before you bite, be sure that the AARP discount you are offered actually undercuts others that are out there (at a standard 10% off the usual rates, sometimes they don't). The well-respected **Elderhostel** (☎ 877/426-8056; www. elderhostel.org) runs many classes and programs, both inside the theme parks and around the Orlando area, designed to authentically delve into literature, history, the arts, and music. Packages last from a day to a week and include lodging, tours, and meals. Some are even multi-generational; bring the grandkids.

ADVICE FOR GAY & LESBIAN TRAVELERS

Orlando still has a conservative streak, but an influx of different types of people from across America, as well as the steady influence of the theme parks (which employ tens of thousands of gay people), have fostered a city in which two ideologically opposed communities coexist. Especially among the younger generation, the two communities mix and play together. See p. 292 for some of the biggest gay and lesbian hangouts in town, including the Parliament House, said to be the largest gay entertainment complex in the world.

Although it's not an officially sanctioned event, Walt Disney World looks the other way when Gay Day events (p. 307) are scheduled. With some 100,000 participants, it's one of the largest annual events in town.

As a consequence of all this mainstream visibility, most visitors to Orlando simply won't need any special resources or assistance. Most hotels aren't troubled in the least by gay couples, and gay people can be themselves anyplace. The most conservative attitudes will be found at the theme parks, which of course are full of people who aren't from Orlando—public displays of affection there are not likely to be greeted warmly by all of the families sharing the park with you. (My advice: Stick to hugs and claim you're cousins on a family reunion.) Use your intuition—and your common sense.

Should you still worry about possible harassment, the **International Gay and Lesbian Travel Association** (☎ 800/448-8550, 954/776-2626; www.traveliglta. com) can connect you with gay-friendly hotels and businesses, but the list is a short one. Most of the Orlando-based gay groups deal mostly with residents' issues. The **Gay, Lesbian & Bisexual Community Center of Central Florida** (946 N. Mills Ave., Orlando; ☎ 407/228-8272; www.glbcc.org) offers the usual support, such as counseling and social groups in an environment where those who seek help are likely to be understood. **Gay Orlando Network** (www.gayorlando.com) lists upcoming events, but they're more likely to be resident-oriented (bowling nights or youth alliances) than tourist-oriented, although it does announce Sunday worship services.

Several publications might lend additional assistance, including the Central Florida edition of *Buzz* (www.buzzpublications.com), a regional giveaway that runs down the parties and includes a map of the biggest gay clubs; *Watermark* (www.watermarkonline.com), which covers state issues; and *Gay Parent* magazine (www.gayparentmag.com), which is sensitive to the issues faced by kids and their same-sex parents.

STAYING WIRED

Getting online isn't hard with your own laptop. Most hotels will have access—sometimes in common areas, sometimes in guest rooms, and sometimes in both places. Strangely, it's the least expensive properties that seem to offer this service for free. Walt Disney World's hotels, for example, charge $10 a day, a pretty standard price. Bring your own Ethernet cable in case your hotel can't produce one. Many home rentals also come with Internet-connected computers. Almost all of the offices of the major home rental agencies maintain computers for guest use.

And those whose hotels don't have access have been known to crib free use by trawling the parking lots of the budget hotels on International Drive or U.S. 192. Many establishments don't password-protect their Wi-Fi signals.

You can also find access at Starbucks (www.starbucks.com), FedEx Kinkos (www.fedex.com) and Panera Bread bakeries (www.panerabread.com).

Those without laptops can usually find at least one taxi computer at their hotel, sometimes for a nominal fee ($2–$5 for 10 minutes of access). Because of this, and the fact that few tourists need to check their e-mail who haven't also brought the means to do it, there are no dedicated Internet cafes to speak of.

Alternatively, locations of the **Orange County Library** (101 E. Central Blvd., Orlando; ☎ 407/835-7323; www.ocls.info) have terminals for public use, although they often require a library card to operate. Use these as a last resort, because you may have to do some sweet-talking.

RECOMMENDED BOOKS & FILMS

Surprisingly, for a city that is so emblematic of American culture and ideals, it's hard to find books that are interested in providing an honest retelling of Orlando's history and its character. Hyperion, a Disney imprint, tends to publish love letters, but it grants extraordinary access to its writers. These works, some of which are out of print, will give you a sense of the city as a place as well as a product:

BOOKS

- *Walt Disney: The Triumph of the American Imagination,* by Neal Gabler. Troubled, distant, driven, brilliant. A portrait of the real man and his business.
- *Since the World Began,* by Jeff Kurtti. One of the few Disney-produced books on park history that doesn't go all misty-eyed and mealy-mouthed.
- *Their Eyes Were Watching God,* by Zora Neale Hurston. Set in Eatonville, 6 miles north of Orlando, this classic novel is about African-American life in Florida at the turn of the last century.
- *Celebration, U.S.A.,* by Douglas Frantz and Catherine Collins. Two journalists are among the first to move into Disney's model community.
- *Inside the Mouse: Work and Play at Disney World,* by The Project on Disney. High-minded academics wander the World and muse on its rhetoric.
- *Team Rodent: How Disney Devours the World,* by Carl Hiaasen. A deeply cynical assault on Disney corporate culture as it pertains to Orlando.
- *30 Eco-Trips in Florida,* by Holly Ambrose. The best book for getting to know the real state of the state.
- *Florida, My Eden,* by Frederic B. Stresau. A classic on Florida horticulture.

FILM & TV

- *Marvin's Room* (1996). As a sign of faith to Miramax, Disney allowed it to be the first movie to shoot in the Magic Kingdom, despite the unpleasant scene.
- *From the Earth to the Moon* (1998). Not only does the HBO miniseries retell the wonders of NASA's missions, it was also shot at Disney–MGM Studios.
- *Jaws 3-D* (1983). Shot at SeaWorld and on land that became Universal.
- *Moon over Miami* (1941) and *Easy to Love* (1953). Shot at Cypress Gardens.

The ABCs of Orlando

Area codes The area code for the Orlando area is **407** (if you're dialing locally, a preceding 1 is not necessary, but the 407 is), although you may encounter the less common **321** code, which is also used on the Atlantic Coast. The **863** area code governs the land between Orlando and Tampa, and the Tampa area uses **813** and **727**. The region west of Orlando uses **352**.

ATMs and currency exchange See "Money Matters," earlier in this chapter.

Business hours Offices are generally open on weekdays between 9am and 5pm, while banks tend to close at 4pm. Typically, stores open between 9 and 10am and close between 6 and 7pm Monday through Saturday, except at malls, which stay open until 9pm. On Sunday, stores generally open at 11am and rarely stay open later than 7pm.

Drinking laws The legal age for the purchase and consumption of alcohol is 21.

Proof of age is almost always requested, even if you look older, so carry photo ID with you at all times. It's illegal to carry open containers of alcohol in any public area that isn't zoned for alcohol consumption (as CityWalk and Pleasure Island are), and the police may ticket you on the spot.

Electricity The United States uses 110–120 volts AC (60 cycles), compared to the 220–240 volts AC (50 cycles) that is standard in Europe, Australia, and New Zealand. If your small appliances use 220–240 volts, buy an adaptor and voltage converter before you leave home, as these are very difficult to find in Orlando.

Embassies & Consulates The nearest embassies are located in the nation's capital, Washington, D.C. Some consulates are located in major U.S. cities, and most nations have a mission to the United Nations in New York City. If your country isn't listed below, call for directory information in Washington, D.C. (☎ 202/555-1212) or log on to www.embassy.org/embassies.

The embassy of Canada is at 501 Pennsylvania Ave. NW, Washington, DC 20001 (☎ 202/682-1740; www.canadianembassy.org). Other Canadian consulates are in Buffalo, Detroit, Los Angeles, New York, and Seattle.

The embassy of Ireland is at 2234 Massachusetts Ave. NW, Washington, DC 20008 (☎ 202/462-3939; www.irelandemb.org). Irish consulates are in Boston, Chicago, New York, San Francisco, and other cities.

The embassy of New Zealand is at 37 Observatory Circle NW, Washington, DC 20008 (☎ 202/328-4800; www.nzemb.org). New Zealand consulates are in Los Angeles, Salt Lake City, San Francisco, and Seattle.

The embassy of the United Kingdom is at 3100 Massachusetts Ave. NW, Washington, DC 20008 (☎ 202/588-7800; www.britainusa.com). Other British consulates are in Atlanta, Boston, Chicago, Cleveland, Houston, Los Angeles, New York, San Francisco, and Seattle.

Emergencies Call ☎ 911 for the police, to report a fire, or to get an ambulance. If you have a medical emergency that does not require an ambulance, you should be able to walk into the nearest hospital emergency room (see "Hospitals," below).

Holidays Banks close on the following holidays: January 1 (New Year's), the third Monday in January (Martin Luther King, Jr., Day), the third Monday in February (Presidents Day), the last Monday in May (Memorial Day), July 4 (Independence Day), the first Monday in September (Labor Day), the second Monday in October (Veterans Day), the fourth Thursday in November (Thanksgiving Day), and December 25. The theme parks are open every day of the year.

Hospitals Orlando Regional Sand Lake Hospital (9400 Turkey Lake Rd., Orlando; ☎ 407/351-8500) is a short drive north up Palm Parkway from Lake Buena Vista. To get to **Celebration Health** (400 Celebration Pl., Celebration; ☎ 407/303-4000), from I-4, take the U.S. 192 exit; then at the first traffic light, turn right onto Celebration Avenue, and at the first stop sign, make another right. In addition, each theme park has its own infirmary capable of handling a range of medical emergencies.

Mail At press time, domestic postage rates were 26¢ for a postcard and 41¢ for a letter. For international mail, a first-class letter of up to 1 ounce costs 90¢ (69¢ to Canada and Mexico); a first-class postcard costs the same as a letter. For more information go to www.usps.com and click on "Calculate Postage."

There's a Post Office at the Mall of Millenia (4200 Conroy Rd., Orlando; ☎ 407/363-3555; Mon–Fri 9am–5pm, Sat 10am–1pm) and at Lake Buena Vista, north of the Downtown Disney area (12133 S. Apopka Vineland Rd., Orlando; ☎ 407/351-2492; Mon–Fri 9am–4pm, Sat 9am–noon). Ask at the theme park Guest Relations desks if mailing your items there will entitle you to a themed postmark.

Newspapers and Magazines Although most hotels distribute that shallow McNewspaper, *USA Today,* to use as your morning doormat, the local paper, the *Orlando Sentinel* (www.orlandosentinel. com), is less widely available but much better for discovering local happenings. *Orlando Magazine* (www.orlando magazine.com) is a glossy that covers trends and upscale restaurants. Also see the box on amateur-run websites covering the theme parks on p. 303; you can usually find more information on those than in professional publications.

Pharmacies As much as I wish there were such a thing as a "local" pharmacy, the tourist area hosts mostly national chains. Walgreens (7650 W. Sand Lake Rd. at Dr. Phillips Boulevard, Orlando ☎ 407/ 345-9497), which has a round-the-clock pharmacy, could, at a stretch, be deemed an outfit with local roots; back in the day, Mr. Walgreen spent the cold months in Winter Park. Turner Drugs (12500 Apopka Vineland Rd., Lake Buena Vista; ☎ 407/828/8125) is not a 24-hour pharmacy, but it delivers prescriptions to most Disney-area accommodations.

Smoking Smoking is generally prohibited in all public indoor spaces, including offices, bars, restaurants, hotel lobbies, and most shops. In general, if you need to smoke, you'll have to go outside into the open air, and in the theme parks there are strictly enforced designated areas.

Taxes A 6.5% to 7% sales tax is charged on all goods with the exception of most edible grocery items and medicines. Hotels add another 2% to 5% in a resort tax, so the total tax on accommodations can run up to 12%. The United States has no Value Added Tax, but the custom is to not list prices with tax, so the final amount that you pay will be slightly higher than the posted price.

Telephone Generally, hotel surcharges on long-distance and local calls are astronomical, so you're better off using your **cellphone** or a **public pay telephone.** Many convenience groceries and packaging services sell **prepaid calling cards** in denominations up to $50; for international visitors these can be the least expensive way to call home. Many public phones at airports now accept American Express, MasterCard, and Visa credit cards. **Local calls** made from public pay phones in most locales cost either 35¢ or 50¢. Pay phones do not accept pennies, and few will take anything larger than a quarter. Make sure you have roaming turned on for your cellphone account.

If you will have high-speed Internet access in your room, you can save on calls by using **Skype** (www.skype.com) or another Web-based calling program, as calls between members cost nothing.

Most long-distance and international calls can be dialed directly from any phone. **For calls within the United States and to Canada,** dial 1 followed by the area code and the seven-digit number. **For other international calls,** first dial 011, then the country code, and then proceed with the number, dropping any leading zeroes.

Calls to area codes **800, 888, 877,** and **866** are toll-free. However, calls to area codes **700** and **900** (chat lines, bulletin boards, "dating" services, and so on) can be very expensive—usually a charge of 95¢ to $3 or more per minute, and they sometimes have minimum charges that can run as high as $15 or more.

For **reversed-charge or collect calls,** and for person-to-person calls, dial the number 0, then the area code and number. An operator will come on the line, and you should specify whether you are calling collect, person-to-person, or both. If your operator-assisted call is international, ask for the overseas operator.

For **local directory assistance** ("information"), dial ☎ 411; for long-distance information, dial 1, then the appropriate area code and 555-1212.

Time The continental United States is divided into four time zones: Eastern

Standard Time (EST), Central Standard Time (CST), Mountain Standard Time (MST), and Pacific Standard Time (PST). Orlando is on Eastern Standard Time, so when it's noon in Orlando, it's 11am in Chicago (CST), 10am in Denver (MST), and 9am in Los Angeles (PST). Daylight saving moves the clock 1 hour ahead of standard time. (A new law extending daylight saving time took effect in 2007; clocks now change the second Sun in Mar and the first Sun in Nov.)

Tipping Tips are customary and should be factored into your budget. Waiters should receive 15% to 20% of the cost of the meal (depending on the quality of the service), bellhops get $1 per bag, chambermaids get $1 to $2 per day for straightening your room (although many people don't do this), and cab drivers should get 15% of the fare. Don't be offended if you are reminded about tipping—waitstaff are used to dealing with international visitors who don't participate in the custom back home.

Toilets Each theme park has dozens of clean restrooms. Outside of the parks, every fast-food place, and there are hundreds, should have a restroom you can use. Barring those, many large hotel lobbies also have some.

Index

See also Accommodations and Restaurant indexes, below.

GENERAL INDEX

AAA (American Automobile Association), 30, 96, 318
AARP, 215, 325
ABC Super Soap Weekend, 309
Accommodations, 20–59. *See also* Accommodations Index
  average prices, 31
  bargaining on rates, 29–30, 31, 48
  B&Bs, 32–33
  best, 5
  downtown Orlando, 58–59
  home rentals, 20–27
  International Drive, 52–58
  Lake Buena Vista, 49–52
  shuttle buses, 10–11, 58, 315
  taxes, 31
  timeshares, 27
  Universal Orlando, 42–43
  U.S. 192 & south of Disney, 43–49
  Walt Disney World, 33–42
    advantages and disadvantages of, 33, 36
    deluxe resorts, 40–42
    "Good Neighbor" policy, 41
    moderate resorts, 38–40
    pricing, 36–37
    value resorts, 37–38
  Web discounts, 29
Adventure Camps at SeaWorld, 249
Adventure Express Tour, 251
Adventure Island (Tampa), 216
Adventureland, 109, 110–112
  restaurants, 127
Adventurers Club, 277, 278, 280
The Affection Section, 162
Africa (Animal Kingdom), 161
Airboat tours, 268–271
Airlines, 312–313
Air (aviation) museum, 234
Airports, 312–316
Albin Polasek Museum and Sculpture Gardens (Winter Park), 236–237
All About Kids, 67
Alligators, 231, 234, 239, 266, 269, 270

Altamonte Mall, 297
The Amazing Adventures of Spider-Man, 192
Ambassador II, 271
AMC Pleasure Island Cinema, 281
The American Adventure, 141
American Airlines, 29
American Antiques and Militaria, 299
American Automobile Association (AAA), 30, 96, 318
American Express, 318
Amtrak, 313, 316–317
Amway Arena, 285
Anheuser-Busch Hospitality Center, 210
Animal Actors on Location!, 184–185
Animal Kingdom. *See* Disney's Animal Kingdom
Animation Courtyard, 153–156
Annie Russell Theatre (Winter Park), 236
Antiques, shopping for, 299–300
Apollo/Saturn V Center (Titusville), 238
Apple Vacations, 29
Area codes, 327
Arena football, 285
Ariel's Grotto, 118
Arnold Palmer's Bay Hill Club & Lodge, 272
Around the World at Epcot, 247
Art museums, 229–230, 234–235, 236–237
Asia (Animal Kingdom), 162–163
Astronaut Encounter, 251
Astronaut Hall of Fame, 237–238
Astronaut Memorial, 239
Astronaut Training Program, 252
Astro Orbiter, 124
A+T Antiques, 299
Atlanta Braves, 254
Atlantic Dance Hall, 282
Atlantis Bayside Stadium, 211
ATM machines, 317
Audubon Center for Birds of Prey (Maitland), 237

Babysitting, 67
Back Booth, 292
Backstage Magic, 245
Backstage Safari, 248
Bald eagles, 163, 269, 271
Ballet, 287
Ballooning, 275
The Band, 256
Banks, 318
Barnes & Noble Booksellers, 301
The Barnstormer at Goofy's Wiseacre Farm, 122
Bars, 289–291
  gay, 292–294
Baseball, 254–255
Basketball, 285
Bass Pro Shops Outdoor World, 296
Bay Hill Shopping Plaza, restaurants, 76–77
Bay Lake, 16, 42, 128, 244, 275
Beaches, Canaveral National Seashore, 267
Beauty and the Beast-Live on Stage, 152
Bed & breakfasts (B&Bs), 32–33
Beetlejuice's Graveyard Revue, 182
Behind the Seeds at Epcot, 247
Believe, 205–206
Beluga Interaction Program, 250
Betty Boop Store, 194
Bibbidi Bobbidi Boutique, 170
BiddingForTravel.com, 48
Big Thunder Mountain Railroad, 113
Bijutsu-kan Gallery, 142
Billy Boy's Tickets, 322
Bird Gardens (Busch Gardens), 217
  restaurants, 220
Birding, 163, 231, 237, 266–267
Blizzard Beach, 166–167
Blue Horizons, 206, 208
Blue Man Group, 284
Blue Spring State Park, 265
The Blues Brothers, 181
Blue Water Balloons, 275
Boardwalk Baseball, 214

Boat tours and cruises, 268–271
    from Port Canaveral,
    240–241
Bob Carr Performing Arts Centre,
    287, 288
Bob Marley—A Tribute to
    Freedom, 68, 283
Body Wars, 134
Boggy Creek Airboat Rides, 270
Bok Tower (Lake Wales), 236,
    264
Bonanza Mini Golf, 233
The Boneyard, 163
Bonkerz Comedy Club, 284
Books, recommended, 327
Bookstores, 257, 300–301
Borders, 300–301
Botanical gardens, 263–264
Broadway Across America, 287
Bruce's Sub House, 136
Busch Gardens Africa, 215–220
    arrival in, 216
    basics cost at, 219
    best of, 215
    restaurants, 220
    tickets, 215
    tours, 252–253
Busch Gardens Africa Skyride,
    218, 219–220
Buses, 10–12, 58, 315
Business hours, 327
Butterfly and Knot Herb Garden,
    143
Buzz Lightyear's AstroBlaster,
    170
Buzz Lightyear's Space Ranger
    Spin, 123–124

Cabs, 12–13, 315–316
Camping, at Walt Disney World,
    40
Camp Jurassic, 195
Camp Minnie-Mickey, 164–165
Campus Crusade for Christ, 260
Canada (World Showcase),
    144–145
    restaurants, 147
Canaveral National Seashore,
    267
Capital One Bowl, 305
Carnival Cruise Lines, 240
Caro-Seuss-el, 198–199
Carousel of Progress, 124–125,
    303
Car racing, 255
Car rentals, 9–10, 314–315
Casey's on Central, 291–292
Cassadaga, 19, 258–259

Cassadaga Camp Bookstore, 259
Cassadaga Hotel, 259
Castaway Creek, 169
The Cat in the Hat, 199
Celebration, 14, 257–258
Celebration Golf Course, 273
Center Street, 107, 126
Central Florida Property
    Managers Association, 22
Central Florida Regional
    Transportation Authority,
    11–12
Chain of Lakes Park (Winter
    Haven), 254
ChampionsGate Golf Resort, 272
Champs Sports Bowl, 310
Character meals, 90–92, 277
Charitable help, 261–262
Charles Hosmer Morse Museum
    of American Art (Winter Park),
    234–235
Charles Rice Family Bookstore
    and Café (Winter Park),
    235–236
Cheetah Chase, 218
Chester & Hester's Dino-Rama,
    163
Children, families with
    babysitting, 67
    nightlife, 277
    travel advice, 323–324
Child Swap, 323
China (World Showcase),
    139–140
    restaurants, 146
Christian sights of interest, 226,
    228, 258–259, 260–261
Christmas, Florida, 239
Churches, 260–261
Cinderella Castle, 108
Cinderella's Golden Carrousel,
    119
The Circle of Life, 137
Circus World, 214
Cirque du Soleil, 281
Citrus Bowl, 305
Citrus Tower, 236
CityArts Factory, 230
City Hall (Magic Kingdom), 106
CityJazz, 283–284
CityWalk, 67, 282–285
    restaurants, 67–70
CityWalk Party Pass, 282
Cleveland Indians, 254
Climate, 304–305
The Club, 294
The Club at Firestone, 290
Club Paris, 291
Clydesdale Hamlet, 210, 220

Clyde & Seamore Take Pirate
    Island, 206
Colby Memorial Temple
    (Cassadaga), 259
Coleman, Bessie, 230
College Park, 256
    restaurants, 83, 84
Colonial Town, 18
Comedy clubs, 288–289
Comedy Warehouse, 277, 280
Comic Book Shop, 192–193
Commissary Lane, 152–153
    restaurants, 157
Concerts, 286–288
Condominium rentals, 20–27
Congo (Busch Gardens), 218
Congo River Adventure Golf, 232
Congo River Rapids, 218
Conservation Station, 162
Consulates, 328
Convention Center
    accommodations, 55–58
    restaurants near, 74–79
Cornell Fine Arts Museum
    (Winter Park), 235
Country Bear Jamboree, 115,
    303
Cranium Command, 134
Credit cards, 317–318
Cross Country Creek, 167
Crown Colony, 219–220
    restaurants, 220
Cruise Brothers, 241
Cruise Compete, 241
Cruise ships and lines, 240–241
Cruises Only, 241
Cruise Value Center, 241
Crush 'n' Gusher, 168
Crystal River Manatee Dive and
    Tour, 266
Cunningham, Earl, 229–230
Curious George Goes to Town,
    185–186
Customs regulations, 311–312
Cyberspace Mountain, 170
Cypress Gardens Adventure Park
    (Winter Haven), 232–234

Dance clubs, 289–291
Dance performances, 286–288
A Day in the Park with Barney,
    185
Déjà Vu, 299
Delancey Street Preview Center,
    181
DeLeon Springs State Recreation
    Area (Deland), 265
Delta Airlines, 29

Detroit Tigers, 254–255
Diamond Cab Company, 13
Dine with a Disney Imagineer, 245
Dining, 60–92. *See also*
  Restaurants Index
  best, 5–6
  Busch Gardens Africa, 220
  dinnertainment (dinner shows), 86–90, 277
  D.I.Y. Dinner, 84
  Downtown Orlando, 79–85
  International Drive, 74–79
  Lake Buena Vista & U.S. 192, 70–74
  luaus, 89–90
  Orlando Magical Dining Event, 61
  pricing symbols, 61
  SeaWorld Orlando, 90, 211–212
  Universal Orlando, 67–70
    Islands of Adventure, 199–201
    Universal Studios, 187–189
  Walt Disney World, 61–67
    Animal Kingdom, 66, 165
    character meals, 90–92, 277
    Disney Dining Plan, 99
    Disney-MGM Studios, 156–158
    Disney's Boardwalk, 66–67
    Downtown Disney, 65–66
    Epcot, 145–147
    Magic Kingdom, 126–127, 129
    money-saving tips, 144
    Pleasure Island, 65–66
    reservations, 61, 90, 94
  Winter Park, 85–86
Dinnertainment (dinner shows), 86–90, 277
Dinoland U.S.A. (Animal Kingdom), 163–164
  restaurants, 165
Dinosaur World (Plant City), 234
Dinostore (Islands of Adventure), 196
Dino-Sue, 164
Disabilities, travelers with, 324–325. *See also* Wheelchair rentals
Discovery Cove, 213–214
Discovery Island, 160–161
  restaurants, 165

Discovery Island Trails, 160
Disney, Roy O., 2, 106
Disney, Walt, 2, 93, 99, 106, 107–108, 129, 154–155, 157
Disney characters, dining with, 90–92, 277
Disney Cruise Line, 240
Disney Dollars, 101, 318
Disney Logic, 168
Disney Look, 99
Disney-MGM Studios, 147–158
  best of, 148
  character greetings, 114–158
  restaurants, 156–158
Disney-MGM Studios Backlot Tour, 155–156
DisneyQuest, 170
Disney's Animal Kingdom, 14, 158–165
  accommodations, 42, 64, 128
  arrival in, 158
  best of, 160
  character greetings, 114
  restaurants, 66, 165
  tours, 248
Disney's BoardWalk
  nightlife, 278, 280, 281–282
  restaurants, 66–67
Disney's Character Premiere, 298
Disney's Family Magic Tour, 246
Disney's Fantasia Gardens, 233
Disney's Pirate & Princess Party, 305–306
Disney's West Side. *See*
  Downtown Disney West Side
Disney's Wide World of Sports, 171
  restaurants, 67
  spring training, 254
Disney's Winter Summerland, 233
Disney Transportation System (DTS), 10–11, 58, 315
Disney Vacation Club (DVC), 27
Disney Wilderness Preserve, 267–268
D.I.Y. Dinner, 84
Dr. Doom's Fearfall, 192
Dolphin Cove (SeaWorld), 208
Dolphin Nursery (SeaWorld), 207
Dolphins, swimming with, 213–314, 248
Donald's Boat, 122
Dottie's Orlando Comedy Theatre, 288–289
Downhill Double Dipper, 167

Downtown Disney, 169–170
  nightlife, 278, 280–282
  restaurants, 65–66
Downtown Disney Marketplace, 169–170
  nightlife, 280–282
  restaurants, 66
Downtown Disney West Side, 169–170
  nightlife, 280–282
  restaurants, 66, 90
Downtown Orlando, 17–18
  accommodations, 58–59
  restaurants, 79–85
  sights and attractions, 226–230
Dragon Legend Acrobats, 139
Dream Along with Mickey, 108–109
Drinking laws, 327–328
Drive-in movies, 253
Drugstores, 329
Dudley Do-Right's Ripsaw Falls, 194
Dueling Dragons, 196–197
Dumbo the Flying Elephant, 119
Dylan's Candy Bar, 296

Earthquake: The Big One, 182
Eating, 60–92. *See also*
  Restaurants Index
  best, 5–6
  Busch Gardens Africa, 220
  dinnertainment (dinner shows), 86–90, 277
  D.I.Y. Dinner, 84
  Downtown Orlando, 79–85
  International Drive, 74–79
  Lake Buena Vista & U.S. 192, 70–74
  luaus, 89–90
  Orlando Magical Dining Event, 61
  pricing symbols, 61
  SeaWorld Orlando, 90, 211–212
  Universal Orlando, 67–70
    Islands of Adventure, 199–201
    Universal Studios, 187–189
  Walt Disney World, 61–67
    Animal Kingdom, 66, 165
    character meals, 90–92, 277
    Disney Dining Plan, 99
    Disney-MGM Studios, 156–158

Eating
  Walt Disney World *(cont.)*
    Disney's Boardwalk,
      66–67
    Downtown Disney,
      65–66
    Epcot, 145–147
    Magic Kingdom,
      126–127, 129
    money-saving tips, 144
    Pleasure Island, 65–66
    reservations, 61, 90, 94
    Winter Park, 85–86
Echo Lake, 148, 150
  restaurants, 156–157
Edge of Africa (Busch Gardens),
  220
Egypt (Busch Gardens),
  219–220
  restaurants, 220
The Eighth Voyage of Sindbad
  Stunt Show, 197
8TRAX, 280
Elderhostel, 325
Electrical Boat Parade, 128, 277
Electricity, 328
eLeisureLink, 29
Eli's Orange World, 300
Elmo and the Bookaneers, 207
Embassies, 328
Emergencies, 328
Enchanted Tiki Room, 111
Entertainment and nightlife,
  276–294
  current events, 276, 305
  dinnertainment, 86–90, 277
  gay and lesbian, 292–294
  performing arts, 285–289
  Universal Orlando, 282–285
  Walt Disney World, 278,
    280–282
Entry requirements, 310–311
The Enzian Theater, 289, 306
Epcot, 129–147
  best of, 130
  character greetings, 114
  hours, 130
  navigation tips, 100
  restaurants, 145–147
  special events, 306–309
  time-saving tips, 120–121
  tours, 246–248
Epcot DiveQuest, 247
Epcot International Flower &
  Garden Festival, 306
Epcot International Food &
  Wine Festival, 307–308
Epcot Seas Aqua Tour, 247–248
Errol Estate Country Club, 273

E.T. Adventure, 185
E-tickets, 123
Expedition Everest, 162
Extra Magic Hours, 33, 121

Factory outlets, 297–298
Fairytale Garden, 118
Families with children
  babysitting, 67
  nightlife, 277
  travel advice, 323–324
Fantasmic!, 152, 277
Fantasyland, 109, 117–119
  restaurants, 127
Fantasy of Flight (Polk City),
  234
Farmer's markets, 236, 299
Fastpass system, 109, 120, 121
Fear Factor Live, 183
Ferries, 10, 33, 100, 128
Festival Bay, 296
Festival of Orchestras, 288
Festival of the Lion King, 164
Festivals, 305–310
Fez House, 142
Fievel's Playland, 185
Finding Nemo—The Musical, 163
Fire Museum, Orlando, 229
Fire Station (Magic Kingdom),
  106
Fireworks, 126, 145, 207, 277
First Baptist Church of Orlando,
  260–261
Fishing, 268
Flamingo Island, 217
Flea markets, 298–299
FlexTicket, 321
Flights of Wonder, 163
Florida Film Festival, 306
Florida Mall, 295–296, 301
  restaurants, 77
Florida Music Festival, 307
Florida Seals, 285
The Flying Fiddler, 210
Flying Unicorn, 196
Football, 305, 310
  arena, 285
Fox & Hound Antiques, 299
France (World Showcase), 143
  restaurants, 147
Frontierland, 109, 112–115
  restaurants, 127
Frontierland Shootin' Arcade,
  115
Full Moon Saloon, 294
Full Speed Race & Golf, 226
FUNAI Classic at Walt Disney
  World Resort, 308

Funjet, 29
Fun Spot Action Park, 225
Future World, 129–137
  tours, 246–247

**The Gallery of Arts and
  History, 142**
Gallery of the Whispering
  Willow, 139–140
Gambling cruises, 271
Gardens, 263–264
Gasoline Alley, 194
Gatorland, 231, 270
Gay and lesbian travelers
  advice for, 325–326
  bars and nightclubs,
    292–294
Gay Day, 307, 325
Gaylord Palms, 270, 309
Germany (World Showcase), 140
  restaurants, 146
G-Force, 226
Golden Phoenix Antiques, 299
Golf, 271–274
Gol Stave Church Gallery, 139
Gooding's, 73
"Good Neighbor" hotels, 41
Go Orlando Card, 322
Grad Nites, 306
Gran Fiesta Tour Starring The
  Three Caballeros, 138–139
The Great Movie Ride, 150
Green Meadows Petting Farm,
  226
Green Swamp, 19, 268
Grocery stores, 73, 301
The groove, 284
Gwazi (Busch Gardens), 217

Habitat Habit!, 161–162
Hall of Presidents, 116
Halloween Horror Nights, 308
Halloween Spooktacular, 308
Hands On Orlando, 261–262
Hang gliding, 275
Happy Limo, 315
Hard Rock Live, 284
Harmony Barber Shop, 106
Harry P. Leu Gardens, 263–264
The Haunted Mansion, 115–116,
  303
Hawaiian Rumble Adventure
  Golf, 233
Hawk's Landing Golf Club, 273
Health concerns, 318–321
Hidden Mickeys, 99, 246
The High in the Sky Seuss
  Trolley Train Ride!, 198

Highlands Reserve Golf Club, 273
Hilo Hattie, 296
Historic Bok Sanctuary (Lake Wales), 236, 264
Hockey, 285
Holidays, 36–37, 328
Hollywood (Universal Studios), 184
    restaurants, 189
Hollywood Boulevard, 148, 150–151
    restaurants, 156–157
Holy Land Experience, 226, 228
Homelessness, 261–262
Home rentals, 20–27
Homosassa Springs Wildlife State Park, 266
Honey, I Shrunk the Audience, 137
Honey, I Shrunk the Kids Movie Set Adventure, 153
Horseback riding, 274
Horse World Riding Stables, 274
Hospitals, 328
Hostel, 43–44
Hot air ballooning, 275
Hotels, 20–59. *See also* Accommodations Index
    average prices, 31
    bargaining on rates, 29–30, 31, 48
    B&Bs, 32–33
    best, 5
    downtown Orlando, 58–59
    home rentals, 20–27
    International Drive, 52–58
    Lake Buena Vista, 49–52
    shuttle buses, 10–11, 58, 315
    taxes, 31
    timeshares, 27
    Universal Orlando, 42–43
    U.S. 192 & south of Disney, 43–49
    Walt Disney World, 33–42
        advantages and disad-
            vantages of, 33, 36
        deluxe resorts, 40–42
        "Good Neighbor" policy, 41
        moderate resorts, 38–40
        pricing, 36–37
        value resorts, 37–38
    Web discounts, 29
House of Blues, 90, 281
Houston Astros, 254

Howl at the Moon Saloon, 291
Humbugs, 299
Hunter's Creek Golf Course, 274
Hunting, 268
Hurston, Zora Neale, 305, 327

Ice!, 309
If I Ran the Zoo, 199
IllumiNations: Reflections of Earth, 130, 145, 277
Imagination!, 137
Impressions de France, 143
Incredible Hulk Coaster, 190
Independence Day, 307
Independent Bar, 290
Indiana Jones Epic Stunt Spectacular, 150
Information, 302–304
    Universal Orlando, 173
    Walt Disney World, 94, 303
Innoventions, 132
    restaurants, 146
International Drive (I-Drive), 17
    accommodations, 52–58
    grocery stores, 73
    restaurants, 74–79
    sights and attractions, 221–225
    trolley, 11, 17, 298
International Flower & Garden Festival (Epcot), 306
International Food & Wine Festival (Epcot), 307–308
International Gateway, 143, 145
International Space Station Center (Titusville), 238–239
International visitors
    customs regulations, 311–312
    entry requirements, 310–311
Internet access, 326
Interstate 4 (I-4), 7–8
I-Ride Trolley, 11, 17, 298
Irlo Bronson Memorial Highway, 16
Islands of Adventure, 189–201
    best of, 193
    restaurants, 199–201
Italy (World Showcase), 140–141
    restaurants, 146
Itineraries, suggested, 3–5
It's A Small World, 117
It's Tough to Be a Bug!, 160–161
IVillage Live, 193

Jai alai, 285
Japan (World Showcase), 141–142
    restaurants, 146
Jaws, 182–183, 186–187, 303
Jellyrolls, 282
Jesus Film Project Studio Tour, 260
Jimmy Neutron's Nicktoon Blast, 177, 180
John F. Kennedy Space Center. *See* Kennedy Space Center
Joker Merchant Stadium (Lakeland), 254–255
Journey into Imagination with Figment, 137
Journey into Narnia: Creating The Lion, The Witch, and The Wardrobe, 155
Journey to Atlantis, 208
Joy Lan Drive-In, 253
Jungle Adventures Nature Park (Christmas), 239
Jungle Cruise, 110–111
JungleLand Zoo, 214
Jurassic Park, 195–196
    restaurants, 200
Jurassic Park Discovery Center, 196
Jurassic Park River Adventure, 195–196

Kali River Rapids, 162
KaTonga: Musical Tales from the Jungle, 216
Kelly, Melissa, 78–79
Kennedy Space Center, 237–239
    tours, 251–252
Kerouac, Jack, 256
Kerouac Project, 256
Ketchakiddee Creek, 169
Keys to the Kingdom Tour, 246
Key West at SeaWorld, 208
Kidcot, 135
Kids Nite Out, 67
Kidzone, 184–186
    restaurants, 189
Kilimanjaro Safaris, 161
Kissimmee, 16
    accommodations, 43–49
    grocery stores, 73
    information, 302
    shopping, 298–299
Kissimmee Convention and Visitors Bureau, 302, 303
Kraken, 208–209
Kumba, 218

Lagasse, Emeril, 69–70
Lake Buena Vista, 16–17, 256
   accommodations, 49–52
   restaurants, 70–74
Lake Buena Vista Factory Stores,
   298
Lake Eola Park, 18, 271
Lake Louisa State Park, 268
The Land, 136–137
   restaurants, 145
Land of the Dragons, 217
La Nouba, 281
Lava Lounge, 293
Layout of Orlando, 7–8, 13–19
Le Chapeau, 107
Lectures, 257
Leu (Harry P.) Gardens, 263–264
Liberty Bell, 116–117
Liberty Square, 109, 115–117
   restaurants, 126, 127
Liberty Square Riverboat, 116
Liberty Tree, 116–117
Lights, Motors, Action! Extreme
   Stunt Show, 152–153
Liquor laws, 327–328
Live music venues, 289–292
Living with the Land, 136–137
Lockers
   SeaWorld, 211
   Universal Orlando, 176
   Walt Disney World, 97
Lodging. See Accommodations;
   Accommodations Index
Loews Universal Cineplex, 285
Lost and found
   Universal Orlando, 173
   Walt Disney World, 94
The Lost Continent, 196–198
   restaurants, 200–201
Luaus, 89–90
Lucy a Tribute, 184
LYNX system, 11–12

McElligot's Pool, 199
Mad Cow Theatre Company, 286
Mad Tea Party, 119
Maelstrom, 139
Magical Midway, 224–225
Magic Behind Our Steam Trains
   Tour, 246
Magic Carpets of Aladdin, 111
Magic Kingdom, 102–127. See
   also specific rides
   arrival in, 102–103
   best of, 103
   character greetings, 114
   guest services, 106

hours, 102
navigation tips, 100
parades and fireworks, 277
restaurants, 126–127, 129
special events, 277,
   305–308
time-saving tips, 120–121
tours, 246
The Magic of Disney Animation,
   154
Magic Sunrise Ballooning, 275
Magic Your Way ticketing sys-
   tem, 94–95, 96
Maharajah Jungle Trek, 163
Mail, 328
Maingate Flea Market, 299
Main Street, U.S.A., 103,
   106–108
   restaurants, 127
Majesty Building, 261
Making of Me, 134
Mall at Millenia, 296, 328
Malls
   outlet, 297–298
   retail, 295–297
Manatee Rescue (SeaWorld), 208
M&M's World, 295
Mannequins Dance Palace, 278
Manuel, Richard, 256
The Many Adventures of Winnie
   the Pooh, 119
Map & Globe, 8
Maple Leaf Tickets, 322
Mardi Gras at Universal Studios,
   306
Marine Mammal Keeper
   Experience, 250–251
Marvel Super Hero Island, 190,
   192–193
   restaurants, 200
Mayan Ceremonial Hall, 139
Mead Gardens (Winter Park),
   264
Meal and Movie Deal (Universal
   Orlando), 67–68
Mears Transportation, 315
Me Ship, the Olive, 195
Medical requirements, 311
Melt Away Bay, 167
Men in Black: Alien Attack,
   183–184
Mennello Museum of American
   Art, 229–230
Merritt Island National Wildlife
   Refuge, 266–267
MetroWest Golf Club, 274
Mexico (World Showcase),
   138–139
   restaurants, 146

Mickey Avenue, 153–156
Mickey's Country House, 122
Mickey's Jammin' Jungle Parade,
   165
Mickey's Magical Milestones
   Tour, 246
Mickey's Not-So-Scary Halloween
   Party, 308
Mickey's PhilharMagic, 118
Mickey's Toontown Fair, 109,
   122
Mickey's Very Merry Christmas
   Party, 309
Military families, accommoda-
   tions, 39
Millenia Fine Art, 230
Miniature golf, 226, 232–233
Minnie's Country House, 122
Mission: SPACE, 133
Mistify, 207, 211
Mitsukoshi Department Store,
   142
Miyuki, 142
Money matters, 317–318
Money-saving tips, 321–323
   accommodations, 29–30,
      31, 48
   car rentals, 9
   cruises, 241
   dinner shows, 86
   Walt Disney World
      nightlife, 280
      restaurants, 144
      tickets, 96, 98
Monorail, 10, 33, 100, 128,
   130, 244
Monsters Inc. Laugh Floor, 125
Montu, 220
Monument of States
   (Kissimmee), 236
Morocco (Busch Gardens), 216
Morocco (World Showcase), 142
   restaurants, 146–147
Morse (Charles Hosmer) Museum
   of American Art (Winter Park),
   234–235
Motion, 278
Mount Dora, 19
TheMouseforLess.com, 30, 241
MouseGear, 132
MouseSavers, 30, 241, 303
Mouse Surplus, 300
Movies, recommended, 327
MuppetVision 3-D, 153
Myombe Reserve, 218–219
Mystic Dunes Golf Club, 273
The Mystic Fountain, 197

Nairobi (Busch Gardens), 218–219
Nairobi Field Station, 219
NASA. *See* Kennedy Space Center
NASCAR, 69, 255
Natural springs, 264–266
Nature reserves, 266–268
Nautilus Theater, 210
Neighborhoods, 13–19. *See also specific neighborhoods*
Network for Good, 262
Newspapers, 329
New Year's Eve, 310
New York (Universal Studios), 180–182
  restaurants, 188
Nightlife, 276–294
  current events, 276, 305
  dinnertainment, 86–90, 277
  gay and lesbian, 292–294
  performing arts, 285–289
  Universal Orlando, 282–285
  Walt Disney World, 278, 280–282
Night of Joy, 307
No Expiration ticket, 95–96
Northland Church (Longwood), 261
North Shore Golf Club, 274
Northwest Mercantile, 145
Norway (World Showcase), 139
  restaurants, 146

The Oasis, 158, 160
Ocala Drive-In, 253
Ocean Commotion, 210
Odyssea, 207, 210
Odyssey Center, 134
Oldies but Goodies, 300
Old Town, 225
One Fish, Two Fish, Red Fish, Blue Fish, 199
Opera, 287
Orange Avenue, shopping, 299–300
Orange Blossom Balloons, 275
Orange County National Golf Center and Lodge, 273
Orange County Public Library, 326
  restaurant, 82
Orange County Regional History Center, 228
Orange Lake Resort & Country Club, 273–274
Orlampa, 19
Orlando Ballet, 287

Orlando Beer Festival at Universal CityWalk, 308–309
Orlando Brewing and Taproom, 292
Orlando City Hall, 257
Orlando Convention and Visitors Bureau, 8, 303
Orlando Film Festival, 308
Orlando Fire Museum, 229
Orlando Improv, 289
Orlando International Airport (MCO), 312–316
Orlando International Fringe Festival, 306–307
Orlando Magic, 285
Orlando Magical Dining Event, 61
Orlando Magicard, 271, 321–322
Orlando Museum of Art, 229
Orlando Official Visitor Center, 30, 302
Orlando Opera, 287
Orlando Philharmonic Orchestra, 287
Orlando Predators, 285
Orlando Premium Outlets, 297–298
Orlando Repertory Theatre, 277, 286–287
Orlando Sanford International Airport, 314
Orlando Science Center, 228–229
Orlando Sentinel, 276, 302, 305, 329
Orlando Speedworld, 255
Orlando Theatre Project, 288
Orlando-UCF Shakespeare Festival, 286
Orlando Weekly, 257, 276, 305
Orlando Wetlands Park, 268
Osborne Family Spectacle of Dancing Lights, 309
Osceola County Stadium, 254
Osceola Flea and Farmers Market, 299
Osprey Eco Tours, 271
Outdoor activities, 263–275
Outlet malls, 297–298
Outpost (World Showcase), 140

Pacific Point Preserve, 209
Package deals, 29, 96–97, 173
Packing tips, 320, 321
Pal Mickey, 135
Pangani Forest Exploration Trail, 161

Parades, 112, 120–121, 165, 277
Park Avenue Area Association, 297
Parking, 10
  SeaWorld, 211
  Universal Orlando, 176
  Walt Disney World, 33, 97, 100, 130
Parliament House, 293
Partners, 108
Passports, 310–311
Peabody Orlando, 270
Penguin Encounter, 209
People's Theatre, 288
Performing arts, 285–289
Peter Pan's Flight, 118
Pets Ahoy!, 206–207
Pharmacies, 329
Phoenix, 218
Photographers, at Walt Disney World, 101–102
PhotoPass, 101–102
Pickpockets, 318–319
Pine Hills, 256
Pinocchio's Marionette Theater (Winter Park), 287
Pirate's Cove, 232
Pirates 4-D, 218
Pirates of the Caribbean, 111–112, 170, 303
Plantation Inn Dive Shop, 266
Playhouse Disney-Live on Stage!, 154
Playmobil FunPark, 296
Plaza Theatre, 277, 288
Pleasure Island, 277, 278, 280
  restaurants, 65–66
Pocahontas and Her Forest Friends, 164
Pointe Orlando, 297
Polasek (Albin) Museum and Sculpture Gardens (Winter Park), 236–237
Pooh's Playful Spot, 118
Popeye & Bluto's Bilge-Rat Barges, 194–195
Port Canaveral, 240–241, 271
Port of Entry (Islands of Adventure), 189
  restaurants, 200
Poseidon's Fury, 197–198
Post offices, 328
Priceline.com, 9, 29, 48
Prime Outlets Orlando, 298
Primeval Whirl, 163
Production Central, 177, 180
  restaurants, 187

Professional sports, 254–255, 285
Pteranodon Flyers, 195
Publix, 73
Pulse, 293

Quicksilver Tours, 315

Rafiki's Planet Watch, 161–162
Rainfall, average, 305
Rainforest Cafe, 66, 165
Rainy-day sights and attractions, best, 4–5
Readings, 257
Red Coconut Club, 283
Reflections of China, 139
Rental properties, 20–27
Reptile World Serpentarium (St. Cloud), 231
Restaurants, 60–92. See also Restaurants Index
best, 5–6
Busch Gardens Africa, 220
dinnertainment (dinner shows), 86–90, 277
D.I.Y. Dinner, 84
Downtown Orlando, 79–85
International Drive, 74–79
Lake Buena Vista & U.S. 192, 70–74
luaus, 89–90
Orlando Magical Dining Event, 61
pricing symbols, 61
SeaWorld Orlando, 90, 211–212
Universal Orlando, 67–70
    Islands of Adventure, 199–201
    Universal Studios, 187–189
Walt Disney World, 61–67
    Animal Kingdom, 66, 165
    character meals, 90–92, 277
    Disney Dining Plan, 99
    Disney-MGM Studios, 156–158
    Disney's Boardwalk, 66–67
    Downtown Disney, 65–66
    Epcot, 145–147
    Magic Kingdom, 126–127, 129

money-saving tips, 144
Pleasure Island, 65–66
reservations, 61, 90, 94
Winter Park, 85–86
Reunion Resort & Club, 272
Revenge of the Mummy, 180–181
Rhino Rally, 219
Richard Petty Driving Experience, 255
Ride the Comix, 170
Ripley's Believe it or Not! Odditorium, 225
Ritz-Carlton Golf Club Orlando, 272
River Country, 214
Rock 'n' Roll Beach Club, 278
Rock 'n' Roller Coaster Starring Aerosmith, 152
Rock & Roll Heaven, 300
Rock the Universe, 307
Rollins College (Winter Park), 235–236
Rollins Walk of Fame (Winter Park), 235
Ron Jon Surfpark, 296
Royal Caribbean International, 240
Royal St. Cloud Golf Links, 273
Runoff Rapids, 167

Safety concerns, 318–321
SAK Comedy Lab, 288
San Francisco/Amity (Universal Studios), 182–183
restaurants, 188
SaveRite, 73
Scorpion (Busch Gardens), 218
Scuba diving, 168–169, 247–248, 265–266
Sea Carousel, 210
Seaport Theatre, 209–210
Seasons, 36–37, 304–305
The Seas with Nemo & Friends, 135–136, 145–146
SeaWorld Orlando, 201–214
basics cost at, 211
best of, 205
for disabled travelers, 324
restaurants, 90, 211–212
special events, 306–310
tours, 249–251
SeaWorld's Bud & BBQ, 306
SeaWorld's Halloween Spooktacular, 308
SeaWorld's Holiday Celebration, 309–310

Senior travelers, 325
Serengeti Railway, 218, 219
Serengeti Safari, 252
Seuss Landing, 198–199
restaurants, 201
Seven Seas Lagoon, 102, 128, 244, 275
Shakespeare Festival, 286
Shamu, 204, 206, 210, 303
Shamu Stadium, 210, 250
Shark Encounter (SeaWorld Orlando), 209
Shark Reef (Typhoon Lagoon), 168–169
Sharks Deep Dive (SeaWorld Orlando), 251
SheiKra, 217
Sheplers, 296
Sherbeth Road, 14
Shingle Creek Golf, 272
Shopping, 295–301
antiques, 299–300
flea markets, 298–299
interesting stores, 300–301
outlet malls, 297–298
retail malls, 295–297
Show Jumping Hall of Fame, 220
Shrek 4-D, 180
Shuttle buses, 10–11, 58, 315
Shuttle Express, 216
Sights and attractions. See also specific sights and attractions
best, 3–5
suggested itineraries, 3–5
Silver Moon Drive-In (Lakeland), 253
Silver Spurs Rodeo of Champions, 306
Ski Patrol, 167
SkyCoaster, 226
Sky60, 290
Sky Tower (SeaWorld), 210
SkyVenture, 222, 224
Sleepovers at SeaWorld, 249
Slush Gusher, 167
Smoking, 329
Snorkeling, 168–169, 247–248, 265–266
Snow Stormers, 167
Snow White's Scary Adventures, 118
Soarin', 136
The Social, 291
Sorcerer Mickey Hat, 148, 150
Sounds Dangerous—Starring Drew Carey, 150
Southern Nights, 293
Southwest Vacations, 29

Space Mountain, 123
Spaceship Earth, 130–131
Special events, 305–310
Spectator sports, 254–255, 285
SpectroMagic, 126
Speed World Dragway, 255
Spider-Man, 190, 192
Spirit of America, 141
Splash Mountain, 113
Splendid China, 214
Spring training, 254–255
Stanley Falls Flume, 217–218
Stanleyville (Busch Gardens),
  217–218
  restaurants, 220
Star Taxi, 13
Star Tours, 151
Star Wars Weekends, 307
State Department, U.S., 310
Sterling Casino Lines, 271
Stingray Lagoon, 208
Stitch's Great Escape!, 125
Stoneybrook Golf Club, 274
Storm Force Accelatron, 190
Storm Slides, 168
Streets of America, 152–153
  restaurants, 158
Strollers, 135, 319
  SeaWorld, 211
  Universal Orlando, 176
  Walt Disney World, 97, 135
Summit Plummet, 166–167
SunCruz Casino, 271
Sunscreen, 101, 320
Sunset Boulevard, 151–152
  restaurants, 158
Swan Boats at Lake Eola Park,
  271
Swiss Family Treehouse, 110

Tabu, 290
Tampa International Airport,
  314
Tanganyika Tidal Wave, 218
Taxes, 31, 329
Taxis, 12–13, 315–316
Teamboat Springs, 167
Telephone, 329
Temperatures, average, 305
Terminator 2: 3-D Battle Across
  Time, 184
Terrific Tuesdays Seminars, 249
Test Track, 134
Theater, 286–288
  dinnertainment, 86–90, 277
Theatre Downtown, 286
Thornton Park, 18
Tibet-Butler Preserve, 267

Tickets
  Busch Gardens Africa, 215
  money-saving tips, 321–322
  SeaWorld Orlando, 204
  Universal Orlando, 175–176
  Walt Disney World, 94–98
    Fastpass, 109, 120, 121
    money-saving tips, 96,
      98
Tiffany, Louis Comfort, 234–235
Tiffany Towncar, 315
Tike's Peak, 167
Tiki Island Volcano Golf,
  232–233
Timacuan Golf and Country Club,
  274
Timbuktu, 218
  restaurants, 220
Time-saving tips, 120–121
Timeshares, 27
Time zone, 329–330
Tipping, 330
Titanic: The Experience, 224
Toboggan Racers, 167
Toilets, 330
Tomorrowland, 109, 122–126
  restaurants, 127, 129
Tomorrowland Indy Speedway,
  122
Tomorrowland Transit Authority,
  124
Tom Sawyer Island, 113–115
Toon Lagoon, 193–195
  restaurants, 200
Toontown Hall of Fame Tent,
  122
Tourist information. *See*
  Information
Tours
  Busch Gardens Africa,
    252–253
  Kennedy Space Center,
    251–252
  SeaWorld Orlando, 249–251
  Universal Orlando, 248–249
  Walt Disney World, 243–248
Town Square Exposition Hall,
  106–107
Toy Story Mania, 155
Train travel, 313, 316–317
Transportation, 8–13, 312–317
Traveler's checks, 318
Travel insurance, 316
The Treasures of Morocco, 142
The Tree of Life, 160
TriceraTop Spin, 163
Turkey legs, 127, 144, 212
Turtle Talk With Crush, 136
The Twilight Zone Tower of
  Terror, 151

Twister . . . Ride It Out, 180
Typhoon Lagoon, 166, 167–169

**Ubanga-Banga Bumper Cars,
  218**
UnDISCOVERed Future World,
  246–247
United Kingdom (World
  Showcase), 143–144
  restaurants, 147
Universal Horror Make-Up Show,
  184
Universal Meal Deal, 188
Universal Orlando, 172–189. *See
  also* Islands of Adventure;
  Universal Studios Florida
  accommodations, 42–43
  basics cost at, 176
  for disabled travelers, 324
  vs. Disney, 174–175
  information, 173
  luaus, 90
  nightlife, 282–285
  restaurants, 67–70
    Islands of Adventure,
      199–201
    Universal Studios,
      187–189
  special events, 306–309
  tickets, 175–176
  tours, 248–249
  transportation, 8, 11
Universal Studios Florida,
  172–189
  arrival in, 176
  best of, 181
  restaurants, 187–189
Universe of Energy, 132–133,
  303
University Club (Winter Park),
  257
Unmasking the Horror, 249
Urban Think Bookstore, 257,
  300
U.S.A. (World Showcase), 141
  restaurants, 146
USA International Speedway
  (Lakeland), 255

Vacation Express, 29
Vans Skatepark, 296
Velvet Lounge, 284
Velvet Sessions, 291
Villas of Grand Cypress, 272
Vimi (Vietnamese district), 18
  eating, 83
V.I.P Tour Experience, 248–249

340 Index

Virgin Holidays, 29

Virtual Jungle Cruise, 170

Visas, 310

Visitor information. *See* Information

Visitors Flea Market, 299

Vista Way, 17

Volunteer Match, 262

The Voyage of the Little Mermaid, 153

Wallaby Ranch (Davenport), 275

Wall Street Plaza, 290

Wal-Mart Supercenter, 73

Walt Disney: One Man's Dream, 154–155

Walt Disney's Carousel of Progress, 124–125, 303

Walt Disney World (WDW), 13–14, 93–171. *See also specific sights and attractions*
  accommodations, 33–42
    advantages and disadvantages of, 33, 36
    deluxe resorts, 40–42
    "Good Neighbor" policy, 41
    moderate resorts, 38–40
    pricing seasons, 36–37
    value resorts, 37–38
  basics cost at, 97
  best sights and attractions, 3–5, 6
  buses, 10–11, 58
  character greetings, 114
  child care, 67
  dinner shows, 89–90
  for travelers with disabilities 324
  eating on site, 98–100
  entertainment districts, 278, 280–282
  Freebies at, 128
  golf courses, 272
  history of, 93
  information, 94, 303
  miniature golf, 233
  navigation tips, 100–101
  optional park services, 101–102
  parades, 112, 120–121, 165, 277
  parking, 33, 97, 100, 130
  restaurants, 61–67
    Animal Kingdom, 66, 165
    character meals, 90–92, 277

Disney Dining Plan, 99

Disney-MGM Studios, 156–158

  Epcot, 145–147

  Magic Kingdom, 126–127, 129

  money-saving tips, 144

  reservations, 61, 90, 94

  six biggest mistakes, 101

  special events, 305–310

  tickets, 94–98

    Fastpass, 109, 120, 121

    money-saving tips, 96, 98

  time-saving tips, 120–121

  tours, 243–248

  vs. Universal, 174–175

  vocabulary of terms, 12

  water parks, 166–169

Walt Disney World Railroad, 103, 106, 113

Waterfront at SeaWorld, 209

Water Park Fun & More (WPF&M) ticket, 95

Water parks, 221–222

  Walt Disney World, 166–169

Water Ski Hall of Fame and Experience (Polk City), 275

Water-skiing, 275

Weather, 94, 304–305

Websites, 303

Wekiwa Springs State Park, 265–266

Wekiwa Springs State Park Nature Adventures, 266

Wells' Built Museum, 230

Western Way, 14

West Side. *See* Downtown Disney West Side

Wet 'n Wild, 221–222

What If Labs, 137

Wheelchair rentals, 324

  SeaWorld, 211

  Universal Orlando, 176

  Walt Disney World, 97

Wide World of Sports. *See* Disney's Wide World of Sports

Wi-Fi access, 326

Wild Arctic, 210–211

Wild By Design, 248

Wildlife Express Train, 161

Winn-Dixie Marketplace, 73

Winter Park, 18–19, 256, 257

  boat tours, 268–271

  restaurants, 74, 85–86

  shopping, 297

  sights and attractions, 234–237

Winter Park Bach Festival, 306

Winter Park Garden Club, 264

Winter Park Historical Museum, 236

Wishes fireworks show, 126, 277

Women's Club of Winter Park, 257

Wonders of Life, 133–134

WonderWorks, 224

Woody Woodpecker's Kidzone, 184–186

Woody Woodpecker's Nuthouse Coaster, 185

WordSpring Discovery Center, 260

World Expo (Universal Studios), 183–184

  restaurants, 188

World Fellowship Fountain, 132

World Market, 301

World of Disney, 169–170

A World of Orchids, 264

World Showcase, 129–130, 137–145

  hours, 130

  restaurants, 146–147

Xanadu, 214

Xcursions, 217

Yellow/City/Checker, 13

Yuletide Fantasy, 245–246

Zora Neale Hurston Festival (Eatonville), 305

ACCOMMODATIONS

Alexander Holiday Homes, 23

All-Star Resorts, 38

All Star Vacation Homes, 23

Award Vacation Homes, 24

Bahama Bay Resort, 25–26

Best Western Kissimmee, 46

Buena Vista Suites, 50

Celebrity Resorts Lake Buena Vista, 27

Clarion Hotel Universal, 56

Comfort Inn International, 55

Comfort Suites Maingate Resort, 46

Country Inn & Suites Orlando Maingate at Calypso Cay Resort, 48–49

Courtyard at Lake Buena Vista, 50–51

Courtyard at Lake Lucerne, 32

Days Inn, 44
Disney's Animal Kingdom Lodge, 42, 64, 128
Disney's Caribbean Beach Resort, 39–40
Disney's Contemporary Resort, 40–42, 64
Disney's Coronado Springs Resort, 39
Disney's Fort Wilderness Resort, 40, 89, 138
Disney's Polynesian Resort, 89, 128
Disney's Pop Century Resort, 37
Doubletree Castle Hotel, 56–57
Doubletree Guest Suites in the Walt Disney World Resort, 52
Encantada Resort, 26
The Enclave Suites Resort, 26
Fairfield Inn (Lake Buena Vista), 50–51
Fairfield Inn & Suites Orlando International Drive, 55
Florida Sun Vacation Homes, 23–24
Gaylord Palms, 49
Grand Bohemian Hotel— Orlando, 59
Grand Floridian Resort and Spa, 40, 64, 128
Hampton Inn Orlando Convention Center, 55
Hampton Inn Universal, 54
Hard Rock Hotel, 43, 284, 291
Hawthorne Suites Orlando Convention Center, 56
Holiday Inn Express Lake Buena Vista, 50
Holiday Inn Sunspree Resort Lake Buena Vista, 51
Holiday Villas, 26
Inn at Oak Plantation, 25
IPG Florida Vacation Homes, 24
J.W. Marriott Grande Lakes Orlando, 57
Lake Suites Hotel, 47
La Quinta Calypso Cay, 46
La Quinta Inn & Suites Orlando Convention Center, 55
La Quinta Inn International Drive, 55
Lowery's Vacation Homes, 24
Marriott Village at Lake Buena Vista, 50–51
Nickelodeon Family Suites, 51–52
Oak Plantation, 25
Palm Lakefront Resort & Hostel, 43–44

Palomino Suites, 49–50
Peabody Orlando, 270
The Perri House, 32
Portofino Bay Resort, 43, 284–285
Port Orleans Riverside and French Quarter, 39
Quality Inn Maingate West, 47
Quality Inn Plaza International Drive, 54
Quality Suites Maingate East, 46–47
Rodeway Inn at International Drive, 54
Rosen Shingle Creek, 57–58
Royal Pacific Resort, 42–43, 70, 90
Seralago Hotel & Suites, 44
Shades of Green, 39
Sheraton Studio City, 56
SpringHill Suites, 50–51
Staybridge Suites Lake Buena Vista, 51
Tropical Palms FunResort, 25
The Veranda Bed and Breakfast, 32–33
VillaDirect, 24
Village at Town Center All Suite Resort, 26
Walt Disney World Dolphin, 41, 65
Walt Disney World Swan, 41
Windsor Palms, 26–27

RESTAURANTS
ABC Commissary, 157
Akershus Royal Banquet Hall, 146
Alchemy Bar, 201
Arabian Nights, 87
Asia Bagus, 72
Bahama Breeze, 74
Beverly Hills Boulangerie, 189
Biergarten Restaurant, 146
Bistro de Paris, 147
Blondie's, 200
bluezoo, 65
Bob Marley—A Tribute to Freedom, 68, 283
Boma, 64
Bongos Cuban Cafe, 66
Boulangerie Patisserie, 147
Bravissimo Wine Bar Café, 83–84
Briarpatch Restaurant & Ice Cream Parlor, 85
Bruno's Italian Restaurant, 70
Bubba Gump Shrimp Co., 69

Bubbalou's Bodacious Bar-B-Que, 74
Between the Buns, 81–82
The Burger Digs, 200
Cafe 4, 200
Café La Bamba, 189
Café Tu Tu Tango, 76
California Grill, 64
Cantina de San Angel, 146
Cap'n Jack's Restaurant, 66
Capone's Dinner & Show, 89
Captain America Diner, 200
Casey's Corner, 127
Chefs de France, 147
Christo's Café, 80
Cinderella's Royal Table, 92, 108, 126
Cinnabon, 200
Circus McGurkus Cafe Stoo-pen-dous!, 201
Columbia Harbour House, 127
Comic Strip Cafe, 200
Confisco Grille, 200
Coral Reef Restaurant, 145–146
Cosmic Ray's Starlight Cafe, 127, 129
Cracker Barrel, 71
Cricketers Arms Pub, 76
Croissant Moon Bakery, 200
Crooked Bayou, 80–81
Crown Colony House, 220
Crystal Palace, 126, 127
Cuban Cafe, 85
Cypress Bakery, 212
Dandelion Communitea Cafe, 79–80
Desert Grill Restaurant, 220
The Dessert Lady, 74, 76
Disney's Spirit of Aloha Show, 89
Dolly Parton's Dixie Stampede, 87
Donald's Breakfastosaurus, 165
Earl of Sandwich, 65
Electric Umbrella, 146
El Pirata y el Perico Restaurante, 127
Emeril's Restaurant Orlando, 69–70
Emeril's Tchoup Chop, 70
Enchanted Oak Tavern, 201
Eola Wine Company, 85
ESPN Club, 66–67
50's Prime Time Café, 156
Finnegan's Bar & Grill, 188
Fiorino New York Pizza World, 71
Fire Eaters' Grill, 201
Flame Tree Barbecue, 165

Fountain View Espresso and Bakery, 146
Fulton's Crab House, 66
Garden Grill (Epcot), 145
Garden View Restaurant (Grand Floridian), 64
Golden Corral, 72, 74
Gospel Brunch (House of Blues), 90
The Green Eggs and Ham Cafe, 201
Harambe Market, 165
Hard Rock Cafe, 68, 301
Hollywood & Vine, 156
Hollywood Brown Derby, 157
Hoop-Dee-Doo Musical Revue, 89
Hop on Pop Ice Cream Shop, 201
Hospitality Deli, 212
Hu Hot, 77
International Food and Film Festival, 188
Jimmy Buffett's Margaritaville, 68, 282
Johnson's Diner, 80
Jungle Jim's Restaurant and Bar, 71
Kaki-Gori, 146
Kid Zone Pizza Company, 189
Kringla Bakeri Og Kafe, 146
The Last Chance Fruit Stand, 200
Latin Quarter, 69
Le Cellier Steakhouse, 147
Le Coq Au Vin, 85
Liberty Inn (Epcot), 146
Liberty Tree Tavern (Magic Kingdom), 126
Little Saigon, 83
Lollicup, 82
Lombard's Seafood Grille, 188
L'Originale Alfredo di Roma Ristorante, 146
Lotus Blossom Café, 146
Louie's Italian Restaurant, 188
Magical Mealtime, 84

Makahiki Luau, 90
Mama Melrose's Ristorante Italiano, 158
Mama's Kitchen, 211–212
Mango Joe's Cafe, 212
Medieval Times, 88
Mel's Drive-In, 189
Memories of India, 76–77
Mickey's Backyard Barbecue, 89
Miller's Orlando Ale House, 71
Ming Court, 78
Monster's Cafe, 187
Mythos, 200–201
Narcoossee's, 64
NASCAR Sports Grille, 69
NBA City, 69
Nine Dragons Restaurant, 146
Official All-Star Café, 67
Old Spanish Sugar Mill Grill and Griddle House (Deland), 265
The Outta Control Magic Show, 88
Pastamoré Ristorante & Market, 69
Pat O'Brien's, 68, 283
Pecos Bill Tall Tale Inn and Cafe, 127
Phó 88, 83
Pinocchio's Village Haus, 127
Pirate's Dinner Adventure, 87–88
Pizzafari, 165
Pizza Predattoria, 200
Ponderosa, 72
Primo, 78–79
Qdoba Mexican Grill, 70
Race Rock, 78
Raglan Road, 65–66
Rainforest Cafe, 66, 165
Restaurant Marrakesh, 147
Restaurantosaurus, 165
Rice Paper, 76
Richter's Burger Co., 188
Rose & Crown Pub, 147
Rosie's All-American Cafe, 158
Safari Barbecue, 165
Sally Lunn Tea, 64

San Angel Inn Restaurante, 146
San Francisco Pastry Co., 188
Schwab's, 189
Sci-Fi Dine-In Theater Restaurant, 157
Seafire Inn, 212
Seasons 52, 77
Sharks Underwater Grill, 212
Sleepy Hollow, 127
Sleuth's Mystery Dinner Show, 88
Smoky Creek, 212
Smuggler's Feasts, 212
Spice Mill Cafe, 212
Spoodles, 67
Stardust Video & Coffee, 82
Studio Catering Co. Flatbread Grill, 158
Sunshine Seasons, 145
Sunshine Tree Terrace, 127
Tangierine Café, 146–147
Taste, 83
Texas de Brazil, 79
Thai Thani, 77
Tijuana Flats, 80
Timpano Chophouse & Martini Bar, 78
Toluca Legs Turkey Co., 158
Tony's Town Square Restaurant, 106, 127
Toy Story Pizza Planet Arcade, 158
Truffles and Trifles, 84
Tusker House Restaurant, 165
Victoria & Albert's, 61
Voyagers, 212
Wantilan Luau, 90
White Wolf Café, 299
Wimpy's, 200
The Wine Room on Park Avenue, 86
Wolfgang Puck Express, 65
Yak & Yeti, 165
Yakitori House, 146
Yorkshire County Fish Shop, 147
Zambia Smokehouse, 220
Z-Café at Orange County Public Library, 8